Law and Families

The International Library of Essays in Law and Society
Series Editor: Austin Sarat

Titles in the Series:

Law and Religion
Gad Barzilai

Police and Policing Law
Jeannine Bell

Law and Society Approaches to Cyberspace
Paul Schiff Berman

Law and Families
Susan B. Boyd and Helen Rhoades

Rhetoric of Law
Marianne Constable and Felipe Gutterriez

Law in Social Theory
Roger Cotterrell

Ethnography and Law
Eve Darian-Smith

International Law and Society
Laura Dickinson

Legal Lives of Private Organizations
Lauren Edelman and Mark C. Suchman

Courts and Judges
Lee Epstein

Consciousness and Ideology
Patricia Ewick

Prosecutors and Prosecution
Lisa Frohmann

Intellectual Property
William T. Gallagher

Human Rights, Law and Society
Lisa Hajjar

Race, Law and Society
Ian Haney Lopéz

The Jury System
Valerie P. Hans

Crime and Criminal Justice
William T. Lyons, Jr.

Regulation and Regulatory Processes
Robert Kagan and Cary Coglianese

Law and Social Movements
Michael McCann

Colonial and Post-Colonial Law
Sally Merry

Social Science in Law
Elizabeth Mertz

Sexuality and Identity
Leslie J. Moran

Law and Poverty
Frank Munger

Rights
Laura Beth Nielsen

Governing Risks
Pat O'Malley

Lawyers and the Legal Profession, Volumes I and II
Tanina Rostain

Capital Punishment, Volumes I and II
Austin Sarat

Legality and Democracy
Stuart A. Scheingold

The Law and Society Canon
Carroll Seron

Popular Culture and Law
Richard K. Sherwin

Law and Science
Susan Silbey

Immigration
Susan Sterett

Gender and Feminist Theory in Law and Society
Madhavi Sunder

Procedural Justice, Volumes I and II
Tom R. Tyler

Trials
Martha Merrill Umphrey

Law and Families

Edited by

Susan B. Boyd and Helen Rhoades

University of British Columbia, Canada and University of Melbourne, Australia

Routledge
Taylor & Francis Group
LONDON AND NEW YORK

First published 2006 by Ashgate Publishing

Reissued 2018 by Routledge
2 Park Square, Milton Park, Abingdon, Oxon, OX14 4RN
711 Third Avenue, New York, NY 10017, USA

Routledge is an imprint of the Taylor & Francis Group, an informa business

Publisher's Note
The publisher has gone to great lengths to ensure the quality of this reprint but points out that some imperfections in the original copies may be apparent.

Disclaimer
The publisher has made every effort to trace copyright holders and welcomes correspondence from those they have been unable to contact.

ISBN 13: 978-0-815-39015-2 (hbk)
ISBN 13: 978-1-351-15424-6 (ebk)

Contents

Acknowledgements *vii*
Series Preface *ix*
Introduction *xi*

PART I THINKING ABOUT FAMILIES AND LAW

1 Frances E. Olsen (1985), 'The Myth of State Intervention in the Family', *University of Michigan Journal of Law Reform*, **18**, pp. 835–64. 3
2 Nikolas Rose (1987), 'Beyond the Public/Private Division: Law, Power and the Family', *Journal of Law and Society*, **14**, pp. 61–76. 33
3 Twila L. Perry (1999), 'Race Matters: Change, Choice, and Family Law at the Millennium', *Family Law Quarterly*, **33**, pp. 461–74. 49
4 Brenda Cossman (1994), 'Family Inside/Out', *University of Toronto Law Journal*, **44**, pp. 1–39. 63

PART II SHAPING FAMILY PRACTICES

5 John Eekelaar and Mavis Maclean (2004), 'Marriage and the Moral Bases of Personal Relationships', *Journal of Law and Society*, **31**, pp. 510–38. 105
6 Belinda Fehlberg (1997), 'Money and Marriage: Sexually Transmitted Debt in England', *International Journal of Law, Policy and the Family*, **11**, pp. 320–43. 135
7 Carol Smart (1991), 'The Legal and Moral Ordering of Child Custody', *Journal of Law and Society*, **18**, pp. 485–500. 159
8 Richard Collier (1995), '"Waiting Till Father Gets Home": The Reconstruction of Fatherhood in Family Law', *Social and Legal Studies*, **4**, pp. 5–30. 175
9 Katherine O'Donovan (2002), '"Real" Mothers for Abandoned Children', *Law and Society Review*, **36**, pp. 347–77. 201

PART III DELIVERING SOCIAL JUSTICE

10 Grania Sheehan (2002), 'Financial Aspects of the Divorce Transition in Australia: Recent Empirical Findings', *International Journal of Law, Policy and the Family*, **16**, pp. 95–126. 235
11 Mary Jane Mossman (1997), 'Child Support or Support for Children? Re-Thinking "Public" and "Private" in Family Law', *University of New Brunswick Law Journal*, **46**, pp. 63–85. 267

12 Marlee Kline (1992), 'Child Welfare Law, "Best Interests of the Child" Ideology, and First Nations', *Osgoode Hall Law Journal*, **30**, pp. 375–425. 291
13 Archana Parashar (2002), 'Just Family Law: A Basic Human Right of All Indian Women', *Delhi Law Review*, **24**, pp. 1–21. 343

PART IV RESOLVING FAMILY DISPUTES

14 Marcia Neave (1994), 'Resolving the Dilemma of Difference: A Critique of "The Role of Private Ordering in Family Law"', *University of Toronto Law Journal*, **44**, pp. 97–131. 367
15 Shelley Day Sclater (1997), 'Narratives of Divorce', *Journal of Social Welfare and Family Law*, **19**, pp. 423–41. 403
16 Martha Fineman (1988), 'Dominant Discourse, Professional Language, and Legal Change in Child Custody Decisionmaking', *Harvard Law Review*, **101**, pp. 727–74. 423
17 Cathy Humphreys and Ravi K. Thiara (2003), 'Neither Justice nor Protection: Women's Experiences of Post-Separation Violence', *Journal of Social Welfare and Family Law*, **25**, pp. 195–214. 471
18 Felicity Kaganas and Alison Diduck (2004), 'Incomplete Citizens: Changing Images of Post-Separation Children', *Modern Law Review*, **67**, pp. 959–81. 491

Name Index 515

Acknowledgements

The editors and publishers wish to thank the following for permission to use copyright material.

Blackwell Publishing for the essays: Nikolas Rose (1987), 'Beyond the Public/Private Division: Law, Power and the Family', *Journal of Law and Society*, **14**, pp. 61–76. Copyright © 1987 Blackwell Publishing; John Eekelaar and Mavis Maclean (2004), 'Marriage and the Moral Bases of Personal Relationships', *Journal of Law and Society*, **31**, pp. 510–38. Copyright © 2004 Blackwell Publishing; Carol Smart (1991), 'The Legal and Moral Ordering of Child Custody', *Journal of Law and Society*, **18**, pp. 485–500. Copyright © 1991 Blackwell Publishing; Katherine O'Donovan (2002), '"Real" Mothers for Abandoned Children', *Law and Society Review*, **36**, pp. 347–77. Copyright © 2002 Law and Society Association; Felicity Kaganas and Alison Diduck (2004), 'Incomplete Citizens: Changing Images of Post-Separation Children', *Modern Law Review*, **67**, pp. 959–81. Copyright © 2004 Modern Law Review.

Harvard Law Review for the essay: Martha Fineman (1988), 'Dominant Discourse, Professional Language, and Legal Change in Child Custody Decisionmaking', *Harvard Law Review*, **101**, pp. 727–74.

Oxford University Press for the essays: Belinda Fehlberg (1997), 'Money and Marriage: Sexually Transmitted Debt in England', *International Journal of Law, Policy and the Family*, **11**, pp. 320–43. Copyright © 1997 Oxford University Press; Grania Sheehan (2002), 'Financial Aspects of the Divorce Transition in Australia: Recent Empirical Findings', *International Journal of Law, Policy and the Family*, **16**, pp. 95–126. Copyright © 2002 Oxford University Press.

Sage Publications for the essay: Richard Collier (1995), '"Waiting Till Father Gets Home": The Reconstruction of Fatherhood in Family Law', *Social and Legal Studies*, **4**, pp. 5–30. Copyright © 1995 Sage Publications.

Taylor and Francis Ltd for the essays: Shelley Day Sclater (1997), 'Narratives of Divorce', *Journal of Social Welfare and Family Law*, **19**, pp. 423–41. Copyright © 1997 Routledge; Cathy Humphreys and Ravi K. Thiara (2003), 'Neither Justice nor Protection: Women's Experiences of Post-Separation Violence', *Journal of Social Welfare and Family Law*, **25**, pp. 195–214. Copyright © 2003 Taylor and Francis Ltd.

University of Michigan Journal of Law Reform for the essay: Frances E. Olsen (1985), 'The Myth of State Intervention in the Family', *University of Michigan Journal of Law Reform*, **18**, pp. 835–64.

University of New Brunswick Law Journal for the essay: Mary Jane Mossman (1997), 'Child Support or Support for Children? Re-Thinking "Public" and "Private" in Family Law', *University of New Brunswick Law Journal*, **46**, pp. 63–85.

University of Toronto Press for the essays: Brenda Cossman (1994), 'Family Inside/Out', *University of Toronto Law Journal*, **44**, pp. 1–39; Marcia Neave (1994), 'Resolving the Dilemma of Difference: A Critique of "The Role of Private Ordering in Family Law"', *University of Toronto Law Journal*, **44**, pp. 97–131.

Every effort has been made to trace all the copyright holders, but if any have been inadvertently overlooked the publishers will be pleased to make the necessary arrangement at the first opportunity.

Series Preface

The International Library of Essays in Law and Society is designed to provide a broad overview of this important field of interdisciplinary inquiry. Titles in the series will provide access to the best existing scholarship on a wide variety of subjects integral to the understanding of how legal institutions work in and through social arrangements. They collect and synthesize research published in the leading journals of the law and society field. Taken together, these volumes show the richness and complexity of inquiry into law's social life.

Each volume is edited by a recognized expert who has selected a range of scholarship designed to illustrate the most important questions, theoretical approaches, and methods in her/his area of expertise. Each has written an introductory essay which both outlines those questions, approaches, and methods and provides a distinctive analysis of the scholarship presented in the book. Each was asked to identify approximately 20 pieces of work for inclusion in their volume. This has necessitated hard choices since law and society inquiry is vibrant and flourishing.

The International Library of Essays in Law and Society brings together scholars representing different disciplinary traditions and working in different cultural contexts. Since law and society is itself an international field of inquiry it is appropriate that the editors of the volumes in this series come from many different nations and academic contexts. The work of the editors both charts a tradition and opens up new questions. It is my hope that this work will provide a valuable resource for longtime practitioners of law and society scholarship and newcomers to the field.

AUSTIN SARAT
William Nelson Cromwell Professor of Jurisprudence and Political Science
Amherst College

Introduction

The turning of the twenty-first century prompted numerous family law scholars to assess the state of family law and, in particular, to identify the trends and contradictions in modern family law and family law reform (for example, Boyd, 2004; Dewar, 2000; Dewar, 2003; Graycar, 2000; Mason, Fine and Carnochan, 2001; Perry, 1999). This volume represents a similar exercise, but with a focus on highlighting important scholarly contributions that have, over time, captured key insights on family law from a law and society perspective specifically. Our effort to highlight these contributions is two-fold. First, we reproduce a selection of these contributions in full in this volume. Second, this Introduction reviews the reproduced essays as well as other key works that we were not able to reproduce. In so doing, we hope to offer a picture of key intellectual and methodological developments in the field, dating from the 1970s through to the twenty-first century.

The increasingly broad range of family law scholarship in recent years reflects the fact that 'the family' has become an issue of intense political debate and sociological interest, especially over the last two decades of the twentieth century as family practices have increasingly diversified. As John Dewar has suggested (1998: p. 468), family law is perhaps more 'cognitively open to its social environment' than other areas of law. The very definition of 'family' was challenged, notably through the struggle of gays and lesbians for inclusion in the family law system (for example, Cossman, Chapter 4). Taken for granted concepts such as motherhood and fatherhood became 'problematized' (for example, Smart, Chapter 7; Collier, Chapter 8), as did the nuclear or exclusive form of family (Harvison Young, 2001). The family and family law emerged as a matter of theoretical and empirical interest to sociologists, as the form of family relationships increasingly diversified (for example, Smart and Neale, 1999; Giddens, 1992; Beck and Beck-Gernsheim, 1995; Morgan, 1996). Childhood itself became the focus of inquiry (Smart, Neale and Wade, 2001) and children's rights were increasingly highlighted in both national and international law, especially with the International Convention on the Rights of the Child, and in scholarly journals such as *Childhood* and the *International Journal of Children's Rights*.

The focus of this volume is on 'law and society' approaches to families and law. Defining a law and society approach is a fraught endeavour (Sarat, 2004), and we have taken a pluralist approach. We have featured authors who bring critical perspectives to their topics, asking new questions about the field and eschewing a positivist approach. Many law and society authors have used the perspectives, methods, and data of social sciences to better understand family law and to expose the gap between the 'law on the books' and 'law in action' in order to propose more effective social policies (Neilson, 2002). The sociological interest in families and law is reflected by the inclusion in this volume of a number of pieces by scholars who work outside the legal academy, such as Nikolas Rose, Carol Smart, Mavis Maclean and Grania Sheehan, whose (primary) training is in the social sciences. Also, we note that legal academics are increasingly employing social science methods in their own studies of family relations (for example, Eekelaar and Maclean, Chapter 5; Rhoades, 2002; Fehlberg, Chapter 6) rather than simply relying on the research of others to provide data.

This collection also takes account of the move towards deconstructivism both from within and without legal realism, a move that offered greater skepticism about the capacity of law to resolve social problems (Sarat, 2004). Several of our authors adopt a complex and critical approach to the role of law in relation to social change and, in particular, social justice, implicating law in the very problems that it is often invoked to resolve (for example, Olsen, Chapter 1; Mossman, Chapter 11). This shift in analytical framing has occurred alongside the 'decline of the social', as the principles of economic rationalism and neo-liberalism have replaced a focus on social welfare and social and state activism (Sarat, 2004). Law is both implicated in this transition and influenced by it (Cossman and Fudge, 2002), with family law in particular reflecting both neo-liberalism and neo-conservatism (Cossman, 2002).

This 'decline of the social' has certainly not indicated the death of law and society approaches to family law. Rather, methodologies have shifted in a manner that reflects the influence of the humanities in addition to the social sciences, as well as an attempt to emphasize the role of race, gender, culture, and sexual orientation. Authors use techniques such as narrative, storytelling, and interpretation/deconstruction, often in combination with other methods (for example, Day Sclater, Chapter 15; Grillo, 1991; Roberts, 1995). Some authors also look to history to understand current developments (Lessard, 2001) while others use comparative methods to analyze the influence of international and global trends (Rhoades and Boyd, 2004; O'Donovan, Chapter 9).

As with all volumes of this ilk, the selection of essays has reflected a process of compromise and a difficult balancing of topics, authors, geographies, and historical periods. We have excluded some authors and essays that have been foundational in our own thinking, sometimes due to space concerns,[1] or not wishing to over-represent certain topics, or because an essay has been so frequently cited and/or reprinted that we felt it need not be reproduced in full in this volume (for example, Mnookin and Kornhauser, 1979). However, we have tried to take a broad approach to the subject matter, highlighting the diversity of family relations and practices and their relationship with law. No one family form is relevant to law, as is increasingly clear with the proliferation of unmarried couples, same-sex relationships, and families created by choice and social ties rather than biological or genetic links. Like many socio-legal scholars, we reject a narrow definition of family law that includes only marriage, divorce, property, maintenance, and child custody (Graycar, 2000; Mossman, 2004: v). Nevertheless, the essays we have reproduced disproportionately reflect these topics, due to space limitations. Moreover, we have barely scratched the surface of the burgeoning field of children's rights with our inclusion of Marlee Kline (Chapter 12), Felicity Kaganas and Alison

1 In particular, we have excluded numerous important essays published in American law journals, due to their length. A bias in favour of essays published in UK journals has resulted, in part due to their pithiness, but also due to the groundbreaking nature of much UK research over the past two decades, which has influenced family law research in other countries, such as Canada and Australia. Socio-legal researchers such as Mavis Maclean, John Eekelaar, Katherine O'Donovan, Carol Smart, and Christine Piper have been leaders in family law research in terms of critical thinking, empirical research and policy-oriented work. A new generation of scholars such as Richard Collier, Alison Diduck, Felicity Kaganas and Shelley Day Sclater, all represented in this volume, have moved family law research and debates forward in innovative ways.

Diduck (Chapter 18), and Katherine O'Donovan (Chapter 9). There is now a vast socio-legal literature dealing with children's citizenship – for example, analyses of the conflicts between children's and parents' rights (for example, Monk, 2004) and of the constructions of childhood in legal discourses (for example, Piper, 1996; Rwezaura, 1998) – which we have been unable to represent in this collection.

Many areas of the law use legal definitions of family as reference points. As a result, a volume on law and families could well have offered examples drawn from fields such as tax law, social welfare law, immigration law, health law, or tort law. The legal system touches and regulates families in many different ways, most of which this volume cannot cover. Entitlement or disentitlement to public financial supports, for instance social assistance or tax credits, is often determined by who is defined as 'family', in particular who is a legal spouse (for example, Gavigan, 1999), and damages awards for personal injuries may depend on how a judge values a wife's work in the home (for example, Graycar, 1997). At a larger level, law plays a role in facilitating economic policy at any given time, which often rests on certain assumptions about the privatized responsibility that families ought to take for the economic security of their members (Boyd, 1999; Cossman and Fudge, 2002; Fineman, 2000). In the end, we have retained family law as our focus, while trying to offer literature that highlights the significance of familial relations to law, and law to families, in a way that is relevant to broader legal fields.

Thinking about Families and Law

Socio-legal scholars have excelled at analysis of the definitional power of law and the way that law 'sees' families. They have highlighted the contradictions between the types of relationships that are regarded as 'private' and those that are treated as 'public', and explored the divisions that law draws, including who is 'in' or who is 'out' of definitions such as 'spouse' or 'parent'. Increasingly, the relative weight of genetic versus social ties in determining legal parenthood has been critically assessed.

A burst of work by critically minded scholars during the late 1970s and early 1980s shook the foundations of thinking in relation to family law. In particular, sociological, historical, and theoretical approaches challenged notions that the family was, or ever could be, an unregulated private sphere (for example, Eekelaar, 1978, 1984; Freeman, 1984; O'Donovan, 1985; Olsen, 1983; Rose, 1987; Smart, 1984). Earlier functionalist accounts such as Eekelaar's quickly gave way to constructionist approaches under the influence of feminism and post-structuralism. It was increasingly clear that calling for more or less state intervention into the family missed the complex relationship between state, market, and family, and the ideological nature of the public/private divide.

In this collection, Frances Olsen (Chapter 1) and Nikolas Rose (Chapter 2) provide two examples of the 1980s reconsideration of the relationship between family and law. These two essays reflect a debate about how best to think about regulation of family relations. Feminist legal scholars such as Olsen (1983, 1985) were first to point out the ideological nature of the public/private divide so key to legal liberalism and the way it placed the family on the private side of the divide, positing it as a realm where laissez-faire was appropriate. Olsen and others such as Katherine O'Donovan (1985) and Michael Freeman (1984) made it patently clear that even legal policies that purported to avoid intervention in family relations in fact represented a form of intervention, often by reinforcing unequal relations within the family on the lines of gender. In another groundbreaking work of the 1980s, Carol Smart (1984) went well beyond a critique of the public/private divide and the question of whether family law either reflected or influenced social relations such as patriarchy to offer a complex exploration of the ideological role of law and legal regulation. This work, along with that of other British socio-legal scholars of the 1980s, was highly influential in other countries such as Canada (for example, Boyd, 1989; Chunn, 1992; Gavigan, 1993; Kline, 1992, 1993; Mossman, 1994).

Where feminist scholars exposed the artificiality of the public/private divide, others such as Nikolas Rose (Chapter 2) in turn quickly challenged some of the feminist analysis. Drawing on the work of Michel Foucault (1978) and Jacques Donzelot (1979), Rose sought to disrupt the certainties of categories such as 'family' and 'family law', and reveal their fragmentary and incoherent nature. In emphasizing legal pluralism and a genealogical approach, Rose argued for a reconceptualization of the relationship between power and the state, including law. Like Carol Smart (1989), he suggested the need to de-centre law in any analysis of regulatory strategies (1987: p. 39). This analytical approach has influenced much socio-legal scholarship on the family, such as Richard Collier's examination of 'new fatherhood' policies in the UK (Collier, 2001).

These early definitional analyses of family law often focused on the issue of gender. Reg Graycar's explorations of judicial practices, for example, revealed the power of judges to define women's private lives, and cautioned us 'to pay careful attention to what judges know about the world' and 'how the things they know translate into their activity as judges' (1995: p. 267). But the elusive divide between public and private depends on other variables besides gender. Twila Perry's essay (Chapter 3) compellingly demonstrates how race matters to a wide range of modern family law issues, including no-fault divorce, pre-nuptial agreements, adoption, and regulation of single motherhood. For example, African–American families, due to their generally precarious material circumstances, experience developments such as the availability of reproductive technology in a different manner than many Americans. Perry shows that 'choice', which is re-emerging in many aspects of family law, for instance in relation to reproductive freedom or private ordering, is constrained for many African–Americans, as it is for '[w]omen, members of other minority groups, and virtually all poor people' (p. 50). Moreover, the family lives of African–Americans are constrainded more by public regulation than by private ordering (pp. 60–1), so that inviting state intervention to address a partner's abusive behaviour may not be an attractive strategy for an African–American woman, given the racial history of the United States (p. 55).

One development that Perry identifies as reflecting the increased emphasis on freedom of choice in family law is the expanding legal recognition of unmarried cohabitation alongside marriage (see Lewis, 2001; Martin and Thery, 2001), and in particular of gay or lesbian headed families (for example, Millbank and Graycar 2000). This sea change in family law, which has challenged the centrality of the heterosexual, nuclear family, has of course been contested, not least as countries such as Canada, the Netherlands, Belgium, and Spain legalized same-sex marriage early in the twenty-first century. Family law scholars have interrogated the meaning of the redrawing of boundaries concerning who is defined as inside or outside of family law. As a result, inclusion within the family has been contested not only by social conservatives who resist extending the legal definition of family to those living outside the heterosexual norm, but also by scholars who are supportive of struggles against heteronormativity in law.

Brenda Cossman's essay (Chapter 4) captures this debate about the meaning of the lesbian and gay demand that their relationships be legally defined as family.

Some scholars have raised concerns that inclusion in family law might lead to the 'domestication' of lesbians and gay men within an oppressive institution of the patriarchal state (Robson, 1994), which has perpetuated the oppression of women and other groups. Many such arguments are evocative of Carol Smart's earlier work (1984), where she suggested that marriage, as a patriarchal institution that reproduces and reinforces the dependency of women, might not be retrievable by feminists. Smart astutely noted that marriage was 'as significant to the unmarried as to the married and to the homosexual as to the heterosexual' (1984: p. 143). Marriage as an ideological 'enclosure' prioritizes coupledom as a norm against which all else is measured and becomes the privileged context for the reproduction of children.

But not all research is focused on marriage. Several authors (for example, Boyd, 1999; Gavigan, 1992; and Robson, 1994) have suggested that other means of expanding recognition of spousal or family relations to include same-sex partners may be a limited strategy that avoids key questions, such as how society organizes the redistribution of economic well-being and the continued privatization of responsibility for economic well-being and care-giving within the family. Cossman's essay (Chapter 4) both identifies many of these debates and critically analyses the terms of the debate, which denies the possibility of contradictory or complex responses to the family.

Martha Fineman has moved these debates forward in another way (1995; 2000), challenging the primacy in law and social policy on adult dyads (the sexual family) and proposing instead a focus on care-giving and dependency, in particular, the paradigmatic mother–child relationship. Her work, while addressing many issues traditionally defined as 'family law', such as child custody, has also challenged the way that we should think about family and related questions such as inevitable and derivative dependency. These types of questions, including increasingly sophisticated consideration of the 'work–family conflict', have increasingly preoccupied American feminist legal scholars (for example, Williams, 2000).

Rethinking the determinants of legal parenthood has also preoccupied socio-legal scholars. Reproductive technologies have disturbed the earlier 'easy' presumptions of parenthood based on birth and marriage, under which the marriage tie between a man and a woman who gave birth largely determined legal fatherhood (Smart, 1987). Reproductive technologies and DNA testing made genetic ties more determinable and raised numerous questions about the relative weight that genetic ties, intention to parent, and social parenting ought to have in determining legal parenthood for various purposes such as birth registration and naming (Lessard, 2004), adoption (Shanley, 2001), and child support (Sheldon, 2003). The rights of children to know their genetic parentage also arose (O'Donovan, 1988; Wallbank, 2004).

Perhaps the clearest example of the tension between affirming genetic ties versus the social ties of care-giving arise in the brave new world of lesbian-headed families and the legal status of sperm donors. Authors such as Katherine Arnup and Susan Boyd (1995) and Fiona Kelly (2004) question whether these families offer the opportunity to break away from a nuclear or exclusive family focus by affirming the possibility of multiple parents (Harvison Young, 1998), or whether recognition of the legal parenthood of sperm donors problematically reinforces the impetus to 'find fathers' for children regardless of the circumstances.

This type of work has highlighted the socially constructed nature of parenthood. In 1995, when surrogate motherhood was being hotly debated, Dorothy Roberts illuminated the racialized history of the genetic tie, which intersects with its patriarchal history. In this volume, Twila Perry draws on Roberts' detailed examination, and argues that given the standard of beauty in the US (White), the availability of reproductive technologies, and differential economic resources of Black and White women, 'the genetic material of Blacks is essentially worthless' (Perry Chapter 3: p.472). The choices available to people about how to construct their families that have arisen as a result of technological developments remain constrained, and shaped, by gender, race, class, and sexual orientation.

Although much of the literature on legal parenthood addresses the vexed question of the status of fathers in law, Katherine O'Donovan's recent work (Chapter 9) reproduced in this volume challenges taken-for-granted assumptions about legal motherhood through a cross-cultural examination of the ways in which England, France and Germany deal with abandoned children. O'Donovan found that even in an era that emphasizes the retention of ties with birth families, open adoption, and children's rights to identity, some countries provide legal safeguards for mothers to abandon their children anonymously. This research highlights not only that the determination of legal motherhood does vary from jurisdiction to jurisdiction, making a distinction between maternity and motherhood significant, but also that different countries that have ratified the Convention on the Rights of the Child treat a child's right to identity differently. This insight about the role of law in shaping definitions of family leads to our next topic: how law shapes family practices.

Shaping Family Practices

A distinction between the images and norms of families produced by law and its regulatory mechanisms (for instance, in judicial decision-making, lawyers' advice, dispute resolution approaches) and actual family practices has been identified by socio-legal scholars, who have inquired into the relationship between the two. Alison Diduck (2003: Chapter 2), for instance, articulates a distinction between the families we live *by* (for example, the norms embedded within family law) and the families we live *with* (actual family practices), drawing on Gillis's work on the families we live by and Morgan's work on family practices (John Gillis, 1997; David Morgan, 1996). As we have already seen, law plays a key role in deciding whether an intimate personal relationship constitutes a 'family' and whether a person's nurturance of a child qualifies them as a 'parent'.

This volume includes a number of studies that examine the gaps between the 'ideal' families of law and the diverse and 'messy' lived realities of family life, and the extent to which law motivates the choices we make about our family structure. John Eekelaar and Mavis Maclean's recent empirical study (Chapter 5) investigated the reasons given by intimate partners for their decisions to marry or not, as well as the extent to which the partners shared resources and felt that they owed reciprocal obligations. Their findings illustrate the many variations in family practice among those who are married, as well as the many similarities between unmarried and married couples. They also challenge any notion that a restrictive legal definition of marriage can dictate actual family practices or that the diminishing of marriage as a privileged institution has led to a diminution in the sense of personal obligation between intimate partners.

Other scholarship in this section also focuses on the limits of the law as a regulatory device. Belinda Fehlberg's essay (Chapter 6) explores the dynamics of suretyship by loved ones, and the impact of legal interventions on a woman's decision to provide financial security for her husband's business loans. Fehlberg's examination of 'surety wives' in England contrasts with the image of the self-interested risk-assessor assumed by judges, and highlights the extent to which women act against their own interests while their relationship is intact, despite the existence of legal protections. Like many socio-legal researchers, Fehlberg concludes that law may have only a minor role to play in resolving social problems such as sexually transmitted debt, as long as economic inequality between husbands and wives remains a feature of our society (see also Neave, Chapter 14).

More recently, John Dewar's much-cited essay, 'The Normal Chaos of Family Law' (1998), proposed that modern attempts to shape family practices adopt a more subtle form, with governments seeking to modify behaviour by 'radiating messages' rather than laying down bright-line rules. For Dewar, family law's normative confusion at the end of the twentieth century provides a paradigm example of what Marc Galanter (1992) calls 'new legalism', by which law operates through indirect symbolic controls (Dewar, 1998: p. 470). In family law, these messages are received and interpreted differently by their various audiences: courts, parents, legal advisers, counsellors, and mediators (p. 474; Dewar and Parker, 1999). The simultaneous delegalization of family law processes alongside a move towards family law engaging in behaviour modification has been elaborated recently in Helen Reece's *Divorcing Responsibly* (2003). For Reece, the focus on reflection and mediation encouraged by new divorce reform initiatives is a form of 'civic education' for separating parents, an attempt to 'inculcate virtue' by 'persuasion rather than regulation'. The use of messages is particularly apparent in relation to post-divorce parenting, where the language of the welfare of the child and anxieties about father-absence have seen 'responsible parenting' become synonymous with cooperation and constrained mothers' ability to raise concerns about a father's capacity to care for the children (for example, Smart, 1995; Day Sclater and Piper, 2001; Rhoades, 2002; Kaganas and Day Sclater, 2004).

There has been considerable attention in the literature to the 'constitution of the mother in legal discourse' (Smart, Chapter 7, p. 159). In this volume, the works by Martha Fineman (Chapter 16) and Carol Smart (Chapter 7) illustrate the ways in which the language of maternal care has become discredited in the context of divorce proceedings, depriving women of a legitimate voice with which to express their experience of caring for children. The changes that have resulted in mothers not being heard within the modern family law system include trends towards gender neutrality, parental equality, reliance on the 'psy' professional discourses, and the use of mediation as the preferred way to resolve disputes, especially those involving children (Fineman, Chapter 16; Day Sclater and Piper, 2001). These trends have had normative as well as process implications (Dewar, 2000: p. 75). Of course, the dominance of the ideology of motherhood in earlier periods did not empower mothers as such, but rather supported a normative image of motherhood as selfless, pure, full-time carers of children within the heterosexual nuclear family (Boyd, 1996). But the resonance of this norm lost its power in law near the end of the twentieth century, as mother love became an increasingly 'exhausted script' (Smart, 1991: p. 486).

Beginning in the early 1990s, Carol Smart's empirical work in the UK (1991, 1995) showed that mothers more often expressed their taken for granted activity of caring for children as 'caring for', whereas fathers talked about 'caring about' children, which 'can produce a sentimental rush of concern and can be instrumental in producing legislative reforms' (Smart,

Chapter 7: p. 163). Smart's examinations of the evolving family law system showed that 'caring about' is placed above 'caring for' in the moral register, meaning that fathers' claims in relation to children are heard positively while mothers' claims about 'caring for' appear as self-interested. Moreover, mothers who failed to take on the work of facilitating paternal contact with children after divorce became identified as bad or vindictive mothers. Thus, the image of the 'no-contact mother', whose anxieties about contact are read as selfishness, was born (Rhoades, 2002).

Although this work by Smart and others produced many insights about fatherhood in addition to motherhood, Richard Collier drew effectively from masculinity studies to detail more specifically the normative reconstruction of fatherhood in family law policy from the late nineteenth century to the 1990s (Chapter 8; and 2001). Collier showed that after the earlier times of father right, fatherhood was first and foremost constructed as an economic resource, such that the physical *absence* of breadwinner fathers from the family domain has been justified in family law (p. 185). Modern family law, however, increasingly requires a father to be an equal partner in the 'symmetrical family' (p. 191), such that some father presence is required. Fathers must, then, be rehabilitated, and paternal masculinity modernized. Collier suggests that this modern father must be present, but in a specific way that conveys paternal heterosexual authority: 'The family man of legal discourse is heterosexual, disciplined, economically responsible and perhaps above all he embodies a particular kind of authority over women and children in the family' (p. 190). This new paternal presence in the family thus rests on still gendered assumptions, and how these assumptions play out in post-divorce parenting law has been the subject of numerous studies. As several authors have documented, the idea that contact with a father is necessary for children's well-being seems to have acquired the status of uncontestable truth (for example, Boyd, 2003; Fineman, 1988; Kaganas and Day Sclater, 2004; Smart, 1995).

Although a more persuasive indirect governance approach can now be detected in some family law fields as they generate new norms of the family in law, a coercive element remains (Reece, 2003). The new focus on process is not entirely agnostic, as we will see further below. Research on other fields of family law, such as child protection, has also identified a coercive element, due to the fact that the legal system participates in the surveillance of families and what Dorothy Chunn has called 'socialized legal coercion' (1992). Sometimes, of course, law is implicated not only in monitoring but also in the disruption of family relations (Kline, Chapter 12). The next section addresses some of these questions and the issues of social justice they raise.

Delivering Social Justice

Different types of families are often dealt with in uneven ways by law, and individuals are also situated differently within families, often in ways that reflect social inequalities. Law and society approaches to family law have of necessity addressed the politics of the family (for example, Barrett and McIntosh, 1982) and related questions of gender, race, class, and sexual orientation. Family law has been studied in relation to its potential for achieving social justice for vulnerable family members and its potential as an agent of broader social change. The notion of rights has increasingly been invoked in family law (Parker 1992), including the rise of children as rights-bearers with the adoption of the UN Convention on the Rights of the Child (Rwezaura, 1998), the claims of lesbians and gay men to spousal recognition, and recognition of the cultural identity claims and needs of Indigenous families. As well, reforms designed to redistribute economic benefits among family members have been sought, such as the development of child support reforms in a number of countries. The recognition of (or failure to recognize) the impact of domestic violence on women's safety and their financial position on relationship breakdown has been an ongoing concern in the literature. Most recently, questions of how to respect cultural and religious pluralism have raised complex concerns of social justice in relation to family law dispute resolution.

During the 1980s and early 1990s, many works documented the extent to which women's economic inequality in society was reproduced, or even exacerbated, by family law. The failure of gender neutral norms to address women's continuing economic disadvantage was a particular focus, with Lenore Weitzman (1985) often being cited in support of the trend for women's standard of living to plummet after divorce, while men's rose. Although Weitzman's findings have been challenged in terms of the extent of the disproportionate financial impact, subsequent studies, including Grania Sheehan's (Chapter 10), affirm that this trend holds true despite various law reform initiatives. Sheehan draws on recent empirical findings in Australia to show that the emphasis on financial contributions to a marriage rather than financial needs generates ongoing economic hardship for women, especially sole mothers, older women living alone, and women who have experienced spousal abuse.

Sheehan is careful to point out that the limited asset wealth available to a large minority of couples on separation is partly responsible for the shortfall that women experience after divorce. As Belinda Fehlberg did in relation to sexually transmitted debt (Chapter 6), Sheehan and others stress the inability of family law alone to effect meaningful social change or to redress the poverty of women and children (see also Eichler, 1990; Pulkingham, 1994). Mary Jane Mossman's essay (Chapter 11) represents this line of inquiry through her examination of the rationales underlying child support law reform in Canada. As has been the case in other countries, the social problem that child support is meant to deal with was defined as 'deadbeat dads', rather than broader questions of economic inequality. Because of the identification of this problem as individual and private, the remedy for it was also privatized and pinned on the income of the payer father. Mossman suggests that this type of privatized remedy will not address the real social problem, which is child poverty. Instead a publicly based remedy embodying social responsibility and government and public support is required. Working from a different angle, Sally Sheldon (2003) too has required readers to consider the assumptions underlying paternal child support obligations. Bringing her research on abortion to bear on this question, Sheldon considers whether a man's act of having sex with a woman necessarily implies that he has voluntarily created need. Ultimately Sheldon finds that voluntary creation of need is an inadequate basis for child support liability and argues for a more collective responsibility for the economic well-being of children, ending up in a similar position as Mossman.

Somewhat ironically, just at the time when various jurisdictions have strengthened their family law norms in relation to the sharing of the economic advantages and disadvantages of marriage and divorce, often in response to feminist arguments (for example, Fineman, 1989-90) a debate has emerged about the primacy of such norms. Countries with diverse cultural and religious communities within their borders have increasingly grappled with the extent to which legal pluralism should be permitted within family law in order to protect multicultural practices in the face of sometimes insensitive imposition by judges of majoritarian opinion and secular norms on ethnic and religious minority communities (Fournier, 2001). Scholars have in turn examined the extent to which affirmation of accommodationist policies may exacerbate the inequality of vulnerable members within a minority community, notably women (for example, Fishbayn, 1999; Shachar, 1998). In this volume, we offer Archana Parashar's (Chapter 13) examination of this question of how to balance claims in the name of religious autonomy with other rights in relation to the various systems of religious personal laws in India. Finding that minority religious leaders in India have invariably strengthened patriarchal control over women in the name of Islam, Parashar argues strenuously for a just family law that would promote gender equality for women. Furthermore, she suggests that gender justice can be achieved only through state or secular law, which should provide a minimum set of norms against which religious personal laws must be measured.

Although Parashar's argument is compelling in the context she addresses, Marlee Kline's research on Indigenous children and child welfare law (Chapter 12) explains why minority cultures and communities might legitimately argue for autonomous legal systems outside of the secular, national system. Offering a careful analysis of the ways in which the 'best interests of the child' principle operates ideologically to structure judicial decision-making in relation to child welfare and First Nations children in Canada, Kline shows how the removal of individual children from their families and communities is rationalized and legitimated, while the history of racial oppression, colonization, and poverty is minimized. Exposing the operation of liberal legality in relation to First Nations communities assists in an understanding of why various non-dominant cultural communities might support legal pluralism. This insight renders of primary importance the debates addressed by Parashar and others concerning which norms should guide dispute resolution processes in this context, particularly in the wake of backlash against Muslim communities since the attacks of September 11, 2001 in the United States and the London bombings of 2005.

As noted earlier, another significant social justice development has been the articulation of children as rights-bearers, encompassing both procedural rights, such as the right to participate in decision-making processes (discussed in the next section on 'Resolving Family Disputes'), as well as substantive rights. With the increasing use of assisted reproductive technologies by families, debates have focused on the question of whether children should be accorded a right to know their genetic history (Wilson, 1997; Wallbank, 2004). Earlier research on adults who had been adopted as children highlighted the harm caused by closed adoption policies, and suggested that children need information about their biological parentage in order to establish a coherent sense of identity (Triseliotis, 1973). On the other hand, feminist scholars challenged the idea of a necessary relationship between children and the donors of their genetic material, with its marginalization of the commitment involved in raising a child (O'Donovan, 1988; Kelly, 2004). Reflecting these different perspectives, Julie Wallbank's recent examination (2004) reveals family law's fragmented and inconsistent approach to protecting the child's right to know her 'genetic identity', where the priority given to it depends upon the political aims underlying the law. For example, regulation in the UK governing donor insemination has favoured protection of the child's social family and the anonymity of the donor, whereas a children's rights approach has tended to prevail in paternity testing decision-making, where concern for biological certainty merges with the policy goal of securing the father–child relationship.

Finally, legal interventions designed to safeguard women and children from violence in the aftermath of relationship breakdown have been the source of a substantial scholarly analysis. Law is engaged on a number of levels in this project, providing avenues of protection for individual women and children as well as attempting broader 'behaviour modification' endeavours. Socio-legal research has contributed critical insights into the effectiveness of these initiatives. Unfortunately much of the picture revealed by this scholarship suggests the law has failed to deliver social justice for the families it is meant to protect. Cathy Humphreys and Ravi Thiara's investigation (Chapter 17) found a high level of ongoing exposure to abuse among the British women they surveyed because of inadequate support for legal protections such as non-molestation orders and anti-stalking legislation. Mirroring the findings of studies from other countries, this work reveals a reluctance among police to prosecute breaches of protection orders where there are 'family law' matters in dispute (for example, Katzen, 2000), and that the promotion of a child's right to have contact with their father has facilitated abusive men's continuing access to mothers (for example, Kaye, Stubbs and Tolmie, 2003; Neilson, 2002). These issues are taken up in the next section.

Resolving Family Disputes

The previous section showed that questions of process are sometimes a part of socio-legal treatments of social justice issues within family law. In fact, authors such as John Dewar (1998) and Helen Reece (2003) have recently suggested that modern family law has become more focused on process rather than on substantive legal norms. As well, private ordering, always an issue in family law literature, has been subjected to renewed inquiry in part due to the trend towards use of alternative dispute resolution processes in family law disputes.

The precise role of legal norms in dispute resolution was questioned by Robert Mnookin and Lewis Kornhauser in their classic 1979 *Bargaining in the Shadow of the Law*, which informed much subsequent research and is still a frequently cited work. This essay affirmed the value of private ordering, but against the backdrop of fair standards that provide a framework for divorcing couples. Still remarkably relevant in many of its observations, it provides an overview of standard divorce issues and how they play out in bargaining. Mnookin and Kornhauser note, for example, that the bargaining power of husbands increased when custody law shifted away from a maternal preference towards a gender neutral best interests standard (see also Mnookin, 1975) and limits were placed on the extent and availability of permanent alimony (1979: p. 978). They also examined the way that a controversial proposal by Goldstein, Freud and Solnit (1973) – much discussed in the 1970s – would impact on private ordering. These authors had proposed that once the custodial parent was determined, either by agreement or by court order, that parent and not the court would be empowered to decide under what conditions he or she wished to raise the child, including the rights of the access parent (p. 38).

Since Mnookin and Kornhauser asserted the primacy of private ordering in 1979, authors, particularly feminist scholars, have raised challenging questions about power and the bargaining process, particularly given women's inequality economically. Marcia Neave in this volume (Chapter 14) responds to Michael Trebilcock and Rosemin Keshvani's (1991) endorsement of private ordering as a means to enhance women's self-determination after marriage breakdown. Neave's essay engages with and challenges the paradigmatic arguments supporting private ordering: that consensual arrangements are more likely to be complied with than imposed solutions, that the parties to a marriage are best placed to judge their own interests, and that private agreements minimize transaction costs. Drawing on empirical research conducted in Australia, Neave shows that these arguments take insufficient account of the evidence that men and women who negotiate agreements are differently situated, and that women have fared poorly under private ordering in the past, both during and after marriage. But rather than making a plea for formal processes to determine post-separation financial entitlements, Neave favours the larger political project of reshaping the relationship between family responsibilities and paid workforce participation (p. 369).

Reflecting much literature prior to the 1980s, spousal abuse was not mentioned by Mnookin and Kornhauser (1979), though they did reference other factors between spouses that might affect bargaining, such as spite, distrust, distaste, or hatred. The ways in which spousal abuse can affect various stages of the family law process, from negotiation to mediation to litigation, have now been subjected to much careful scrutiny and critical analysis (for example, Grillo, 1991; Mahoney, 1991; Neilson, 2002). Analyses of mediation processes have shown that mediators marginalized the issue of domestic abuse when it was raised (Greatbatch and Dingwall, 1999), and that women have felt pressured to reach agreements with abusive former partners for the sake of their children (Hunter, 2003; Kaye, Stubbs and Tolmie, 2003). More broadly, Shelley Day Sclater's narrative analysis of women's divorce stories (Chapter 15) suggests that mediation, like litigation, pays insufficient attention to the need to revisit and make sense of the past. In common with other researchers of post-separation disputes, Day Sclater is critical of the tendency among divorce professionals to circumscribe what may legitimately be said in dispute resolution fora, and their advocacy of amicable cooperation (for example, Neale and Smart, 1997). In the case of family mediation, techniques such as 'reframing', which borrows from family therapy, are used to direct parties away from talking about the history of their relationship and to focus squarely on the future. Day Sclater's study suggests that there may be dangers in this approach and that couples need to air their grievances in order to preserve a sense of 'self' and move on with their lives.

Many socio-legal and feminist scholars have pointed to the relationship between the failure of the legal system to deal with the implications of spousal abuse and shifting norms in post-separation parenting law. As discussed above under 'Shaping Family Practices', the normative assumption that contact with a father is necessary for a child's well-being has increasingly become embedded in the family law system. This normative imperative has particular process implications, which may have a disproportionately negative impact on women (Smart, 1995; Rhoades, 2002). Studies of professional practices in the family law system show that a shift has occurred in the making of contact orders, such that contact between father and child is now rarely refused even when there are concerns about violence (Dewar and Parker, 1999; Rhoades, 2002; Humphreys and Harrison, 2003), while other research has provided insights into the material effects of this development for women and children (for example, Kaye, Stubbs and Tolmie, 2003). Humphreys and Thiara's investigation (Chapter 17) reveals, for example, that the introduction of the child's right to ongoing contact with their father has compromised women's ability to relocate to a secret address as a safety strategy, and suggests that its prominence in decision-making has become a key barrier to protecting mothers and children from post-separation violence.

Mnookin and Kornhauser also noted the role of lawyers in the divorce process and since they wrote, socio-legal research on lawyering in family law has expanded. Proponents of mediation often suggest that the participation of lawyers in the divorce process generates more disputes and higher costs (see Fineman Chapter 16: pp. 754-756, on the 'horror story'). However, research has shown that (as signaled by Mnookin and Kornhauser, 1979: pp.986-7), lawyers differ enormously and may, by and large, facilitate dispute settlement out of court (Eekelaar et al, 2000; Hunter, 2003). Some research in the UK suggests that family lawyers may acknowledge a place in their practices for traditional non-legal discourses such as welfare and morality, operationalizing these discourses in legal terms (for example, Neale and Smart, 1997). In contrast, Austin Sarat and William Felstiner's research in the US (1995) suggests that lawyers may resist engaging with their clients' emotional and moral processes, although they do participate in the process of their client's forging of an identity in the divorce process. As Smart suggested in 1995, the new norms of parenting law have been promoted not only by mediators but also by many lawyers who have embraced these norms (see also Neilson, 2002).

The most significant challenge to Mnookin and Kornhauser's 1979 insights has perhaps been in relation to the notion that private ordering happens in 'the shadow of the law'. Recent studies suggest that modern family law is characterized by complexity, fragmentation, and a variety of processes and it is therefore increasingly difficult to state at any level of generality its nature and effects. The top-down quality of the 'shadow of the law' notion assumes that parties pay attention to legal norms and attend to law in the same way. Yet this assumption may not reflect the current complexity of family law processes, nor the extent to which law's shadow is mediated by many other factors, including social location as well as legal aid policies, court procedures, professional styles (Dewar and Parker, 1999) and communities of legal practice (Mather et al., 2001). As John Dewar points out (2000: p. 74), 'the very meaning given to legal rules may vary according to where in the system they are being applied', whether in private ordering or litigation, whether with or without legal advice. Dewar also argues that the new role for family law challenges Mnookin and Kornhauser's 'shadow of the law' metaphor: 'gone is the idea that the role of law is to facilitate and implement private decisions: it now seeks to influence the decisions themselves' (Dewar, 1998: p. 477). Helen Reece has provided a basis for this argument in *Divorcing Responsibly*.

Finally, a new addition to scholarship in this area focuses on the role of children in dispute resolution processes. This development has been influenced by the burgeoning socio-legal research on children's experiences of divorce, which indicates that children value the opportunity to participate in post-separation decision-making and feel disempowered when they are not consulted about arrangements that affect them (Smith, Taylor and Tapp, 2003; Smart, Neale and Wade, 2001). Based on these findings, researchers criticized the legal system's failure to listen to children's voices or provide a space for children's agency (James and Richards, 1999; Smart, 2002). Family law scholarship also challenged the paternalism of the welfare discourse underpinning custody laws and its construction of children as inevitable victims of divorce (Smart, Neale and Wade, 2001), suggesting that exclusion of children from decision-making processes was more about 'containing' adult anxieties than protecting children (Day Sclater and Piper, 2001; Smith, Taylor and Tapp, 2003). Since then, a number of countries have developed child-inclusive dispute resolution policies, including mediation practices that incorporate children's views into the negotiation process (McIntosh, 2004; Day

Sclater and Piper, 2001). Despite these shifts, Felicity Kaganas and Alson Diduck (Chapter 18) argue that children's citizenship remains 'incomplete'. Their examination reveals that recent regulatory strategies around post-separation parenting involve a blending of paradigms, which combines the traditional image of the child as a passive victim of parental choices with a more modern idea of children as active citizens with power to shape their environment. Kaganas and Diduck's review suggests that while children are beginning to be included in the legal process, the role afforded them remains well short of constituting a 'radical reconstruction' of childhood in family law (Kaganas and Diduck, p. 512).

Conclusion

The tendency for family law debates to be subject to political influences rather than attentive to research (Graycar, 2000; Hunter, 2003) has been highlighted in recent years, and is evidenced by the impact that the fathers' rights lobby has had on family law reform (Boyd and Young, 2002; Kaye and Tolmie, 1998; Smart, 2004). Socio-legal research on family law has the potential to redress demands for inappropriate legal responses, and indeed we have argued previously that research can temper the extent to which policy reforms respond to the anecdotes and anger of disaffected consumers of the family law system (Rhoades and Boyd, 2004). This kind of work has proved increasingly important to policymakers who draw on the research insights of socio-legal scholars to inform their design of regulatory strategies. For example, as our population ages, governments will need to know how families provide care for their members and who they see as worthy of this care (Maclean and Eekelaar, 2004), and with the rise of active parenting by fathers, lawmakers look to the studies of post-separation families to understand the factors that make shared custody a viable arrangement for children (Smart, 2002).

The scholarship represented in this volume captures some of the key thinking and debates of the past thirty years about law and the family, including questions of who is a family and how should law support them. The selected essays cover a broad range of projects with which law has been engaged, from recognizing relationship status to promoting responsible behaviour, constraining maternal discourses to containing parental anxieties. Socio-legal analyses have examined the multiple ways in which law shapes our ideas about what families are and our understandings of what families do, critically engaging with proposed policy goals and exposing the material effects of past legal interventions, and revealing the gaps between law's assumptions and the lived realities of those affected by it. The work represented here also reflects on wider social injustices that come within the purview of family law, challenging the resort to law and legal processes as the solution to structural inequalities faced by family members. As we hope this volume illustrates, the relationship between the family in law and family practices is a complex one that law and society scholars are especially well-equipped to study.

References

Arnup, Katherine and Susan Boyd (1995), 'Familial Disputes? Sperm Donors, Lesbian Mothers, and Legal Parenthood', in Didi Herman and Carl Stychin, (eds) *Legal Inversions: Lesbians, Gay Men, and the Politics of Law*. Philadelphia: Temple University Press, 77–101.

Barrett, Michèle and Mary McIntosh (1982), *The Anti-Social Family*. London: Verso.
Beck, Ulrich and Elisabeth Beck-Gernsheim (1995), *The Normal Chaos of Love*. Cambridge: Polity Press.
Boyd, Susan B. (1989), 'Child Custody, Ideologies and Employment', 3(1) *Canadian Journal of Women and the Law*, 111–133.
Boyd, Susan B. (1996), 'Is There an Ideology of Motherhood in (Post)Modern Child Custody Law?' 5(4) *Social and Legal Studies*, 495–521.
Boyd, Susan B. (1999), 'Family, Law and Sexuality: Feminist Engagements', 8(3) *Social and Legal Studies*, 369–390.
Boyd, Susan B. (2004), 'Legal Regulation of Families in Changing Societies', in Austin Sarat, (ed.) *The Blackwell Companion to Law and Society*, Malden, MA: Blackwell Publishing, 255–270.
Cammack, Mark, Lawrence A. Young, and Tim Heaton (1996),. 'Legislating Social Change in an Islamic Society – Indonesia's Marriage Law', 44 *The American Journal of Comparative Law*, 45–73.
Carbone, June (2000), *From Partners to Parents: The Second Revolution in Family Law*. New York: Columbia University Press.
Chunn, Dorothy (1992), *From Punishment to Doing Good: Family Courts and Socialized Justice in Ontario, 1880-1940*, Toronto: University of Toronto Press.
Collier, Richard (2001), 'In Search of the "Good Father": Law, Family Practices and the Normative Reconstruction of Parenthood' 22 *Studies in Law, Politics and Society,* 133–169.
Collier, Richard (1995). '"Waiting Till Father Gets Home": The Reconstruction of Fatherhood in Family Law', 4 *Social & Legal Studies* 5–30.
Cossman, Brenda (1994). 'Family Inside/Out', 44(1) *University of Toronto Law Journal*, 1–39.
Cossman, Brenda (2002). 'Family Feuds: Neo-Liberal and Neo-Conservative Visions of the Reprivatization Project', in Brenda Cossman and Judy Fudge (2002), *Privatization, Law, and the Challenge to Feminism*, Toronto: University of Toronto Press, 169–217.
Cossman, Brenda and Judy Fudge (2002), *Privatization, Law, and the Challenge to Feminism*, Toronto: University of Toronto Press.
Day Sclater, Shelley (1997). 'Narratives of Divorce', 19 *Journal of Social Welfare and Family Law*, 423–441.
Day Sclater, Shelley and Christine Piper (2001), 'Social Exclusion and the Welfare of the Child', *Journal of Law and Society*, 409–429.
Dewar, John (1998), 'The Normal Chaos of Family Law', 61(4) *Modern Law Review*, 467–485.
Dewar, John (2000), 'Family Law and Its Discontents', 14 *International Journal of Law, Policy and the Family*, 59–85.
Dewar, John (2003). 'Families', in Peter Cane and Mark Tushnet, (eds), *The Oxford Handbook of Legal Studies*, Oxford: Oxford University Press, 413–434.
Dewar, John and Stephen Parker (1999), 'The impact of the new Part VII Family Law Act 1975', 13 *Australian Journal of Family Law*, 96–116.
Diduck, Alison (2003), *Law's Families*, London: LexisNexis Butterworths.
Donzelot, Jacques (1979), *The Policing of Families*, New York: Pantheon. Translated by Robert Hurley.
Eekelaar, John (1978), *Family Law and Social Policy*, London: Weidenfeld & Nicholson.
Eekelaar, John and Mavis Maclean (2004), 'Marriage and the Moral Bases of Personal Relationships', 31 *Journal of Law and Society*, 510–538.
Eekelaar, John, Mavis Maclean, and Sarah Beinart (2000), *Family Lawyers: The Divorce Work of Solicitors*, Oxford: Hart Publishing.
Fineman, Martha (1988), 'Dominant Discourse, Professional Language, and Legal Change in Child Custody Decisionmaking', 101 *Harvard Law Review*, 727–774.

Fineman, Martha L. (1989–1990), 'Societal Factors Affecting the Creation of Legal Rules for Distribution of Property at Divorce', 23 *Family Law Quarterly*, 279–299.
Fehlberg, Belinda (1997), 'Money and Marriage: Sexually Transmitted Debt in England', 11 *International Journal of Law, Policy and the Family*, 320–343.
Fishbayn, Lisa (1999), 'Litigating the Right to Culture: Family Law in the New South Africa', 13 *International Journal of Law, Policy and the Family*, 147–173.
Foucault, Michel (1978), *History of Sexuality, Vol. I: An Introduction*, New York: Random House. Translation by Robert Hurley.
Fournier, Pascale (2001), 'The Erasure of Islamic Difference in Canadian and American Family Law Adjudication', 10 *Journal of Law and Policy*, 51–95.
Freeman, Michael D.A. (1985). 'Towards a Critical Theory of Family Law', 38 *Current Legal Problems*, 153–185.
Galanter, Marc (1992), 'Law Abounding: Legalisation around the North Atlantic', 55 *Modern Law Review*, 1–24.
Gavigan, Shelley A.M. (1993), 'Paradise Lost, Paradox Revisited: The Implications of Familial Ideology for Feminist, Lesbian and Gay Engagement to Law', 31(3) *Osgoode Hall Law Journal*, 589–624.
Gavigan, Shelley A.M. (1999), 'Legal Forms, Family Forms, Gendered Norms: What is a Spouse?' 14(1) *Canadian Journal of Law and Society*, 127–157.
Giddens, Anthony (1992), *The Transformation of Intimacy*, Cambridge: Polity Press.
Gillis, John (1997), *A World of Their Own Making: A History of Myth and Ritual in Family Life*, Oxford and New York: Oxford University Press.
Goldstein, Joseph, Anna Freud and Albert J. Solnit (1973), *Beyond the Best Interests of the Child*, New York: Free Press.
Graycar, Reg (1995), 'The Gender of Judgments: An Introduction', in Margaret Thornton (ed.) *Public and Private: Feminist Legal Debates*, Melbourne: Oxford University Press.
Graycar, Reg (1997), 'Hoovering as a Hobby and Other Stories: Gendered Assessment of Personal Injury Damages', 31 *University of British Columbia Law Review*, 17–35.
Graycar, Reg (2000), 'Law Reform by Frozen Chook: Family Law Reform for the New Millennium?', 24 *Melbourne University Law Review*, 737–755.
Greatbatch, David and Robert Dingwall (1999), 'The Marginalization of Domestic Violence in Divorce Mediation', 13 *International Journal of Law Policy and the Family*, 174–190.
Grillo, Trina (1991), 'The mediation alternative: process dangers for women', 100 *Yale Law Journal*, 1545–1610.
Harvison Young, Alison (1998), 'Reconceiving the Family: Challenging the Paradigm of the Exclusive Family', 6 *American University Journal of Gender & Law*, 505–554.
Harvison Young, Alison (2001), 'The changing family, rights discourse and the Supreme Court of Canada', 80 *Canadian BarReview*, 750–792.
Herman, Didi (1990), 'Are We Family? Lesbian Rights and Women's Liberation', 28(4) *Osgoode Hall Law Journal*, 789–815.
Hunter, Rosemary (2003), 'Adversarial Mythologies: Policy Assumptions and Research Evidence in Family Law', 30 *Journal of Law and Society*, 156–176.
Humphreys, Cathy and Ravi K. Thiara (2003), 'Neither Justice nor Protection: Women's Experiences of Post-Separation Violence', 25 *Journal of Social Welfare and Family Law*, 195–214.
Humphreys, Cathy and Christine Harrison (2003), 'Squaring the Circle – Contact and Domestic Violence', *Family Law*, 419–423.
James, Adrian L. and Martin P.M. Richards (1999), 'Sociological perspectives, family policy, family law and children: Adult thinking and sociological tinkering', 21 *Journal of Social Welfare and Family Law*, 23–39.

Kaganas, Felicity and Alison Diduck (2004), 'Incomplete Citizens: Changing Images of Post-Separation Children', 67 *Modern Law Review*, 959–981.

Kaganas, Felicity and Shelley Day Sclater (2004), 'Contact Disputes: Narrative Constructions of 'Good' Parents', 12 *Feminist Legal Studies*, 1–27.

Katzen, Hayley (2000), 'It's a Family Matter, not a Police Matter: The Enforcement of Protection Orders', 14 *Australian Journal of Family Law*, 119–141.

Kaye, Miranda and Julia Tolmie (1998), 'Fathers' Rights Groups in Australia and their Engagement with Issues in Family Law', 12 *Australian Journal of Family Law* 19–68.

Kaye, Miranda, Julie Stubbs and Julia Tolmie (2003). 'Domestic violence and child contact arrangements', 17 *Australian Journal of Family Law*, 93–133.

Kelly, Fiona (2004), 'Nuclear Norms or Fluid Families? Incorporating Lesbian and Gay Parents and their Children into Canadian Family Law', 21(1) *Canadian Journal of Family Law*, 133–178.

Kline, Marlee (1992), 'Child Welfare Law, "Best Interests of the Child" Ideology, and First Nations', 30 *Osgoode Hall Law Journal*, 375–425.

Kline, Marlee (1993), 'Complicating the Ideology of Motherhood: Child Welfare Law and First Nation Women', 18 *Queen's Law Journal*, 306–342.

Law Commission of Canada, *Beyond Conjugality: Recognizing and Supporting Close Personal Adult Relationships*, Ottawa: Law Commission of Canada.

Lessard, Hester (2001), 'The Empire of the Lone Mother: Parental Rights, Child Welfare, and State Restructuring', 39 *Osgoode Hall Law Journal*, 717–770.

Lessard, Hester (2004). 'Mothers, Fathers, and Naming: Reflections on the *Law* Equality Framework and *Trociuk* v. *British Columbia (Attorney General)*', 16(1) *Canadian Journal of Women and the Law*, 165–211.

Lewis, Jane (2001), 'Debates and Issues Regarding Marriage and Cohabitation in the British and American Literature', 15 *International Journal of Law, Policy and the Family*, 159–184.

Maclean, Mavis and John Eekelaar (2004), 'The Obligations and Expectations of Couples Within Families: Three Modes of Interaction', 26 *Journal of Social Welfare and Family Law*, 117–130.

Mahoney, Martha (1991), 'Legal images of battered women: Redefining the issue of separation', 90 *Michigan Law Review* 1–94.

Martin, Claude and Irene Thery (2001), 'The PACS and Marriage and Cohabitation in France', 15 *International Journal of Law, Policy and the Family*, 135–158.

Mason, Mary Ann, Mark A. Fine, and Sarah Carnochan (2001), 'Family Law in the New Millennium: For Whose Families?' 22(7) *Journal of Family Issues*, 859–881.

McIntosh, Jennifer (2000), 'Child-Inclusive Divorce Mediation: Report on a Qualitative Research Study', 18 *Mediation Quarterly*, 55–69.

Millbank, Jenni and Reg Graycar (2000), 'The Bride Wore Pink...to the Property (Relationships) Act', 17 *Canadian Journal of Family Law*, 227–282.

Millbank, Jenni (1997), 'Lesbians, Child Custody, and the Long Lingering Gaze of the Law', in S.B. Boyd, (ed.), *Challenging the Public/Private Divide: Feminism, Law, and Public Policy*, Toronto: University of Toronto Press, 280–303.

Morgan, David (1996), *Family Connections*, Cambridge: Polity Press.

Mnookin, Robert H. (1975), 'Child-Custody Adjudication: Judicial Functions in the Face of Indeterminacy', 39 *Law and Contemporary Problems*, 226–93.

Mnookin, Robert H. and Lewis Kornhauser (1979), 'Bargaining in the Shadow of the Law: The case of divorce', 88 *Yale Law Journal*, 950–997.

Monk, Daniel (2004), 'Problematising Home Education: Challenging "Parental Rights" and "Socialisation"', 24(4) *Legal Studies*, 568–598.

Mosoff, Judith (1997), '"A Jury Dressed in Medical White and Judicial Black": Mothers with Mental Health Histories in Child Welfare and Custody', in S.B. Boyd, (ed.), *Challenging the Public/Private Divide: Feminism, Law, and Public Policy*, Toronto: University of Toronto Press, 227–252.

Mossman, Mary Jane (1997), 'Child Support or Support of Children? Re-Thinking "Public" and "Private" in Family Law', 46 *University of New Brunswick Law Journal*, 63.

Mossman, Mary Jane (2004), *Families and the Law in Canada: Cases and Commentary*, Toronto: Emond Montgomery Publications Limited.

Mossman, Mary Jane (1994), 'Running Hard to Stand Still: The Paradox of Family Law Reform', 17 *Dalhousie Law Journal*, 5–34.

Neale, Bren and Carol Smart (1997),. '"Good" and "Bad" Lawyers? Struggling in the Shadow of the New Law', 19 *Journal of Social Welfare and Family Law*, 377–402.

Neave, Marcia (1994). 'Resolving the dilemma of difference: A critique of "The role of private ordering in family law"', 44 *University of Toronto Law Journal*, 97–131.

Neilson, Linda C. (2002), 'Comparative Analysis of Law in Theory and Law in Action in Partner Abuse Cases: What do the Data Tell Us?' 26 *Studies in Law, Politics, and Society*, 141–187.

O'Donovan, Katherine (2002), '"Real" Mothers for Abandoned Children', 36 *Law & Society Review*, 347–377.

O'Donovan, Katherine (1988), 'A Right to Know One's Genetic Parentage?' 2 *International Journal of Law & the Family*, 27–45.

O'Donovan, Katherine (1985), *Sexual Divisions in Law*, London: Weidenfeld and Nicholson.

Olsen, Frances E. (1983), 'The Family and the Market: A Study of Ideology and Legal Reform', 96 *Harvard Law Review*, 1497–1578.

Olsen, Frances E. (1985), 'The Myth of State Intervention in the Family', 18 *University of Michigan Journal of Law Reform*, 835–64.

Parashar, Archana (2002), 'Just Family Law: A Basic Human Right of All Indian Women', 24 *Delhi Law Review*, **1–21.**

Parker, Stephen (1992), 'Rights and Utility in Anglo-Australian Family Law', 55 *Modern Law Review*, 311–330.

Perry, Twila L. (1999), 'Race matters: change, choice, and family law at the millennium', 33 *Family Law Quarterly*, 461–474.

Piper, Christine (1996), 'Divorce Reform and the Image of the Child', 23 *Journal of Law and Society*, 364–382.

Polikoff, Nancy D. (1989/90), 'This Child Does Have Two Mothers: Redefining Parenthood to Meet the Needs of Children in Lesbian-Mother and Other Nontraditional Families', 78 *Georgetown Law Journal*, 459–575.

Reece, Helen (2003), *Divorcing Responsibly*, Oxford: Hart Publishing.

Rhoades, Helen (2002), 'The "No Contact Mother": Reconstructions of Motherhood in the Era of the "New Father"', 16 *International Journal of Law, Policy and the Family*, 71–94.

Rhoades, Helen and Susan B. Boyd (2004), 'Reforming Custody Laws: A Comparative Study', 18 *International Journal of Law, Policy and the Family*, 119–146.

Roberts, Dorothy E. (1995), 'The Genetic Tie', 62 *University of Chicago Law Review*, 209–273.

Robson, Ruthann (1994), 'Resisting the family: Repositioning lesbians in legal theory', 19 *Signs*, 975–96.

Rose, Nikolas (1987), 'Beyond the public/private division: Law, power and the family', 14 *Journal of Law and Society*, 61–76.

Rwezaura, Bart (1998), 'Competing "Images" of Childhood in the Social and Legal Systems of Contemporary Sub-Saharan Africa', 12 *International Journal of Law, Policy and the Family*, 253–278.

Sarat, Austin (2004), 'Vitality Amidst Fragmentation: On the Emergence of Postrealist Law and Society Scholarship', in Austin Sarat, (ed.) *The Blackwell Companion to Law and Society*, Malden, MA: Blackwell Publishing, 1–11.

Sarat, Austin and William Felstiner (1995), *Divorce Lawyers and Their Clients: Power and Meaning in the Legal Process,* New York: Oxford University Press.

Shachar, Ayelet (1998), 'Group Identity and Women's Rights in Family Law: The Perils of Multicultural Accommodation', 6(3) *Journal of Political Philosophy*, 285–305.

Shanley, Mary Lyndon (2001), *Making Babies, Making Families: What Matters Most in an Age of Reproductive Technologies, Surrogacy, Adoption, and Same-Sex and Unwed Parents*, Boston: Beacon Press.

Sheehan, Grania (2002), 'Financial Aspects of the Divorce Transition in Australia: Recent Empirical Findings', 16 *International Journal of Law, Policy and the Family*, 95–126.

Sheldon, Sally (2003), 'Unwilling Fathers and Abortion: Terminating Men's Child Support Obligations', 66 *Modern Law Review*, 175–194.

Smart, Carol (1989), *Feminism and the Power of Law*, London: Routledge.

Smart, Carol (2004), 'Equal shares: rights for fathers or recognition for children?' 24(4) *Critical Social Policy*, 484–503.

Smart, Carol (2002). 'From Children's Shoes to Children's Voices', 40 *Family Court Review*, 305–317.

Smart, Carol (1991), 'The Legal and Moral Ordering of Child Custody', 18 *Journal of Law & Society*, 485–500.

Smart, Carol (1995), 'Losing the Battle for Another Voice? The Case of Family Law', 18(2) *Dalhousie Law Journal*, 173–195.

Smart, Carol (1984), *The Ties That Bind: Law, Marriage and the Reproduction of Patriarchal Relations*, London: Routledge and Kegan Paul.

Smart, Carol (1987). '"There is of course the distinction dictated by nature": Law and the Problem of Paternity', in Michelle Stanworth, (ed.) *Reproductive Technologies: Gender, Motherhood and Medicine*, Minneapolis: University of Minnesota Press, 98–117.

Smart, Carol and Bren Neale (1999), *Family Fragments?* Cambridge: Polity Press.

Smart, Carol, Bren Neale and Amanda Wade (2001), *The Changing Experience of Childhood: Families and Divorce*, Cambridge: Polity Press.

Smith, Anne B., Nicola J. Taylor, and Pauline Tapp (2003), 'Rethinking children's involvement in decision-making after parental separation', 10 *Childhood*, 203–218.

Thery, Irene (1986), '"The Interest of the Child" and the Regulation of the Post-divorce Family', 14 *International Journal of the Sociology of Law*, 341–358.

Trebilcock, Michael J. and Rosemin Keshvani (1991), 'The Role of Private Ordering in Family Law: A Law and Economics Perspective', 41 *University of Toronto Law Journal*, 533–591.

Triseliotis, John (1973), In Search of Origins, London: Routledge and Kegan Paul.

Wallbank, Julie (2004), 'The Role of Rights and Utility in Instituting a Child's Rights to Know Her Genetic History', 13(2) *Social and Legal Studies*, 245–264.

Weitzman, Lenore (1985), *The Divorce Revolution: The Unintended Social and Economic Consequences for Women and Children in America*, New York: Free Press.

Williams, Joan (2000), *Unbending Gender: Why Family and Work Conflict and What to Do About It*, New York: Oxford University Press.

Wilson, Sarah (1997), 'Identity, Genealogy and the Social Family: The Case of Donor Insemination', 11 *International Journal of Law, Policy and the Family*, 270–297.

Part I
Thinking about Families and Law

[1]

THE MYTH OF STATE INTERVENTION IN THE FAMILY

Frances E. Olsen*

Most people concede that there are times when state officials should intervene in the private family. Doctrines of family privacy are no longer thought to justify societal neglect of beaten wives or abused children. Yet society continues to use the ideal of the private family to orient policy. It seems important therefore to examine the concept of state intervention in the private family. In this essay, I argue that the private family is an incoherent ideal and that the rhetoric of nonintervention is more harmful than helpful.

Although most people accept in general the assertion that the state should not intervene in the family, they qualify the assertion with the caveat that the state should sometimes intervene in order to correct inequality or prevent abuse. I refer to this widely-accepted caveat as the "protective intervention argument" against nonintervention in the family.

This essay presents a different argument against the policy of nonintervention in the family. It suggests that the terms "intervention" and "nonintervention" are largely meaningless. The terms do not accurately describe any set of policies, and as general principles, "intervention" and "nonintervention" are indeterminate. I refer to this argument as the "incoherence argument."

A useful comparison can be drawn between arguments against a policy of nonintervention in the private family and arguments against a policy of nonintervention in the free market.[1] The pol-

---

* Acting Professor of Law, University of California at Los Angeles. B.A., 1968, Goddard College; J.D., 1971, University of Colorado; S.J.D., 1984, Harvard University.

I am grateful to Mary Joe Frug, Grace Blumberg, and Bill Alford for helpful comments on earlier drafts. I would also like to express my appreciation to the summer, 1984, Fellows of the University of Wisconsin Legal History Colloquium sponsored by the National Endowment for the Humanities for convincing me that more had to be said about state intervention in the family; to the editors of the *University of Michigan Journal of Law Reform* who, with grace and good humor, coaxed and badgered me into writing this essay; to Ken Kimmel for his research assistance; and to the Research Committee of the UCLA Academic Senate for financial support.

1. I originally drew this comparison in Olsen, *The Family and the Market: A Study of Ideology and Legal Reform*, 96 HARV. L. REV. 1497 (1983).

icy of nonintervention in the free market, often referred to as laissez faire, was pursued by many American courts in the nineteenth and early twentieth centuries. The group of scholars known as legal realists played an important role in discrediting the legal theories that supported laissez faire. Their arguments form a useful contrast and resource for the arguments I present in this essay.

The protective intervention argument applies in a similar manner to both laissez faire and nonintervention in the family: whenever either the market or the family misfunctions, the state should intervene to correct inequality and protect the defenseless. The most common and easily accepted argument against laissez faire is that the free market sometimes breaks down or works to the serious disadvantage of particular individuals or groups; state intervention is then necessary to protect the interests of the weaker economic actors and of society in general. This parallels the protective intervention argument regarding the family. Sometimes the family misfunctions; instead of being a haven that protects and nurtures family members, the family may become a center of oppression and exploitation.[2] When this happens the state should step in to prevent abuse and to protect the rights of the individual family members. Both the market version and the family version of this protective intervention argument presuppose that it would be possible for the state to remain neutral, but present reasons that the state should not do so.

The incoherence argument against nonintervention in the family parallels the legal realists' argument against laissez faire. Both laissez faire and nonintervention in the family are false ideals. As long as a state exists and enforces any laws at all, it makes political choices. The state cannot be neutral or remain uninvolved, nor would anyone want the state to do so. The staunchest supporters of laissez faire always insisted that the state protect their property interests and that courts enforce contracts and adjudicate torts.[3] They took this state action for granted and chose not to consider such protection a form of state intervention. Yet the so-called "free market" does not function except for such laws; the free market could not exist independently of the state. The enforcement of property, tort, and contract law requires constant political choices that may

2. *See* Minow, *Beyond State Intervention in the Family: For Baby Jane Doe*, 18 U. MICH. J.L. REF. 933, 948-50 (1985).

3. *See* Cohen, *The Basis of Contract*, 46 HARV. L. REV. 553, 561-62 (1933).

benefit one economic actor, usually at the expense of another. As Robert Hale pointed out more than a half century ago, these legal decisions "are bound to affect the distribution of income and the direction of economic activities."[4] Any choice the courts make will affect the market, and there is seldom any meaningful way to label one choice intervention and the other laissez faire. When the state enforces any of these laws it must make political decisions that affect society.

Similarly, the staunchest opponents of state intervention in the family will insist that the state reinforce parents' authority over their children. Familiar examples of this reinforcement include state officials returning runaway children and courts ordering incorrigible children to obey their parents or face incarceration in juvenile facilities. These state actions are not only widely supported, they are generally not considered state intervention in the family. Another category of state policies is even less likely to be thought of as intervention. Supporters of nonintervention insist that the state protect families from third-party interference. Imagine their reaction if the state stood idly by while doctors performed non-emergency surgery without the knowledge or permission of a ten-year-old patient's parents, or if neighbors prepared to take the child on their vacation against the wishes of the parents, or if the child decided to go live with his fourth grade teacher. Once the state undertakes to prevent such third-party action, the state must make numerous policy choices, such as what human grouping constitutes a family and what happens if parents disagree. These choices are bound to affect the decisions people make about forming families, the distribution of power within the family, and the assignment of tasks and roles among family members. The state is responsible for the background rules that affect people's domestic behaviors. Because the state is deeply implicated in the formation and functioning of families, it is nonsense to talk about whether the state does or does not intervene in the family. Neither "intervention" nor "nonintervention" is an accurate description of any particular set of policies, and the terms obscure rather than clarify the policy choices that society makes.

---

4. Hale, *Coercion and Distribution in a Supposedly Non-Coercive State*, 38 POL. SCI. Q. 470 (1923). *See* Kennedy, *Form and Substance in Private Law Adjudication*, 89 HARV. L. REV. 1685, 1748-49 (1976).

I. THE PROTECTIVE INTERVENTION ARGUMENT

To understand the incoherence argument, it is useful to examine in more detail the protective intervention argument—the argument that nonintervention would be possible but is not always a good idea. The protective intervention argument is an argument in favor of selective intervention.[5] In exceptional situations, the state should intervene in the family to protect the interests of society and of the family members who may be at risk; aside from such exceptional situations, state intervention should ordinarily be limited to routine matters such as setting formal requirements for marriage licenses and providing public schooling for children.[6]

According to the usual version of the protective intervention argument, state intervention beyond routine matters should be carefully limited. Excessive or unnecessary intervention jeopardizes people's freedom and interferes with family intimacy. Because of the risks inherent in state intervention, say proponents of protective intervention, safeguards should be devised to protect against government abuse and to prevent unnecessary expansion of state intervention. As long as proper safeguards exist, however, state intervention can be useful—an important force for good.

---

5. The protective intervention argument presupposes that the concept of state intervention in the family is coherent and meaningful. I argue that the concept is instead incoherent and meaningless.

First, it makes no logical sense to consider the policies referred to as "nonintervention" any less interventionist than many policies referred to as "intervention." By and large, policies supporting the status quo are referred to as nonintervention and attempts to change the status quo are called intervention; "intervention" and "nonintervention" are inappropriate and misleading terms to use to characterize these policies. Moreover, the policies referred to as "intervention" and "nonintervention" have a wide range of overlap; the same policy will be referred to as intervention by some and nonintervention by others. There is no objective or rational basis upon which to determine who is correct, because there is no logical basis for considering any particular set of policies nonintervention.

The protective intervention argument, however, presupposes that there is a basis for distinguishing intervention from nonintervention and that the terms have meaning. In my discussion of the protective intervention argument, I find it convenient occasionally to use the term "intervention" as though it had meaning. When I use the term, I intend for it to convey the range of contradictory meanings that people assign in everyday use of language.

6. As I argue *infra*, pp. 848-54, these "routine" matters can have an important influence on family roles and power relations within the family.

A. *Families Can Malfunction*

The argument in favor of selective state intervention is based on the notion that although families ought to be safe, supportive, and loving, some families at some times are not.[7] The family is supposed to be a warm, nurturant enclave governed by an ethic of altruism and caring—a haven protecting its members from the dangers of an authoritarian state and from the anarchistic intrusions of private third parties. Proponents of protective intervention recognize that in some unfortunate situations, the family can cease to be a haven and become instead, "a center of oppression, raw will and authority, violence and brutality, where the powerful economically and sexually subordinate and exploit the powerless."[8]

B. *State Protection of Individuals*

When a family malfunctions it may be important for the state to protect an individual from the private oppression that members of families sometimes inflict on each other. The protective intervention argument justifies state intervention in the family to protect children from abuse or serious neglect. State officials can remove children from their families if the children have been physically or sexually abused. In cases of child neglect, the state may send social workers into the children's homes or remove the children, temporarily or permanently, for their protection. Such state protection can include ordering medical care, even against the parents' religious scruples. These policies are generally considered to be a form of state intervention in the family, but accepted as intervention that is justified, indeed necessary.

Until recent years, state protection for battered wives was also considered state intervention in the family—again, perhaps justified intervention, but intervention nonetheless. The protective intervention argument characterizes such state protection as a

7. A more radical strand of criticism might argue that the nuclear family is a seething hothouse or an oppressive structure that will *often* become destructive of individual members.

8. Minow, *supra* note 2, at 948. Professor Gerald Frug describes the city similarly as an enclave protecting individual freedom or alternatively a threat jeopardizing individual freedom. *See* Frug, *The City as a Legal Concept*, 93 HARV. L. REV. 1057, 1121 (1980). He suggests that "any form of group power intermediate between a centralized state and the individual" may have a precarious existence in a liberal political state. *See id.*

beneficial and necessary form of intervention into a family that has problems. Few people today would openly oppose state enforcement of rape and battery laws against spouses.[9] If providing shelter houses and legal aid to battered wives constitutes state intervention, many argue that such intervention is fully justified to protect individual wives from being oppressed by their husbands. In the exceptional cases in which families misfunction, the state should step in to protect the powerless.

This protective intervention argument begins to blend into the incoherence argument when people dispute whether such protection should be considered intervention at all. Some people would assert that when the family relationship has broken down, so has any justifiable claim to family privacy, and that state protection of the individual no longer constitutes intervention into the family. Indeed, proponents of this view might argue that it would be state intervention to try to keep the family together—for example, not to allow estranged spouses to get a divorce. In such arguments, the idea that the privacy of the family unit should be protected from state intervention begins to be replaced by the notion that what merits protection is the privacy of the individual regarding sexuality, procreation, and the formation of intimate, family-like relationships.[10] I consider this

---

9. People struggling to eliminate the marriage exemption from rape laws tell me, however, that they find a great many people who *do* oppose the enforcement of rape laws against husbands. The National Clearinghouse on Marital Rape sent me a packet of newspaper clippings from all over the country that are filled with amazing quotations from state legislators. Opposition to marital rape laws range from assertions that "sex is part of the [marriage] contract," Tex. Rep. Patricia Hill, *quoted in* the Times-Herald, May 21, 1985 (Dallas, Tex.), and "I don't know how you can have a sexual act and call it forcible rape in a marriage situation," Alaska Sen. Paul Fischer, *quoted in* Daily News, Mar. 21, 1985 (Juneau, Alaska), to concerns with false charges and "blackmail." Legislators argue that the "state shouldn't be going behind the bedroom doors." Tex. Rep. Patricia Hill, *quoted in* Times-Herald, *supra. See also* S.D. Rep. Joe Barnett, *reported in* Argus Leader, Mar. 2, 1985 (Sioux Falls, S.D.) (keep government out of the bedroom). Spousal rape laws are "an absolute intrusion into family life," S.D. Sen. Thomas Ruby, *quoted in* Capital Journal, Mar. 15, 1985, (Pierre, S.D.). They would pit family members against one another, S.D. Rep. Bernie Christenson, *reported in* Capital Journal, Feb. 14, 1985 (Pierre, S.D.) and "erode at family life," S.D. Sen. Harold Halverson, *quoted in* Argus Leader, Feb. 28, 1985 (Sioux Falls, S.D.). "I still believe in the old traditional bond of marriage." Alaska Sen. Paul Fischer, *quoted in* Daily News, *supra* (copies of all clippings on file with U. MICH. J.L. REF.).

10. This shift from the concept of a private family into which the state should not intervene to the concept of individual privacy regarding intimate relationships corresponds to a more general shift I have referred to as the "liberalization of the family." *See* Olsen, *The Politics of Family Law,* 2 LAW AND INEQUALITY 1, 6-8 (1984). There I discuss the shift that has taken place from seeing the family as an organic group to seeing it as a contract among individuals. *See id.* at 11-12.

For an argument that this individual privacy right should be grounded in individual autonomy and not in marriage and family, see Eichbaum, *Towards an Autonomy-Based*

concept of individual privacy to be part of the protective intervention argument—that state intervention is sometimes justified—because although the privacy argument redefines state intervention, it still considers intervention and nonintervention coherent, meaningful concepts.

C. *Safeguards Against Excessive Intervention*

The protective intervention argument usually treats nonintervention as the norm and intervention as an exception.[11] As one jurist put it: "The normal behavior of husband and wife or parents and children towards each other is beyond the law—as long as the family is 'healthy.' The law comes in when things go wrong."[12]

People who support selective state intervention often assert that safeguards are necessary to protect families from excessive state intervention—attempts by the state to offer protection when it is not really necessary. Child abuse and neglect statutes typically provide that until behaviors pass some threshold, the family is to remain private and the state should not intrude. The Constitution has been held to supply additional protection to family privacy by requiring a clear and convincing showing of abuse or neglect before parental rights may be severed.[13] Physical or sexual abuse or serious neglect is usually necessary to trigger state intervention. This possibility of state intervention, even if it actually occurs only in rare exceptional cases, can play a significant role in keeping family behavior within reasonable bounds of decency.[14]

Divorce or legal separation may also be considered a sufficient trigger to justify state intervention that would otherwise not be allowed. For example, many people who would oppose such policies in an ongoing family believe that if parents separate, the

---

Theory of Constitutional Privacy: Beyond the Ideology of Familial Privacy, 14 HARV. C.R.-C.L. L. REV. 361 (1979).

11. A more radical version of the protective intervention argument might maintain that state intervention is frequently or always necessary to protect individuals from the inherent oppressiveness of the nuclear family. *See supra* note 7.

12. Kahn-Freund, *Editorial Foreword* to J. EEKELAAR, FAMILY SECURITY AND FAMILY BREAKDOWN at 7 (1971), *quoted in* Freeman, *Violence Against Women: Does the Legal System Provide Solutions or Itself Constitute the Problem?,* 3 CAN. J.F.L. 377, 387 (1980).

13. Santosky v. Kramer, 455 U.S. 745, 768-70 (1982).

14. The possibility of state action in more extreme cases can have a significant influence on everyday behavior within the family. *See, e.g.,* Minow, *supra* note 2, at 952-53.

state should order the noncustodial parent to provide financial support for his or her child in case the parent would not do so without a court order.[15] As long as they see safeguards, such as thresholds of family misbehavior or breakdown, to protect against excessive intervention, most people today support a certain level of protective intervention by the state.

II. THE INCOHERENCE ARGUMENT

The incoherence argument goes further and I believe is more fundamental than the protective intervention argument. The protective intervention argument treats nonintervention as a fully possible but sometimes unwise choice; the incoherence argument questions the basic coherence of the concepts intervention and nonintervention. The state defines the family and sets roles within the family; it is meaningless to talk about intervention or nonintervention, because the state constantly defines and redefines the family and adjusts and readjusts family roles. Nonintervention is a false ideal because it has no coherent meaning.

For example, suppose a good-natured, intelligent sovereign were to ascend the throne with a commitment to end state intervention in the family. Rather than being obvious, the policies she should pursue would be hopelessly ambiguous. Is she intervening if she makes divorces difficult, or intervening if she makes them easy? Does it constitute intervention or nonintervention to grant divorce at all? If a child runs away from her parents to go live with her aunt, would nonintervention require the sovereign to grant or to deny the parents' request for legal assistance to reclaim their child? Because complete agreement on family roles does not exist, and because these roles undergo change over time, the state cannot be said simply to ratify preexisting family roles. The state is continuously affecting the family by influencing the distribution of power among individuals.

The incoherence argument is more complex with regard to the family than with regard to the market. Because nonintervention in the family has been understood as a variety of things, demon-

15. *Compare, e.g.*, Anderson v. Anderson, 437 S.W.2d 704 (Mo. Ct. App. 1969) (ordering divorced father to pay for daughter's college education) *with* Roe v. Doe, 29 N.Y.2d 188, 272 N.E.2d 567, 324 N.Y.S.2d 71 (1971) (refusing to order father to support daughter's college education). In McGuire v. McGuire, 157 Neb. 226, 59 N.W.2d 336 (1953) the court refused to order spousal support for the wife in an ongoing marriage, although the circumstances of the parties were such that the court might well have awarded spousal support had there been a legal separation.

strating its incoherence becomes more complicated than demonstrating that laissez faire is incoherent with respect to the market. Laissez faire is incoherent because no apolitical or neutral way exists to enforce property, contract, or tort law; once the state undertakes to enforce any of these laws, courts are forced to make political choices that cannot help but have important effects on the market and on the direction of economic activities. The alternative of not enforcing any property, contract, and tort law—creating a "state of nature"—is unacceptable in the marketplace. Once one rules out a state of nature, the government can no longer keep "hands off" the market; the question becomes simply which particular policies the government shall support.

The greater complexity of the incoherence argument with respect to the family than with respect to the market makes it initially easier to see that the state is not a neutral arbiter when it deals with the family. Historically, the state bolstered the power of the father over his family. A policy-based refusal to bolster this power might well be considered "intervention"—whether justified under the protective intervention argument or considered obtrusive and unjustified.[16] Even today the state is often expected to enforce parents' authority over their children. To many who endorse hierarchical family relations, "nonintervention" seems to mean simply state support for the family member with power. "Nonintervention" loses much of its appeal if one thinks of it as mere reinforcement of the status quo. Moreover, because the status quo undergoes continual change, nonintervention in the hierarchical family cannot be coherent. Even if state officials attempted simply to support the status quo they would still be forced to make political choices that have important effects on the distribution of roles and power within a family.

In recent years, the state has been expected to treat the members of the family—especially the husband and wife—more as equals. With increasing juridical equality within the family, the parallel between laissez faire with respect to the market and nonintervention with respect to the family becomes closer. Complete juridical equality would require a new concept of state intervention and nonintervention. At least two radically different concepts are possible, though neither would be acceptable to most people and, as I will demonstrate, neither is coherent. One possibility, which I refer to as the Market Model, is based on

16. *See infra* p. 850.

enforcement of all laws, just as they are enforced in the market. Under this model, all rights and obligations would be enforced between family members the same way laws are enforced between strangers. In this manner the state could avoid direct support for family hierarchy. Nonintervention under the Market Model would be incoherent for the same reasons laissez faire is incoherent: enforcement of any property, tort, or contract law, whether between family members or strangers, requires political choices that necessarily affect the power of the individuals and groups involved and the direction of both their intimate and their commercial relations.

A second possible model of state "nonintervention" in a juridically equal family is non-enforcement or delegalization—no rights or obligations to be enforced between family members. I refer to this construct as the State of Nature Model. Unlike the situation regarding the market,[17] something approaching this model is acceptable to many as a form of "nonintervention" in the family. It can be demonstrated, however, that nonintervention under the State of Nature Model is also incoherent. First, because the "state of nature" would exist only within the family, the state would have to decide the boundaries of family. In addition, if the state of nature within the family were partial instead of complete, the state would have to decide which rights and obligations it would enforce within the family. These decisions require political choices that necessarily affect the roles and power within a family. Once the state undertakes to enforce some but not all rights and obligations, the state cannot avoid policy choices that will affect family life. No logical basis exists for identifying these state choices as either intervention or nonintervention.

A. *Introduction: Laissez Faire and Nonintervention*

As I have suggested, the incoherence argument against nonintervention in the family is both simpler and more complex than the corresponding argument against laissez faire in the market. An important claim of laissez faire was that the state could and should treat market actors as juridical equals and enforce evenhandedly uncontroversial neutral ground rules that would en-

17. In the market, virtually no one would find a state of nature acceptable. People insist that some form of tort, contract, and property law be enforced. *See supra* p. 836.

sure the protection of all.[18] The incoherence argument against laissez faire demonstrated that the ground rules were not and could not be made neutral and that they could not be enforced even-handedly. Opponents of laissez faire showed that policy issues arose constantly within every aspect of tort and contract law doctrine—that the kind of apolitical legal system that laissez faire envisioned and depended upon was a myth.[19]

In the case of the market, laissez faire seemed at least to produce a kind of state neutrality, because courts treated people as juridical equals. Workers and bosses were said to have identical rights to freedom of contract.[20] Legal formalism or conceptualism presupposed that it was possible for a legal system to be rational, objective, and principled—scientific rather than political. The failure of legal formalism or conceptualism rendered laissez faire incoherent.[21] Had it really been true that law could be apolitical, that contract law could simply enforce the will of the parties, and tort law simply require those at fault to compensate their victims, laissez faire might well have been coherent.[22] No one has come up with any plausible method for removing the need for political choice from law, however, and I consider it highly unlikely that any such method exists or could be devised.[23]

B. Nonintervention and the Hierarchical Family

The notion of nonintervention in the family is in a sense less plausible than laissez faire in the market. The ideal laissez-faire state would treat market actors as juridical equals; the state does not treat members of a family as juridical equals. Further,

18. I refer to laissez faire in the past tense because I am speaking of its classical form, which came to seem implausible many years ago. *See* Kennedy, *supra* note 4, at 1746-48.

19. *See id.* at 1748-49.

20. *See, e.g.,* Lochner v. New York, 198 U.S. 45, 52-58 (1905).

21. *See* Kennedy, *supra* note 4, at 1731-32.

22. Under these circumstances, the incoherence argument would fall, and the important question would be the one raised by the protective intervention argument—whether the free market led to injustice and needless suffering in particular cases that could properly be relieved through selective state intervention.

23. My agnosticism regarding the possible existence of an apolitical jurisprudence is based primarily on the difficulty of proving a negative. It is relatively easy to show that particular attempts to ground judicial decision-making on apolitical bases fail—for example, that the law-and-economics field does not offer such a basis, *see* Horwitz, *Law and Economics: Science or Politics?*, 8 HOFSTRA L. REV. 905 (1980) (arguing that law-and-economics claims to present such an apolitical basis but cannot)—but it would be very difficult to prove that all possible attempts are bound to fail.

the constitutive role of law in creating the market is less obvious than law's constitutive role in creating and defining the family. Laws establish who is married to whom and who shall be considered the child of whom.

The existence of this "legal-positivist" view of the family should not, however, obscure the coexisting and competing "natural law" belief that the family exists as a natural human formation, not created but merely recognized (or not recognized) by the state. Such a notion is implicit in the sense shared by most of us that some families exist that are not legally recognized. In fact, a great deal of family law doctrine can be seen as a response to the problems caused by the disjunction between legally recognized or de jure families and "natural" or de facto families—the gap between the legal definition of family and the sense people have of what a family really is.[24]

Although the state defines and reinforces specific roles and a particular hierarchy within the family, these policies are often considered nonintervention; indeed, a refusal to bolster family hierarchy has sometimes been considered state intervention in the family.[25] The idea that the state can intervene or not intervene in the family, and particularly that the state practices a policy of nonintervention when it bolsters family hierarchy, would seem to depend upon the belief that a natural family exists separate from legal regulations, and that the hierarchy the state enforces is a natural hierarchy, created by God or by nature, not by law.[26]

---

24. Common law marriage, putative marriage, and a variety of presumptions that legitimate bigamous second or third marriages all serve to enable courts to treat established (real) families like legal families. *See also, e.g.*, Stanley v. Illinois, 405 U.S. 645, 651-52 (1972) (invalidating state law denying unwed father legal rights of parent); Glona v. American Guar. & Liab. Ins. Co., 391 U.S. 73, 75-76 (1968) (limiting state's discretion to base wrongful death law on legal rather than biological relationships).

25. *See infra* p. 850.

26. In response, it might be argued that the state can adopt a meaningful policy of "nonintervention" even towards a "family" that it plays the major part in defining. Proponents of this view might acknowledge that their policy of selective nonintervention departs from the literal meaning of the term but assert that a distinction between the roles the state must play before the family can be legally recognized and other roles it might play lends coherence to their use of the term. On this view, the state plays one role as ground rule maker—policing the borders of the definition of "family" and protecting that family from intruding third parties. This role might be said to be sufficiently noncontroversial that it may be distinguished from numerous other roles—such as providing contraception or abortion—that the state may choose to avoid under a policy of "nonintervention."

The standard and most obvious difficulty with this approach appears when one tries to select which functions are so "noncontroversial" that they come within the state's role as ground rule maker, and which functions are objectionable enough that the state should abjure them under its general policy of "nonintervention." While there may be some

1. *The concept of a natural family*— Last century the idea that wives were naturally dependent upon their husbands was believed by some people as firmly as the idea that children are naturally dependent upon their parents is believed now. The state was expected to bolster the husband's power over his wife whenever it was threatened. The husband chose the family domicile and the wife was essentially forced to live there, just as children are today. As expressed in a nineteenth-century treatise on domestic relations: "The domicile of the wife follows that of the husband; the domicile of the infant may be changed by the parent. Thus does the law of domicile conform to the law of nature."[27] Natural law or "Divine Providence" was thought to be the origin of our laws regarding the family.[28] "[P]ositive law but enforces the mandates of the law of nature, and develops rather than creates a system."[29] Although there have been changes in what is considered natural within the family, the basic notion that family relations are natural relations has not changed that much. Today women may no longer be considered naturally dependent on their husbands, but children are still considered naturally dependent on their parents.[30]

A similar concept of a natural family finds expression in constitutional law. At least since 1944, the Supreme Court has recognized a constitutionally-protected right of family privacy—a "private realm of family life which the state cannot enter."[31]

---

functions—for example, requiring blood tests of marrying couples—that most would agree fit the first category, the great bulk of decisions will be objectionable to a number of putative "family" members. Given the inevitability of substantial disagreement over which family policies are neutral ground rules and which are objectionable intervention, labelling any such set of policies "nonintervention" robs the term of any sensible meaning. These family policies in fact arise from politics and do not flow logically from neutral principles.

A second and more fundamental difficulty defeats the project of distinguishing the establishment of neutral ground rules from other state activities. Any ground rules that are sufficiently noncontroversial that they might plausibly be considered neutral would be too general to settle concrete disputes. Policies may well be internally consistent but still be indeterminate. No policies "flow logically" from principles, even if principles could be neutral. This argument parallels the arguments of some legal realists that laissez faire was incoherent because the state could not enforce even-handedly uncontroversial neutral ground rules. *See supra* pp. 844-45.

27. J. SCHOULER, A TREATISE ON THE LAW OF THE DOMESTIC RELATIONS § 3, at 9 (5th ed. 1895). The author later criticizes as "judicial interference" the policy of some courts to relieve the wife of her obligation to follow her husband where his choice of domicile is unreasonable. *See id.* § 38, at 69.

28. *See id.* § 3, at 8.

29. *Id.* § 2, at 5.

30. *See infra* pp. 851-52 & note 46.

31. Prince v. Massachusetts, 321 U.S. 158, 166 (1944). The right to family privacy is often traced back to Meyer v. Nebraska, 262 U.S. 390 (1923) and Pierce v. Society of

The source of this family privacy has recently been said to be "not in state law, but in intrinsic human rights."[32] The Supreme Court clearly envisions a concept of family relationship that is not dependent upon state law: "Nor has the [Constitution] refused to recognize those family relationships unlegitimized by a marriage ceremony."[33] The family has its "origins entirely apart from the power of the State."[34] Thus, for purposes of constitutional adjudication, "[t]he legal status of families has never been regarded as controlling."[35] The nineteenth century concept of a natural family has continued into the twentieth century. We now recognize law's important role in creating the nineteenth-century family. I would hope we will not have to wait until the twenty-first century to recognize the constitutive role of law in the twentieth-century family.

2. *State enforced hierarchy: Not intervention?*— Nonintervention would seem to have meaning against a backdrop of preexisting prescribed social roles within the family. State-created background rules shape and reinforce these social roles by assigning power and responsibility within the family. These background rules are not usually thought of as state intervention, but they implicate the state in the prescribed family roles and undermine claims of nonintervention. The setting of the roles requires political choices that can hardly be considered nonintervention. The state whose policy choices have had such a great effect upon these family roles certainly cannot be considered neutral, nor should the label "nonintervention" be used to conceal or confuse the political nature of the choices society makes.

Moreover, the enforcement of these family roles, which is what many people mean by "nonintervention," requires the state to make continual policy choices about the scope and

---

Sisters, 268 U.S. 510 (1925). *Meyer* invalidated a statute that forbade the teaching of any modern language other than English in the first eight grades, and *Pierce* overruled a law that required children to attend public schools. Both statutes were found to be unwarranted intrusions into parents' liberty to raise their children. The cases were decided on the basis of the individual right to liberty, once granted substantive protection by the due process clause of the fourteenth amendment. Although the Court has abandoned many of its substantive due process cases from the same period, it has reaffirmed *Meyer* and *Pierce*. *See Developments in the Law—The Constitution and the Family*, 93 Harv. L. Rev. 1157, 1161-63 (1980).

32. Smith v. Organization of Foster Families, 431 U.S. 816, 845 (1977) (footnote omitted).

33. Stanley v. Illinois, 405 U.S. 645, 651 (1972). The *Stanley* Court was dealing with the biological father-child relationship, but it also emphasized Mr. Stanley's role in *raising* his children.

34. Smith v. Organization of Foster Families, 431 U.S. 816, 845 (1977).

35. *Id.* at 845 n.52.

meaning of the roles it is enforcing. The content of family roles has changed over the years and there has never been complete agreement about the authority husbands and parents have over wives and children or about the responsibilities that go along with the authority. State officials must determine borderline questions about the nature and extent of family hierarchy on a case-by-case basis, and pursuing a policy of "nonintervention" cannot relieve state officials from having to make ad hoc political decisions about the family.

a. The Family Head Model: Direct empowerment of superior— Last century some people believed that by empowering the head of the family—the husband and father—to act for the family and to settle intrafamily disputes, the state could avoid intervening in the family. I refer to this policy as the Family Head Model. In theory, this model would relieve the state of making case-by-case decisions regarding the family.

During the early nineteenth century, the husband was the juridical head of the family, entitled to control the wife and children. He was also the financial head of the family. The common law, enforced by the state, provided that a wife's property belonged to her husband. Any personal property to which the wife held legal title was transferred automatically, by operation of law, to her husband; and the husband was given a life estate in her real property.[36] He was entitled to the services of his wife and children. If they received wages, these wages belonged to him; even if they worked without pay, the father could recover the value of services they provided to third parties.[37] Although he could not legally sell the sexual services of his wife and minor

36. This dramatic imposition was not considered state intervention. The transfer of the wife's property was sometimes characterized as a "gift," *see* J. SCHOULER, *supra* note 27, § 80, at 132, but the wife had no choice about conferring it. Even if the couple agreed that the wife could keep her property, their contract would have been invalid. Complicated rules applied to certain incorporeal interests of the wife. The husband's title to choses in action and certain real property interests was considered conditional and he would have to complete certain acts in order to appropriate the choses to himself or to carry out his right of reduction into possession. *See id.* §§ 80-159, at 131-248.

37. *See* Benson v. Remington, 2 Mass. 113 (1806) (ordering neighbors who had allowed a teenager to live with them to pay her father wages for the value of the services she performed or might have performed for them). Probably the neighbors would not have resisted the father's claim and appealed the decision in his favor had it not been for the peculiar facts of the *Benson* case. Several years before, the father had abandoned his family and left them in "extreme poverty." *Id.* at 113. The neighbors found the daughter in a "very helpless condition," *id.*, and took her into their home. Three years before he brought the lawsuit, the father had returned and made a similar demand of money from the neighbors, but community pressure forced him to compromise his claim. This history suggests that in the *Benson* case, the state was empowering the father and not just enforcing the agreed norms of society.

daughters, he could recover money from any man who had sexual intercourse with them without his permission.[38] Some people objected to these policies, but there is no evidence that anyone considered the policies state intervention.

Moreover, the nineteenth-century concept of nonintervention might require the state to bolster the authority of the father. If the wife were to leave and take the children with her, the courts would ordinarily be expected to grant a habeas corpus writ ordering her to return them to him. For courts to refuse to issue such a writ would be considered state intervention in the family.[39]

Today courts are less expected to bolster the power of the husband over the wife, but they are still expected to reinforce parents' authority over children. Many states have a procedure whereby courts can label a child "incorrigible" or "in need of supervision" and order the child to obey the parents or be locked up in the functional equivalent of jail.[40] Parents also have considerable power over whether their child will be institutionalized as mentally defective or troubled.[41] My point is not that such situations are very common, but that these state policies that empower parents are not considered state intervention in the family.

In more subtle ways, also, the state directly authorizes parents to act on behalf of the child. The parents are empowered by the state, as well as by custom, to name the child and to change its name if they wish. They determine the state of which the child shall be a legal citizen. They enroll the child in school. These powers are established by state regulations, regulations that define family roles but are hardly noticed and certainly not considered state intervention.

b. Creating economic dependence— The social interaction within a family can be significantly affected by the economic dependence of wives on husbands and of children on parents. It is obvious to us today that laws and regulations in force early last century made the wife economically dependent upon the husband, and an adolescent economically dependent on his father,

---

38. The husband's action would be for "criminal conversation" if the man had intercourse with his wife and for loss of services if with the daughter. Many commentators have considered this action for loss of the daughter's services to be a legal fiction that allowed the father to recover for his loss of honor or hurt feelings.

39. *See* Olsen, *supra* note 1, at 1505 & n.30.

40. *See* Katz & Teitelbaum, *PINS Jurisdiction, the Vagueness Doctrine, and the Rule of Law*, 53 Ind. L.J. 1 (1977-1978).

41. *See* Parham v. J.R., 442 U.S. 584, 600-04 (1979).

typically until age twenty-one. Neither married women nor minors could carry on a trade or business except under the authority of the husband and father; their services belonged to him and he could collect any wages they might earn. Last century this dependency seemed natural to many people.

Today the state's role in reinforcing economic dependency is less obvious but it is still significant. Although state laws no longer require women to perform unpaid work for their husbands as part of the marriage contract, as in previous centuries, federal tax laws still provide a significant economic incentive for domestic labor to remain unpaid.[42] An additional basis for women's economic dependency is low pay; statistically, women's wages are only sixty-one percent of men's.[43] Although state laws that in the past encouraged or required sex discrimination in employment have been preempted by federal antidiscrimination laws,[44] a number of government agencies save many thousands of dollars by paying lower salaries for jobs held mainly by women than for jobs of comparable worth that men perform.[45]

A child's economic dependence on her parent reinforces and increases the parent's power over the child. Although young children might not be capable of independence,[46] as children grow

42. If a taxpayer pays to have housework done, the cost is generally not a tax deduction. If, however, he marries someone who keeps house for him, he can file a joint return with her and they need not include as income the value of her housekeeping services. Or, suppose two taxpayers each did paid housework for the other. Their tax liabilities would be greater than if they each did their own housework.

43. NATIONAL COMMITTEE ON PAY EQUITY & NATIONAL INSTITUTE FOR WOMEN OF COLOR, WOMEN OF COLOR AND PAY EQUITY, *reprinted in Women in the Workforce: Pay Equity: Hearings Before the Joint Economic Committee*, 98th Cong., 2d Sess. 190, 198 (1984).

44. *See* Olsen, *supra* note 1, at 1548, 1555-59.

45. A number of state governments have undertaken studies and have found that it would be very expensive to enact a program of "comparable worth." Thus they would seem to be reaping a significant economic benefit from taking advantage of women's lower pay. In AFSCME v. State of Washington, Nos. 84-3569, 84-3590 (9th Cir. Sept. 4, 1984) (available September 18, 1985 on LEXIS, Genfed Library, Cases file), the Ninth Circuit struck down a District Court decision that would have required Washington State to make comparable worth payments.

46. It is easy to assume that young children are naturally dependent on their parents. Upon closer examination, however, this assumption seems unjustified. Certainly, human offspring would appear to be as defenseless as other primate young, and in this sense can be said to be naturally dependent. But, in this sense, children would be naturally dependent upon their mother, possibly on their father, and probably upon the larger community. In many parts of the world a mother and infant or a mother, father, and infant could not survive alone.

In civilized society, young children remain dependent. That this dependency is on the child's *parents* is surely based on laws. Laws ensure that most children remain with their parents, although in spite of the law, large numbers of children are separated from their parents. Presumably more children would be taken from their parents were it not for the

older, their dependence is increasingly attributable to state regulations. Child labor laws, however wise as policy, are state regulations that make it difficult for children to gain economic independence.[47] And the state goes further. State laws not only limit a child's opportunity for paid employment, they also require her to attend school—work for which she receives no pay.[48] Finally, when a state pays welfare benefits for a child or orders one parent to pay support for a child, the money does not go to the child herself, but to a custodian, usually the other parent. This maintains the child's economic dependency on her custodian. If we are concerned about the state intervening in the family if it provides free contraceptives to girls without telling their parents, we should not overlook the fact that state policies have made it difficult for girls to pay for contraceptives or to get them any other way.[49]

c. *Eliminating alternative sources of support or nurturance*— Last century a woman was required to live in the home of her husband. He could choose to live anywhere, and she was obliged to follow him. One method of enforcing this requirement was to eliminate alternative living possibilities. Anyone who offered lodging to a runaway wife could be charged with harboring her. Although her father might, as a practical matter, get by with this infraction, it would be difficult for anyone else to do so. Most women would be unable to help her and most men ill-advised to do so.[50] If a runaway wife formed a close relationship with a man, they could be suspected of adultery and treated very harshly. If she actually had sexual relations with another man, she could be recaptured and forced home by her

---

legal (as well as social) disapproval of kidnapping.

Moreover, the period of dependency could be considerably shortened if, for example, property laws were not enforceable against children. One could have a society in which children were allowed to take whatever they needed and to eat food they found as freely as many children eat at home. My point is not that this plan would produce a better society or healthier children, but simply that it would be possible.

47. *See, e.g.*, Cal. Labor Code §§ 1290-1311 (West 1971 & Supp. 1985); Youth Employment Standards Act, Mich. Comp. Laws §§ 409.101-.124 (1979) (restricting and regulating the hours and types of employment for minors).

48. *See, e.g.* Compulsory Education Law, Cal. Educ. Code §§ 48200-48324 (West 1978 & Supp. 1985); Michigan Compulsory School Attendance Law, Mich. Comp. Laws Ann. §§ 380.1561.-1599 (West 1979). Of course, it can be argued that school attendance is non-productive labor and should be considered a benefit rather than a burden. In some societies, however, being a student is considered gainful employment and people are paid to attend school. My point is simply that these state policies are not natural or inevitable and they implicate the state in the economic dependency of youngsters.

49. *See infra* p. 860; Olsen, *supra* note 1, at 1506 & n.33.

50. *See* J. Schouler, *supra* note 27, § 41, at 71-72.

husband.[51] The husband could bring a civil suit and recover money damages from the man for "criminal conversation." The husband would continue to own his wife's property and to be entitled to her services, but he would no longer have to support her. In many cases he could take their children away from her and perhaps even bar her from visiting them.[52]

Today the state will ordinarily not penalize third parties who offer lodging or friendship to a woman without the permission of her husband, but laws continue to penalize those who offer the same to children without the permission of their parents. The state is implicated in the power and role distribution within the family when its laws prevent children from looking to third parties for support. Yet the state is not accused of intervening in the family when it forces children to live with their parents or when it prohibits doctors from treating minors without the parents' knowledge and approval. The child may be required to associate or forbidden from associating with people, at the whim of the parents. Statutes permitting courts to issue grandparent visitation orders that may limit this parental prerogative in certain egregious cases are themselves sometimes criticized as state "intervention" in the family.[53] The state gives parents considerable coercive power over children and then characterizes its refusal to monitor this power as "nonintervention."

d. Limiting state protection— Last century the father was permitted to discipline his wife and children, and this permission often extended to corporal punishment. Behavior that would constitute a criminal offense if directed at a stranger was fully legal against one's children and mere grounds for separation or divorce if directed against one's spouse. Doctrines of intrafamily tort immunity protected the husband and father from civil suits by his beaten wife or children.[54]

---

51. *See id.* § 45, at 76. If a husband discovered his wife in bed with another man and killed them, his crime would be a misdemeanor, not a felony. *See id.* § 45, at 76, n.5.

52. Lord Talfourd's Act, an 1839 reform bill in England that gave courts power to grant mothers child custody and visitation, specifically excluded from its provisions adulterous mothers; and some Lords who opposed the bill still argued that the *risk* that an adulterous mother could benefit from the reform if her adultery could not be proven was so unacceptable that the bill should be defeated. *See* 44 PARL. DEB. (3d ser.) 772, 789 (1838).

53. *See, e.g.*, Olds v. Olds, 356 N.W.2d 571, 574 (Iowa 1984). In some situations, grandparent visitation orders may coerce a child to continue unwanted contact with the grandparents.

54. The same doctrine would, of course, protect the wife and child from civil suit if they were to assault or batter the husband and father, but usually it did not work that way.

Today, intrafamily tort immunity has been widely abolished, but a great deal of behavior that would be criminal or tortious between strangers may still be done with impunity within a family. In many states, the husband may legally force sexual intercourse upon his wife. In most states, spouse abuse is treated differently from other forms of personal violence—sometimes better, often worse. Children are offered limited state protection against their parents. Usually, crimes and torts will be recognized only if a child is badly abused; and even this occasional enforcement is often thought to constitute state intervention—justified, but intervention nonetheless. In theory, parents can be prosecuted for homicide, sexual abuse, serious physical assaults, and child neglect. In practice, however, a child's dependency is so extensive that many crimes, including assault and sexual abuse, often go unprosecuted.

3. *Changes in family hierarchy over time*— The nature and degree of power that the state allows one family member to exercise over another has changed over time and is regularly contested. Reforms that have claimed to provide for juridical equality between men and women have tended to modify the legal role expectations placed on husbands and wives. The role relationship between parent and child has also undergone considerable change over time. Because parents' power over their children is incomplete, the state must adjudicate borderline cases and in doing so necessarily influences the family. At one extreme, state prosecution of a father for intentionally killing his child is universally approved and is unlikely to be considered state intervention in the family; at the other extreme, charging a father with kidnapping for sending a child to her room as a form of punishment would strike most people as serious state intervention in the family. Courts must frequently draw a line between protecting the individual family member and promoting family authority, and different courts would draw the line closer to one or the other of these extremes. Exactly where a court draws the line, or where it would be expected to draw the line, will affect power relations within the family. The choices that courts make will be based on policy considerations and the state cannot avoid making decisions that will influence family relations.

Moreover, when parents disagree, the state has to decide which of the two to empower or to refuse to empower. This choice will in turn influence relations between the parents. Thus, what is frequently referred to as "nonintervention" involves an initial policy choice regarding family roles, followed by further policy choices regarding the details of those roles.

Because nonintervention is understood with reference to specific family roles and the state is expected to take these roles into account in settling disputes, courts must make one choice after another regarding the content and nature of these roles. As long as they do not ratify and enforce *all* assertions of authority by a husband or parent—for example, they prosecute intrafamily murder—courts must decide which behavior they will sanction and which they will not. These decisions require courts to take a stand on complex issues of intergenerational conflict and gender politics. The simple claim that the state should not intervene in the family tends to obscure the genuine problems of ethics and policy that continually arise.

C. Nonintervention and the Egalitarian Family

In theory it would be possible for the state to avoid taking a stand in favor of juridical hierarchy within the family. There are at least two ways the state could settle lawsuits involving families that would avoid ratifying family hierarchy. One would be to treat the family as a miniature state of nature by refusing to enforce any lawsuits between family members; the other would be to treat marriage as nothing more than an express contract and parentage as irrelevant, and enforce all lawsuits between family members just as though the litigants were not related. A consideration of these two contrasting extremes will further illustrate the difficulty with the concept of "nonintervention."

1. State of Nature Model— The state might seem to be able to remain neutral among family members by steadfastly refusing to enforce any tort, contract, or criminal law between members of a family. This approach, if carried to the extreme, would create a "state of nature" within the family, and could be said to take seriously the notion that families should work out their own problems. If a wife were being beaten, it would be up to her to deal with the problem; the state would not "intervene." If she dealt with the problem by shooting her husband, the state would be expected to continue its policy of "nonintervention." If a person were indicted for murder, it would be a sufficient defense to prove that the defendant and the victim were members of the same family. The killing would then be considered a family matter into which the state should not intrude.

As in any imagined state of nature, this approach would seem to benefit the stronger and prejudice the weaker members of a family. In fact, though, it might disempower the physically weak less than the system that seems to operate in some communities—a system that treats intrafamily battery as private, but leaves homicide fully outlawed. Such a system is especially disempowering to wives if spouse abuse is not recognized as a justification for or defense to homicide.[55]

The State of Nature Model would not really enable the state to remain neutral or uninvolved in the family. Even if the state of nature were complete within the family, the state would still have to decide who constituted a family and how to deal with lawsuits involving third parties and members of the family. Also, a complete state of nature would not fit contemporary views of nonintervention in the family. A partial state of nature within the family might be acceptable to many people; but if the state of nature were partial, decisions about what laws to enforce among family members would require additional political choices that would affect authority and roles within families.

2. *Market Model*— A second way the state might seem to be neutral among family members is based on the opposite strategy of enforcement. The state could treat each member of a family as a juridical equal and treat their family status as irrelevant. Marriage and parentage would become private relationships, not recognized by the state. Courts would treat as irrelevant the fact that litigants were married to one another or that one was the parent of the other, and enforce lawsuits as between any unrelated people or strangers. This approach essentially ignores the family relationship and treats family members just as strangers are treated. Such a policy would not fit contemporary views of nonintervention in the family, especially as regards children. For example, under the Market Model, parents who disciplined their children by sending them to their rooms might be guilty of kidnapping and the children could have a valid cause of action for false imprisonment. Parents would have neither an obligation to support children nor a right to keep them from living away from home. Children and parents would be free to cut their own deals. Contracts entered into between children and their parents, or between any other family members, would be just as enforceable as contracts between any unrelated individuals.

The concept of nonintervention based on the Market Model is not only unacceptable to most people, but it is also no more coherent than laissez faire. All the arguments put forth by the legal realists to show the incoherence of laissez faire apply to nonintervention under the Market Model. The neutrality of the

55. *See* Olsen, *supra* note 1, at 1509.

Market Model would be formal neutrality only, even as between adults. The particular tort, contract, and criminal laws the state chose to create and enforce would affect the relative power of individuals and thus the bargains they could negotiate with their spouses, children, or other relatives. For example, strong battery laws are likely to help wives and children; weakened self-defense doctrines limit their ability to protect themselves, and would seem to help husbands.[56]

To illustrate further, consider the laws that forbid prostitution and nullify contracts when sexual services constitute all or part of the consideration on one side of the agreement. In our present society, the effect of nullifying such contracts usually enriches the male at the expense of the female.[57] The public policy against prostitution might have something to do with refusing to reduce women to sex objects, but it might have as much or more to do with preserving for men the economic resources that rein-

---

56. Popular television programs have recently presented sympathetic portrayals of abused wives and children who, unable to enlist police protection against an abusive husband or father, killed their abuser. *See, e.g.*, "The Burning Bed" (dramatized account of abused wife killing husband); "60 Minutes" (news special on boy who shot his abusive father).

57. The case of Marvin v. Marvin, 18 Cal. 3d 660, 557 P.2d 106, 134 Cal. Rptr. 815 (1976), has been widely praised and blamed for the many things it held and refused to hold, but few if any commentators have paid attention to the court's insistence that a contract for sexual services is unenforceable. This seemingly neutral rule is likely in practice to hurt occasional unsophisticated women. Men, sophisticated or unsophisticated, are likely to be benefited or left untouched.

The anti-prostitution rule also limits the right to contract, and it limits it in a way more likely to hurt women than men. It is one thing to say that we will not assume that men necessarily get more out of sexual intercourse than women do, but it is quite another thing to say that courts may not consider and couples may not contract about any differential benefit that may accrue. Given the statistics on present satisfaction with sexual intercourse, I would suggest that this clearly harms women. *See* Leerhsen, Jackson & Bruno, *Ann Landers and 'The Act,'* NEWSWEEK, Jan. 28, 1985, at 76 [hereinafter cited as *Ann Landers*] (reporting survey results that 72% of women were dissatisfied with sex as practiced).

One criticism sometimes made of the *Marvin* case is that it invites courts to inquire into the intimate details of a couple's life. *See, e.g.*, Chambers, *The "Legalization" of the Family: Toward a Policy of Supportive Neutrality*, 18 U. MICH. J.L. REF. 805 (1985). To make "whisperings across the pillows," *id.* at 825, sacred, private, and unrepeatable is to support the sexual status quo. Sex as currently practiced seems to be startlingly more satisfactory to men than to women. *See Ann Landers, supra.* Privatizing sex reduces discussion that might lead to change. Sex is private in part because the state makes it private and because keeping sex private seems to serve the interests of those with power. The taboo on inquiring into the quality of male-female relationships may be based more on a fear of exposing systematic inequality than on anything else. Child custody cases often involve inquiry into the quality of parent-child relationships. Although commentators may criticize courts' ability to judge intimate relationships, child custody cases do suggest that courts can examine intimate relationships without any devastating effects.

force their prestige and power.[58] The result of policies that enrich men and impoverish women is that even if the law were to refuse to permit "family" defenses to contract, tort, or criminal actions, wives would still often bring to the marriage a position lower in the social and economic hierarchy, and thus a weaker bargaining position vis-à-vis their husbands.

III. The Experience of State Intervention

The assertion I have made—that the concepts of state intervention and nonintervention in the family are essentially meaningless—might ring hollow to an impoverished mother struggling to keep the state from taking her children away from her. More tragically, my assertion could sound absurd or seem totally meaningless to many innocent children who live in fear of the juvenile authorities. Hundreds of youngsters, the quality of whose lives has already been diminished by poverty and neglect, have been forced into silence and concealment. The specter of state intervention in the family denies to many of them even the partial relief they might get from sharing their pain and humiliation with a friendly neighbor or sympathetic teacher. Many such children exist, and to them state intervention can seem real and frightening.

There are many other examples of situations in which people experience themselves to be victims of state intervention. In the 1960's a husband and wife in Connecticut were denied legal access to contraceptives until they sued and appealed their case to the United States Supreme Court.[59] Earlier in the century, Lillie and O.B. Williams were prosecuted for bigamous cohabitation and sentenced to jail terms when state officials in North Carolina decided to challenge the Nevada divorces they had obtained from their previous spouses.[60] They too took their case to the United States Supreme Court and won, only to lose on a retrial and second appeal.[61] To both these couples state intervention would seem to be a very real concern.

State intervention may also have considerable meaning to the lover who, upon the death of his beloved, finds himself with no

58. For an elaboration of these ideas, see F. Olsen, Prostitution: The Stigma of Money (Apr. 16, 1985) (transcript of talk given at UCLA Law School) (copy on file with U. Mich. J.L. Ref.).

59. *See* Griswold v. Connecticut, 381 U.S. 479 (1965).

60. *See* Williams v. North Carolina, 317 U.S. 287 (1942).

61. *See* Williams v. North Carolina, 325 U.S. 226 (1945).

status, their jointly shared property snatched away by the beloved's long-estranged parents. The lover has no say about funeral arrangements and cannot even attend services without the permission of the parents. Even if the couple drew up wills, the beloved's testament would once have been routinely set aside for presumed undue influence.[62]

The parents, however, might well consider their family intruded upon if the state were to limit their rights for the sake of their child's lover. Lillie and O.B. Williams's first spouses may have resented the courts of Nevada intervening in their family affairs by granting divorces against them when, under their own state law, they had committed no wrong and would expect to have a right to remain married.[63]

The experience of state intervention in the family can involve either affirmative coercive behavior by state officials, such as physically forcing a child away from his or her parent, or a refusal by state officials to come to the aid of one claiming a family right, such as the state's failure to order foster parents to relinquish a child to her natural parent.[64] From the child's perspective, the transfer of custody to natural parents the child barely knows would seem to be as serious intervention as it would be to take her away from a natural parent.

The experience of intervention depends upon having some expectation disappointed or some sense of entitlement violated. Disappointment and violation are very real experiences. Unfortunately, they cannot be avoided by a simple policy of nonintervention in the family. Moreover, disappointment and violation of hopes and dreams may be as distressing as the disappointment and violation of expectations and entitlements. It is not clear, in the example above, that the state should sacrifice the interests of a lover for the sake of the beloved's parents, just because the parents, under present law, have more settled expectations and entitlements.

Because the notion of state intervention depends upon a conception of proper family roles and these roles are open to dispute, almost any policy may be experienced by someone as state

62. *See In re* Kaufman's Will, 20 A.D.2d 464, 247 N.Y.S.2d 664 (1964), *aff'd,* 15 N.Y.2d 825, 205 N.E.2d 864, 257 N.Y.S.2d 941 (1965). *See also* Sherman, *Undue Influence and the Homosexual Testator,* 42 U. PITT. L. REV. 225, 239-48 (1981) (asserting that homosexuals' wills are subjected to heightened scrutiny for undue influence).

63. For a discussion of the difficulties with such conflicting rights, see Olsen, *Statutory Rape: A Feminist Critique of Rights Analysis,* 63 TEX. L. REV. 387 (1984).

64. *See* Bennet v. Jeffreys, 40 N.Y.2d 543, 356 N.E.2d 277, 387 N.Y.S.2d 821 (1976) (finding long period of separation from natural parent an extraordinary circumstance that can "trigger" the best interests of the child test).

intervention. In many situations, someone's expectations will be disappointed or sense of entitlement violated no matter what action the state takes or refuses to take. One can often argue that in a particular case nonintervention really means whatever one wants the state to do; any policy one dislikes might be labeled intervention.

For example, from one perspective, the state intervenes in the family when it provides contraceptives to minors. The "squeal rule" proposed by the Reagan administration, although not preventing the distribution of contraceptives, would have required that parents be notified that contraceptives had been given to their children.[65] This was supposed to reduce state intervention in the family and to enable parents to counsel their children about the problems of adolescent sex. Opponents feared it would deter the youngsters from obtaining contraceptives (but not from engaging in sex), and argued that this particular intervention in the family was justified.

From another perspective, the "squeal rule" does not reduce state intervention (whether for good or ill), but is itself a crude, abusive form of intervention. The state achieves a virtual monopoly on effective birth control by impoverishing young women and forbidding inexpensive over-the-counter sales of prescription contraceptives.[66] It then proposes to use this monopoly to intrude into the parent-child relationship and pass along information to the parents that the parents have neglected to obtain the old-fashioned way—by talking with their children. The state thus rewards neglectful parents and removes from them an incentive to maintain supportive communication with their children. It encourages parents to neglect their child's sex education and to ignore the pressures put upon their child until after the child has become sexually active and the state so notifies them.

65. *See* 48 Fed. Reg. 3600 (1983) (to be codified at 42 C.F.R. §§ 59.2, 59.5). *See also* N.Y. Times, Feb. 20, 1983, at E5, col. 4. The rule was found unlawful on statutory grounds. *See* Planned Parenthood Fed'n of Am. v. Schweiker, 712 F.2d 650 (D.C. Cir. 1983). Some people have opposed the "squeal rule" on the grounds that certain fathers might demand sex from their daughters if they found out that the daughters were sexually active. Others fear fathers would respond with physical abuse of their daughters.

66. The state's role seems even more intensive and insidious when we consider how reluctant state officials are to prosecute date rape. The state permits unsafe streets that limit a woman's choices: she may stay home (statistically, a remarkably dangerous location for women), go out in a group of people, or go out with one man. Especially if she chooses the one-man option, the female may find herself faced with the further choice of consenting to sexual intercourse or being raped by him without recourse. Thus, women cannot really be said to have the option of refraining from sexual intercourse. Abstinence is not a reliable form of birth control for many women.

Nonintervention arguments can be leveled against laws and regulations that refuse to treat unmarried couples enough like a family[67] or against laws that treat them too much like a family.[68] Nonintervention arguments can be used to keep children from being put into foster care, to remove them from foster care, or to keep them from being removed from foster care.[69] Nonintervention arguments can even be leveled against a policy of enforcing contracts between unwed couples.[70] While one can sympathize with anyone who is disappointed by a state policy, it is hard to see that anything is actually gained by characterizing the cause of that disappointment as state intervention.[71]

IV. WHY IT MATTERS

The protective intervention argument, that the state should intervene in the family when necesary, has gained so much acceptance—just as the protective intervention argument against laissez faire has gained widespread acceptance—that one might wonder why we need the incoherence argument, that intervention and nonintervention are meaningless concepts. First, it is not the case that the exception has swallowed the rule. Under the protective intervention argument, the state is treated as having a policing function—to detect and correct those rare circumstances that disturb and disrupt the family, without questioning any of the basic individualistic foundations of society. The assertion that the state can and should avoid "intervention" in the family plays an important but generally unrecognized ideological role.[72] Further, focusing on "nonintervention" tends to mush and confuse the ethical and political choices we make. It directs our attention to a false issue and obscures genuine issues of ethics and policy. Finally, both laissez faire and nonintervention in

67. *See* Chambers, *supra* note 57.

68. *See id.*; Burt, *Coercive Freedom: A Response to Professor Chambers*, 18 U. MICH. J.L. REF. 829 (1985).

69. *See* Smith v. Organization of Foster Families, 431 U.S. 816 (1977) (acknowledging, but refusing to accept, argument).

70. *See* Burt, *supra* note 68.

71. This is not to deny the ideological significance of the concern, however. To complain that the hassling of your living arrangement (whether through zoning laws, fornication laws, or any other law or regulation) constitutes state intervention in the family is an ideological claim, a claim of entitlement to live the way you choose. For example, successfully characterizing state laws against homosexual relations as state "intervention" in the family tends to legitimate same-sex relationships.

72. For an interesting discussion of the ideological role of family law, see Freeman, *supra* note 12, at 387-401. *See also* Olsen, *supra* note 10.

the family have sprung up in modern versions—law-and-economics in place of laissez faire and the individual right to privacy in place of nonintervention in the family. These new forms, one labeled conservative, the other liberal, are flawed in the same way the originals—laissez faire and nonintervention—are flawed. The standard liberal criticism of law-and-economics and the standard conservative criticism of the right to privacy are both versions of the protective intervention argument. In each instance, I believe the incoherence argument presents a more important critique.[73]

---

73. In the case of privacy, liberals argue that the fundamental principle of individual privacy offers a rational justification or grounding for a great many policies—ranging from access to contraceptives to a disapproval of surveillance over sexual choices. Conservatives often respond by pitting public morality against individual privacy. This is parallel to the protective intervention argument regarding the family. The conservatives assume that privacy is a coherent concept and that the rational elaboration of this principle would lead to the policies supported by the liberals. The argument of the conservatives that public morality justifies limiting privacy is like the argument that the state should intervene in the private family to protect against abuse.

The stronger and more important answer to the liberals' claim would be like the incoherence argument. Privacy is not a coherent concept and it does not lead to any indisputable policy choices. The state is implicated in privacy just as it is in family. Although I support many of the policies they advance in the name of "privacy," I believe the liberals are mistaken to think that they can ground or justify these policies on any rational or apolitical basis.

In the case of law-and-economics, conservatives argue that the concept of efficiency offers a rational justification for a great many policies. In particular, law-and-economics purports to demonstrate that many economic policies supported by liberals simply fail objectively—they will not produce the results the liberals hope to achieve. Liberals often respond by pitting equality, justice, or fairness against efficiency. This is parallel to the protective intervention argument against laissez faire policies toward the free market. Liberals often assume that efficiency is a coherent concept and that a relentless focus on efficiency would lead to the policies supported by the conservatives.

The stronger and more important answer to the conservatives' claim would be like the incoherence argument against laissez faire. "Efficiency" is indeterminate and does *not* lead to the policy choices that conservatives claim it does. Liberals do not have to resort to arguments that pit other goals against efficiency, but can challenge the basic underlying premises of conservative law-and-economics. *See* Kennedy, *Distributive and Paternalist Motives in Contract and Tort, with Special Reference to Compulsory Terms and Unequal Bargaining Power*, 41 MD. L. REV. 563 (1982); Kennedy, *Cost-Benefit Analysis of Entitlement Programs: A Critique*, 33 STAN. L. REV. 387 (1981); Kelman, *Misunderstanding Social Life: A Critique of the Core Premises of Law and Economics*, 33 J. LEGAL EDUC. 274 (1983); Kelman, *Consumption Theory, Production Theory and Ideology in the Coase Theorem*, 52 S. CAL. L. REV. 669 (1979); Kelman, *Choice and Utility*, 1979 WIS. L. REV. 769. *See also* Horwitz, *supra* note 23; Kennedy & Michelman, *Are Property and Contract Efficient?*, 8 HOFSTRA L. REV. 711 (1980).

CONCLUSION

State intervention in the family is an ideological, not an analytic concept. The incoherence argument demonstrates that neither intervention nor nonintervention has a coherent meaning. The protective intervention argument, that the state should intervene in the family whenever necessary to defend the interests of society or of individual oppressed family members, does not go far enough. First, it presupposes that nonintervention is a possible choice; and second, it usually accepts nonintervention as a norm or as an ideal.

The protective intervention argument misperceives the problems caused by unfortunate social policies. For example, the problem with state officials taking children away from poor parents is not really a problem of state "intervention," but a problem of the substance of that state behavior. What the state does is sometimes *so bad* that people would rather it did nothing—which of course is not possible. The effort to get the state to do nothing, even if it were possible, misfocuses attention. It is misguided to treat freedom as the polar opposite of state "intervention" or of government regulation. As Morris Cohen noted in another context, real freedom depends upon opportunities supplied by institutions that involve legal regulation.[74] The attempt to criticize state "intervention" instead of criticizing the particular policies pursued may be especially limiting for poor people, who often have to rely on various government programs and are thus less likely to benefit from any political strategy based on the myth of nonintervention.[75]

Sexual abuse of children provides an example of the inadequacy of the rhetoric of nonintervention. It also illustrates problems with the state giving adults so much authority and power over children.[76] A child's failure to report sexual abuse

---

74. *See* Cohen, *supra* note 3, at 591.

75. *Cf.* MacKinnon, *The Male Ideology of Privacy: A Feminist Perspective*, 17 RADICAL AMERICA, July-Aug. 1983, at 23, 32 (noting that abortion rights are particularly easy to deny to poor women because the right is based on privacy).

76. The state establishes a situation of dependency and then allows as the only alternative a complete severing of the relationship. If you watch television ads for toilet paper and blue jeans, the puzzling question is not why incest is so widespread but rather that sexual abuse of children has any limits. If we make children totally dependent upon one or two adults and allow helplessness and dependency to be eroticized, we should not pretend surprise and outrage at child abuse. The state empowers adults and gives tax deductions for advertising that eroticizes domination. *See generally* J. Kilbourne, Killing Us Softly: Advertising's Image of Women (Cambridge Documentary Films, Inc. 1979) (film examining use of sex in advertising as reflective and partially constitutive of

may often be her best response to a bad situation. Incest deprives a child of autonomy and corrupts the protection the abusing parent offers the child. And when abuse is discovered, instead of empowering the child and making it possible for him or her to resist the adult, state officials tend to move in and take over—sometimes making matters worse. After revealing sexual abuse the child is all too likely to have even less autonomy and fewer options for dealing with his or her vulnerability and hurt. The child may be summarily denied the opportunity to maintain any relationship with the abusing adult, even if the child wants desperately to maintain a relationship. In cases of child abuse, including sexual abuse, state policy should end the abuse or empower the child to end it, not force the child to leave home.[77]

If we think in terms of intervention versus nonintervention, and consider our options to be thus limited, we are less likely to devise effective alternatives.[78] As we become less preoccupied with the myth of state intervention, perhaps we can focus proper attention on the realities of people's lives.

---

culture).

77. How to empower children to end their abuse is a topic for another article. Most of us are not accustomed to thinking about ways to empower victims. For some early thoughts, see Olsen, *supra* note 63, at 407-09, 424, 431. It seems important to explore creative ways to improve the options available to children in difficult home situations. For example, modern technology might enable children to summon help quickly enough that it would be safe for them to stay with abusive parents to whom they are deeply attached.

78. While this essay has focused on the family, its thesis is general. The state cannot be neutral, nor can it be a neutral arbiter of rights. *See* Olsen, *supra* note 63; *Symposium: A Critique of Rights*, 62 TEX. L. REV. 1363 (1984).

[2]

Beyond the Public/Private Division: Law, Power and the Family

NIKOLAS ROSE*

Over the past ten years, the intellectual machinery which radical social analysts have used to produce political intelligibility has begun to fall apart. Faced with the inadequacies of most social theory to cope with the problems of contemporary social reality, two strategies of repair have been noteworthy. The first is to shift the issue of power to the forefront of investigation. Power is no longer seen as the automatic by-product of economic exploitation or social stratification; it is itself the focus of analysis and the stake in political contestation. The second is to use 'history' rather than 'grand theory' as a way of taking apart the self-evidence of the present. The past is used to reveal the socially constructed nature of the present, implying that it can be transformed by conscious political strategy. Yet studies carried out under these auspices find it difficult to abandon the comfort provided by old forms of explanation. Historical investigation often merely projects conventional radical wisdom back onto the past. Power often appears in the repetitive guise of denial, control and repression. The old theories reappear as solutions to their own failure.

The aim of this paper is to recommend a use of the past, and an analysis of power which would disrupt these certainties. I term this approach 'genealogical' in that it uses the analytical devices developed in the 'genealogical' studies of Michel Foucault and his co-workers. Genealogy is not a methodology, but a means of distancing oneself from certain conceptual tools which have a powerful hold over critical thought. I will counterpose genealogy to the most popular radical strategy of all, that of critique. I will focus upon the area where the arguments seem to me to be most advanced: feminism and the critical analysis of 'the family' and 'family law'.

Feminism exploded the boundary lines of traditional socialist politics, and re-inserted questions of family, sexuality, children and domestic life into the heart of progressive political discourse. The analysis of domination was no longer confined to the market, the workplace or the formal institutions of the criminal justice system. A multiplicity of infra-state powers were made visible and contestable. Feminist studies of law and legal regulation often succeeded

* *Department of Human Sciences, Brunel University, Uxbridge, Middlesex UB8 3PH, England.*

This paper was originally given at the First Annual Critical Legal Conference, University of Kent, September 1986. I would like to thank Alan Hunt and Phil Jones for comments and criticism.

almost uniquely in tying up concrete, contingent and local instances of oppression and domination with, on the one hand, more general networks of social power and, on the other hand, specific and immediate strategies for reform.

Recently, however, a certain language of analysis has come to the fore which promises to confer a unity upon the investigations of the diverse social, legal and economic practices within which women are subordinated.[1] Each of these, it is suggested, can be understood in terms of the division and opposition of public and private spheres. In this paper I examine this claim in order to illustrate some basic weaknesses in much contemporary critical analysis of law and politics. I argue that critical analysis must abandon the analytic strategy of critique and rethink some of its fundamental concepts – state, interest, ideology and power. I conclude by sketching out some characteristics of a genealogical approach to family powers, identifying regulatory mechanisms which raise difficult problems for political evaluation.

PUBLIC POWERS AND PRIVATE FREEDOMS?

Contemporary disputes over the boundaries of public powers and private freedoms in issues of morality, sexuality, marriage, reproduction, child care and divorce follow familiar lines. How much should the state intervene into private life? How successful are public authorities in making decisions on care, custody and so forth? What aspects of personal morality are public concerns and what are not? Is there a sphere of private life and personal morality that is, in brief and crude terms, not the law's business? Have welfare professionals colonised the family at the expense of personal liberties and formal legal protections? The debate has been going for a long time; the problems seem both crucial and interminable.

Recently feminist lawyers and critical legal scholars have proposed a new approach to these old disputes.[2] They have argued that the key to resolving the analytical and practical problems lies in understanding the division between public and private spheres. Thus Freeman suggests that "at the root of a critical theory of family law is the public/private dichotomy".[3] It is claimed that such a dichotomy both underpins the present organisation of legal regulation of family relations and that:

> ... many of the reform strategies in the recent past which are conceived within this particular world view are 'cabined, cribbed and confined' by it and that their effectiveness is accordingly limited.[4]

Critical analysis of the public/private distinction is hardly new in legal thought. Throughout the first half of this century jurists attacked the premises lying behind the classification as it underlay the division of law into public and private realms, arguing that so-called 'private' categories of law such as contract actually represented a delegation of public power, entailing a policy decision and enforced by state imposed sanctions.[5] Extending this critique, contemporary critical legal scholars in the U.S.A. argue that the public/

private division is one of a number of homologous distinctions that:

> . . . taken together, constitute the liberal way of thinking about the social world. These distinctions are state/society, public/private, individual/group, right/power, property/sovereignty, contract/tort, law/policy, legislature/judiciary, objective/subjective, reason/fiat, freedom/coercion . . . .[6]

These oppositions, it is argued, shape our consciousness. When incorporated into legal discourse they induce beliefs that existing social arrangements are just, natural, inevitable, legitimate, thereby denying our capacity to conceive of new forms of human relations and to challenge existing forms of domination.[7] Critical legal scholars in the U.S.A. have sought to demonstrate that the public/private distinction has no determinate content in law, that it functions more as an image or metaphor which is able to suture judicial argument to existing values and beliefs, and that it serves less as an analytic tool or means of deciding cases than as a form of political rhetoric used to justify value choices.

These authors argue that the distinction serves or seeks to maintain the belief that social and economic life – business, education, community, family – are outside government and law, simultaneously denying the role of political processes in constituting and maintaining them, and legitimating these arrangements by implying that they have arisen from decisions and choices freely made by individuals. This protects existing hierarchies yet delegitimises alternative forms of group solidarity – unions, universities, communities – which cannot fit within the public/private divide. Hence critical legal theorists regard the public/private distinction as inimical to the construction of democratic, self-governing group life which would transcend the distinction between the state as the *locus* of all legitimate power and the individual as the isolated atom of freedom and rights.

This analytic machinery is deployed by Olsen in her critique of the dichotomies underpinning the subordination of women to men.[8] The central opposition, she claims, is that between the market and the family, which was consolidated in the nineteenth century. This is less a real division of zones and relations than a set of powerful beliefs that structure our ways of conceptualising and evaluating different types of activity. The family/market dichotomy embodies the idea that the market structures our productive lives whilst the family structures our affective lives. This division of experience into two separate and interdependent spheres must be transcended.

Olsen argues that the free market combines an egalitarian ideology with an individualist ethic, whilst the private family combines an hierarchical ideology with an altruistic ethic. When our consciousness is structured by the public/private division we conceive of reforms only in terms of making the market more like the family or the family more like the market. Thus reforms to the market have sought to mitigate individualism but only at the price of creating new hierarchies, and reforms of the family have sought to undermine hierarchy but at the price of creating a spurious equality which promotes individualism, undermines solidarity and altruism, and obscures the real differences in power between women and men. The solution is to transcend the public/private divide, transforming both family and market, and simultaneously transcending the male/female dichotomy – creating what she terms "a new referential system for relating men and women to the world . . . allowing the human personality to break out of the present dichotomised system".[9]

English critics of the public/private divide as it relates to the family have tended to draw upon a different language of critique but come to similar conclusions.[10] The division between public and private is traced back in political and social philosophy at least as far as Aristotle's distinction between *polis* and *oikos* and up to the natural rights theories of John Locke. However, in the eighteenth and nineteenth centuries the distinction is reposed in terms of the division between home and market. It is given a philosophical foundation in the liberal political philosophy of J. S. Mill and his followers, with the opposition between the realm of legitimate public regulation and the realm of freedom from intrusion, personal autonomy and private choice. Writers point to the particular associations in these texts between the public sphere – the world of work, the market, individualism, competition, politics and the state – and men, and the corollary association of women with the private, domestic, intimate, altruistic and humanitarian world of the home.

These feminist histories argue that notions of the home and family relations as private so far as the law was concerned pre-date the constitutional theories of the nineteenth century. Similarly, these authors refuse the earlier Marxist account of the division as a function of the change in production relations associated with the rise of capitalism, arguing not only that it pre-dates capitalism but that its primary function was to support and reinforce male, patriarchal control over women, both in the formulation of laws and regulations pertaining to the public sphere, and in the powers allowed to men in the home and family to control women. It is argued that, in law as elsewhere, this public/private divide, and the conception of the private which it uses, has always functioned to sustain a particular and oppressive set of relations between men and women.[11]

However, most of the authors suggest that the developments within capitalism in the nineteenth century reworked this public/private divide to suit the interests of a ruling, property owning male elite. This can be seen in the emergence of a cult of domesticity with its idealisation of motherhood. Whilst allowing that this allotted certain powers to women, these authors suggest that it did so only in their status as mothers confined to the private sphere, and hence failed fundamentally to challenge either the patriarchal separation of realms, or the economic power which men wielded over the family unit.

Analyses of the legal regulation of marriage, divorce, sexual behaviour and domestic violence are deployed to show that the ideology of individual choice and personal freedom in the private domain of home and family legitimates a refusal by public authorities to intervene into certain places, activities, relationships and feelings. Designating them personal, private and subjective makes them appear to be outside the scope of the law as a fact of nature, whereas in fact non-intervention is a socially contructed, historically variable and inevitably political decision. The state defines as 'private' those aspects of life into which it will not intervene, and then, paradoxically, uses this privacy as the justification for its non-intervention.

Like *laissez faire* in relation to the market, the idea that the family can be private in the sense of outside public regulation is a myth. The state cannot avoid intervening in the shaping of familial relations through decisions as to which types of relation to sanction and codify and which types of dispute to regulate or not regulate. The state establishes the legal framework for conducting legitimate sexual relations and for procreation and privileges certain types of relation through rules of inheritance. Further, the state, through public law, has established complex welfare mechanisms, especially those surrounding the proper development of children. And however potent is the legal ideology of family privacy, in decisions as to the best interests and welfare of children in cases concerning care and custody, and in the division of family property and other aspects of family disputes, legal functionaries operate according to ideological and patriarchal beliefs as to morality, responsibility and family life and what is best for children. On the one hand, the state, representing dominant male interests, chooses the nature and objectives of public regulation; on the other, a domain is constituted outside legal regulation where welfare agencies enforce the ideology of motherhood, and where male power is not even subject to limited protections of the rule of law. The public/private division mystifies these processes.

Amongst the reform strategies discussed and criticised because of their commitment to the public/private dichotomy are those which seek to increase regulation of family relations by public law, those that try to decrease legal regulation of family conflicts by encouraging informal, non-legal forums for dispute resolution such as conciliation and family courts, proposals which advocate that the powers, duties and responsibilities of parties to domestic arrangements should be specified in private contracts enforcible at law, and those that seek to protect the family from excessive state intrusion by establishing a framework of family rights.[12]

For example, conciliation and family courts are frequently advocated as techniques and institutions which will increase the powers, capacities, autonomy and responsibility of the private parties involved, reducing damaging conflict between the parties and respecting their interests.[13] However, the critics of the public/private divide argue that the consequences of the reduction of such controls as flow from formal legal hearings – legal representation, due process and so forth – will be different: ignoring real conflicts in capacities, situations and wishes, denying inequalities in power and, in general, increasing the powers of welfare professionals over family members and of men over women. And the development of conciliation and family courts are viewed as part of a general increase in mechanisms of informal justice whose benign rhetoric disguises an increase of state power, establishing new, less visible channels through which the social control capacities of the state are extended and dispersed.[14]

Arguments for family rights can be similarly undercut. Thus, in an influential book, Goldstein, Freud and Solnit argued:

> The child's need for safety within the confines of the family must be met by law through its recognition of family privacy as the barrier to state instrusion upon parental autonomy in child rearing.[15]

The critical rejoinder is that such proposals gloss over, ignore or obscure the different powers and interests of different members of the family: family privacy is all too often a licence for men to dominate women and children.[16] The very notion of family privacy thus mystifies the extent to which the family is constructed and controlled by the state and its agencies, and obscures the power differences and conflicts amongst family members. Reform proposals which operate in terms of the public/private divide, or which seek to increase an unproblematical family privacy, are thus fundamentally flawed. Critical legal theory must expose the ideological nature of the dichotomy; critical family politics must transcend it in practice.

CRITICISM AND CRITIQUE

The arguments which I have been discussing conceptualise the public/private division as an ideology and subject it to a critique. As in other critiques of ideology, this has a particular form. It seeks to demonstrate the *falsity* of the dichotomy. It aims to reveal the *function* of the dichotomy. It thus appears to *explain* the falsity *in terms of* the function it serves. The public/private division is false because the private realm is not natural but is itself a construction within a particular set of beliefs. And it has at least four functions. It mystifies the fact that the state itself constructs both the boundaries and the limits of privacy. It legitimates the extent to which the state refuses to intervene into certain places or relations through its legal mechanisms. It masks the fact that privacy is all too often the right of men to dominate women and children. And it obscures the degree to which the state empowers welfare professionals to impose social norms on the family lives of certain sections of society, expecially controlling women in their roles as wives and mothers.

This critique of the public/private division is frequently revealing and insightful. But it is hamstrung by the analytic strategy it uses. This limits our understanding of the relations between regulatory systems and conjugal, domestic and child-rearing arrangements and forms of habitation. It fails to grasp the ways in which the private family has, on the one hand, been linked into new forms of political rationality which have developed over the last century, and, on the other hand, has been central to transformations in subjective realities and desires. It thus leads to over-simple criticisms of family policies and proposals for reform. If we are to understand the politics of familialisation, and the transformation of political concerns into personal and familial objectives which it entailed, we need to fragment, disturb and disrupt some of the central explanatory categories of critique.

The first fragmentation must be of 'law' itself. The 'legal system' is neither totalised nor enclosed. There is no unity to the complex of written codes, judgments, institutions and agents and techniques of judgment which make up 'the law'. 'Law' does not operate on 'the family': family law is a creation of textbook writers and legal pedagogy. Different laws – in relation to inheritance, marriage, divorce, custody, the protection of children and so forth – specify their objects and powers in terms of varied statuses which cannot be simply translated into each other: husbands, wives, parents, spouses and so forth. Legal regulation of each of these different relations and processes has emerged at different times and in relation to different concerns. They have defined their terms differently and utilise diverse forms of judgment and mechanisms of enforcement. They do not operate according to a single division of 'public' and 'private' - spaces, activities and relations which are within the scope of regulation for one purpose are outside it for another. Unities and coherences must be analysed in terms of outcomes rather than origins or intentions. Rather than conferring a false unity upon the diversity of legal regulation, critical analysis should treat this diversity as both a clue to the social intelligibility of the law and, perhaps, as the key to a political strategy in relation to law.

Further, law does not exist in isolation from other regulatory systems. Over the past hundred and fifty years we have seen the construction of a new form of 'government', one in which the family was central – or rather in which certain desirable states of affairs – profit, tranquillity, security, health, virtue and efficiency – were to be brought about by governing residential, domestic, sexual and child rearing arrangements in the form of the private family. Government here should be seen in an extended sense, as all those interdictions, urgings, interventions, techniques and evaluations which seek to shape up events towards desired ends. Legal mechanisms need to be relocated within this far wider field of regulatory mechanisms ranging from taxation, through welfare to the design of domestic space. Critical approaches to law must face up to the paradox that, in many cases, analysis of law is the wrong place to start if one wishes to understand regulatory strategies.

Critiques of the law appear ineluctably drawn to a concept of the state which reproduces the terms of constitutionalist doctrines. The state is conceived as the single sovereign source of authoritative regulation in a given, bounded national territory. Power is the state and the law is its voice. What the state does not prohibit, it commands. Power is construed as centralised, wielded by a political elite and directed outwards through the various organs of social control. But we need to take the category of the state as a problem and not a solution. The programmes of regulation of domestic, conjugal and reproductive arrangements, and the projects for the reform of habitation, did not originate with 'the state'. Their initiators, supporters and allies were heterogeneous, the problems which they posed themselves were diverse. They were certainly bound up with systems of domination, if one takes this term in its sense of ruling or governing, shaping events to certain ends. But the ends they sought were not in any simple way functional to the state, to men or to the economy. We should see 'the state' not as the origin but as the outcome of these programmes. Rather than seeing an expansion of state control we should seek to analyse what one might term 'the governmentalisation of the state': a transformation of what could be governed, by whom and in what ways.

We need to take the arguments of political and legal 'pluralism' seriously. Modern societies are shifting networks of agencies, associations, corporations and domestic units, with many distinct and differentiated *loci* of decision, criteria of judgment, bodies of knowledge and expertise. This 'pluralism' entails genuine conflicts of interest, struggles for political ascendancy and labile alliances. Familialised concerns have arisen in relation to different issues across these networks: inheritance of property or of pathology; vice and delinquency; health and efficiency; motherhood and femininity. They have issued in diverse laws concerning anything from testation to video nasties, and have been incorporated into varied regulatory apparatuses ranging from taxation and social security through architecture and town planning to the decisions of judges in relation to the disposal of female offenders. This 'pluralism' is not a mere surface which we must aim to unify through critique; it must be the field of analysis not least because it must also be the sphere of political judgment and policy evaluation.[17]

The new vocabularies and programmes which emerged in the nineteenth and twentieth centuries do, indeed, entail the formation of sectors and zones which are not merely creatures of state power or means of it extending its control. 'Familialisation' was crucial to the means whereby personal capacities and conducts could be socialised, shaped and maximised in a manner which accorded with the moral and political principles of liberal society. It is inadequate to regard the languages of regulatory strategies, the terms within which they thought themselves, the ways in which they formulated their problems and solutions, as ideological. Little will be understood about their rationale or consequences through 'interpreting' them to reveal fundamental processes or contradictions which they dissimulate or suppress.[18] Instead we need to examine the new ways of thinking and acting which these languages of the family have introduced into our reality. Rather than obscuring or legitimating, they actually constituted new sectors of reality, new problems and possibilities for personal investment as well as for public regulation. The familialisation of society operates because it has managed to command considerable subjective commitment from citizens who have come to regulate their own lives according to its terms. To analyse the private family in terms of illusion, mystification or false consciousness is to avoid examining how this new system of regulation operates, the relations of power it installs and, indeed, how we might seek to transform it, if at all.

Finally, we need to re-conceptualise 'power'. It is now a commonplace to assert that power is not merely negative, repressive and inhibitory. But too often this recognition is merely a means of claiming that a given subject of power – the state, capitalism, patriarchy, men – extends their control by ever more wily means into even more nooks and crannies of existence. But power – the ability to exercise mastery over others, to pursue goals against resistance, to mobilise natural or human forces individually or collectively around aims, aspirations and beliefs – does not have any such single subject or repetitive form. Power cannot be calibrated in zero-sum terms, where what is gained by one side is lost by another. The sources of power are multiple – from control over economic, political, cultural or military resources to charisma, erotic attraction and desire.[19] The mechanics of power vary from physical coercion, through the inertial properties of multiply secured social circuits of exchange or hierarchy, to the micro-organisation of technical forms such as military organisation or domestic architecture. And amongst the modes of operation of power, the shaping of wills, desires, aspirations and interests, the formation of subjectivities and collectivities is more typical than the brute domination of one will by another.

If these arguments are accepted, we must recognise that the critical apparatus of radical thought needs more than repair. Indeed, the demarcation of theoretical resources conducted by radical theorists over the past two decades itself needs to be junked. We will find as much insight in Max Weber as in Karl Marx, in Emile Durkheim as in Evgeny Pashukanis, in Robert Dahl as in Antonio Gramsci. If the work of Michel Foucault has been the stalking horse for this rethinking of the role and nature of radical theory, it is perhaps in large part because he posed these problems to us in their starkest form.

THE GENEALOGY OF FAMILY POWERS

What might an alternative critical analysis of family powers look like? Whilst such a task cannot be undertaken here, some important themes can be drawn out of recent genealogical studies which highlight the differences between genealogy and critique.[20]

1. Beyond the State

Katherine O'Donovan concludes her examination of developments in family law from feudalism to the nineteenth century by arguing that, by the end of this long period, although public regulation provided a legal form for conjugal relations, the content of those relations continued to be ordered by patriarchy – the control of women and children by men. Despite the changes in the law bound up with what she terms "the elevation of domesticity", she concludes: "Rather than intervene directly to regulate family relations publicly, the state delegates its power and authority to the husband."[21] The state is seen as, on the one hand, the enunciator of regulation in the form of law and, on the other hand, the embodiment of male interests.

But the ways of thinking about and acting on family life which have developed over the last century do not have the sources, the functionality or the unity which is here ascribed to them and used for evaluating them. To suggest that these transformations originate in the state, and amount to allotting powers to husbands and fathers, or to coercive welfarism rendered benign by ideology, is to obscure the new types of powers and relations between individuals, experts, professionals and authorities which have taken shape over the last century, and the ways in which the subjectivities, responsibilities and aspirations of both women and men have been transformed.

The emergence of an institutionally distinct political domain, the sovereign state, entailed the gradual concentration of formal political, juridical and administrative powers which had hitherto been dispersed amongst a range of authorities – guilds, justices, landowners, religious authorities – and which had contained extensive mechanisms for specifying, monitoring and sanctioning detailed aspects of personal, conjugal, sexual and domestic conduct.[22] This concentration, and the concomitant legitimation and delimitation of political authority by the doctrines of 'rule of law', entailed the conceptualisation of certain domains which were freed from the threat of punitive sanction and detailed internal regulation. In general terms, one sees here the formation of the domains of the economy and the social, as new sectors of existence.

In the same movement as the political domain separates itself out in this way it defines the limits of the social and economic domains and polices certain of their key elements. If the contract is fundamental to the economy, so the family is fundamental to the government of the social. The family, as Donzelot points out, appeared as a positive solution to the problems of the regulation of morality, health and procreation posed by a liberal definition of the limits of legitimate state action.[23] It has been both distinguished from political life, yet defined by law and permeable to both compulsory and voluntary interventions.

Throughout the nineteenth century and into the twentieth one sees a proliferation of hundreds of little and large projects which sought to shape, mould, regulate and utilise the family and 'what goes on' in it, for social ends and to secure social objectives. Thus 'family reform' was central in programmes for the reform of morality, for the elimination of crime and for the maximisation of efficiency through promoting hygiene of body and mind. A wide variety of problems and possibilities were thought about in terms of the family and acted upon by seeking to affect domestic, conjugal and child rearing arrangements. Public authorities were not often the originators of these programmes, but were involved in various ways, for example by providing a legal framework for voluntary action, by establishing key institutional sites, and by supporting private campaigns with funds and information. One needs to think of 'socialisation' less as an anthropological universal than as an historically specific outcome of such diverse programmes for constructing the capacities, habits, ambitions and subjectivities of citizens. These programmes of socialisation were not simply targetted upon evident social threats – prostitutes, vagrants, lunatics, criminals – but also upon those who were not of 'society' in its earlier sense, that is, who were not persons of property and civility. The familialisation of society was a central instrument in constituting what one might call a subjectivity of citizenship.

By the start of the twentieth century, the family is administered and policed by practices and agencies which are neither private – in that their powers are constructed legally, they are the recipients of public funds and their agents are publicly accredited by some form of licensing – nor organs of political power in that their operations and objectives are not specified by the decrees and programmes of political forces but operate under the aegis of moral principles and, increasingly, by professional expertise underpinned by the power of a claim to truth. To claim that the content of family relations is either unregulated or delegated to husbands is to fundamentally mistake the nature of the modern family and its political role, it is to fall victim to the public/private dichotomy not to transcend it.

2. Whose Interests?

These new programmes of government thus cannot be attributed to the actions of an agency termed 'the state'. The state is not a unified and internally coherent entity which is the *locus* of all social power, but a complex set of agencies which are involved to different extents in projects for the regulation of social and economic life whose origins, inspirations and power often come from elsewhere. Nor can one see all these new programmes of government as unified in the interests they served or the objectives they sought. The issues around which forces were mobilised were often surprising and the groupings promoting reform were complex and heterogeneous. For example, moral and sexual scandals such as those over masturbation in the eighteenth and nineteenth centuries or over the breakdown of marriage in the cities in the mid-nineteenth century operated as important relays through which the wishes of individuals could become linked up with the concerns of population regulation. The campaign against masturbation constituted parents as responsible for the supervision and government of the petty habits of children in the names of their own future health.[24] In the campaign for marriage, the legal relation was to promote emotional and economic investment by both men and women into the home, cathecting domesticity at the expense of street life, public bawdiness and vice.[25] But these campaigns were not organised or orchestrated by the state nor by groups seeking to impose the interests of one class or gender upon another. The anti-masturbation campaign was medically inspired and directed primarily towards the bourgeois family concerned about its own lineage. The campaigns to get the urban poor to marry, to reform domestic architecture and to promote domestic hygiene were waged by bourgeois women who sought to extend the benefits of domesticity to their working class sisters and to further their interests by increasing their powers *vis-à-vis* their menfolk.

Women have not been passive victims or duped collaborators in the family reforms of the last century. They have frequently been active campaigners for such reforms, arguing for them from explicitly radical and feminist positions, and conceiving them as in their political interests, in the interests of their sex, or those of children, or vital for the pursuit of more general moral or social objectives. Increasingly over this century, campaigns for family reform have been initiated by professionals and experts, backing their proposals with a claim to authority based in science. Indeed, many of the current campaigns to increase the autonomy of the family have actually reversed this relation between family members and expertise: family members have organised reforming campaigns, and have called upon expertise to back their criticisms and proposals.

Of course, it is still possible to 'interpret' these campaigns, to reveal underlying class, gender or occupational interests. But it is difficult to see what intelligibility is conferred by such *ex post facto* 'explanations' upon the issues, forces, alliances and methods involved. To seek to explain these events *in terms of* interests – as if these interests pre-existed the events and determined their course and pattern – is to miss the point. What is involved is the emergence of new ways of constituting one's own and others' interests, and new mobilisations of forces around them.

3. *Power and Control*

Critical legal scholars conceptualise the new networks of power which link up the private family and personal life with authoritative judgment as extension of the social control apparatus of the state disguised by the ideology of the family as a realm of privacy. For example, recent moves to informalism in the resolution of family disputes are often seen as actually extending the monitoring and controlling of family relations. This is supported by the argument that:

> . . . informal justice increases state power. Informal institutions allow state control to escape the walls of those highly visible centers of coercion . . . and permeate society . . . . But it is possible – and essential – to penetrate the comforting facade of informalism and reveal its political meaning.[26]

The object of critique, then, is to penetrate the facade of privacy and free choice, to reveal the hidden mechanisms of control and to expose the interests served.

But, as I have already argued, there is little empirical evidence for such linkages between strategies of the state, interests in control and the establishment and operation of regulatory systems.[27] Further, social control is a somewhat meagre explanatory device. It 'explains' only at the cost of unifying a vast range of mechanisms, techniques and objectives. It must 'explain away' not only the varied ethical, political and technical motives of social reformers, but also the subjective commitments of the individuals involved to the values and practices which 'control' them.[28]

It is often suggested that women's apparent investment in family matters is actually forcibly imposed upon them.[29] Women are forced into the private domain by the inequities of the structure of the labour market, the wage system and other institutions from education to child care; domesticity and motherhood are portrayed as the sites of female satisfaction, and women's rejection of this role is portrayed as the origins of all sorts of personal and social ills from juvenile delinquency to unemployment. But we can contest the constraints upon choice in domestic arrangements, the lack of child care facilities, the social representations of women and so forth without reducing personal commitments to domestic life, or to the pleasures and pains of caring and intimacy, to a 'coercion of privacy'.

It is misleading to analyse social representations of motherhood, fatherhood, family life and so forth as if they distort experience or impose false consciousness; they are crucial aspects of the processes by which individuals constitute their selves and their lives, and come to establish certain 'personal' aspirations and evaluations. Of course, the construction of subjective values and investments was the aim of many familialising projects of the nineteenth and twentieth centuries. It was an explicit rationale in the moralising philanthropy of the nineteenth century, and in the arguments for universal education. It was also evident in the concern for the health and welfare of children in the early twentieth century. This certainly sought to utilise 'the family' and the relations within it as a kind of social or socialising machine in order to fulfil various objectives: military, industrial and moral. But this was to be done not through the coercive enforcement of control under threat of sanction, but through the construction of mothers who would want their homes and children to be governed according to hygienic norms. The promotion of hygiene and welfare could only be successful to the extent that it managed to solicit the active engagement of individuals in the promotion of their own bodily efficiency. Perhaps the final instalment in the construction of a subjectivity of citizenship comes only with the Second World War and its aftermath, in which films, television and propaganda interpellated those of all ages, sexes and classes as engaged in a common struggle in defence of their country, in which each had their value and each their part.

If the family came to serve social objectives, it was not in spite of the wishes of women and men, but because it came to work as a private, voluntary and responsible agency for the rearing and moralising of children and promoting their physical and mental welfare. Domestic, conjugal and parental conduct is increasingly regulated not by obedience compelled by threat of sanction but through the activation of individual guilt, personal anxiety and private disappointment. Husbands and wives, mothers and fathers themselves regulate their feelings, desires, wishes and emotions and think themselves through the potent images of parenthood, sexual pleasure and quality of life. In the necessary gap between expectation and realisation, between desires and satisfaction, anxiety and disappointment fuel the search for expert assistance. It is this pleasure/anxiety relation that drives the government of personal life; it is this which is both installed by the tutelage of expertise and which provides it with its voluntary relation to its subjects. These kinds of mechanisms, not those of social control, domination and subordination, link up the private family with social, economic and political objectives through the maximisation of consumption, the promotion of subjectivities and the construction of social solidarity through the rituals of personal life.

Indeed, the contemporary family is not the subject of perpetual scrutiny or of totalitarian policing. The repetitive 'scandals' of abused children reveal how diverse and unco-ordinated are the agencies which surround even the 'problem' family, how varied are their values and techniques, how ineffective is their scrutiny. More generally, the variety of expert discourses, the range of sources of advice, the competitiveness of pressure groups, lawyers, psychologists, psychiatrists and other professionals, the proliferation of advice on all aspects of personal relations means that pluralism is more than a myth. What unifies the family machine, as it were, is not the solutions posed to the problem of living healthy, well adjusted and fulfilled life, raising happy children and forming satisfying relationships – it is the terrain established by the problem itself.

CONCLUSION

Critical analysis of family law must relocate legal regulation within the complex network of powers which link up domestic, sexual and parental relations with social, economic and political objectives. Laws and statutory duties, statuses and obligations are very important here, but are neither primary nor constitutive. Certainly coercive regulation of familial relations needs to be understood as just one modality amongst many differentiated modes by which privacy is scrutinised, judged and normalised: we need to analyse its place without regarding it as paradigmatic or determinant. Legal relations and legal sanctions are bound up in different ways in the varied regulatory apparatuses by which social life has become familialised, but an analysis of family policies cannot privilege family law.

In particular we need to appreciate the forms of power flowing from claims to knowledge concerning family life, child rearing, sexual pleasure, health and hygiene, happiness and contentment. The power of expertise installs a new type of relation between authority and its subjects. Expertise is a form of authority bound up with the development of new regulatory techniques. It certainly cannot be compartmentalised according to the public/private opposition but nor can it be evaluated in terms of *state* regulation, social *control* or *male* power. The term 'tutelary' captures the nature of this relationship rather well, with its implications of dependence, subservience, guardianship and instruction.[30]

Characterisations of the family as a site of female subordination, however accurate, fail to capture the complexity of familial powers, of the duties, obligations, pains and pleasures which have been constituted through the familialisation of the subjectivities of both women and men. The programmes for the government of the conduct of families, parents and children, husbands, wives and sexual partners over the last hundred years have actually constituted new forms of social subject committed to a project of subjective fulfillment in which familialism has a central role. This is not to deny the extent to which many aspects of familial relations disadvantage women, or the failure of legislation and enforcement to rectify this disadvantage. But feminist critiques and proposals will be of limited value unless they can provide a positive analysis of the new types of power and authority which have come into existence over the last century and the ways in which they operate. In analysing these forms of subjectification from the perspective of power we need to free ourselves from the belief that this entails only the submission of self to others and allow the possibility that it also involves the way in which we – modern women and men – have become tied to a project of our own identities, a project which binds us to others at the same moment as it binds us to ourselves.

More generally, I have suggested that social analysis needs to break from the techniques of critique which have underpinned its explanatory strategies for so long. Critique has certain advantages for radicals: for it appears simultaneously to explain, to judge and to proffer an alternative. Breaking with critique makes visible a complex of practices and powers that do not lend themselves to global analysis and evaluation. Hence they do not suggest the task of constructing a general theory of power or a programmatic politics of social transformation. Rather, they suggest a more modest task that, starting from definite problems or concerns would seek to uncover the conditions and assumptions which have made them possible and the relations of advantage and disadvantage they entail. Such investigations pose us questions of judgment which cannot be answered by political slogans but require ethical choices that are both difficult and compromising.

NOTES AND REFERENCES

1 For some of this literature see M. Stacey, "The Division of Labour Revisited" in *Development and Diversity: British Sociology 1950-1980* (1981; eds. P. Abrams *et al.*); M. Stacey and M. Price, *Women, Power and Politics* (1981); E. Gamarnikow *et al.* (eds.), *The Public and the Private* (1983). Much of the recent debate refers back to M. Rosaldo, "Women, Culture and Society" in *Women, Culture and Society* (1974; eds. M. Rosaldo and L. Lamphere).

2 F. Olsen, "The Family and the Market: a Study of Ideology and Legal Reform" (1983) 96 *Harvard Law Rev.* p. 1497; K. O'Donovan, *Sexual Divisions in Law* (1985); M. Freeman, "Towards a Critical Theory of Family Law" (1985) 38 *Current Legal Problems* p. 153; A. Bottomley, "Resolving Family Disputes: A Critical View" in *State, Law and the Family* (1984; ed. M. Freeman).

3 Freeman, *op. cit.*, n. 2.

4 *Id.*

5 M. Horwitz, "The History of the Public/Private Distinction" (1982) 130 *University of Pennsylvania Law Rev.* p. 1423.

6 D. Kennedy, "The Stages of the Decline of the Public/Private Distinction" (1982) 130 *University of Pennsylvania Law Rev.* p. 1349.

7 Cf. K. Klare, "The Public/Private Distinction in Labour Law" (1982) 130 *University of Pennsylvania Law Rev.* p. 1349.

8 *Op. cit.*

9 *Id.*, p. 1578.

10 *Supra*, n. 1.

11 See O'Donovan, *op. cit.*, p. 11 and Freeman, *op. cit.*, p. 169.

12 *Supra*, n. 2.

13 E.g., L. Parkinson, "Conciliation: a new approach to family conflict resolution" (1983) 13 *Brit. J. Social Work* p. 19; M. King, "Child Protection and the Search for Justice for Parents and Families" in Freeman, ed., *op. cit.*, n. 2, p. 139.

14 E.g., Bottomley, *op. cit.*, n. 2, pp. 293-300 and Freeman, *op. cit.*, n. 2, pp. 163-65. Cf. R. Abel (ed.), *The Politics of Informal Justice* (1982) 2 Vols.

15 J. Goldstein, A. Freud and A. Solnit, *Beyond the Best Interests of the Child* (1983).

16 Freeman, *op. cit.*, n. 2, p. 171.

17 See the paper by Hirst and Jones in this volume.

18 This is the task Olsen sets herself, wrenching the language of reforming strategies from their context and reinterpreting them in terms of the family/market opposition. What is gained in elegance is lost in intelligibility as to what was at stake in these debates. See Olsen, *op. cit.*, n. 2.

19 For a thought-provoking historical study of power relations with a productive conceptual basis see M. Mann, *The Sources of Social Power* (1986) Vol. 1.

20 See J. Donzelot, *The Policing of Families* (1979); M. Foucault, *History of Sexuality* (1978) Vol. 1; D. Riley, *War in the Nursery* (1983); N. Rose, *The Psychological Complex* (1985); P. Miller and N. Rose (eds.), *The Power of Psychiatry* (1986) especially chap. 2; J. Minson, *Genealogies of Morals* (1985); D. Garland, *Punishment and Welfare* (1985).

21 *Op. cit.*, n. 2, p. 57. See also Freeman, *op. cit.*, and, in a stronger form, C. MacKinnon, "Feminism, Marxism, Method and the State: Towards Feminist Jurisprudence" (1983) 8 *Signs* p. 635.

22 Minson, *op. cit.*, n. 20 has a good discussion drawing on J. Strakosch, *State Absolutism and the Rule of Law* (1967).

23 *Op. cit.*, n. 20.

24 See Foucault, *op. cit.*, n. 20 and Donzelot, *op. cit.*, n. 20, and the discussion in Minson, *op. cit.*, chap. 8.

25 *Id.*; see also Rose, *op. cit.*, n. 20, chap. 6.

26 Abel, *op. cit.*, n. 14, p. 6. Cf. Bottomley, *op. cit.*, n. 2, p. 300; O'Donovan, *op. cit.*, n. 2, p. 195; Freeman, *op. cit.*, n. 2, pp. 163 and 173.

27 See also R. Gordon, "Critical Legal Histories" (1984) 36 *Stanford Law Rev.* p. 57 and D. Sugarman's introduction to *Law, Economy and Society* (1984; eds. G. Rubin and D. Sugarman).

28 Even those sociologists most committed to explanations in terms of social control now have doubts about the utility of the concept; see, for example, A. Scull and S. Cohen (eds.), *Social Control and the State* (1982). But they end up offering revamped versions of social control as a solution to its own failure: see the criticisms in Miller and Rose, *op. cit.*, n. 20.

29 Freeman, *op. cit.*, n. 2; C. Smart, *The Ties That Bind* (1984); T. Dahl and A. Snare, "The Coercion of Privacy" in *Women, Sex and Social Control* (1978; ed. C. Smart); S. Hall, "Reformism and the Legalisation of Consent" in *Permissiveness and Control* (1979; ed. National Deviancy Conference).

30 Cf. Donzelot, *op. cit.*, n. 20.

[3]

Race Matters: Change, Choice, and Family Law at the Millennium

TWILA L. PERRY*

I. Introduction

Beginning in the 1960s, legal regulation of the family began to shift from a system characterized predominately by state regulation of marriage and other intimate relationships, to one in which substantial limits were imposed on state control of many personal life choices. Cases such as *Roe v. Wade,*[1] *Griswold v. Connecticut,*[2] and *Eisenstadt v, Baird,*[3] recognized important rights of privacy with respect to reproductive rights and sexual activity. The increased power of individuals over their intimate lives was also reflected in developments such as the increased recognition by state courts of antenuptial contracts and cohabitation agreements. More recently, innovations in technology have given hope of parenthood to couples who in earlier times would have had to accept infertility as a sad fact of life. Adoption has become more common, and there has been increased recognition of the legitimacy of diverse forms of families, including single-parent families, stepfamilies, and families with parents who are gay or lesbian. There are also new legal options for those who find themselves in unhappy or abusive relationships. For many people, the changes in family law over the last forty years mean that they now have more power than ever to make choices about their personal lives.

Although these changes have affected everyone, not everyone has an equal opportunity to take advantage of the wider range of options. As

---

* Professor of Law, Rutgers University School of Law-Newark.

1. 410 U.S 113 (1973).
2. 381 U.S. 479 (1965).
3. 405 U.S. 438 (1972). *But see* Bowers v. Hardwick, 478 U.S. 186 (1986).

we approach the millennium, it is clear that for many Black Americans, the new freedom to structure choices about family life is often illusory.

This essay will identify and discuss some of the ways in which the factor of race continues to constrain the choices of many African-Americans about family life. Part One will first describe some present realities of Black life in this country. Part Two will focus on two areas: choices concerning intimate relationships between adults, and choices about becoming a parent, to illustrate some of the ways in which the options of many Blacks remain constricted.

Part Three will point out some ways in which this society seems to be moving toward more, rather than less public regulation of the lives of many Black families. Finally, Part Four will briefly note some issues concerning race that family law will need to address in the new millennium.

In focusing, for this symposium, on the de facto limitations on the choices of Black people, I am not suggesting that Blacks are the only group in this country forced to make choices about family life within constraints. Women, members of other minority groups, and virtually all poor people live lives in which choices about family are limited by circumstances over which they have little control. The problems of these groups also deserve more attention, and I hope that scholars will continue to address them.

II. Black Life at the Millennium

There is a stark disparity in this country between the material circumstances of Black people and those of white people. The median income of Black families in the United States is $26,522; for white families it is $44,756.[4] The number of Black men of working age who are unemployed is twice that of white men.[5] In 1997, the median income of employed white men was $24,949, for employed Black men it was $16,491.[6] Of people living below the poverty level, 28.4% are Black—the figure for whites is only 11.2%.[7] Forty-one percent of Black children in America live in families with incomes below the poverty level, while the figure for white children is only 10.5 percent.[8] This country's prisons house more Black men than white men, even though Blacks comprise only 13 percent of the

4. Bureau of the Census, U.S. Department of Commerce, Statistical Abstract of the United States 472 (118 ed., 1998) [hereinafter Census].
5. *Id.* at 425.
6. *Id.* at 476.
7. *Id.* at 478.
8. *Id.* at 478.

population.[9] The infant mortality rates for Black babies is more than twice that of white babies[10] and the maternal mortality rate for Black women is five times that of white women.[11]

As discouraging as these statistics may seem, it is also true that the lives of the majority of Black people in this country are much better now than they were at the close of the last century. A little more than one hundred years ago, the separate but equal doctrine of *Plessy v. Ferguson*[12] enshrined second class citizenship for Black Americans. The results of that U.S. Supreme Court decision included increased racial segregation in public accommodations and education, flagrant violations of Black people's voting rights, and increased physical violence and racial intimidation. One of the most devastating consequences of *Plessy* is that it legitimized racial stigma as a part of American culture. Although there has been substantial progress toward equality during this century, significant problems persist. The choices Black people make and are able to make with respect to family life, and the way in which those choices are viewed by others must be examined in the context of the past and present economic and cultural realities of race in America.

III. Choices Concerning Adult Relationships

For most Americans decreased state regulation of the family has meant increased options in terms of decisions about marriage, divorce and cohabitation. Unhappily married couples can now end their marriages by opting for no-fault divorces, avoiding much of the unpleasantness and embarrassment that were a part of divorce under the fault system. The option of cohabitation contracts, accepted by many states since *Marvin v. Marvin*,[13] permits couples to structure alternatives to marriage which allow them to access some of marriage's benefits, while limiting some of its obligations. The right to bring a tort action against one's spouse and the right to invoke state protection from domestic violence provide remedies that are very different from those which were available a generation ago.

For some Black people, these new options provide the same oppor-

9. *Id.* at 14. Statistics reveal that in 1996, there were 510,900 white male sentenced federal and state prisoners. The figure for black males was 528,200. U.S. DEPARTMENT OF JUSTICE, SOURCEBOOK OF CRIMINAL JUSTICE STATISTICS 494 (1997) [hereinafter CRIMINAL JUSTICE STATISTICS].

10. CENSUS, *supra* note 4, at 99.

11. *Id.* at 98.

12. 163 U.S. 537 (1896).

13. 557 P.2d 106 (Cal. 1976).

464 *Family Law Quarterly, Volume 33, Number 3, Fall 1999*

tunities that they do for other Americans. For other Blacks, however, difficult or marginal economic circumstances mean that the new choices about marriage and divorce have little practical relevance to their lives. For still others, pursuing an option that on its face seems equally available to everyone may be a complicated matter because of political or cultural considerations that they believe are important.

A. Marriage

As an initial matter, for many Black people, choosing to enter into even the most traditional and conservative structure for adult intimate relationships—formal marriage—can be problematic. A major source of difficulty is the sheer disparity in numbers between Black women and Black men at the optimum ages for marriage. At the present time, there is a numerical excess of women over men at every age group in the marriageable years.[14] This means that assuming that most Black women are seeking Black partners for marriage, a substantial number of Black women will probably never marry. In 1997, 17.5 percent of white women over the age of eighteen had never been married. The figure for Black women was 37.2 percent.[15]

A second critical factor affecting the rates of marriage for Black people is the precarious economic situation of many Black men. In this country, Black men are disproportionately unemployed, underemployed, and undereducated.[16] Rates of entanglement with the criminal justice system, poor health, and early death are also substantially higher for Black men than they are for white men of similar ages.[17] These fundamental demographic realities should not be thought of as only constraining marriage choices for Black women—they also constrain the ability of Black men to marry. Although as this century closes, remaining single has gained acceptance as a permanent lifestyle rather than a temporary state, for some people, the realization that marriage is simply not a viable option can be a substantial source of unhappiness. Of all the women in this country, Black women are the least likely to marry, the most likely to be divorced, and the least likely to remarry.[18]

14. William A. Darity, Jr. & Samuel L. Myers, *Family Structure and the Marginalization of Black Men: Policy Implications, in* THE DECLINE IN MARRIAGE AMONG AFRICAN-AMERICANS: CAUSES, CONSEQUENCES AND POLICY IMPLICATIONS 265 (M. Belinda Tucker & Claudia Mitchell-Kernan, eds. 1995) [hereinafter DECLINE IN MARRIAGE].

15. CENSUS, *supra* note 4, at 57.

16. *See generally* YOUNG BLACK AND MALE IN AMERICA: AN ENDANGERED SPECIES (Jewelle Taylor Gibbs, ed. 1988); JOSEPH L. WHITE & JAMES H. CONES III, BLACK MAN EMERGING: FACING THE PAST AND SEIZING A FUTURE IN AMERICA (1999).

17. Darity & Myers, *supra* note 14, at 263, 265.

18. M. Belinda Tucker & Claudia Mitchell-Kernan, *Trends in African-American*

The state of affairs described above affects other choices Black women may make about family life. Sociologists have drawn a correlation between the availability of potential mates for marriage and the number of Black families headed by single women.[19] The decision to bear a child outside of marriage, for example, may represent a particular woman's personal political stance against marriage or a desire to rebel against traditional mores or expectations. But what is often not recognized is that such a division may simply represent a woman's practical response to demographic realities.[20]

B. Divorce

Beginning in the early 1970s, many states began to move from a system in which proof of fault was a requirement for divorce, to a system characterized by no-fault.[21] By making divorce less costly, no-fault has certainly made divorce a more realistic option for people of limited economic means. The alleged downside of no-fault, that it has hurt women economically,[22] clearly has less relevance to the lives of Black women than it does to the lives of white women. Black couples typically have less economic wealth to divide than white couples do, and fewer Black men than white men have the kind of jobs that would make generous alimony awards even a remote possibility.[23]

In this country, the divorce rate for Black couples is higher than it is for white couples.[24] Does this mean that Black couples are more likely to "choose" divorce than white couples, and if so, why is this the case? In thinking about the question of why Blacks divorce more often than whites, attention must be paid to the frank reality that race is a factor which makes marriage an even more fragile institution for Blacks than it is for whites. For Black couples, the normal stresses

Family Formation: A Theoretical and Statistical Overview, in THE DECLINE IN MARRIAGE, *supra* note 14, at 12 (noting lower rates of marriage and higher rates of divorce for Black women); M. Belinda Tucker & Claudia Mitchell-Kernan, *Marital Behavior and Expectation: Ethnic Comparisons of Attitudinal and Structural Correlates, in* THE DECLINE OF MARRIAGE, *supra* note 14, at 167 (noting lower rates of remarriage for Black women).

19. Darity & Myers, *supra* note 14, at 263–89.

20. *Id.* at 263–289.

21. HOMER H. CLARK, THE LAW OF DOMESTIC RELATIONS IN THE UNITED STATES 513–21 (2d ed. 1987).

22. *See, e.g.*, Twila L. Perry, *No-Fault Divorce and Liability Without Fault: Can Family Law Learn from Torts,* 52 OHIO ST. L. J. 55 (1991).

23. Twila L. Perry, *Alimony: Race, Privilege and Dependency in the Search for a Theory,* 82 GEO. L.J. 2481 (1994).

24. Black women divorce at a rate that is twice as high as that for white women. In 1990, for white women the divorce rate was 153 per 1,000 married women. The figure for Black women was 358 per 1,000 married women. *See* M. Belinda Tucker & Claudia Mitchell-Kernan, *Trends in African American Family Formation: A Theoretical and Statistical Overview, in* THE DECLINE IN MARRIAGE, *supra* note 14, at 10, 12.

associated with marriage are multiplied exponentially by the factor of race.

The fragile economic status of many Black men once again is a factor. In a world in which the male is still traditionally expected to be the major breadwinner and greater economic power in a family, the man who cannot fulfill this role is likely to feel diminished, and these feelings almost inevitably lead to marital stress. Although gender roles within marriage are less distinct than was true in the past, the power of patriarchy as a cultural norm in this country should not be underestimated. The fact that many Black men are unable to meet society's cultural expectations about the role of men in marriage undoubtedly contributes to a higher divorce rate among Black couples.

C. Cohabitation, Antenuptial Contracts, and Remedies for Mistreatment

Antenuptial contracts, cohabitation agreements, and newly available remedies for physical and emotional abuse are other contexts in which the likelihood of an individual accessing new options with respect to family life is affected by race. The fact that cohabitation between unmarried people has become more common in recent years[25] has meant increased freedom for a wide range of people to choose this option without apology or shame. Cohabitation without marriage used to be widely thought of as a way of life common only among poor people and/or minorities.[26] The term "common law wife" was considered derogatory,[27] even though common law marriages, if they met certain criteria, have long been formally recognized by the law in a number of states.[28] The fact that in recent years, cohabitation has become common among white middle and upper-middle class people has clearly increased its legitimacy and respectability. Cohabitation no longer has the stigma it had when it was associated with poor people and Black people. Instead, cohabitation is increasingly viewed as a respectable long-term life choice for people of all ages, classes, and races.

Still, in cohabitation, race matters. Couples are unlikely to enter into a formal written cohabitation contract unless the assets that could become the subject of dispute are sufficient to justify the transaction costs

---

25. The 1980 census revealed 1,589,000 unmarried couples of the opposite sex sharing the same household. By 1997, that figure had risen to 4,130,000. CENSUS, *supra* note 4, at 60.

26. CLARK, *supra* note 21, at 45, 59 n. 86 (citing treatises in the 1940s and 1950s noting the prevalence of common law marriage among Blacks and lower class whites).

27. Walter O. Weyraugh, *Informal and Formal Marriage: An Appraisal of Trends in Family Organization,* 28 U. CHI. L. REV. 88, 98–99 (1960).

28. For a discussion of the long history of common law marriage in this country, *see* CLARK, *supra* note 21, at 48–62.

of the contracting process. Since Blacks generally have little economic wealth, such contracts are unlikely to be a part of their cohabitation arrangement.

Anteuptial contracts,[29] which seek to allocate the economic consequences of divorce prior to marriage, are similarly less likely to be entered into by Black couples. Here too, the option of entering into such agreements is meaningful only where there are assets substantial enough to be the subject of litigation in the event of a divorce.

Economic status also plays a role in the decision of one spouse as to whether to bring a tort action against the other at the time of divorce.[30] The demise of interspousal immunity means that one spouse may now seek a money judgment against the other for wrongful acts committed during the course of the marriage. Actions for marital torts, however, are obviously futile where the spouse to be sued has few assets. Therefore, Black women, who, for the most part, are married to Black men, are unlikely plaintiffs in such suits.

Domestic violence is another context in which spouses may seek newly available forms of relief for wrongdoing by their partners. It used to be the case that state concerns for marital privacy deprived wives of protection against physically violent husbands. Today, in most states, marital rape is a crime,[31] and there is a new commitment to addressing the problem of domestic violence.[32] However, choosing to invoke state remedies to address a partner's abusive behavior may be a more complex and troubling choice for a Black woman than for a white one. Black women are well aware that encounters between the police and Black men often result in violence and even death. Black women are also very aware of the disproportionate rates of incarceration of Black men. Because of the racial history of this country, most Black women regard Black men as their brothers in a struggle against a common foe of racism, and many would consider it an act of racial disloyalty to call the police on their husbands or partners.[33] Thus, many Black women may be reluctant to pursue this option even when perhaps, pursuing it would be the wiser choice.

---

29. Beginning in the 1970s, many state courts began to uphold the validity of antenuptial contracts. *See, e.g.,* Posner v. Posner, 233 So. 2d 381 (Fla. 1970); Osborne v. Osborne, 428 N.E.2d 810 (Mass. 1981).

30. *See, e.g.,* Henrikson v. Cameron, 622 A.2d 1135 (Me. 1993); Davis v. Bostick, 580 P.2d 544 (Or. 1978).

31. *See, e.g.,* Warren v. State, 336 S.E. 2d 221 (Ga. 1985); People v. Liberta, 474 N.E.2d 567 (N.Y. 1984).

32. In 1994, for example the federal government enacted the Violence Against Women Act, Pub. L. No. 103-322, Title IV, 108 Stat. 1902-55 (codified in scattered sections of 8 U.S.C.A., 18 U.S.C.A. & 42 U.S.C.A), intended to be a major initiative against domestic violence.

33. *See generally* Kimberle Crenshaw, *Mapping the Margins: Intersectionality, Identity Politics, and Violence Against Women of Color,* 43 STAN. L. REV. 1241 (1991).

468 *Family Law Quarterly, Volume 33, Number 3, Fall 1999*

IV. Choices about Becoming a Parent

One consequence of the move toward more private ordering in family law is that people now have more choices about ways to become parents. Single motherhood, adoption, and the new reproductive technology represent routes to parenthood other than traditional marriage. In each of these contexts, race is a significant a factor in the availability of choices. It is also a factor in how the larger society regards the choices people make.

A. Single Motherhood

One memorable moment in recent public discourse about the family occurred in 1992 when former Vice President Dan Quayle criticized the choice of television sitcom character Murphy Brown to bear a child as a single mother.[34] This incident sparked what became widely known as the "family values" debate. Public discussion focused on the idea of women raising children alone, and quickly moved on to the usual scapegoating of single mothers on public assistance. What was particularly interesting and ironic was the fact that the fictional television character who ignited the debate was a white, well to do, extremely successful, professional woman complete with a townhouse and full-time nanny.

The public discussion about single mothers in the wake of the Murphy Brown incident once again demonstrated that although single motherhood is still somewhat generally stigmatized in this country,[35] for many people, the image of the woman who chooses to bear a child outside of marriage is that of a Black woman rather than a white one. The assumptions are that such a woman is lazy, that she is not interested in marriage, that she doesn't work and doesn't want to work, and that she is likely to go on to have a house full of children who have little chance of becoming law-abiding, productive citizens.

I have already discussed the link sociologists have made between marriage options and the rates of single motherhood in black communities. The fact today, however, is that single motherhood is growing at a faster rate among white women, who have more marriage options, than among Black women. It will be interesting to see whether the fact that increasing numbers of white women are having children outside

34. *See, e.g.*, John E. Yang & Ann Devroy, *Quayle: "Hollywood Doesn't Get It," Adminstration Struggles to Explain Attack on TV's Murphy Brown*, WASH. POST, May 21, 1992, at A1.

35. *See generally* MARTHA ALBERTSON FINEMAN, THE NEUTERED MOTHER, THE SEXUAL FAMILY AND OTHER TWENTIETH CENTURY TRAGEDIES 100–25 (1995).

of marriage[36] will have any effect on how society views Black women who make the same choice. Although women may have different options with respect to marriage, women tend to desire motherhood for similar reasons: to nurture another human being, to pass on a legacy of culture and/or biology. However, the choices women make about becoming a mother are often not given equal respect.

The different ways that society views the choices women make about motherhood extends beyond matters of childbearing to choices about how children will be cared for. The middle class married mother who stays out of the workforce in order to care for her children is often admired as a person who has made a significant personal sacrifice. On the other hand, a single mother on public assistance who chooses to do the same thing is likely to be considered just plain lazy. Society does not respect her choice as to how best care for her children. The main difference between the two women, however, is usually that one is being financially supported by a man and the other is not.[37] But why should the presence or absence of a man define the legitimacy of a mother's decision about what her children need? Rather than passing moral judgments, the society and the government should do more to support all mothers in the choices they make about care for their young children.

B. *Transracial Adoption*

As shocking as it may seem in today's increasingly multiracial society, it was not until the 1967 Supreme Court decision in *Loving v. Virginia*[38] that state statutes prohibiting marriages between Blacks and whites were declared unconstitutional. Until that time, people in this country did not have the basic, simple right to choose to marry a person of a different race. In recent years, the number of interracial marriages has risen dramatically, although such marriages still represent a very small proportion of all marriages entered into in this country.

The public debate about interracial families now often takes place in the context of the controversy over transracial adoption rather than over interracial marriage. The subject of transracial adoption seems to consistently capture the public's attention, probably because it is a symbol of the tensions, misunderstandings, anger, and other complex feelings that persist between whites and Blacks over the issue of race.[39]

36. Census data reveals that in 1980, 48% of births were to unmarried white women. By 1995, that figure had risen to 62.6%. CENSUS, *supra* note 4, at 81.

37. *See* Perry, *supra* note 23, at 2500–2502.

38. 388 U.S. 1 (1967).

39. *See* Twila L. Perry, *The Transracial Adoption Controversy: An Analysis of Discourse and Subordination,* 21 N.Y.U. REV. L. & SOC. ch. 33 (1993–94) [hereinafter *Transracial Adoption*].

470 *Family Law Quarterly, Volume 33, Number 3, Fall 1999*

Much of the attention in the transracial adoption controversy has focused on the question of whether white adoptive parents can raise Black children to be well-adjusted, productive adults with a positive sense of racial identity.[40] There are other issues, such as whether transracial adoption constitutes cultural genocide[41] and whether the Black community has an interest in whether Black children are placed with adoptive parents who are Black.[42] One issue that has not received the attention it deserves is how racial choice plays out differently for Black and for white prospective adoptive parents.

The current structure of transracial adoption is essentially a one-way street in terms of racial choice.[43] Basically, whites are free to adopt children of any race. If a white couple expresses a preference for adopting a white baby, as most whites do, that preference is generally accommodated and its legitimacy is not questioned. At the same time, it is obvious that a Black couple would not be given a white baby even if they requested one. Moreover, when Blacks advocate matching Black parents with Black children, they are often criticized. The National Association of Black Social Workers, for example, has been the subject of a great deal of criticism for the strong position it has taken against transracial adoption and in favor of same-race placements for Black children.[44]

Although as a practical matter, most Black families do not seek to adopt white children, the way in which racial choices are treated in adoption is significant because it is symbolic of the many ways in which racial stigma is alive and well in this country. The current system makes clear that Black families continue to be devalued—one of the reasons the idea of Blacks adopting white children exceeds the nation's cultural imagination is that many whites believe it could never be in the interest for a white child to be adopted by a Black family.

C. Reproductive Rights, Privacy and Reproductive Technology

Obtaining the right to abortion was one of the most important developments in family law during the latter third of the twentieth century.

40. *Id.* at 57–65.
41. *Id.* at 72–77.
42. *Id.* at 65–72.
43. *Id.* For a discussion expanding this analysis, see R. Richard Banks, *The Color of Desire: Fulfilling Adoptive Parents Racial Preferences Through Discriminatory State Action,* 107 YALE L.J. 875 (1998).
44. *Transracial Adoption, supra* note 39, at 46–47. For an example of criticism of the National Association of Black Social Workers and criticism of Black opposition to transracial adoption generally, *see* Elizabeth Bartholet, *Where Do Black Children Belong? The Politics of Race Matching in Transracial Adoption,* 139 U. PA. L. REV. 1163 (1991).

Unfortunately, as the millennium approaches, it is unclear as to what limitations may ultimately be placed on this right,[45] or indeed, whether the right will survive at all.

A different aspect of reproductive freedom is the right of a woman to have her choice to bear a child respected by the larger society. In recent years, many public controversies have made it clear that the choices Black women make about motherhood are easily devalued. Initiatives such as family cap provisions in the context of so-called "welfare reform,"[46] attempts by some judges to condition women's sentences in child abuse cases on their consent to use Norplant,[47] the prosecution in some states of pregnant drug addicts,[48] and the attempt to link the issue of transracial adoption to welfare reform[49] send a clear message: Black women, and especially poor Black women, are bad mothers who need to stop having children. These controversies represent instances in which the state has intruded into some of women's most personal life choices.

At the same time that society seems to discourage Black women from having children, new reproductive technologies have provided the opportunity for more and more white middle and upper middle-class people to choose and experience biological parenthood. These new technologies, which have given hope to so many, raise a myriad of moral and ethical issues. Some of the more troubling but least addressed issues involve race. The new reproductive technology now permits couples to virtually preorder the kind of baby that they want. This means that the genetic material of those with the kind of physical features that are

45. *See, e.g.*, Planned Parenthood v. Casey, 505 U.S. 833 (1992).

46. Dorothy Roberts, Killing the Black Body: Race, Reproduction and the Meaning of Liberty 136–243 (1997).

47. *See, e.g.*, Stacey L. Arthur, *The Norplant Prescription: Birth Control, Woman Control or Crime Control?*, 40 UCLA L. Rev. 1 (1992); Julie Mertus & Simon Heller, *Norplant Meets the New Eugenicists: The Impermissibility of Coerced Contraceptives*, 11 St. Louis Pub. L. Rev. 359 (1992).

48. *See generally* Dorothy E. Roberts, *Punishing Drug Addicts Who Have Babies: Women of Color, Equality and the Right of Privacy*, 104 Harv. L. Rev. 1419 (1991).

49. Some conservatives have sought to link adoption with welfare reform. *See, e.g.*, Charles Murray, *Stop Favoring Unwed Mothers*, N.Y. Times, Jan. 15, 1992, at A3 (contending that welfare removes the financial incentives for poor women to give their children up for adoption.) In congressional testimony in connection with welfare reform legislation, William J. Bennett stated:

> I believe that making adoption easier is an essential and compassionate part of welfare reform. Adoption is the best alternative we have to protect a child's interest in a post-welfare world. . . . Lifting restrictions on interracial adoption and easing age limitations for adoptive parents will help to insure that large numbers of children will be adopted into good, stable, loving homes.

Welfare Revision: Hearing Before the Subcommittee on Human Resources of the Committee on Ways and Means, 104th Cong. 1995 (Testimony of William J. Bennett, Co-Director of Empower America).

472 *Family Law Quarterly, Volume 33, Number 3, Fall 1999*

most desired in this country has become a valuable commodity. Because the standard of beauty in this country is a white one, in the world of reproductive technology, the genetic material of Blacks is essentially worthless.[50]

This new technology provides a new world of choice for people with substantial economic means, but most black people do not have the economic means to take advantage of the new procedures.[51] Assuming that infertility strikes the rich and the poor with equal opportunity, those with less economic means will not have the same chance to become parents.

In addition, the new technology provides other kinds of choices for white women that clearly will not be available to Black women. White women will be able to choose to market their services either as genetic or gestational surrogate mothers. However, Black women, whose genetic material has no market value in the white world of surrogacy, will be limited to functioning as gestational surrogates—which is certain to be the less lucrative form of surrogacy.

The phenomenon of surrogacy also sheds light on the fact that the act of producing children outside of marriage can be an assailed choice, or a respected one, depending on the status of the individuals involved. Affluence not only provides special opportunities—it can also provide a shield against stigma. One fact not often noted is that children born of surrogacy are, in reality, children born outside of marriage. Yet, neither these children nor the parents who have chosen to create them outside of marriage seem to suffer any social stigma associated with so-called "illegitimacy."[52]

V. Black Families and Public Regulation

While many people in this country have increasing freedom to make choices about family life, the family lives of Black people, especially poor Black people, seem to be characterized more and more by public regulation than by private ordering. Poor families are public families. The state intrudes in the lives of poor families through a range of mechanisms: the rules of public housing, the requirements of welfare regulations, the intervention of the child welfare system. The fact that poor women use public clinics subjects them to the possibility of reports

50. For a racial critique of surrogacy, *see* Dorothy E. Roberts, *The Genetic Tie,* 62 U. CHI. L. REV. 209 (1995).

51. *Id.* at 244–45.

52. Since the 1960s, the Supreme Court has invalidated most statutory distinctions between children born within and children born outside of marriage. *See, e.g.*, Trimble v. Gordon, 430 U.S. 762 (1977).

being made to authorities that would never be made if the same women were using private doctors.

In this country, the law attaches a high value to the principle of family autonomy concerning childrearing. The Supreme Court has held that the parent-child relationship is constitutionally protected and that parents have a liberty interest in raising their children without state interference.[53] This means that with respect to the distribution of power between parents and the state, choices about how children are raised rest primarily with the parents, and state intervention is justified only in limited circumstances.

For many Black families, however, state intervention seems to have become the norm rather than the exception. Disproportionate numbers of Black children are under the supervision of child welfare authorities and disproportionate numbers have been removed from their homes and placed in foster care.[54] The high rate of foster care placement for Black children is the result, primarily, of two factors: first, the poor economic circumstances of many Black families, and second, the policies of a child welfare system that undervalues family preservation and devalues Black families. As the millennium approaches, the autonomy and integrity of Black families seems to be under siege by a growing number of factors including draconian welfare reform measures, high unemployment rates in Black communities, and the increasing number of Black women who are incarcerated,[55] many of whom are mothers and are at risk of having their parental rights terminated.

VI. Race and the Future of Family Law

As the millennium approaches, I am reminded of W.E.B. DuBois' statement in 1900 that "the problem of the twentieth century is the problem of the color line."[56] Unfortunately, the same statement could be made at the close of this century about the twenty-first. In some ways, the problem of the color line in the coming century is likely to be even more complex because the debate about race is likely to include people from many different racial and ethnic backgrounds.

53. Meyer v. Nebraska, 262 U.S. 390 (1925); Pierce v. Society of Sisters, 268 U.S. 510 (1925).

54. CHILD WELFARE: AN AFRICENTRIC PERSPECTIVE 2–3 (Joyce E. Everett, Sandra S. Chipungu & Bogard R. Leashore, eds.1991).

55. In 1990, there were 19,700 Black women sentenced prisoners in state and federal prisons. In 1996, that number had risen to 33,900. CRIMINAL JUSTICE STANDARDS, *supra* note 9, at 494.

56. W.E.B. DuBois, "To the Nations of the World," in REPORT OF THE PAN-AFRICAN CONFERENCE, *reproduced in* WRITINGS IN NON-PERIODICAL LITERATURE 11–12 (Herbert Aptheker, ed. 1982), *cited in* DAVID LEVERING LEWIS, W.E.B. DUBOIS: BIOGRAPHY OF A RACE 1868–1919 251 (1993).

There are a number of important issues for the scholarly agenda on the Black family. Work must continue to be both corrective and prescriptive. One critical need is for scholars to insist upon respectful treatment for Black families in the law and in public discourse. Black family life is the reflection of a complex web of factors including individual personalities and choices, as well as remnants of African culture and patterns of survival dating from the period of enslavement. Black family life has also developed in response to a history and a present reality of segregation, discrimination, and racial stigma.[57] Black family life is, therefore, clearly adaptive, and it is complex, but it is not pathological. It deserves more respect than it has been given, and this message must be reinforced in as many ways as possible.

Another critical task for scholars of the Black family is a very practical one—consistent advocacy for the kind of social programs that Black families need in order to survive and thrive. Clearly, programs providing for better health care and child care and better housing and educational opportunities would make an important difference in the circumstances under which most Black families live.

VII. Conclusion

As long as black people live under less favorable economic conditions than white people do, and as long as racial stigma remains a part of this nation's culture, Black people will continue to have fewer choices about many aspects of their lives, including, of course, family life. I am certain that Black families, which have survived under far worse circumstances in the past, will continue to survive, and in many instances, to thrive. Despite the obstacles they continue to confront, Black people, like any other people, will continue to fall in love, to marry, to divorce, and to have and raise children. Like other people, they will make the best of the choices about their lives that are available to them. However, it will only be when there are improved material circumstances and the erasure of racial stigma that Blacks will be able to access and enjoy the same range of choices that many others now take for granted.

57. For extensive discussion of the history and evolution of the Black family, *see* ANDREW BILLINGSLEY, CLIMBING JACOB'S LADDER; THE ENDURING LEGACY OF AFRICAN-AMERICAN FAMILIES (1992); HERBERT G. GUTMAN, THE BLACK FAMILY IN SLAVERY AND FREEDOM 1750–1925 (1976); NIARA SUDARKASA, THE STRENGTH OF OUR MOTHERS: AFRICAN AND AFRICAN-AMERICAN WOMEN & FAMILIES: ESSAYS AND SPEECHES (1996).

[4]

FAMILY INSIDE/OUT†

Brenda Cossman*

I *Introduction*

The battle lines have been drawn in the current debate around lesbian and gay relationships and family status. On one side, under the slogan We Are Family, lesbians and gay men are demanding to be let inside the family, and claim its benefits.[1] They argue that their historic and continuing exclusion is discriminatory, and violates their equality rights guaranteed by human rights legislation and the Constitution. On the other side, under the less catchy slogan We Are Not Family, lesbians and gay men argue that the family is an oppressive and exclusionary institution. Some argue against the assimilationist politic of claiming that we are the same, on the basis that it obscures the diversity of relationships within lesbian and gay communities, establishes a hierarchy of socially legitimate relationships, and negates the ways in which our relationships are different and subversive. Others focus more specifically on the role of the family in the oppression of women, in terms of sexuality, reproduction, and division of labour. Gays and lesbians on this side of the debate argue that we should not be trying to get inside family, but should be trying to decentre, deconstruct, and/or otherwise destroy it.

This is no longer just a debate within lesbian and gay communities. Nor is it just a matter of words. Increasingly, the claim that We Are Family is being framed in legal discourse, as courageous lesbians and gay men take their lives to court.[2] Indeed, the Supreme Court of Canada

* Osgoode Hall Law School.

† With thanks to Susan Boyd, Annie Bunting, Jody Freeman, Judy Fudge, Shelley Gavigan, Allan Hutchinson, Ratna Kapur, Marlee Kline, Denise Réaume, and Bruce Ryder.

1 The We Are Family campaign was coined in the Canadian context by Karen Andrews, in her groundbreaking struggle to obtain health insurance benefits for her partner. See Karen Andrews 'We Are Family' (1989) Fall: 18 *Healthsharing*, *Andrews* v. *Ontario (Minister of Health)* 1988 49 DLR (4th) 584 (Ont. HC).

2 See Andrews, supra note 1; Brian Mossop in *Mossop* v. *Canada (Secretary of State)* (1989) 10 CHRR D/6064; overruled in *Canada (Attorney General)* v. *Mossop* 71 DLR (4th) 661 (Fed. CA); *Canada (Attorney-General)* v. *Mossop* [1993] SCR 554 (SC); *Leshner* v. *Ontario (No. 2)* (1992) 16 CHRR D/184 at D/223; *Veysey* v. *Canada (Commissioner of Correctional Services)* 29 FTR 74, aff'd on other grounds 109 NR 300 (FCA); *Knodel* v. *British Columbia* (Medical Series Com.) 1991 58 BCLR (2d) 356

recently decided its first gay rights case.[3] The stakes are high. A loss in the courts risks the further marginalization of gays and lesbians in society. Yet even a win is not always on our own terms. My own concern is with the effect that this increasing legalization of lesbian and gay struggles is having on us. For our legal strategies, we have to argue that we are, or are not, family.[4] And the more we translate our position into

(BCSC); *Egan and Nesbit* v. *The Queen* (Man. QB); *Brown* v. *British Columbia* (Minister of Health) (1990) 42 BCLR (2d) 294 (BCSC). It is not only in the context of family status, however, that lesbians and gay men have taken their lives to court. See *Re Haig et al. and the Queen in right of Canada et al.* (1972) 86 DLR (4th) 617; aff'd Ontario Court of Appeal, 6 August 1992 (unreported), in which Joshua Birch, who was dismissed from the Armed Forces and was precluded from seeking redress under the Canadian Human Rights Act, SC 1976–77, c. 33 since the legislation did not prohibit discrimination on the basis of sexual orientation, successfully sought a declaration that the absence of sexual orientation from the Act violated the equality guarantees in section 15 of the Canadian Charter of Rights and Freedoms.

3 *Canada (Attorney-General)* v. *Mossop* [1993] 1 SCR 554 (SCC) (hereinafter *Mossop*).

4 I have deliberately chosen to use the term 'we' throughout my text, although it is problematic. First, my use of 'we' is not entirely consistent. It is at times used simply as part of the discourse in which the debate around family has been framed; at other times, it is used to refer to lesbians and gay men; at yet other times, 'we' is intended to engage the reader in the challenges and dilemmas that require participation. Martha Minow in 'Foreword: Justice Engendered' (1987) 101 *Harv. LR* 10, 15 writes: 'My use of "we" ... represents an invitation to the reader to assent, to disagree, but above all, to engage with this focus. I use "we," moreover, to emphasize the human authorship of the problems and solutions at hand and to avoid locutions that eliminate human pronouns.' Secondly, the use of 'we' within feminist scholarship has been criticized for suggesting a unitary and homogenous experience and community of women, which obscures the diversity of women. The same criticism can be directed at any attempt to use 'we' within lesbian and gay theory – that is, it suggests a homogeneity of experience and community that does not exist, and that obscures or even negates the diversity of experience of gays and lesbians of colour, disabled lesbians and gays, and others. Further, the term 'we,' like the term 'woman' or 'lesbian' or 'gay,' may reinforce static and universalistic notions of identity and community, as well as the very categorical and binary oppositions that we should be deconstructing. See Denise Riley *'Am I That Name?': Feminism and the Category of 'Women' in History* (Minneapolis: University of Minnesota 1988) and Judith Butler *Gender Trouble, Feminism and the Subversion of Identity* (New York: Routledge 1990) exploring the need to deconstruct the identity categories of 'woman' and 'gender.' Ed Cohen explores some of these issues in the problematic constructions of lesbian and gay identity in his essay 'Who Are We? Gay "Identity" as Political (E) motion' in Dianna Fuss (ed.) *Inside/Out: Lesbian Theories, Gay Theories* (New York: Routledge 1991): '[U]nproblematically hinging 'our' political/group identity upon idealized notions of sexuality, and the body, the aggregation of 'gay' and 'lesbian' as epistemological, social and political categories frequently occludes the very difficulties that both bring us together and keep us at odds time and time again – ie, the force of our difference(s).'

legal language – the more we argue that we are or we are not family on law's terrain – the more entrenched we become in our positions. The increasing legalization is further entrenching the dichotomization of the debate. We increasingly find ourselves having to decide whether we believe that we are family, or not. We have to take a side. The choice is constructed as one between two mutually exclusive categories – between family and its opposition, not family.

For some time now, I have found myself uncomfortably positioned on both sides of the debate, agreeing, on the one hand, that the strategy for inclusion is important and subversive, while also maintaining, on the other, that any appeal to the discourse of family is, at least for women, deeply problematic. My apparently contradictory position left me feeling unable to enter the debate in a meaningful way. I was, for whatever reason, unable to commit myself. I have only recently realized that it is precisely from this contradictory position that I want to enter the debate. The problem was not with my contradictory experience of family, but the construction of the debate in terms that deny the possibility of contradiction.

In this article, I will attempt to use the insights of recent feminist postmodern scholarship to develop an approach to family/not family that recognizes multiplicity and contradiction.[5] By examining our con-

It might thus seem unwise to inhabit the category of 'we.' Yet, I know of no other way to avoid the false objectivism of the detached author, and to capture the sense of perspective, location, and participation that is essential for scholarship and for the resolution of the dilemmas that confront us. Further, my shifting use of 'we,' rather than simply being inconsistent, is intended to avoid the reification of any one meaning of the term.

5 Postmodernism, and poststructuralism with which it is often conflated, elude any simple definition. As Susan Boyd has written in 'Some Postmodernist Challenges to Feminist Analyses of Law, Family and State: Ideology and Discourse in Child Custody Law' (1991) 10 *Can. J. of Fam. Law* 79, 81: 'Postmodernism seems to mean many things to many people.' Judith Butler in 'Contingent Foundations, Feminism and the Question of "Postmodernism"' in Judith Butler and Joan Scott (eds) *Feminists Theorize the Political* (New York: Routledge 1991) elaborates on this point, arguing that various positions are ascribed to 'postmodernism or poststructuralism, which are often conflated with each other and sometimes conflated with deconstruction, and sometimes understood as an indiscriminate assemblage of French feminism, deconstruction, Lacanian psychoanalysis, Foucaultian analysis, Rorty's conversationalism and cultural studies.' As Butler notes, there are enormous differences and disagreements between and among these various positions, and to attempt to conflate these 'positions with a single stroke' obscures far more than it elucidates.

While I therefore do not propose to define postmodernism in any general sense, I will briefly review the particular debates within feminism and postmodernism that I believe to be relevant to understanding the current debates around family within

tradictory experiences of family, we may be able to further deconstruct and displace the dichotomization of family/not family. I will argue that it is within such an analysis of our experiences of family that we can see that we are both family and not family, and that our position on the inside/out of family at any particular moment depends on our location, as well as the location of others who judge, on a broad range of discursive practices. Moreover, an understanding of subjectivity as shifting and contradictory will allow for, and indeed necessitate, strategies of resistance that are shifting and contradictory. I will argue that such an approach that reveals the ways in which our subjectivities are constituted in and through multiple and often conflicting discourses, may help us move beyond the current We Are Family/We Are Not Family debate. I will, at the same time, argue that the insights of postmodernism must be balanced with an analysis of material relations, particularly relations of power and oppression.

II *Deconstrucing the inside/out*

Lesbians and gay men are currently faced with a dilemma.[6] Either we are family, or we are not. Like most dilemmas, at least part of the

gay and lesbian communities, and of evaluating competing strategies for our political struggles. It is my intention, and my hope, that I will make this work sufficiently accessible for readers who are not familiar with postmodernism to follow and assess my arguments. For an excellent overview of the principles of poststructuralism, and its potential for feminism, see Chris Weedon *Feminist Practice and Poststructuralist Theory* (Oxford: Basil Blackwell 1987); see also Linda Nicholson (ed.) *Feminism/Postmodernism* (New York: Routledge 1990). For an overview of the problems and potentials of postmodernism in the context of law, see Alan Hunt 'The Big Fear: Law Confronts Postmodernism' (1990) 35 *McGill LJ* 507–40; in the context of feminism and law, see Susan Boyd, supra. See also Zillah Eisenstein *The Female Body and the Law* (Berkeley: University of California Press 1988) and Carol Smart *Feminism and the Power of Law* (London: Routledge 1989).

6 I have chosen to speak of both lesbians and gay men in my text, although I have questioned the appropriateness of this choice. In addition to the problems of community discussed supra note 4 suggested by this term, I have questioned whether I am really speaking about lesbians and gay men, or just about lesbians. On the one hand, the debate regarding family status is one which affects the lesbian and gay community as a whole. It has been both lesbians and gay men who have been excluded from family, and who have taken their claims to family status into the political and legal arena. It is also both lesbians and gay men who have resisted the appeal to family status. However, there is a specifically feminist dimension to the resistance to the discourse of family which has highlighted the extent to which women and men are differently located within the family. Feminist criticism has illustrated the ways in which family and familial ideology has contributed to, and indeed has been central to, women's oppression. See discussion infra, at notes 24–30.

difficulty lies with its very construction. And also like most dilemmas, its construction as a dichotomous choice as an either/or represents a false polarization. In this section, I will attempt to illustrate that part of the problems with this construction is that it assumes that each of us can be unproblematically located either inside or outside the family and that the very distinction between inside and outside the family makes sense. I will begin by reviewing the family debate in some detail to illustrate the complexity and heterogeneity of the arguments on each side. Relying on the deconstructive techniques adopted by some recent feminist post-structuralism,[7] I will then attempt to deconstruct the family/not family debate and go on to illustrate the way in which these complex arguments are reduced to a simple either/or of family or not family.

A. WE ARE FAMILY

The We Are Family campaign was launched by Karen Andrews, in her legal battle to obtain provincial health insurance benefits for her partner.[8] Ms Andrews argued that she and her partner, along with her partner's children, were a family and thus entitled to family benefits. She argued that same-sex couples were the same as opposite-sex couples. The We Are Family side of the debate has since expanded to include

In taking this criticism seriously, it suggests that lesbians and gay men might part ways in their relationship to the family. Insofar as (heterosexual, white, middle-class) men have not been harmed by their location within familial ideology, (white, middle-class) gay men would seem to have less at risk in demanding to be let into the family.

This argument is not to suggest that all feminists and all lesbians take this position, nor that no gay men are concerned with the oppression of women within the family. It is only to suggest that lesbians and gay men may be located at different subject positions within the discourse of family. As a result, it would seem that my own comments are more specifically directed at lesbians and family status. Further, my analysis is firmly situated within feminist scholarship, and the focus of this scholarship more generally is on women. I am, however, uncomfortable, particularly at this moment in time, to advocate further fragmentation on the basis of identity, since the Right sees little difference in its assault on gays and lesbians; since fragmentation may only facilitate their attack; since it is a time when coalition politics must take us beyond identity politics in our struggles. It is in this light that I have chosen to speak of both lesbians and gay men.

7 For a discussion of deconstruction, see Christopher Norris *Deconstruction Theory and Practice* (Routledge: London 1991); for a discussion of feminist deconstruction, see Susan Hekman *Gender and Knowledge: Elements of Postmodern Feminist* (Boston: Northeastern University Press 1990); and Joan Scott *Gender and the Politics of History* (New York: Columbia University Press 1988).

8 Andrews, supra note 1.

other gays and lesbians who are demanding legal recognition of their relationships as family, and entitlement to family benefits.[9] Some have argued on the basis of a functional approach to the family,[10] whereas others, more recently, have shifted away from basing their challenges on a definition of the family.[11] Generally, the We Are Family arguments are cast in the discourse of equality, that is, it is argued that the exclusion of same-sex couples from family benefits is discriminatory.[12] The denial of

9 See, for example, *Mossop* supra note 2. For an excellent review of the Canadian case law, see Bruce Ryder 'Equality Rights and Sexual Orientation: Confronting Heterosexual Family Privilege' (1990) 9 *Can. J. of Fam. Law* 39–97. In the American context, see Editors of the Harvard Law Review *Sexual Orientation and the Law* (Cambridge: Harvard University Press 1990). In the United States, the arguments have played out more specifically in the context of same-sex marriage. For an argument in favour of same-sex marriage, see also Thomas Stoddar 'Why Gay People Should Seek the Right to Marry' (1989) 6 *Outlook* 9; Alissa Friedman 'The Necessity for State Recognition of Same Sex Marriage: Constitutional Requirements and Evolving Notions of Family' (1987–88) 3 *Berkeley Women's LJ* 134; and Claudia Lewis 'From This Day Forward: A Feminine Moral Discourse on Homosexual Marriage' (1983) 97 *Yale LR*, arguing that the right to marry will help eliminate discrimination against gays and lesbians.

10 The functional approach to the family was adopted by the Canadian Human Rights Tribunal in the *Mossop* case, supra note 2, which held that same-sex relationships were included within 'family status,' and that the denial of bereavement leave to Mossop to attend the funeral of his partner's father violated s.10(b) of the Canadian Human Rights Act. The tribunal rejected a narrow definition of family and family status, stating that such concepts 'must be tested in today's world, against an understanding of how people are living and how language reflects reality.' However, this functional approach was rejected by the Federal Court of Appeal, which held that family status did not include same-sex relationships. According to the court, family is a concept with a clear and core meaning – a meaning that was in its view missed by the tribunal's functional approach, ibid. 34: 'It seems to me that what was done by the Tribunal was to take some attributes usually ascribed to families, such as mutual love between members, mutual assistance, joint residence, emotional support, sharing of domestic tasks, sexual relations and treat them as being the essence of the concept itself being signified.' For a further discussion of the Mossop case, see Jody Freeman 'Defining Family in *Mossop* v. *DSS*: The Challenge of Anti-Essentialism and Interactive Discrimination for Human Rights Litigation' this issue, and Didi Herman '"Sociologically Speaking": Law, Sexuality and Social Change' (1991) 2: 2 *J. of Human Justice* 57–71. For an example of the functional approach in the American context, see *Braschi* v. *Stahl Assocs. Co.* 74 NY (2d) 201, 543 NE (2d) 49 (NY CA).

11 On appeal to the Supreme Court of Canada, Brian Mossop's argument shifted away from a functional approach to the family. The intervenors' factum in the *Mossop* appeal declined to provide a definition of the family, arguing instead that people must be free to make their own choices of family, and that these choices must be respected. See Freeman, supra note 10.

12 See Ryder, supra note 9; Nitya Duclos 'Some Complicating Thoughts on Same Sex Marriage' 1 *Law and Sexuality* 31; Editors of the Harvard Law Review, supra note 9;

benefits violates human rights codes that prohibit discrimination on the basis of sexual orientation,[13] family and marital status,[14] and/or sex. The denial of family benefits is also argued to violate the equality guarantees of the Canadian Charter of Rights and Freedoms.[15]

Some lesbians and gay men base their arguments on the need for public legitimation of their relationships and are unapologetically assimilationist in their arguments and objectives.[16] Others on this side of the debate argue that their demands to be let inside the family are fundamentally subversive. Despite the language of sameness in which the arguments are cast, they argue that their position is not assimilationist, but rather, that their inclusion within family radically transforms the nature of the institution and subverts the traditional gender roles within the institution.[17] From a different perspective, some gay men and

Factum in *Mossop* submitted by the intervenors, Equality for Gays and Lesbians Everywhere, the Canadian Rights and Liberties Federation, the National Association of Women and the Law, the Canadian Disability Rights Council, and the National Action Committee on the Status of Women (hereinafter EGALE et al.).

13 Ontario Human Rights Code, 1981, SO 1981, c. 53 as amended by SO 1984, c. 58, s. 39, and SO 1986, c. 64, s. 18; Quebec Charter of Human Rights and Freedoms RSQ 1977, c. C–12, s. 10; Manitoba Human Rights Code, SM 1987–88, c. 45, s. 9(2)(h); Yukon Human Rights Act, SY 1987, c. 3, s. 6(g).

14 The Federal Human Rights Code, which did not include sexual orientation as a prohibited ground, did include family and marital status, and is the basis of the challenge by Brian Mossop. In December 1992, the federal government introduced amendments to the Federal Human Rights Code to include sexual orientation. The amendments, however, also include a definition of marriage as requiring opposite sexes.

15 The federal government has taken the position that sexual orientation is a non-enumerated ground included within section 15 of the Charter. Report of the Parliamentary Committee on Equality Rights, Equality for All (Ottawa: Queen's Printer 1985); Canada, Department of Justice, Toward Equality: The Response to the Report of the Parliamentary Committee on Equality Rights (Ottawa: Queen's Printer 1986).

16 This public legitimation argument is represented by Lewis, supra note 9, who argues, at 1798, in the context of gay and lesbian marriage: 'The public function of marriage is particularly important to homosexual couples seeking social acceptance of their relationships. Public expression of commitment through marriage triggers recognition by and consequent protection from the State thus promoting a sense of belonging to the community through mutual identification.

17 Conversation with Karen Andrews. In the context of the American marriage debates, Nan Hunter argues in 'Marriage, Law and Gender: A Feminist Inquiry' (1991) 1 *Law and Sexuality* 9, 17 that the legalization of gay and lesbian marriage 'has a fascinating potential for denaturalizing the gender structure of marriage for heterosexual couples' and 'destabili[zing] the cultural meaning of marriage.' She further argues, at 29, that we need to be careful in the discourse that we adopt in these legalization struggles, insofar as the popular understanding of legal reform may be more significant for social change than the rules themselves: 'The social meaning of the

lesbians of colour argue that for them the family has not been an oppressive institution, but rather, an important source of support and refuge from a racist world.[18]

B. WE ARE NOT FAMILY

On the other side of the debate, lesbians and gay men argue that the family is an oppressive and exclusionary institution, and that lesbian and gay couples should not be trying to claim its benefits. At its most general, this position argues that our relationships are different, and any attempt to argue that we are family undermines the importance of our differences. The claim to family and family status is seen as assimilationist, and thereby deradicalizing.[19] There are, however, significant divergences of opinion within this side of the debate regarding the nature of these differences. Two positions are identifiable – a radical pluralist position and a feminist position.[20] The radical pluralist position argues that our relationships do not fit the model of the heterosexual family.[21] Gay and lesbian relationships are not functionally equivalent to heterosexual relationships – they are not necessarily based on sexual monogamy or emotional exclusivity. These relationships do not necessarily involve a high degree of interaction among the various dimensions of family life.[22]

legalization of lesbian and gay marriage, for example, would be enormously different if legalization resulted from political efforts framed as ending gendered roles between spouses rather than if it were the outcome of a campaign valorizing the institution of marriage, even if the ultimate "holding" is the same.' See also Friedman, supra note 9.

18 See Didi Herman 'Are We Family?: Lesbian Rights and Women's Liberation' (1990) 28 *Osgoode Hall LJ* 789.

19 See ibid. on the dangers of arguing that we are the same; see also Duclos, supra note 12.

20 My labelling of these two position is somewhat problematic and artificial, insofar as it constructs the radical pluralist position in opposition to a feminist perspective. In fact, many lesbian feminists adopt the radical pluralist position, and there seems to be a specifically lesbian feminist perspective within the radical pluralist position. See infra note 24. However, I believe that there are some important theoretical differences between these two positions, which I attempt to highlight by distinguishing between them.

21 Mary Eaton's LLM thesis (Queen's University); Carol Allen 'Family Ties' (June 1992) *Quota.*

22 See generally Margaret Eichler *Families in Canada Today: Recent Changes and Their Policy Consequences* (Toronto: Gage 1988) who speaks of the dimensions of familial interaction, rather than the functions of family. She argues at 6 that the most significant dimensions have been reproductive, sexual, emotional, economic, residential, social. Eichler argues at 10 that the monolithic approach to the family 'is characterized by the assumption that high interaction in one dimension coincides

In this view, any attempt by lesbian and gay couples who do fit the more traditional family model to obtain family benefits by arguing that they are the same will simply establish a hierarchy of relationships. Lesbians and gay men who are not sexually monogamous, lesbians and gay men who are not in relationships, will be further marginalized.[23]

The feminist position focuses more specifically on the role of the family in the oppression of women. Early feminist reformers pointed to the role of the family in women's subordination.[24] More recently, socialist feminists have argued that the family and familial ideology is the primary site of women's subordination.[25] Michelle Barrett and Mary MacIntosh have argued that the family is a major site of the reproduction of the social inequalities of both gender and class.[26] Michelle Barrett has argued:[27]

with high interaction in all other dimensions of familial interplay ... By contrast, the multidimensional approach to families is characterized by the assumption that interaction in any one of the dimensions identified can vary independently.'

23 Allen, supra note 22. In the context of the marriage debates in the United States, Ruthann Robson and S.E. Valentine 'Lov(h)ers: Lesbians as Intimate Partners and Lesbian Legal Theory' (1990) 63 *Temple LR* 511 argue at 538 that 'the prospect of lesbian marriage is detrimental because it creates a two-tier system of "good" and "bad" lesbians that elevates married lesbian couples over other varieties of lesbian relationships.' See also Paula Ettelbrick 'Since When Is Marriage a Path to Liberation?' (1989) 6 *Outlook* 9; Joan Nestle *A Restricted Country* (London: Sheba Feminist 1987). Robson represents the more specifically lesbian feminist pluralist approach, which cautions against 'hetero-relationalizing' lesbian relationships. Her position integrates the arguments of both the radical pluralist and feminist critique of marriage, and concludes by arguing that lesbians should be working to abolish marriage.

24 The first wave of the women's movement, from the mid-nineteenth to early twentieth century, identified women's position in the family as an important factor in women's inequality. These feminists struggled for formal equality rights in the family through, for example, the Married Women's Property Acts. Again, in the second wave of the feminist movement beginning in the 1960s, the family was again identified as an important factor in women's inequality. Early radical feminists likened marriage to slavery and/or prostitution. See, for example Kathleen, Barry *Female Sexual Slavery* (New York: New York University Press 1971); Roberta Hamilton 'Women, Wives and Mothers' in Nancy Mandel and Ann Duffy (eds) *Reconstructing the Canadian Family: Feminist Perspectives* (Toronto: Butterworths 1988).

25 Michelle Barrett *Women's Oppression Today: Problems of Marxist Feminist Analysis* (London: Verso 1980); Michelle Barrett and Mary MacIntosh *The Anti-Social Family* (London: Verso 1982); Shelley Gavigan 'Law, Gender, Ideology' in Anne Bayefsky (ed.) *Legal Theory Meets Legal Practice* (Edmonton: Academic Printing and Publishing 1988) and 'Paradox Revisited' ibid.

26 Supra note 25, 163.

27 Ibid. 211.

The family-household constitutes both the ideological ground on which gender difference and women's oppression are constructed, and the material relations in which men and women are differentially engaged in wage labour and the class structure. Women's dependence on men is reproduced ideologically, but also in material relationship, and there is a mutually strengthening relationship between them.[28]

The ideology of the nuclear, heterosexual, patriarchal family reproduces, and is reproduced by, the sexual division of labour, the family wage, and the public/private distinction, all of which are central to the subordination of women. It has been further argued that this ideology of family is reproduced and reinforced in law.[29] In the context of lesbian and gay struggles, Didi Herman has pointed out that '[b]y appropriating familial ideology, lesbian and gay men may be supporting the very institutional structures that create and perpetuate women's oppression.'[30]

C. DECONSTRUCTING FAMILY/NOT FAMILY

When translated into legal and political arguments, however, these heterogeneous arguments are collapsed and the debate becomes one of family or not family. The We Are Family/We Are Not Family debate becomes seen as yet another sameness/difference debate. We Are Family is an appeal to sameness, while We Are Not Family is an appeal to difference.[31] As such, we have much to learn from the feminist debates

28 Ibid.

29 See Gavigan 'Law, Gender, Ideology' supra note 25, who argues at 294 that the law 'assumes and therefore ensures, that there is but one family form and that despite the ideology of family privacy, the dominant family is in large measure defined and created by law.'

30 Herman, supra note 18, 797; See also Gavigan 'Paradox Revisited' supra note 25. Nancy Polikoff in 'Lesbians Choosing Children: The Personal Is Political Revisited' in S. Pollack and J. Vaughn (eds) *Politics of the Heart* (Ithaca: Firebrand Books 1987) raises some of these concerns about the role of motherhood and the family in the oppression of women in the context of lesbian parenting. For an argument directly in contrast to Polikoff, see Baba Copper 'The Radical Potential in Lesbian Mothering of Daughters' in Pollack and Vaughn, supra.

31 Cohen, supra note 4, 73 describes this tension between identity/sameness and difference within gay and lesbian politics: 'For while some would try to constitute "identity" as the ground for claiming larger social inclusion (e.g., we are the same as everybody else and hence should not be treated differently) others would use "difference" as a strategy to interrupt the hegemony of dominant social/sexual arrangements (e.g., we are different and difference will resist those practices that try to make us the same).' See also John D'Emilio *Sexual Politics, Sexual Communities: The Making of a Homosexual Minority in the United Sates, 1940–70* (Chicago: University of Chicago Press 1983).

that have already raged around sameness and difference.[32] Unlike the first stage of feminist legal scholarship, with its emphasis on gender sameness and formal equality, and the second stage, with its emphasis on gender difference and substantive equality, in the third stage, feminists have attempted to move beyond this sameness/difference debate.[33] Joan Scott, for example, has argued: 'When equality and difference are paired dichotomously, they structure an impossible choice. If one opts for equality, one is forced to accept the notion that difference is antithetical to it. If one opts for difference, one admits that equality is unattainable.'[34] Similarly, when we structure the choice between family or not family as dichotomous pairs, we are presenting ourselves with an impossible choice. Either we are the same and we are family, and thereby forced to accept that difference is antithetical to family; or we are not family, and thereby forced to relinquish any claim to equality.

Joan Scott, along with others, argues that we have to move beyond these either/or constructions of the debate, to move beyond accepting such binary pairs as 'timeless and true and start asking how the dichotomous pairing of equality and difference works.'[35] She argues that these

32 For a discussion of the sameness/difference debates within feminist scholarship, see Lucinda Finely 'Transcending Equality Theory,' (1986) 86 *Colum. LR* 1118; Catharine MacKinnon 'Difference and Dominance' in *Feminism Unmodified* (Cambridge: Harvard University Press 1987); Ann Scales 'The Emergence of Feminist Jurisprudence' (1986) 95 *Yale LJ* 1371; Joan Scott 'Deconstructing Equality-Versus-Difference or the Uses of Poststructuralist Theory for Feminism' (1988) 14 *Feminist Studies* 33.

33 See Martha Minow 'Introduction: Finding our Paradoxes, Affirming our Beyond,' (1989) 24 *Harv. CR–CLR* 1, 2 for a discussion of these three stages of feminist scholarship. For a discussion of the dilemmas of difference, see Martha Minow *Making All the Difference, Inclusion, Exclusion and American Law* (Ithaca, NY: Cornell University Press 1990); Brenda Cossman 'A Matter of Difference' (1990) 28 *Osgoode Hall LJ* 303.

34 Supra note 7, 172. See also Minow, *Making All The Difference* supra note 33; and Minow 'Justice Engendered' supra note 4 arguing that we can deconstruct the dilemma of difference by recognizing the ways in which difference is relational.

35 Supra note 33. Scott argues that our response must be twofold: 'the unmasking of the power relationship constructed by posing equality as the antithesis of difference, and the refusal of its consequent dichotomous construction of political choices.' Scott, supra note 7, 172. She further argues that definitions are based as much on what they exclude as what they include: 'Positive definitions rest always, in this view, on the negation or repression of something represented as antithetical to it. And categorial oppositions repress the internal ambiguities of either category. Any unitary concept rests – contains – repressed or negated material and so is unstable, not unified ... Fixed oppositions conceal the heterogeneity of either category, the extent to which terms presented as oppositional are interdependent – that is, derive their

concepts and their dichotomous pairing must be deconstructed. We need then to be asking how the dichotomization of family and not family works, and exploring the power relationships that sustain this opposition. In this respect, the deconstructive work of Dianna Fuss is very helpful.[36] She argues that the inside/out figure – a binary opposition that she argues underlies other such oppositions as heterosexual and homosexual – is central to contemporary lesbian and gay theory.

> To the extent that the denotation of any term is always dependent on what is exterior to it (heterosexuality, for example, typically defines itself in critical opposition to that which it is not: homosexuality), the inside/outside polarity is an indispensable model for helping us to understand the complicated workings of semiosis. Inside/outside functions as the very figure for signification and the mechanisms of meaning production.[37]

This inside/out figure, at the same time, 'also designates the structure of exclusion, oppression, and repudiation' – a structure which she argues has been particularly 'insistent to subjects routinely relegated to the right of the virgule – to the outside of systems of power authority and cultural legitimacy.'[38] Fuss argues that we are always situated both inside and out: 'The problem, of course, with the inside/outside rhetoric, if it remains undeconstructed, is that such polemics disguise the fact that most of us are both inside and outside at the same time.'[39]

The debate around the family can be seen as such an inside/out opposition. We Are Family means that we are out, but we should be in. We Are Not Family means that we are in and we should be out, or we are out, and we should stay there. What this construction fails to reveal, and which we must begin to reveal, are the ways in which our positions on the inside/out of family are multiple. We are not in any absolute way located outside family, nor inside. We are both. We are neither. We are in. We are out.

meaning from internally established contrast rather from some inherent or pure antithesis.'

36 Fuss, supra note 4, Introduction.

37 Ibid. 1.

38 Ibid. 2: 'Interrogating the position of outsiderness is where much recent lesbian and gay theory begins, implicitly if not always directly raising the questions of the complicated process by which sexual borders are constructed, sexual identities assigned and sexual politics formulated.'

39 Ibid. 5.

III *The constituted subject*

The family/not family debate can be seen to be informed by an understanding of the subject as coherent and self constituting – that is, a subject which can firmly locate itself at a position of its choosing either inside or outside of the family.[40] Deconstructing this debate, and the binary oppositions on which it is predicated, involves the substitution of a more complex and contradictory understanding of subjectivity. One of the many themes of poststructuralism is the critique of the subject.[41] The stable, coherent, self constituting subject of the Enlightment has been deconstructed, decentred, and rejected.[42] According to poststruc-

40 This liberal humanist construction of the subject within the debate does not apply to all the scholarship that this debate would seem to embrace. For example, it does not apply to socialist feminist work, which is characterized by a much more sophisticated understanding of the subject as constituted through ideology. Rather, the humanist construction of the subject seems to inform the ways in which the debate is becoming increasingly reified in political and legal forums.

41 Just as postmodernism/poststructuralism elude any simple definition, so too does the poststructuralist critique of the subject. The various positions share a common object of critique – that is, the subject of the Enlightment – the humanist, Cartesian transcendent subject. However, as Susan Hekman 'Reconstituting the Subject: Feminism, Modernism, and Postmodernism' (Summer 1991) *Hypatia* 6: 2 44–63 writes, at 45: 'There is no one "postmodern" critique of the subject.' Rather, as she explains, 'Foucault's treatise on the "death of man," Derrida's decentering of the subject, and the Lacanian-inspired discussions of the "subject in process," despite their differences, have all called into question the major tenets of the subject-centered epistemology of modernity.' It is, however, the Foucaultian critique of the subject that has been most influential in the feminist poststructuralism of Chris Weedon, supra note 5; Susan Hekman, supra note 7; and others relied on herein. See also Jane Flax *Thinking Fragments: Psychoanalysis, Feminism, and Postmodernism in the Contemporary West* (Berkeley: University of California Press 1990).

42 It is both the humanist subject and the Cartesian subject that has been the subject of the poststructuralist critique. Weedon, supra note 5, describes this humanist subject, at 80: 'The distinguishing feature of humanist discourse is their assumption that each individual woman or man possesses a unique essence of human nature.' Hekman, supra note 41, describes the Cartesian subject as the knowing, self constituting subject, at 62: 'For Descartes, and, hence, for modernity, the subject is the self conscious guarantor of all knowledge.' Eleanor MacDonald 'The Trouble with Subjects' Feminism, Marxism and the Questions of Poststructuralism' (1991) 35 *Studies in Pol. Econ.* 43 further describes at 45 this Cartesian subject: 'Descartes ... sought to establish the subjects' self certainty. He did this by asserting the ability of subjects to reason their own existence. Out of this arose a theory of the subject as unitary, autonomous, individualist, and rational. The subject's use of reason ... presumed the possibility of an unproblematic relationship between reality and its accurate representation in thought.'

turalism, the subject does not exist prior to language or discourse, but rather, is constituted in and through multiple and conflicting discourses. 'Subjectivity is produced in a whole range of discursive practices – economic, social, and political – the meanings of which are a constant site of struggle over power.'[43] As Chris Weedon describes, 'poststructuralism proposes a subjectivity which is precarious, contradictory and in process, constantly being reconstituted in discourse each time we think or speak.'[44]

Many feminists, along with other social theorists, remain highly suspicious of this poststructuralist critique of the subject. It has been argued that the rejection of the Enlightenment subject undermines any possibility of agency on the part of the feminist subject, an agency which is central to a feminist politics of resistance and change.[45] A central question for feminism's engagement with poststructuralism is thus whether we can use its insights, while retaining a sense of agency for the subject, and the possibility of feminist politics.

Feminists engaged with poststructuralism have argued that we can in fact do so; that the rejection of the Enlightenment subject does not

Poststructuralism rejects both the idea of an essential human nature, and of a subject that exists prior to language. Reason is seen as simply an effect of discourse, not an essential characteristic of a transcendent subject. This is a critique of the epistemology of the Enlightenment, and a rejection of the subject/object distinction on which it is based. Hekman describes this critique as twofold, at 63: 'First, postmoderns argue that knowledge is not acquired through the abstraction of an autonomous subject from a separate object, but, rather, that knowledge, along with subjects and objects, is constituted collectively through forms of discourse. Second, they challenge the notion that there is only one, true method by which knowledge is acquired. Instead they define knowledge as plural and heterogenous; there are "truths," not Truth.' For an excellent discussion of the poststructuralist critique of the subject, see Hekman, supra note 7. See also Flax, supra note 42.

43 Weedon, supra note 5, 21.

44 Ibid. 3.

45 Daryl McGowan Tress, for example, in 'Comment' (1988) 14 *Signs* 196, 197 has argued that 'without the possibility of a coherent self, liberation becomes impossible. There is no one who persists, who remembers, whose experience and suffering counts; there is no one to emancipate.' Nancy Hartstock remains highly suspicious of poststructuralism's critique of the subject and asks, 'Why is it that just at the moment when so many of us who have been silenced begin to demand the right to name ourselves, to act as subjects rather than objects of history, that just then the concept of subjecthood becomes problematic?' 'Foucault on Power: A Theory for Theory' in *Feminism/Postmodernism* supra note 5, 163. She concludes that poststructuralism 'represents a dangerous approach for any marginalized group to adopt.' Ibid. 160. See also N. Hartsock 'Rethinking Modernism: Minority vs. Majority Theories' *Cultural Critique* 187–206.

involve a negation of the subject, nor a negation of agency. First, as Judith Butler has argued, the poststructuralist critique of the subject 'is not a negation or repudiation but, rather, a way of interrogating its construction as a pregiven or foundationist premise.'[46] Of the much acclaimed death of the subject, Butler rhetorically asks 'but which subject is that?'[47] The poststructuralist decentring of the Enlightenment subject does not negate the subject, but rather, redirects our attention to the question of how subjects are produced. Pierre Schlag has written, 'The interesting version of the problem of the subject is not whether there are subjects, but rather, how there are subjects and what those subjects are like.'[48]

Nor does the poststructural critique of the subject necessarily involve a repudiation of agency.[49] Several feminists engaged with poststructuralism have argued that it is the very ways in which subjects are constituted in and through multiple and contradictory discursive fields that allows for the subject's agency. Both Judith Butler and Susan Hekman argue that we must break away from understanding agency as opposed to construction, and see the latter instead as 'the necessary scene of agency, the very terms in which agency is articulated.'[50] The

46 Butler 'Contingent Foundations' supra note 5, 9.

47 Ibid.

48 Pierre Schlag 'Stances' (1991) 139 *U. Pa LR* 1059, 1060. See also Schlag 'The Problem of the Subject' (1991) 60 *Tex. LR* 1627.

49 The dilemmas of agency presented by the critique of the humanist subject is not only a problem within poststructuralist theories. Rather, the humanist subject has been critiqued from a number of different perspectives, including feminist and Marxist. The contemporary struggle of feminists engaged with poststructuralism to reinsert the agency of the constituted subject is not dissimilar to the dilemma within some Marxist scholarship of attempting to balance agency and determinism. See, for example, the response of E.P. Thompson in *The Poverty of Theory* to Althusserian Marxism. For a detailed discussion of the problematic nature of the subject within Althusser's theory of ideology, see Terry Eagleton *Ideology* 136–44. For a discussion of the similar problems facing both poststructuralism and Marxism in terms of the rejection of the humanist subject, see Kate Sopher *Troubled Pleasures: Writing on Politics, Gender and Hedonism* (London: Verso 1990), particularly her essay entitled 'Constructing Ergo Sum?' See also Eleanor MacDonald 'The Trouble with Subjects: Feminism, Marxism and the Question of Postmodernism' observing both the parallels and contrasts in poststructuralist, Marxist and feminist critiques of the Enlightenment subject. Summer 1991 *Studies in Pol. Econ.* 35.

50 Butler *Gender Trouble* supra note 4, 147; Hekman, supra 41, 59. Butler at 12 further argues: 'We may be tempted to think that to assume the subject in advance is necessary in order to safeguard the *agency* of the subject. But to claim that the subject is constituted is not to claim that it is determined; on the contrary, the constituted character of the subject is the very precondition of its agency.' See also Bell Hooks

discursively constituted subject creates the possibilities for creativity, agency and resistance: '[T]he result of the forces that create subjectivity is not a seamless whole. There are gaps and ambiguities with the interstices of language that prevent a uniform determination of subjectivity. It is these gaps and these ambiguities that create the possibility for both change and resistance.'[51] As Chris Weedon describes, neither the subject, nor the subject's agency are negated:

> [A]lthough the subject in poststructuralism is socially constructed in discursive practices, she none the less exists as a thinking, feeling subject and social agent, capable of resistance and innovations produced out of the clash between contradictory subject positions and practices. She is also a subject able to reflect upon the discursive relations which constitute her and the society in which she lives, and able to choose from the options available.[52]

The multiple and conflicting discursive practices through which the subject is constituted give rise to the very possibility of agency and resistance. Our subjectivities are never fixed, but always in the process of being reconstituted. We negotiate our way through the multiplicity of discursive fields, capable of reflection, choice, action – although our agency is constituted within and limited by our particular positions within the web of intersecting and conflicting discursive fields.

Recognizing our shifting and multiple subject positions does not, however, mean that we are always free to shift our positions. As Chris Weedon tells us, discourses take on concrete forms within particular social contexts:

> To subscribe to the provisional nature of meaning is not to imply that it does not have real effects ... [F]eminist poststructuralism, concerned as it must be with power, looks to historically and socially specific discursive production of conflicting and competing meanings. These meanings are only fixed temporarily, but this temporary fixing has important social implications.[53]

'Postmodern Blackness' in *Yearning* (Toronto: Between the Lines 1990) 28 arguing that postmodern insights on identity and subjectivity can be useful for disadvantaged groups, and African Americans in particular: 'Postmodern critiques of essentialism which challenge notions of universality and static overdetermined identity within mass culture and mass consciousness can open up new possibilities for the construction of self and the assertion of agency.'

51 Hekman, supra note 41, 59. Joan Scott 'Experiences' in Butler and Scott (eds) supra note 5, 34 similarly argues: 'Subjects are constituted discursively, but there are conflicts among discursive systems, contradictions within any one of them, multiple meanings possible for the concepts they deploy. And subjects have agency. They are not unified.'

52 Weedon, supra note 5, 125.

53 Ibid. 86.

Not only do discourses take on important social implications, but some discourses become dominant. As Susan Boyd argues in her recent work, 'at particular historical moments, one discourse may assume more power than another, or may dictate the extent to which counter discourses can enter the public consciousness in a meaningful way.'[54] She further argues that 'we need to retain a sense of the ways in which power flows from material (economic and social) circumstances in order to understand the hierarchy of discourse.'

The concept of ideology may take us some distance in attempting to explain the ways in which some discourses become dominant.[55] Ideology explores the processes through which meaning is produced,[56] and through which our ideas and beliefs are universalized and naturalized.[57] Further, ideology explores the relationship 'between ideas, attitudes and beliefs on the one hand, and economic and political interests on the other.'[58]

The relationship between ideology and discourse is highly contested. Many writers have insisted on the fundamental differences in the philosophical tradition from which these concepts derive, and particularly on the epistemological incompatibility between ideology and discourse.[59] Discourse rejects the subject/object distinction on which

54 Supra note 5, 104.

55 The concept of ideology is a contested one, with many competing definitions and usages. For an excellent review of the competing understandings of ideology, see Terry Eagleton *Ideology: An Introduction* (London: Verso), particularly 1–31. In the context of law and ideology see generally C. Sumner *Reading Ideologies: An Investigation into the Marxist Theory of Ideology and Law* (London: Academic Press 1979); Alan Hunt 'The Ideology of Law: Advances and Problems in Recent Applications of the Concept of Ideology to the Analysis of Law' (1985) 19 *Law and Soc. Rev.* 11; Gavigan 'Law, Gender and Ideology' supra note 25; Jennie Abell *Bringing It All Back Home: Feminist Struggle, Feminist Theory and Feminist Engagement With Law – The Case of Wife Battering* (LLM thesis, York University 1991).

56 Michele Barrett in *Women's Oppression Today* supra note 25, 97 described the concept of ideology as referring 'to those processes which have to do with consciousness, motive, emotionality; it can best be located in the category of meaning. Ideology is a generic term for the processes by which meaning is produced, challenged, reproduced, transformed. Ideology is embedded historically in material practice but it does not follow either that ideology is theoretically indistinguishable from material practices or that it bears any direct relationship to them.'

57 Marlee Kline in 'The Colour of Law: Ideological Representations of First Nations in Legal Discourse' *Soc. & Legal Studies* (forthcoming) writes: 'Ideology is, in part, a representational process whereby beliefs, images, attributions and explanations are constructed historically in conjunction with, and in relation to, material and cultural conditions and power relations, but are presented as natural, inevitable and necessary in the current conjuncture.'

58 Hunt, supra note 55, 13.

59 See for example Zillah Eisenstein, supra note 5, 15: '[T]here is no moment "outside" discourse – whereas there is an "outside" to ideology. This is the significant

modernist epistemology is based, arguing that both subjects and objects, and thus, our knowledge of both, are constituted in and through discourse.[60] Ideology, by contrast, is seen to be informed by a modernist epistemology, based on the distinctions between subject and object, and material and ideal. Zillan Eisenstein writes, for example:

> Ideology particularly in its classic Marxist meaning, presumes a notion of the real that is clearly differentiated from the ideal (meaning a false reality). Ideology supposedly inverts the real and represents it in an untrue form. It presents reality from the bourgeois standpoint; for example, alienated labour is seen as private property ... The distinction between 'true' and 'false' gives the term 'ideology' its meaning.[61]

difference between the two philosophic traditions encompassed in the terms "ideology" and "discourse." The latter has a pluralist epistemology regarding the status of truth and the relations between language and power.'

Foucault, in developing his theory of discourse, argued that ideology 'always stands in virtual opposition to something else which is supposed to count as truth. Now I believe that the problem which falls under the category of scientificity or truth, and that which comes under some other category, but in seeing historically how effects of truth are produced within discourses which in themselves are neither true nor false.' Colin Gordon (ed.) *Power/Knowledge: Selected Interviews and Other Writings, 1972–1977* (Brighton: Harvester 1980) 115. Foucault further argued that the concept of ideology was inadequate insofar as it was based on a humanist concept of the subject, and the determinism of the base/superstructure distinction. Following this and other passages, many have argued that Foucault developed his theory of discourse in opposition to Marxist theories of ideology, and that it is important to distinguish these concepts. See Alan Hunt 'Living Dangerously on the Deconstructive Edge' (1988) 26 *Osgoode Hall LJ* 867 and Michele Barrett in *The Politics of Truth: From Marx to Foucault* (Stanford: Stanford University Press 1991).

60 Hekman, supra note 7, 63 describes the postmodern challenge to modern epistemology as involving two interrelated arguments: 'First, postmoderns argue that knowledge is not acquired through the abstraction of an autonomous subject from a separate object, but, rather, that knowledge, along with subjects and objects, is constituted collectively through forms of discourse. Second, they challenge the notion that there is only one, true method by which knowledge is acquired. Instead they define knowledge as plural and heterogenous; there are 'truths' not 'truth.' See Barry Hindess and Paul Hirst *Pre-Capitalist Modes of Production* (London 1975) and *Mode of Production and Social Formation* (London 1977) rejecting the modernist distinctions between material/ideal, and object/subject, and arguing that objects must be seen not as external to and reflected in discourse, but as constituted in discourse. They argue, for example, that 'the relation between discourse and its "objects" need not be represented in terms of both a distinction and correlation between a realm of discourse and an independently existing realm of objects ... The question of the "reality" of the external world is not the issue ... [T]he entities discourse refers to are constituted in it and by it.' *Mode of Production* (1977), 20.

61 Eisenstein, supra note 5, 13.

Other writers have rejected the notion of ideology as necessarily based on falsity, arguing that this distinction between truth and falsity is too simplistic, and in so doing, have further complicated the relationship between ideology and discourse.[62] Indeed, those who have insisted on ideology as the lived experience of subjects have gone considerable distance in closing the epistemological gap between ideology and discourse, and have suggested that we can use both in our analyses. Terry Eagleton, for example, drawing on the works of Pecheux and Voloshinov suggests that we might understand 'ideology as a discursive or semiotic phenomenon ... [which would] at once emphasize its materiality and preserves the sense that it is essentially concerned with meanings.' He argues that '[i]t may help to view ideology less as a particular set of discourses, than as a particular set of effects within discourse.'[63] Stuart Hall, drawing more explicitly on the insights of Foucault, has attempted to develop a 'discursive understanding of ideology, which mediates the link between ideas and social forces through language and representation' and suggests that we understand that 'the arena or medium in which ideology functions in one of signification, representation, discursive practice.'[64] Susan Boyd in her

62 See Hunt, supra note 56, 13 who argues that 'the idea that ideology necessarily entails some sort of "false consciousness" should ... be discarded because it removes the empirically important issue of the association between ideas and interests.' See also Gavigan, supra note 25, and Boyd, supra note 5. Eagleton, supra note 49, while arguing that ideologies may but do not necessarily involve falsity and distortion, writes at 26: 'Those who oppose the idea of ideology as false consciousness are right to see that ideology is no baseless illusion but a solid reality, an active material force which must have at least enough cognitive content to help organize the practical lives of human beings.'

63 Eagleton, supra note 49, 194. He further argues that 'Ideology is a matter of "discourse" rather than language – of certain concrete discursive effects, rather than of signification as such. It represents the points where power impacts upon certain utterances and inscribes itself tacitly within them ... [It] aims to disclose something of the relation between an utterance and its material conditions of possibility, when those conditions of possibility are viewed in the light of certain power struggles central to the reproduction of a whole form of social life.' Ibid. 223. See also Diane Macdonell *Theories of Discourse: An Introduction* (Oxford: Basil Blackwell 1986) who also attempts to trace a specifically Marxist and thus materialist tradition of discourse analysis, relying particularly on the work of Althusser and Pecheux.

64 Stuart Hall 'The Toad in the Garden: Thatcherism among the Theorists' 73. At 51 he writes: 'No social practice exists outside of the domain of the semiotic – the practices and production of meaning.' While drawing on some of the insights of Foucault's work on discourse, Hall is explicitly concerned with highlighting the limitations of Foucault. At 53, he argues: 'The problem with Foucault, to put it brusquely, is a conception of difference without a conception of articulation, that is, a conception of power within a conception of hegemony.'

recent work argues that we can and indeed should be able to use the insights from both the concepts of discourse and ideology:

Ideology cannot be reduced to discourse because one loses a sense of how discourses have wider ramifications and connections with material relations. Nor can discourse be reduced to ideology, as the concept of discourse allows us to focus on sites in which particular knowledges, including counter discourses, are produced, and is a more particularistic concept in this regard.[65]

It is not my intention to resolve the theoretical dilemmas of the relationship between discourse and ideology. Rather, my intention is simply to raise the tensions, and highlight the need to retain a focus on material relations. Some argue that this can be done within discourse analysis; others argue that disclosure is simply not up to this kind of analysis; and yet others argue that we need to reintroduce the concept of ideology in order to accomplish this task. But the point of agreement is that we must retain a focus on the material. The important inquiry is not the primacy of the ideological or the discursive, nor the primacy of the material or the ideal. Rather, it is to pursue an analysis that allows us to pay adequate attention to the relationship between them. Some would do so by maintaining the distinction and arguing that we must find the dialectical interaction between them;[66] others would do so by collapsing the very polarity of the distinction.[67] Moreover, it may be that we will not be able to resolve the tensions between these theoretical perspectives at an abstract and theoretical level, but only in concrete analyses of particular social relations.[68]

While my use of discourse is not one that is in opposition to the material, I am persuaded that it may still be useful to invoke the notion of ideology, if only to serve as a reminder of the need to consider dominant discourses, inscribed in material practices. Further, it allows

65 Boyd, supra note 5, 98. Discourse alone, she argues, fails to reveal the ways in which 'discourses are constituted and reproduced, nor how some discourses come to be more powerful and privileged than others.' See also Sopher, supra note 49.

66 Boyd, supra note 5; Sopher, supra note 49.

67 Laclau and Mouffe in *Hegemony and Socialist Strategy: Towards a Radical Democratic Politics* (London: Verso 1985) 108 insist on 'the material character of every discursive structure.' They argue that the discursive practice of articulation 'cannot consist of purely linguistic phenomena, but must instead pierce the entire material density of the multifarious institutions, rituals, and practices through which a discursive formation is structured.' See also Eisenstein, supra note 5; Barrett, supra note 59.

68 I again agree with Susan Boyd, supra note 5, who has noted that 'in concrete analysis, there may often be very little difference in practice' as between discourse and ideology.

us to speak of ideologically dominant discourses, that is, of discourses that have become dominant and that 'mediate the relationship between groups that are fundamentally unequal in terms of power.'[69] It is in this respect that attention to ideology, and to material relations of oppression may provide an important complement to discourse analysis. It allows us to recognize that not all discourses are equal in power; that some discourses are institutionally inscribed in ways that others are not. Moreover, it allows us to recognize that some discourses reinforce relations of domination in ways that others do not. Despite the multiple ways in which we are constituted in and through discourse, ideologically dominant discourses and the material relations in which they are inscribed resist the free play of shifting subjectivities.

IV *Multiple subject positions of family*

Within this framework of the constituted subject we can reveal how our subject position is constituted not through a unitary disclosure of family, but, rather, in and through multiple and potentially conflicting discourses of family. In this section, I will argue that some discursive practices locate us inside family, while others operate to exclude us. The way in which we, as constituted subjects, negotiate our way through these multiple and contradictory discourses affects our own position inside or out, and our understanding of the political position of the inside/out.

The idea of multiple and contradictory experiences of family is not new. Michael Anderson, in the context of family history, has written:

> [T]he one unambiguous fact which has emerged in the last twenty years is that there can be no simple history of *the* Western family since the sixteenth century because there is not, nor ever has there been a single family system. The West has always been characterized by diversity of family forms, by diversity of family functions and by diversity in attitudes to family relationships not only over time but at any one point in time.[70]

This diversity of family forms and experiences has become an important theme in recent feminist scholarship, particularly by women of colour. In response to the feminist critique of the family as a site of women's

69 Marlee Kline, manuscript on file with author.

70 Michael Anderson *Approaches to the History of the Western Family 1500–1914* (London 1980) 14. See also Leonore Davidoff and Catherine Hall *Family Fortunes: Men and Women of the English Middle Class, 1780–1850* (London: Hutchinson 1987); Barrett and MacIntosh, supra note 25.

oppression, some women of colour have argued that the family is a site of contradiction and multiple experiences.[71] Some have argued, for example, that 'the Black family has been a site of political and cultural resistance to racism.'[72] This critique has led to a more general emphasis on the diversity of families, including the diversity of families within gay and lesbian communities. Nitya Duclos, for example, in developing her anti-essentialist approach to gay and lesbian marriage, has argued that there is no universal family.[73] Didi Herman, in considering this diversity within the context of gay and lesbian relationships, has argued that while 'for some families the oppositional familial ideologies are important sites of resistance and affirmation,' for others, family is experienced as oppressive and not at all radical.[74] She concludes: 'Families are sites of contradictions; the very word means different things to different people.'[75] This emphasis on diversity has been important in directing our attention to some of the different ways in which we live in and experience families, and in highlighting the ways in which our experiences of family are constituted by different discursive and ideological relations, including those of sexism, racism, and homophobia. I will argue, however, that in order to deconstruct and ultimately move beyond the family/not family debate, we need to further this analysis in two important and seemingly contradictory ways. First, we need to further explore and deconstruct our multiple and conflicting experiences of family, and the discourses that constitute these experiences. While families do mean different things to different people, we need also to consider the ways in which families can mean different things to the same

71 Hazel Carby 'White Women Listen! Black Feminism and the Boundaries of Sisterhood' in *The Empire Strikes Back: Race and Racism in the 70s Britain* (London: Hutchinson 1982); Jewelle Gomez 'Repeat After Me: We Are Different; We Are the Same' (1986) 14 *Rev. of Law and Soc. Change* 935; Patricia Hill Collins *Black Feminist Thought: Knowledge, Consciousness and the Politics of Empowerment* (New York: Routledge 1991); Kum-Kum Bhavani and Margaret Coulson 'Transforming Socialist Feminism: The Challenge of Racism' (1986) *Feminist Rev.* 26; Marlee Kline 'Race, Racism and Feminist Legal Theory' (1989) 12 *Harv. Women's LJ* 115.

72 Carby, supra note 71, 214–5.

73 Duclos, supra note 12: 'The search for a universal family law is misdirected because there is no universal family for it to regulate.'

74 Herman, supra note 18.

75 Ibid. It is similarly this emphasis on the increasing diversity of Canadian families and on the need to respect different family choices, including gay and lesbian families, that informs the factum of the Intervenors, EGALE et al. in *Mossop*. See for example Submission 46: 'In reality, the dominant conception of the nuclear family does not accurately reflect the way a great many people live. There are numerous family forms in Canadian Society ...'

people. Secondly, we need to move beyond an emphasis on multiple and diverse experiences to explore the discursive and material relations that produce these experiences. We need to contextualize these multiple experiences within the broader framework of ideologically dominant discourses.

A. THE INS AND OUTS OF FAMILY

An understanding of the discursively constituted subject allows us to further deconstruct the claims that We Are Family/We Are Not Family and reveal the complexities and contradictions that otherwise remain submerged. We can further interrogate the meaning of these political claims. What do we mean when we make these political claims? What and/or who do we exclude when we make these political claims? It is the erasures and internal ambiguities that we must also reveal in the family/not family. For example, in considering these claims, we must interrogate who the 'we' is, what 'family' we are talking about, and to whom we are talking. When we claim that 'We Are Family,' the 'we' is gay and lesbian couples, and their dependent children. The claim is being asserted by gay and lesbian couples about gay and lesbian couples. The 'family' within this claim is first and foremost the marital/spousal-like family – it is the voluntary creation of a family-like unit by two adults.[76] It may or may not also be nuclear-like family – that is, it may include the children of one or both of the adults. The unstated subject within this claim, as Nitya Duclos has pointed out, is the state.[77]

In the claim that We Are Not Family, the 'we' remains constant, but the unstated subject changes. At least to date, this claim seems to be more directed to the lesbian and gay community itself. It is an effort to

76 The family status cases have virtually all been claims to spousal benefits, and thus, specifically, to the claim that same-sex partners are spouses.

77 Duclos, supra note 12, 42. Duclos's observation is specifically with regard to the question of 'should homosexuals be allowed to enter a legal marriage.' She argues that: 'The hidden subject of this sentence is the state: it gets to give or withhold permission.' Duclos argues that we would shift the perspective from which we ask our questions. Shifting perspectives means changing the subject of the sentence and opening up the file of responses. We could ask something like 'will lesbians and gay men or some of them benefit from legal recognition of their relationships through the marriage system?' While I agree with Duclos that this shift would be an important improvement by focusing on lesbians and gay men, I am not convinced that it has ultimately removed the state as the hidden subject, which does still at the end of the day get to give or withhold permission. The same holds for the claim that We Are Family – although lesbians and gay men are the explicit subjects, it is still the state that is the intended recipient, and which gets to give or withhold permission.

persuade lesbians and gay men of the need to rethink a politics based on family. 'Not family,' within this claim, is simply the negation of the claim to family – we are not spousal-like. At a deeper level, this claim can be seen to have both a descriptive and a normative component. It could mean that the claim to family is not descriptively accurate, insofar as (some, many, most) gay and lesbian relationships are not based on sexual and intimate exclusivity. As a more normative claim, it could mean that heterosexuality and family is an inappropriate normative model for gay and lesbian relationships. In both its descriptive and normative forms, however, the claim that we are not family assumes meaning in relation to, albeit in negative relation, and understanding of family as spousal. In this respect, the understanding of family is the same on both sides of the family/not family opposition. It focuses on the way we are constituted in families as spouses.

Yet, these are not the only ways in which we live as family and in which the claim that we are family/we are not family acquires meaning. We live in a myriad of less than voluntary family subject positions. We are daughters, sisters, mothers, cousins, aunts ... And neither we (lesbian and gay couples) nor the state are the only ones who have the power to assert whether we are or are not family. Our families, whomever that may include, give meaning to who is family every day.[78] If we are 'out' as lesbians and gays, are we still inside family? Is our partner family? The definitional boundaries of who's inside/out are drawn in and through the lived experiences and interaction of family members. The process of inclusion and exclusion is a complicated and potentially contradictory one. Some members of our family may include us, while other members may not. A sister or a cousin may accept our partner as family, yet a parent may not. We are, then, both inside and outside family at the same time. The power of inclusion and exclusion is diffuse, shifting, and, often, the site of conflict. Whether we are inside or outside family in any particular context depends on particular configurations of power, and thus on who has the power to set the definitional boundary within that context. It is important to recognize that this power of inclusion and exclusion, which affects our position on the inside/out of family, is

78 Martha Minow 'Identities' (1991) 3 *Yale J. of Law and Humanities* 97, 119 writes: '[W]ithin any given period of time, family roles have acquired meaning through a complex process of interpretation by the people who fill them. Family identities are unavoidably relational ... [A] woman is a mother in relation to a child; a boy is a brother in relation to a sibling; they are a family in relation to one another. None of these relationships is intrinsic to a single person; each depends upon the patterns of connection between individuals, and between those people and the larger society and culture within which they live and make meaning of their lives.'

missed by the construction of We Are Family as spoken only by gay and lesbian couples, about lesbian and gay couples.

Moreover, the definitional boundaries of who's inside/out may or may not correspond to our own position on the political claim that We Are Family. Indeed, our own experience in this regard may be completely contradictory. We may never claim that We Are Family – that is, never claim its privileges in law, nor claim that it has meaning for us, in spousal-like terms. Yet, at the same time, our positions within our broader families may have enormous meaning – it is here that it may be important that our family bring our partner into its fold. It is important *not* that we claim that we are family, but that each of our families claim that we are family – that our partner is family – a claim with a very different meaning. It is a claim that is not contingent on spousal relationships. Alternatively, we may claim that we are family precisely because our families have refused to take our relationships into their fold. We may even lose our own family status within this process. Our claim to family is often in response to those definitional boundaries which have excluded us from family. It is a challenge to those with the power of inclusion and exclusion to name ourselves as family in the face of others' refusal to do so.[79]

B. BEYOND EXPERIENCE

This deconstruction of the multiple and conflicting discourses that constitute our experiences of family can help us move beyond the polarization of we are family/we are not family, by illustrating the extent to which we are inside/out. However, this emphasis on the diversity of our experience of family cannot be the end of the story. Indeed, an overemphasis on the diversity of familial experiences has some problematic implications. First, it risks reifying experience as a claim to truth, rather than locating experience as a product of the subject position within a broad range of discursive practices. Indeed, this is an increasing tendency within the current debate around family. One form is the assertion of experience as a basis for grounding the truth of each side of the debate.[80] Arguments are heard, both for and against the recognition of gay and lesbian relationships, on the basis of personal experience.

79 Kath Weston *Families We Choose: Lesbians, Gays, Kinship* (New York: Columbia University Press 1991) traces the historical shift, arguing that it was denial of gay and lesbian relationships as family that eventually gave rise to the claim to family.

80 It is not, however, the case that all those on the We Are Not Family side of the debate would adopt this reductionist approach to experience. Indeed, the socialist feminist work of Shelley Gavigan is extremely critical of any such unmediated uses of experience. Gavigan, supra note 25.

This personal experience is asserted as the basis of the truth or authenticity of the political position. Its second, and even more disturbing form is the assertion of experience as a basis for dismissing the non-truth of the other side of the debate. It is an attempt to use experience to delegitimize the subject within the debate by illustrating the contradictions between their experience and their politics. Arguments are heard, for example, dismissing anti-family politics on the ground that some of its advocates live within a clearly defined family unit, and take advantage for its privileges. There might be an important point to glean from such an apparent contradiction – but dismissal and delegitimization is not it. The reliance on experience as a claim to truth is problematic. Chris Weedon has argued that this approach to experience is premised on a humanist conception of the subject, that is, 'on the liberal humanist assumption that subjectivity is the coherent, authentic source of the interpretation of the meaning of reality,'[81] and thus of experience as 'the source of true knowledge.'[82] This reification of the experience obscures the extent to which our subjectivities are constituted by a broad range of discursive practices. It obscures the way in which our experience is a product of our location in a broad range of social relations: it is mediated, partial, and contradictory.[83]

Our experience of family is the product of our location at a broad range of intersecting relationships – including our positions on the inside/out figure of family. We all have our own stories of family, stories that inform who we are and what we believe. Our stories revolve around inside/out, around our relative inclusion and exclusion of family. We are in and we want to be out. We are out and we want to be in. We are never one or the other. We have to recognize that our stories of family are

81 Weedon, supra note 5, 8.

82 Ibid.

83 For a further discussion of the mediated and partial nature of experience, see Scott, supra note 51; Cossman and Kapur 'Trespass, Impasse, Collaboration: Doing Research on Women's Rights in India' (Spring 1991) 2: 2 *J. of Human Justice* 102–8; Mary Hawkesworth 'Knowers, Knowing, Known: Feminist Theory and Claims of Truth' (1989) 114: 3 *Signs* 533–57; Martha Minow 'Partial Justice: Law and Minorities' in Austin Sarat (ed.) *Amherst Lecture Collection*; Diana Fuss *Essentially Speaking, Feminism, Nature and Difference* (New York: Routledge 1989). For a discussion from a socialist feminist perspective, see Linda Brisken 'Identity Politics and the Hierarchy of Oppressions: A Comment' (Summer 1990) 35 *Feminist Rev.* and Gavigan, supra note 26. For a discussion from a postcolonial, socialist feminist perspective, see Himani Bannerji 'But Who Speaks for Us? Experience and Agency in Conventional Feminist Paradigms' in Bannerji et al. *Unsettling Relations* (Toronto: Women's Press 1991).

situated at point of contradiction and inconsistency, and that our experiences of family are mediated by our subject positions on this, and other, inside/out figures.

The mediated and partial nature of experience suggests that we need to move beyond the mere identification of different experiences. As Joan Scott argues, we need to attend to the question of how difference is constituted: 'to the historical processes that, through discourse, position subjects and produce their experience.'[84] We must do more than expose the different experiences of family of different groups. The fact that some or many lesbians and gay men experience their relationships as family is not the end of the story, but merely its beginning; as Scott writes, this experience is 'not the authoritative evidence that grounds what is known, but rather, that which we seek to explain.'[85] The experience of gay men and lesbians on the inside/out of family must be further interrogated and explained.

Kath Weston's recent work is useful in providing some of the social and historical context from which the claim to and experience of family has emerged.[86] She traces an ideological shift in gay and lesbian location to the family. Until recently, gay and lesbian identity was constructed in opposition to family – to be gay or lesbian meant exclusion from one's biological family, and the impossibility of constructing one's own. Within the last decade, however, lesbians and gay men have begun to contest this dominant cultural representation, and to 'inscribe themselves within the domain of kinship' by laying claim 'to a distinctive type of family characterized as families we choose or create.'[87]

The claim to family can thus be seen as a contest to the categorical and hierarchical oppositions of straight/gay and family/not family. Lesbians and gays who claim that We Are Family have challenged the way in which the gay/straight opposition has rested on the negation and exclusion of lesbians and gays from family. These gays and lesbians are contesting the cultural meaning of gay/lesbian identity and family, which were both based on the location of gays and lesbians outside of

84 Scott, supra note 51, 25.
85 Ibid.
86 Weston, supra note 79.
87 Ibid. 28–9. She attempts, at 29, to trace the sociohistorical developments that gave rise to this transformation of gay and lesbian relationships: '[C]hanges in the context for disclosing a lesbian or gay identity to others, attempts to build urban gay "community," cultural inferences about relationships between "same gender" partners and the lesbian boom associated with alternative inseminations' were all significant factors in the emergence of a discourse on gay and lesbian families.

the family. And in so doing, this contest over meaning resulted in the emergence of a new conception of family – families we choose.

Lesbian and gay couples who experience their relationships as family, and as subversive of family, must not be seen as the victims of 'false consciousness' or delusion.[88] Rather, this claim makes sense when situated within its broader historical and social context. However, attention to the broader historical and material processes that produce different experiences reminds us that these experiences are partial. We need to examine not only what we experience, but what we do not experience; that is, we must also be attentive to the silences, gaps, and omissions in our experience. We must again return to the question of what is excluded by the claim that We Are Family. While the claim that We Are Family pushes at the margins of family by challenging its exclusive and restrictive borders, and the ostensible 'naturalness' of its heterosexual form, the claim has not challenged the hierarchical opposition between family and not family. On the contrary, family remains the dominant and positive social value.

It is at this point that the concept of ideologically dominant discourses may be helpful. This concept reminds us that some discourses become dominant, inscribed in institutional practices, and reinforce relations of domination.[89] In the context of family, we need to recognize that the multiplicity of discourses of family does not mean that each of these discourses carries equal weight in terms of social meaning. Rather, one discourse of the family has become and remains dominant. We have already seen that there is not, nor has there ever been, a single and universal family. There has, however, been a dominant image of family – a white, middle-class, heterosexual, nuclear family, comprising a wage-earning husband, an economically dependent wife, and their biological children. Notwithstanding the historical and material specificity of this family form and the fact that it has never accurately described the way in which the vast majority of people live, even in the West, this image of

88 See supra note 62.

89 The question of the relationship between familial biology and familial discourse is as complicated as the relationship between ideology and discourse more generally discussed supra. Michelle Barrett, in her introduction to the new edition of *Women's Oppression Today* supra note 25, writes at xiv of her reluctance to 'abandon the idea of "familial ideology" ... Somehow familial ideology can have you by the throat in a way that a discourse of familialism is simply not up to. This is because the concept of ideology, whatever its undoubted and manifest failings, speaks both to and beyond the experience of the individual subject.' My own tentative resolution of the relationship, following my discussion of the relationship between discourse and ideology, is to speak of the ideologically dominant discourse of family and/or familialism.

the family continues to prevail today.[90] It is the image that continues to inform both the cultural representation and the legal regulation of the family. As Shelley Gavigan writes: '"The family" is presented both in law and in popular culture as the basic unit in society, a sacred, timeless and so natural an institution that its definition is self-evident.'[91] The claim that We Are Family, while pushing at the borders of this dominant image of the family, does no more to question or challenge this 'sacred, timeless and so natural' institution. Indeed the claim makes sense only in the context of the continuing hegemony of this ideologically dominant discourse of the family.

The broader historical and material process within which the claim that We Are Family is situated also limits the social meaning and implications of our experience. We must remember that the shifting and multiple nature of our subject positions of family does not mean that we are always free to shift our positions. We cannot assume that we can undermine the ideologically dominant discourse of family simply by deconstructing it, or redefining it. The diversity of family forms and experiences has not negated the ideologically dominant discourse of family. As both Susan Boyd and Shelley Gavigan have argued, while experiences of family may be different, these different familial forms and experiences continue to be affected and regulated in and through the dominant ideological form.[92] Gavigan argues that despite the 'dissonance between many people's lived experience and the dominant ideology of family ... the ideology of the patriarchal nuclear family provides the prism through which relationships are examined, and the measure against which they are judged, notwithstanding a shifting demography which indicates that the idealized nuclear family household may be becoming increasingly less typical.'[93] As Gavigan argues, the assertion of different experiences of family does not displace this dominant form.

We need therefore to be able to grasp, all at once, the contradictory ways in which the experience of family makes sense, the ways in which that experience is subversive of the cultural construction of family, and the ways in which the assertion of that experience is partial and does not displace the ideologically dominant discourse of the family.

90 The image has allowed some variation, such as wives who work outside the home and adoptive children.

91 Gavigan, supra note 25, 293.

92 Boyd, supra note 5; Gavigan, supra note 25.

93 Gavigan, supra note 25, 15–6.

V *Strategies of resistance*

The family/not family dilemma begins to dissolve when we refuse to accept the dilemma on its own terms, when we reject its either/or, and recognize that we are both. Exploring the contradictory nature of subjectivity can help us begin to reveal the ways in which we live at multiple and conflicting sites of family, and the ways in which the increasing dichotomization of the debate obscures and negates the complexities of our lives. But contradiction is much more difficult for legal politics. Legal categories do not allow for contradiction. As Mary Joe Frug has observed:

> Law requires all legal claimants to assume a particular posture – a partial identity – in seeking judicial assistance; we must leave aside much of the multiplicity and complexity of our lives in order to engage in legal discourse.[94]

When we return to law, which eludes attempts to work with life's intricacies and inconsistencies, we risk reinscribing the dilemma.

When presented with the question of what all of this has to do with law, it is at one level tempting to conclude, the less the better. If it is law that has got us into this dilemma, it is perhaps unrealistic to expect that law can get us out. Yet, at another level, this is unrealistic. First, it is important to recognize that it is not only law that has created the dilemma. The dominant cultural representations of family, and lesbian and gay identity, have been constituted and reconstituted by a multiplicity of non-legal discourses as well. We must neither look to law as the exclusive site of the problem, nor the exclusive site of the solution. However, it is at the same time important not to ignore law. Attention to the dispersion of power should not preclude attention to the ways in which power is also centralized, and to the continuing power of law as constituting discourses.[95] Legal discourses may be only one among many

94 Mary Joe Frug 'Law and Postmodernism: The Politics of Marriage' (1991) 62 *U. of Colorado LR* 483, 487. As Patricia Williams has observed: 'That life is complicated is a fact of great analytic importance. Law too often seeks to avoid this truth by making up its own breed of narrower, simpler, but hypnotically powerful rhetorical truths.' *The Alchemy of Race and Rights Diary of a Law Professor* (Cambridge: Harvard University Press 1991) 10.

95 See Eisenstein, supra note 5; Alan Hunt 'Foucault's Expulsion of Law: Toward a Retrieval' (1992) 17 *Law and Social Inquiry* 1; and Carol Smart *Feminism and the Power of Law* (London: Routledge 1989) who argue in response to Foucault that notwithstanding the dispersion of power in and through a multiplicity of non-legal discourses, law and juridical power remain an important sign of power, and that we need to explore the relationships between these juridical and non-juridical forms of regulation and discipline. See also Annie Bunting 'Feminism, Foucault and Law'

constituting discourses.[96] Yet, these legal discourses are important and potentially hegemonic in ways that other discourses are not. We ignore them at our own peril. Legal discourses continue to constitute and reconstitute lesbians and gay men through regulation and exclusion.[97] While lesbians and gay men must be careful about engaging with law on law's terms, we cannot afford to ignore law altogether. Law remains a powerful site, and must thereby remain a site of resistance.[98] We have to challenge law, engage with law, and resist law. The question of strategy becomes when, and on whose terms.

How can we evaluate strategies for resistance? More specifically, how can we evaluate and choose between the competing strategies of resistance by gay men and lesbians – between the We Are Family strategy that appeals to the liberal discourse of equality, and the We Are Not Family strategy, which relies on the feminist discourse and critique of family? First, we need to stop looking for simple or definitive answers. Perhaps the most insightful message of postmodernism for law is that we admit the contingency and partiality of our perspectives, and, thus, of our strategies.[99] As Scott argues, if we historicize and relativize the meaning of our concepts,

> it means we must also recognize the contingent and specific nature of our political claims. Political strategies then will rest on analyses of the utility of certain arguments in certain discursive contexts, without, however, invoking absolute qualities ...[100]

(1992) 15 *Alta LR* 829 arguing that Foucault does not suggest that the legal system, with its multifarious forms and mechanisms of power, is declining in importance as a site for the exercise of power.

96 See Smart, supra note 95, and Hunt, supra note 95, on the plurality of law and legal discourse. Hunt, at 32, writes: 'It is important to insist on the fundamental tenet of legal pluralism that law has never been a unitary discourse but has always involved a range of discourses connected to and competing with a range of extra legal discourses.'

97 For a comprehensive discussion of the ways in which Canadian law 'stigmatizes lesbian and gay existence by exclusion' see Ryder, supra note 9. He argues at 47–8 that '[t]he legal exclusion of gays and lesbians operates on a number of levels. On an ideological level, it constructs heterosexuality as the norm and gays and lesbians as deviant ... More concretely, the law is a source of material and psychic oppression for gays and lesbians. Gays and lesbians are deprived of the advantages and power afforded by laws aimed at improving the emotional and material security of heterosexual family units.'

98 Smart, supra note 95.

99 See Cossman, supra note 33, 353–4.

100 Scott, supra note 7, 175. She argues, for example, that while political strategies may in one context require arguments based on a recognition of women's roles as mothers, it must be done without arguing that womanhood *is* motherhood.

Similarly, if we relativize the meaning of family, we must also recognize that our political demands will be contingent and specific. We must evaluate the potential of our demands within specific discursive contexts, contexts which include a consideration of the material and ideological relations of the discourse.

In developing and evaluating strategies for resistance, we need then to consider the relative power of competing discourses and the extent to which resistance at a particular gap or cleavage is likely to affect institutionally inscribed social practices. In the context of lesbians, gay men, and family status, we need to consider the possible effects of the competing discursive strategies on actual social practices. The discourse of equality – that is, the challenge to discrimination and exclusion, heterosexism, and homophobia which lesbians and gay men face every day and which continue to be key discursive elements in the prevailing construction of lesbians and gay men as inferior, deviant, other – is important. In many respects, it is the powerful resonance of the liberal discourse of equality that has legitimized gay and lesbian struggles.[101] It is this powerful discourse that has brought cases like Brian Mossop's to the Supreme Court of Canada. As long as the dominant cultural representation of lesbians and gay men remains one of deviance and otherness, worthy only of social contempt, the claim to equal rights and equal respect of our relationships remains subversive. The increasing incidents of gay bashing and related hate crimes[102] suggests that claims based on sameness and social respectability should not be so easily dismissed as assimilationist.[103]

Yet, strategies of resistance based on the discourse of equality – inclusion within the family – leaves virtually untouched the discourse of

101 See Laclau and Mouffe, supra note 68, on the opening of democratic space for new social movements such as gay and lesbian rights through the principles of equality and liberty.

102 The National Gay and Lesbian Task Force Policy Institute reports that anti-gay harassment and violence increased by 31 per cent in 1991 in five major American cities. See 'Gays Under Fire' *Newsweek* 14 September 1992. In Oregon, gay bashing is reported to have increased by 300 per cent since Measure 9, the anti–gay and lesbian ordinance, has been introduced. See Donna Minkowitz 'Immodest Proposals' *Village Voice* 13 October 1992.

103 Martha Minow in 'Identities' supra note 78, 115 argues that we should not so easily dismiss strategies based on assimilation by individuals within minority communities as inherently deradicalizing: 'Signs of assimilation by a group treated as less powerful than the majority deserve a second look because they may indicate subtle acts of resistance and accommodation by people seeking to retain an independent identity without risking conflict or further suppression.'

family, and the way in which this discourse oppresses not only by exclusion, but also by inclusion. Resistance only at the level of equality discourse leaves intact the dominant discourse of family that continues to constitute subjects in deeply problematic and oppressive ways. Some advocates of this approach may respond that equality rights are important to those who do not have them, and that the fight to obtain equality rights, although perhaps limited, is the necessary first step in gay and lesbian struggles.[104]

It is important, however, to look beyond the immediacy of this discursive struggle, and evaluate its potential for bringing about change within the broader context of the complex web of legal and non-legal discourse that constitute the family. It is important to consider how the discourse of equality will interact, react, counteract with competing and conflicting discourses. Feminist reflections on women's struggles for equality rights may be instructive in this regard. Carol Smart and Susan Boyd, for example, have explored the impact of the realization of equality rights within the family, specifically, within child custody determinations, and found that the realization of equality rights can transform rather than eliminate the ways in which women are oppressed

104 A review of the rights debate and the question of the role of law in struggles for social change is beyond the scope of this paper. The debate between family and not family, while in some ways paralleling it, should not be reduced to the debate for and against rights. Although the We Are Family position more explicitly bases its legal arguments on equality rights discourse, the We Are Not Family position does not necessarily reject the rule of law in struggling for its political objectives. For a discussion of the rights debate, see generally Joel Bakan 'Constitutional Interpretation and Social Change: You Can't Always Get What You Want (Nor What You Need)' (1991) *Can. Bar Rev.*; Judy Fudge and Harry Glasbeek 'The Politics of Rights: A Politics With Little Class' (1992) 1 *Soc. and Legal Studies* 45; Alan Hunt 'Rights and Social Movements' (1991) 17 *J. of Law and Soc.* 309; Amy Bartholemew and Alan Hunt 'What's Wrong With Rights?' (1990) 9 *Law and Inequality* 1; Williams, supra note 94; Elizabeth Schneider 'The Dialectics of Rights and Politics: Perspectives from the Women's Movement' (1986) 61 *NYU LR* 589, arguing for a reconceptualization of rights that locates rights within broader political strategies. As I have argued elsewhere, I believe that we must complicate our understanding of rights to embrace both their possibilities and limitations in our struggles. B. Cossman 'Dancing in the Dark' *Windsor Access to Justice Yearbook*; B. Cossman and R. Kapur 'Women and Poverty in India: Law, Legal Literacy and Social Change' *Can. J. of Women & Law* (forthcoming). In the context of lesbian and gay struggles, see Herman 'Are We Family' supra note 10; Becky Ross 'Sexual Dis/Orientation or Playing House: To Be or Not to Be Coded Human' Sharon Dale Stone (ed.) *Lesbians in Canada* (Toronto: Between the Lines 1990).

through law.[105] Boyd has illustrated how the advent of liberal ideology of equality in the context of child custody did not simply displace the more traditional familial ideology such as the ideology of motherhood. Rather, the interaction of these two ideologies – of women as equal and of women as mothers – has 'created an almost impossible situation' for women trying to win custody of their children.[106] Notwithstanding the shift towards the liberal ideology of equality, the traditional ideology of motherhood, and the dominant ideology of the family on which it is based, continues to inform child custody determinations.

Gay and lesbian struggles can gain important insight from this history. First, the advent of the liberal ideology of equality did not displace the ideology of the family, but rather, transformed the very nature of the ideological struggle. In the same way, it may be unrealistic to expect that the struggle for and realization of formal equality rights within lesbian and gay relationships is likely to displace the traditional and dominant familial discourses. It may be more realistic to expect that the discourse of equality will interact with these and other competing discourses, and produce quite unanticipated consequences. This is not to imply that the struggle for formal equality rights is not important, or ought not to be pursued. It is only to suggest that our project must include an attempt to anticipate the unanticipated, to explore how these discourses are likely to interact, and to highlight the way in which we cannot afford to ignore the ideologically dominant discourse of family, lest it comes back to haunt us.[107]

105 Susan Boyd 'Child Custody, Ideologies and Employment' (1989) 3 *Can. J. Women & Law* 111–33; 'Child Custody and Working Mothers' in S. Martin and K. Mahoney (eds) *Equality and Judicial Neutrality* (Toronto: Carswell 1987) 168–83; 'From Gender-Specificity to Gender-Neutrality? Ideologies in Canadian Child Custody Law' in Carol Smart and Selma Sevenhuijsen (eds) *Child Custody and the Politics of Gender* (London: Routledge 1989) 126–57; Carol Smart, supra note 95.

106 Boyd, supra note 5.

107 Any evaluation of strategy must necessarily be historically and contextually specific. For example, the legal legacy of *Bowers* v. *Hardwick* 478 US 186 (1986), in the United States, in which the United States Supreme Court upheld a Georgia state law criminalizing sodomy and thereby refused to extend constitutional protection to consensual sexual relations between persons of the same sex, stands in stark opposition to the Canadian legal context where sodomy was removed from the Criminal Code in 1968, and where gay rights litigation is beginning to make some inroads in the courts. The continued criminalization of gay relationships in many states suggests that the struggle for the most basic of equality rights for gays and lesbians – the legalization of same-sex relationships – remains an overwhelmingly important one. Further, in *Bowers* Justice White, writing for the majority, affirmed the cultural representation of gays and lesbians as not family, in holding at 191: 'No

We must similarly explore the potential of strategies based on We Are Not Family, that is, based on resistance to the discourse of family, to effect social practices. There is good reason to resist the allure of family. As Shelley Gavigan has powerfully argued, the ideology of family continues to reinforce women's subordination, and strategies of resistance are required that 'chip away at the ideological assumptions about the family.' Campaigns to disarticulate social rights and benefits from family status have been and must continue to be a central focus of feminist struggles. As Gavigan encourages us, we must think creatively about waging 'defamilializing' campaigns, even at this moment when the family is being so firmly retrenched by the Right, and other political organizations and parties are being forced to appeal to its powerful rhetoric.[108]

The refusal to lay claim to family must be seen as an important discursive challenge to the hierarchal opposition of family/not family. In this strategy, the contest over the meaning of lesbian and gay identity involves challenging the opposition between gay and straight not by including gay men and lesbians within family, but rather, by challenging the hierarchical opposition of family over not family. In this deconstructive strategy, the hierarchies are inverted in an attempt to displace the normative assumption that family is necessarily the better way.

However, resisting only at the level of the ideologically dominant discourse of family leaves in place a discourse of discrimination and exclusion that constitutes us as other. As long at the hierarchical opposition of family/not family remains in place, the cultural representation of lesbians and gay men as not family continues to constitute gays

connection between family, marriage, or procreation on the one hand and homosexual activity on the other has been demonstrated.' As Claudia Lewis has argued, supra note 9, 1790, in so doing, 'the Court failed to acknowledge that only state prohibitions – legal constructs – bar homosexuals from marrying and raising families. Such blindness reinforces the "naturalness" of the stereotype of homosexuality as antithetical to family values.' This negation of any legitimacy to gay and lesbian relationships suggests that challenges to the dominant cultural representations of gays and lesbians as not family remains a very radical strategy.

108 The currency of 'family values' in the 1992 United States presidential election campaign exemplifies this tendency. See Priscilla Painton 'After Willie Horton: Are Gays Next' *Time* 3 August 1992, 26 arguing that behind the Republican Party's rhetoric on family values is an attack on gay rights and on Democrats for supporting gay rights. See also Andrew Rosenthal 'Family Values: Bush Tries to Recoup from Harsh Tone on "Values"' *The New York Times* 21 September 1992; 'Just Folks: What's Meant and What's Mean in the "Family Values" Battle' *The New York Times* 26 July 1992; Chris Bull 'Why Bush Hates You: The Religious Right's Stranglehold on the Residence and the GOP' *The Advocate* 20 October 1992, 39–47; Jeffrey Schmalz 'Gay Politics Goes Mainstream' *The New York Times Magazine* 11 October 1992.

and lesbians as deviant, inferior, other. As long as family is a dominant social value, and lesbians and gay men are not family, we remain trapped within (or perhaps, with/out) an exclusionary discourse. Moreover, beyond the contest for cultural meaning and identity, the continuing ideological dominance of the discourse of family has very immediate economic effects on the lives of lesbians and gay men.[109] The reprivatization of the family, an essential component of the conservative strategy of dismantling the welfare state, may further increase the stakes of opposing family.[110] As individuals are increasingly forced to rely on their families for economic and social support, turning back the clock on the advances made in the socialization of these functions through the welfare state, the continued denial of family status leaves lesbians and gay men with nowhere to turn. The ways in which familial discourse remains inscribed in concrete social practices continues to constitute and reconstitute lesbians and gay men outside family in real and painful ways. A failure to highlight and challenge this discrimination and exclusion only reinforces and is reinforced by the heterosexism and homophobia that plague our lives – day in and out.

In conclusion, we can see that no one strategy in and of itself will be sufficient to challenge adequately the complex way in which we are located both inside and outside family. Our multiple and contradictory position on the inside/out of family requires that we pursue multiple and potentially contradictory strategies. Since we are both inside and out, then we need to be struggling to get in, and we need to be struggling to decentre and deconstruct the inside.

The final and perhaps most difficult question of all is how we actually set out to do two contradictory strategies at the same time. One option is just to let each side pursue its own political agenda and strategies, and attempt to create an environment of tolerance and respect for the each other's choices of both family and politics. In so doing, we might try to ensure that our strategies do not undermine the strategies of others. We

109 Supra note 18.

110 See Judy Fudge 'The Privatization of the Costs of Social Reproduction: Some Recent Charter Cases' (1989) 3 *Can. J. of Women & Law* 246; 'The Public/Private Distinction: The Possibilities of and the Limits to the Use of Charter Litigation To Further Feminist Struggles' (1987) 25 *Osgoode Hall LJ* 485, 72; Davina Cooper and Didi Herman 'Getting "The Family" Right: Legislating Heterosexuality in Britain, 1986–1991' (1991) 10 *Can. J. of Fam. Law* 41; Mary Morton 'Dividing the Wealth, sharing the Poverty: The Re-formation of "Family" in Law in Ontario' (1988) 25 *Can. Rev. of Soc. and Anthrop.* 257.

might refrain from publicly arguing against the validity and legitimacy of the strategies of others. Beyond this respect of the political agendas of others, we might try to consider the extent to which our own approach could learn and adapt from the strategies of others. We might, for example, consider in any particular context whether we could not accommodate some of the insights of the other. Rather than attempting to resolve the dilemma of family or not family, we might attempt to evaluate the relative merit of each argument within specific contexts. In any given context, we should ask whether there is any potential for disaggregating the benefit from family status. We could consult with one another, to consider if we can frame our arguments in ways that minimize the dangers of an uncritical acceptance of the ideologically dominant familial discourse. Is there room to make a claim for entitlement that is not based on family status? Can we individualize the claim? Can we make a claim based on discrimination on the basis of sexual orientation, rather than family status? Can we reduce the extent to which we rely on the ideologically dominant family discourse? Can we resist the temptation to provide the courts/legislatures with a definition of family? Many of the consultative strategies were successfully pursued[111] in *Mossop*, wherein the intervenors resisted providing any definition of family and sought relief in non-familial terms.[112]

When we pursue strategies of resisting the ideologically dominant discourse of family, and work, for example, towards disaggregating benefits from family status, we need to ensure that we are not erasing the lives of lesbians and gay men. Arguments that focus on the oppressive nature of the family, and on the need to deconstruct the family, do not tend to focus much attention on the discrimination and homophobia to which lesbians and gay men are subject, beyond their exclusion.[113]

111 By 'successfully pursued' I am referring to and evaluating the consultative strategy used by the intervenors EGALE et al., and to the factum that was written as a result of this process, and not to the result of the Supreme Court of Canada decision. For a further discussion of these arguments, see Freeman, supra note 10.

112 The EGALE et al. intervenors' factum in *Mossop* is an excellent example of attempting to consider and accommodate the arguments of the other side of the debate, and thereby minimize the risk of an uncritical acceptance of the discourse of family. See Freeman, supra note 10. It is important to recognize at the same time that notwithstanding the adoption of an anti-essentialist approach to the family, the argument remains steeped in the discourse of sameness.

113 Barrett and McIntosh, supra note 25, 9, in noting the absence of any consideration on the relationship between the family and sexual preference, write: 'It would be ironic for us to be accused of reproducing the hegemonic heterosexism of our culture. Nevertheless we have to some extent inevitably done this, as we believe the

We must therefore be careful in pursuing strategies intended to deconstruct the privileged heterosexual family form that our arguments do not become 'so steeped in heterosexism'[114] that we deflect attention away from the lives and struggles of gay men and lesbians. We can try to ensure that our arguments bring those lives and struggles to the centre of our engagement with the ideologically dominant discourse of family.

Paradoxically, the strategy of the New Right confirms, and may indeed exacerbate, this contradictory nature of our struggles. In its efforts to shore up the family, the Right is staging a virulent attack on gay men and lesbians as anti-family.[115] Their objective is a rearticulation and reinscription of the traditional and patriarchal family, with all its trappings, including the traditional and subordinate position of women within this family. And an important discursive strategy in achieving this objective is the attack on and exclusion of gay men and lesbians from family. It is an effort on the part of the Right to rearticulate the meaning of gay and lesbian as anti-family. In Canada, this pro-family agenda of the New Right has permeated mainstream political parties. The family caucus of the Progressive Conservative Party is involved in a save-the-family campaign.[116] The caucus fears 'that the traditional family unit is crumbling under pressure from feminists, homosexuals, activist judges,

present ideology of the family to be so steeped in heterosexism that any realistic engagement with familialism must locate the discussion within that framework.'

114 Ibid.

115 For a discussion of the New Right in Canada, and its attacks on gay and lesbian rights, see Didi Herman 'Beyond the Rights Debate: A Reply to Judy Fudge and Harry Glasbeek' *Soc. and Legal Studies* (forthcoming). In the United States, this attack has found official sanction in the 1992 platform of the Republican Party, as well as in the anti–gay rights referendums in Oregon, Colorado, and Maine. While Measure 9 was defeated in Oregon, the anti–gay rights reference won in Colorado. In July 1993, however, the Supreme Court of Colorado held that such referendums are unconstitutional. Heather Rhoads 'Cruel Crusade: The Holy War Against Lesbians and Gays' *The Progressive* March 1993, 18–23. See Bull, supra note 108.

116 Geoffrey York 'Tory Politicians Form Family Compact' *The Globe and Mail* 3 June 1992. The family caucus has been lobbying to amend federal laws to include an official definition of the family. Don Blenkarn, a member of the caucus, states: 'It should define a family as a male and female, living together to raise children. And that's the only kind of family that ought to be defined.' The normative vision of the family is constructed explicitly in opposition to gay and lesbian rights. The committee is, at the same time, involved in a campaign to block the amendment to the Federal Human Rights Act that would prohibit discrimination on the basis of sexual orientation. Stanley Wilbee, one of the group's founding members, states: 'You've got the feminists, the gays and lesbians, all the various alternative lifestyles that are demanding attention. But we feel that the family is the basic cornerstone of Canadian life.'

special interest groups and the Charter of Rights.'[117] No doubt, each side of the family/not family debate will claim that the current assault vindicates their position. The We Are Family advocates will argue that their strategy has been so subversive of the family as to antagonize the Right. The We Are Not Family advocates will argue that it is the very ideological force of the family that fuels the fire of the Right's assault. The problem, again, is that both sides are right. Indeed it seems as if the family caucus, like other right-wing organizations, understand how to pursue contradictory strategies at the same time, albeit from a different, and chilling, direction. They are arguing *against* equality, and they are arguing *for* family. They are trying to meet both of our strategies, even before we have figured out exactly what our strategies are.

The agenda and increasing political legitimacy of the New Right and its discourse on gay men, lesbians, and family only heightens the urgency of our project – a project that we must accept as ridden with multiple and contradictory tasks. In a world in which the dominant cultural representation of lesbians and gay men is in opposition to family, laying claim to family is a politically significant and subversive strategy. In a world in which the dominant ideological form of family continues to contribute to the oppression of women, laying claim to family is a politically dangerous and potentially reactionary strategy. The problem we face is that the world we live in is both. To move beyond the opposition, the either/or, the inside/out, we have to recognize that we are family and we are not; we are inside and we are out. We must be able to pursue these multiple and contradictory strategies at the same time, for it is the only way that we will be able to challenge the multiple and contradictory discourses that constitute us.

117 Ibid.

Part II
Shaping Family Practices

[5]

Marriage and the Moral Bases of Personal Relationships

JOHN EEKELAAR* AND MAVIS MACLEAN**

Marriage is a legal institution. Current debates about whether it should be extended beyond its traditional heterosexual constitution, and whether many of its legal incidents should apply to couples who live together without marrying, and about the introduction of civil partnership (modelled closely on marriage) for same-sex couples, make an examination of its contemporary role particularly timely. This article is about the interplay between the institution of marriage and ideas of obligation within personal relationships. It takes as its starting point some commonly held opinions. First, that the sense of obligation which hitherto guided people's behaviour in their personal relationships has much diminished or even disappeared. Second, that this diminution is reflected in the decline in marriage. We will then examine what the evidence of an empirical study conducted by the Oxford Centre for Family Law and Policy reveals about the way people in married and unmarried relationships understand the nature of their personal obligations. In doing this it will be seen that the moral bases which underpin people's personal relationships is complex and does not correspond in a simple way with formal, external social categories.

I. THE DECLINE OF OBLIGATION[1]

Prior to formulating an argument (to which we will return) that the obligations created by marriage constitute a human good, Scott Fitzgibbon asserts that 'the twentieth century brought a crisis of obligation'.[2] He cites little evidence for

* *Pembroke College, St Aldates, Oxford OX1 1DW, England*
** *Department of Social Policy and Social Work, University of Oxford, Barnett House, 32 Wellington Square, Oxford OX1 2ER, England*

1 This has been covered at greater length in J. Eekelaar, 'Personal Obligations' in *Family Law and Family Values*, ed. M. Maclean (2003).

2 S. Fitzgibbon, 'Marriage and the Good of Obligation' (2002) 47 *Am. J. of Jurisprudence* 41–69, at 47.

this proposition,[3] but the sentiment is common enough. Gilles Lipovetsky has referred to the alleged phenomenon as '*le crépuscule du devoir*'[4] and Zygmunt Bauman has described postmodern sociality as one which 'knows not and hears not of rights, obligations, contracts or legal entitlements'.[5] The 'culprit' (if such there be) for this state of affairs is said to be the rise of 'individualism'. Thus, in 1985, Robert Bellah and colleagues[6] identified 'individualism' as 'the first language in which Americans tend to think about their lives', leading them to value 'independence' and 'self-reliance' above all else.[7] For these authors, individualism seems to denote a kind of self-centred indulgence, to be contrasted with a disposition towards 'commitment' and recognition of 'obligations'. But it is not so simple. Some writers have argued that the sense of obligation to others has been replaced by a sense of obligation to oneself to live a authentic life.[8] In a more complex analysis, Giddens in 1992[9] and Beck and Beck-Gernsheim in 1995,[10] drawing on a wide range of contemporary literature (in Giddens' case, especially psychoanalytical discourses), developed a more complex version. According to Giddens:

> Confluent love is not necessarily monogamous ... What holds the pure relationship together is the acceptance of each partner 'until further notice', that each gains sufficient benefit from the relationship to make its continuation worthwhile.[11]

3 His cites only the rise in bankruptcy filings by individuals and families in the United States of America, an assertion by Allan Bloom that American students have impoverished ideas of friendship (A. Bloom, *The Closing of the American Mind* (1987) 82–140), and the claim by Patrick Atiyah that respect for promises has declined in English life, see P.S. Atiyah, *The Rise and Fall of Freedom of Contract* (1979) 649–59.

4 G. Lipovetsky, *Le Crépuscule du Devoir* (1992).

5 Z. Bauman, *Postmodern Ethics* (1993) 130.

6 R.E. Bellah, R. Madsen, W.M. Sulian, A. Swindler, and S.M. Tipton, *Habits of the Heart: Individualism and Commitment in American Life* (1985, updated 1996).

7 id., p. viii. This was a very broad-brush analysis. Much of the discussion on values in the private sphere centres around four individuals chosen as paradigms, who speak in very general terms about their 'philosophies of life'. The authors found that they had difficulty in 'justifying the goals of a morally good life'; they were confused about defining 'the nature of success, the meaning of freedom and the requirements of justice.' Since these are issues with which philosophers and theologians have wrestled for centuries, the problems of the respondents are very understandable. Similarly, their observation that 'Americans are ... torn between love as an expression of spontaneous inner freedom, a deeply personal, but necessarily somewhat arbitrary, choice, and the image of love as a firmly planted, permanent commitment, embodying obligations' does not do other than take up an age-old theme, whether expressed in terms of conflict between individual passion and obligations to wider family, country or spouse.

8 For an excellent discussion, see H. Reece, *Divorcing Responsibly* (2003) 84–92.

9 A. Giddens, *The Transformation of Intimacy: Sexuality, Love and Eroticism in Modern Societies* (1992).

10 U. Beck and E. Beck-Gernsheim, *The Normal Chaos of Love* (1995).

11 Giddens, op. cit., n. 9, p. 63.

Central to this is the role of 'negotiation'. The rights and obligations arising from the relationship are subject to negotiation.[12] Even sexuality is a matter of negotiation, whether it be the matter of sexual exclusivity, or even the nature of the sexuality itself.[13] Beck and Beck-Gernsheim describe the same phenomenon. They call it, creating a 'do-it-yourself life history'.[14] In daily life, 'more and more things have to be negotiated, planned, personally brought about'.[15] The organization of life after divorce 'has to be negotiated, often fought over'.[16]

This new individualism is hardly a world of 'do as I please'. Autonomy may have become a newly important value, but it is restrained by the necessity of coexisting with other people who are exercising the same value. Coexistence is made possible through negotiation. But this analysis throws up new problems. What is meant by negotiation? It surely does not occur within a vacuum. How, then, is it affected by the social or moral context in which it occurs? *Is* there such a context? Janet Finch, in an important analysis of what negotiation might mean in this context, saw it not as being the equivalent to conscious bargaining, but as an *understanding* which emerged over time 'that there are certain things which they would do for each other if necessary'.[17] But Finch was clear that such 'negotiation' takes place within 'external structures'. It is these structures which create 'shared understandings' absorbed through membership of society that underlie the negotiations, for example (as Finch explains):

> most people, both sons and daughters, acknowledge some responsibility for their parents in old age; daughters are commonly thought to be the people most suited to provide nursing care, for their mothers especially; men do not give up their jobs to care for a parent.[18]

This reference acknowledges the role of 'social rules', which Finch describes as not being so much 'moral' rules 'concerned with determining how someone "ought" to behave, as common perceptions of "how the world works".'[19]

In 1999 Carol Smart and Bren Neale reported on a study of post-separation parenting involving 31 women and 29 men interviewed twice during 1994–6, at twelve and eighteen months after their separation. The purpose was to detect whether there were 'newly emergent forms of responsibilities, caring patterns and ethical codes'.[20] Smart and Neale concluded that indeed there were. These

12 id., p. 191.
13 id., pp. 63, 96.
14 U. Beck and E. Beck-Gernsheim, *Individualization* (2001).
15 id., p. 91.
16 id., p. 94.
17 J. Finch, *Family Obligations and Social Change* (1989) 181.
18 id., p. 183.
19 id.
20 C. Smart and B. Neale, *Family Fragments?* (1999) 40.

people were not acting amorally, in the sense that they reflected on their decisions and weighed up their consequences. They argued that the mothers exhibited an ethic of care, in the sense that, for them, their decisions about what 'should be done' were solutions to specific problems in which the primary guideline was the practical manifestation of 'care' for another, in this case, the children. The fathers, by contrast, tended to proclaim an 'ethic of justice', which was abstract and rights-based, and they used the rhetoric of equality.

The circumstances of post-separation parenting is of course a good context in which to examine the norms to which people have reference when determining what their personal obligations are. But it is a very special context, which arises only after shared living has finished. We still need to know more about the norms to which shared living may give rise. Jane Lewis has made an important contribution to this knowledge.[21] Lewis accepts that the advent of individualism 'does not mean that there will be no consciousness of "ought", but it is no longer imposed but has to be negotiated'.[22] To discover more about such negotiation, she interviewed 17 married couples with children and 17 unmarried couples with children, aged between 27 and 50, recruited by advertisement in nursing, teaching, and social work publications. In order to provide a generational perspective, 72 of their parents were also interviewed. This was clearly not a 'representative' sample of the general population, and was not intended to be because one of the main objectives was to explore areas 'likely to reveal the balance between attention to self, as opposed to attention to other and to the relationship',[23] and the sample was designed to further that objective. However, some further questions (but not interviews) were posed to 777 people drawn from an Omnibus Survey by the Office for National Statistics, which was representative. Lewis describes the central issue as revolving around the idea of 'commitment'. The unmarried had tended to 'drift' into long-term unmarried cohabitation. They had lived together for so long they saw little point in marrying.[24] They saw their 'commitment' as being 'private' rather than 'public'. Half of the unmarried and one-quarter of the married said they had no obligations to one another, or had not thought about them; but for the rest, they saw the obligation as coming from 'within' and not externally imposed:

> The crucial thing ... was seen to be the existence of commitment rather than its manifestation. Given that ... it is not surprising that most people in the sample also felt that it was proper to treat married and cohabiting parents the same.[25]

The picture is one of pragmatic compromise, and, although Lewis herself does not emphasize the concept, a sense of the importance of mutual *respect*.

21 J. Lewis, *The End of Marriage? Individualism and Intimate Relationships* (2001).
22 id., p. 126.
23 id., p. 128.
24 id., pp. 135–6.
25 id., p. 145.

THE GROWTH OF 'RIGHTS'?

When we consider the character of interpersonal relationships, the question arises how far, if at all, ideas of 'rights' are present or indeed appropriate. We should say, immediately, that we are not primarily referring to legal rights here. Whether A has a legal right against B is in principle, if not always in practice, a straightforward matter. The answer lies in the legal texts and legal practice. But can we also imagine that people have rights of a different kind, moral or ethical, to the way the other party to a relationship should behave?

Some people have thought that the very idea of rights in personal relationships is meaningless, or even dangerous. For example, the judge, Sir John Laws, expressed this view in a lecture in 2002.[26] For him, the content of morality was contained entirely in the realm of duties. To make a moral claim was to assert what you, or someone else, ought to do with regard to another person: in other words, to assert the existence of a duty. In contrast, this view holds that to claim a right is entirely self-centred, and therefore not a moral claim except perhaps in the trivial sense that it refers indirectly to duties of others. Others have expressed similar views.[27] By way of contrast, Giddens considered that concepts of rights and obligations were very important in postmodern 'intimate' relationships. Indeed, he writes that 'intimacy should not be seen as an interactional description but as a cluster of prerogatives and responsibilities that define agendas of practical activity' and notes that the importance of rights as a means of achieving intimacy can be seen from women's struggle to achieve equal status in marriage.[28] John Dewar and Stephen Parker have suggested that family law has progressed from a 'formal' era (from about 1857 to the 1960s), when 'there was a strong sense of spouses as rights-holders', through a functionalist era to the present 'complex' or 'chaotic' era. But complexity has not reduced the role of rights; indeed:

> there is now a greater emphasis on rights, but the rights-claims are more diverse and stem not from marriage itself ... but from other states, mainly to do with childhood or parenthood.[29]

These contrasting views do not take into account the perceptions which individuals in relationships themselves hold about rights. Even if one does

26 Sir J. Laws, 'Beyond Rights' (2003) 23 *Ox. J. of Legal Studies* 265–280. Laws argued that the language of rights was only appropriately used to refer to legal claims against the state.

27 For example: M.A. Glendon, *Rights Talk: The Impoverishment of Political Discourse* (1991); A. Etzioni, *The New Golden Rule: Community and Morality in a Democratic Society* (1996); M.C. Regan Jr., *Alone Together: Law and the Meanings of Marriage* (1999).

28 Giddens, op. cit., n. 9, p. 190.

29 J. Dewar and S. Parker, 'English Family Law since World War II: From Status to Chaos' in *Cross Currents: Family Law and Policy in the US and England*, eds. S.N. Katz, J. Eekelaar, and M. Maclean (2000) ch. 6.

not expect such individuals to have engaged in sophisticated conceptual analysis, perceptions of rights can be a powerful driver of behaviour. It seemed important to explore this issue.

A FURTHER INVESTIGATION: STRUCTURE OF THE RESEARCH

We wished to tap into that generation which experienced its childhood during the years when the 'great disruption'[30] began to first make its impact on family life. These would be people born between the late 1960s and late 1970s, who are now between their late 20s and early 40s. We wanted to include only people who were likely to have had the opportunity to experience extended relationships. We also wished to obtain a sample drawn from a fully representative base, and were fortunate in obtaining the consent of the Office of National Statistics to introduce a screening question into its Omnibus Sample on family change.[31] This question allowed us to identify respondents who were within the desired age range and who had experienced partnerships of some kind. We interviewed 39 individuals, 18 men and 21 women. Two were under 29, and the rest between 30 and 45; 26 were married, nine currently cohabiting, two were now living alone and two were 'living apart together' (in a current relationship but living in separate homes). One of the last was the only gay relationship in the sample.

Since we also wished to examine whether ethnic diversity was a significant factor in the responses, we were also able to weight our sample so as to ensure such diversity among the respondents. Sixteen respondents were from ethnic minority groups (in which we include White Irish). In presenting our data, we have followed the categories used by the ONS in indicating ethnicity. We have indicated the ethnicity of the respondents in what follows, but will explore issues of ethnicity directly in a later article. The study should be seen as a qualitative one, indicating the range of perceptions, values and behaviours relevant to personal relationships which people hold in contemporary British society. We cannot make quantitative extrapolations from our data about the extent to which any particular type of response is held in the general population.

Our questions were designed to discover how the respondents reacted to certain key events in what is often called the family life cycle, but which, in more individualist mode, might be called their personal lives, and, above all, *why* they responded as they did. The key events are forming a co-residential unit, marrying, becoming a parent, leaving a co-residential unit, experiencing

30 The expression used by Francis Fukuyama to describe the transformation in family and personal relationships described in the text: F. Fukuyama, *The Great Disruption* (1999).

31 We express our special thanks to John Haskey of the Office of National Statistics for much assistance on this.

the departure of children from home, and feeling the first effects of the dependency of elderly parents. Not every respondent will have experienced all these events.

The respondents were asked both about the effect of such events on their actual behaviour and their reasons for such behaviour. The latter questions raised certain difficulties. It was difficult to know how people would react. However, whatever people may say, they must act for a reason. We notice the proposition[32] that, while at some level we can talk about acting on one's desires (eating when hungry; sleeping when tired), this turns out to be a very limited way of accounting for behaviour. It is not simply that there are many occasions when we do not in fact act on our desires, crudely conceived. It assumes that the only way we can decide between conflicting desires is to choose the strongest desire (although the expression 'choose' seems inappropriate, for the image seems closer to the stronger desire dictating the choice). In such a scenario, you would not need to, perhaps could not, weigh up all your desires. Your action would just 'happen', flowing from the desire. But that seems a strange way to explain behaviour. While people sometimes do lose control and act on urges alone, those are generally considered to be pathological cases. You can also sometimes want things, but have no reason to have them (you already have enough, for example). In such cases acquiring them can be some form of addiction. It therefore seems more plausible to say that in the standard case the action you choose you choose for a reason.

Uncovering the reasons for action has not only an explanatory purpose. A reason must refer to something which is of value to the actor. To act for a reason which holds no value for the actor is to act for no reason at all. As Raz has put it: 'reasons are rooted in values'.[33] This is of particular importance in this context, for by reflecting on people's reasons for acting, we may access the values they hold. An important goal was to gain an insight into the values people hold in conducting their personal lives. We were initially unsure whether subjects would find it easy to articulate such reasons, and they sometimes struggled to formulate them. Our work is not one of psychoanalysis, and we do not claim to have accessed unconscious motivations. The articulated reasons nevertheless provide indicators of those values which the respondents were prepared to lay some claim to.

32 J. Raz, *Engaging Reason* (2000) 51-6. T.M. Scanlon, *What we Owe to Each other* (1998) argues that even when quenching 'brute' wants, satisfaction of the desires are not reasons for action but the future pleasures which the desires point towards (pp. 41–49). See, also, J. Dancy, *Practical Reality* (2000) 35–8.

33 Raz, id., p. 252; '. . . one can only want something because of a good one believes the thing to have' (p. 261).

THE ANALYSIS

In what follows, for reasons of space, the evidence supporting the analysis is selective. The evidence is set out in full in an Occasional Paper of the Oxford Centre for Family Law and Policy (OXFLAP). We start with an account of the reasons those respondents who had married gave for choosing to marry rather than live together without marrying. This was not an outlandish choice for these people, since most of the respondents will have been partnering during the 1980s, and, while in 1971, 97 out of every 1000 single women over 16 were married, this ratio had fallen to 56:1000 in 1987. The proportion of all women who had never married and were cohabiting outside marriage increased from 8 to 17 per cent between 1978 and 1987. 53 per cent of women who married in 1987 had lived together with their partner before marriage.[34] Clearly, the generation of people who were entering into personal partnerships during the 1980s faced a realistic choice between marriage and (continuation of) living together without marrying.

But why did the married marry? The answers should give some indication about what values they thought marrying held for them. This might further reveal what importance it had in respect to their relationships, and allow inferences to be drawn about how they viewed the relationships. But inference is not enough. We also needed to ask directly how they considered marriage, or the other life events described earlier, affected their sense of how they felt they should behave towards their partner. We did not direct our questions solely at the relationship between the partners, for we wanted to know whether the partnership (married or not) could provide a source for a sense of obligations to certain other people (in particular, to in-laws), and, if so, why that was so. We will make some reference to these responses here, but a fuller treatment will be the subject of another paper.[35] At present we will direct attention at the relationship between the partners themselves, married and unmarried.

REASONS FOR MARRYING

Of our 39 respondents, nine were currently living in a partnership but had not married their partner, and two were living singly after having cohabited. Of these, four had been married earlier. Two further respondents were in the position sometimes described as 'living-apart-together', which, for these purposes, we will include among the unmarried cohabitants. We will return to this group later, but will start by looking at both all those who were now

34 See J. Eekelaar, *Regulating Divorce* (1991) 53.

35 See M. Maclean and J. Eekelaar, 'The Obligations and Expectations of Couples within Families: Three Modes of Interaction' (2004) 26 *J. of Social Welfare and Family Law* 117–30.

married, and also those of the first group who had been married before their subsequent cohabitation. This constitutes 32 respondents.

This large group had all married at some time. We have divided their reasons for marrying into three main categories. The first are entirely *pragmatic* (three cases). Marriage was entered into to achieve some collateral objective, and not by reason of any value attaching to marriage itself. The second group of reasons we call *conventional* (18 cases). This is because the respondent refers to some social source, external to the respondent, whether it be in the form of the practice of others, or the opinions of others, which are recounted as being significant in determining his or her decision. The respondent in these cases can be seen as placing value in *conforming* to some kind of convention. The third group of reasons we term *internal* (18 cases). Here the respondent perceives the institution of marriage as allowing the respondent to realize or promote a goal which is important to himself or herself. The respondent does not seek to satisfy external demands, but his or her internal goals. Of course respondents could hold more than one reason, so some cases appear in more than one category. The overlap between cases in the conventional and internal categories is of particular interest. Two cases could not be allocated to any category.

1. Pragmatic reasons

There were three examples:

> Int. Why get married?
> R. My husband went to work in [middle eastern country] and the only way I could go out there was if we were married ... I wouldn't say it was the only reason but that is what precipitated it at that time; we were happy as we were. (Female, 39, Cohabiting after previous marriage ended in divorce; White British, speaking of first marriage) [13].

> Int. Why marry after living together?
> R. It just happened; we were going to emigrate and it was easier with all the papers.
> (Female, 34, Married, White Irish) [26].

> Int. Why marry at this time?
> R. Inheritance tax. My husband saw this Panorama programme on TV last October.
> (Female, 39, Afro-Caribbean) [38].

2. Conventional reasons

Curiously, the number of cases in this category (18) turned out to be the same as the number in the 'internal' category, discussed below. But there were nine cases of overlap between them, and we will give these special attention when we discuss the internal category. The conventional reasons given were: following religious prescription, following parental wishes, and following social or cultural practice.

In two cases religious prescription was cited as a sufficient reason in itself:

> Int. Why marry rather than live together?
> R. I'm a Catholic ... a practising Catholic. My wife isn't. She is C of E. My family is Catholic.
> (Male, 38, married, White British) [32].

> Int. Why marry?
> R. I'm a practising Muslim; my wife was born a Muslim but knew nothing about it ... she converted to Islam and gave me an ultimatum: live the Muslim way and marry ... after a year of the marriage I came to Islam, it took a year, studying; before we lived by society's rules, now I live as a Muslim.
> (Male, 24, Afghani, Muslim) [33].

In the second case, the religious prescription governed the wife's behaviour rather than the husband's: becoming a Muslim and marrying was the only way he could have a relationship with this woman. Nevertheless, it was the religious prescription which led to the marriage.

In three other cases, parental prescription was afforded similar status. For example:

> (We) did not live together before marriage.
> Int. What view did you take about living together before marrying?
> R. Personally I would not have had a problem with it but my father would not have countenanced it at all; there would have been no way my Dad would have allowed it.
> (Female, 43, Married, White British) [20].

Two respondents combined this with religious prescription. Here is one:

> I am a practising Catholic ... my Dad told us to get married ...
> (Female, 38, married, Black African) [35].

A number of respondents regarded the social conventions of their community as exerting a considerable force on their behaviour. But this tended to be combined with religious practice and parental wishes. For example:

> R. I think it was a cultural thing to do with it, and expectations of parents ... back home, if you start living together you get married ... we are Christians ...
> Int. Would you say part of the reason was a religious reason?
> R. It is difficult to say, isn't it ... it is both cultural and religious.
> (Male, 45, married, Black African) [19].

Another way of expressing this was to say that it was 'the thing to do at the time' (male, 39, married, White British) [14] or 'because that's what you did and maybe it's because what your parents did as well' (female, 44, married, White British) [17] or 'I was brought up you didn't do it until married' (female, 42, married, White British) [27] or 'I didn't want a baby and not to be married. It was 1980 ... still a bit of a stigma' [29].

These expressions indicate an acceptance of the prescriptions of religion, cultural practices or family expectations as sufficient reason to enter marriage. The extent to which respondents cited their desire to conform to the wishes of their parents was striking and took us somewhat by surprise. These, after all, were people who would have been marrying in the 1980s. However, it was noticeable that when cultural and family expectations were cited as relevant factors, some respondents appeared to wish to distance themselves from the appearance of treating those as exclusive determinants of their decision. For example:

> Int. There was a wish you would get married?
> R. Absolutely ...
> Int. What were your own feelings about that?
> R. Mmmm ... well, because in Ireland at the time family expectations were of a church marriage ... I would say for me it was something I owed my parents ... for my wife, she's more religious, very religious parents ... though I can't say it was just for the parents. I think we ourselves were traditional enough to believe that commitment would involve marriage.
> (Male, 41, married, White Irish, Roman Catholic) [11].

Here the respondent recognizes a duty towards both his and his wife's parents, as well as to his wife's religion, but introduces a new element which is neither expressly anchored in religion nor in filial duty: it is 'tradition'. Tradition has a compromise quality to it. Following a tradition suggests a lifestyle choice, freely entered, rather than being subject to prescriptions by reason of one's membership of a community which one may not have freely chosen. This perspective could be adopted in the absence of any, or any strong, religious motivation. Giving as a reason for marrying that one is 'old-fashioned' (female, 40, married, White British) [31] seems to be adopting a similar viewpoint.

3. *Internal reasons*

The value which marriage was seen to hold by these respondents all related to the idea of commitment. But they seemed to do so in slightly different ways, which we describe as confirmation (four cases), completion (eight cases), and construction (six cases). As we will explain, some of these cases overlapped with those in the 'conventional' category.

(a) Confirmation
Here marriage appeared to hold a purely symbolic significance for the respondent. It was important for the respondent in so far as it demonstrated, usually to the outside world, a state of affairs already reached by the parties. In itself it made no difference to the relationship as these respondents perceived it, but was seen to confirm what already existed. For example, one respondent, who, when asked why he married his cohabiting partner, said:

> It's the final thing, really, plus the legalities ... it was just the final thing to do.
> (Male, 32, married, Black British) [37].

Another:

> It makes everything in place, din't?
> (Male, 39, married, White British) [12].

In these cases, marriage appears to be no more than a single event – indeed, as one said – a 'party', with no further implications in itself, though representative of responsibilities already felt or assumed. It is perhaps not surprising that none of them overlapped with those in the 'conventional' category. The symbolic effect of the marriage was indeed a matter of value, but since it was symbolic only, these respondents did not feel that external conventions provided any reason in themselves for going through the ceremony.

(b) Completion

There were eight cases, however, where marriage seemed to play a more significant role from the internal point of view. It was more than merely a public display undertaken mostly for others, but assumed a more personal nature, and provided in itself an added impetus for, or source of, further commitment. In this sense it was a significant element in completing the sense of commitment which the parties already felt. But it is interesting that five out of the eight cases in this category overlapped with the 'conventional' category. As will be noted, the respondents who combined conventional and internal reasons were able to reconcile their individualistic aspirations with their acceptance of the external conventions. Perhaps they found the two aspects mutually reinforcing.

An example was the following:

> Cohabitation is not a full committment. My parents wouldn't be happy with us living together, but only because we wanted to.
> (Female, 31, married, Asian British) [16].

The strongest version of this attitude was where marriage had provided a catalyst, some kind of turning point; it forced the respondent (or both parties) into a decision that their relationship really was for life; that they should settle into a more permanent mode of living:

> Marriage for me is the point at which it moves from being 'This is very nice now' to 'we've got to make a life together with a view to being together for as long as you last, ultimately probably having children, etc.' In that sense it's a deeper commitment.
> (Male, 41, married, White Irish, Roman Catholic) [11].

A further case showed a strong personally held view that marriage 'completes' the personal commitment. The respondent had expressly insisted that they should enter into marriage, despite her pregnancy, but only if her partner 'wanted' it:

> [Partner] proposed when I was pregnant; he said we ought to get married. I said 'no', only if you want to get married; we had discussed having a family and agreed we wanted it ... a proper family is mum and dad and married.
> (Female, 42, married, White British) [15].

These cases all show marriage operating as an event which seals, or raises to a new level, a relationship which has been maturing over time. It is often consistent with seeing marriage as mandated by external convention. No doubt the parties believe the relationship will continue to grow after the marriage, but marriage is essentially seen as the event which has an independent effect in completing the fundamental nature of the partnership.

(c) Construction

But there is another reason for marrying, also associated with the idea of commitment, but this time it represents an earlier stage in the relationship: it sets up a framework within which the partners *work towards* the deeper commitment which, for the earlier group, marriage already signified. We see the significance of marriage here as constructing a framework within which the partners consciously strive to achieve a still deeper commitment. Usually that deeper commitment occurs on the birth of a child. As in the 'completion' cases, it was possible for respondents to combine the use of marriage as a framework for deepening their relationship with accepting conventional reasons for marrying, and three did so (cases [2], [21], and [22]).

Typical construction cases are the following:

> Int. Why marry at all?
> R. I don't know. I s'pose we just wanted to ... it was like a way of saying 'I want to be with you for ever' ... [but] when you're married, you've always got a get-out, not that you hope to divorce, but you're not bonded in the same way. The real commitment is having kids, not the marriage. Then you're connected to that person further.
> (Female, 38, married, White British) [4].

> We both wanted children and we wanted to get married first before we had any children.
> (Female, 32, married, White British) [9].

This use of marriage as a framework for deepening a commitment which was completed on the birth of a child could have operated as an additional or subsidiary reason in some cases where the primary reason seemed to be conventional. For example, the Hindu respondent who explained that he had married out of conformity to cultural traditions and parental expectations, added:

> Although you see each other during the day [before marriage] it's totally different living together ... most people have children in two years, we delayed it until five years ... I think the delay for settling down and having

> children was just to make sure that we were compatible and knew what way we were heading.
> (Male, 36, married, Asian British, Hindu) [21].

This was a respondent to whom cultural factors were important. It is possible that the very fact that such respondents were subject to strong conventional prescriptions to marry, so that the act of marriage did not necessarily fully coincide with a sense of confirmation of emotional commitment (as in the completion cases), *encouraged* the perception of the marriage being a framework within which commitment grows. Unlike the overlap cases in the completion category, where the respondents were able to synthesize their own ethical motivations with conformity to convention, these overlap cases show respondents using the convention as a resource for promoting a sense of commitment, which would normally be confirmed by a later event, typically the birth of a child.

REASONS FOR NOT MARRYING

There were ten respondents in current relationships outside marriage. Some had strong negative views of marriage:

> I would never marry again ... it's like bungee jumping ... once is enough, it was not a nice time; we're fine now and don't want to change it.
> (Female, 42, White Irish, cohabitant after marriage involving violence) [29].

In four cases, the respondent equated marriage with 'the wedding': it was no more than a one-day event, with no apparent further significance, and was therefore irrelevant. For example:

> Int. Do you see yourselves marrying in the future?
> R. That's a very difficult question. The answer is yes, but it's financial ... finances permitting. At the end of the day, we don't want to just go down to the Registry Office and do it for £10. If you want to do it properly it costs something like £15,000, especially because me and (my partner) have both got massive families ... I could always see a better way of spending £15,000 than sunnying around in a white dress, personally.
> (Male, 38, cohabitant, White British) [1].

It seems that these respondents could be considered as having a very similar approach to marriage as two who had married for pragmatic reasons ([13] and [26]).

Reasons people have for marrying, and for not marrying, are important indications of the role marriage plays in contemporary life. For many, marriage is undertaken as a matter of conformity: to parents' wishes, to religious prescription or to cultural norms. But marriage was just as widely used by people to express a personal value: this might be an achieved state of commitment or a mode of clearing the pathway towards such commitment. It is quite possible, of course, that people could see these goals as being independent of each other. That is, that marriage may be undertaken for conventional reasons, but not be seen as having any relevance to whatever internal reasons a person may have for entering a relationship. But, as we have seen, a significant number of people see the state of marriage in itself as contributing in some way to enhancing an internal attitude.

However, the internal reasons we have been examining are attitudes towards *marriage*. They do, of course, reflect, and have implications for, the respondents' attitudes towards the other partner. But we thought that issue demanded a separate inquiry. We did this by asking how various events, namely, beginning to live together, getting married and having a child, affected their sense of 'what they owed' to their partner.

PERCEPTION OF RESPONSIBILITIES BETWEEN PARTNERS

In analysing the data we will break the reasons people gave for explaining their behaviour towards their partner into three types: first, when the behaviour is ascribed to following duties which derive from a source external to the parties. We will call this the 'external-duty' approach. The second sees the source of obligations as being embedded in the relationship itself. It is seen as something that builds up over time, and is coterminous with the relationship. This idea seems to be closely related to a particularist view of ethics. The behaviour just follows from the nature of the circumstances. Being in a relationship simply *means* acting in a supportive way towards one another, and the more so the longer the relationship has lasted. We will dub this the 'evolutionary' approach. The third perception appeals more directly to certain ethical principles. We will call this the 'ethical' approach. This might seem very similar to the second group. For those respondents in the second group who cited the relationship itself, or being in a relationship, rather than making a direct appeal to an ethical principle, such as love or care, as the reason for acting supportively towards their partner, did not, of course, mean that they did not act lovingly or caringly, or did not see these as virtues. But they saw the virtues as being intrinsically tied to what one did if one had a working relationship. Those in the third group seemed to express a commitment to the ethical principle which was independent of the relationship, although, as we will see, it was possible for elements of more than one perspective to be held.

1. The external-duty approach

One might anticipate that those who undertook marriage for conventional reasons would be inclined to see the relationship as being dominated by rules or obligations set by the marriage itself. There was some indication of that. For example, a fundamentalist Christian said, in answer to the question whether he thought it was his duty to share, or whether they just wanted to do it that way:

> I am a Christian ... God say there is no man and there is no woman ... man and woman is one, not two ... so why think differently ... everything belong to me belong to her; not I must do, I think I should do ...
> (Male, 38, married, Brazilian, Christian) [24].

Although the respondent distinguished between 'I must do' (which he rejected) and 'I think I should do' (which he accepted), it seemed clear that his acceptance of the obligation derived from his Christianity-based view of marriage: 'man and woman is one, not two'. So here we have a link, which we might expect, between an external-duty approach and a strongly conventional reason for marrying.

Similarly, a Muslim respondent said:

> There are rules about marriage ... it tells you how to live together and keeps us happy.
> (Male, 24, married, Afghani, Muslim) [33].

Such respondents had a strong conventional element in their reasons for marrying. But it was not only those with a religious background who adopted the external duty approach, although for these others it seems to have played a weaker role. One, for whom concern over parental disapproval had motivated marriage, but who admitted to being 'old-fashioned' about it, had even gone to a solicitor while she was still living together with her husband to get a letter demanding he give her money (female, 40, cohabiting after divorce) [31].

2. The evolutionary approach

As explained above, these respondents see the nature of their behaviour as being inherently determined by the nature and progress of the relationship. Paradigmatically, one would be inclined to associate this primarily with unmarried cohabitants. There was certainly a strong example from that group:

> Int. Would your partner have any right [against you, now]?
> R. I wouldn't have seen it as a right ... it sounds almost contractual ... I'm trying to search for a softer word than a right ... again, obligation is quite a strong word ... it's part of being in a relationship.
> (Male, 33, cohabitant, White British) [8].

Such responses show that those adopting this approach can be reluctant to concede they are under an obligation. Yet the relationship seems to exert some kind of normative force. For example, a respondent who had married for pragmatic reasons said:

> Being together should be mutually supportive ... now people provide support in different ways depending on their personality or on their ... how they are equipped within the relationship ... so a mutual supportive role ... otherwise you are just living with a friend ... it's a developmental relationship ... I don't think I had a right to financial support ... emotional support though ... ummm ... I think you have a right for somebody to support you if you are in a long-term committed relationship.
> (Female, 39, cohabiting after previous marriage ended in divorce; White British) [13].

That respondent went as far as to see a long-term relationship as capable of giving a 'right' of some kind. This approach is found also in other categories, such as those who saw marriage as a confirmation of the relationship. Another respondent, whose partner had a teenage son, when asked whether she had any obligations towards the boy, replied:

> We have made a family, the way I want it, there is no 'ought' about taking on [son] I can't see [son] as anything other than part of the relationship with [partner] ... we are no different from married ... it all depends on the quality of the relationship, not legal status ... maybe commitment should contain the length of time together ... but that should apply to marriage too ...
> (Female, 45, cohabitant planning to marry, White British) [34].

This response introduces an important additional element to this perception. The respondent characterized her attitude towards her stepson as *an element of her relationship with her partner*. To complicate matters further, the evolutionary approach was also articulated by some who had conventional reasons for marrying. This was a respondent who married for a multiplicity of conventional reasons, including seeing it as a completion of the relationship. The obligation is expressed here in terms of the 'right' of the partner:

> I think if you're making that degree of commitment to somebody, then I think at some level they have a right to expect you to behave ... there is an implicit contract somewhere in that ... this is where an awful lot depends on the quality of the relationship because I don't think any of these things flow from a system of law ... it's a betrayal of the relationship ... so there's a right on the basis of the evolution of the relationship.
> (Male, 41, married, White Irish, Roman Catholic) [11].

We conclude that, while people who had strong conventional reasons for marrying would often see the obligations flowing from the conventions they were following as having some, sometimes strong or exclusive, force in directing their behaviour in their relationship, people marrying without such conventional reasons (but also some who *did* have such reasons) very often also saw their behaviour as being prescribed by the fact of being in the relationship itself rather than from the marriage. And of course this could be true for those who did not marry.

3. The 'ethical' approach

There were pervasive responses, spread among all 'types' of marriage, and among those who were not married, where the respondents referred to some independent ethical value in explaining the way they thought they should behave in their relationships.

(a) The golden rule

The most commonly cited 'ethical' basis for behaving towards a partner was the so-called 'golden' rule: do unto others as you would have them do unto you. This might look like a manifestation of the reciprocal or reflexive relationships which Giddens identified as being characteristic of modern intimate relationships. But there is a difference. The reflexive relationship is one in which (at least theoretically) the relationship is kept constantly under review and renegotiation so as to keep the interests of each partner in balance. There were indeed some examples of this. Here is one from a married woman, a Roman Catholic, whose relationship had clearly weakened. But even this deviates from the Giddens model because she was bringing into the calculation the effect of her behaviour on others, notably her children:

> Even when I first got married, I was never one of those to tempt fate and say that it was so fantastic that we were never going to break up. I don't like saying that because I've seen too much go wrong for other people. Long-term relationships are very difficult and it depends how much compromise you want to do. However, the flipside is how much devastation you cause if you do break up. The price of having an affair for your family is high. Basically, I've found that price too high to pay at the moment ... If I didn't have children the whole thing would be different . . , I think I'd get out of a relationship much quicker, or at least have a cooling off period, where you could find out whether you still wanted to be together or not.

This respondent had initially expressed an ethic in terms of the 'golden rule', but went on to suggest that her view had changed. Perhaps the respondent felt that she had now made more of a contribution to the family: she was not just taking, but contributing (or was in a better position to contribute). But this must also be seen in the context of the weakening relationship:

> When somebody's been supporting the whole family as long as he has, you don't feel in quite as strong a position to argue 'well, I want to do this' because you feel selfish, when somebody else has been working all these hours and [my husband's] not just going off and doing what he wants either. But now, I've changed ... I've re-educated myself and gone to university, my horizons have broadened ...
> (Female, 40, married, White British) [5].

But reciprocity was more likely to be expressed in terms that indicated the acceptance of an obligation towards the other from the fact that the other had given benefits to the respondent, or had undertaken detriments. The obligation this generated was a continuing one (though presumably not immutable):

> I think at the back of my mind I must have felt, he's working so hard, if I just stayed at home doing nothing, that would have been very unfair on him; if it had been the other way around, and I'd been working all day long, coming back, and my husband having a nap all day, I would not be very happy.
> (Female, 43, cohabiting after divorce, discussing former marriage undertaken for strong conventional reasons, Japanese) [10].

A cohabitant who expressed the 'evolutionary' paradigm strongly seemed to trace the source of his responsibilities to his partner to the fact that she had moved to his 'territory':

> Int. The reason you gave for your responsibilities ... [you indicated that] it was because she'd moved?
> R. Because previously we had been on neutral territory ... and it was shifting the balance to go one way or the other way or to stay in a neutral town, so the very fact that [she] made the move ... I expect it was a case of appreciating what she'd done ... I would do anything to support her decision to move.
> (Male, 33, cohabitant, White British) [8].

Another cohabitant, who put great weight on the birth of the child in cementing the relationship ('Now it's a very firm bond. I'm one half of a whole, whereas before there was that bit of independence'*)*, had expressed the 'golden rule' as governing his attitude to his partner's parents:

> Int. Would you help your partner's parents?
> R. Yeah
> Int. Why?
> R. To be honest, they're nice people, but more importantly ... you should do unto others as you'd have done unto yourself. They've helped me in the past and I would like to reciprocate if it was required.
> (Male, 30, cohabitant, White British) [1].

It is interesting that this open reference to the golden rule appeared more prominent in unmarried cohabitations than in married ones. It is possible that, for the married, the ethic simply became absorbed in the duties of marriage, or the conceptualization of the relationship.

(b) Trust building
Another expressed ethic drew on the idea of trust. We saw this expressed in the context of both marriage and cohabiting relationships. This could be seen as a form of reflexivity, but it is more than simply adjusting to find the maximum benefit for each partner: the goal is an ethical one of mutual confidence.

> I think [financial arrangements] was simply a more sensible way of doing things ... I suppose, in a way, in the early part it was a bit like saying, well, let's start working together and tying ourselves up more ... it's that sort of trust building; to say it's trust building sounds like there's a suspicion, but it's more a natural step that far along ... we have separate accounts as well as the joint account ... we try to keep the separateness but togetherness.
> (Male, 44, married, White British, Buddhist) [2].

> Int. If you were still living together with your new partner and got into need, would your partner have a responsibility to you?
> R. I don't know if it is a responsibility but I would probably expect something from him, some help, I don't know in what way; but if he ignores (me) I don't trust him any more.
> (Female, 43, cohabitant after divorce, Japanese, describing cohabitation relationship) [10].

In this last example, the reciprocal element is reversed, for under the golden rule the respondent's sense of obligation rests on benefits received or the other party's detriments undergone, whereas here the respondent reposes trust in the other in the expectation that it will be honoured. But it is a mutual process.

(c) Love, respect, and care

It is perhaps surprising that respondents did not mention love as a reason for their behaviour more often. This does not, of course, imply that love was absent in cases where it was not mentioned. Failure to mention it may indicate some coyness about putting what might be thought of as an emotional response up-front to an interviewer. But three male respondents had no such difficulty. It is interesting (but not necessarily significant) that all three had married according to strong conventional reasons. Here are two examples:

> Int. When you started to live together having got married, how did that change things ...?
> R. Well, I think it both started with love ... and respect to each other and if you have that then we see we have better productive if you do things together. I think the foundation was I say love then respect and you build on it: that's how I see it.
> (Male, 45, married, Black African, Christian) [19].

> Int. You think you've got responsibilities to your wife primarily because you're married to her: that would be our reason ...
> R. No ... I married her because I love her, that would be (the reason) ...
> (Male, 38, married, British Asian, Sikh) [22].

Three women ([9], [17], and [31], all White British) also mentioned love as being a reason for marrying in the first place. Two of these ([17], [31]) coupled it with strong conventional reasons. It is curious that it was only the married who referred to 'love' as a basis for behaviour. Perhaps it is because it appeared as a reason for marrying, and of course the cohabitants did not marry. Yet the cohabitants failed to refer to it as a reason which explained the way they behaved towards their partners. Jane Lewis[36] also did not refer to 'love' in discussing the way her respondents, both married and unmarried, viewed their relationship. However, 'caring' was referred to by two women as being an important feature of their relationship and a cohabiting woman, who had had a (literally) bruising experience of marriage, said simply:

> Int. What kind of support can you expect from your partner; do you have any rights?
> R. Rights don't come into it. I expect him to treat me with respect; that's all.
> (Female, 42, cohabiting after divorce, White British) [29].

36 Lewis, op. cit., n. 21.

PERCEPTIONS OF RIGHTS

Having considered the way in which respondents saw their duties or responsibilities, we now turn to consider specifically the extent to which respondents felt the language of rights was appropriate within their relationship. We recall that a number of authors have expressed scepticism about the appropriateness of using concepts of rights within personal relationships, but also that we see claims about rights as attempts to secure the application of duties by others in accordance with certain background moral principles.

1. Discomfort with ideas of rights

We found evidence that respondents indeed had discomfort about speaking in terms of rights. This was so for cohabitants and for married people.

> Int. Do you think you have a right to expect certain behaviour of your partner?
> R. I don't think 'expect' is the right word. No ... obviously I would like certain things to be done, but I'm understanding in the circumstances, how difficult it is to get things done when you have a child. So if I come home and dinner is not on the table ... that's not a problem.
> (Male, 30, cohabitant, White British) [1].

> Int. Would she have a right (to support from you)?
> R. I wouldn't have seen it as a right ... it sounds almost contractual ... I'd have thought more of a ... I'm trying to search for a softer word than right ... it's part of being in a relationship.
> (Male, 33, cohabitant, White British) [8].

> It doesn't mean you would not provide it (support), but it's different about whether it's a right ... I don't think right is a word I would use anyway ... I don't think people have a right to things ... it's about consideration.
> (Female, 39, cohabiting after divorce, White British, talking about position in her former marriage) [13].

So while, as one might expect, we can find those who adopted the 'evolutionary' approach to their sense of responsibilities to have particular reluctance to speak about rights ([8], [3], [12], and [13]), we find similar reluctance among those who were willing to acknowledge an ethical basis for *responsibilities* ([1], [2], [8], and [29]) and even one who saw duties being externally imposed ([22]).

2. Rights seen as respecting the interests of the partner

Yet there were contexts in which some respondents did find the expression appropriate. One was where the respondent expressly acknowledged an interest of the partner. This might be for personal space:

> My wife has a right to go out and visit her sisters and her friends and go out to work: I can't say, you stay in, you can't go out to work.
> (Male, 45, married, Black African, Christian) [19].

Or it might be an acknowledgement of the partner's interests to consideration:

> Ummm ... I'm quite easy going, so I'd say she has a right to be happy, that's the only thing I'd say ... it's up to me in some sort of way to make sure she is happy ... I don't feel I've got any rights from her.
> (Male, 32, cohabitant, White British) [23].

One interpreted the word as referring to her own interest in a degree of independence:

> I think I should have a right to say ... 'I'm going out' ... and then, if he's got any plans, we can sort it out, find a babysitter, whatever. He shouldn't be saying, 'no you can't go'.
> (Female, 38, married, White British) [4].

It might be significant that this was uttered in the context of what appeared to be a deteriorating relationship.

3. Association of rights with economic contributions

Interestingly, some linked this idea of rights to the fact they had made economic contributions. For example:

> Int. Do you think the right, which you say you feel you now have, is linked to any responsibilities?
> R. Because if you're earning as well, you have more power, you have more say: 'I'm going to do this because I'm contributing to the house'. But when somebody's been contributing to the whole family, you don't feel in quite as strong a position to argue: 'well, I want to do this', because you feel selfish, when somebody else has been working all these hours.
> (Female, 40, married, White British) [5].

The fact that they were making economic contributions also led some women to the thought that they had some right to support from their husbands or partners. For example, respondent [13] thought she had some right to share in his pension for that reason. Similarly, in replying to the question whether she had a right to support from her husband, a respondent said:

> We're both working: so a bit of a right, yes.
> (Female, 31, married, White British) [16].

But women were ready to concede that their husbands or partners had rights to expect support from them, when the husband was providing all the economic support. For example, a Japanese respondent attributed her feeling that her former husband had rights against her to the fact that he supported her. This was recognized even where the woman was working:

> Int. Did your partner have any right to ask you to help him out financially when you were in transitional stage (i.e. living together before marriage)?
> R. Yeah, because in effect I was living there, so I don't see why not ... we were both working, so I'd say you split things up.
> (Female, 26, married, White British) [6].

However, one male respondent cited the fact of economic contributions as a reason against his wife having rights to support:

> Int. Do you see yourself or your wife as having a right to the kind of support you talked about?
> R. It depends ... if you're both working, both looking after the children ... I don't see one has got a right over the other ... when she's not working there is an obligation on me to support her.
> (Male, 43, married, White British) [30].

4. *Rights based on convention*

Certain respondents saw themselves as having some kind of right flowing from the rules related to marriage. such as a right to the security of the home [17]. One woman had gone to a solicitor to have her right to support enforced while the marriage was ongoing. Those respondents for whom the conventional aspects of marriage were important were not surprisingly inclined to see rights and duties as flowing naturally from the convention. For example:

> I think it goes without saying ... both of us have a right to each other and responsibility to each other as well.
> (Male, 45, married, Black African, Christian) [19].

Another, whose marriage was in the conventional category:

> Both sides have rights, in a family, both sides have got responsibilities ... I got rights, she got rights.
> (Male, 42, married, Indian) [18].

However, this respondent seemed later to place a particular restraint on this by saying this did not 'come from the marriage' but rather from the duty towards children. Even if 'rights' were not specifically referred to, they must have been implicit in the response which stated that marriage laid down 'rules' (male, 24, married, Afghani, Muslim) [33]. But that was not an inevitable response from those who married for conventional reasons.

> Int. Would you have felt you had a right to that (knowledge about finances)?
> R. I don't know whether it's a right or not; it's always been for us ... I wouldn't say that ... had we wished to keep that personal I wouldn't say I had a right ... but we were in a partnership and, yeah, we shared everything.
> Int. So you would not have thought he had rights against you or you had rights against him ...?
> R. No ... not at all.
> (Female, 43, married, White British) [20].

However, that respondent did say 'we would expect' financial support from one another if they split up 'just because we've been married for 24 years'.

COMMUNALITY

It is sometimes said that people in unmarried cohabitation are less inclined to share resources than the married.[37] In our data, some cohabitants did seem inclined towards retaining a degree of economic independence, but this seemed to be related to the fact that the cohabitant had experienced difficulties in an earlier relationship. However, it was possible to find cohabitants who had a strong sharing ethic:

> I don't think we see it as each other's property, we see it as our property, we find it very difficult to say, that's mine, that's yours.
> (Male, 33, cohabitant, White British, first cohabitation) [8].

Another placed this approach as arising after the birth of a child, when:

> It really became a situation of 'what's mine is hers' and vice versa.
> (Male, 30, cohabitant, White British) [1].

Others, who had now married, had adopted a sharing approach from the time their pre-marital cohabitation started:

> R. We share everything.
> Int. You did that right from the beginning (i.e. when moved in together before marrying)?
> R. Yes ... money ... everything ... cars ... whatever ...
> (Male, 39, married, White British) [12].

Some married respondents also expressed a strong sharing ethic:

> I was quite surprised to see friends of ours that had separate accounts and kept them. I find that extremely strange.
> (Female, 40, married, White British) [5].

> We work together as a team ...
> (Male, 45, married, Black African) [19].

Others retained a degree of independence. In one case, where the parties kept separate accounts for their own purposes, the wife kept a secret stash because the husband was bad with money ([6]). Two other married couples had a similar arrangement ([7], [16]). In another, a full-time mum received 'an allowance' ([15]).

DISCUSSION: MARRIAGE, RELATIONSHIPS, AND THE 'GOOD' OF OBLIGATION

We referred earlier to the paper by Scott Fitzgibbon in which the author expresses the view that obligation is non-instrumentally good as an instantiation of the good of steadfastness and stability'[38] and that 'marriage

37 See L.J. Waite and M. Gallagher, *The Case for Marriage* (2000) 39.
38 Fitzgibbon, op. cit., n. 2, at p. 64.

is a drama of mutual reinforcement of obligation'.[39] The point seems to be that acknowledgment of obligation to another is a manifestation of 'steadfastness' and 'stability' (which are goods for both the person displaying these characteristics and the one towards whom they are displayed), and that marriage generates such obligation. We would not wish to dissent from the idea of steadfastness and stability as being goods. Reflecting on our data, however, we are led to wonder whether the sense of obligation can come only from an external source and therefore to doubt whether marriage is either a necessary or sufficient context for the acceptance of personal obligation.

As far as expectations of endurance of the relationship is concerned, cohabitants could express as much incomprehension at the thought of possible future separation as married people. It was so unthinkable that they could not easily contemplate how the eventuality should be dealt with:

> Int. If things went wrong, would either have any rights or a claim?
> R. I don't know ... I've never considered it ...
> Int. In terms of splitting up, would having a child make a difference?
> R. I'm sure it would, though in our case it's not something we've given any consideration at all ...
> Int. Should people think about it?
> R. Yes and no ... The probability is so low on the scale ... it's not something to consider.
> Int. You would see this relationship lasting for life?
> R. Yes.
> (Male, 33, cohabitant, White British) [8].

A respondent who was now married made it clear that he had expected the relationship to be for life from the moment pre-marital cohabitation began:

> Int. Is it your feeling that this relationship will go on for the rest of your life?
> R. Yes, I'd expect that.
> Int. From the beginning ...
> R. From the beginning of what ... marriage or when we were together?
> Int. When you were first together.
> R. Yes, you would expect that, yeah.
> (Male, 39, married, White British) [12].

One did have very low expectations:

> I tend not to live too much in the future to be honest ... yeah, I would say my expectations are less as far as the future is concerned ... a more short-term assessment.
> (Female, 39, cohabitant undergoing divorce, White British) [13].

However, this was true of some married respondents too. Here are two:

> Int. Do you imagine remaining married for life?
> R. No ... we just argue so much ... when it becomes detrimental to the children.
> (Female, 38, married, White British) [4].

39 id., at p. 66.

> Int. What of the future … would you see yourself being married for life?
> R. Erm … I don't know … even when I first got married, I was never one of those to tempt fate and say it was so fantastic that we were never going to break up … the flipside is how much devastation you cause if you do break up. The price of having an affair for our family is high. Basically, I have found that price too high to pay at the moment.
> (Female, 40, married, White British) [5].

We are not suggesting that this was characteristic of the married; on the contrary, they too could find splitting up so remote as to be out of range:

> Int. What if you and (wife) were to separate?
> R. I find this very hard to imagine … if it did happen I would have to be not myself … it's so hard to say …
> (Male, 39, married, White British) [14].

Of course the above evidence shows only what the respondents' expectations were and it might be said that to identify the sense of obligation so closely with the persistence of the relationship is to rob it of prescriptive effect, because each individual is free to terminate the relationship. At most, the obligation is treated as an *instrumental* good: valuable to the extent that it is necessary to keep the relationship going (but disposable along with the relationship), rather than as a good in itself which nurtures the relationship. However, the respondents who expressed themselves in this way did also indicate an attitude which showed a desire to invest efforts in making the relationship work in event of difficulty. The relationship exercised a normative 'pull':

> I would have to … I don't know: to struggle on the best we can [23].

> We're both difficult people. If we married it might spoil it [34].

In addition, cohabitants frequently referred to some additional factor, such as having a child, or some ethical principle, which reinforced this normative position, and would have commended steadfastness:

> R. The only thing that's ever changed our relationship has been the baby … before the baby came along we were always independent financially, but since the baby came along that just changed instantaneously, and it really became a situation of 'what's mine is hers' and vice versa … I think it's now a very firm bond. I'm one half of a whole, whereas before there was that bit of independence.
> (Male, 30, cohabitant, White British) [1].

> Int. Does marriage make any difference to people's responsibilities in relationships?
> R. No … um … no maybe people around us expect differently, but I don't think it makes much difference really.
> Int. Then what is important, if not marriage, what things are important for you?
> R. Trust and care …
> (Female, 43, cohabitant after divorce, Japanese, describing cohabitation relationship) [10].

In any case, married people also expressed the 'evolutionary' approach (cases [6], [12], [34]), and also appealed directly to 'ethical' principles ([2], [5], [6], [10], [11], [14], [19], [22]) and having a child ([9], [15], [16], [21], [33]) as sources of obligations. So, while married people had an additional source available from which to derive their obligation, many of them referred to the same ones as the non-married. It becomes increasingly difficult to identify being married in itself as *necessarily*, or even *characteristically*, constituting a significant source of personal obligations in the eyes of the participants in such relationships. Nor can we say that we found evidence, either among the married or the unmarried, that our respondents saw their sense of obligation as primarily owed to themselves. The conventional and ethical bases of obligation are clearly inconsistent with this, and, while the 'evolutionary' approach might appear to have some similarities to that view, it was really very different because the obligations were seen to be owed to the other, albeit that they arose out of the 'situation', as 'situational' ethicists would put it. All in all, the evidence showed rich and diverse sources for perceptions of obligations, which suggests that the thrust of much of the literature reviewed at the beginning of this article should be re-evaluated.

Finally, we revert to the role of rights, and the interrelationship with perceptions of obligation. We must stress that we were not focusing on how people might perceive their rights if the relationship came to an end. The conclusion seems to be that, as far as people's perceptions of their ongoing relationships is concerned, ideas of rights are not prominent. This appears to be somewhat at odds with the Giddens view of relationships being in a continual state of renegotiation. However, while not prominent, they are not necessarily absent. They seem to be part of the conceptual means by which partners recognize the interests of the other, which is inconsistent with the perception that ideas of rights are necessarily self-centred. They also seem to be associated with two specific factors. One is where the respondent sees the marriage in strongly conventional terms. Of course such respondents will associate responsibilities with such terms as well, but it appears that in these cases they will also be conscious of their 'own' entitlements. This sits uneasily with claims that marriage pre-eminently instantiates ***obligations***. Of course it does that, but can also prompt a 'rights-based' view of aspects of the relationship, whereas the unmarried cohabitants, many (but not all) of whom grounded their sense of obligations in either the normative pull of the relationship itself or in ethical values, were less inclined to think in terms of rights as protecting their self-interest. The other factor is in connection with a perception of economic contribution, either by the respondent or the partner. As far as allocation of capital on divorce is concerned, the English courts have only recently proclaimed that financial and non-financial contributions to a marriage should be seen as having equal worth,[40] and the principle is

40 *White* v. *White* [2001] 1 All E.R. 1.

still not acknowledged if the couple are not married.[41] We should not be too hasty to extrapolate from these responses to the view that partners who do not contribute financially should not have rights on separation, for, as we have said, the present context did not assume separation. Rather, it suggests to us an unwillingness in most respondents to see their role in personal relationships as one which places demands on the other. They accept obligations on themselves and these tend to be related to background moral values like recognizing what the other has done for them, care, and respect, or are seen as necessary ingredients for making a relationship work, something which held value in itself. Rights, in the sense of claims on the other, seemed to have special resonance where economic contributions may have entered the calculation.

On the whole, though, we found that being married was consistent with a range of attitudes, both to marriage itself, and also to the relationship within it. For some people, it was an important catalyst for their relationship, either as providing some kind of seal to the state of commitment they had already reached, or a framework in which an even deeper sense of commitment, usually reached by the birth of a child, would be attained, or a reinforcement of their internal goals. But it could also play other roles, such as the purely symbolic, or openly instrumental. So marriage is useful and important to many people in a number of ways. But when we examine the way people think about their relationships, we find that there are many variations between those who are married, and many similarities with those who are not. Cutting across them all, though, we find a range of values which are held in common, and which have a substantial effect on generating ideas of personal obligation.

This conclusion should lead to caution over claims that marriage is *uniquely* capable of producing certain 'goods'. The picture is more complex. Whether marriage delivers those 'goods' more successfully than when people live together without marrying[42] is also hard to substantiate. It appears to be true that, statistically, married relationships last longer than unmarried ones.[43] But it is also true that, at times when marriage was more widespread than it is now, the marriages of the young, the poor, and the remarried were at much higher risk of breaking up than those of older, more financially secure, first-time married people.[44] Those risk categories may now be being substantially filled by unmarried cohabitants,[45] so the reasons

41 *Lloyd's Bank* v. *Rosset* [1991] 1 A.C. 107.

42 Arguments of this kind have been put forward most notably by Waite and Gallagher, op. cit., n. 37.

43 This is demonstrated, and discussed fully, in M. Maclean and J. Eekelaar, *The Parental Obligation: A Study of Parenthood across Households* (2000).

44 The evidence is summarized by C. Gibson, 'Changing Family Patterns in England' and D. Ruane Morrison, 'A Century of the American Family' in Katz, Eekelaar, and Maclean, op. cit., n. 29, chs. 2 and 3.

45 This seems to be true for the United Kingdom with respect to unmarried cohabitants who have children: see Maclean and Eekelaar, op. cit., n. 43, p. 20.

why married people who were in those circumstances were more likely to separate than others probably apply disproportionately to unmarried cohabitants. Our evidence shows that married and unmarried people who are living together share many values. Indeed, the similarities in the normative determinants of their behaviour may be greater than the dissimilarities. This is a intriguing perspective on a society in which, outwardly, the form personal relationships take seems to be becoming increasingly diverse.

[6]

MONEY AND MARRIAGE: SEXUALLY TRANSMITTED DEBT IN ENGLAND

BELINDA FEHLBERG*

ABSTRACT

In recent years of economic recession, the problems faced by spouses and partners (especially wives) who provide third party loan security (usually a second mortgage over the family home) for the business debts of their spouse or partner has emerged as an increasing evidence social and legal problem, especially in the United Kingdom, and also Australia (where the problem has become know as 'sexually transmitted debt'). In this article, the central findings of the first major empirical study of 'sexually transmitted debt' are discussed, after first placing the problem in its legal and social context.

1. INTRODUCTION

Lawyers deal with people's problems every day. When a social problem confronts a lawyer, however, the lawyer is unlikely to recognize it as such. Even if the lawyer does recognize the social problem, the lawyer will not see her or his role as involving curing that social problem. The lawyer will see a lawyer's role as identifying the legal issues and working out who should win the particular competition. Linkages between personal troubles and 'the public issues of social structure' remain unexplored.[1]

This research focused on a particular social and legal problem, known in Australia as 'sexually transmitted debt'.[2] I wanted to look at how people suffering from the problem saw their experiences, and to consider their interpretations in the light of sociological research on money and marriage, how the law dealt with their experiences, and how others close to the problem saw those experiences. In this way, I could explore the personal troubles of a particular group of people and their intersections within wider society.[3]

* Lecturer, Law School, University of Melbourne, Parkville, 3054, Australia. The author would like to thank Mavis Maclean, Centre for Socio-Legal Studies, Oxford, John Eekelaar, Pembroke College, Oxford, Gerry Bean, Phillips Fox, Melbourne and Swee Yue Tan (for research assistance). This article is based on a paper presented at the fifth Australian Family Research Conference, Brisbane, 27–29 November 1996.

This project was undertaken between 1992 and 1995 in England at the Centre for Socio-Legal Studies, and comprised my DPhil law thesis.[4] It is the first empirical research specifically on sexually transmitted debt.[5] This was a small-scale, qualitative study, and exploratory in nature.

Before the findings are considered, a context for understanding the research is provided by considering the meaning of the term 'sexually transmitted debt', and placing the problem in its legal and social context.

2. 'SEXUALLY TRANSMITTTED DEBT'

'Sexually transmitted debt' occurs when a spouse or partner (called a 'surety', and usually a wife in the reported law cases) provides 'security' (often a second mortgage over the family home) to a lender (usually a bank) for the business debts of her husband (or partner) (the 'debtor').

Providing security represents a specific example of how major financial decisions are made between couples. One difference is that this decision extends beyond the purely domestic sphere. The private, personal relationship is used by an outsider, the bank, to protect its own interests. Legally, the wife agrees to repay to the bank money owed by her husband (or his business) if he does not pay. The security – usually the family home – is sold by the bank. This issue, then, can be viewed as an example of how the hazy boundary between the 'private' and the 'public' can be used to advantage banks.[6] This theme emerges more clearly below, when the research findings are discussed.

It would be too simple, though, to say that only the bank gains when a wife provides security. By providing security, the wife helps her husband to obtain a loan for his business. The wife may also assist herself, especially if she is financially dependent on her husband, his business is successful, and their relationship remains intact. This possibility of some advantage to the wife is one reason why 'sexually transmitted debt' is a particularly difficult problem – why shouldn't the wife have to take the risk of business failure along with the possibility of its success? A problem that judges often fail to see is that any advantage to the wife is likely to be less direct than the advantage enjoyed by other parties to the transaction: the bank and the husband. If the wife is not involved in managing the business, she will have no control over its success. Also, any advantage she gains from the business will be dependent on her marriage continuing. In contrast, her liability to the bank does not automatically end if husband and wife separate – a point that women often fail to realize. Lawyers often see sexually transmitted debt cases in troubled times, either on separation or divorce as an aspect of property settlement, or on business failure.

3. SOCIAL CONTEXT AND THE LEGAL RESPONSE

There is nothing new about sexually transmitted debt, but it is a problem which has received the increasing attention of judges, commentators and law reformers not only in Australia,[7] but also in the United Kingdom,[8] and to a lesser extent in Canada.[9] The immediate social background has been economic recession and a corresponding rise in house possession actions by banks.[10] It is also one aspect of the wider trend in which the banker/customer relationship has come under increasing scrutiny.[11]

In recent English and Australian cases, judges have been prepared to acknowledge that they are, indeed, faced with a social problem. For example, in *Barclays Bank plc* v *O'Brien*,[12] (in which a surety wife won her case against the Bank) the House of Lords considered that in many families, the wife follows her husband's advice on business matters without independent thought.[13] This is consistent with sociological research which suggests that the power to make major financial decisions rests with husbands rather than wives,[14] and that women are particularly likely to act in a way which prioritizes the continuance of close relationships over furthering their individual interests.[15] In the end, though, the approach taken by judges usually involves little more than flagging the social problem before getting on with the task of identifying the legal issues and deciding the winner of the case. To do this, judges deciding sexually transmitted debt cases in England (and also Australia and Canada) take, in essence, a two-step approach. First the judge decides whether the husband or the bank is guilty of any legal wrong toward the wife. Then if (as is generally the case) the husband rather than the bank is guilty of a legal wrong (such as pressuring her to sign or misleading her about the transaction), the judge decides whether the bank should be held responsible for that behaviour. The bank may be considered responsible if, for example, the bank relied on the husband to inform the wife about the transaction, rather than insisting that she receive independent legal advice from a solicitor.

Underlying the application of this judicial approach are a number of assumptions which I wanted to test by doing this research. For example, in many of the cases judges appear to assume that financial resources are adequately shared between couples.[16] On that basis, it can be assumed that wives choose to provide security because they may benefit financially if the business is successful.[17] Judges tend to take an essentially objective, commercial view which downplays other factors which constrain the exercise of 'free choice'. For example, judges are reluctant to hold banks responsible for subtle emotional pressure brought to bear by husbands on their wives. The assumption seems to be that the threshold of legally acceptable emotional pressure is higher between husbands and wives than between other parties who enter contracts. For example, in *Barclays Bank plc* v *O'Brien*, referred to above, the pressure exerted by Mr O'Brien on Mrs O'Brien, (emotional scenes and insistence that she sign) was not considered by Scott LJ in the Court of Appeal to amount to undue influence 'in the context of the normal husband and wife relationship and bearing in mind Mrs O'Brien's character and capabilities'.[18]

This perspective is understandable from the point of view of banks, who will often know very little about the private circumstances between husband and wife. The problem is that the prevailing perspective reflects a lender's eye-view of the problem, with women being judged by that standard. Women's descriptions of their experiences thus appear in a variety of ways to be marginalized in the law cases. In contrast, the main aim of this research was to consider the experience of providing security from sureties' perspectives.

4. THE SURETY SAMPLE

The empirical part of this research comprised forty-nine, in-depth, personal interviews with sureties (twenty-two, including two men), debtors (five, including two women), lenders (nine) and lawyers (thirteen). By including within the sample sureties, debtors, lenders and lawyers, a balance was maintained between reflecting the views of sureties, and acknowledging that those views are interpretations of an event likely to be viewed differently by others involved.

Surety interviewees were contacted mainly (twenty) through a bank pressure group formed to agitate for changes in relation to a wide range of banking issues including suretyship. The absence of a sampling frame meant that it was not possible to base the study on a random sample of sureties. The resulting sample was then by definition a group of people discontented with their present circumstances. Indeed, all described business problems and half were separated or divorced at the time of interview. Clearly, there was the risk that business and relationship problems described were likely to result in negative perception of the experience of providing security. Conversely, the willingness of sureties to acknowledge this issue and to attempt to deal with it by distinguishing between their position in the past rather than at the time of interview tends to support the veracity of the findings: 'Looking back . . . it didn't seem rather bad at the time. I wasn't unhappy' (Mrs Bond).[19] In this respect, the findings support the observation of sociologists that barriers to talking about money, (especially financial power),[20] and unconscious concealment about household finances break down when a marriage is under threat or ended.[21]

As regard other sample characteristics, the surety sample was predominantly female, middle-aged, British, moderately to highly educated (half held a degree or had higher education below degree level and in only six cases was the formal education received by the surety lower than that of their spouse),[22] and with dependent children. In terms of socio-economic group, the surety sample was characterized by two main groups: 'professionals' (mainly teachers and health care professionals, and including both males), and 'intermediate and junior non-manual' employees (mainly involved in clerical work).[23] In contrast, their spouses and partners were mainly self-employed non-professionals, who often held a trade or non-professional qualification. In most cases (sixteen out of twenty-two) the male was described as the main breadwinner during the relationship. The majority of sureties described themselves as having a modest to comfortable (although in most cases not affluent) lifestyle prior to the onset of their financial problems. Most (eighteen out of twenty-two) were married to the debtor for whom they gave security; the remainder were cohabitees.

All sureties had a husband or partner who had been 'self-employed' in their own business during at least part of the relevant relationship. Most went into business after spending a significant period in (often very successful) full-time employment (fifteen out of twenty-two). Most of the businesses were successful for a period (although six businesses had never been profitable enough to provide the main source of income for the family on an on-going basis, and a further three had never made a profit), but all had experienced financial problems in recent years.

5. MONEY, MARRIAGE AND THE 'FAMILY' BUSINESS

Sureties (and debtors) were asked about their domestic financial arrangements in order to provide an indication of the financial dynamics underlying surety and debtor relationships, and thus the more specific experience of a major financial decision: providing security.

When Jan Pahl's typologies of management and control were applied,[24] all sureties had some management role over domestic finances. Most also perceived themselves as having a significant role in the control of domestic finances. Yet sureties consistently described themselves as ultimately having less financial power than debtors. This was supported by evidence that sureties would accede to the debtor's view if there was a dispute over an important financial decision, and were less likely to appropriate financial resources for their personal use.[25]

Significantly, only three sureties (including one male) thought that they and their spouse had a similar attitude towards money. Female sureties (seventeen out of twenty) consistently emphasized that their approach to money was more moderate, cautious, and responsible compared to debtors, who were often described as risk-takers who were inclined to 'speculate and accumulate' (Mrs Kirby). Sureties, in contrast, emphasized their more domestic focus, and the importance of a reliable income in order to provide for the family:

He sees his priorities differently than I do. My priorities are keeping my kids fed and clothed and looking nice and providing for them how I feel they should be provided for. Whereas [my partner] if he's got £500 in his bank account and someone's driving him crazy for £250 of that, he'll say to me, 'Right. No more new shoes [for the children]. We'll just have to eat mince all week. I've got to get that guy off my back. He's driving me crazy'. (Ms Owen)

The complexity of the conjugal contract was underlined by the fact that while sureties often considered debtors to be, in negative terms, less financially responsible and realistic than themselves, they also viewed them in positive terms, as more entrepreneurial and business-minded. Debtors' financial priorities reflected a different view of what was in the family's interests:

[My husband is] an optimist and I'm a pessimist. I try to remain a cheerful pessimist, it's always been this way. So if he ever asks me anything, he knows he's going to get a pessimistic answer. . . . I think I'm more realistic, really. Had he listened to me, he'd never have gone into business and had 20 successful years. (Mrs Morris)

On one view, acquiescing to an entrepreneurial debtor's sense of adventure in the form of a new business venture could offer sureties the possibility of benefiting from that risk and the excuse, if anything went wrong, that it was not their idea. However, sureties' general insistence that they were happier to face fewer financial risks even if their income was less should not be lightly disregarded, particularly when viewed in the context of their strong sense of family responsibility, which was consistent with a cautious approach that emphasized the value of financial security.

In contrast with domestic finances, the business was very clearly the province of the debtor. The marked divide between family and business financial decisions was conveyed clearly by one couple:

Mr Upton: I follow her advice.
Mrs Upton: No, you never do. That's your problem. In domestic arrangements, possibly. But not in your business at work; you've never followed my advice.

Significantly, both surety and debtor interviewees took the view that the business was the debtor's business. Only four sureties (all wives who had worked in the business) viewed the business as a 'family' business, even though eleven sureties (all wives) had an active role within the business (cleaning the office, deliveries, clerical and receptionist work, and bookkeeping, often in addition to holding a formal office such as company director or secretary). Sureties consistently described their strategic decision-making role in the business as negligible or non-existent:

I had no say in any management decision. People were just spending money on things that I didn't think were very relevant to the business and I just saw money being thrown away all the time by other directors. The other directors had good salaries, company cars, expense accounts, yet they had no responsibilities. And there was I, basically just an accounts clerk. (Mrs Hayes)

At best, the position of sureties resembled the 'informed powerlessness' described in Singh's Australian study of women, information and the family business.[26]

Sureties shared in the business profits but invariably at the debtor's discretion. Where sureties did derive some income directly from the business it was minimal, being below the tax threshold. Where businesses were profitable, families often lived modestly while profit was poured back into the business by debtors who were often described as having an emotional investment in the success of the enterprise which went beyond the welfare of the family. Sureties said they supported debtors out of loyalty, love and economic necessity, but, as noted above, generally expressed a preference for a lower but more reliable breadwinner income. Despite their objections to the way the business was run, the possibility of sureties using formal legal rights as a company director or shareholder to exert a greater influence within the business was understandably not contemplated in this context. Rather, sureties who held formal offices (such as company director or secretary) emphasized that their role on paper did not correspond with their position in reality, and those who held shares invariably did not know the extent of their shareholding.

The findings on domestic and business financial arrangements revealed that the judicial (and social) assumption that a surety will necessarily share in the profits of the business is questionable, especially where the assumption is that the wife will independently enjoy a substantial rather than token share in the financial profits or benefits from the business. Businesses were not always profitable, and any benefit that women shared was, on their interpretation, paid for highly, in terms of reduced breadwinner income, reduced family time, and increased family responsibilities.

6. PROVIDING SECURITY

All of the sureties had provided security for a husband or partner's business loan, mainly in the form of a second mortgage over the family home. Most had provided security more than once (fifteen out of twenty-two).

There was no requirement that sureties included in this study be experiencing problems with the security provided, but all of the sureties described problems with their security or securities. The focus of this research was on the security which the surety was most unhappy about having signed, although securities which were not a source of complaint were also discussed. It became clear during the interviews that sureties were far more likely to complain about a security provided in the context of financial and/or relationship difficulties.

Sureties' descriptions of providing security were considered under four headings. These were: (A) involvement (how involved was the surety in planning the transaction?); (B) understanding (did the surety understand what she (or he) was signing?); (C) choice (did the surety feel that she had any choice about signing?); and (D) potential gain (what did the surety think she could gain from signing?). This approach reflected the concerns of the courts when deciding competitions between sureties and banks, outlined above.

A. Involvement

Most sureties said they were not involved in planning the transaction. This was consistent with the House of Lords' view of such transactions in *Barclays Bank plc* v *O'Brien*. I wanted to explore how that lack of involvement come about.

Most sureties were told one week or longer before signing that they would be required to provide security (fifteen out of twenty-two). At least in theory, then, most had the opportunity to become involved in planning the transaction. Other factors, however, countered strongly against this. Sureties were usually told of the transaction by the debtor. They were given the impression that the decision to go ahead with the transaction had been made. Given their lack of involvement at a decision-making level within the business, sureties were unlikely to consider that they had the opportunity to become involved: 'I was the cavalry, over there' (Ms Fenwick).

Sureties' descriptions of themselves as playing only a support role were reflected in the approach of banks, who relied on debtors to supply the necessary personal information about sureties, and did not treat them as independent contracting parties:

> There is a bank manager's note of the meeting that [my now ex-husband] went to, which of course I didn't go to. And in that meeting it was discussed that . . . I had a cottage and some bonds from my mother. But I was not aware that [my husband] discussed that with [the bank manager]. I was not aware at the time that [the cottage and the bonds] were discussed, because I thought that those were mine and therefore not part of the equation. (Mrs Parkes)

Sureties were often not particularly interested in the financial details of the business, and even if they were interested, considered that debtors were not always willing to consider their views. There was a tendency for sureties, including Mrs Parkes, to emphasize that they had been busy concentrating on their own specific concerns (such as employment or childraising), and in the course of doing so had turned a blind eye to potential problems. This was the view taken by the Judge in the bank's possession proceedings for Mrs Parkes' cottage: 'I am sure the Defendant was aware of [her husband's] capabilities and equally sure that she was carried away by his enthusiasm. I believe that to some degree she closed her eyes to the true situation'.[27]

The somewhat contradictory picture to emerge was that while sureties never considered the prospect that ill would befall them as a result of signing, most said they had felt concerned about providing security. Similarly, a number preferred to trust optimistic debtors, but had little faith in the debtor's financial abilities. This was consistent with surety views regarding domestic finances, particularly sureties' own high sense of financial responsibility compared with debtor irresponsibility, noted above. Sureties' unwillingness to focus on relationship or financial problems that could arise in the future[28] and thus to protect their individual positions is in marked contrast with the clear-sighted, self-interested assessment of risk expected of commercial contracting parties.

B. Understanding

Recent cases in England, Australia and Canada have consistently emphasized the importance of independent legal advice in protecting banks in sexually transmitted debt cases. Even if there has been some legal wrong by a husband, a bank is unlikely to be held responsible if the wife has consulted an independent solicitor.[29] I was interested to find out whether sureties benefit to the same extent as banks from this process.

Most sureties (nineteen out of twenty-two) said that they had known in broad terms at the time of signing why security was required. Usually, sureties obtained this information from the debtor. Most (twenty out of twenty-two) also said they had some understanding of the legal effect of the security provided, although in nine cases the surety had misunderstood the amount being secured. This sort of misunderstanding could amount to a legal wrong (in the form of a misrepresentation) if it was caused by the debtor or the bank.

Eleven sureties met with a solicitor before signing. There was, however, apparently some confusion about the role of solicitors. Sureties who signed before a solicitor consistently said they believed at the time that the purpose of the appointment was merely to have the documents witnessed. None was aware that she was attending to receive 'independent legal advice' (if that was indeed the case). This is significant because a person who is unaware of the reason for their contact with a professional is unlikely to utilize that professional's expertise in her own interests:

> The phrase 'independent legal advice' I had never heard until I actually ended up in court. And the question whether I had had independent legal advice was discussed at length. But the concept was entirely new to me; I'd never come across it before. (Mrs Parkes)

Crucially, regardless of their actual role, solicitors appeared to give the impression that their function was merely to witness the documents:

> [The solicitor] said, 'Take a seat. I've got all the documents here for you to sign. Would you just like to sign on that line?' And I said to him, 'Hang on a minute. I'm not one hundred per cent sure what I'm signing'. And he said, 'Well, I thought all this had been outlined to you at the Bank'. And he was very brusque, as if to say, 'Why are you wasting my time with all of this?' And he said, 'What you've got to understand is that if the overdraft is not repaid for whatever reason, the Bank can repossess your house'. (Ms Owen)

The prospect thus began to emerge that judges may be categorizing as 'independent advice' meetings which were not perceived at the time by the actors as involving any more than the witnessing of a signature.

The independence of solicitors was also questionable. Appointments with solicitors were usually organized by the debtor, and often with a solicitor known to the debtor but not to the surety. Sureties were thus not aware that the solicitor was acting for them, rather than for the business or the bank. Debtors usually attended meetings between sureties and solicitors (seven out of eleven). In no case did the surety pay for the solicitor's services, which also suggested that the solicitor's client was not the surety. The problem, as sureties often pointed out, was finding an independent solicitor who would be in a position to provide both informed and independent advice: '*Real* informed, independent advice would have been a great help but who would have been qualified to give it? All those who knew the state of the business were on the same side' (Mrs Parkes).

In fact, it seemed when solicitors themselves were interviewed that independent advice is a misnomer. Solicitors saw their role as strictly being limited to explanation, not business advice. Consistent with this, sureties consistently claimed that solicitors' comments did not involve advice about the wisdom of providing the security, but at most a brief explanation of its legal effect: 'Do you realize you will be putting your house at risk?' (solicitor to Mrs Elliot). The Judge's view in Mrs Parkes' case reveals the gap between surety and judicial expectations of independent advice:

> [The solicitor] told her that if the company was wound down she would lose the cottage. What advice should have been given? It is not his duty to advise on the business efficacy of the transaction.[30]

A further dimension to the conundrum of 'independent legal advice' became evident when sureties were asked whether, if they had received adequate independent advice, this would have made any difference to their decision to sign. Significantly, only six sureties were confident that independent advice would have resulted in their refusal to sign. The willingness of sureties to admit a point which was potentially very damaging to their case[31] once again supports the reliability of the findings. More often, sureties considered that truly independent advice would have encouraged them think more carefully about signing and to discuss the issue further with the debtor, but would not necessarily have changed their ultimate decision:

If I'd had independent advice, I'd still have had no choice. . . . I hadn't found that part of me that even thought I *should* have a choice. So that's not looking good, in a way, if the law was changed, because there will be women about who are harnessed by things other than paper to their husbands. (Mrs Inness)

This view was supported by the experiences of two sureties who had received truly independent advice not to sign, and had still gone ahead and provided the security: 'It made me restless. I was torn between my own feelings and what my husband needed' (Mrs Kirby).

Sureties' experiences of dealing with professionals reinforced that 'independent legal advice' is a triumph of legal form over substance which is more likely to protect banks than sureties. Although most sureties had previous experience with home loan transactions as mortgagors, the unfamiliar setting of a business meeting with a solicitor or banker was recalled as a highly intimidating experience. As a result, sureties typically did not ask questions or read the documents they signed. Their chances of doing either of these were reduced by the fact that most (twenty-one out of twenty-two) said they had not seen the documents before the signing, and were not given a real opportunity to read them before being asked to sign. Sureties often said that they felt uncomfortable about keeping others waiting, and did not want to appear stupid by asking questions:

I'd start looking at the print . . . I would start reading through . . . I'd probably get half a minute into reading something like that, [indicating one of the documents]. [My husband] would shuffle and sigh, somebody would bang a pen on the table as if to say, 'Are you actually going to read through the six pages of this document while we sit here, because [the solicitor] has another appointment in half an hour'. You look at page three or four and it continues, [reads] 'The mortgagor hereby agrees to indemnify the mortgagee as a separate covenant' and you think, 'It's ridiculous, I haven't got the faintest idea what I'm reading'. (Mrs Dean)

Sureties, due to their lack of business experience, did not know the questions to ask. Their decision to sign was a decision based on trust in the debtor and the bank, rather than a commercial decision:

[Seeing the bank manager was] very similar to sitting in front of a doctor. You don't question it. . . . It's not something that you are in a position to question because you wouldn't know what to ask, anyway. When you are as inexperienced as we were, it's like going to a foreign country. (Mr Gibson)

Partly as a result of the authority which bank managers and solicitors were perceived to have, most sureties said they did nothing to alert professionals to the 'private' difficulties described during research interviews (in particular, anxiety, lack of understanding, and the need to take the document away to read it). Rather, they often considered that these were 'private' problems which should not be revealed in 'public and would be of no relevance to banks or solicitors:

> [In court] the solicitor said there was nothing in my demeanour to suggest that I needed to go away and think again. He said he does get women coming in who are clearly emotionally upset. He said there was absolutely no way he could have told that I was unwilling. And I was forced to admit that I never gave him any reason to suppose I was unwilling. (Mrs Parkes)

The minority of sureties who described themselves as being obviously upset about did not consider that the business-like solicitors and bankers they met with had noticed, or wanted to notice, that they were upset: 'The whole thing was an absolute nightmare. I was literally dragged to the solicitor's office. I was asked to sign it and I was crying at the time' (Mrs Dean). The tendency of professionals not to deal with 'private' emotions of sureties was acknowledged in a light-hearted fashion by one of the solicitors interviewed: 'You're talking about an English solicitor who would pretend not to notice'. According to this solicitor, the typical response to a surety who was upset would be for the solicitor to remain detached and to offer the surety coffee. Interviews with solicitors suggested that this response resulted from a combination of factors, including lawyers' discomfort in challenging couples who presented together for the wife's 'independent advice', the view that '[i]f people want that money they'll sign anything for it', the awareness that surety transactions did not always work out badly, and the minimal fee charged for their service. Solicitors' apparent low level of involvement arguably protected the interests of all concerned (at least in the short term) by allowing for the expeditious and relatively untroubled conduct of daily business.[32] Unfortunately, given the reluctance of sureties to reveal their private feelings, and the equal reluctance of professionals to notice, the likelihood of sureties signing without their problems being revealed or addressed was high.

C. Choice

Sureties consistently said that at the time of signing, they felt they had no choice about whether or not to sign. I found that the factors inhibiting choice were more fundamental than is often acknowledged in the law cases.

Five sureties said that the idea that they had a choice had never entered their minds. It was just assumed by themselves, and by those around them, that they would sign. For female sureties who were either economically inactive or working for the debtor's business at the time of signing (fourteen out of twenty), economic dependence was a crucial factor making the issue of choice became largely irrelevant:

It was a devastating shock, and I was really upset about it. . . . In reality there was very little that one is able to do about it in circumstances like that. . . . They would stop [my husband's] business from trading, our income would disappear, and we would have no means of support, particularly as I wasn't earning an income at that time. (Mrs Upton)

Added to economic considerations was the emotional pressure invariably described by sureties, which ranged from subtle forms of pressure inherent in the conjugal relationship, to emotional blackmail and extreme physical abuse:

In retrospect, obviously I had a choice about signing. If I had simply refused, he wouldn't have got my signature. But the circumstances were such that I didn't feel I had any choice because he attacked me when I was pregnant with my little boy there, and it had been going on over and over again, every morning and every night he started and he'd be in a temper. I couldn't live with it and I decided that I had to get away from him. I couldn't take any more – that's the only way I can explain it. . . . Basically, God knows why, I still loved [my husband] and I suppose I still felt an obligation to him as his wife . . . I hated not trusting him . . . I hated him and I loved him . . . I think in the end I signed because I loved him. (Mrs Dean)

The violence described by Mrs Deane was severe enough to amount to a legal wrong in contractual terms (duress or undue influence), but the pressure described by sureties was not always so obvious, often being inherent in the situation, rather than exerted overtly by the debtor:

To other people, the pressure that [my husband] put me under wouldn't have been particularly great. He didn't hit me, he didn't scream at me, he didn't do anything like that. [But] because of the relationship we had, the pressure was considerable, looking at it from my point of view. And I had thought, very very carefully, about what the alternatives would actually mean. And again, although we didn't separate until very long after, bear in mind that at this stage it had never crossed my mind that we were going to [separate]. I thought I'd got to live with it, and if I had to live with it, having done that [refusing to sign], things weren't going to be so very hot. And it didn't seem to me very likely at that stage that there was going to be something pulled out of a hat to rescue me. It looked as though I'd got it to do. Practically, there was no real choice at all. (Mrs Parkes)

Married sureties were particularly inclined to emphasize their perception at the time of signing that their marriage was for life, and that, as a result, they felt bound to support their spouse. The concern to preserve the relationship was particularly acute for the five female sureties who were divorced and provided security for a second husband, and also for the three cohabiting, previously divorced female sureties. Having experienced the break-up of a previous union, these women were fearful of risking a second relationship, and vulnerable because of this.

Added to this emotional pressure was the fact that eleven sureties had been experiencing significant relationship difficulties before signing. Those difficulties had resulted in various changed living arrangements, including separation under the one roof, one party moving out, instituting divorce proceedings, and divorce. Significantly, sureties in this position did not consider that the apparent disintegration of their relationships left them with a greater choice not to sign. Rather, lack of choice resulted from a combination of physical abuse, economic dependence and a complicated on-going emotional commitment to the debtor.

D. Potential Gain

Most sureties considered that by signing, they could 'benefit' to the extent that their pre-signing position would be maintained, both financially and in terms of the relationship. Most, however, viewed this as a neutral or negative benefit, because they were in effect sacrificing in order to maintain their pre-security position. Perceptions of negative benefit were particularly evident where the relationship or the business (and sometimes both) were experiencing difficulties: 'I didn't want him to lose his business. There was never any question of losing him. I didn't want it to be a situation of him being dependent on me; didn't want him to lose face in the community in which he moved' (Ms Fenwick).

The perceptions of sureties are in stark contrast with judicial perceptions, outlined above. Courts have often regarded a security given by a wife to save her husband's business as being for her potential benefit.[33] There is no indication in the case law that the courts make any distinction at all between 'start-up' security and 'rescue' security: both are considered to represent a potential financial benefit to the surety. While this is arguable in cases where the surety is economically dependent on the business, the descriptions of sureties conveyed, as Ms Fenwick suggests, a more complex series of emotional and economic motivations.

7. SURETY MEN

As noted above, the surety sample included two men who had provided security for their female counterparts. Separate consideration of the male surety interviewees underlines the particular economic vulnerability of surety women.

In particular, neither of the surety men viewed their female partner's business as the main source of income for the family. Rather, the business was a means of increasing the family's income, while providing an interest for the woman: 'My idea with [my wife's] business was that it was her business, and it was something that was bringing in money which was good, but it didn't interfere and the family didn't depend on it' (Mr Neill).

While eleven surety wives worked for the business, neither of the surety men was involved in the business, apart from providing security. Both were professionals engaged in full-time employment at the time when the debtor was in business. The position of male sureties remained that of supportive outsiders, rather than that of economic dependants. As a result, providing security was more the result of emotional commitment within the relationship, rather than the more complex web of economic and social factors which impacted on surety women.

Particular individual factors were also relevant to surety males. In one case, the surety male was many years younger than his debtor partner; the surety commented that he had grown up while living with her. The second surety male had been supported throughout his university degree by his wife, who had always controlled their financial affairs. These factors help to explain why they had provided security, apparently a predominantly female pursuit.

8. DEBTORS' VIEWS ON PROVIDING SECURITY

As noted above, five debtors (three males and two females) were interviewed for this research. These interviews provide additional perspectives to the surety interviews discussed above.

A strong theme to emerge from interviews with debtors was their perception that they often faced similar problems to those described by sureties. However, while sureties had tended to criticize themselves, the conduct of debtors,[34] lenders and solicitors, debtors were more inclined to view the lender as ultimately responsible regarding both the transaction and subsequent events. A circle of blame-shifting began to emerge:

> [The bank manager] called me in and said for the company to continue trading, he would need more security. And the only security I had at that time was my house. I knew him quite well. But then again . . . I think it was the Bank's policy decision. (Mr Upton)

The tendency for debtors and sureties in intact relationships to view the lender as responsible for their problems was significant but not surprising. By allocating responsibility to the lender, outside the 'private' relationship, the debtor's sense of responsibility was reduced and feelings of betrayal were alleviated. The relationship between surety and debtor could thus survive, although the surety's trust and confidence in the debtor were often severely undermined. Arguably, however, the tendency of debtors to view the lender as responsible would be likely whether the relationship was intact or not.

Debtors consistently described themselves as having a greater *involvement* than sureties, but no real influence, in the planning of transactions.

Taking security was the lender's idea, and organized by the lender, with debtors merely doing as they were asked. There were, however, indications that debtors at least had the opportunity to negotiate the form of security provided. For example, two debtors, Mr Morris and Mr Upton, were both so unhappy about their previous experience of providing a second mortgage over the family home that they refused to do so again. Instead, Mr Upton gave two personal guarantees, and Mr and Mrs Morris each gave two further guarantees when the Bank required security. This influence undermines the notion that debtors had no involvement in or influence over the planning of transactions.

More serious was the consistent claim of debtors that they had little *understanding* about the legal implications of the documents which they and sureties, usually at their suggestion, signed:

> I think that most entrepreneurs are not fully aware of some of the things that happen, and the powers that the banks have. . . . I think if they said to you, 'We need this guarantee from you. How would you intend to pay it if it was called back?', I think that would be a stunning question. I think that many people have signed guarantees not knowing the powers which the banks have to claim their money back. (Mr Upton)

This situation was particularly striking given that most of debtor interviewees had been in business for many years.

Despite their apparent lack of understanding, none of the debtors had the benefit of explanation or independent advice. The danger of ill-informed debtors was well illustrated by Mr Morris and Mr Upton, who had both believed that giving a guarantee was preferable to a second mortgage. As a result, as noted above, guarantees had been provided instead. Both were facing enforcement action by their Bank at the time of interview, with the family home being the only asset available to satisfy the debt.

A further significant gap in the understanding of debtors was their failure to appreciate the risk involved in the transaction. Debtors also consistently said they had not considered the possibility of economic downturn. Debtors making this claim included Mrs Neill, who had her own real estate and insurance business: 'You never know what the future will hold, do you? I mean, when I [asked my husband to sign] my business was good, it was going forward, nothing was ever going to happen. Then the recession hit. You can't predict that' (Mrs Neill). This perspective was consistent with surety descriptions of optimistic debtors who lived for the day.

Debtors also emphasized that while they recognized the difficult position of the surety, they experienced a similar lack of *choice* about providing security:

> In most cases where the banks ask you for guarantees or something else, it's 'gun to your head' time, really. You either give it to them or they say, 'Well,

we withdraw our support'. It upset [my wife] a lot. And also, I didn't like it as much as [my wife]. I can understand women saying it's a bitter blow to them; it's a bitter blow to a husband as well. (Mr Upton)

Consistent with this, debtors emphasized that it was the bank who *benefited* from the transaction and not themselves. For most debtors, this had come as a bitter realization. Debtors consistently said that while the business was going well, they had been regarded very favourably by the bank. As a result, they had regarded their relationship with the bank as a business relationship involving some mutual gain, respect, and, above all, support for the business. With the arrival of the recession and business problems, this arguably naïve perception had proved ill-founded. The realization of the unequal commercial positions of debtor and bank often led to a sense of disbelief, followed by bitterness, on the part of debtors. The unequal bargaining positions of banks and debtors were apparently not fully revealed until a situation of crisis arose.

While debtors understood the grievances of sureties, they also emphasized their own vulnerability, and that living with the consequences of their actions was not easy:

You can imagine the guilt and terror in me that I've done this to him. I know that the Bank was the one that caused it to happen, but if I hadn't had this wretched idea in the first place, none of this would have happened. So it isn't just myself that I've hurt, I have ruined [him] (Ms Gibson).

Although debtors emphasized their mutual vulnerability with sureties, rather than dwelling upon sureties' vulnerability, the greater involvement of debtors in planning transactions compared with sureties (whether they took the leading role or not), their ability to influence the form of the transaction, and their greater involvement in and knowledge of the financial position of the business, meant that debtors were invariably in a stronger position than sureties. Thus, as Ms Gibson said, the unfortunate reality was that 'It's hard that it always comes back to me. It's not nice to feel that it's always down to me'.

9. LENDERS' AND LAWYERS' VIEWS ON PROVIDING SECURITY

As noted above, nine lenders and thirteen lawyers were also interviewed for this study.

The sample of nine lenders was the result of an initial mail-out to the legal departments of twenty lending institutions of varying size and activities, including all high street banks, and (using the sampling frame provided by the Yellow Pages listing for 'banking and financial institutions'), a number of smaller banks, building societies and finance houses. More small banks and finance houses were contacted by letter at the suggestion of lenders interviewed (a 'snowball' approach). This sampling technique resulted in a sample of lenders derived from the policy level within lending institutions, rather than employees at branch level who typically deal directly with sureties and debtors when security is provided. The problem of ensuring that policy is reflected in practice was a significant concern of the lenders interviewed and was addressed in depth during interviews.

The sample of lawyers comprised thirteen practising lawyers (three barristers and ten solicitors) and was accessed by a number of different methods. Letters written to practising lawyers who had published articles or books dealing with surety wives resulted in interviews with three solicitors and one barrister. As a result of contact with the bank pressure group, contact was made with two solicitors who often acted for Group members. Also interviewed were seven of the lawyers (five solicitors and two barristers) who acted for sureties interviewed. This approach had the advantage of allowing comparability of data in specific cases (the surety's experience as perceived by both the surety and her or his solicitor), while also allowing the collection of data on how lawyers go about giving independent legal advice.

In essence, interviews with lenders and lawyers underlined the gap between 'private' troubles, 'public' interpretations of those troubles, and willingness to take responsibility for those troubles. In particular, while the problems experienced by sureties were acknowledged by lenders and lawyers, those problems were ultimately either viewed as an individual problem of the surety and debtor or as part of a wider social problem, both which were beyond the power of lenders or lawyers to resolve. This stance was understandable but undoubtedly provided a rationalization for lenders and lawyers not doing more to protect sureties than was necessary to protect themselves.

This approach was revealed most obviously when lenders' procedures for taking security were analysed. At least in the past, it appeared that procedures were generally reactive rather than proactive, reflecting community expectations, case law developments, and in recent times, and the introduction of the Code of Banking Practice.[35] As a result, it did appear that procedures had improved (although more research would be needed to examine the implementation of these at branch level), with lenders either following the *Barclays Bank plc* v *O'Brien* approach of having a private (and scripted) meeting between lending manager and surety in the absence of the debtor,[36] or insisting that the surety meet with a solicitor who, although nominated and paid for by the surety, would provide an endorsement to the lender that the transaction had been explained to the surety. A more pro-active approach was evident in a minority of cases, for example, the increasing disinclination to take unlimited guarantees, and moves towards plain English security documentation. These changes were, however, arguably prompted by the impending implementation in the United Kingdom of the European

Directive on Unfair Terms in Consumer Contracts.[37] Consistent with sureties' descriptions, past and present procedures were focused on providing information rather than advice, and were understandably dictated by the need to acquire an enforceable security whilst avoiding liability for negligent misstatement.

As discussed above, solicitors similarly described giving information to sureties in the form of a basic legal explanation of the security, rather than any advice regarding whether the surety should sign. The providing of advice was impossible in the usual situation where the solicitor had no information regarding the wider aspects of the relationship or transaction (for example, previous dealings with the parties or information about the business), and usually no training when it came to interpreting business financial information even if it were available. In any case, the minimal fee charged did not warrant solicitors taking on the risk of an advisory role.

Thus although providing security involved points of contact between sureties and debtors (the 'private') with lenders and lawyers (the 'public'), such contact, where it did occur, was more illustrative of irreconcilable interests. As surety interviews revealed, the partnership of marriage or cohabitation dictated that sureties act in accordance with a 'private' ethic of community, mingled with the self-interest involved in the preservation of their relationship with the debtor and the family's financial livelihood. In contrast, the commercial interests of lenders (and, to a lesser extent, lawyers) dictated that they act in accordance with an ethic of materialistic self-interest characteristic of contract law. The resulting 'assistance' to sureties was thus strictly circumscribed by the need of professionals to protect themselves in the course of conducting their daily business.

10. POST-SECURITY EXPERIENCE: SHIFTING THE BLAME, WEARING THE RESPONSIBILITY

As a result of interviewing debtors, lenders and lawyers as well as sureties, a circle of blame-shifting emerged, with sureties tending to blame themselves, debtors (especially where the relationship was not intact), lenders, and lawyers. Debtors tended to blame banks. Lenders and lawyers viewed sureties as being ultimately responsible for their own actions.

Sureties' accounts of their post-security experiences completed the circle of blame shifting by indicating that in real terms, and accordance with the law of suretyship, sureties (rather than banks and debtors) paid the larger personal price for business failure. Seven sureties described their spouse or partner as bankrupt at the time of interview, but no surety was bankrupt. Sureties were more inclined to stay solvent and pay the price. This was consistent with sureties' perceptions of their own sense of financial responsibility compared to that of debtors, discussed above, and meant that sureties were indeed ideal candidates for the role.

Divorced and separated wives were especially disadvantaged when the on-going contractual obligation involved in providing a security outlasted the intimate relationship between debtor and surety.[38] Although most sureties (nineteen out of twenty-two) were facing some sort of enforcement action by the bank, divorced or separated sureties had the doubly traumatic situation of coping with their grief over a broken relationship:

> It's made me think back and think that I should have thought more about myself and my own life, really, and thought what to do if I ever became single again. I'd need a career to fall back on. I should have thought more about doing things for myself. And when I think about it I think I basically brought the children up, and my husband could not have done that without me, but at least he's now able to set up another business and carry on. He's just moved on. He's struggling on, but he's got something there. (Mrs Hayes)

Sureties in intact relationships generally described themselves as being in a better state of emotional and physical well-being that those who were divorced, separated or widowed. They had a person with whom to share (or blame for) their problems, and were not as isolated as sureties who dealt with their problems alone. However, the trust and confidence between couples had in some cases been severely undermined by problems with the security: 'Our relationship is threadbare' (Ms Gibson).

11. PROSPECTS FOR REFORM

This research suggests that the law currently fails to recognize and address the problems that sureties face, in particular their lack of involvement, choice, understanding, and direct benefit from providing security. But what instruments of reform could be useful?

Reforms directed at banning suretyship or limiting the use of the family home as business loan security seem unlikely to gain support from lawmakers at present. This is due to the general view that it would not be good for families or for commerce if people were prevented from 'choosing' to use the family home as security for business borrowing.[39] Most of the sureties interviewed would not want the law to be changed to prevent others doing what they had done, although some suggested limitations on choice, for example, when a couple had dependent children. Although greater consideration is now being given by banks to their procedures (for example, fewer banks now take security for an unlimited amount), suretyship by loved ones is still regarded as an important way of financing small businesses.

Law reform which helps sureties to help themselves may be more acceptable (for example, ensuring that sureties have access to information about the business and adequate independent advice). Other reforms could focus on the security as a contract, and could include both specific measures (for example, cooling-off periods, which allow a change of heart within a certain period after signing) and broad measures (for example, the Contracts Review Act 1980 (NSW), which aims to remove general unfairness).[40]

The problem is that such options for law reform will not resolve the fundamental problems, especially lack of choice, facing many sureties due to the existence of economic dependence and emotional commitment. In the end, changing public attitudes rather than legal change may prove a more effective, and appropriate, way of assisting sureties. While it is in everybody's interests to ensure that small businesses have access to the capital they need, there is a need to undermine the link between suretyship by loved ones and business financing.[41] There is some evidence that this is already occurring in Australia, where it has been reported[42] that one major bank, the Commonwealth Bank, will make business loans more widely available to small businesses on the basis of cash-producing assets without the need to use the family home. Of course, this development will only assist small businesses with solid financial histories and sound business plans, rather than businesses starting out or in poor financial circumstances – as were often described throughout this research as the circumstances where security was required. The real challenge lies in assisting sureties who provide security in these situations, which are inherently more risky – as lenders well appreciate. The beginnings of that change may well lie in encouraging couples (not just sureties) to consider before security is provided whose interests the surety is really being asked to serve.

NOTES

1 Wright Mills (1959, ch 1).

2 Lawton (1991, 7). While the term 'emotionally transmitted debt' has been preferred by some commentators (for example, Baron (1995)), 'sexually transmitted debt' most clearly reflects the focus of this research: suretyship within intimate relationships. The term 'emotionally transmitted debt' may, however, more closely reflect the motivation of sureties, and similar issues do arise outside the context of relationships between couples. A surety may, for example, be a close relation (particularly a parent) of the debtor and the application of emotional pressure may be significant in such circumstances. While this study does not extend beyond spouses and partners, a similar analysis may apply in other relationship contexts.

3 Wright Mills (1959, 12).

4 Fehlberg (1995).

5 The closest Australian counterpart to this study is Singh (1995).

6 See further on the public/private dichotomy: Olsen (1983), Eekelaar (1983), and Lacey (1993).

7 Recent examples of judicial consideration include *Akins* v *National Australia Bank* (1994) 34 NSWLR 155 (NSW CA), *National Australia Bank Limited* v *Garcia* (1996) ASC 56-354 (NSW CA), and *Teachers Health Investments Pty Limited* v *Wynne* (1996) ASC 56-356 (NSW CA)). Examples of recent commentary include Baron (1995), Fehlberg (1996A), and Howell (1994). Examples of

recent investigations of the problem by consumer and law reform bodies include: *Report of the Expert Group on Family Financial Vulnerability* (1996), the Australian Law Reform Commission (1994), and the Women and Credit Task Group (1990).

[8] In the United Kingdom, see *Barclays Bank plc* v *O'Brien* [1994] 1 AC 180 (HL) and its aftermath in terms of commentary, including Berg (1994), Cretney (1994), Hooley (1995), Fehlberg (1994) and (1996), Lawson (1995), and Oldham (1995).

[9] In Canada, in the wider context of consumer guarantors (including surety wives), see Hasson (1995). See also in the specific context of surety spouses: *Kerr Controls Limited* v *Waldick* (1994), 133 NSR 207 (SC), *Manulife Bank of Canada* v *Conlin* (1996) 139 DLR 4th 426 (surety husband), *Mackay* v *Bank of Novia Scotia* (1994), 20 OR (3d) 698 (Gen Div) (surety mother), and Ogilvie (1996).

[10] See *Housing Finance* No 20 November 1993, 33 (reported 31,780 property possessions for the first half of 1993, compared with 15,810 for the whole of 1989). This Table also reveals that possession rates are now falling: there were 38,930 possessions for the first part of 1991, cf 31,780 for the first part of 1993.

[11] E.g. the Jack Committee Report (1989).

[12] [1994] 1 AC 180.

[13] Ibid at 188.

[14] E.g. Pahl (1989), Volger (1994), Wilson (1987), Edgell (1980). In Australia, see Edwards (1984), Singh (1995) and Littlefield (1996).

[15] Gilligan (1982).

[16] English examples include *Bank of Credit and Commerce International SA* v *Aboody* [1990] 1 QB 923 (CA). Australian examples include *Akins* v *National Australia Bank* (1994) 34 NSWLR 155. (For further discussion of this case, see Fehlberg (1996A).) Cf to the contrary, sociological research suggesting a lack of equal sharing between couples: Brannen and Wilson (1987, 16), Pahl (1989, 170), and Volger (1994, 234).

[17] In terms of social theory, this judicial tendency resembles an 'exchange theory' approach – that is, the assumption that individuals choose between lines of action in such a way as to minimize their costs and maximize their rewards, and should engage in action only if it is profitable for them to do so: See further Cheal (1991, 134–5). Alternatively, the judicial tendency resembles 'rational choice theory', to the effect that 'agents have complete and consistent preference ordering and can calculate perfectly the probability of events': Jordon, Redley and James (1994, 9). See also Carling (1992, 106). See also the law and economics approach to surety wives: Trebilcock and Elliot (forthcoming), and Richardson (1996).

[18] *Barclays Bank* v *O'Brien* [1993] QB 109 (CA) at 141.

[19] Pseudonyms are used throughout this paper in place of sureties' real names.

[20] E.g. Edwards (1984, 131), and Wilson (1987, 141): '[f]inancial power was an area that many women preferred to avoid'.

[21] Edwards (1984, 143).

[22] This is unusual. Martin and Roberts (1984, 99), for example, found that 34 per cent of husbands in their sample were better qualified than their wives in contrast with 17 per cent of wives who were better qualified than their husbands.

[23] Applying the Office of Population Censuses and Surveys *General Household Survey 1992* approach of defining socio-economic group by using as a basis the current employment or last employment position of the sureties and debtors.

[24] 'Management' describes the actual handling of money and the making of payments, 'control' involves having 'an overall influence over all but minor purchasing decisions': M. Edwards (1984, 127–8), adopting Pahl's typologies: Pahl (1989). 'Power' in contrast, involves the ability to influence and control another person's behaviour: C. Safilios-Rothschild (1970).

[25] Cf Singh (1995). Most of Singh's survey group (73 per cent) said that decisions regarding major domestic purchases and expenditure were made jointly: at 62. Perhaps one reason for the difference is that Singh's survey involved women in continuing businesses and relationships, whereas the sureties interviewed for this study were usually experiencing business problems and in some cases, relationship problems at the time of interview.

[26] Singh (1995, 71), meaning the situation of being informed about the business but unable to influence decisions.

[27] County Court Judgment, 11/4/94.

[28] Consistent with observations made by Singh (1995, 90–1).

[29] See further Fehlberg (1995). For a recent case reinforcing this point, see *Barclays Bank plc* v *Thomson* (CA, Lord Justice Simon Brown, Lord Justice Waite, and Lord Justice Morritt, 15 November 1996) *The Independent*, 15 November 1996.

30 County Court Judgment, 11/4/94.

31 *BCCI* v *Aboody* [1990] 1 QB 923 at 970–1 (dicta of Slade LJ: 'at least in ordinary circumstances, it would not be appropriate for the court to exercise [the undue influence] jurisdiction in a case where the evidence establishes that on a balance of probabilities the complainant would have entered the transaction in any event'.

32 See further: Strong (1988).

33 E.g. *National Westminster Bank plc* v *Morgan* [1985] 1 AC 686 (HL).

34 Although to a lesser extent when the relationship was intact.

35 British Bankers' Association (et al), (1992, 2nd edn 1994).

36 At which the surety is told the extent of her liability under the security, warned of the risk she is running, and urged to take independent advice: [1994] AC 180 at 196.

37 European Union Directive on Unfair Terms in Consumer Contracts, Council Directive 93/13/EEC of 5 April 1993, OJ L 95/29, 21 April 1993; Implementing Statutory Instrument: The Unfair Terms in Consumer Contracts Regulations 1994, SI, No 3159.

38 The high cost of caring described is consistent with the work of Maclean (1991), Funder (1992) and Folbre (1993).

39 *Barclays Bank plc* v *O'Brien* [1994] 1 AC 180 at 188.

40 Although this legislation has often not been applied in a manner which protects sureties. See further: Howell (1994) and Baron (1995).

41 See also Hasson (1995).

42 *The Age*, 16 September 1996, 'New business loan that takes pressure off the family home', C4.

REFERENCES

Australian Law Reform Commission (1995) *Equality Before the Law: Women's Equality*, Report No 69 (Canberra, AGPS).

Baron, P. (1995) 'The Free Exercise of Her Will: Women and Emotionally Transmitted Debt', 13 *Law in Context* 23.

Berg, A.G.J. (1994) ' "Wives" Guarantees: Constructive Knowledge and Undue Influence', *LMCLQ* 34.

Brannen, J. and Wilson, G. (eds) (1987) *Give and Take in Families* (London, Allen and Unwin).

British Bankers' Association (*et al*), (1992, 2nd edn 1994) *Good Banking – Code of Practice* to be observed by banks, building societies and card issuers when dealing with personal customers.

Carling, A. (1992) 'Rational Choice and Household Division' in C. Marsh and S. Arber (eds) *Families and Households: Divisions and Change* (London, Macmillan).

Cheal, D. (1994) *Family and the State of Theory* (Hempel Hemstead, Harvester Wheatshaft).

Cretney, S. (1994) 'Mere Puppets, Folly and Imprudence: Undue Influence for the Twenty-First Century', *Restitution Law Review* 3.

Edgell, S. (1980) *Middle Class Couples* (London, Allen and Unwin).

Edwards, M. (1984) *The Income Unit in the Australian Tax and Social Security Systems* (Melbourne, Australian Institute of Family Studies).

Eekelaar, J. (1989) 'What is Critical Family Law?', 105 *LQR* 224.

Fehlberg, B. (1994) 'The Husband, the Bank, the Wife and Her Signature', 57 *MLR* 467.

Fehlberg, B. (1995) 'Securities and Guarantees: Another Perspective on Money and Marriage', DPhil thesis, University of Oxford, published as (1997) *Sexually Transmitted Debt: Surety Experience and English Law* (Oxford, Oxford University Press).

Fehlberg, B. (1996) 'The Husband, the Bank, the Wife and her Signature – the Sequel', 59 *MLR* 675.

Fehlberg, B. (1996A) 'Surety Wives and Australian Law: *Akins* v *National Australia Bank*', 11.3 BFLR 449.

Folbre, N. (1993) *Who Pays for the Kids?: Gender and the Structures of Constraint* (London, Routledge).

Funder, K. (1992) 'Australia: A Proposal for Reform' in L. Weitzman and M. Maclean (eds), *Economic Consequences of Divorce: The International Perspective* (Oxford, Clarendon Press).

Gilligan, C. (1982) *In a Different Voice* (Cambridge, Mass, Harvard University Press).

Hasson, R. (1995) 'Darkness at Noon – A Comment on the Consumer Guarantee Law in Ontario', 11.1 *BFLR* 141.

Hooley, R. (1995) 'Taking Security After O'Brien', *LMCLQ* 346.

Howell, N. (1994) ' "Sexually Transmitted Debt", A Feminist Analysis of Laws Regulating Guarantors and Co-Borrowers', 4 *The Australian Feminist Law Journal* 93.

Jack Committee Report (1989) *Report of the Review Committee on Banking Services Law, Banking Services: Law and Practice* (Chair: Professor R.B. Jack) Cmnd 622 (HMSO).

Jordon B., Redley M., and James, S. (1994), *Putting the Family First* (London, UCL Press Limited).

Lacey, N. (1993) 'Theory into Practice? Pornography and the Public/Private Dichotomy', 20 *Journal of Law and Society* 93

Lawson, A. (1995), '*O'Brien* and its Legacy: Principle, Equity and Certainty?', *CLJ* 280.

Lawton, J. (1991), 'What is Sexually Transmitted Debt?', in R. Meikle (ed) *Women and Credit: A Forum on Sexually Transmitted Debt Summary of Proceedings* (Melbourne, Ministry of Consumer Affairs).

Littlefield, L. (1996) 'Who Has the Power to Make Decisions in Current Couple Relationships?', Paper presented at the Fifth Australian Family Research Conference, (Australian Institute of Family Studies, Melbourne).

Maclean, M. (1991) *Surviving Divorce* (London, Macmillan).

Martin J., and Roberts C. (1984) *Women and Employment: A Lifetime Perspective, the Report of the 1980 DE/OPCS Women and Employment Survey* (HMSO).

Office of Population Censuses and Surveys (1994) *1992 General Household Survey*, GHS no 23 (London, Government Statistical Service).

Ogilvie, M. (1996) ' "Special Tenderness for Sexually Contracted Debt": A Feminist Banking Law in Embryo?: *Del Grande* v *Toronto Dominion Bank*', 11.3 *BFLR* 447.

Oldham, M. (1995) 'Neither a Borrower nor a Lender Be – the Life of O'Brien', 7 *Child and Family Law Quarterly* 104.

Olsen, F. (1983) 'The Family and the Market: A Study of Ideology and Legal Reform', 96 *Harvard Law Review* 1497.

Pahl, J. (1989) *Money and Marriage* (London, Macmillan).

Report of the Expert Group on Family Financial Vulnerability (1996) *Good Relations, High Risks: Financial Transactions Within Families and Between Friends* (Canberra, AGPS).

Richardson, M. (1996) 'Protecting Women Who Provide Security for a Husband's, Partner's or Child's Debts: The Value and Limits of an Economic Perspective', 16 *Legal Studies* 368.

Safilios-Rothschild, C. (1970) 'The Study of Family Power Structure: A Review 1960–1969', 32 *Journal of Marriage and the Family* 539.

Singh, S. (1995) *For Love not Money: Women, Information and the Family Business* (Melbourne, Consumer Advocacy and Financial Counselling Association of Victoria).

Strong, P. (1988) 'Minor Courtesies and Macro Structures' in P. Drew and A. Wootten (eds) *Erving Goffman: Explaining the Interaction Order* (Cambridge, Polity Press).

Trebilcock, M.J., and Elliot, S.B. (forthcoming) 'The Scope and Limits of Legal Paternalism: Intra-Familial Financial Arrangements and Gatekeeper Responsibilities', in P. Benson (ed) *Essays in Contract Law* (Cambridge, Cambridge University Press).

Volger, C. (1994) 'Money in the Household' in M. Anderson, F. Bechhofer and J. Gershuny (eds), *The Social and Political Economy of the Household* (Oxford, Oxford University Press).

Wilson, G. (1987) 'Money: Patterns of Responsibility and Irresponsibility in Marriage', in J. Brannen and G. Wilson (eds) *Give and Take in Families* (London, Allen & Unwin).

Women and Credit Task Group (1990) *How to Get Out of Sexually Transmitted Debt* (Melbourne, Consumer Credit Legal Service).

Wright Mills, C. (1959) *The Sociological Imagination* (London, Penguin).

[7]

The Legal and Moral Ordering of Child Custody

CAROL SMART*

INTRODUCTION

This paper is based upon a small empirical study of divorced and divorcing parents and how they 'negotiated' the question of child custody.[1] However, before I discuss the 'findings' of the research, I propose to outline my theoretical perspective and to clarify certain concepts which have come into use in the field of feminist philosophy but which may be less familar elsewhere.

My interest in law is in terms of law as a discourse which brings into practice or operation the feminine legal subject. The specific feminine legal subject I am concerned with here is the mother who, in legal texts, takes shape in various forms and guises. We need not assume in advance that there will be, or has been, a consistency in the legal subject mother. She is constituted variously, but we might also recognize that, at specific historical moments, a dominant construction emerges which could almost be said to over-determine legal policy or decision making, or at least structures the debates which give rise to new policy formations.

The constitution of the mother in legal discourse is not, of course, merely iconographic. Discourse produces not only the subject but subjectivity. Thus we should understand subjectivity to include both the social processes by which the individual is constructed (or even becomes conceptually possible) and the processes by which the individual comes to recognize herself or to claim an identity. This double meaning of subjectivity is perhaps contentious in that it often presumes an easy access to the interior subjectivity of individuals and how identities might change within a person's lifetime or across generations. Yet we can see how this has operated in fields like homosexuality and lesbianism with clearly shifting modes of expressing identity[2]. More recently, we might remark that the status of fatherhood has taken on a new meaning such that, for many, to be a father carries very different meanings, emotions and behaviours than in the pre-war period. Such changes have coincided with legal changes in which the father has lost his legal authority whilst being regarded as more and more central to the family in emotional and psychological terms. The father as constituted in legal discourse is no longer the paterfamilias, he is the producer of normal,

* *Department of Sociology, University of Warwick, Coventry CV4 7AL, England*

heterosexual children, the stabilizing anti-delinquency agent, and the bringer of realistic values and the desire for achievement.

This is not to suggest that this has been brought about by shifting legal discourse alone. Crucial to this have been the 'psy' discourses which in the 1950s and 1960s constructed the mother as vital to the child's well-being, and which in the 1980s and 1990s are doing the same for the father. However, law and discussions of legal policy play a vital part in taking up and legitimizing certain discursive constructs (which may have their genesis elsewhere) and in providing a legitimizing language in which to voice the newly experienced subjectivity.

At the same time that law (in its various manifestations) may be encapsulating and legitimating a new subjectivity; it also may deploy power to relegate or disperse other subjectivities. In embracing certain subject positions as central, others are marginalized. Thus the central and determining metaphors in family law have become the welfare of the child and the importances of the father as an instrument of welfare and as an individual who earns legal standing.[3] The mother seems to lose her standing. My point is not, of course, that courts or legal policy ignore mothers, nor that mothers have no part to play in the legal proceedings. However, it is not clear to me that there is any longer a language available for mothers to voice their subject position in law. There is an erasure taking place which is based on a form of silencing which arises out of giving the legitimate modes of expression to those who speak of welfare (psy professions now rather than mothers) and those who speak of the significance of fatherhood (fathers and the psy professions – but also many mothers).

This does not mean that mothers are saying nothing, only that what they say in relation to motherhood cannot be heard or will not register because legitimate speech is in the mouths of those whose subject position has been freshly constituted. Mothers may make recourse to the previously acceptable language of maternal love or instinct, but this is now discredited and is made to appear as self-interest speaking.[4] Thus the very language that was so powerful in many women's claims to children on divorce[5] and which judges and other legal actors routinely mouthed, has come to indicate an unjustified special pleading made at the cost of the superior claims of welfare (which has been largely divorced from maternal ideology) and of fatherhood.

The problem, then, that faces mothers is how to be heard because, although the repertoire of maternal instinct is alive and well in everyday life, it is increasingly an exhausted script in the divorce courts and solicitors' offices. I shall turn to this after discussing the development of ideas about the morality of care in feminist philosophy.

THE SUBJUGATED MORAL DISCOURSE OF CARE

I want to argue, on the basis of my interviews with mothers and fathers, that a mode of speaking about being a mother is being silenced by the dominant discourses of contemporary family law. This silenced discourse is what may be referred to as the moral discourse of care.

Family law has more or less eschewed any discussion of morality in the last twenty years. At least, this is so at the level of policy, and whilst moral norms may well underlie concepts of welfare, they are rarely acknowledged as such. This rejection of morality as a corner of the debate in divorce matters has been seen as progressive and those who want to bring morality back in are often identified as reactionary or instilled with a religious dogma. However, this polarization of moral issues into progressive and reactionary is possible only if we assume that morality is a term that stands for (improper) sexual behaviour or the sanctioning of 'bad' behaviour. Thus, bringing morality back in is thought to reflect a desire to reintroduce punishments for adultery and the desire to apportion blame. However, we need not constrain our thinking into such rigid categories, nor need we assume that a claim which is based on a form of moral argument seeks to demolish all other claims by attributing rightfulness to one party and banishing or vanquishing the other. It is often enough for a moral claim to be recognized as legitimate in and of itself.

In suggesting that a moral discourse has been silenced or subjugated I am not therefore implying that parents wanted a return to the old system of matrimonial fault. I am using the concept of morality of care as it has arisen out of feminist discussions on the limits of moral philososphy and judicial reasoning. Thus, Tronto argues:

> Caring suggests an alternative moral attitude. From the perspective of caring, what is important is not arriving at the fair decision, understood as how the abstract indivual in this situation would want to be treated, but at meeting the needs of particular others or preserving the relationships of care that exist. In this way, moral theory becomes much more closely connected to the concrete needs of others.[6]

What Tronto is arguing is that a schema of moral values can be derived from the work of caring which may be different from those that arise from processes of abstract thought. Typically legal reasoning is thought to reflect the latter (even if it does not always live up to the principles of objectivity, neutrality and so on).

Now family law, as a 'soft' form of law has not, in recent years, been constrained by rigid interpretations of legal method and principles. Yet the shift away from the relatively rigid or doctrinaire reading of law which perhaps characterized family law in the last century is not to be understood in terms of a rush to embrace an alternative code of moral reasoning, but in terms of the acceptance of psychological principles of child welfare.

This means that the dichotomy between the ethic of justice and the ethic of care originally proposed by Gilligan[7] does not work easily in the field of family law.[8] Instead, I think we need to begin with a more complex schema with three overlapping elements, namely: the ethic of justice (equality, equity, impartiality); the welfare principle (as largely determined outside legal and moral thinking), and the ethic of care (which as yet has little standing). The content of the ethic of care, as defined by Gilligan, is connectedness, the preservation of relationships, and the avoidance of harm. Yet this is precisely where I part company with Gilligan and prefer the orientation of Tronto above[9] (which I discuss further below).

Gilligan's thesis is that two modes of moral reasoning, which are typically idenitifed as masculine and feminine, arise from differential psycho-social development patterns in childhood. The ethic of caring is therefore not a female attribute but a feminine one and, as such, may be found in males but is more typical of girls/women. Similarly the ethic of justice is masculine but not male. This is not therefore a biologically reductionist argument, but a form of argument similar to the neo-object relations school of psychoanalysis. This argues that 'connectedness' arises from the experience of being mothered, followed by identification with the mother figure if you are a female child, needing therefore no distancing. 'Disconnectedness', on the other hand, arises from the process of identification with the father after having formed an initial bond with the mother, necessitating distancing.[10] It is this distancing which is thought to give rise to impartiality, neutrality and the primacy of logic in 'masculine' moral reasoning.

Gilligan's now familiar argument is that the 'masculine' form of moral reasoning has been mistakenly taken to be the highest possible form of ethics, whilst the 'feminine' form has been treated as a lower stage on the road to the desired pinnacle. She argues, in contradistinction, that both forms are equally valid. Moreover, she argues that law in Western societies is based on the principles of the ethic of justice and thus fails to reflect the ethical code more typical of the feminine. Thus, she argues that we must introduce the feminine mode into legal practice.

It may seem that this is what I am also advocating when raising the issue of a silenced discourse on the morality of caring. The logic would seem to be that wanting to give voice to the subjugated discourse must be synonymous with the Gilligan project. However, if we approach the morality of caring from a philosophical and a sociological stance we may find that what is being advocated is quite different.

Tronto[11] argues that we should start with the practices of caring to see what moral questions are posed. Her critique of moral reasoning is based on its tendency to start with abstract concepts and to discuss moral values in abstract terms. Thus she makes a vital disctinction between 'caring about' and 'caring for'. 'Caring about', she suggests, is what has concerned moral philosophers. Questions about whether one 'cares about' the suffering of others or 'cares about' the environment are typical moral issues. What has no entry into this traditional debate is 'caring for', the physical work of caring as opposed to the intellectual concern which may not be focused on a specific or concrete subject. Now, whilst these two states may coincide, Tronto argues that in differentiating them we can see that the activities of women have been typically left outside debates on moral issues. Her thesis, therefore, is that we need to see 'caring for' as a moral practice not something outside the moral domain. This argument is, in turn, linked to the argument of sociologists like Graham, Finch and Groves[12] who have been striving for the recognition of caring as form of work with specific material consequences rather than as a natural activity arising simply from gender differences. Thus whilst Tronto appears to be arguing that we must cease to take the practice of care for granted in moral philosophy, Graham and others are attempting to rescue the work of care from sentimentalized mists which render the activity and its costs invisible to all but those who do it (and sometimes even to them). It is precisely because 'caring for' has been discursively constructed as a natural outpouring of that supposedly natural substance, maternal love/instinct, that it could be so taken-for-granted and rendered so invisible. It is interesting, for example, to consider that women who do not care, or who refuse to care, are regarded as 'unnatural' rather than as moral agents making moral choices, or as economic agents recognizing the potential opportunity costs of caring.[13] The supposed 'naturalness' of the activity of caring is precisely what has taken it outside moral philsophy and indeed out of the perusal of the sociologist.

We are now in a position to recognize the complexity of the concept of 'care' and to appreciate that it is not simply a natural outpouring of instinctual love but a *moral practice*. Moreover, I want to stress that the relationship of gender to care is quite different in the formulations of Tronto, Graham, Finch, and others from the formulation in Gilligan. To reiterate, Gilligan links the ethic of justice and the ethic of care to the childhood processes of becoming masculine and feminine. Thus, they are not biologically given, but they nonetheless become seen as virtual personality attributes of femininity and masculinity. For Tronto and the sociologists, the morality and value of care comes from the activity of caring. Now, all these authors acknowledge that women typically do far more of the work of caring than do men; they might therefore posit that women occupy a different position or standpoint and may thus see the world differently. But this difference arises out of social structural difference, not out of a psychological process in the formation of personalities. So the latter would not say that women *are* more caring, but that they usually *do* more caring and that this gives rise to a moral position and social perspective.[14] We might also add that it gives rise to an identity or subjectivity which, whilst it is in part a psychic process, does not hark back to a process occurring in infancy as the over-determining moment in gender differentiation.

Thus, although 'caring for' is both valuable work and a moral practice, we are left with a situation in which we have no legitimate mode of expressing this and in which claims of fatherhood which are often (although not always[15]) based solely on biological status or on 'caring about' can produce a sentimental rush of concern and can be instrumental in producing legislative reforms.[16] I therefore want to turn to how parents themselves speak about children, care and custody.

THE STUDY

In 1990 I interviewed twenty-one women and sixteen men as part of a small-scale pilot study of how parents negotiated the issue of custody on divorce.[17]

Most parents were contacted through solicitors, others through a local conciliation service and through a process of networking. The average age of the women was thirty-four and the men thirty-seven. The majority of children involved were under ten at the time of the interview although they may have been up to two years younger at the time of their parents' separation. The aim of the study was to see how parents came to agree or disagree on future plans for their children, how these arrangements reflected prior child-care arrangements (if at all), how expectations changed over the process of divorce, and how encounters with the legal profession, conciliation services, and courts helped or hindered the process. The interviews were therefore open-ended and parents basically told their 'stories'. I was not concerned with narrow questions of truth and falsehood, but with how parents constructed their accounts. I relied on the old, but still remarkably useful dictum from W.I. Thomas that 'if men [sic] define situations as real they are real in their consequences'.[18] What follows is a mere fragment of the stories I was told.

USING A 'RIGHTS DISCOURSE'

Having rights was expressed as an almost exclusively masculine prerogative. That is to say that whereas some men thought and spoke in terms of 'fathers' rights', only one mother mentioned the concept of 'mothers' rights'. On the other hand mothers did speak in terms of their husbands and children having rights. I want to suggest, tentatively, that motherhood is always already constructed as antithetical to claims based on 'rights', whilst these were legitimate claims if made by fathers or on behalf of children. For example:

> I think that, despite the fact that we had split up, I thought joint custody would give me exactly the same rights as when I was living there . . . I couldn't see why that should change, I couldn't see why I should forfeit anything. (Frederick)

> OK, it ebbs and flows. Until 1973 fathers had most of the rights when it came to custody. From 1973 it seems to have flipped to the completely opposite end of the spectrum. It is actually quite rare now for the father to get custody. As far as I can see, fathers are in a much worse position and that's why we have groups agitating for the rights of fathers. (Allen)

> I think the whole system is very unfair . . . What really angers me is you see a lot of these equal rights and things, but they fall far far short of what they should be. And the man is nearly always the victim regardless of whether he has been right or wrong in the relationship.(William)

But compare the following:

> I'm so glad now that I didn't – as perhaps in my heart, for my own selfish reasons, I didn't want him to get to know her because I've brought her up all alone, with the help of mum and dad. But at the same time I knew I couldn't stop her from seeing him. It's her right, it's her father. (Jane)

The point is that even angry, bitter and disappointed mothers did not speak in terms of having too few rights themselves. They were more likely to express anger and bewilderment at a legal system that could give joint custody or unlimited access to a father who might 'care about', but who had not done any of the 'caring for'. But it would be a mistake to imagine that it was only disappointed mothers who made this distinction. On the contrary, what distinguished between mothers was not whether they could see the difference between 'caring about' and 'caring for', but whether some felt that 'caring about' was enough. For example:

> He said he hadn't been a bad father and he didn't see why any judge would say to him that he couldn't have joint custody. I thought he had quite a good point really because he hadn't been a bad father. He *had* left them, but before that he wasn't cruel or vindictive and we didn't go short of anything so really I couldn't say that he had abused the children in any way. (Maureen)

> Yes, (the children) are a great part of his life. Although he never did what I consider to be a lot for them as other dads do – taking them to the park and just being with them a lot, and playing. It's the same as with me, he has never treated me particularly nicely, but I have never really had much doubt that he hasn't loved me . . . *He's their father, I hope I can speak pleasantly of him when they come home.* (Alison, who was subjected to physical violence by her husband)

Both of these mothers felt that their husbands cared about their children. They were in fairly traditional marriages in that they had given up work or were working part-time in order to accommodate their caring responsibilties. They both wanted the fathers to have good relationships with their children and could see that joint legal custiody was a fair reflection of the moral order that had been established in their households. However, neither Maureen nor Alison would have tolerated the idea of joint physical custody or care and control going to their husbands.

> I would have fought tooth and nail that he couldn't have them. There is no way he would have taken the children off me because I am a good mother and I love my children . . . Yes, I think mothers and fathers feel differently about their children and a mother's love is a strong deep love and even though they are boys, and boys are supposed to be closer to their father, I think in a stable background I would give them the best stability and love in their lives until they are old enough to go on their own. (Maureen)

Now, we can dismiss this as special pleading based on an outdated ideology of motherhood and mother love. It might even be that she is mistaken and that she can not give her sons what they most need. But this is not the point. She was making a moral claim which had its foundations in the years of care she had given to her sons.

If we say this is nothing, or that it counts for little, we are adopting a position which affirms that the act of 'caring for' has no moral value in our culture. We continue to place 'caring about' above 'caring for' and *turn the moral claims which rest on acts of caring into self-interest.*

In her statement Maureen is obviously associating the moral claim that arises out of caring with gender identity. That is to say, she does use the language of the ideology of motherhood which is held as suspect in many quarters. Indeed, one of the main claims of fathers' rights groups as well as many feminists is that there is nothing intrinsic to being a woman/mother which means you can *automatically* love deeply and care well. However, whilst we can accept that there is nothing intrinsically caring about being a woman, this does not imply that we should reject the meanings that arise from providing care and nurture. Indeed, this research project has indicated quite clearly that as soon as men begin to 'care for' children, dramatic changes can occur. They become, metaphorically, 'born again'[19] They enter into a different moral domain where they have new responsibilities and their priorities are reordered. This transformation might have been initiated by the shock of discovery that their marriage was about to end, but it also became more firmly rooted in many cases when fathers actually started to do a lot of the 'caring for'. For example:

> I feel Ryan and his dad have a much better relationship now than they ever did when we were a family. His dad didn't have a great interest in him as a baby which I don't think a lot of men do. You can't blame him for that, they are boring little things . . . By the time he came home from work, and he'd go out four or five nights a week playing squash and other sports pursuits, and he didn't see a lot of Ryan any way. The best thing that happened to their relationship was us splitting up because it made such a difference. (Helen)

> When they first went to stay he had a real shock because he had to do so much. But it also brought them closer together and their relationship has improved tremendously, particularly with the youngest one who he'd had very little to do with in many ways. It has been a positive step, they are closer to him than ever before. (Caroline)

> I probably play more with them now than I did then. I actually devote more energy to them. They were around before and it was a bit like having the TV on, you become blasé, oblivious and indifferent to a degree, and something has to happen to wake you up. (Frederick)

> Time that has been dropped from the working week is now spent with the kids. (What does that mean for your quality of life?) It has improved. Financially, I am no worse off because my wife's income has increased in the meantime. I feel much fuller, much more complete now that I am relating to the kids nore. (Tom)

> I was a bit unsure in the beginning about how much I could trust him to pull his weight on (caring for the children). But I've been very impressed by his level of commitment. (Shirley)

THE MORAL DISCOURSE OF CARE

Tronto's argument is that 'caring for' gives rise to moral issues and, indeed, that it is a moral practice. In this study it would seem that the work of 'caring for' gave rise to a moral ordering in households which both women and men recognized much of the time. If this moral order was undisturbed, negotiations over the children did not seem especially problematic. This meant that where parents had been sharing the 'caring for' they seemed (in this sample at least) to feel they would continue this commitment beyond the end of the marriage.

> It came about as the logical continuation of the way we've always parented because we'd always shared the parenting. So when I decided that for me the marriage was over I was also very concerned to protect his relationship to them and their relationship to him . . . We talked a lot about how we could manage it in a way which would minimize the disruption to the children. (Shirley)

> Because we brought the kids up to believe that we shared responsibility for them in everything in the house and outside . . . I think we saw us splitting up as not diminishing in any way our individual relationships with the kids . . . it was just that it was clear that both of us were also so fond of, and involved with the kids that we wanted their interests to be first. (Brian)

Both Shirley and her former husband, and Brian and his former wife asked the courts for joint legal and physical custody but were denied it. In Shirley's case, she was awarded joint legal custody with care and control, and in Brian's case, he got joint legal custody and the care and control. This outcome was deeply problematic for both of them as they had worked so hard to sustain a moral (and emotional) equilibrium.[20] Their feeling was not just that the courts had not acted in the best interests of the children, but that an injustice had been done to a partner who had been doing the work of 'caring for'.

In households where the mothers had done the bulk of the 'caring for' it seemed clear that they felt that this work 'counted' for something. What is interesting is that, although Maureen (above) expressed herself through the narrative of maternal love, many of the mothers and fathers actually acknowledged the work of caring rather than invoking the term 'love' which could imply a fairly passive state (as with 'caring about'). This work of caring did seem to indicate a moral claim.

> I did feel he'd be better off with me, all mothers would I suppose, but as I say he hadn't had much of a relationship with his dad up until that point anyway and he'd known me for 14 hours a day, 7 days a week . . . *I'd always been there for him.* (Helen)

> Her relationship to the children was very good. *She was always there when they needed her.* (Frederick)

> The main stability has been me, there was no question that they wouldn't come with me at all. I mean, he never questioned it at all, He felt their place was with me. (Caroline)

> I feel quite sorry for the husband from that point of view, but I think that in our situation it was most probably a bit different in that *the children come first to me.* (Heather)

> I fell into the role of being a mum even though I went straight back to work . . . As a mum you are responsible. I am not particularly baby-minded, but you look after the silly things like 'Have you got ear-buds?' 'Do his toe-nails need cutting?' (When he's been at Collin's for two weeks his toe-nails aren't cut). *I think there are still things that you do as a mum.* (Christine)

These comments reveal the practicalities of caring and ultimately the responsibility of caring which women feel more often than men because they are more likely to be doing the 'caring for'. They could be compared with statements made on fathering in a traditional household.

> I think a child needs his mother more than his father really in their growing years. (Do you think there is a closeness or that mothers can provide something special?) In order to provide, especially in my instance. *My wife is much more practical regarding bringing up a child than I am.* I would sooner walk him up to the park and have a pint with him. (Peter)

This father is expressing his preference for relationships based on friendship or 'caring about' rather than 'caring for'. At the same time he obviously felt the 'caring for' was a rather easy option as he asserted that if he had a part-time job he 'could cope with it quite easily'. The work of caring remained invisible and he saw it as a matter of personality. He describes his wife as patient as if this was just a given rather than a moral attitude which might be acquired through the work of caring.

However, I do want to acknowledge that fathers who were actively engaged in 'caring for' children from an early stage spoke quite differently, talking of intimacy, pleasure and the drudgery of everyday caring. Yet the point I wish to make here is that where we witness a traditional division of labour, a distinctive moral ordering occurs which arises out of the work women do as carers. This moral ordering does not preclude co-operation and even quite extensive shared parenting after divorce. However, where there is a conflict, there is a tendency for the welfare principle to make the moral claims made by these mothers, based on the work of 'caring for', appear to be statements of self-interest. Equally, the fathers' rights principle makes such claims appear to resemble the unacceptable and 'old-fashioned' appeal to biological motherhood which is now renounced in favour of a policy of equality. The consequence is that such claims are disregarded or silenced. Moreover, the mother is constituted as selfish and self-serving.

There is, moreover, a tendency to defeat these tentative moral claims by reference to the fact that men are perfectly capable of 'caring for' as if this *projected capacity* should carry the same moral weight as the *actual activity*. Once again, the tendency to do this reflects the extent to which we view women's caring work as a natural attribute which requires little or no substantive acknowledgement, while men's expression of 'caring about' seems increasingly to occupy a sentimental and sacred place in the dominant moral and legal order. This is part of the discursive re-construction of fatherhood mentioned above.

OTHER DIMENSIONS OF MORALITY AND CARING

It has been suggested that shared parenting after divorce can only be successful if parents view their children's interests and welfare as separate from their own wishes and if there exists a positive regard for the other parent.[21] The combination of these two factors is important because, while family law seeks to ignore the circumstances which lead up to a separation, these may be vital to the way in which parents regard each other. Part of the process of establishing some degree of mutual regard after divorce hinges on the ability to distinguish between the other- as-spouse and the other-as-parent. Hence it was not uncommon to hear wives say a man was awful as a husband but fine as a father. The same was often said of women. The device of separating the qualities of spouse and parent is now used extensively to try to help parties accommodate to a new regime after divorce. Parents who make this distinction are regarded as mature and able to make the transition to post-divorce parenting, while those who do not are regarded as remaining trapped within the emotional orbit of their marriage, as failing to acknowledge the needs of their children, and as morally immature.[22]

I shall consider the parents who apparently had made this transition and were able to speak of one another with care and concern. I shall then consider how the other parents spoke of one another or of their children and will raise questions about why there is a tendency to treat different moral codes as if they are symptomatic of cognitive or emotional immaturity.

1. *Caring for the Other Parent*

The clearest expressions of care, regard or respect for the other parent were made by parents who were operating a form of shared parenting. Brian and Shirley, quoted above, are good examples, but Helen also expressed this form of care.

> It must have been difficult for him having to give his child up . . . We went for joint custody which was only fair. I felt that, any major decisions, my ex-husband would have to be involved in . . . We like each other quite a lot but we had made a mistake in marrying. We were more like brother and sister than husband and wife. (Helen)

What is noticeable about these comments is the way in which the parents talk in terms of 'we'. It is clear that they are still engaged in a joint project of child rearing even if their marriages have finished. Not surprisingly, the ability to feel part of a joint project is easier when the breakdown is mutual, or at least where both partners come to accept the wisdom of separation fairly quickly. However, this ability to continue to care for the other parent, or at least to give priority to co-operation rather than conflict, was also achieved in more difficult contexts.

> At the end of the day, she is my daughter as well as hers so it's not fair for Nicole to be deprived of whatever affection I can give. I also think (my wife) has gradually realized that – although her initial insincts were to say, 'No, no, you are not having her', which, in all fairness, I didn't think would happen – but looking back on it, it was a very natural reaction. So things have got a lot better. (Wesley)

> So I don't think it is easy for my husband, to be perfectly honest. It is not easy for any of us. (Maureen)

> That is probably why I am sympathetic to their father. I saw all my poor brother went through and how he was treated and taken for everything, and left with nothing, and a wife who wouldn't let him see the children. I think that is unkind . . . you can't chop your partner off, put him in a box and send him away, because he is still the father of your children. Somehow you have got to work it out. (Tina)

These three quotations reflect three different ways of arriving at a new post-divorce relationship. In the first case, Wesley experienced his wife's bitterness because he left her shortly after the birth of their daughter. He also expressed anger at the possibility of being denied access, but was able to understand his wife's responses and did not reject them as spite or self-interest.

Maureen had been devastated when her husband left her just when her children had reached their teens and she remained extraordinarily sad at the turn of events she had endured. Notwithstanding her pain, she was able to see how hard it was for her husband to (re)form and sustain his relationship to their sons and she was working hard to make this possible even though she was not prepared to include the 'other' woman in her efforts.

Finally, Tina was faced with a husband who was doubly dependent, on drugs and alcohol. Her reaction was one of sympathy rather than mutual understanding; nonetheless, she regarded her husband in a caring way and was prepared to work to sustain his role as father even though it had been entirely minimal until that time. Once again, however, it is important to realize that this caring for the other parent involved work.

It came as a shock to many parents who had had little involvement in 'caring for' children during a marriage that there is emotional work required to sustain relationships after divorce. This work relates to sustaining a relationship with the children, to the spouses' relationship with the children, and to the relationship between the adults. The parents who were successfully sharing parenting after divorce shared this invisible work. That is to say, they took on an extra dimension of planning and negotiating in order to make it work. For example, summer holidays and Christmases had to be organized long in advance, dates of school meetings had to be co-ordinated, flexibility was required in cases of sickness and so on. This was arduous but regarded as essential.

The parents who had 'cared about' but done little 'caring for' often seemed angry at the emotional and practical work that appeared to be 'suddenly' required. One father remarked that he could not see why things could not be just like they were during their marriage. He did not want to do the emotional work that was necessary to keep things going nor did he want to alter his schedules to accommodate another adult who had been so easily taken for granted before. In other cases, the mothers merely took on all the work of keeping access going. They prepared the children emotionally for their fathers, they consoled the children when their fathers left, they kept up the flow of information, they packed the bags and did the washing on return, and so on. The work of 'caring for' merely extended beyond the boundaries of divorce, and dealing with access was an additional dimension.

The work of sustaining the image of their former husbands as adequate fathers also became an additional task in the repertoire of post-divorce care giving. It is interesting that when mothers refuse to take on this extra work they become identified as bad or vindictive mothers. It would seem that the work of sustaining access is like housework: it is only visible when it is not done. When it is done it is expected, like virtue, to be its own reward, but when it is not done, the mother becomes morally blameworthy or denounced as emotionally immature.

If we accept that sustaining parenting after divorce is hard work, that it extends the invisible work of caring as well as adding a new dimension of collaboration which is not strictly necessary during an ongoing marriage, we need to consider that there may be circumstances in which parents are reluctant to do the extra work without regarding this as a moral failure or as emotional immaturity on their part.

2. *'Failing' to Do the Caring Work*

Typically, mothers ceased to do the work of sustaining access when they felt that their husbands had abrogated their duties as both husbands and fathers, Tricia, for example, felt that her husband's departure, which coincided with the bank foreclosing on the mortgage because of his fraudulent business arrangements, the arrival of the bailiffs and her rapid descent into homelessness and acute poverty indicated that her husband cared little for what happened to his children. She felt a deep sense of injustice when the court gave her husband joint custody of the children as she regarded him as totally irresponsible and uncaring. There had followed many disputes over access and maintenance but Tricia's strategy – if it can be called that – was not to obstruct access but simply not to do the work that it is assumed mothers will do to retain fathers' status in the eyes of their children. Wendy and Sonia followed similar lines in that they refused to represent their children's fathers to them in a positive light. That is not to say that they necessarily maligned the fathers; rather, they ceased to 'cover up'. Thus when a father failed to contact the children and they asked whether their father really cared for them, one mother advised her son to ask his father himself since he was old enough to do so.

It is sometimes surprising that mothers are prepared to go to extremes to 'cover up' for fathers. Margaret, for example, refused to accept her parents' evaluation of her husband's fathering qualities when he consistenly failed to keep to arrangements to see his two-year-old son. Alison was intent on preserving her husband's relationship with their sons in spite of his violence towards her which she felt was damaging to the children. These mothers set almost impossible standards against which other, less altruistic, mothers are judged and found wanting. In other words, it is assumed that children need fathers so badly that mothers must be prepared to tolerate almost any behaviour. In this form of reasoning, the welfare principle overrides any moral principle arising form the activities of caring, and diverts attention away from the problem of the 'bad' father by creating in its place the 'bad' mother.

Indeed, the welfare imperative had cretaed a situation in which the 'bad' father is almost inconceivable. For some of the women in this sample it was impossible to represent their husbands to me as bad fathers as this seemed to break an ethical code.

> I think in his way he loves the children. (Wendy)

> He's a very good father, he's a lot better than me in a lot of ways. He will take time and explain things to them where . . . I'm a bit thick. (She later explained that he had seen the children approximately six times in the last two years.) . . . They still, to this day, don't know that Mike doesn't give me anything towards their upkeep. As far as Mike is concerned, I will always say he is a brilliant father to them and I will support him if he shouts at them and I will always support him in front of them. (Heather)

It would be impossible to describe a woman who saw her children six times in two years as a good mother no matter how marvellous she was on those occasions.

Regarding the woman who does not meet with enthusiasm the work of sustaining access or shared parenting after divorce as an inadequate or morally incompetent mother ignores the way in which questions of justice, welfare and morality interweave. It also ignores just how hard the work is. Parents who share the care speak volumes on what they go through to set up a system and to keep it operating smoothly. The negotiations never end, and as circumstances change, ground rules have to keep changing. To expect that this should be taken on in a one-sided way and then to criticize the carer who refuses to co-operate because of her perception of the situation (that is, her notions of morality and justice) returns us to a situation in which the work of caring is disregarded or treated as a sort of reflex which requires no human resouces. Yet, if shared parenting is hard where there *is* co-operation, it takes little imagination to think of its costs where there is none.

One of the most potentially damaging factors which could disrupt the moral domain of child care established during marriage was the assertion of rights as a way of reaching decisions about children. Although mothers recognized fathers's rights, there were always rights which were delineated by an established moral code of caring. Whilst mothers did not think in terms of rights for themselves, many of the fathers interviewed were angry with what they saw as the disproportionate rights accorded to mothers. What is interesting is that many of these fathers could not see the moral claim that mothers might have arising out of the work of 'caring for' children. This moral dimension was as invisible to them as the actual work of caring had been. Rather, they saw a legal discrimination which had to be tackled legally. The consequence was often that they decided to fight, 'lost' custody and therefore their belief in discrimination was confirmed. Alternatively, the issue became transformed by solicitors and conciliators into a question of welfare, the children were put centre stage thus quite marginalizing the mother and avoiding any discussion of pre-divorce child care arrangements. This could deflect conflict but it still rendered the work of 'caring for' an unspoken and unspeakable element in the debate.

CONCLUSION

This small-scale study raised a number of issues. It 'confirmed' that there was a considerable sensitivity over the position of fathers in the process of divorce. More surprisingly perhaps, it 'revealed' an often-stated concern to preserve relationships after divorce for the sake of the children. But it also 'showed' that because 'caring for' as a form of work is invisible and yet also collapsed into the moral category of 'caring about', mothers who 'care for' have no legitimate voice unless they speak the language of equal rights (for fathers) or welfare (for children).

At the same time, the taken-for-grantedness of 'caring for' during a marriage distorts our perception of the work of shared parenting after divorce. In this process there is an ironical echo from the work of Gilligan. She has pointed out that orthodox psychology has taken the moral reasoning of girls/

women as a lower form of morality, arising from the arrested psychological development of the feminine. It would seem that family law may be following this practice. While *fatherhood* now represents equality (an element of the higher moral reasoning) and *welfare* represents the interest of the child or weakest member, *motherhood* represents some atavistic, pre-new enlightenment claim which would drag us back into selfish emotion and a satisfaction of the senses rather than a meeting of objective needs.[23] I may be graphically overstating the case here, but I would argue that metaphor is a large part of the construction of all contemporary folk devils. The lone or divorced mother is undoubtedly such a one. Such constructions can become over-determining and part of a newly formed – yet apparently timeless – common sense which then has practical implications. It is, however, possible to understand what mothers (and many caring fathers) are saying about 'caring for' children if we have a different conceptual framework in which to interpret or hear what is said. In other words, we should cease to treat statements of 'caring for' as synonymous with 'caring about', and we should equally cease to hear such statements as if they reiterate an ideology of motherhood and maternal instinct. The moral discourse of care is such a framework and while it does not promise a solution to the difficulties of divorce and child custody, at least it allows all the parties a legitimate voice.

NOTES AND REFERENCES

1 This research was funded by the Nuffield Foundation Small Grants Scheme. A full report of the study is available from the author.

2 See M. Foucault, *The History of Sexuality* Vol. I (1979); J. Weeks, *Sex, Politics and Society* (1981); L. Faderman, *Surpassing the Love of Men* (1985).

3 In using the term 'legal standing' I am not trying to indicate the strictly legal sense of this term as someone who has the status to bring a legal action to court. Rather, I am trying to imply a person of some significance in a social or psychological sense in a legal forum.

4 See S. Sevenhuijsen, 'Fatherhood and the Political Theory of Rights: theoretical perspectives of feminism' 14 (1986) *International J. of the Sociology of Law* 329–40.

5 It is not uncontroversial to argue that some mothers could exercise a degree of power in making claims based on maternal instincts. Maternal instincts and the ideology of motherhood have been seen as oppressive of women and I would not demur from this point of view. However, as Brophy has argued, such claims made inroads into absolute paternal authority over children (J. Brophy, 'Parental Rights and Children's Welfare: some problems of feminists' strategy in the 1920s' 10 (1982) *International J. of the Sociology of Law* 149–68). However, so-called adulterous wives in the 1950s and 1960s, and lesbian mothers were and are less eligible to make such claims. From a different perspective, see S. Maidment, *Child Custody: What Chance for Fathers?* (1984) which argues that the power of this claim led to a bias against fathers who were treated as less worthy as parents than mothers in the 1970s.

6 J. Tronto, 'Women and Caring: What Can Feminists Learn about Morality from Caring?' in *Gender/Body/Knowledge*, eds. A. Jaggar and S. Bordo (1989).

7 C. Gilligan, *In a Different Voice* (1982).

8 See K. Daly, 'Criminal justice ideologies and practices in different voices: some feminist questions about justice' 17 (1989) *International J. of the Sociology of Law* 1–18. Daly has made this point in relation to juvenile justice also. That is to say that the ethic of justice has been compromised for a considerable time by individuated sentencing and the promotion of treatment over punishment. It is, of course, also possible to argue that because law makes

claims to operate according to an ethic of justice we should not be taken in by this 'appearance' but should look to the reality of practice. However, this is an empirical argument which has some power but is inappropriate when used against an argument really concerned with metaphor.

9 Tronto, op. cit., n. 6.

10 N. Chodorow, *The Reproduction of Mothering* (1978).

11 Tronto, op. cit., n. 6.

12 J. Finch and D. Groves (eds.), *A Labour of Love* (1983) and, in particular, H. Graham, 'Caring: a labour of love' in the above; J. Finch, *Married to the Job* (1983).

13 H. Joshi, 'The Cost of Caring' in *Women and Poverty in Britain*, eds. C. Glendinning and J. Millar (1987).

14 I hope I am not forcing the argument of these authors unduly but it is important to recognize the difference between their use of the term care or morality of care, and the Gilligan type of approach.

15 I want to stress that fathers as well as mothers may 'care for' as well as 'care about'. Indeed, where fathers did the work of caring, I would argue that they also deployed the moral discourse of care. However, the claims that fathers could make, which would be heard just as readily, were claims based on the mere fact of biological fatherhood.

16 It is important to acknowledge that the English Law Commission (*Review of Child Law: Guardianship and Custody* (1988; working paper no. 172)) did not respond slavishly to the pressures of the Fathers' Rights Group in its deliberations on the law on child custody. However, it would also be fair to suggest that the father was a determining absence in the text of the report because of the concern to address the perceived problem of the disengaging non-custodial parent (which is a gender-neutral term for fathers) and the desire to reduce hostility which was perceived to arise from custody orders which, on the face of it at least, gave all rights to a sole legal custodian (which is a gender-neutral term for mother).

17 A fuller discussion of the methodology can be found in my research report to the Nuffield Foundation. It should be noted that the research was deliberately carried out before the Children Act 1989 was enacted in order to allow for possible comparisons with the new regime at a later stage.

18 W.I. Thomas, *The Child in America* (1928).

19 Issues of justice are, of course, raised when fathers' discovery of this new realm of moral relationships takes precedence over the taken-for-granted care that mothers have more typically given. Fathers in this situation are regarded much like the prodigal son and mothers feel a serious sense of injustice when the work and loyalty they have demonstrated over many years is treated so lightly by comparison.

20 In fact the courts could not really award joint physical custody at this time, but this had not been explained to any of the parents who felt that their careful plans for their children and the delicate equilibrium they had achieved were undermined.

21 S.B. Steinman et al., 'A Study of Parents who Sought Joint Custody Following Divorce: Who Reaches Agreement and Sustains Joint Custody, and Who Returns to Court' (1985) 24 *J. Am. Academy of Child Psychiatry* 554–62.

22 I. Thery, ' "The Interests of the Child" and the Regulation of the Post-divorce Family' in *Child Custody and the Politics of Gender*, eds. C. Smart and S. Sevenhuijsen (1989); C. Piper, 'Divorce Conciliation in the UK: How Responsible are Parents?' 16 (1988) *International J. of the Sociology of Law* 477–94.

23 Thery (id.) has spoken of the construction in contemporary psychology of the figure of the 'vampire' mother who suffocates and overprotects her offspring, living through them and allowing them no independent existence.

[8]

'WAITING TILL FATHER GETS HOME': THE RECONSTRUCTION OF FATHERHOOD IN FAMILY LAW

RICHARD COLLIER

University of Newcastle-Upon-Tyne

INTRODUCTION

THIS ARTICLE is about how the law has constructed fatherhood. It starts from a belief that in order to understand how ideas of 'absent', 'good' and 'errant' fathers have been reproduced in recent debates around family law reform, we need first to address the problematic concept of 'fatherhood' in law itself. In England and Wales contested ideas of paternal masculinities, and the question of whether families do indeed 'need fathers', has been central to government rhetoric around 'back to basics' and 'family values' in the early 1990s. Running through a succession of ministerial comments about single mothers,[1] and in the linking of family breakdown, absent fatherhood and rising crime as major 'social problems of the day',[2] has been one recurring issue: what are fathers for? In debates around reproductive technologies facilitating 'motherhood without men' through to the high-profile campaigns of fathers and second families against the Child Support Act 1991[3] one idea, spanning the political spectrum," has been central: the feeling that the problem with families is really a problem with *men*. At the heart of these debates, though it is seldom addressed as such, is the question of what being a 'father' actually involves.

In this article I shall argue that fatherhood has, from the late nineteenth century to the present day, been reconstructed in law and that in this process it has in important respects been rendered 'safe'. I wish to explore how the familiar (but taken for granted) idea of the 'good father', the fatherhood of the 'companionate marriage' and the egalitarian 'symmetrical' family, emerged at a specific historical moment. In particular I shall investigate how the potent idea of the *family man* has been constituted through reference to the economic and familial order of gender hierarchy and compulsory heterosexuality. It is through reference to this ideal, I shall argue, that a particular male heterosexual subject position continues to be privileged in law. The heterosexual economy of legal marriage has been constructed through dichotomies and hierarchies more complex than a simple hetero/homosexual dualism. The 'modernizing'[5] of fatherhood has involved an appeal to the reconstituted masculinity of the ideal 'family man'; but it is an ideal which, we shall see, is at the present moment as fragile as it is misleading.

In the context of debates about family law in the early 1990s, feminism is frequently singled out as the 'cause' of a number of tensions around fatherhood and masculinity.[6] Yet the issues about paternal masculinity raised by recent debates around father-absence have a long history. They can, I want to suggest, be traced back to the very contours of the reconstruction of fatherhood in law and the ways in which a range of changes in the division between public and private reconstituted the meaning of what it was to be a 'family man' in law. For all the law's endeavours to bifurcate masculine subjectivities, ideas of 'dangerous' and 'familial/safe' masculinities share much more than is commonly acknowledged. It is the aim of this article to explore the nature of these connections through investigating the archaeology of the 'family man' in legal discourse.

'MEN'S STUDIES' AND 'NEW FATHERS': CONSTRUCTING A CLIMATE OF CHANGE AND CRISIS

To begin to unpack this history of fatherhood it is worthwhile to first locate it in the context of the burgeoning scholarship on masculinity which has emerged during the 1980s and 1990s. This literature has no one politics or method and it would be erroneous to group together a disparate collection of texts and practices under one umbrella (be it 'men's studies', the 'sociology' or 'critical study' of masculinity). It is, rather, marked by a heterogeneity which encompasses both explicitly pro- and anti-feminist accounts of modern masculinities. It also involves a variety of approaches to the legal status of fathers. In academic texts addressing masculinity, where the interest appears perhaps most marked, a wide range of intellectual fields have been traversed. These texts have frequently embraced an interdisciplinary eclectism which is both suitably postmodern and is also, perhaps, indicative of wider shifts in social theory; for some male academics the deconstruction of masculinity and masculinist discourses[7] has provided, following the collapse of previously comforting meta-narratives, a (convenient?) paradigm for ostensibly 'critical' scholarship to continue.

Notwithstanding the diversity of these writings, however, it is possible to identify a number of themes which recur in the construction of what I shall term the 'masculinity problematic'. In both explicitly pro-feminist accounts (such as those within the 'men against sexism' tradition; see Rutherford, 1992: 2–11), as well as explicitly anti-feminist and 'men's liberation' texts, we can find an underlying assumption that masculinity is undergoing a profound change. Where the pro-feminist and men's liberationist accounts tend to differ is in their analyses of the causes and consequences of this change. In a stronger version of the thesis it is argued that we are in fact undergoing a *contemporary crisis* in masculinity (Brittan, 1989: 25–36; Connell, 1987: 183–6; Hearn, 1987: 16–31); and, crucially, that this is a crisis which has a specifically *legal* dimension.

It is, in essence, around a perceived breakdown of traditional masculine authority in relation to the family and men's relationships with women and children that the idea of a masculine crisis has been constructed.[8] If we stand back from the topicality and apparent newsworthiness of the 'redundant man' discourse[9] we can see that debates such as these around legal changes are in fact a well-established part of the politics of family law reform. The student of family law, for example, will be familiar with the long history of men's resistance to the equalizing of parental rights in relation to children (Brophy, 1985). More recently, from the Campaign for Justice on Divorce in the late 1970s and early 1980s through to the continued (and increasingly controversial) campaigns of Families Need Fathers in the 1990s,[10] is the recurring issue of the perceived diminution of men's legal rights in relation to women, children and property. It is this which is seen as undermining the role of men in the family; the law, it is argued, has now swung too far in favour of its 'spoilt darling'.

In the early 1990s we have seen the focus of these debates shift. Prompted in part by a pervasive and powerful (if empirically questionable) ideology of the 'new fatherhood' (Lewis, 1986; Lewis and O'Brien, 1987; Smart, 1989b) the politics of both family law and fatherhood have not so much become enmeshed within debates around masculinity, social change and feminism; they have become central to the arguments of those who have sought to expound a particularly bitter and vituperative anti-feminism (frequently employing an ostensibly 'progressive' men's liberationist rhetoric: e.g. Lyndon, 1992). Utilizing a rhetoric of 'political correctness'[11] in a critique of liberal ideology, a correlation between father-absence and a range of 'social problems' (e.g. welfare spending, criminality, moral relativism) has been constructed in which ideas of 'change' and 'crisis' in men's lives have become common currency. One result of this has been to make it difficult to see just what the politics of both the 'new fatherhood' *and* the developing 'sociology of masculinity' may be at a time when attacks on perceived feminist legal 'gains' have been gaining ground (Faludi, 1992: Roberts, 1992).

THE EXAMPLE OF CHILD CUSTODY

This brings us to one of the paradoxes of the developing critique of masculinity, exemplified by (in pre-Children Act 1989 terms) legal responses to child custody. In recent years analysis of the gendered juridification of child custody

(Sevenhuijsen, 1992) has prompted feminists to question the masculinism of law and the gendering of legal assessments of parenting capacity (Smart and Sevenhuijsen, 1989). In England and Wales before the 1989 Children Act, research produced the generally consistent finding that it was mainly mothers who both claimed and obtained custody of children whatever their status in the divorce petition. It is also clear that contested custody cases were very much the exception. Maintaining continuity of care was of 'overwhelming importance' (Bromley and Lowe, 1987: 327) in this vast majority of cases, with the courts not so much determining whether the mother or father is the more 'appropriate' parent as simply making orders confirming the existing situation (Eekelaar et al., 1977). Prompted by a succession of feminist analyses, the practice and substance of custody law have become an important part of the politics of family law (Brophy and Smart, 1985; Sevenhuijsen, 1986; Smart and Sevenhuijsen, 1989).

This is an issue which cuts to the heart of men's responses to feminism, however. On the one hand, explicitly anti-feminist organizations such as Families Need Fathers and Dads After Divorce have drawn on the rhetoric of 'men's liberation' and, in the name of 'equal rights', have sought to extend the rights of fathers (Brophy, 1985). In the context of post-separation maintenance arrangements in England and Wales recent concerns about the operation of the Child Support Act 1991 have similarly served as the focus of this more general disquiet about how the law treats fathers (Collier, 1994).[12] At the same time, however, a range of anti-sexist critiques of masculinism have also sought to challenge traditional notions of parenting and encourage men to take a greater role in childcare.[13] What is important to recognize at this point is how, in relation to each perspective, the idea of a masculine 'crisis' has been constructed through reference to the formal legal rights of men and women. It has not been concerned with seeking to analyse and understand the historical background to a range of contemporary cultural insecurities around sexuality and gender (and, importantly, under the sign of AIDS). Instead, what has tended to take place has been an elision of the ideas of 'men's studies' and 'new fatherhood'; the idea that they are both part and parcel of a qualitative change in men's lives.

This has had two consequences; first, it has legitimated a reading of the historical development of fatherhood within the terms of a classic liberal legal concern with the rights, entitlements and prerogatives of individual men and women. Thus men may be constructed as the 'victims' of a feminism which has gone 'too far' in unbalancing hitherto 'equal' rights (the father's rights position). Second, it has served to deflect attention from the cultural climate in which the gender configurations of legal discourse, as well as shifting representations of fatherhood, have themselves been produced. It is these cultural configurations in which discourses of masculinity are constructed which, I will argue, must be tackled if we are to address historical change in ideas of fatherhood in law.

What we are dealing with here are debates about gender and power which are central to matrimonial politics. Discourses of paternal masculinity and ideas of what might constitute a 'normal father's love' have become the currency in which issues about law reform are being articulated. However 'fatherhood' is at once both a public and a private concept. Through exploring its *historical* constitution in legal discourse it becomes possible to open out to analysis an important, though curiously neglected, part of how the ideological division between men's public and private citizenship has been constructed in law. If fathers have been curiously absent in recent debates around single parenthood then it is in part because it is male heterosexuality itself which the perceptual grid of law has systematically rendered invisible.

Constructing Fatherhood in Law: From Father-Right to Father-Absence

'Fatherhood' is a social construct through which the law has historically sought to attach men to children (Sevenhuijsen, 1992). It is not a unitary concept and there is no one fatherhood in law (Smart, 1987). Thus contemporary debates about the legal contours of fatherhood do not float free. To begin to make sense of the tensions and contradictions which surround contemporary fatherhood, and which are testified to by the plethora of recent texts addressing the subject,[14] it is worthwhile looking at how the law has historically constructed fatherhood, authority and male economic power – and how, through the processes of naturalizing masculinity, men continue to be constituted as subjects of a particular discourse of familial masculinity.

What do we mean by this phrase 'discourse of masculinity'? In order to assign any particular significance to the idea of historically specific representations of masculinity it becomes necessary to address the social relations within which these representations are reproduced at any given historical moment (Middleton, 1992: 142). Outside of such an institutional context the idea of a 'discourse of masculinity' has no self-evident meaning. Thus

> To speak legitimately of a discourse of masculinity it would be necessary to show that a particular set of usages was located structurally within a clearly defined institution with its own methods, objects and practices. Otherwise the reference to discourses of masculinity is simply a reference to repeated patterns of linguistic usage, which may be significant, but cannot be theorized .... Masculinity is produced within some discourses in the stricter theoretical sense, but most examples of 'masculine' utterance are not discourses. (Middleton, 1992: 142)

Law provides just such a set of usages for discourses of masculinity which can be located structurally. Law also provides clearly defined institutions with their own (doctrinal exegetical) method, objects and practices. Discourses of masculinity, in other words, have had an established and entrenched link with the histories of power and knowledge both in and of law; and, as a wealth of feminist jurisprudential scholarship has stressed, analyses of the gendering of law do not stop at the substantive level. They must also embrace a critique of the very method, language and logic of law. The task becomes one of deconstructing what it is that the law has had to say about masculinity in the past and, in the present context, to locate these readings in relation to how legal discourse continues to disqualify those knowledges which might seek to challenge its pervasive familialism. To this end, and with this in mind, it is useful to explore further the historical background to married fathers' rights. A paternal masculinity which has tended to be associated in the past with the married man has increasingly served to valorize all men's subjectivities[15] while, by sleight of hand, rendering the overarching masculinity of the 'family man' invisible. It is, we shall see, misleading to read the legal history of heterosexual masculinity in family law in terms of such a distinction between the rights of married and unmarried fathers. At issue here are changes in understandings of paternal masculinities per se.

A HISTORICAL SNAPSHOT: THE 'GOLDEN AGE' OF FATHERS' RIGHTS

The rights and obligations which married men[16] have historically had over 'their' children must be located in the context of the changes in family structure which resulted from the transformations of the agricultural and industrial revolutions of the eighteenth and nineteenth centuries. Writing in the eighteenth century, Sir William Blackstone, in his *Commentaries on the Laws of England* (1765), declared that at the time when the child reaches the age of 21 the 'empire of the father . . . gives place to the empire of reason'. However until that time the 'empire of the father continues even after his death' (*Blackstone's Commentaries on the Law of England*, Vol. 1:453, quoted in McKee and O'Brien, 1982:27). The mother, in contrast, 'is entitled to no power, but only to reverence and respect'.

By the time of the late nineteenth century the law had already began, albeit slowly, to move away from this common law 'empire of the father' position declared by Blackstone. Although a succession of legal reforms had gradually brought increased legal rights to the mother, however, it is important to remember that it was not to be until the 1970s that the formal rights of mothers and fathers were finally equalized in law (see further Brophy, 1985). Contemporary family law textbooks continue to cite, as the apotheosis of 'absolute father right', the 1883 case of *Agar-Ellis* v. *Lascelles*. This, of all the nineteenth-century cases, perhaps best illustrates the nature of the married fathers' rights at the time. Almost a century later Lord Upjohn, in *J* v. *C*, commented that he could 'only describe as dreadful' the decision in *Agar-Ellis*. Nonetheless it is interesting how the reasons given by Brett M. R., the trial judge, to endorse his view of the legal rights of the father continue to be echoed in contemporary appeals to the 'natural' quality of a father's role in the family.

In this case the father, a Protestant, had agreed at the time of his marriage that any children of the marriage would be brought up Roman Catholic. At the birth of the first child he changed his mind. The mother proceeded to teach the children Catholicism and, when the children later refused to go to a Protestant church, the father made the children wards of court. This prevented the mother from taking the children to confession and left the father in control of the 'spiritual welfare' of the children. He proceeded to remove the children from the mother, placing them with others, and he censored the mother's letters and restricted her visits to the children to once a month. The daughter had written to the judge begging to be allowed to live with her mother and to practise her religion but the father continued to refuse. The daughter and mother petitioned to the court to allow them a two-month holiday together and free correspondence and access. The father opposed, fearing that the mother would alienate him from the affections of the child (although by this time the desire of the daughter to be with her mother was beyond doubt). He continued to refuse to allow the daughter to visit the mother and for the daughter and mother to correspond except on the condition that the letters were to be shown to himself or third parties (*Agar-Ellis*: p. 325).

The appeal against a first instance decision in favour of the father was dismissed on the ground that the court had no jurisdiction in a case such as this to interfere with the legal right of a father to control the custody and education of his children. Father right was, first and foremost, natural and based on the reciprocity of obligation and paternal prerogative (per Brett M. R. in *Agar-Ellis*: pp. 327–8). Fathers' rights were 'sacred' rights with which, given their natural ordination, a court 'whatever be its authority or jurisdiction, has no right to interfere with ' (per Vice-Chancellor Bacon in *Re Plomley*: 'the Court must never forget, and will never forget . . . the rights of family life, which are sacred' (p. 337; see also *In Re Curtis*) It was the sacred quality of these rights which Brett M. R. stated in *Agar-Ellis* he 'endeavoured to express' (p. 329) in his judgment_ 'on account of the general trust which the law reposes in the natural affection of the father this case is not brought within any of the rules which authorize the Court to interfere' (p. 329). In an argument which continues to be made by advocates of fathers' rights, paternal authority is made inseparable from a perceived threat to both familial and social order.

> To neglect the natural jurisdiction of the father over the child until the age of twenty-one would be really to set aside the whole course and order of nature, and it seems to me it would disturb the very foundation of family life. (p. 336)

Masculine authority in this case is *naturalized*; it needs no explanation, justification or further deliberation – it is impervious to questioning. To interfere with the rights of the father 'would be to ignore the one principle which is the most fundamental of all in this history of mankind, and owing to the full play of which man has become what he is' (p. 337). It is a similar naturalizing of masculinity which continues, of course, to pervade representations of masculinity and male sexuality.[17]

How might we read a case such as this? How might we present a 'critical genealogy of the naturalization of sex and of bodies' which occurs in this case (Butler, 1990: 147)? What does it tell us about public and private, property and power? *Agar-Ellis* provides us with a historically specific construction of masculinity in law. Yet the paternal masculinity Brett M. R. invokes (broadly, one of the Victorian paterfamilias) only related to the lives of some fathers socialized into the 'civilized self-control . . . rigidity of character structure' which marked the middle-class Victorian Man (Cominos, 1963, quoted in Richards, 1987: 27). Class, geographic (e.g. rural/urban), religious and ethnic differences all divested the legal authority of the father (as well as beliefs about sexuality) in different ways. The cases which came to court at the time in this area involved wealthy families. Divorce was heavily restricted and permeated by a sexual double standard.[18] It would be misleading, therefore to simply assume that the sacramental bourgeois family depicted in the case, and to which this masculinity is seen as fundamental, was unproblematically diffused throughout the social order (Weeks, 1981: 38).

The 'separate spheres' ideology which underlay the depiction of domestic arrangements in *Agar-Ellis* did not necessarily apply universally. The passionate homilies of judges with regard to the symbolic good of 'the family', be they from the 1880s or 1990s, can be seen as prescriptive rather than descriptive. Historically, and bearing in mind occupational and regional differences in family structures, 'it is difficult to find any support for either a universal progressive democratization of family life or of the thesis of general cultural diffusion' (McKee and O'Brien, 1982: 18). This is not, however, to claim that as a concept within legal discourse 'fatherhood' has no heuristic purpose; nor, indeed, is it to state that the concept of 'masculinity' is itself redundant in the light of the fragmentation which has followed the recognition of the contingencies of class, sexuality and ethnicity in constructing men's subjectivities in law.[19]

It is possible, rather, to see this masculinity in the context of those strategies aimed at containing the 'dangerous' sexualities of the lower orders (e.g. of the moral purity and temperance movements of the late nineteenth century);[20] that is, to locate this fatherhood in relation to a more general concern to 'domesticate' men to the moral, sexual and economic strictures of the family which were taking place at the time (Davidoff and Hall, 1987; Hey, 1984). The familial masculinity which emerged around the mid to late nineteenth century was also, however, infused with the values of participation, investment and commitment to the ethics of the developing capitalist order of the times; and the gendered subject of legal discourse – the 'man of law' (Naffine, 1990: 116) – was itself established around the same time as urbanization, industrialization and capital accumulation were transforming pre-industrial conceptions of civil society and, crucially, of ideals of parenthood itself.

Together these changes brought about no less than a reconstitution of familial, household and gender relations – just at the same time as men's power within the 'public' domain of work, the market and industrial capitalism was being entrenched through the incorporation of distinctly 'public' masculinities (Hearn, 1992) and the values of the 'man of law' as an ideal-typical gendered legal subject (Naffine, 1990). Far from constructing any unitary and universal model of masculinity from legal cases (which would continue to assign to law an epistemological significance of which it is undeserving) I would suggest it is more worthwhile to ask some different questions of law. How did the particular familial masculinity to be seen in *Agar-Ellis* emerge at the time it did? How was it legitimated and promulgated 'through the printed word and via prestigious and proliferating educational institutions?' (Mangan and Walvin, 1987: 1); and how, as one discourse of masculinity among many, has this binding of fatherhood/authority and economic power continued to inform legal constructs of family relations? In the remainder of this article I shall seek to answer these questions.

TOWARDS THE 'BEST INTERESTS OF THE CHILD'

Let us move forward a century to the 1980s. The 'sacred rights' of a father no longer exist as formal legal justiciable rights which he can assert in relation to 'his' children (or, indeed, 'his' wife). During the nineteenth century a change took place in social attitudes to children which was well under way by the time of *Agar-Ellis* (Ariès, 1973). From a hitherto valuing of children by reference to their skilled labour capacities the increasing power of a range of ideologies began to stress the 'special' and distinct quality of pre-adult years (Pinchbeck and Hewitt, 1969). Alongside a succession of legal reforms (not least child protection legislation), childcare 'changed from a valuable family burden that men wished to control to a costly family asset that men wished to avoid' (Brown, 1981: 242, quoted in Hearn, 1992: 55).

In the reconstitution of the familial ideal as a distinctly modern and egalitarian household unit the emergence in law of the 'welfare principle' made it necessary to ascertain just what the 'best interests of the child' as a 'paramount consideration' might actually be in any particular case (Guardianship of Infants Act 1925, section 1; Children Act 1989, section 1). By the 1920s, and following the entrenching of the welfare principle in the 1925 Act, the father's role had already become increasingly problematic. Informed by a succession of childcare manuals the role of the wife/mother was being emphasized in a celebration of the values of the family and marriage (Richards, 1987: 32). Influenced by 'scientific' paediatric discourses and shifting ideologies of childcare, as well as their own and all too evident personal prejudices, judges had begun from the late nineteenth century onwards to detail a range of factors which together have constituted the 'welfare principle' in law and the 'best interests of the child' (Bromley and Lowe, 1987: 317). To this day family law textbooks continue to list the 'factors' (such as employment and remarriage prospects) established in a succession of frequently contradictory Appeal cases which determine the 'welfare principle' at a particular historical moment (e.g. see *Re L* (1962); *Re K (Minors) (Wardship: Care and Control)* [1979]).

One effect of the increasing influence of the welfare principle throughout the twentieth century has been to politicize fatherhood and to bring men's involvement in childcare into the *public* domain (Hearn, 1992). If families do 'need fathers', then why do they? What is it about fatherhood which renders it 'in the interests of the child'? The emerging welfare principle fractured the hitherto 'natural' basis of the father-right of *Agar-Ellis* through providing an alternative and child-centred moral imperative – and in doing so fatherhood was itself brought into the public and political domain through a reassessing of whether families do indeed 'need' fathers. On one level the idea of the companionate marriage had presumed an increased joint activity on the part of both husband and wife. However, in reality tasks remained segregated on gender lines with the father a detached and often absent figure (see below). From the language of metaphysically ordained 'father's rights', the best interests of the child moves on to centre stage; but this process did not mean that fatherhood no longer involved claims to power and authority *or* that the paternal masculinity of the family man was no longer naturalized.

To understand how this transformation took place it is first necessary to address how marriage has ceased to be the central vehicle of family law in the process of safeguarding (legal) fatherhood (Sevenhuijsen, 1992: 80). Other legal concepts and techniques now, sometimes with great difficulty, seek to walk the tightrope of doctrinal coherence in attaching men to children (Smart, 1987). Yet these developments have not meant that legal discourse no longer continues to protect fatherhood. It does so, not through granting to the father his hitherto formal legal *rights* in relation to other family members, but through

> taking mothers and fathers as degendered persons or simply 'parents', and then bring[ing] them under the jurisdiction of human rights reasoning and equality reasoning. Family law treats these persons *as if* they are equal. . . . Equality then comes down to equal treatment or consistency . . . (Sevenhuijsen 1992: 80)

It is hard to refute the justice of the equal rights claim, the language through which the contemporary international fathers' rights movement and advocates of men's liberation have pitched their argument, without denying the fundamental premise of liberal legal order (Brophy, 1985; Smart, 1989a). The men and women involved in disputes over childcare articulate their claims through this language of equal rights (Smart, 1991). One effect of this, however, has been to depoliticize the gendering of male and female subjectivities in the first place; and analysis of this would involve rejecting the conceptual baggage of liberal legalism (turning, in a sense, away from law) just at the same time as legal rights are assuming an increased significance in debates around family law and father-absence (or turning 'to' the law).

Parents do not come before the law as ungendered bearers of abstracted legal rights but as gendered beings subjectively committed to identities and institutions within which they might find themselves both powerful and powerless. The possibility of agency, however, remains ever present in opening out alternative discursive routes or 'ways of being' (Butler, 1990: 143).The meaning of fatherhood, like heterosexuality and homosexuality, is fluid; and if parents accord that a child is 'better off' with the day-to-day care of the mother (as the majority appear to do), or if it is given that a man's primary commitment is to work and not to childcare (for which he is 'naturally' unsuited), then this does not mean that these beliefs are then beyond theory or 'trapped within the unnecessary binarism of free-will and determinism' (Butler, 1990: 147). It becomes, rather, necessary to explore how these gendered subjectivities have been constituted through discourse in the first place and, in particular, how such beliefs are presented as 'natural' and thus inviolable. In so doing it is revealing to consider further how the law has constructed the modern 'good father' as a desirable presence in the family.

FATHER-ABSENCE AND THE 'MASCULINE ACHIEVER'

Central to the idea of the 'good father' in law is the correlation between men and work. We have seen that any legal authority the modern father may have is no longer justified by reference to the 'natural' rights he may possess by virtue simply of being a father (as per *Agar-Ellis*). What we find instead is that it has been through a primary reference to work and his capacity for paid employment that masculine subjectivities have been constructed in family law. The idea that the family sphere has been legally structured as the location for the exercise of power, authority and dominance by men has, of course, been central to much feminist legal scholarship on the family (e.g. Atkins and Hoggett, 1984; O'Donovan, 1993, 1985; Okin, 1989; Smart, 1984, 1989a). Yet feminism has also, through rejecting sociology's traditional sexual divisions of public/work and private/home, in turn questioned such a gendered definition of 'work' as an a priori public-related activity. In so doing, an apparently seamless web of masculine authority has been revealed which encompasses the familial and institutional terrains of interpersonal relationships, employment, the state and the 'public spaces' of leisure and the street. This means that any ideas we may have of masculine 'authority' per se can no longer be confined to the familial domain or conceived through reference to the public/private dichotomy. They should be seen as embracing aspects of *both* private (men at home) and public (men at work) masculinities, as well as the relation between the two.

This involves recognizing that the historical division of masculinity into 'public' and 'private' lives discussed above is itself an ideological construct which has been premised on the dualisms of liberal legal discourse (public/private, work/home, etc.). However, it is precisely through reference to that division and, in particular, to the idea that masculinity is first and foremost something to be mobilized as an economic resource, that the physical *absence* of fathers from the family domain (because they are or should be 'at work') has been justified in family law. We have seen above how fatherhood was rendered problematic just as the welfare principle was stressing the paramountcy of the child's interests. If the father is absent then what is his primary familial 'function' or 'role' in this discourse? That, as the reduction of fathering to an economic nexus in the Child Support Act 1991 makes all too clear, is to 'provide', to be 'responsible' financially (Simpson et al, 1993:48).[21] This mobilizing of masculinity as an economic resource continues to be central to the legal regulation of post-divorce financial and property relations whilst paternal masculinity continues to be defined in law primarily through reference to men's capacities to provide economically for 'their' families.

The idea that paid employment has a central place in the maintenance of masculine identity and status has appeared in a succession of legal cases (e.g. *Allington* v. *Allington*; *B* v. *B*; *Greer* v. *Greer*; *Ives* v. *Ives*; *S (BD)* v. *S (DJ)*). It is also very much in evidence in sociological research on the family (e.g. Komarovsky, 1964; Tolson, 1977; Willmott and Young, 1962). This is in marked contrast to legal constructions of the correspondence between maternity, childcare and women's familial role, where ideas of the 'natural' parenting abilities of fathers and mothers continue to prove pervasive;[22] after all, 'however good a sort of man he may be he could not perform the functions which a mother performs by nature in relation to a little girl' (*M* v. *M*, per Stamp L. J.). The corollary of these natural abilities of the mother is, or course, the belief that a man should be engaged in employment and, even within the home, a physical definition of masculinity has been sustained through a legally endorsed sexual division of domestic tasks (Atkins and Hoggett, 1984; O'Donovan, 1985). In the cases of *Wachtel* v. *Wachtel*, *Cooke* v. *Head* and *Eves* v. *Eves* a gendered division of domestic labour is constructed in such a way as to assess (and ultimately devalue) domestic tasks seen as 'female'. 'Male' jobs, in contrast, require strength and certain traditionally masculine skills such as building, repairs, constructing the garden, digging, maintaining household machinery and maintaining cars (see also *Burns* v. *Burns*; *Langston* v. *AUEW*). In these cases the legal construction of 'housekeeping' takes place from a vantage point in which gendered roles for male and female are assumed (on the gendered narrative in these cases see Bottomley, 1993).

This form of breadwinner masculinity has clearly been endorsed in law. The 'problem' in the present climate is that it involves a correlation between men and work which is coming under increasing attack. A range of cultural and economic developments have recently combined to render the social consequences of this construct of father as economic provider increasingly problematic. The impact of feminism, the increasing proportion of women in the workforce, wider shifts in employment patterns resulting from economic restructuring, mass unemployment and shifts from industrial based to service economies (as well as an increasing cultural valorization of leisure time) have all thrown into question the traditional ideas of paternal subjectivity based on the centrality of work.[23] We have seen that the breadwinner ideal involves a physical absence from the family which has been sanctioned in law. We have also seen how it involves a man in 'providing' for his family. When it comes to those men who, for differing reasons, have rejected the fundamental premise of this masculinity, or else cannot so 'provide', then the response of the law is very different.

THE MAN WHO DOES NOT WORK: CONSTRUCTING PATERNAL MASCULINITY IN LAW

The case of the man who chooses not to work in order to be involved in childcare brings together the ideas of historical change in masculinity, 'men's liberation' and 'new' fatherhood discussed above. A central problem facing men who choose to take on primary childcare responsibilities has been identified as 'the practical problem of fathers being able to cope' because of the demands of their full-time employment (Lowe, 1982: 35). In two cases from the 1980s, both called *B* v. *B*, just such a situation occurred.

In the first *B* v. *B (Custody of Child)* a case subsequently cited with approval by Families Need Fathers, a central question for the court was how the father could maintain contact with his child. To keep up his contact he had to make arrangements to see that his son did not suffer in any way from the fact he had to go to work. He thus delegated day-to-day responsibility for childcare to his family, his mother and then sister (thus reproducing a traditional sexual division of labour). This case was not one of 'a father who has deliberately given up work in order to go on social security: circumstances have forced him to give up work . . . he is now unemployed and is likely to be for some time'. Unlike those fathers who 'choose' to go on social security *this* father's hand was forced through his employer's demands. A differentiation is thus made between different classes of deserving/undeserving fathers.

In the second *B* v. *B* the father decided that he *did* wish to live on social security so that he would be able to care for the child. At first instance the trial judge was unequivocal. He stated that the primary role of the father was to go to work and generate the resources whereby he would be able to provide support for himself and the child. It would be 'plainly wrong and silly if the father were to remain unemployed in order to look after one 4-year-old boy' (p. 177). Indeed, he continued, 'I shall take a great deal of convincing that it is right that an adult male should be permanently unemployed in order to look after one small boy' (p. 174). Moreover

> a healthy young man like you must generate resources by your work to support your child and yourself . . . rather than have other people supporting you . . . through the tax payer. (p. 174)
>
> The father's primary role must be by his work to generate resources which provide for the support and maintenance of his child and himself, rather than remain at home performing what traditionally is regarded as the mother's role. (p. 177–8)

The Court of Appeal subsequently allowed the father's appeal and awarded care and control to the father with reasonable access to the mother. However they explicitly did not reject the construction of the relation between men and work that the trial judge considered so important. Indeed the Court went to great lengths to stress that they were not in disagreement with his reasoning in the case:

> I do not for a moment wish to be thought unsympathetic to, or critical of, the judge's viewpoint that a young and able-bodied man ought to work; indeed, other things being equal, it is a view that I personally wholeheartedly subscribe to. (p. 179)

Moreover, 'the prospect of an able-bodied man being permanently unemployed is . . . a relevant consideration' (p. 179) particularly where a father seemed 'fit and vigorous in appearance and manner' (p. 177). The second *B* v. *B* does not, therefore, involve a rejection of the idea that men should work to support their families or that a young child is best in the day-to-day care of the mother: 'It is not just the ties and incidence of nature. It is a hundred and one practical, common sense reasons' (p. 182).

Perhaps above all it was the *special* circumstance of this case, stressed throughout, which reveal that this father was quite unusual and not like other fathers. He 'lives in a kind of social cocoon . . . some day he is going to emerge from it'. In both *B* v. *B* cases, as in a succession of other custody cases, what is striking is the judicial concern with the necessary arrangements he would have to make to maintain contact with children (and thus not disturb the man/work bond). In *May* v. *May* a father made a similar arrangement with his employer to work restricted hours which would enable him to take the children to school and be available to collect them or be at home when they came home. In *Re C (A), C* v. *C* the father was 'usually at home at the time the infant gets back from school', whilst in *Re W (A Minor)* the judge noted that the father 'had the advantage of working in his own father's business which made it possible for him to arrange more flexible working hours than would be feasible for most men'.[24] In the second *B* v. *B* case the father was 'trying to start a one-parent father's club' (p. 181) (presumably whilst living in his 'kind of social cocoon') but he was also assisted by a 'family circle living locally upon which he can call for assistance' (p. 182). He had available a wider network of support from his own relations 'and if necessary from other relations in the extended family' (as was also the case in *May* v. *May* (p. 329). in *Re W* the father also 'had the advantage of support from a number of members of his family who helped him with the onerous obligation . . .'. Fathers, it would seem, might need a familial support and assistance with the parenting role that single mothers do not. Such assistance might then help them out with the 'onerous obligation' of childcare.

The benign influence of an appropriate paternal masculinity might even be ascribed a temporal dimension. In *May* v. *May*, Ackner L. J. stated that the crucial period when parents might have influence over their children is

> before they go to school and when they come home. Before they go to school there is the important training as to punctuality, tidiness, assistance in the household and the like, and when they come home there is the difficult conflict . . . between the time to be spent on homework, the time to be spent on television, and the time at which the child or children should go to bed. It seems to me that the father was given this crucial period during which he could exercise his influence . . . (p. 330)

This crucial period, interestingly, corresponds with the times of the paternal presence whilst the presumably more routine 'day-to-day' care may be left to the mother (or other family members). Even the quality of the paternal presence has been assessed by judges through reference to ideals of what are, and what are not, desirable masculine role models. In *May* v. *May* the central issue was a conflict of values between the potential fathers who differed in their views on how to bring up the two boys, aged 8 and 6. The competence of the mother and father in caring for the children was beyond question. Both parents 'by all standards have done a marvellous job together in bringing up these little boys' (p. 326). However, the mother and her new partner, a Mr Mitchell ('who had himself been divorced and since that divorce had lived with two other ladies'; p. 326), were adjudged by the court to have

> a much freer and easier approach to life, and his approach to the discipline of the children (the time they should spend working, the time they should spend watching

television and the like) and the emphasis on academic achievement would be significantly different from that of Mr May. (p. 328)

The natural father, in contrast, thought it appropriate 'to stimulate them from the educational point of view and to develop their character' (p. 329). Mr May placed greater emphasis 'on fostering academic achievement. He would also inculcate different values – for example he chose to put some of Russell's birthday money in a building society account; Mrs. May felt he should be allowed to spend it all.' It was noted, continuing the curious tradition of judicial interest in ideals of physical manliness, that both Mr May and Mr Mitchell were, according to the welfare report, 'keen sportsmen and can foster athletic development' in the boy (p. 328). However 'Mrs. May, because of her quiet nature, will need the support of her partner as the boys grow to test parental discipline' (p. 328). Implicitly she would need some man to help her. Extra-judicial input also, it would seem, reproduces familiar ideas of masculinity/authority and work.

There is a clear class dimension to the assessment of paternal masculinities in *May* v. *May*. What we are dealing with here are 'respectable' middle-class values. It is through reference to these that the appropriate paternal masculinity is assessed – the concern is with academic achievement, promoting an environment of discipline and ability to 'foster athletic development' and so forth. Judges have consistently related to such a 'middle-class conception of masculinity in the sense that middle-class male intellectuals have tended to find these qualities themselves' (Naffine, 1990: 116). In *May* v. *May*, by stressing the contrast with the lax, free and easy and 'different' atmosphere of the mother's house, the need for paternal discipline in a case concerning two boys was heightened; 'discipline was . . . very much in the mind of the father, the discipline meaning learning to discipline and organize one's own life' (p. 328–9). The conclusion followed that it was in the best interests of the children to be brought up by the standards of the father as opposed to the mother.

What emerges from these cases, and family law generally, is not just the class-based version of familial masculinity so evident in recent debates surrounding the Child Support Act 1991.[25] It is also a valorization of the masculinity/work relation, albeit with some flexibility around working hours. It is this which negates the value of men's involvement in childcare at the same time as it promotes the ideal of breadwinner masculinity. The courts have, whatever the arguments of the fathers' rights movement to the contrary, shown considerable sympathy with some fathers who wish to care for their children. With flexible working hours and a wider network of support (usually from female relatives) judges have constructed paternal masculinity as a positive influence in the lives of children (so long, that is, as it is heterosexual). The paternal masculinity here invoked remains premised on existing social structures and familial arrangements, on a heterosexual familialism and a clear notion of what are 'appropriate' male/female relations with children. Whether a man works or not is not so much a moral choice as something which is presumed. As a father his natural primary duty is *to employment and not to childcare*. This means that the man who actually gives up employment to care for children is not seen as acting on any 'natural' nurturing instinct but is, rather, acting against this natural breadwinner masculinity.

'FAMILY VALUES' AND FATHER-ABSENCE: THE MODERNIZING OF PATERNAL MASCULINITY:

How might we make sense of the above cases? To recap: we have seen constructions of paternal masculinity in law at two historical moments a century apart. We have moved, in a sense, from a concern with *father-right (Agar-Ellis)* to the construction of a problematic of *father-absence* (the latter all too evident in recent debates around single mothers and crime). The presence of the father continues to be seen as a signifier of stability, 'normality' and the 'healthy' adjustment of children. Educational under-achievement, confused sexual identity, crime, aggressiveness, promiscuity and poor verbal skills have all been laid at the door of the absent father as the genesis of social delinquency (e.g. Anderson and Dawson, 1986a; Dennis and Erdos, 1992). For some government ministers and newspaper editorials in Britain the greatest social problem of the day is this 'scrounging' single mother – the woman who rejects the 'normal love' of the responsible 'good father'.[26]

Yet the question remains to be answered – what is this 'father's normal love'? We can begin to find an answer when we consider the nature of the paternal *presence* in the family. This is clearly not a physical presence (given the primary obligation to paid employment). The familial masculinity which pervades legal discourse, and that which has been attacked by the 'hostility of vociferous minorities to the presence of men in families' (Anderson and Dawson, 1986b: 14), is a presence of a certain kind. It is the presence of paternal heterosexual authority. In short, not *any* father will do. The family man of legal discourse is heterosexual, disciplined, economically responsible and perhaps above all he embodies a particular kind of authority over women and children in the family. I have argued above that a historical transformation took place in family law whereby the father of the 'pre-modern' *paterfamilias* became the 'modern' father of the purportedly 'symmetrical' egalitarian family. To understand the *empowering of the paternal presence* in law we now need to look at this process in more detail.There have been two elements to this modernizing of paternal masculinity.

First, it has been necessary to construct father-presence as desirable and father-absence as problematic. This has been achieved through reference to their presumed utility as appropriate 'role models', utilizing primarily a crude and intellectually flawed variant of sex role theory. The construction of father-absence as problematic in legal discourse has involved the mobilizing of discourses which have established fatherhood as a desirable presence during marriage in the first place. Throughout the twentieth century the belief that families need fathers for the social, psychological and economic well-being of *all* the members of the family unit has historically underscored judicial hostility to autonomous motherhood. It is this belief which has been articulated most clearly through the welfare principle and the juridical assessment of maternal capability – the judging of the 'good' and 'bad' mother (Brophy, 1985; Smart, 1992).

In the 1990s the centrality of fatherhood in the process of defining 'the familial' in law, and in negating the viability of extra-familial households, continues. It is evident in developments around reproductive technology[27] and in the law's continued and frequently convoluted attempts to attach unmarried men to children. The law continues to ascribe the status of 'dysfunctional' to those families in which an appropriate paternal masculinity is either (a) absent (for example in the case of lesbian motherhood) or else is (b) far removed from the hegemonic heterosexual ideal considered to be desirable (as in the case of the male homosexual parent). As we approach the year 2000 – and as more and more jobs created will be what were traditionally termed 'women's jobs' – it is ironic that the economic rationality of capitalism means that being a 'good' father in fact involves a considerable physical absence from families for increasing numbers of men in work (while a government which seeks to promote 'family values' continues to pursue policies which are, in so many ways, detrimental to 'family life').[28]

The second element of the modernizing of paternal masculinity has involved rendering fatherhood 'safe'; or, more accurately, making a division between the law's construction of familial paternal masculinities and other 'dangerous' masculinities. If this father is to be an equal partner in the 'symmetrical family' it is important that he no longer embodies the threat of the undomesticated male. The process of domesticating masculinity (referred to above) involved ridding masculinity of that which has been seen to be the perceived essence of maleness – the 'natural' force of male sexuality, authority and power. Such a dichotomy between ideas of respectable/dangerous masculinities is not just a thing of the past however; it continues to function to divert attention from the problematic nature of masculinity per se and, in particular, to obfuscate the socially destructive nature of masculinities *inside* the family. How could a 'family man' be deceitful, disloyal or even dangerous to those he loves? How could he be violent? How could he be 'secretly' gay?[29] Yet even a cursory glance at the sexual politics of both the late nineteenth and twentieth centuries would reveal that the distance between the myths and the realities of 'family men' continue to be considerable. This ideological split between the familial/safe and dangerous/ extra-familial remains with us today just as important aspects of what might be termed 'pre-modern' paternal masculinities continue to appear in legal discourse. Imaging the family man as dangerous, of course, remains profoundly difficult so long as he appears to be, a priori, the antithesis of that danger.

The historical transformation of fatherhood involved in each of these developments took place in a dialectical relation to the institutional incorporation of 'public' masculinities around the late nineteenth and early twentieth centuries. In particular it was the period 1870–1920 (remembering that *Agar-Ellis* dates from 1883) in which 'men and masculinities came from the heroic "heights" of industrial capitalism in the mid-nineteenth century to become "modern men" of this century' (Hearn, 1992: 96). The period of around 1870–1920, we must remember, witnessed not just the emergence of the welfare principle but also a succession of those legal reforms which brought about the diminution of men's formal legal rights in the family. Fatherhood in law was transformed as

> men in the private domains came to be defined less as fathers and more as husbands. . . . The state was sponsoring the means to be uninvolved in active fathering or active parenting – and instead was assisting the creation of the detached father and the status of husband. (Hearn, 1992: 114)

It is (some) of the contours of this 'detached' modern father which I have sought to explore in this article. The masculinity of the 'family man' continues to be enmeshed with class-based notions of economic and sexual propriety and authority. We have seen how authority and (legitimate/at work) absence, bonded by the breadwinner ideology, remain central to the status of the father in legal discourse. The late nineteenth and early twentieth centuries witnessed the emergence of this 'family man' or 'detached father' in legal discourse. He is marked by all the trappings of a benign and safe/domesticated masculinity – a masculinity pervaded by the dualism of a public/private divide which legitimated his absence from childcare whilst simultaneously maintaining the structural supports whence he derived his economic power.

Concluding Remarks

How does all this relate to matrimonial politics in the 1990s? What does this tell us about 'family values'? I have argued that these changes did not mean that men ceased to be powerful in families simply because they had less formal 'rights' than before. In constructing the modern family the gendered subjectivities of women and men were themselves transformed through the disciplinary mechanisms of the new governmental order in such a way that mobilizing paternal power no longer depended on resorting to juridical 'right'. This reconstruction of fatherhood assigned to the extra-familial domain, values which did not accord with this image of the modern and safe father. It is these signifiers of deviance which in turn render the married father safe and desirable. Masculinities *outside* the familial matrix are thus sexualized: we have the 'promiscuous' homosexual, the 'irresponsible' or 'errant' unmarried father who evades his responsibilities, the sexually suspect male who fails to marry after 'sowing his wild oats' and the 'family man' whose tragic death spoke of his 'secret life'. Each involve complex and sometimes overlapping ideas of promiscuity, respectability, uncleanliness and notions of male sexuality as a threat to children. All are, in a sense, the 'other side of the coin' from the safe, purged, family man as dominant motif in family law. They are indivisible. When a 'family man' is revealed by a prurient press to be homosexual it is saying more than that he may be hypocritical; within the terms of the family man discourse, he is not really a man at all.

Ultimately those who 'fail' to attain the economic power or sexual orientation to enter the comforting world of familial heterosexuality, with all its complex codes of courtship, coupledom and irretrievable breakdown, continue to speak in tongues alien to dominant notions of economic and sexual propriety. What recent debates around single parents, absent fathers and 'back to basics' signify is how this culture is itself fracturing under the weight of the demands and voices of those it excludes. The home may be permeated with the codes of heterosexual familialism but the multivarious subjectivities which have proliferated outside this gender order testify to a diversity which undermines any claims to 'normality' for the globalizing heterosexual subject. In order to challenge the law's foreclosure of alternative subject positions it is necessary to fragment the purported unity of this heterosexual identity and reveal its contingent sociality.

Legal representations of masculinity, male sexuality and fatherhood in family law continue to articulate a male subjectivity which remains premised on the coherent unified, univocal and rational essence of liberal humanism. It is a masculinity which confines emotion and vulnerability to (heterosexual) familial relations, which valorizes calculative rationality and, my focus in this article, a competitive economic individualism which is in the end – as celebrated in longer working hours, material gain and the striving for economic 'success' – destructive of men's relationships with both women, other men and the children they appear to so rarely see.

NOTES

1. Families and the meaning of 'family values' are at present central to political debates in the UK. At the 1992 Conservative Party conference the Secretary of State for Social Security had, in a parody of *The Mikado*, spoken of 'young ladies who get pregnant just to jump the housing list and dads who won't support the ladies they have . . . kissed'. In July 1993 another government minister, John Redwood, suggested that some single women were deliberately becoming pregnant, with no intention of marrying, in the knowledge that they would then be supported by the state. He declared that lone mothers should not receive state benefit until the 'errant father' had been found and forced to return to the family. Redwood was not simply suggesting that fathers should make a financial contribution to the upkeep of their child. He was also requiring that fathers return to the household so that they might offer what he called 'the normal love and support that fathers have offered down the ages'. Further statements from ministers appeared to suggest that the Prime Minister was happy for a high-profile debate about single parents and 'family breakdown' to take place at a time of public spending cuts.
2. John Redwood referred to single parenthood as 'one of the greatest social problems of our day'. The ensuing controversy scapegoated single mothers as 'undeserving' poor whilst, conveniently, placing on the political agenda the possibility of further cuts in welfare benefits. However this 'family values' agenda can be traced back to Margaret Thatcher's speech to the National Children's Home in January 1990 when she had declared: 'Children are in danger of seeing life without the father, not as the exception, but as the rule. This is a new kind of threat to our way of life, the long-term implications of which we cannot grasp.' The argument that 'no father should be able to escape from his responsibilities' laid the ground for what was to become the Child Support Act 1991. By the time of the Conservative Party Conference during the autumn of 1993 this debate over family values was intensified as, under an ill-defined and ultimately misguided notion of 'back to basics', a range of social ills were now laid at the door of the single-parent family and the absent father.

3. On the ways in which the campaign against the Child Support Agency (CSA) is playing out these ideas see Collier (1994). The continued political purchase of such terms as 'feckless' single mothers and 'errant', 'irresponsible' fathers is all too evident in debates surrounding the operation of the Agency.
4. This widespread and continuing opposition to the Child Support Act 1991 and in particular at the inflexible way it has worked, has cut across the political divide. Yet when the agency began work on 1 April 1993 there was a remarkable level of agreement that it was desirable that a state-backed system take the place of the courts, assess the man's income and dock maintenance in the process. This was notwithstanding evidence of the problems which would inevitably arise through such a reduction of emotional relationships to a financial calculation ('No One Listened Over Child Support' *Independent on Sunday*, 7 November 1993). Perhaps not surprisingly, given the high media profile and middle-class constituency of the campaign against the Agency, the political sensitivity of the Child Support Act has not been lost on the government: on the Social Security Committee recommendations, see Eekelaar (1994). Media reporting of the CSA has tended to take the perspective of the individual father: for an alternative view see the Legal Action for Women Handbook *The Child Support Act: Your Rights and How to Defend Them* (available from the King's Cross Women's Centre, 71 Tonbridge Street, London WC1H 9DZ).
5. This idea of the modernizing of masculinity borrows heavily from the argument of Carrigan et al. (1985) and Connell (1987). This stressing of the historical *continuity* of men's power, albeit in different forms, stands as a useful corrective to the current emphasizing of the idea of a rupture or break denoted by the idea of masculine 'crisis'. See also the notion of 'synthetic introspection' in men's responses to feminism (Mars-Jones, 1990: 2).
6. In the North American context note the 'backlash' thesis of Faludi (1992). In Britain the media has paid considerable attention to what is seen to be the impact of modern (frequently North American) feminism (e.g. A. Gill 'Sister Act: Sex, Fear and Feminism' *Sunday Times*, 23 January 1994). In so doing it has highlighted what it sees as divisions within feminism whilst constructing feminism per se as a threat to men and, in particular, a 'natural' male sexuality. It is questionable to what extent the idea of an anti-feminist 'backlash' applies to Britain (see Franklin et al., 1991; also Walby, 1993). Nonetheless the language of 'sex war', and the considerable British media attention given to the 'men's liberationist' polemics of Lyndon (1992), Thomas (1993) and Farrell (1993), do appear to indicate a shift in perceptions of feminism – the echoes of which can be seen in recent constructions of the CSA as an 'attack' on fatherhood and, ultimately, on all men.
7. It is possible that the growth of masculinity studies has been prompted in part by a disillusionment with traditional critical theory (and in particular Marxism) whereby for postmodernist nihilist and post-Marxist alike:

> The experience of being left out, on the sidelines, was the new and threatening reality for many a young male radical, no longer feeling as certain as he had in the 1960s of his own participation in the making of history. (Segal, 1990: 280)

   On the problematic nature of the 'men's studies' genre generally see further Canaan and Griffin (1990) and Moore (1991).
8. Roger Whitcombe, a self-styled 'men's rights activist', captures this idea in his call for men to strike back against a 'growing feminist tidal wave . . . a sustained and remorseless attack on the institution of marriage and the patriarchal family based on it' (*Guardian*, 24 January 1994). The particular object of Whitcombe's anger is what

he calls 'lone mother pseudo-families'. Jim Parton of Families Need Fathers similarly insists that 'however unworthy the natural parent is, he is best and should be involved as much as possible. . . . The absence of a male role model leads to crime' (*Guardian*, 20 September 1993).

9. A confusion around the 'role' of or 'need for' men is never far below the surface of debates around the changing family and has been particularly clear in the scapegoating of single mothers as 'folk devils'. On the UK men's movement as a response to these doubts see P. Baker. 'Who's Afraid of the Big Bad Woman?' (*Guardian*, 24 January 1994). The fear that men are becoming the 'disposable sex' is particularly clear in the work of Farrell (1993). In the week preceding the 'International Man's Day' (Monday 7 February 1994) the British media's appetite for the 'myths of masculinity' appeared limitless (see Marina Warner's 1994 Reith Lectures, 'Myths and Monsters'; A. Karpf, *Guardian*, 19 January 1994). It certainly seems clear that the support groups against the Child Support Agency being set up across the country are feeding into a 'men's rights' consciousness.
10. Recent accusations that they encourage child abduction have thrown into question the charitable status of Families Need Fathers. See Sally Weale 'Paternal Rights and Wrongs' (*Guardian* 7 April 1993).
11. Though not comparable in scale or intensity with debates in North America, ideas of 'Political Correctness' have been very much part of the 'pro-family' government stance. A succession of ministerial statements followed John Redwood's lead (note 1 above) in blaming the numbers of single mothers on such diverse influences as the church, 'politically correct' ideas and a feminist movement which 'has given encouragement to the concept that it is all right to have a child and bring the child up on your own. . .' (Graham Riddick, *Guardian*, 6 July 1993); according to John Perry, Institute of Housing Policy Director, there is in fact no evidence that single parents on waiting lists are allocated better housing more quickly. Attacking a purported 'politically correct' feminist mentality has proved a powerful weapon for those seeking to defend the 'traditional' nuclear family and male sexual prerogative. These ideas have recently come together in Britain around the issues of women's sexual harassment of men (heightened by the UK publication of Michael Crichton's novel *Disclosure*) and 'politically correct' comments on heterosexism within education (e.g. 'Theatre of the Absurd', *Sunday Times*, 23 January 1994). In the United States the Lorena Bobbitt trial proved a similar focus of concerns about shifting sexual attitudes.
12. See note 4, above. The stated aim of the Child Support Agency, set up under the 1991 Act, is preventing maintenance becoming a source of conflict between parents and securing the day-to-day maintenance costs of children. The Child Support Act 1991 itself is marked by confused ideas of fatherhood. Is it primarily an economic bond between father and child? How does enforcing this bond reinforce or disturb familial relations? The hand of the state remains curiously absent in such debates about child maintenance.
13. This tension is illustrated in the pages of the British 'radical men's magazine', *Achilles Heel*, where an editorial critical of the fathers' rights movement (Winter, 1992/3) has prompted accusations that this 'anti-sexist' stance misreads the politics of groups such as Families Need Fathers (J. Allbar 'Supporting Families Need Fathers', *Achilles Heel* 15[Summer] 1993: 5).
14. For example, see French (1992), Lee (1991), Hoyland (1992). It is curious that what are ostensibly books about fatherhood frequently emerge as confessionals about the experience of sonhood – a very different thing.
15. On unmarried fathers' legal position see Smart (1987). The relationship between unmarried fatherhood and ideas of 'errant' and 'irresponsible' masculinities is explored further in Collier, (1995).

16. This article addresses the law relating to married men. The modernization of paternal masculinity which I shall argue has taken place has also involved treating the unmarried father increasingly *as if* he were married. However there remain important differences between the legal position of the married and unmarried father.
17. On changes in constructions of male heterosexuality from the nineteenth to the late twentieth century see Collier (1992) and Moran (1990). A belief in the natural, and inviolable, nature of male sexuality recurs, of course, in a succession of judicial statements from the nineteenth century to the present day.
18. Divorce itself did not become a civil matter till 1857, incorporating principles hitherto used in private acts of Parliament. A similar double standard is entrenched in the history of family law. The 1839 Custody of Infants Act, for example, only gave a discretion to the court to grant to the mother custody of her children. Any decision was to be dependent on her sexual behaviour and adultery would bar her from any custody entitlement. On the development of family law see further Smart (1984).
19. The epistemological implications of the fragmentation of masculinity into 'masculinities' is considered in more detail by Morgan (1992: 45).
20. Strategies aimed, of course, at both women and men; see Walkowitz (1980) and Mort (1987).
21. The reduction of emotional relationships to a financial equation by the CSA, however objectionable in theory, tells us much about how law has constructed the family man. The problem for those contesting the CSA assessments, and the perceived reduction of men to 'cheque-signing machines without rights' (Roger Whitcombe, *Guardian*, 24 January 1994), is that in law 'being' a father frequently does appear to come down to an economic link with children.
22. More detailed discussion can be found in O'Donovan (1993), Smart (1984) and Brophy (1985). In the legal treatment of lesbian mothers in contested custody cases the idea of the 'good' and 'bad' mother has been particularly clear (Rights of Women, 1984).
23. The 'nuclear family', to which this breadwinner masculinity is central, was very much a phenomenon of the post-war years. The social conditions which supported it have now gone; however a central problem – still seldom addressed – is the continued desirability of full-time life-long employment supported by women's unpaid work at home. British men, interestingly continue to work the longest hours in the European Community (Hewitt and Leach, 1993).
24. Facilitating arrangements whereby fathers might care for children clearly depends on the nature of his employment. On this and other factors which might make men more inclined to take on childcare tasks see Segal (1990: 49–59).
25. See further Collier 1994. A number of commentators noted the class-based nature of the campaign against the Child Support Act 1991. James Pirrie of the Solicitor's Family Law Association captures well this aspect of the protest: 'Looking back, the most astounding thing about this fiasco is how middle-class left- and right-wingers created the mythical bogeyman of the absent father who wandered around council estates, siring children without a care in the world'(*Independent on Sunday* 1 July 1993). For many fathers this was their first experience of the welfare benefit system; the comparison with the Campaign for Justice on Divorce is revealing with regard to just who was protesting (Alcock, 1984). Again, the government appears to listen to the complaints of middle-class men in a way it fails to do with other groups in society.
26. Note 1 above. The connection between absent fathers and crime has been repeatedly made by the Home Secretary, Michael Howard (drawing, in particular, on the research of Dennis and Erdos [1992]) and has constituted a significant part of

his 'law and order' criminal justice policy since 1993: at a fringe meeting at the 1993 Party Conference he stated that 'children born in these circumstances learn to get their own way. With few adult male role models around they are all too likely to . . . emulate the most aggressive and most rebellious boys in the neighbourhood.' This is one of a number of misconceptions which have pervaded the public debate about single parents in 1993 (see e.g. 'Separation: Fiction and the Facts', P. Ghazi and L. Gerard, *Observer* 11 July 1993; 'Single Mothers: How Many Are There? What Do They Cost the State? Are the Children Likelier to go Astray?' R. Waterhouse *Independent on Sunday*, 14 November 1993). Of such single mothers who have never married, half are older than 25. Whilst it is true that the number of never-married lone mothers has risen sharply (representing in 1993 6.4 percent of all families compared with 1.2 percent in 1971) changes in family structures have meant that around 20 percent of all households are made up of single parents of which 1.4 percent are headed by men. On the gendering of the underclass debate see further Mann and Roseneil (1994).

27. Particularly clear in the UK in relation to the practice of artificially inseminating 'virgin mothers'. The objection of the 'pro-family' right appeared to be that the practice involved motherhood without men (or, specifically, without intercourse, see e.g. *Guardian*, 12 March 1991; *Daily Mail*, 12 March 1991).
28. What is in effect a moral panic around lone parents has served to distract attention from the real needs of children. Benefit cuts, the withdrawal of public housing and granting of new responsibilities to grandparents to maintain their grandchildren are all being canvassed by the British government at the time of writing. At the same time it is estimated that one in five children in Britain live in poverty (Hewitt and Leach, 1993).
29. Prostitution serves as an interesting example of how the 'family man' discourse is reproduced. This was particularly clear in Britain following the resignation of the Director of Public Prosecutions after he had been charged with kerb-crawling: the media questioned the 'Fatal Attraction of Prostitutes' and the seeming perennial problem of 'Men Who Fall From the Kerb' (*The Times*, 4 October 1991). Implicitly it was asked: how could a family man act in such a way?

CASES CITED

Agar-Ellis v. *Lascelles* (1883) 24 Ch.D 317.
Allington v. *Allington* [1985] FLR 586.
B v. *B* (1985) FLR 166.
B v. *B (Custody of Child)* [1985] FLR 462.
Burns v. *Burn* [1984] a All. E.R. 244.
Re C (A), C v. *C* [1970] 1 All. E.R. 309.
Cooke v. *Head* [1972] 2 All. E.
Re Curtis [1859] 28 L.J 458.
Eves v. *Eves* [1975] 3 All. E.R. 768.
Greer v. *Greer* (1974) 4 Fam. Law 187.
Ives v. *Ives* (1973) 4 Fam. Law 16.
J v. *C* [1970] AC 668.
Re K (Minors) (Wardship: Care and Control) [1979] 1 All. E.R. 647.
Re L (1962) 1 WLR 886.
Langston v. *AUEW* [1974] 1 All. E.R. 980.
M v. *M* (1979) 9 Fam. Law 16.
May v. *May* [1986] FLR 325.

Re Plomley (1882) 47 L.T. 284.
Re W (A Minor) FLR 492, 13 Fam. Law 47.
S (BD) v. *S (DJ) (Infants: Care and Consent)* All. E.R. 1 [1977] 656.
Wachtel v. *Wachtel* [1973] 1 All. E.R. 829.

REFERENCES

Alcock, P. (1984) 'Renumeration or Remarriage? The Matrimonial and Family Proceedings Act 1984', *Journal of Law and Society* 11(3): 357–65.

Anderson, D. and G. Dawson (1986a) 'Popular but Unrepresented: The Curious Case of the Normal Family', in D. Anderson and G. Dawson (eds), *Family Portraits*. London: Social Affairs Unit.

Anderson, D. and G. Dawson (eds) (1986b) *Family Portraits*. London: Social Affairs Unit.

Ariès, P. (1973) *Centuries of Childhood*. Harmondsworth: Penguin.

Atkins, S. and B. Hoggett (1984) *Women in Law*. Oxford: Blackwell.

Bottomley, A. (1993) 'Self and Subjectivities: Languages of Claim in Property', in A. Bottomley and J. Conaghan (eds), *Feminist Theory and Legal Strategy: Journal of Law and Society: Special Issue*. Oxford: Blackwell.

Brittan, A. (1989) *Masculinity and Power*. Oxford: Blackwell.

Bromley, P. and N. Lowe (1987) *Family Law*, 7th edn. London: Butterworth.

Brophy, J. (1985) 'Child Care and the Growth of Power', in J. Brophy and C. Smart (eds), *Women in Law; Explorations in Family, Law and Sexuality*. London: Routledge.

Brophy, J. and C. Smart (eds) (1985) *Women in Law, Explorations in Family Law and Sexuality*. London: Routledge.

Brown, C. (1981) 'Mothers, Fathers and Children: From Private to Public Patriarchy', in L. Sargent (ed.), *Women and Revolution: The Unhappy Marriage of Marxism and Feminism*. London: Pluto.

Butler, J. (1990) *Gender Trouble: Feminism and the Subversion of Identity*. London: Routledge.

Canaan, J. E. and C. Griffin (1990) 'The New Men's Studies: Part of the Problem or Part of the Solution?' in J. Hearn and D. Morgan (eds), *Men, Masculinities and Social Theory*. London: Unwin Hyman.

Carrigan, T., R. Connell and J. Lee (1985) 'Towards a New Sociology of Masculinity' *Theory and Society* 14: 551–604.

Collier, R. (1992) '"The Art of Living the Married Life": Representations of Male Heterosexuality in Law', *Social & Legal Studies* 1: 543–63.

Collier, R. (1994) 'The Campaign Against the Child Support Act 1991: "Errant Fathers" and "Family Men"', *Family Law* July: 384–7.

Collier, R. (1995) *Masculinity, Law and the Family*. London: Routledge.

Cominos, P. (1963) 'Late-Victorian Sexual Respectability and the Social System', *International Review of Social History* 8: 18–48, 216–50.

Connell, R. (1987) *Gender and Power*. Cambridge: Polity Press.

Davidoff, L. and C. Hall (1987) *Family Fortunes*. London: Hutchinson.

Dennis, N. and G. Erdos (1992) *Families Without Fatherhood*. London: Institute of Economic Affairs.

Eekelaar, J. (1994) 'Third Thoughts on Child Support', *Family Law* February: 99–102.

Eekelaar, J., K. Clark, E. Clive and S. Raikes (1977) *Custody After Divorce*. Oxford: Centre for Socio-Legal Studies, Wolfson College.

Faludi, S. (1992) *Backlash: The Undeclared War Against Women*. London: Chatto & Windus.

Farrell, K. W. (1993) *The Myth of Male Power: Why Men Are the Disposable Sex*. New York: Simon & Schuster.

Franklin, S., C. Lury and J. Stacey (eds) (1991) *Off-Centre: Feminism and Cultural Studies*. London: Harper Collins.
French, S. (1992) *Fathers and Sons*. London: Faber.
Hearn, J. (1987) *The Gender of Oppression*. Brighton: Wheatsheaf.
Hearn, J. (1992) *Men in the Public Eye*. London: Routledge.
Hewitt, P. and P. Leach (1993) *Social Justice, Children and Families*. London: Institute for Public Policy Research.
Hey, V. (1984) *Patriarchy and Pub Culture*. London: Tavistock.
Hoyland, D. (ed.) (1992) *Fathers and Sons*. London: Serpents Tree.
Komarovsky, M. (1964) *Blue-Collar Marriage*. New York: Vintage.
Lee, J. (1991) *At My Father's Wedding*. London: Piatkus.
Lewis, C. (1986) *Becoming a Father*. Milton Keynes: Open University Press.
Lewis, C. and M. O'Brien (1987) *Reassessing Fatherhood: New Observations on Fathers and the Modern Family*. London: Sage.
Lowe, N. (1982) 'Fathers and the Law', in L. McKee and M. O'Brien (eds), *The Father Figure*. London: Tavistock.
Lyndon, N. (1992) *No More Sex War*. London: Sinclair Stevenson.
Mangan, J. and J. Walvin (eds) (1987) *Manliness and Morality: Middle-class Masculinity in Britain and America 1800–1940*. Manchester: Manchester University Press.
Mann, K. and S. Roseneil (1994) 'Some Mothers Do 'Ave 'Em': Backlash and the Gender Politics of the Underclass Debate, paper delivered to the 'Good Enough Mothering? Feminist Perspectives on Lone Motherhood' Conference, Gender Analysis and Policy Unit, University of Leeds, May.
Mars-Jones, A. (1990) *Venus Envy*. London: Chatto & Windus.
McKee, L. and M. O'Brien (eds) (1982) *The Father Figure*. London: Tavistock.
Middleton, P. (1992) *The Inward Gaze: Masculinity and Subjectivity in Modern Culture*. London: Routledge.
Moore, S. (1991) 'Trivial Pursuits of Stags at Bay', *Observer*, 9 January.
Moran, L. (1990) 'A Study of the History of Male Sexuality in Law: Non-consummation', *Law and Critique* 1(2): 155–71
Morgan, D. (1992) *Discovering Men*. London: Routledge.
Mort, F. (1987) *Dangerous Sexualities: Medico-Moral Politics in England since 1830*. London: Routledge.
Naffine, N. (1990) *Law and the Sexes: Explorations in Feminist Jurisprudence*. London: Routledge.
O'Donovan, K. (1985) *Sexual Divisions in Law*. London. Weidenfeld & Nicolson.
O'Donovan, K. (1993) *Family Law Matters*. London: Pluto.
Okin, S. M. (1989) *Justice, Gender and the Family*. London: Basic Harper Collins.
Pinchbeck, I. and M. Hewitt (1969) *Children in English Society, Vol. 1: From Tudor times Till the Eighteenth Century*. London: Routledge & Kegan Paul.
Richards, M. (1987) 'Fatherhood, Marriage and Sexuality: Some Speculations on the English Middle-Class Family', in C. Lewis and M. O'Brien (eds) *Reassessing Fatherhood: New Observations on Fathers and the Modern Family*. London: Sage.
Rights of Women (1984) *Lesbian Mothers on Trial: A Report on Lesbian Mothers and Child Custody*. London: Rights of Women.
Roberts, Y. (1992) *Mad About Women*. London: Virago.
Rutherford, J. (1992) *Men's Silences*. London: Routledge.
Segal, L. (1990) *Slow Motion: Changing Masculinities, Changing Men*. London: Virago.
Sevenhuijsen, S. (1986) 'Fatherhood and the Political Theory of Rights: Theoretical Perspectives of Feminism', *International Journal of the Sociology of Law*, 14(3–4): 329.
Sevenhuijsen, S. (1992) 'The Gendered Juridification of Parenthood', *Social & Legal Studies* 1: 71–83.

Simpson, B., J. Vorlyon, P. McArthy and J. Walker (1993) *Post-divorce Fatherhood: Discussion Document*. Family and Community Dispute Research Centre, University of Newcastle Upon Tyne.
Smart, C. (1984) *The Ties That Bind*. London: Routledge.
Smart, C. (1987) 'There Is, of course, a Distinction Dictated by Nature: Law and the Problem of Paternity', in M. Stanworth (ed.), *Reproductive Technologies*. Cambridge: Polity Press.
Smart, C. (1989a) *Feminism and the Power of Law*. London: Routledge.
Smart, C. (1989b) 'Power and the Politics of Child Custody', in C. Smart and S. Sevenhuijsen (eds), *Child Custody and the Politics of Gender*. London: Routledge.
Smart, C. (1991) 'The Legal and Moral Ordering of Child Custody', *Journal of Law and Society* 18(4): 485–500.
Smart C. (ed.) (1992) *Regulating Womanhood: Historical Essays on Marriage, Motherhood and Sexuality*. London: Routledge.
Smart, C. and S. Sevenhuijsen (eds) (1989) *Child Custody and the Politics of Gender*. London: Routledge.
Thomas, D. (1992) *Not Guilty*. London: Weidenfeld & Nicolson.
Tolson, A. (1973) *The Limits of Masculinity*. London: Tavistock.
Toynbee, P. (1994) 'Family Fortunes', *Guardian*, 2 February.
Walby, S. (1993) '"Backlash" in Historical Context', in M. Kennedy, C. Lubelska and V. Walsh (eds), *Making Connections: Women's Studies, Women's Movements, Women's Lives*. London: Taylor & Francis.
Walkowitz, J. (1980) *Prostitution and Victorian Society: Women, Class and the State*. Cambridge: Cambridge University Press.
Weeks, J. (1981) *Sex, Politics and Society: The Regulation of Sexuality Since 1800*. London: Longman.
Wilmott, P. and M. Young (1962) *Family and Kinship in East London*. Harmondsworth: Penguin.

[9]

"Real" Mothers for Abandoned Children

Katherine O'Donovan

Drawing on the laws and practices of three countries—England, France, and Germany—this article examines the constructions of narratives of abandoned children. Although the three countries share the values of the United Nations Convention on the Rights of the Child, having ratified it, their laws and practices with regard to the child's identity rights have little in common. Explaining the different approaches to abandonment, the article argues that these are justified by stories about the birth giver as the "real" mother, stories that vary according to place and culture. This leads to different conceptions of the child's identity and of motherhood, to exclusions and stigma. Focusing on the justifications offered in each country for its laws and practices, the article analyzes discourses of nature (England), juridical constructs (France), and pragmatic concerns for the child's life (Germany). The article concludes that, given the myriad of family forms and of life experiences, it is not surprising to find that countries governed by a shared international convention give very different accounts of the meanings of identity and motherhood.

Introduction

Abandoning a child is a crime in most legal systems. Yet some jurisdictions permit a form of legal abandonment in which the mother remains anonymous, a legal form that goes beyond placement for adoption. Despite current open adoption policies that emphasize the retention of ties with birth families and children's identity rights, a contrary tendency is emerging—the development of legal safeguards for anonymous abandonment, even in jurisdictions with open adoption policies. This is evidently a policy that contradicts openness. Contradictory tendencies have to be supported by differentiating discourses in order to develop. Thus the contradiction between permitting anony-

I am grateful for the generosity of the Nuffield Foundation, which provided financial assistance for visits to France and Germany for this research. Charlotte Augst gave assistance with translations and advice on the part of this article that deals with Germany. The translations from French are my own.

The research on which this paper is based is funded by the Nuffield Trust. Address correspondence to Katherine O'Donovan, Department of Law, Queen Mary, University of London, Mile End Road, London E1 4NS (e-mail: k.odonovan@qmul.ac.uk).

mous abandonment in which a child will not know his or her origins and open adoption, which emphasizes the retention of ties with the biological family, reveals tensions. This article concerns the issues of abandonment and identity rights in three European jurisdictions: England, France, and Germany. Contrasts among the legal policies on child abandonment both within and among these countries illuminates the difficulties of making coherent and consistent policies when faced with human problems for which law has few answers.

A summary of the law on abandonment in the three jurisdictions under investigation can name England as a case of denial, France as creating a legal right of anonymous maternity, and Germany as accepting anonymous abandonment as a pragmatic necessity. In other words, English law does not permit the giving up of parental responsibility by birth parents except through a legal process, such as consent to adoption. Even when a child is taken into the care of the state, parental responsibility is retained by parents and shared with the local authorities (Children Act 1989). France, however, in various forms has protected the right of a woman to give birth anonymously since the Revolution of the 18th century (Dreifuss-Netter 1994). A distinction is made between maternity and motherhood, the latter state being assumed through registration of the mother/child relationship after the child's birth and requiring further elements of proof (Rubellin-Devichi 1991). In Germany the law appears to tolerate "Babyklappen" (baby flaps), which have appeared in twenty-five cities, enabling the placement therein of infants without indication of birth registration or other details of identity of child or parents. What these jurisdictions have in common is that all three have ratified the United Nations Convention on the Rights of the Child, which contains two Articles (see Appendix A) protecting the child's identity (Le Blanc 1995:chap. 4).

We know from research on adopted children that genetic identity is important to some, whether for medical, psychological, or material reasons (Triselotis 1973; Wayne Carp 1998). Interest in genealogy is seen as natural, although the adoption search movement has been critiqued as introducing a new negativity into adoption (Bartholet 1993:37). The failure to understand "experiences of adoption as rooted in conflicting cultural conceptions of the natural and the social aspects of kinship" (Wegar 1997:16) must raise questions about claims that the search for genitors is a universal need. The institutions, policies, and discourses that constitute family, kinship, and adoption all play a part in the construction of "a right to know one's genetic parents." Care has to be taken not to stigmatize those who cannot, or do not wish to, search for their genitors (O'Donovan 1988). Open adoption policies contained in legislation in many jurisdictions show acceptance of blood ties as important, yet this investigation has not found that genetic identity is central in the discourses concerning abandonment under present investigation. The reasons are explored below.

A preliminary question when examining the discourses surrounding abandonment is whether the concern is with children or mothers. In discussions in England and France the focus is on the mother. It is the construction of her actions, combined with theories of motherhood, that provide the basis for the formulation of policies. Given the early stage of development of infants, it might be thought inevitable that the focus is on adult motivations. Yet the discourse in Germany provides a contrast in that there is neither speculation about the mother's state of mind, as in England, nor an emphasis on the rights of autonomy, as in France, but pragmatic talk of child protection, admittedly by adults who have taken on the role of protectors. In all three jurisdictions issues of the child's identity rights remain subordinate. Given these countries' shared participation in the UN Convention on the Rights of the Child, these discourses reveal not only the tensions involved in the constructions of maternity and motherhood and a lack of priority given to children's rights but also the localization of interpretations.

In choosing particular typifications of three jurisdictions, above, I do not intend to suggest that these are ideal types, nor that one is preferable to another. Instead, I argue that, faced with the complexities and the messiness of human lives, and with international obligations and domestic traditions, legislators find that consistency is difficult to achieve. In the making of laws ideals are expressed, but those ideals do not always meet the ambivalences of emotional attitudes concerning maternity and motherhood, nor do those whose imaginings form the basis of policies necessarily have the experiences on which to found them. One can easily find differences in discourses. Some discussions emphasize blood, genetic ties, in which the "real" mother is the one who gives birth. As Yngvesson (1997:37) observes,

> the concept of a "birth" mother or of an "adoptive" mother is oxymoronic in the context of a blood institution that defines a "real" mother as a woman who is connected to her child by blood ties that can neither be severed (a mother who gives her child away is unthinkable, she is a "monster") nor "artificially" created.

The discourse of "real" mother is often found in English popular language of adoption and abandonment and is much less prevalent in the French discourse.[1] It is tempting to conclude that this situation exists because of the construction in French law of both motherhood and fatherhood as juridical concepts,

[1] The German discourse of abandonment is so recent that no general conclusions can yet be drawn.

with consequences in terms of property and succession rights.[2] But this is too neat an explanation; it does not fully explain the ambiguities and ambivalences identified in this research project, although legal constructions and micro-institutional policies play an important part. Large claims about differences in national laws as emblematic of broader cultural differences are not made here. The object is to bring out the contradictory beliefs that surround abandoned children and to illustrate constructions of genetic and social relationships for children brought about by those outside the family of birth.

This article examines the question of how discourses are constructed to justify outcomes that are internally inconsistent and also at odds with laws and policies in other jurisdictions governed by the same international conventions that take differing views of children's rights. It makes sense to account for such discourses as containing taken-for-granted assumptions embedded in culture and history and in terms of social tensions to which the legislator attempts to respond. Throughout the article I will make a distinction between maternity and motherhood, in order to mark the different meanings given to the latter word, which can denote giving birth, genetic relationship, or raising a child. Maternity will be used only to denote birth giving. Separating these situations from one another helps the clarity of the analysis and challenges the taken-for-granted assumption that the three states are inevitably connected. The use of the term "birth giver" is intended as a recognition that maternity involves giving, just as mothering does.

Part One explores the United Nations Convention on the Rights of the Child, which contains two Articles on the protection of the child's identity rights (Appendix A). The legislative history of Articles 7 and 8 of the Convention gives evidence of an initial notion of identity as genetic, but an open definition that gives an illustrative rather than an exhaustive list of aspects leaves space for other interpretations.

Part Two considers how the three jurisdictions examined, England, France, and Germany, formulate and justify their legal responses to maternity and abandonment. The justifications offered by texts in each jurisdiction are different, not only in the reasons offered for policies but also because the texts emanate from non-comparable sources. For example, there is no public or official discussion of abandonment in England, nor is there social research, whereas in France a discourse participated in by legislators, pressure groups, and academics—with two important research studies—is available, despite containing contested views. In Germany the texts available emanate from those who have set

[2] Yngvesson (1997:37) argues that in the American social order, motherhood is culturally interpreted as "fundamentally outside the law," grounded in biology, whereas fatherhood is fundamentally within the law, grounded in property rights.

up the Babyklappen, who appear to have negotiated a silent assent to their activities from the local state authorities.

Part Three explores the discoursive constructions of the women who abandon their infants or who give birth anonymously. As these constructions are used to justify policies and laws explored in Part Two, the purpose of this further exploration is to understand the contradictions in legal policies within jurisdictions and the differing interpretations of international obligations.

This article is the result of my own interpretation and construction, through a series of choices. This is the nature of academic writing, just as it is the nature of lawmaking. A narrative structure is the method of proceeding in both. It is for the writer to support her constructions from research evidence, and for the reader to judge whether these constructions are convincing. I have used a conventional structure for this article; however, in an earlier article on the history of English law on abandonment, I found that an indirect methodology of using fairytales resolved the question of how to convey the emotions and anxieties aroused in people by this subject, of which I remain strongly aware (O'Donovan 2000).

Part One

Children's Identity Rights Protected by the UN Convention on the Rights of the Child

The United Nations Convention on the Rights of the Child (the Child Convention)[3] contains Articles 7 and 8, devoted to identity rights. Article 7 provides for registration of a child after birth, and rights to name, nationality, and "as far as possible, the right to know and be cared for by his parents." To many commentators Article 7 creates rights to know the identities of genetic parents (Fortin 1998; Freeman 1996; Masson & Harrison 1996). But as we shall see, domestic laws do not necessarily carry this through. Article 8 protects "the right of the child to preserve his or her identity, . . . including family relations" (Appendix A). As such, it may cover broader aspects of identity than the preceding Article. The history of these two Articles suggests that they were developed to deal with the problems of children caught up in political struggles and armed conflict, and with refugees. Nevertheless, subsequent history and the interpretations by the United Nations Committee charged with enforcement of the Convention show that the Articles may be read more broadly to cover a variety of aspects of identity.

[3] The drafting of the Convention was completed in 1989. It is the most successful Convention in the history of the United Nations, having been ratified by 191 states. Only two members of the United Nations have failed to ratify it (Lansdown 2000:113).

The legislative history of Article 8 shows that it originated as a response to the "disappearances" in Argentina under the military dictatorship of 1975 and 1983. An estimated 30% of those who disappeared were women, some with children. It is known that 3% of the women were pregnant (Van Bueren 1995:chap. 4). The full account of what happened to the children is missing, but state orphanages, abduction, and illegal adoption all played a part. Some children, born in military detention centers, often by cesarean operations, were immediately removed without having been registered or named (Fisher 1989). The activities of the grandmothers of Plaza de Mayo in drawing attention to the disappearance of their children and grandchildren are well known. Domestic law in Argentina did not provide a remedy in terms of state action to restore children to their families, giving rise to a belief that international law was necessary to create such an obligation.

With the creation of a National Commission on Disappeared People, a genetic bank with facilities to undertake DNA analysis was established. The genetic data of all families with disappeared children are stored there, and a number of children have been returned to their grandparents on this evidence. Article 8 of the Convention was sponsored by Argentina. As explained by the Argentinian proposer:

> On the basis of these painful experiences, the Argentine Delegation tried to introduce a new legal concept so that future national legislatures could provide for this phenomenon and at the same time the children affected and their families would have access to appropriate legal mechanisms for the purpose of reestablishing genuine blood ties. (Cerda 1990:115)

Initial objections by other delegates that Article 8 is superfluous, particularly in light of Article 7, were withdrawn out of respect and sympathy for what has been a national trauma, and the proposers believe that a new form of human right has been created (Cerda 1990). Specific objections from other states referred to existing domestic legislation granting anonymity to donors of gametes and embryos for medically assisted procreation, and reservations to Article 8 were made by a number of states on this point.[4] Commentators argued that Article 8 is weak and that the concept of identity is imprecise (Stewart 1992), although the sponsors intended the concept to be open and the elements of nationality, name, and family relations listed in the Article to be illustrative rather than exhaustive. More troubling, however, is the implied assertion in the Article itself—and the clear statement in the original draft, which refers to a "true and genuine identity" and to "restoring the child to his blood relations," that

[4] The United Kingdom, the Czech Republic, Luxembourg, and Poland have made reservations.

identity is genetic.[5] It is evident that, for a small child, identity may be almost entirely linked to genes, but being abandoned, adopted, or cared for by a particular nurturing other also constitutes identity, even for the smallest of persons.

Nowhere does the Child Convention define "identity," leaving a wide margin for interpretation in domestic law. This has been acknowledged by the sponsor of Article 8, who says

> the nature of the new right created by this article will, in fact, depend on the development of the legal systems of the countries concerned rather than on the specific phenomenon that initially prompted the sponsoring countries to introduce this new idea. (Cerda 1990:117)

It can be argued that Articles 7 and 8 provide protection to collective identities, particularly of those groups subjected to state policies based on the concealment of their origins and culture for purposes of assimilation or elimination.[6] The cases of children "exported" from Britain during the colonial era (Bean & Melville 1989; Eekelaar 1996; Humphries 1994), of Irish children removed to the United States for adoption without their mothers' consents (Milotte 1997), and of native peoples whose children were forced into boarding schools provide ample evidence of the need for protection (Australian Human Rights Commission 1997). Debates in the United States on the Indian Welfare Act provide further examples (Kunesh 1996).[7]

Although identity rights are not mentioned specifically in the European Convention on Human Rights, Article 8, which protects "private and family life" has been interpreted by the European Court of Human Rights as a right to one's own lifestory. In *Gaskin v. UK* (1989) the issue was access to personal files on his childhood by a person who had remained in the care of the state until the age of majority. The right in question was enunciated as "persons in the position of the applicant have a vital interest, protected by the Convention, in receiving the information necessary to know and understand their childhood and early development."

---

5 However, as Cerda (1990) points out, the wording of the proposed Article 8 that referred to "blood ties" was modified during negotiations in the Working Group on the Draft Convention. The original wording of the proposed Article was "The child has an inalienable right to retain his true and genuine personal, legal and family identity. In the event that a child has been fraudulently deprived of some or all of the elements of his identity, the State must give him special protection and assistance with a view to re-establishing his true and genuine identity as soon as possible. In particular, this obligation of the State includes restoring the child to his blood relations to be brought up" (Stewart 1992:223).

6 Article 11 of the Genocide Convention (1948) provides that the forcible transfer of children of a group "with intent to destroy, in whole or in part, a national, ethnic, racial or religious group" is genocide.

7 An emphasis on blood as creating membership of family, clan, or group identity inevitably introduces issues of exclusion. See MacKinnon (1987:chap.4).

The files on a childhood in public care were accepted by a majority of the Court as a substitute for parental memory, normally available to children brought up within the family. Notwithstanding the specificity of the application for access to information, the potential for a wider reading of "lifestory" is evident. Interpretation of Article 8 in this case had two results. The first was the imposition on states of a positive obligation to allow independent evaluation of requests for personal files classified as "confidential." The second was new legislation introduced by the United Kingdom, the Access to Personal Files Act of 1987.[8]

Concern with personal history and genetic identity can call on The Hague Convention on Inter country Adoption of 1993 for support. The Convention regulates the adoption of children across national boundaries and is intended to protect children and birth mothers. Article 30 of this Convention gives protection to a child's rights to information by placing an obligation on the member state authorities to conserve the information on the origins of the child, particularly that which relates to the identity of the parents, as well as details of the medical history of the child and his or her family. Under certain conditions and in accordance with local law, the child is to have access to this information upon becoming an adult. The qualification of this right by reference to local laws, however, diminishes its potential application. During the discussion preceding the drafting of the Hague Convention, some delegates wished to give the child an absolute right of access to the documentation about his or her birth and adoption. However, other delegates opposed this access on grounds that there are dangers to the life of both woman and child in that the former is perceived to have violated norms of honor codes of her community through pregnancy and birth.[9] On the grounds that the right to life is more important than knowledge of identity, if only because the life is necessary for identity, the reference to local laws was included in the Convention (Parra-Aranguren Report 1993). The effect of this inclusion has been to place an obstacle in the way of some children adopted abroad in tracing their genetic heritage.

In ratifying the UN Child Convention, the United Kingdom made a declaration limiting the reference to "parent" to those persons who, by national law, are treated as parents.[10] This limitation was put in place because legal motherhood, through giving birth, does not necessarily coincide with genetic mother-

[8] The Act is also a response to demands for freedom of information. It gives a general right of access to personal information held by authorities, subject to restrictions contained in subordinate regulations.

[9] The Sri Lankan delegate was particularly strong on this point. Interview with Professor William Duncan, the Irish delegate to the Hague Conference, June 1989.

[10] United Nations, *Convention on the Rights of the Child.* C/Rev. 2, para. 33. See Hodgkin & Newell (1998) p. 104.

hood, since egg and embryo donation are permitted under English law. Thus "parent" does not necessarily mean "genetic parent," and some children only have one parent. The Czech Republic, Luxembourg, and Poland have also made reservations on this point.[11] Notwithstanding the above, the United Nations Committee charged with the enforcement of the Convention on the Rights of the Child is critical of these reservations. The United Nations–sponsored *Implementation Handbook for the Convention on the Rights of the Child* states that it is a reasonable assumption that the child's right to know his or her parents includes genetic, birth, and psychological parents (Hodgkin & Newell 1998:105).

Some interpretations of Article 7 give rights not only to know the identities of genetic parents but also to have contact with them. The word "know" is taken to refer not only to knowledge of genetic identities but also to acquaintance through personal contact (Fortin 1998). The laws of State Parties may be ambivalent on knowledge of parents, however defined. On reaching the age of eighteen, adopted children may have rights of access to their original birth certificates.[12] Official help is available to the adopted in attempting to establish the identities of their birth parents, and attempting to contact them, but this is not in accordance with the Convention, as the right only arises on reaching the age of majority. Thus the sealed records debate, unlike that of the United States, has been concluded in favor of openness, but only when childhood is officially over.

The commitment of States Parties to children's identity rights can be tested by considering legal provisions on anonymity of donors of gametes and embryos for use in medically assisted conception. Children conceived by donation do not have rights to know the identities of their genitors in many countries, because it is believed that donors need protection. A possible explanation of this provision is that donors are not legal parents, whereas a woman who gives birth is. However, this explanation is unsatisfactory, as it raises, but does not answer, the issue of the connection between "identity" and genetic origin.

The UN Committee on the Rights of the Child, charged with implementation of the Convention, notes the possible contradiction between "the rights of the child to know his or her origins" and the policies of State Parties "in relation to artificial insemination; namely, in keeping the identity of sperm donors secret"

[11] United Nations, *Convention on the Rights of the Child*. C/Rev. 2, paras. 16, 24, & 29. See Hodgkin & Newell (1998) p. 104. Hodgkin & Newell (1998), writing on the implementation of the Convention for the United Nations, note that France, Norway, and Denmark maintain secrecy of identity of sperm donors. Practice among State Parties with regard to a right to know one's parents varies.

[12] E.g., under English law, access to birth certificates at the age of eighteen, help with contacting birth parents, and an adoption contact register have been established (Adoption Act 1976, ss. 51 & 51A).

(Hodgkin & Newell 1998:107). France, Norway, Denmark, the Czech Republic, Luxembourg, Poland, and the United Kingdom,[13] among others, maintain donor anonymity. Reasons given focus on the child's best interests and donor anxiety. Rights to know genetic parentage are said to conflict with best interests rights guaranteed by Article 3 of the Convention, but this argument seems more appropriate to the young child. The Convention applies to children under eighteen, and adolescent best interests may require an openness about genetics. Utilitarian points are made about deterrence of donors, the happiness of the future child, and the happiness of childless couples. In France, importance is attached to medical confidentiality in assisted conception (Code Civil, Art. 311–20; Code de la sante publique, Art. L.151).

Protecting identity rights is a simple term for a complex issue requiring clarification of the distinction between identifying and non-identifying information on genitors. Of the three jurisdictions under investigation, not one treats the requirements of the UN Child Convention as absolute in terms of safeguarding information about the genetic origins of the child. Whether the route out of absolutism is a reservation to the Convention, as in England; or a compromise of rights, as in France; or a limiting interpretation of the obligation, as in Germany, it seems that an understanding of identity is not confined to genetic origins. The tensions between conflicting cultural conceptions of "the natural" and "the social" remain.

Part Two

England: A Case of Denial

In England, newspaper reports on abandoned babies, usually neonates, emphasize the police search for the birth giver: She "may be in need of medical attention . . . and we would ask her to come forward as soon as possible" (*The Guardian*, Dec. 27, 1996, p. 6). The language concerns the mother who may have given birth alone. "Our prime concern is her care and welfare. She may need medical attention, and she will be dealt with with the utmost consideration. Our aim is to reunite her with her child" (Jones 1998:5). It is noteworthy that in the course of my research and interviews with social workers I have found no references in England to the identity rights of the child.[14] The picture

[13] See Hodgkin & Newell (1998:105–6). Judicial rhetoric in England and Wales upholds a child's right to know its genetic origins (*Re H (a minor) (blood tests)* 1996; *Re G (parentage) (blood sample)* 1997).

[14] Research on abandonment is, by its nature, difficult. Research on the issue does not exist, and no reliable figures for abandonment are available. I have done a survey of newspaper reports for 1999 and 2000, but these cannot be relied upon as comprehensive. I have also interviewed social workers and have interviewed adults who were abandoned

presented is of the desperate circumstances of the birth giver rather than her choice. There are assumptions that woman and child are one, and that reunion is best for both. The friendly police words of encouragement to come forward contain assumptions about maternity and motherhood that appear to be shared by a large majority of the population of England. Yet annual figures show that a small group of women who have given birth remain hidden and silent after abandoning a neonate. In 1997, 65 neonates were abandoned, and 52 women were traced by the police (Home Office 1996:5.11; Hall 1998:5). Caution in the interpretation of the official statistics is required here. Although abandonment is against the law, the police view of the abandonment of infants is that this is a welfare rather than a criminal law issue. Thus when a newborn was discovered behind a kebab shop, the police stated, "Our main concern is for the mother. There is nothing for her to be worried about as far as the police are concerned" (*The Guardian*, June 29, 2001, p. 6). Since the official figures only deal with cautions and prosecutions, if no action has been taken the case will not be recorded.

In 1861 it became a crime in England to abandon an infant under two years when, as the text of the law specifies, the life of the child is endangered or there is permanent injury to the health of the child (Offences Against the Person Act of 1861, s. 27). This Act was not new law in that it codified case law. At common law, if the child survived abandonment, conviction of the birth giver did not necessarily follow. In *R v. Renshaw* (1847) a woman left her child of ten days at the bottom of a ditch along which ran a path. The judge, Baron Parke, said that

> there were no marks of violence on the child, and it does not appear, in the result, that the child actually experienced any inconvenience, as it was providentially found soon after it was exposed; and therefore, although it is said in some of the books that an exposure to the inclemency of the weather may amount to an assault, yet if that be so at all, it can only be when the person suffers a hurt or injury of some kind or other from the exposure. (p. 28)

Other reported cases from the mid-19th century also emphasize the baby's endangerment to life or health (*R v. March* [1844]; *R v. Cooper* [1849]; *R v. Hogan* [1851]), and there was reluctance to convict without evidence of physical injury. When

as babies. The only official figures I have come from the Home Office. These have to be treated with caution, as all abandonments are not recorded in the same way, particularly when the infant is dead, or no prosecution results. What the newspaper reports suggest is that the police are brought in immediately when a child is found. Public requests by the police for the birth giver to come forward generally follow the formula of "she may be in need of medical attention." Dr. Lorraine Sherr, a clinical psychologist, reported to the British Psychological Society on her work on abandonment over ten years. Her findings are that 16% of those abandoned between 1989 and 1999 were left to die, and that two-thirds of birth givers were not located (*The Independent*, Sept. 8, 2000, p.7).

the 1861 legislation was presented to Parliament, the Solicitor-General stated that it was a measure to codify case law, and very little debate took place (Hansard 1860:vol. 159, para. 270). Subsequent cases show that the insistence on physical injury continued (*R v. Falkingham* [1870]), and this reflects the requirement of danger to life or physical injury contained in the Offences Against the Person Act of 1861.

Since the introduction of a more general act on child cruelty in 1933, most prosecutions for abandonment have taken place under that legislation, which covers all minor children (Children and Young Persons Act of 1933, s.1). When neonates are abandoned, sympathy for the birth giver continues. According to the Department of Health, "Women who have abandoned their children are given counselling before their children are returned to them, for as long as deemed necessary" (Cox 1998:5). Instead of a criminal charge, the public effort is to persuade the woman to learn to mother. A typical comment is the following from a clinical psychologist: "There needs to be an assessment to unearth what led her to do this, because she won't be feeling very good about herself" (Cox 1998:5).

Amongst the assumptions about a woman who abandons a neonate is that she needs social assistance. She is depicted as a victim herself, who can be helped to come to terms with motherhood. On one hand she is to become a mother, but on the other she is already a mother by virtue of giving birth. An idyllic view of biological mother love underpins English attitudes, and the recent delivery of a baby provides an excuse for the birth giver's failure to come to terms with motherhood, particularly since medicalized terms are used in explanation. Comparisons with the history of leniency toward infanticide in English law show a similar pattern (O'Donovan 1984; Wilczynski 1997; Ward 1999). However, when a mother abandons an older child, her violation of "maternal emotion" outrages public opinion. Abandoning an older child is cruelty in terms of law and public attitudes. Thus a woman who left her child, aged three, in the middle of a wood, was sentenced to five years' imprisonment. The Crown court judge told her: "You went against the basis of all maternal emotion and abandoned your child to its fate" (*The Guardian*, May 22, 1999. p. 5).

This analysis is not intended to underplay the fear a young child may experience on being separated from security and familiarity, nor the dangers to a neonate left abandoned. Of interest is the notion of maternal emotion, and the assumption that a particular form of love follows from giving birth, that is, that the mother and child automatically bond and should be together. Biology and love are linked, although it is believed that hormonal disturbances may temporarily disrupt this connection. A discourse of "the natural" enters in, containing assumptions about mother love. The "natural" has various aspects: blood and genes, but also a construction of maternal behavior. It is an "unnatural" or a sick woman who abandons her child. The idea that this action might be a choice in taking control of one's life, or an exercise of reproductive autonomy, does not enter the discourse, perhaps because it is too threatening.[15] Yet issues of "intention" have been tolerated in legal and popular discussions elsewhere; for example, discussions of new reproductive technologies, or surrogacy. So it seems that when the intentions from the outset of conception are to help other adults, the discourse of "real" mother does not arise. This absence suggests that the discourse is concerned not only with blood but also with a construction of how a "natural" woman behaves on giving birth.

There is something slightly ominous in the English discourse surrounding women who abandon neonates. In people's minds, the assumptions about these women's mental states are linked to the states of mind of women who commit infanticide. A sane woman will not abandon her child. Such an act is taken by a woman suffering post-partum depression; therefore, counseling and treatment, for as long as it takes, will reconcile the woman to her fate as mother. This treatment does seem to succeed in that most of the women who abandon their babies do come forward on police appeals. As noted above, 52 out of 65 cases of abandonment in 1997 resulted in temporary or permanent reunion.

Maternity and motherhood are conflated in English law and public opinion. Law follows from biology, and only biology is real. In discussions of adoption, identity, and the establishment of contact on reaching adulthood, popular parlance refers to the birth giver as the "real" mother. It is not clear what this notion of "real" comports. It does not refer to material expectation, nor to existing ties, both of which can be expected from adoptive parents. It can only be understood in the context of cultural interpretations that blood makes relationships real. The English discourse and cultural assumptions appear to bear out this idea more closely than does the French or the American research on adoptive kinship (Bartholet 1993; Modell 1994; Yngvesson 1997).

English law contains internal inconsistencies on people's access to identifying information about their genetic parents. As noted earlier, despite existing rights of access to information about genetic parentage given to the adopted, children conceived through donated gametes have no such rights. Giving birth makes a woman a mother in English law, under both common law and statute, notwithstanding that the child may have no genetic connection with her. Regardless of intention or blood,

[15] This view seems also to be the case for the United States. In a critique of adoption policies, Barthloet (1993:xxi) says "For women, adoption can be seen as an important part of reproductive autonomy;" and on p. 45 she says, "Adoption can give birth parents a chance to gain control over their lives."

parturition makes motherhood. Fatherhood is accepted as a legal fiction when donated sperm helps a man's wife or partner to conceive. Nevertheless, there is a legal obligation, sanctioned by criminal law, on the birth giver and on those who assist her, to enter her name as mother on the birth certificate. It is not sufficient to record that an infant has been born on a particular date in a particular place. Yet there is no absolute requirement that the names on the birth certificate be those of the genitors. Although a new birth certificate may be issued on adoption or in the case of surrogacy on court parental order, the original certificate remains on record as a historic document. To give up her child officially, the birth giver must consent, and a court order must be obtained (Adoption Act of 1976; Human Fertilization and Embryology Act of 1990, ss. 27–30).

A woman in England who does not wish to be a mother may choose abortion, provided she satisfies the requirements of the Abortion Act of 1976. What she cannot do is to give birth and refuse legal motherhood. She cannot refuse to be named on the birth certificate, nor can she "legally" abandon her child. Abortion is available upon medical certification during the first twenty-four weeks of pregnancy, and in some cases up to term. If the woman's opportunity to abort is missed or rejected, however, giving birth makes her a "real" mother, whose identity will be secret only if she abandons her child illegally.

I found no research on abandonment in English law. The history of abandonment in Europe has been documented (Boswell 1988; Gavitt 1990), and there is an English study dealing with one institution, a foundling hospital (McClure 1981). A small beginning has been made (O'Donovan 2000). The evidence is that abandonment is not a matter of public or social concern and that the current legal position is considered satisfactory. This view reflects the popular belief that blood ties and biological mother love are the natural, and best, situations for child rearing. In this belief, other family forms are considered second best and are to be avoided. Identity and blood are synonomous.

France: Legal Protection of Anonymous Birthing

Law in France, as in both Italy and Luxembourg,[16] offers women the choice to give birth anonymously. Women who avail themselves of this choice do not become legal mothers. They may enter a hospital when delivery of their baby is imminent, and may opt for anonymity. In French law this is a right that is pro-

[16] Luxembourg entered a declaration and reservation to the UN Child Convention in relation to Article 7, as follows: "The government of Luxembourg believes that Article 7 of the Convention presents no obstacle to the legal process in respect of anonymous births, which is deemed to be in the interest of the child, as provided under Article 3 of the Convention" (Hodgkin & Newell 1998, p. 104).

tected by Article 341-1 of France's Civil code, whereby, "at the time of her delivery a mother may demand that the secret of her admission and of her identity be preserved." This right, added to the Civil Code in 1993, has existed in one form or another since 1793 when, under The National Convention of the French Revolution, secret pregnancy and birth were protected by law (Bonnet, 1995:20). It has given rise to a lively debate in France, which recently culminated in a reform bill preserving the woman's right, while simultaneously recognizing that the child born to an anonymous mother may wish to know his or her own genetic heritage. An explanation of this seeming paradox follows.

The right to give birth anonymously in France is known as "accouchement sous X," because the birth giver will be recorded on the birth certificate as X. Article 341 of the Civil Code, introduced in 1993, precludes a child born to X from establishing any legal tie to the mother, even if her identity should be discovered. This Article is important in a civil law system where automatic rights of succession arise from legal ties to parents. Therefore, the action to establish a legal bond with a mother (action en recherche de maternite) cannot be instituted by a child born to X since he or she is legally barred, but the action of researching paternity remains open (Code Civil, Article 340).

Official estimates are that approximately 600 women a year in France give birth anonymously (Dekeuwer-Defossez 1999). A recent study shows a decrease in the numbers of women who do so, from about 780 in 1991 to about 560 in 1999 (Lefaucheur 2000). The reasons for denying children of X the action to establish the identity of the woman who gave birth to them lie in French history and in legal conceptions of parent/child relationships, although the latter aspect is changing (O'Donovan 2000).

France's legal reasoning contains a step between birthing and mothering. The traditional notion of family membership for those born outside marriage was that parental choice rather than birth was determinative. Thus men not married to the woman who gave birth to their genetic child could refuse to legally recognize the child, until recently (Rubellin-Devichi 1999). Although this tradition has changed with the increased emphasis on children's rights, there remain cases where the child's father is known but no affiliation takes place because of legal difficulties (Dekeuwer-Defossez 1999:43–44). Furthermore, a distinction has always been made between a child who is illegitimate and a child born from an adulterous relationship, with the latter excluded from the family of the adulterer. Perhaps this notion of admittance to the family through parental choice can be seen most clearly in the case of a single woman who gives birth. Her child, notwithstanding his or her acceptance through registration at birth, cannot establish filiation based on this alone; further proof of the baby's acceptance by the mother into her family is necessary, although this proof is subject to possible reform (Dekeuwer-Defossez 1999).

The establishment of legal parenthood in France is subject to a series of prior concepts, which include elements of choice for genitors. My interviews in 1999 with young French women studying for post-graduate diplomas in family law show that they perceive anonymity as a choice open to all women giving birth in France. Notwithstanding a heated public debate on the subject, particularly based on the rights of the child, this choice persists in the law. In French discourse on *accouchement sous X,* the notion of "real" mother, prevalent in cultures that link biology and parenthood, is not evident.[17] Discursive emphasis is placed on the rights, autonomy, and privacy of the woman. However, the concept of autonomy is subject to differing interpretations of what constitutes autonomous action, as will be explored in Part Three.

To the outsider not familiar with a legal culture of patrimonial succession rights, it might seem that there is a clear distinction between a right to know one's genetic origins and a right of membership in a particular family. Evidence indicates that the great majority of children of X are fully adopted very quickly after birth and acquire patrimonial rights in their adoptive families.[18] The issues of filiation and knowledge have been entangled in the French debate because an established, as opposed to an empty, filiation has significance for rights under family law.

The debate that took place in France in 1993 on the implementation of the UN Child Convention largely resulted in a rewriting of family law to recognize the rights of the child (Rubellin-Devichi 1999:3739). Subsequently, anonymous birthing was the subject of a passionate argument for more than eight years. In the 1993 legislative debate members divided into two groups. There were those who, in the interests of the child's identity rights, advocated the abolition of the right to give birth anonymously, at that time contained in the Family Code and arising from an earlier tradition (Code de l'action sociale et des familles, Art. L. 222-6). Opposed were those in favor of anonymous birthing as a woman's right. Their answer to those who cited obligations under the UN Child Convention was to point to the words "as far as possible" qualifying the Convention's protection of a child's rights to know his or her parents under Article 7. The

---

[17] It is worth noting that in France, in accordance with notions of *egalite,* there is much less emphasis on mirroring the biological family than there is in the United Kingdom. For instance, once parents are accepted as candidates to adopt, their names go on a waiting list and children are allocated on a basis of the list. "Matching" child to parents is not a major concern.

[18] French law makes a distinction between *adoption simple* and *adoption pleniere.* Under adoption simple, links are retained to the family of birth, and no patrimonial rights are acquired in the adoptive family. By contrast, adoption pleniere is full adoption, with absolute rights of financial succession on death of an adoptive parent.

outcome of the debate was the strengthening of the woman's right to give birth anonymously by the insertion of a new article in the Civil Code prohibiting the establishment of a baby's filiation tie to the birth giver.

Later debates in France led to the commissioning of two reports, and a new law was passed in January 2002. Participants in these debates include those born from X mothers who have lobbied for change, as well as legislators, academics, and commentators of various kinds. The issue has divided feminists. Two empirical studies provide information. The first was undertaken between 1986 and 1989 (Bonnet 1991). The resulting book, *Gesture of Love,* argues that the right to give birth anonymously is a fundamental freedom. This argument cites the woman's rights to privacy and a right to renounce forever the motherhood of a particular child as autonomous choices. Pragmatic arguments about infanticide, exposure of infants, and patriarchal attitudes in some communities that regard birth outside marriage as a female crime against family honor were also advanced in justification (Bonnet 1995; Trillat 1994). The second study, by Nadine Lefaucheur, was published in 2000.

The ideal of a right to give birth anonymously was put into question by two reports. Thery (1998), a feminist sociologist, challenges the absolute right of a woman to hide her maternity as negating the objective fact of giving birth and as contrary to children's rights of knowledge of their origins. Part of Thery's argument turns on the reforms of 1993, giving rights to a child born outside marriage to establish a legal tie to the father. Anonymous maternity is seen as undoing this reform (Thery 1998:9). To Thery, the child born to X suffers an "empty filiation" through having no tie to genitors. This fact, and the secret organized by law in allowing anonymity, are a source of acute suffering to children born thus. "Perhaps it is worse to know that the effacement of one's origins was organised by society, than to be faced with the silence of the unknown, as with lost children" (1998:179).

A compromise is offered by the Dekeuwer-Defossez (1999) report, which considers anonymous birthing in the context of wider issues of parentage. It proposes that existing distinctions in the child's filiation rights, according to the sex of the parent, be eliminated, where possible (1999:36). However, it also proposes to retain the woman's right to give birth anonymously, and merely to remove the bar to establishing a legal tie, should the identity of the birth giver become known, thus placing genitors in a position of equality in the establishment of parenthood, regardless of sex.

It is clear that an understanding of French law in relation to filiation depends on knowledge of concepts and history. Traditions of family law in France have been of collective family rights, particularly in relation to succession, with admittance to the family for the most part dependent on the will of the patriarch. France's law of parentage has long been based on voluntary parental acceptance and has hesitated to allow children free access in establishing ties to birth parents. Court actions for the establishment of parentage "have been surrounded by a luxury of precautions and restrictions which have given way little by little" (Dekeuwer-Defossez 1999:36). Presently, when a single woman gives birth and registers the child in her name, this action is insufficient to establish filiation without evidence of her acceptance of the child (Code Civil, Art. 57). It is proposed that the registration alone should suffice (Dekeuwer-Defossez 1999:58–59, 67).

A patriarchal conception of the family is beginning to change, despite suspicions on the part of the family of intrusions by non-marital children over its threshold. The proposals contained in this report attempt a compromise between the genitors' choice to accept a non-marital child and the child's rights to belong to the family of birth.

Although the reports by Thery and Dekeuwer-Defossez set the discussion of anonymous birthing in the wider context of family and parentage, the law passed in January 2002 deals with one issue only. The right of a woman to give birth anonymously was retained, but attempts were made to reconcile this right with the UN Convention on the Rights of the Child. The new law is based on a clarification of different concepts of anonymity. Since 1996, French law has permitted that either non-identifying information about his or her origins be given to a child of eighteen about parental characteristics, culture, and social and family situation, or that the birth giver's identity be made known, when she has agreed (Law of 5 July 1996). The intention behind the new law is to build on this access to information through the creation of a national council for access to personal origins.

The right of *accouchement sous X* remains inscribed in France's Civil Code, despite the new legislation; however, the woman will be invited to identify herself under secret seal in such a way as to enable the child on reaching adulthood to know his or her own origins. When presenting this reform the Minister for Family and Children explained as follows:

> In the matter of divulging the secret of identity, for this to happen there must be a meeting of wills, that of the child looking for the identity of the birth mother, and that of the birth mother, sought by the council charged with the delicate mission of seeking her express consent to this divulging of the secret. This will be the most delicate aspect of the mission of the council. It must act with respect for the privacy of the birth mother, with discretion, in the hope of accompanying both parties in finding an agreement by mediation. (Royal 2000:4)

For the present, the French authorities are open in their acknowledgment that the identity rights deriving from the UN Child Convention are not fully observed. They explain this by their reliance on the wording of the text itself and by the notion of a balancing of rights of the mother with those of the child. It is clear, however, that genetic arguments are gaining force.

The identity articles contained in the UN Child Convention placed alongside France's right of women to give birth anonymously have caused much soul-searching in France. The new law of 2002 has attempted a compromise. The right of access to genetic origins has not become an absolute right. It has been presented to the public in terms of evolution. As explained by the Minister for Family and Children, two new social rules are developing. On one hand maternal delivery is not solely a private event, and society is right to ask women to reveal their personal identities for the sake of their children. On the other hand, "this evolution takes into account the point of view of women hoping to give birth as X, who have generally experienced dramatic situations. There will not be 'police' control: the woman is only 'invited' to consign her identity under secret seal at the time of birth" (Royal 2000:4). Thus the new French law is merely educative, rather than requiring a compulsory revelation of the birth giver's identity. In terms of a child's right to know the identity of his or her birth mother, there is very little change.

Germany: Acceptance of Anonymous Abandonment as a Lesser Evil

Baby flaps (Babyklappen) are a recent innovation in Germany. Hamburg, the city that inaugurated this idea in December 1999, has two. They provide safe places in which a woman who has given birth can leave an infant, with the knowledge that the baby will be taken care of. One "flap" is similar to a very large mailbox, behind which is a heated cot. As soon as a baby is left, a bell rings alerting a security company, which then telephones the Babyklappen worker on duty in another part of the building that also houses a day nursery. The flap is not easily visible from the pavement, and there is some privacy for the woman who wishes to deposit a baby. Thus anonymous abandonment is possible and seems to be accepted by the appropriate authorities. According to my interviews in July 2001 in Hamburg with the Findelbaby group—which inaugurated the baby flaps—and with local state authorities, no legal obstacle to this anonymous giving up of children exists, although new legislation is proposed to clarify this practice and to introduce the French system of anonymous birthing.

The Findelbaby project started in Hamburg after four cases of infanticide by unknown persons. It has now spread to 25 German cities, and a flap was opened in Austria in February 2001.

The group negotiated with the public prosecutor and with the courts and received agreement for the project to proceed, as confirmed by local legal authorities (interview with Youth Dept., July 2001).

A press release (Feb. 15, 2001) issued by the Hamburg Findelbaby group states that the woman's right to dignity, autonomy, and privacy (Personlichskeit, under the German Constitution) is balanced against the child's right to roots and heritage (Abstammung). One right competes with another. Since interpretations of rights in German law on the issue of abortion give priority to the woman over the fetus, it follows that this priority will also exist in the case of Babyklappen. A further argument is that the child's life can only be protected with the consent of the mother, who may otherwise commit infanticide or abort. This view thus concerns the morality of "pragmatic reasoning," as identity rights only make sense if the child is born and survives.

In terms of the UN Child Convention, the Findelbaby project is justified by reference to the words "as far as possible" in Article 7, modifying the child's right to know his or her parents. The Convention is said not to be directly applicable in Germany, and in any case, it gives priority to the right to life under Article 6. However, it is legally arguable that Articles 2 and 1 of the German Constitution, which contain the *allgemeines Personlichkeitsrecht,* do protect identity rights, in addition to the UN Child Convention. Article 1 protects personal life, including aspects such as identity and privacy, against intrusion. "Personal individuality" depends on one's knowing one's "constituting factors," including heritage, background, and origin (*Abstammung*). The German Constitutional Court has given three decisions on the child's right to know his or her origins, but the interpretation of the right has been restrictive. In a case concerning paternity and the identification of the legal father through the courts, it was held that the obligation on the state is to disclose information it has, and not to interfere with the child's search (BVerfG FamRZ, 1989:255). In effect, this case restricts the child's rights in that it merely requires the opening of information that is available on the child's origins. There is no obligation for the government to be active in giving assistance to the child, and the recording of information at birth has not been pronounced upon.

German law contains requirements for the registration of births in the *Personenstandsgesetz.* The birth of a child must be registered within a week. The primary duty falls first on the father, if he has parental responsibility, and then on those in attendance at the birth: midwife, doctor, or any other birth attendant, and finally on the woman who gave birth (para. 16). In the case of birth in a public institution, there is an obligation by that institution also (para. 18); when a baby is found, there is a duty to report this fact to the police within a day (para. 25).

The Penal Code (*Strafgesetzbuch*) criminalizes the failure to support (para. 170) and the failure to care for one's child (para. 171). Abandonment (*Aussetzung*) is a serious crime for parents whereby someone helpless is exposed to imminent danger (para. 221). However, under the Babyklappen system, according to the Findelbaby group, this sanction does not apply because the infant is handed over to the care of an organization, and not left exposed.

As the German developments are recent, academic commentary is sparse, and no cases have been tested in the courts. Barlein and Rixen argue that the only possibility of criminal liability for the mother is the failure to register a birth, and that the only obligation on a hospital is to report a birth without identifying the mother (2001:54–56). Neuheuser argues that the criminal prosecutor is obliged to investigate whether a crime has been committed, and that the woman may have violated the provisions on birth registration and on duty of child support (2001: 175–78).

At present, it seems that the Babyklappen system is tolerated in Germany and that the proponents' negotiations with the legal authorities have not led to challenges. The child's identity rights are not central to discussion, and it seems to be accepted that informing the authorities that a child has been born is sufficient to satisfy the requirements of the law, without identifying information on the genitors or birth giver. Yet, if the provisions of the UN Child Convention are to be read in this manner then the notion of identity does not necessarily refer to genetic identity. This raises the question of what else the word "identity" can refer to in relation to a baby. Establishing a personal identity is the work of childhood, even perhaps of a lifetime. Therefore, it seems that the German authorities read "identity" as encompassing the circumstances of birth, the giving of a name, nationality, and being a Findelbaby, an X child, a foundling, or an *enfant trouve,* as in medieval times.

In Germany the UN Convention is said to be respected on one hand because of adopted children's access to the register of original birth certificates. On the other hand, the state does not have an active role in ensuring that the genetic identities of all children born in the jurisdiction are established. Children born through donated sperm, the only form of medically assisted procreation permitted, have, in theory, a right to know their genetic origins. However, no system has been organized to give access to information about donors. And abandonment becomes a crime only when the child is in danger in terms of survival, but not when the abandonment is anonymous. Thus, although the principle of access to information has been recognized, the means for putting this access into effect does not exist, and it seems that the federal and local states have no positive duty to make it so.

Issues of the child's identity rights are dealt with by leaving a letter for the woman in the heated cot, behind the flap into which the baby is placed. In this letter she is advised that she can change her mind about abandoning her baby during the next eight weeks, that she can get help with no questions asked, and that she can leave a letter for her child to be opened at the age of 18.

Part Three

Discursive Constructions of "Real" Mothers and Other Mothers

Constructing the birth giver's actions in England and France provides the justification for policies in those countries, either by depicting her as ill, or by bestowing a particular right on her. Yet this view gives rise to tensions because of the resonances of mothers as persons who *give* to their children. In order to retain motherhood as a state of continuous giving, the reasons mothers give away their children have to be explained away. Barbara Yngvesson's work illuminates the negotiations of identity that birth mothers and children go through when open adoption is practiced, and she has chosen a research methodology that brings out people's contradictions, subjectivities, disjunctions, and silences (Yngvesson 1997). Her work, and that of other American researchers, emphasizes the tension between cultural conceptions of the natural and the social (Modell 1994; Wegar 1997). This tension may offer an explanation for English law, but may have only a small role in accounting for policies in France and Germany.

Popular discourse and legal policies concerning motherhood in England stem from a shared idealization of motherhood and the family based on biology, in the face of much evidence to the contrary of family breakdown and conflict. Explanations of many kinds may be offered for this idealization, including the late advent of the legal institution of adoption in 1926, and later creations of statutes. Policies mimicking the "natural family" when matching children to parents to conceal adoption, the idea "that adoption not only mirrors biology but also upholds a cultural interpretation of biological, or genealogical kinship" (Modell 1994:3), even the adoptee's search movement,[19] all play a part. Freedom of testacy in England means that children have no automatic claim on family assets, in contrast to France and Germany. A juridical notion of parenthood is still under development there

[19] The evidence in England and Wales is that the majority of adoptees do not search. Of those who obtain a copy of their original birth certificates, the majority do not contact the birth parents. If searching takes place in the context of openness of adoption laws and culture, there should be less pain for all involved.

and is unlikely to take the same shape as in the civil codes of France and Germany

Constructions of maternity, biology, identity, and love are influenced by many factors, including laws and institutional policies. The constructions and meanings are chosen, at least to a degree. But women who successfully give up a child through abandonment rarely explain their reasons; they remain silent as they act in secret, and they seek anonymity. It is others who construct their own identities, and it is perhaps these others who call on their own conceptions of what they believe to be natural, both in the genetic sense and in how a "natural" woman behaves on giving birth. Yet people may also construct such women as autonomous agents who make choices in taking control of their lives, as in France. It might seem that meanings attached to narratives are predetermined by the discourses available. Yet England, France, and Germany, having accepted the obligations contained in the UN Convention on the Rights of the Child, offer contrasting emphases in the discourses concerning the abandonment of infants.

Scholars who study childhood agree on its constructed nature throughout history (Aries 1973; De Mause 1976). Being a child does not have and has not had the same meaning according to time and space (Jenks 1996; Prout & James 1990). The same appears to be true of maternity and motherhood. Whereas some cultures assume that biology makes motherhood, others see parenthood as a social, biological, and legal construct. The exclusion of "illegitimate" and "adulterine" children from family membership in the past looks discriminatory today, and it is unlawful under international treaty obligations.

The distinction in popular speech between the "real" mother, generally the woman who gave birth, and the adoptive, or "pretend," mother is based on the assumption that biology creates motherhood. In this age of egg, sperm, and embryo donation such assumptions may have to be revised. But even more damaging to the adoptive and non-genetic family is the stigmatization of relationships implied in this language. The plurality and diversity of family forms, as well as advances in medically assisted conception in the 21st century, cause us to question the notion that a "real" parent is necessarily a biological parent.

The UN Child Convention has become an almost universally accepted standard for children's rights. Although governed by the same text, a country's interpretations of the Convention may differ according to its history, culture, and domestic legal arrangements, and this may lead to different consequences. As Claire Neirinck says, "To take the measure of *accouchment sous X* today it is not enough to describe it. One must analyse the significance for the woman and for the child to whom she gave birth" (1993:90). Thus the significance and meanings attached to "maternity in difficulty" in France are different from those of the United Kingdom.

The first empirical study of X mothers in France showed that many were young, at school or university, not yet employed, and financially dependent on their families (Bonnet 1991). The majority discovered they were pregnant in the second or third trimester of pregnancy, and therefore outside the period when French law permits the autonomous choice of abortion without medical reason (Law of 17 January, 1975). Bonnet (1991) offers a psychosocial explanation for respondents' failure to notice the changes in their bodies while pregnant. She examines the childhoods of the women involved and very often finds that physical, sexual, emotional abuse, or parental neglect blocked the women's capacity to anticipate the future as a sexual being or as a mother. These misfortunes made their awareness of pregnancy a late discovery, and created the possibility that they would commit infanticide. To Bonnet, *accouchement sous X* protects both child and woman, particularly when the latter comes from a community that cannot accept her sexuality outside marriage.

From Bonnet's work, a particular construction of X women emerges. The majority of the X women do not wish to reveal their identity and do not see themselves as mothers. They believe that adoption is the best solution for the child, and they do not wish to meet later in life. Adoption pressure groups support this position, since children of anonymous women can be placed for adoption without the fear of later withdrawal of consent by the mother (Dekeuwer-Defossez 1999:61). These women are not only victims but also autonomous agents with rights. They take advantage of the possibilities offered by the law. To Bonnet, giving birth anonymously and surrendering their child is a "gesture of love," the title she gives her book.

Nevertheless, Nadine Lefaucheur's study, concluded in 1999, shows that constructions of women in France are changing. Her study adopts a different tone of voice and finds a different view of autonomy. It shows that two-thirds of the women were less than 25 years old, more than a quarter were students, half were unemployed, and a significant minority were from the middle-class. Her results indicate that four-fifths were unmarried, one-quarter lived at home, between 4% and 10% were rape victims, about 12% were living with partners, and that 10% were separated or divorced, over 35, with existing families. In this study there is more emphasis on hardships of various kinds experienced by the women involved: lack of autonomy and resources, fear of parental reaction, pressure by parents from a religious or conservative background, personal problems, inability to cope with another child, domestic violence, or existing large families in socioeconomic difficulties. Lefaucheur (2000:6) concludes as follows:

> From a sociological point of view, the situation of women who request secrecy of identity and delivery arises today *essentially* from a lack of autonomy and from problems of youth and actual difficulties in entering a family and professional life, from the precariousness of immigration status, and from the "double constraint" of the isolation and material difficulties of single parent families, as well as domestic violence (emphasis mine).

To Lefaucheur, it is precisely because the X women lack autonomy that they seek anonymity and the consequent adopting out of their child. For Bonnet, however, such action is a mark of choice and freedom, and is a woman's right. Both use the word autonomy but come up with different definitions. The link between interpretation of research findings and the construction placed thereon is manifest.

Constructions do not take place in an abstract, nor in an *essential*, context. They exist in a climate of many factors, material and discursive. These factors shape attitudes and ways of seeing. As the discourse of children's identity rights gains ground in France, the constructions placed on the actions of the woman who gives birth anonymously change.

A considerable amount of material has been put into the public domain by the Findelbaby group in Germany (www.findelbaby.de). What runs through the discourse is the trumping argument that the protection of the child's life is more important than the protection of the child's identity. At an expert hearing before the German Parliament (*Bundestag*), Dr. Jurgen Moyisch, one of the founders of the Findelbaby project, argued a pragmatic case, based on existing actions by women who have given birth: 250 cases a year of women giving false names when on maternity confinement in Germany, with a resultant trade in babies. Infanticide figures, based on press reports, were also cited in evidence: 34 in 1999 and 39 in 2000. Moyisch's argument is that these facts justify not only the actions taken so far in setting up the Babyklappen but also that legislation on anonymous birthing should be introduced as the best protection for women and babies facing the social reality he has outlined (Findelbaby press release, May 20, 2001). The pragmatism of the argument that calls on social facts in support and that uses a "for want of anything better" strategy is notable.

The proposal to introduce the French concept of anonymous birthing to Germany is said on one hand to be legal but on the other to require legislation for clarification. In legal terms, the German proposal differs markedly from the law in France. Anonymous births already take place in German hospitals, which run the risk of prosecution. At present, the Civil Status Code (para. 16) makes it an offense for a hospital to fail to report the birth of a child. The idea is to change this statute to make it an offense to fail to report what is known, thus obligating the hospital to make a report that an anonymous birth has occurred, but without identifying details of the mother.

The Penal Code changes required are to para. 169, containing the offense of *Personenstanzfalschung*, which is a false report on the civil status of an infant. This paragraph should be amended to permit anonymous birth. However, a certain unease in the discourse is discernable: "The anonymous birth will remain the exception. Most women look forward to their child and would not give it up for any reason" (Findelbaby press release, February 15, 2001). It is proposed that the period for registration of the birth of a child be left open for eight weeks to allow the woman to change her mind. She is to be encouraged to leave a secret letter for the child to be opened by the latter at the age of 16.

Although respect for the woman's autonomy is mentioned, particularly in the context of an analogy with abortion law, it is clear that the German discourse is not framed in terms of rights but in that of protection. It is said that anonymous abandonment should not be a matter of the woman's choice or rights, but a matter of necessity. Germany's avoidance of the language of choice, which is the language of autonomy, seems to reflect the fear of being accused of encouraging abandonment. Therefore, the emphasis is on giving help and protection. The Findelbaby group has established five safe houses in which pregnant women can take refuge and, without pressure, consider what their futures hold after giving birth (July 2001 interviews with Findelbaby group, Hamburg; Findelbaby press release, May 30, 2001).

The language involved is not specifically legal; it is the discourse of social workers who see the law as a tool that can be changed to meet the needs of clients. At the same time, there seems to be a lack of clarity as to what exactly is the law. It permits the practice of Babyklappen, yet it may need clarification. Uneasiness is evident in the German discourse. Justification is expressed in terms of saving the baby from infanticide, with the woman's privacy and autonomy—as established in abortion rights—a secondary argument. Much of the emphasis is on helping pregnant women prior to a birth that may result in abandonment. The help is said to be non-judgmental, and women may or may not have the child adopted subsequently.

Notwithstanding the pragmatism of the justifications for the Findelbaby project, some constructions of the women's actions emerge. The average age of the woman who gives up her child is 23, and some are much younger. The reasons for abandonment or taking refuge are youth, pressure from the family, immigration status, dishonor and rape, or, in the case of women who already have children or who plan to do so in the future, being classified as a "bad mother" (interview, Hamburg, July 2001). So, although constructions of the woman as ill, or as an autonomous rights-bearer, are not drawn upon in the German discourse, it is deemed necessary to give some account for her actions, depicting her as a victim.

Underlying all three discourses is the assumption that if the woman who gives birth were not a victim, or ill, she would not abandon her child and that giving up one's baby is unnatural for a "real" mother—that is, a woman who has given birth. Her actions therefore have to be constructed in such a way as to assuage people's anxieties about mothers, about what is natural, and about love.

Conclusion

Stories about children's abandonment, mistaken identity, the finding of children in a basket of rushes, and changelings are particularly central to the canon not only of Western literature but also of oral traditions throughout the globe. The narratives constructed correspond to anxieties that lie deep yet involve people's hopes for a successful outcome (Boswell 1988; O'Donovan 2000). People's expectations of consistency in family law must be modified where law "engages with areas of social life, feeling, emotion, pain and identity, that are themselves riven with contradiction and paradox" (Morgan 2001:35). There are inconsistencies in the creation and content of law in its response to the demands of different constituencies, and also in its application. The best interests of the child may be given differing interpretations, or may take priority over law enforcement.

"We can acknowledge the ongoing grief of a woman who has given up a baby without saying that makes her the real mother, or more the mother than the adoptive mother or father who gives ongoing love and care" (Rothman 1989:126). In this article my use of the concept "real" mother has been examined and found to contain the implication that there are other kinds of mothers. I have critiqued the assumptions of universal traits of women and motherhood, of what is natural, in terms of the discursive constructions of women who go through maternity without proceeding to motherhood. The varying experiences of children and women and the self-understanding that creates a narrative of self-identity are suppressed in the constructions of "real" mothers. The emphasis on genetic ties contained in this discourse not only stigmatizes those who cannot conform to the idea of a "normal family," but it is out of touch with the myriad of family forms today.

When justifying the policies in the three jurisdictions explored in this article, policymakers' discussions of abandonment are individualized, decontextualized, and depoliticized. Yet motherhood, like other social institutions, takes place within larger society. Motherhood has been presented in the past as an institution where "failure to fulfil social norms and ideals of motherhood has traditionally been regarded as a primary indicator of a woman's social irresponsibility and social ineptitude" (Wegar 1997:124). This focus on individuals rather than on the larger changes in traditional social identities merely stigmatizes the identities of children, and of the women who look after them through pregnancy and childhood.

Despite undertaking international obligations to protect the child's identity rights, it is evident from this research that legislators have been unable to develop consistent policies for these rights, nor have they been able to put institutional mechanisms in place to guarantee protection. To say this is not to castigate legislators, but rather to draw attention to the complexities of the issues involved. Maternity and motherhood are idealized *and* complex. Instead of loading these terms with the expectations and demands of culturally prescribed standards, maybe we should study the contests and politics of motherhood and maternity as institutions.

References

Aries, Philippe (1973) *Centuries of Childhood.* London: Cape.

Australian Human Rights Commission (1997) *Bringing Them Home: Report of the National Inquiry into the Separation of Aboriginal and Torres Strait Islander Children from their Families,* Canberra, Commonwealth of Australia.

Barlein, Michael, & Stephen Rixen (2001) "Babywiegen—ein Hilfskonzept eigener Art," *Kriminalstik* 54–56.

Bartholet, Elizabeth (1993) *Family Bonds: Adoption and the Politics of Parenting.* Boston: Houghton-Mifflin.

Bean, Philip, & Jay Melville (1989) *Lost Children of the Empire.* London: Unwin.

Bisset-Johnson, Alastair (1996) "Qualifications of Signatories to the United Nations Convention on the Rights of the Child," in N. Lowe & G. Douglas, eds., *Families Across Frontiers.* Dordrecht, The Netherlands: Kluwer.

Bonnet, Catherine (1991) *Geste d'Amour* (Gester of Love). Paris: Editions Odile Jacob.

——— (1995) "La loi de l'accouchement secret," 228 *Les dossiers de l'obstetrique* 20–26.

Boswell, John (1988) *The Kindness of Strangers: The Abandonment of Children in Western Europe from Late Antiquity to the Renaissance.* London: Pantheon Books.

Cerda, Jaime (1990) "The Draft Convention on the Rights of the Child: New Rights," 12 *Human Rights Q.* 115–19.

Cox, Kathleen (1998) *The Guardian,* London, England, 2 Jan. p. 5.

Dekeuwer-Defossez, Francoise (1999) *Renover le droit de la famille: propositions pour un droit adapte aux realites de aux aspirations de notre temps.* Paris: Ministry of Justice, Documentation Française.

De Mause, Louis (1976) *The History of Childhood.* London: Souvenir Press.

Dreifuss-Netter, Frederique (1994) "L'accouchement sous X," *Liber amicorum a la memoire de Daniele Huet-Weiler.* Paris: PUS/LGDJ.

Eekelaar, John (1996) "'The Chief Glory': The Export of Children from the United Kingdom," in N. Lowe & G. Douglas, eds. *Families Across Frontiers.* Dordrecht, The Netherlands: Kluwer.

Fisher, Jo (1989) *Mothers of the Disappeared.* Boston: South End Press.

Fortin, Jane (1998) *Children's Rights: The Developing Law.* London: Butterworth.
Freeman, Michael (1996) "The New Birth Right?" 1 *International J. of Children's Rights* 1–28.
Gaskin v. UK (1989) 12 European Human Rights Reports 36.
Gavitt, Philip (1990) *Charity and Children in Late Renaissance Florence.* Ann Arbor, MI: Univ. of Michigan Press.
Hall, Sarah (1998) *The Guardian,* Jan. 2, p. 5.
Hansard, Rachel (1860) 159 Parl. Deb. (3rd ser.) 270.
Hodgkin, Rachel, & Peter Newell (1998) *Implementation Handbook for the Convention on the Rights of the Child.* London: UNICEF.
Humphries, Margaret (1994) *Empty Cradles.* London: Corgi.
Jenks, Chris (1996) *Childhood.* London: Routledge.
Jones, Phil (police spokesperson) (1998) *The Guardian,* January 2, p. 5.
Kunesh, Patricia (1996) "Transcending Frontiers: Indian Child Welfare in the United States," in N. Lowe & G. Douglas, eds., *Families Across Frontiers.* Dordrecht, The Netherlands: Kluwer.
Lansdown, Gerison (2000) "The Reporting Process under the Convention on the Rights of the Child," in P. Alston & J. Crawford, eds., *The Future of the UN Treaty: Rights Monitoring.* Cambridge: Cambridge Univ. Press.
Le Blanc, Louis (1995) *The Convention on the Rights of the Child.* Lincoln: Univ. of Nebraska Press.
Lefaucheur, Nadine (2000) *Etude —enfants nes sous X.* Paris: CNRS–IRESCO.
Maclean, Sarah & Mavis Maclean (1996) "Keeping Secrets in Assisted Reproduction," 8 *Child & Family Law Q.* 243–51.
McClure, Ruth (1981) *Corum's Child.* New Haven: Yale Univ. Press.
MacKinnon, Catharine (1987) *Feminism Unmodified.* Cambridge: Harvard Univ. Press.
Masson, Judith, & Catharine Harrison (1996) "Identity: Mapping the Frontiers," in N. Lowe & G. Douglas, eds., *Families Across Frontiers.* Dordrecht, The Netherlands: Kluwer.
Milotte, Mike (1997) *Banished Babies.* Dublin: New Island Books.
Modell, Judith (1994) *Kinship with Strangers: Adoption and Interpretations of Kinship in American Culture.* Berkeley: Univ. of California Press.
Morgan, Derek (2001) *Issues in Medical Law and Ethics.* London: Cavendish.
Neirinck, Claire (1993) "L'accouchement sous X," 392 *La Semaine Juridique* 143–56.
Neuheuser, Stephan (2001) "Begrundet Weggabe eines Neuborenen in Babyklappe den Anfangsvedacht einer Straftat?" *Neue Strafrechtszeitung,* 175–78.
O'Donovan, Katherine (1984) "The Medicalisation of Infanticide," *Criminal Law Rev.* 259–71.
——— (1988) "A Right to Know One's Genetic Parentage?" 2 *International J. of Law & the Family* 27–45.
——— (2000) "Enfants Trouves, Anonymous Mothers and Children's Identity Rights," in K. O'Donovan & G. R. Rubin, eds., *Human Rights and Legal History.* Oxford: Oxford University Press.
Parra-Aranguren Report (1993) "Report of the Drafting Committee on Convention on Inter-Country Adoption," The Hague.
Prout, Alan & Allison James, eds., (1990) *Constructing and Reconstructing Childhood.* Basington, England: Falmer Press.
Rothman, Barbara (1989) *Recreating Motherhood: Ideology and Technology in a Patriarchal Society.* New York: Norton.
Royal, Segoline (2000) Conference de presse de Sogolene Royal ministre deleguee a la Famille et a l'Enfance, Dec. 14 2000.
Rubellin-Devichi, Jacqueline (1991) "Droits de la mere et droits de l'enfant: reflexions sur les formes de l'abandon," 90 *Revue trimestrielle de droit civil* 4–11.

——— (1994) "The Principle of the Welfare of the Child in French Law and Practice," 8 *International J. of Law & the Family* 269–85.
——— (1999) *Droit de la Famille.* Paris: Dalloz.
Stewart, George A. (1992) "Interpreting the Child's Right to Identity in the UN Convention on the Rights of the Child," 26 *Family Law Q.* 221–33.
Thery, Irene (1998) *Couple, filiation et parente aujourd'hui.* Paris: Editions Odile Jacob.
Trillat, Brigitte (1994) "La loi de l'accouchement anaonyme: De l'opporbre a la consecration," *Liber amicorum a la memoire de Daniele huet-Weiler.* Paris: PUS/LGDJ.
Triselotis, John (1973) *In search of Origins: The Experiences of Adopted People.* London: Routledge.
Van Bueren, Geraldine (1995) *The International Law on the Rights of the Child.* The Hague: Nijhoff.
Ward, Tony (1999) "The Sad subject of Infanticide," 8 *Social & Legal Studies* 163–80.
Wayne Carp, E. (1998) *Family Matters: Secrecy and Disclosure in the History of Adoption.* Cambridge: Harvard Univ. Press.
Wegar, Katarina (1997) *Adoption, Identity and Kinship.* New Haven: Yale Univ. Press.
Wilczynski, Anna (1997) *Child Homicide.* London: Greenwich Medical Media.
Yngvesson, Barbara (1997) "Negotiating Motherhood: Identity and Difference in 'Open' Adoptions," 31 *Law & Society Rev.* 31–80.

Cases Cited

Gaskin v. UK (1989) 12 European Human Rights Reports 36.
The Queen v. Cooper (1849) 1 Den. 459, 169 Eng. Rep. 326.
The Queen v. Falkingham (1870) L.R. 1 C.C.R. 222, 39 L.J.M.C. 47.
The Queen v. Hogan (1851) 2 Den. 277, 169 Eng. Rep. 504.
The Queen v. March (1844) 1 Car. & Kir. 496, 174 Eng. Rep. 909.
The Queen v. Renshaw (1847) 2 Cox's Criminal Law Cases, vol. 2, 285.
Re G (parentage) (blood sample) [1997] 1 Family Law Reports 360.
Re H (a minor) (blood tests) [1996] 2 Family Law Reports 65.

Statutes and International Conventions

Access to Personal Files Act of 1987, ch. 37 (Eng.).
Access to Personal Files (Social Services) Regulations 1989, SI 1989/206 (Eng.).
Adoption Act of 1976, ch. 36 (Eng.).
Children and Young Person's Act of 1933, ch. 12 (Eng.).
Children Act of 1989, ch. 20 (Eng.).
Code Civil (France) Paris, Dalloz, edition 2001.
Code de la famille et de l'aide sociale (France) Decr. No. 56-149 du 24 janv. 1956, Dalloz, C. civ. Edition 2001, 343.
Code de la sante publique (France) Decr. no. 53-1001 du 5 oct. 1953.
European Convention for the Protection of Human Rights and Fundamental Freedoms (1950) Council of Europe, 87 United Nations Treaty Series 103; European Treaty Series 5.
Grundgesetz (Federal Constitution of Germany).
Hague Convention on Intercountry Adoption (1993) Hague Convention on Private International Law: Final Act of the 17th session, Including the Convention on Protection of children and Co-operation in Respect of Intercountry Adoption, May 29, 1993.
Human Fertilization and Embryology Act of 1990, ch. 37 (Eng.).
Loi 17 janv. 1975 (France) Dalloz, C. civ. Edition 2001, 342.

Loi n. 93-22 du 8 janv. 1993 (France) Dalloz, C. civ. Edition 2001, 342.
Offences Against the Person Act of 1861, 24 & 25 Vict. Ch. 100 (Eng.).
Personenstandgesetz (Civil Status Code, Germany).
Strafgesetzbuch (German Penal Code).
United Nations Convention on the Prevention and Punishment of the Crime of Genocide (1948), 78 U.N. Treaty Ser. 277.
United Nations Convention on the Rights of the Child, G. A. Res. 44/256, U.N. GAOR, 44th Sess., Supp. No. 49, U.N. Doc. A/44/736 (1989).
United Nations Convention on the Rights of the Child, Committee on the Rights of the Child, U.N. Doc. CRC/C/2/Rev.2.

Part III
Delivering Social Justice

[10]

FINANCIAL ASPECTS OF THE DIVORCE TRANSITION IN AUSTRALIA: RECENT EMPIRICAL FINDINGS

GRANIA SHEEHAN*

ABSTRACT

In this article, an overview of recent empirical findings on the financial aspects of the divorce transition is provided. The findings are drawn from the *Australian Divorce Transitions Project* – a national random survey of 650 divorced Australians, conducted in late 1997 by the Australian Institute of Family Studies. The overview presents key findings on how property is divided (including the treatment of superannuation and spousal maintenance), living standards post-separation and divorce and pathways out of poverty such as family reformation, and the relevance of spousal violence to post-separation financial outcomes (including property division, living standards and work history).

The data suggest that little has changed over the past decade in the way the financial aspects of the divorce transition are effected. The way women and men divide their property on divorce primarily reflects the financial contributions made to the marriage, and concern for the future welfare of the children. The future financial needs of a former spouse are overlooked by parties when allocating property and financial resources – a shortfall that, in part, reflects the constraints imposed by the limited asset wealth available to a large minority of couples on separation. This shortfall is, however, inappropriate given the significant and enduring financial hardship experienced post-separation and divorce by sole mothers, older women living alone, and women who have experienced spousal violence.

1. INTRODUCTION

A. Background: Divorce Transition in Australia

In Australia, as elsewhere, there are considerable risks associated with relationship breakdown and subsequent transition in peoples' lives.

*Socio-Legal Research Centre, Griffith University, Nathan 4111, QLD, Australia. email: g.sheehan@mailbox.gu.edu.au. This paper draws heavily on work undertaken by the author while employed at the Australian Institute of Family Studies. It is an overview of core findings from a study conducted at the Institute titled the *Australian Divorce Transitions Project* (1996–2001). The *Australian Divorce Transitions Project* (ADTP) was conceptualized by the late Kate Funder and conducted by a project team comprising Kate Funder, Grania Sheehan and Bruce Smyth. Many other colleagues at the Australian Institute of Family Studies (Belinda Fehlberg, Jody Hughes, Christine Kilmartin, Ruth Weston and Ilene Wolcott) and elsewhere (Juliet Behrens, John Dewar and Bruce

These risks translate into social and economic costs, personal suffering and ill-being of varying degrees for men, women and children. For some families the emotional and financial impact of separation and divorce can resonate for many years after the separation, and the impact of this distress on the community and public resources can be considerable.[1]

Since, in Australia, two in five marriages will end in divorce, and divorce will affect one in five children during their dependent years,[2] marriage and relationship breakdown where children are involved is a common occurrence. Rates of relationship dissolution are even higher for second marriages and de facto relationships.[3] These patterns are not unique to Australia, but reflect broad based demographic trends in evidence across many affluent Western societies.[4] The expectation is that high relationship dissolution rates in developed countries, including Australia, will continue.[5] Despite the prevalence of relationship breakdown in the community and the associated risks, when measured against the passage of history, we are still at a very early point in our experience of high divorce rates and, as a society, must continue to adjust our family law and social policy response to this situation.[6]

B. Project Aims

The central purpose of the *Australian Divorce Transitions Project* (ADTP) was to improve understanding of how divorce can be made a functional transition for families in Australia, and to build on the previous work in this area by the Australian Institute of Family Studies (AIFS), particularly research on the economic consequences of marriage breakdown carried out in the 1980s and early 1990s and described in *Settling Up* and *Settling Down*.[7] In seeking to examine the complexity of the divorce transition and identify those factors that make a family's passage particularly difficult (or particularly easy), this project had a number of specific aims.

First, precedence was given to securing national data on the financial aspects of the divorce transition. Data generated from a national representative sample[8] can be used to calculate the probability that the patterns observed in the sample will exist in (or generalize to) the wider population of divorced women and men. Deriving data from a national representative sample is important, given that population estimates are a fundamental plank in any agenda for family law reform or for the review of services and support provisions. Prior to ADTP, there was no such national data available in Australia that covered the financial aspects of the divorce transition.

Headey) assisted with the analysis of the data and the dissemination of the project findings. The author acknowledges that the interpretation of ADTP data presented here represents the views of the author and not those of the Australian Institute of Family Studies. This paper is dedicated to Kate Funder whose untimely death is a great loss to family studies in Australia.

As there is great variation in the ways in which the divorce transition is effected, a second and complementary aim was to identify particularly vulnerable groups among those divorcing so that the diversity in this population could be recognized. The provision of detailed information about certain groups (perhaps relatively rare in the population) was also considered important in that some of these groups consume a large proportion of the time and resources of the Family Court, and other agencies within the family law system. In this category are highly conflicted divorces, which consume enormous public and private financial resources, and involve considerable suffering and personal distress for adults and children. This is particularly the case for families where domestic violence and/or child abuse have been a characteristic of past and ongoing relations between family members.[9] Other groups are distinguished by their financial vulnerability post-separation and divorce. For example, single parents, older women and men from long-term marriages warrant focused study directed at the early detection of difficulties related to immediate and future financial security.

Third, the project was designed to enable trend analysis by comparing recent divorce transitions with those that took place in the early 1980s and described in *Settling Up* and *Settling Down*.[10] Since this early research was conducted, there have been a number of important policy, economic, and demographic changes in Australia that may have influenced the way in which the financial aspects of divorce are experienced by men, women, and children.

These changes included the introduction of the Child Support Scheme[11] – a major legislative reform that arguably eased the financial burden of divorce for single parents, and reduced the need for the day-to-day support of children to be taken into account in property proceedings. The full effects of the Child Support Scheme were not evident in earlier AIFS research due to the timing of the introduction of the Scheme.

At an even broader level, there have been a number of economic and demographic changes in Australia that may have increased financial resilience post-separation and divorce by reducing the 'opportunity costs' of marriage for women. A core change is the continued growth in women's workforce participation prior to and during marriage, particularly in the area of part-time and casual employment.[12] Concomitant with an increase in women's educational attainment,[13] these kinds of changes may have improved women's chances of being in, or finding, paid work when marriage ends, thereby reducing the economic toll of separation and divorce.

In addition, changes in fertility and the nature of relationships may also have led to some mitigation of the economic costs of separation and divorce for women. The increasing tendency for couples to live together before marriage, to marry at a later age, and have fewer children,[14] creates demographic shifts that may extend the period of time in which women lead financially independent lives. However, this is not to say that we expected the adverse economic consequences of divorce for women to have all but disappeared.

There is clearly a need for up-to-date information on the financial aspects of the divorce transition in Australia, especially in light of the policy, economic and demographic changes that have occurred in the past ten years or so. Drawing on data from two national surveys of divorced women and men conducted by the author in association with Funder, Hughes and Smyth, and the ADTP teams' analysis and interpretation of these data, this paper presents an overview of the key findings on: (a) the nature of asset wealth on divorce and the ways in which this wealth is divided; (b) the economic circumstances of women and men post-separation and divorce; and (c) the impact of spousal violence and other factors such as repartnering on these circumstances. Before presenting the key findings the methodology for ADTP is briefly discussed.

2. METHODOLOGY

A. Sample

Data on the financial aspects of the divorce transition are derived from two surveys – the main *Divorce Transitions Survey*, and a subsidiary *Domestic Violence Survey*.

The first and larger survey – the *Divorce Transitions Survey* – was a random national telephone survey of 650 divorced Australians, conducted in late 1997 by the AIFS. Two samples (stratified by gender and geographical location) were drawn from the population of Australian households with telephones. Households from Western Australia were not sampled due to some differences then in the law on child-related issues between this state and the rest of Australia.[15]

The first sample comprised 513 parents (284 women, 229 men) who were divorced under Australian law, were separated after January 1988, and who had a child under eighteen years of age at the time of separation. This sample is referred to in the paper as the 'young parent' sample. The respondents in the second sample were also divorced under Australian law but comprised 137 older women and men from 'long-term' marriages of at least fifteen years duration where the age of the wife at separation was between forty-five to sixty-five years (seventy-seven women, sixty men). Although respondents' status as a parent was not a specific criterion for inclusion in the long-term marriage sample, it is noteworthy that half the respondents in this sample had at least one child under the age of eighteen years at the time of separation. For most of the analyses reported using ADTP data, these two samples are combined. The exception to this is the analysis of post-separation and divorce living standards where the financial circumstances of older women from long-term marriages are a focus.

A subsidiary survey that focused on spousal violence was also conducted. The *Spousal Violence Survey* was a follow up telephone survey of 398 of the participants who were involved in the *Divorce Transitions Survey*.

The focus of ADTP was thus on those who had experienced divorce; data were not collected from those who had been in *de facto* relationships. No assumption was made that project results generalized to cohabiting relationships.

B. Response Rate

Data were collected by computer assisted telephone interview. Respondents for the *Divorce Transitions Survey* were randomly selected from the Australian 1997 residential telephone directory. Of the 881 households contacted that contained a person who fitted the sampling criteria,[16] 74 per cent of respondents completed the interview (26 per cent refused to participate). However, the true response rate would have been somewhat lower than this because some of the refusals, which occurred during the screening interview, would have met the various sampling criteria (most refusals occurred before interviewers could determine the eligibility of respondents for the study).

At the time of the *Divorce Transitions Survey* interviews, 593 (332 women and 261 men) gave their permission to be recontacted.[17] All 593 *Divorce Transitions Survey* respondents were recontacted and asked if they would like to participate in a survey on spousal violence: 398 respondents agreed (245 women, 153 men). The completion rate for the *Spousal Violence Survey* thus was 67 per cent of those who gave permission to be recontacted: 74 per cent for women, 59 per cent for men. The under-representation of male respondents in this sample should be noted and may, in part, reflect several well-known patterns of non-response on the part of men.[18]

C. Demographic Profile

As a result of stratified sampling, 63 per cent of respondents who completed the *Divorce Transitions Survey* lived in urban centres. Women and men were of a similar age (the mean age of women was forty-three, and the mean age of men was forty-nine years), had been married for an average of fourteen years, and had been separated for six years on average. The largest proportions of women and men indicated that they had no post-secondary school qualifications (58 per cent as opposed to 46 per cent). Women were less likely than men to report that they had received a diploma or vocational training (18 per cent as opposed to 34 per cent), were less likely to be in paid work (68 per cent as opposed to 78 per cent), and were marginally more likely to indicate that they were tertiary graduates (24 per cent as opposed to 20 per cent). Women were also more likely than men to rely on social security as their main source of income (33 per cent as opposed to 12 per cent), and to have significantly lower personal and household incomes (for example, median personal annual gross income $20,000 as opposed to $30,000). These differences are consistent with prior research conducted by the Australian Institute of Family Studies.[19]

The divorced women and men who were involved in the *Spousal Violence Survey* have similar demographic profiles to that described above for the base sample. For all intents and purposes both samples are deemed representative of the Australian population of divorced women and men, with the one exception. Men's reports of domestic violence may not be representative of the Australian divorced male population's experience.

D. Survey Content

The *Divorce Transitions Survey* content covered a broad range of issues that are of relevance to the financial aspects of the divorce transition including, among other issues: child support, property division and spousal maintenance, education, training and work history, and income and housing. The *Spousal Violence Survey* covered, among other things: history and types of domestic violence (ie, physical, sexual and emotional abuse, and post-separation harassment such as stalking), and the nature of the negotiations that took place regarding the division of property.

In combination, these two surveys provide a comprehensive picture of the financial arrangements and economic circumstances of couples who divorce in Australia, and the inter-personal context in which these financial arrangements were made.

E. Methodological and Conceptual Issues

As with most studies of divorce, our data were based on retrospective self-reports. The accuracy of the information is thus dependent not only on respondents' candour, but on recollections of events that may have occurred many years before and at a time when respondents were under much stress.

Three more general methodological limitations should also be noted. First, while the cross-sectional nature of the survey design can detect associations (for example, between the share of property received and the time spent out of paid work to have and care for children), it cannot determine the direction of these associations. Thus no claim can be made that certain factors *lead to* specific property and economic outcomes.

Second, the unit of analysis was a spouse – not a couple – from a dissolved marital union; and only scant information was obtained about the respondent's former spouse. As a consequence, there are limits to checking the accuracy of the data. The absence of couple data also limits our ability to determine the proportion of marriages in the divorcing population where one party has the financial capacity to redress (or compensate for) the post-separation financial hardship experienced by the former spouse.

Finally, since not everyone is accessible by telephone, the omission of certain groups of people in the population available through telephone surveys sets limits on the generalizations that can be made from the data to the Australian population at large. Among those who are often systematically excluded in such surveys are the very poor, those with unlisted numbers, those who live in geographically remote areas, and those who have hearing or English language difficulties. Of particular note in the present study is that women and men who have been the victims of serious violence may have unlisted numbers and are consequently likely to be under-represented in the sample.

Nonetheless, few approaches enable national estimates to be obtained across the spectrum of the divorcing population, and especially of both court registered and private financial arrangements. The ADTP provides the most recent national estimates that we have of divorcing Australians and their financial circumstances.

3. CORE RESEARCH FINDINGS

A. *Overview*

Because of the breadth of coverage of the ADTP, the project served as an umbrella under which a number of subsidiary studies have been undertaken. The following section presents core findings from those subsidiary studies which have covered how property and financial resources are divided (including the treatment of superannuation and spousal maintenance), living standards post-separation and divorce and pathways out of poverty such as family reformation, and the relevance of spousal violence to post-separation financial outcomes (including property division, living standards and work history).[20] These findings will be presented in three parts. First, details on the nature of asset wealth on divorce and the ways in which this wealth is divided are presented. This is followed by an examination of the current economic circumstances of women and men some six years after separation. Third, links between domestic violence, property settlement outcomes, and the economic circumstances (post-divorce financial living standards and workforce participation) of divorced men and women are explored.

In essence, the ADTP data suggest that little has changed since the publication of *Settling Up* and *Settling Down*, conducted by the AIFS in the 1980s,[21] in the way the financial aspects of the divorce transition are effected. The way women and men divide their property on divorce primarily reflects the financial contributions made to the marriage, and concern for the future welfare of the children. This translates into men receiving the vast majority of the non-domestic assets of the marriage such as businesses, farms and investments, and the couple's primary financial resource – the husband's superannuation. Women on the other hand, receive the lion's share of the domestic (or house and garden assets) such as the family home and contents.

The future financial needs of the former spouse may, however, have been overlooked by parties when allocating property – a shortfall that, in part, reflects the constraints imposed by the limited wealth available to a large minority of couples on separation. This shortfall is not being compensated for through alternative methods of financial transfer between the parties such as spousal maintenance. It is also inconsistent with the degree of financial hardship that continues to be experienced by sole mothers and older women living alone some six years post-separation and divorce. The strongest evidence of this failure to take account of the future financial need of women is found for women who have experienced severe spousal violence. These women receive well below the average share of property to the wife for the sample, despite evidence of significant and enduring financial hardship post-separation and divorce.

These findings are now considered in more detail.

B. Asset Wealth on Divorce

Sheehan and Hughes' analysis of the data on asset wealth from the ADTP suggest that the asset wealth at separation of a large minority of divorced couples is insufficient to meet the immediate financial needs of the respective parties. Nor can it be relied on to offset any longer-term financial hardship.[22]

The financial hardship experienced post-separation and divorce is for some a continuation of the ongoing financial hardship that characterized the marriage. Recent Australian research indicates that separation and divorce is more likely among couples experiencing financial hardship during their relationship as compared to others.[23] This finding is consistent with longitudinal research from the United States, Finland and the United Kingdom which links economic stress with low marital satisfaction and reduced couple resilience to relationship breakdown.[24] Separation and divorce can thus both result in, and be a consequence of, financial hardship.

The greater incidence of divorce amongst those with a weak economic base is evidenced in the value and nature of asset wealth at separation of the women and men interviewed for the ADTP. The median net asset wealth excluding superannuation was $124,101. This value is well below the average value of assets for the general population of Australian couples for a comparable age cohort (ie, a difference of around $100,000).[25] The vast majority of couples (79 per cent) had wealth levels that placed them below the cut off for the 1997 Social Security Pensions Assets test (ie, $268,500), and around half the sample (46 per cent) had net asset wealth valued at less than $114,000).[26] Further, for these women and men from 'low asset' marriages, this wealth was almost entirely concentrated in the family home (of which there was substantial mortgage obligation – on average 50 per cent of the value of the property) and household goods, the family car and superannuation.

The general nature of the assets owned by parties on separation and divorce appears to have remained largely consistent with the patterns of asset wealth identified in the early 1980s by McDonald,[27] with one exception. There has been a substantial increase in the importance of superannuation as an aspect of family wealth. Dewar, Sheehan and Hughes' analysis of the ADTP data indicate that around 81 per cent of all cases involved at least one superannuation policy (usually the husband's).[28] This represents a substantial increase on the rate of 55 per cent cited by McDonald in the 1980s.[29] The value of this superannuation relative to the other assets owned by the parties at separation has also increased significantly, and accounts on average for 25 per cent of the parties' total asset wealth – up from roughly 14 per cent in the 1980s. This trend offers striking confirmation of what theorists some time ago described as the rise of 'new property'.[30] It is also consistent with the shift in Government policy in Australia during the late 1980s and 1990s towards promoting savings in the form of superannuation.[31]

This composition of asset wealth – limited wealth in non-domestic assets, a high proportion of wealth in immediately inaccessible assets such as superannuation, and high levels of debt – suggests that it would be difficult for a large minority of women and men to divide their assets in a way that would allow both parties access to immediate financial resources post-settlement, and secure the family home for the resident parent and children. The restricted nature of this wealth is consistent with recent research findings that ownership of non-domestic assets such as non-pension stocks and bonds, and non-owner-occupied real estate, is highly concentrated. The majority of Australian households have little or no wealth in such assets, and a minority of households have a great deal.[32]

This profile of the asset wealth of couples at separation highlights the challenges faced by parties and legal practitioners in distributing what little asset wealth there is available in a way that is fair, and eases the immediate and longer-term financial consequences of divorce. The extent to which this is achieved by Australian women and men is now considered.

C. *The Allocation of Assets on Divorce*

(i) Legal framework

The Australian system for dividing the matrimonial assets on divorce is a 'separate' property regime. Separation entails no assumption of community or joint ownership of family property. The starting point when dividing property is that each spouse retains ownership of the property legally his or hers. This is, however, only a starting point. Under the financial provisions of the Family Law Act (Cth) 1975, the Family Court has the discretionary power to alter parties' property interests on marriage breakdown if it is satisfied that, in all the circumstances, it is just and equitable to make the order. Exercising this power requires the court to consider the parties' respective contributions to the property, and other factors including their future financial needs. Where spousal support is sought in addition to a property order, it becomes the final stage in the process. (*In the Marriage of Clauson* [1995] FLC 92–595).

More specifically, when dividing the property the Court is directed to take account of the financial and non-financial contributions made to the property and to the welfare of the family. Non-financial contributions in particular include any labour that may have increased the value of the property as well as contributions made to the welfare of the family through unpaid work at home and care of the children (s 79(4)). Having determined the respective shares of property based on these contributions, the Court then makes an adjustment to take account of other factors including the future financial needs of each of the parties. The estimation of this adjustment is based on factors or circumstances of a broadly financial nature such as the age and health of the parties, employment prospects and financial resources, responsibility for the care of children post-separation and divorce, the duration of the marriage and the extent to which it has affected the future earning capacity of the parties. In all there are fifteen largely prospective factors for consideration covering what each party is likely to need and what each is able to pay to support the other (the factors are set out in s 75(2)).[33]

While simplified above, the detailed financial provisions that govern the allocation of property on divorce in Australia are inherently complex and there is broad scope for disagreement amongst the judiciary and the parties themselves as to the interpretation of these provisions.[34] This is not surprising given that the law confers wide discretion in settling property matters. In such an environment, dividing property on divorce is a difficult task, and one that is made even harder for the sizeable minority of women and men who settle their property matters without formal legal representation.[35] There is, therefore, significant potential for wide variation in settlement outcomes amongst divorcing couples, discordance between the provisions of the law described above, and the application of these provisions by women and men who 'bargain in its shadow'.[36]

Australian Divorce Transitions Project findings suggest that current practice in dividing property does not reflect the full ambit of these legislative provisions. Non-financial contributions to non-domestic assets and financial resources (such as businesses and farms, investments and superannuation) were unlikely to be reflected in the share of property received. As regards future needs, the needs of dependent children appear to have been the most important consideration, and the financial need of a former spouse may have been overlooked.

(ii) Financial contributions count

At first glance, ADTP findings are consistent with the notion that the current discretionary system allows for substantial variation in settlement outcomes. Sheehan and Hughes' analysis of the ADTP data on property division showed that shares are not heavily bunched in the 40 to 60 per cent *share to the wife* range. In around 71 per cent of the cases, the share received by the former wife was outside this range.[37] This degree of variation in settlement outcomes is consistent with that reported by McDonald in the 1980s.[38] This is not surprising given that the financial provisions of the Family Law Act have not changed in this period.

However, upon closer examination the data reveal a surprising degree of consistency in the way in which assets are being allocated on divorce. As Figure 1 shows, irrespective of the asset wealth of the marriage, the former wife receives around two-thirds of the couple's domestic (or house and garden) assets (such as the family home and its contents), and around one quarter or less of the non-domestic assets and financial resources of the marriage (for example, superannuation, businesses and farms, and investments such as real estate and shares).[39]

The striking consistency in the allocation of assets between husband and wife across the different asset wealth groups suggests that despite the discretionary framework for property division under the Family Law Act, some distinct and powerful norms apply when property and financial arrangements are made on divorce. In particular, it appears that consideration of women's contributions and future needs is usually done within the parameters of the domestic asset pool, while men's contributions and future needs are addressed by recourse to other property, and financial resources such as superannuation – a result that mirrors McDonald's findings a decade earlier.[40]

This pattern translates into very different settlement outcomes for women from *low asset wealth* marriages (net asset wealth valued at less than $114,000) compared to women from *high asset wealth* marriages (net asset wealth valued at more than $268,500). While the share of domestic and non-domestic assets and financial resources received by

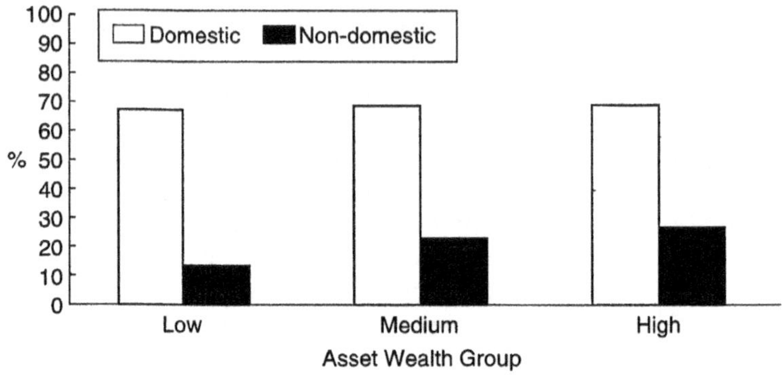

Figure 1: Mean Percentage Share to the Wife: Domestic Assets and Non-Domestic Assets (Including Financial Resources), by Asset Wealth Group (n = 190) (Source: AIFS, G. Sheehan and J. Hughes, 2001(20)).

Notes:

1. A subsample of 190 men and women were used in this analysis. These women and men included those who: (a) reported the value of all asset items and the corresponding value of the share of each asset received by each party; and (b) had a child under the age of 18 years at the time of separation. Restricting this subsample to respondents with a child under 18 years at the time of separation ensures that, for each case, the welfare of the children and the future financial needs of the resident parent may have been considered when dividing the property, along with an assessment of any contributions made in the form of caring for the children of the marriage.
2. Respondents were categorized according to the level of asset wealth of the couple at the time of separation. The 1997 social security non-home owner Pension Assets Test was used to assess the reported net asset wealth levels of the couple at the time of separation. As all calculations of assets include the value of couples' net equity in their home, the test for all assets was used rather than the test that excludes the value for the owner-occupied home. This involved deriving the value of the couple's total net assets excluding superannuation, as superannuation is excluded from calculation of the 1997 social security non-home owner Pension Assets Test. This value was then adjusted to 1997 dollars using the Consumer Price Index to determine whether the real value of assets was above or below the Asset Test cut off: $268,500. The following three categories of asset wealth were created based on the 1997 social security non-home owner Pension Assets Test: (a) the *high* asset wealth group where asset wealth was greater than the cut off for the assets test (that is, $268,500), (b) the *medium* asset wealth group with asset wealth valued at between $114,000 and $268,500, and (c) the *low* asset wealth group with asset wealth valued at below $114,000. The two 'low asset' groups were determined by a median split for those cases where assets were valued at less than $268,500.
3. To determine the share of property received by respondents at division, the total net amount (summed across all domestic assets or non-domestic assets including superannuation) received by respondents was divided by the total net value of the domestic (or non-domestic) property. This amount was then calculated as a percentage share received for each respondent.
4. The three asset wealth groups are not significantly different from one another in the share of domestic assets the wife received. However, the three asset wealth groups are significantly different from one another in the share of non-domestic assets and financial resources the wife received ($F(2,187) = 3.42$, $p<.05$). The mean difference driving this effect is that between the low asset and the high asset wealth group.

women changes very little across the respective asset wealth groups, the extent of the couples' asset wealth bound up in non-domestic assets does change. The greater the asset wealth of the marriage the higher the proportion of total asset wealth accounted for by non-domestic assets. Receipt of a minority share of non-domestic assets thus has the capacity to depress the overall share received by the wife in wealthy marriages because wealth of this nature makes up the majority of the couple's total asset wealth.[41] Conversely, receipt of a minority share of non-domestic assets by women from low asset marriages has little effect on reducing the overall share of property these women receive because assets of this nature make up a small proportion of these couple's total asset wealth.

There are a number of different reasons why property is being divided this way. For example, the allocation of non-domestic asset wealth and financial resources to the husband may reflect the significant weight given to husbands' initial contributions of non-domestic assets owned prior to the marriage, the husbands' inheritance of non-domestic assets such as businesses and farms, and the Family Court's inability to split superannuation at the time of divorce.[42] Particularly in the case of those from wealthier marriages, such a finding may suggest that additional weighting was given to the husbands' contributions in cases where the husband's business activities involved the exercise of special skills, enterprise or expertise (*In the Marriage of Ferrero* [1992] 111 FLR 170, 173). In regards to those from low asset marriages, where the family home and husband's superannuation make up the bulk of the couple's wealth, such a finding may simply reflect that the husband's share comprised his superannuation alone.

While each of these possible explanations may have played a role in the way parties' allocated their property on divorce, it is not the complete story. When the influence of assets acquired prior to marriage, and gender differences in inherited wealth are statistically taken into account in the analysis, the pattern of findings remains the same, although the effect is somewhat weaker.[43] This suggests that there is a further reason why non-domestic assets are predominantly allocated to the husband, namely that non-financial contributions made to these assets, particularly the domestic activities performed by one spouse that free the other spouse to work directly for financial reward, have been undervalued when the property was divided. This could happen if the homemaker contribution was undervalued by the judiciary[44] and/or the parties themselves.[45] It may also be a function of the practical difficulties involved in assessing and comparing contributions that are fundamentally different from one another, and in the case of non-financial contributions, notoriously difficult to quantify in monetary terms.

(iii) Children first: the consideration of future financial need

As outlined earlier, after contributions, the second part of the property division equation is future needs. The ADTP data suggest that of the s

75(2) factors tested, responsibility for the care of dependent children is the most influential in predicting the share of property a party receives.[46] This is despite its equal weighting in the Family Law Act with each of the remaining s 75(2) factors.

Further, the s 75(2) factors were not taken into account in a way that unduly favoured women at the expense of men – a criticism frequently directed at the Government by men's rights groups in reference to property reform.[47] Irrespective of whether it was the former husband or former wife who was the resident parent, the share received shifted in favour of the resident parent. This occurred even if other needs did not appear significant. For example, resident fathers reported receipt of 15 per cent more of the property than non-resident fathers even though the vast majority of these resident men had spent no time out of the work force during marriage (76 per cent) and were in paid work at the time of separation (89 per cent).[48] This suggests that the 'future needs' adjustment is being driven by the needs of the children, not necessarily those of the former spouse. Such a finding is not surprising given the increasing legislative emphasis in Australia over the past decade on protecting the interests of the children of the marriage, the continuing responsibility of both parents to look after their children, and on reducing state costs in their upbringing when the marriage ends.

In contrast, responsibility for the future needs of the spouse (independent of concerns for the welfare of the children) had very little impact on the allocation of property on divorce. The length of the marriage, the extent of the wife's involvement in paid work during the marriage and at the time of separation, and responsibilities taken for unpaid work in the home and the care of the children during the marriage, generally did little to increase her share of the property. For example, women who had spent more than one third of the time they were married out of paid work, and those women who were out of paid work at the time of separation received less than the average share to the wife for the total sample (41 per cent and 36 per cent respectively as opposed to 55 per cent).[49]

Nor were the future needs of the wife taken into consideration via the payment of spousal maintenance. Behrens and Smyth's analysis of the ADTP data indicate that for the women and men interviewed 'periodic spousal support [is] . . . rare (spousal maintenance was paid in fewer than seven per cent of cases), minimal (support averaged about $6,640 per annum or $128 per week), and brief (support typically lasted about two years)', and was predominantly paid out as bridging-finance until the property matters were finalized, rather than as a form of ongoing financial support for the former wife.[50]

These findings may, in part, reflect the practical difficulties faced by women and men in allocating their property in a way that satisfies the needs of all parties. The restricted nature of the wealth available for division in a large minority of marriages means that, once the family home has been secured for the use of the children and the resident parent, there is little left over to address the future needs of either party. So while on average women receive a majority share of the matrimonial property (55 per cent) the actual value of this property may be low. Alternatively, these findings may, in part, reflect that notions of responsibility for the future needs of the spouse, are governed by a very different ideology – that of a *clean break* and the cessation of any ongoing responsibility for one another's welfare on divorce.

(iv) Real value of share received

Sheehan and Hughes' analysis of the ADTP data provides insight into the actual amount of finance made available to women and men post divorce through property distribution, and the extent to which this finance could supplement current income from other sources. To obtain an estimate of the 'relative value' of the share of property women and men receive, a comparison was made between the annual investment return on the dollar share of property received at settlement and the respondent's current annual income.[51] Figure 2 presents the median ratio of income generated from the share of property received at settlement to the median annual income for women and men from the respective asset wealth groups.

Not surprisingly, Figure 2 shows that the greater the asset wealth of the parties at separation the greater the potential of the assets received to ease any financial hardship experienced post-separation and divorce. More specifically, the comparison of women's annual investment income from the property settlement with current annual income shows that on average women's share of the property may provide an additional 12 per cent (estimated annual income from share received: $2,090/current annual income: $17,500) of annual income for women from low asset marriages through to an additional 46 per cent ($14,370/ $31,200) of annual income for women from high asset marriages. Thus, while women from low asset marriages generally receive a majority share,[52] the *relative value* of the share they receive is low. These women are clearly not *asset rich* and *income poor*. In contrast, while women from high asset marriages generally receive an equal share,[53] the *relative value* of the share they receive is substantial.

A similar pattern to that for women was found for the men. Men's share of property interests could potentially provide an additional 8 per cent ($2,316/$29,000) of annual income for men from low asset marriages through to an additional 39 per cent ($16,366/$41,840) of annual income for men from high asset marriages. These figures suggest that the capacity of the share received to supplement the post-separation income of men from low asset marriages is constrained. Further, the

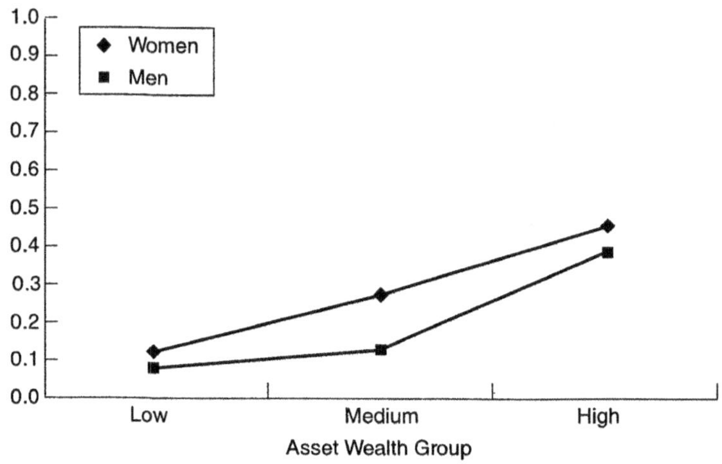

Figure 2: Median Ratio of Income Generated from the Share of Property Received at Settlement to the Annual Income of Women and Men from Different Asset Wealth Groups (n = 174) (Source: AIFS, G. Sheehan and J. Hughes, 2001(20)).
Notes:
1. A subsample of men and women were used in this analysis. These women and men included those who: (a) reported the value of all asset items and the corresponding value of the share of each asset received by each party; and (b) had a child under the age of 18 years at the time of separation. Cases with a net shortfall on the total value of assets, excluding superannuation, where respondent received no property, or where respondent received debt only were excluded form this analysis bringing the sample size for this analysis to n = 174.
2. The ratio of estimated annual income from share received to post-divorce annual income was calculated by first estimating the annual income that the respondent would receive if he or she had been able to invest their full share of the property. To calculate these values the assumption was made that the dollar share of assets received at settlement, if invested, would yield an income of a simple 7.9 per cent per year (the all ordinaries return on investments for the calender year 1997: Monthly Index Analysis, December, 1997). The annual income return on these invested assets was then compared with the party's current individual gross annual income (including any child support received).

share these men receive might be represented mainly in superannuation that cannot be relied on to meet housing and other more immediate day-to-day financial needs. Reducing the share of property these men receive in favour of the wife will thus provide her with little real financial assistance. The same cannot be said for men from high asset marriages.

To put these findings in perspective, a recent estimate of the earnings that an Australian woman forgoes as the result of taking on the role of homemaker and caring for children amounts to 28 per cent of her lifetime earnings or $200,000 for the birth of one child.[54] It is of note that only one quarter of the mothers in the sample received a share of the couple's asset wealth to the value of at least $200,000.

However, as was demonstrated earlier, this is largely due to assets of this amount not being there in the first place.

These findings, while helpful in ascertaining the limits of property division in Australia as a method of addressing post-separation financial hardship (or as a method of directly compensating women for the forgone earnings from having and caring for children), do not inform whether a clear gender disparity exists between the post-divorce financial resources available to former spouses. In the absence of couple data, such an analysis is beyond the scope of the ADTP. The *Australian Divorce Transitions Project* data can, however, be relied on to identify particular groups of women and men in the divorcing population that are particularly financially disadvantaged (or particularly well off) post-separation and divorce. *Australian Divorce Transitions Project* data that inform the current financial circumstances of divorced women and men in Australia are now presented.

D. Current Financial Circumstances

An important aspect of any enquiry into the financial aspects of the divorce transition is the relative financial circumstances of men and women post-divorce. Historically, women have tended to experience greater economic vulnerability across the life course than men.[55] This vulnerability is clearly evident upon marital separation. Past research by the AIFS suggests that women are at a considerable disadvantage compared to men in terms of their financial circumstances following marital dissolution.[56]

Women's greater economic vulnerability post-separation can be attributed to a combination of social and economic factors, many of which operate independently of marriage. These factors include women's weaker position in, and attachment to, the labour market and their relatively lower earnings compared with similarly aged men.[57] Other factors, by contrast, relate more specifically to the role some women adopt during and after marriage, and in particular to the time they spend out of paid work to have and care for children.[58] For example, during marriage the couple may decide that the husband's income earning capacity will be promoted while the wife assumes greater responsibility for caring for children and home making. Given the needs of children and men's usually higher earning capacity, this arrangement can work well – unless the marriage ends. On separation the costs of this division of labour during the marriage, such as loss of immediate earnings and reduced ability to earn income in the future, place these women in economically precarious circumstances post-separation and divorce.[59] On this particular issue, ADTP findings suggest that women are more financially disadvantaged than men on divorce, and divorced single older women and sole mothers are likely to be particularly financially disadvantaged – a pattern that is consistent with previous AIFS research.[60]

(i) Living standards post-separation and divorce

Smyth and Weston's analysis of the ADTP data, shows that women are still more likely than men to experience financial hardship after divorce, and the hardship they experience is considerable.[61] Specifically, close to half (45 per cent) the women and around one quarter of the men (24 per cent) were classified as living below the Henderson poverty line some six years post-separation.[62] This gender difference remained in evidence when more stringent measures of financial disadvantage were employed (ie, current household income of less than 73 per cent of the Henderson Poverty line).[63]

(ii) Pathways out of poverty

Smyth and Weston's analysis of the ADTP data also suggests that while gender is a significant determinant of post-divorce circumstances, it is not the sole determinant. A key pathway out of this hardship is repartnering. This is because repartnering brings with it access to the benefits of a second income. In particular, women living alone (single older women from long-term marriages and sole mothers) are the most likely group to be classified as financially disadvantaged post-divorce regardless of the threshold of poverty adopted.[64] Specifically, the majority of older women from long-term marriages, living alone, have incomes below the poverty line. The highest rate of disadvantage was found for older women who live alone (65 per cent) followed by older women who are sole parents (59 per cent).[65] In addition, a disproportionate number (44 per cent) of younger sole mothers were also living below the poverty line.[66]

Smyth and Weston also note that, like the patterns for women, the most disadvantaged men were those living alone or as sole fathers. Indeed, one third of the men living alone, and one quarter of the sole fathers, had incomes below the Henderson poverty line.[67] The position of these particular groups of men is in stark contrast to financial circumstances of the younger men who have repartnered and who don't have children living with them. Two thirds of this group had incomes at the highest level (ie, greater than 200 per cent of the poverty line), and only 11 per cent had incomes below the poverty line.[68]

The ability or desire to repartner is itself constrained by factors related to gender and ongoing child-care responsibilities. The various constraints to repartnering were explored in detail by Hughes. Drawing on ADTP data, Hughes shows that those who are most in need of the financial and social support provided by a new relationship – women with the primary responsibility for the care of young children, older women, and women and men from *asset poor marriages* who have access to limited financial resources on separation – are the least likely to have repartnered some six years after divorce.[69]

Hughes argues that women's and men's involvement in the paid workforce is an important catalyst for repartnering, and that the difficulties that these particular groups of women and men face in finding and continuing in the paid workforce, in part, explains these patterns in the propensity to repartner post-separation and divorce.[70] Thus two of the key pathways out of poverty, repartnering and re-entry into the paid workforce, are linked. Access to either pathway, is in part, determined by a person's gender, the extent of their responsibilities for the care of dependent children, and their financial circumstances.

In combination these findings indicate that a range of factors combine to effect post-divorce economic disadvantage, but that the most significant of these is having had throughout the marriage, and continuing to have, the primary responsibility for young children. Taking primary responsibility for the care of children post-separation and divorce impacts on men's and women's access to a range of social and economic pathways that can lead them out of this economic disadvantage.

There is, however, a further important factor in this complex clustering of social and economic circumstances that creates and maintains financial disadvantage post-separation and divorce, namely spousal violence. *Australian Divorce Transitions Project* findings that inform the link between spousal violence and the financial aspects of the divorce transition are now presented.

E. Spousal Violence and Financial Disadvantage

Until recently, spousal violence and post-separation financial disadvantage were issues that had been considered in isolation. Spousal violence has traditionally been considered in the context of making arrangements for the children on separation and divorce, while post-separation financial hardship has traditionally been considered in the context of making the arrangements for property. However, concerns expressed about the post-separation financial consequences of spousal violence and debate about its importance as an issue in property division have been growing.[71]

Many of the concerns that have been raised are, however, based on case law or anecdotal evidence about the disadvantages women experience in negotiating a fair property settlement when they have been the victim of spousal violence,[72] and the impact such violence has on contributions to the marriage and future financial need.[73] This important debate is, however, incomplete in the absence of reliable empirical evidence of the association between spousal violence and the financial aspects of the divorce transition.

Sheehan and Smyth's analysis of the ADTP data demonstrates that the relationship context in which women and men negotiate the divorce transition, as well as the relationship context that pre-empted the marriage ending, are important considerations in identifying and understanding financially vulnerable groups. Spousal violence amongst those who separate and divorce is a common occurrence, and the more severe the violence experienced, the greater the disadvantage evidenced across three domains of financial disadvantage: living standards post-separation and divorce, the ability to move back into paid work post-separation, and the share of property received at settlement.[74] These particular findings are discussed in more detail below.

(i) Prevalence of spousal violence amongst the divorced

Retrospective surveys suggest that couples whose marriages have ended are more likely than continuously married couples to have experienced spousal violence at some stage during the relationship.[75] In many ways, this evidence is not surprising. Spousal violence may result in marital separation.[76] It may also be precipitated by the process of separation as the relationship *sours*,[77] or result from post-separation negotiations. Negotiations about children, property, or both can act as a *lightning rod* for many pent up emotions – particularly those negotiations developing in the context of an adversarial legal process. So too can a unilateral decision by one spouse to end the relationship, especially where the relationship is characterized by notions of power and a *terroristic* control of one party by the other party.[78]

The ADTP findings confirm this commonality of spousal violence amongst those who divorce. When broadly defined, spousal violence is not an exceptional circumstance for divorced women and men but rather the norm. A majority of women (65 per cent) and a majority of men (55 per cent) reported experiencing some form of physically abusive or threatening behaviour during the marriage and/or post-separation.[79] Even when the severity of this violence is taken into account, rates for women remain very high. Around one third (30 per cent) of the women interviewed reported having experienced severe and ongoing violence. In contrast, only 5 per cent of the men interviewed reported having experienced such violence.[80] This means that amongst divorcing women and men violence in varying degrees is characteristic of the relationship context in which separating couples negotiate (legally and otherwise) the financial aspects of the divorce transition.

(ii) Financial living standards and workforce participation

Violence is reported to be more common among those who are financially disadvantaged. Many studies indicate that spousal violence is more likely to occur in low-income, low socio-economic status families,[81] suggesting that a reciprocal relation between violence and economic hardship exists. In other words, an amalgam of socio-demographic stressors acts as a *pressure cooker* that can result in violence. The violence, in turn, can exacerbate the strained financial circumstances in which the victim lives. Determining whether spousal violence caused these financial circumstances is a difficult task because of the complexity of social reality. To do so requires a more sensitive research design to the one employed for the ADTP. The ADTP data, nevertheless, provide confirmation of the link between violence and post-separation financial disadvantage. In regards to post-separation living standards, Sheehan and Smyth's analysis of the ADTP data indicates that increased levels of spousal violence are associated with economic disadvantage post-divorce for women.[82]

In order to compare the financial outcomes of divorced women and men who report different levels of violence, respondents were classified into one of four categories,[83] which together form a continuum of increasing violence severity. The criteria used to classify cases into these categories are summarized below:

—No physical violence: no physical violence and/or sexual abuse (actual or threatened) reported. The respondents did not fear for their safety or well-being.

—Physical violence: physical and/or sexual abuse (actual or threatened) reported but this violence did not cause fear.

—Moderate violence: one or two domains of abuse reported (ie, physical/sexual, emotional, post-separation harassment) that caused the respondent to fear for his or her safety and well-being.

—Severe violence: all three domains of abuse reported (ie, physical/sexual, emotional, post-separation harassment), and the abuse experienced in each domain caused the respondent to fear for his or her safety and well-being.

Women who reported experiencing severe violence were significantly more likely than women who indicated no physical violence to have household incomes below 120 per cent of the Henderson poverty line at the time of interview (66 per cent as opposed to 43 per cent).[84] Furthermore, financial disadvantage seemed to increase in direct proportion with the apparent severity of reported violence (43 per cent as opposed to 50 per cent as opposed to 62 per cent as opposed to 66 per cent) – confirming that financial disadvantage and spousal violence go hand in hand. Nevertheless, the experience of severe abuse was not restricted to women who were financially disadvantaged.

Women's pattern of workforce participation also appeared to be related to the level of spousal violence reported.[85] Figure 3 illustrates the percentage of women in paid work prior to marriage, at separation and at interview for each of the four categories of violence.

Women who reported severe abuse showed the lowest rate of employment at the time of interview – on average some six years post-separation. Surprisingly, violence was not related to a reduction in the rate of employment at separation, and was unrelated to the rate of

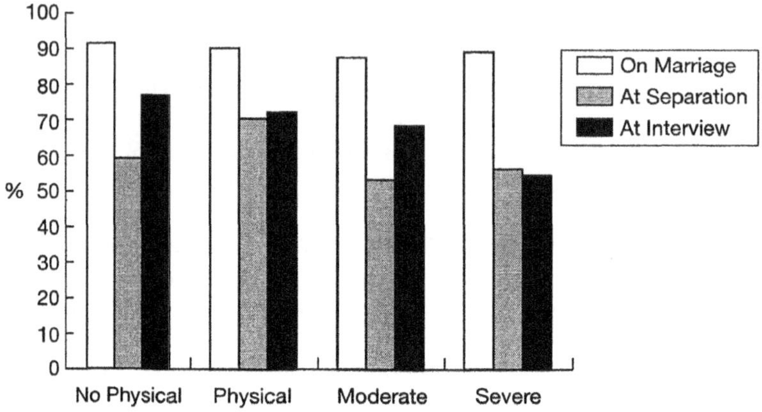

Figure 3: Paid Workforce Participation by Level of Violence: Percentage of Women ($n = 235$) (Source: Australian Journal of Family Law, G. Sheehan and B. Smyth, 2000 (20)).

Notes:

1. Number of missing cases = 9.
2. There are no significant differences between the four violence groups in the proportion of women in paid work at marriage and at separation. There is a significant difference between the four violence groups in the proportion of women in paid work at the time of interview – on average six years post-separation ($p<.05$). The group difference driving this effect is that between the 'no physical violence' group and the 'severe violence' group.

employment at marriage and the time spent out of paid work during marriage. Thus, while there is little difference between the women in the four violence groups with regard to their paid workforce participation prior to and during the marriage, those who report severe violence appear less able to move back into the paid workforce post-separation.

This relationship between spousal violence and current workforce participation, however, may have been related to women's age and education. Women who reported that they had experienced severe violence were inclined to be younger and have young children in their care (ie, under forty years) and less educated (ie, less likely to have a tertiary education) than women who indicated no physical violence.[86] These factors were, in turn, related to employment status at the time of interview. Thus, these factors (along with others that have not been examined) may, in part, explain the observed pattern for this group of women.

The experience of spousal violence by men was not significantly associated with living standards or labour market disadvantage.[87] There are a number of reasons why this might be the case. First, men typically have a stronger position in the labour market and a higher earning capacity than women (and thus are less likely to be financially disadvantaged) – especially on divorce. Second, men are less likely than women to have young children in their households immediately following separation, and to take time out of paid work during marriage to care for children. Third, men are less likely to experience severe spousal violence. In summary, men's greater earning capacity and participation in the paid workforce, and the nature of the violence that they report experiencing might mitigate the economic effects of spousal violence.

(iv) Share of property received

A women's experience of violence also places her at a disadvantage when dividing the matrimonial property. Sheehan and Smyth's analysis of the ADTP data indicates that women who reported experiencing severe violence were around three times as likely as women who reported no physical violence to indicate receipt of a minor share (less than a 40 per cent share) of the total property (17 per cent as opposed to 49 per cent), and of the domestic assets (12 per cent as opposed to 37 per cent).[88] These findings are striking given the circumstances of these women at separation. Almost half of the women who reported severe violence were out of work at separation, more than half the women had spent one third of the time they were married out of the workforce, and almost all had primary responsibility for the care of dependent children after separation and divorce. Further, this group of women were the most likely to have left the family home soon after separation which, in turn, predicted receipt of a lower share of property. Such findings suggest that these women give safety precedence over their right to a fair share of the matrimonial property.

Surprisingly, women who indicated having experienced moderate violence were more similar to the no physical violence group in the reported share of property received (17 per cent of the women in the *no physical violence* group reported receipt of a minor share of the property as opposed to 26 per cent of the women in the *moderate violence* group). This finding may, in part, be explained by the type of property agreement that these women had with their former spouse. Women from the moderate violence group were the least likely of all women to have made a private agreement for property settlement (28 per cent as opposed to 37 per cent through to 39 per cent for the remaining three groups). It appears that the majority of these women were in a relatively strong position to argue for a fair share of the property. The reasons why this particular group of women utilized court resources to settle their property matters more than the other three groups are unclear. This finding does suggest, however, that access to the Family Court and legal assistance on property matters may make a difference to the settlement outcome for women who have experienced violence.

For the majority of men – in contrast to the findings for women – there was no significant relation between their experience of spousal violence and the share of property they reportedly received, with most men indicating receipt of less than 40 per cent of the property (total and domestic assets).[89] The gender difference in the relationship between spousal violence and property division outcomes may, in part, be explained by the different baseline of 'share of property received' for women and men. The majority of men surveyed were non-resident parents, had a strong position in the labour market, and had a greater income and earning capacity as compared with women. This helps explain the tendency for most men to indicate receipt of less than 40 per cent of the property. This means, however, that the relation between spousal violence and men's property settlement outcomes may be less pronounced than for women. Furthermore, the small proportion of men who reported severe levels of violence (ie, 5 per cent of men as opposed to 30 per cent of women) inhibits a true estimate of the relation between spousal violence and men's property settlement outcomes.

When the financial living standards and work history findings are considered in conjunction with the findings for share of property received, a clear pattern emerges: many women who reported experiencing spousal violence appear to have been denied their right to a just and equitable share of property on divorce, despite their disadvantaged economic circumstances and their ongoing responsibility for the care of children post-separation and divorce. Ensuring that the basic property rights of women who experience spousal violence are met is thus a matter of urgency in Australia.

4. CONCLUSIONS

For many years, concern has been expressed in Australia about the financial circumstances of those who separate and divorce, and there has been ongoing debate about its importance as an issue in property reform and social security provision. Unfortunately, over the past decade, there has been no broad-based empirical evidence available on the financial aspects of the divorce transition with which to inform this important debate. The ADTP sought to fill this gap by providing detailed information on the financial aspects of the divorce transition, based on a national survey of a representative sample of divorced women and men. The findings presented here provide an up-to-date overview of the economic and social factors that are reported to make a family's passage through the divorce transition particularly arduous (or relatively easy).

The study is, however, limited in its ability to conclude that characteristics of the marriage (such as time spent out of the paid workforce to have and care for children and spousal violence), the Family Law Act and the legal process, in any way *caused* the parties' financial circumstances. There is such a complex relationship between the factors surrounding the way in which the financial aspects of the divorce transition are played out that disentangling the relative influence of any one factor from another is a formidable task – one that is beyond the methodological capacity of the ADTP. An alternative research design that is based on couple data, and which can track the changing financial and social circumstances of men and women over time would be better placed to answer questions of cause and effect. The ADTP data do, however, lead to the following conclusions.

Over the past decade, little has changed in the way that the financial aspects of the divorce transition are effected. The 'feminization of poverty' post-separation and divorce remains an important issue for family law and social policy in Australia. This is despite significant advances in social policy such as the introduction of the Child Support Scheme, and the growing awareness amongst legal practitioners, policy makers and the community of the financial consequences of separation and divorce, particularly for women and the children in their care.

There is, however, a substantial diversity of financial needs amongst those who separate and divorce. Those most in need of assistance are characterized by a clustering of factors that disadvantage them financially in making the divorce transition. These include, living alone, responsibility for the care of young children post-separation, low asset wealth and the resulting limited access to financial resources on separation, difficulty moving back into the workforce, and spousal violence. Financial supports and services designed to help disadvantaged groups of women and men to get back on their feet financially have to be broadly-based and multi-purpose in their approach to providing assistance.

The ADTP findings regarding property division indicate that the current practice in dividing property is at odds with the disadvantaged financial circumstances of many divorced women post-separation and divorce. Further, current practice in dividing property does not reflect the full ambit of the legislative provisions. Non-financial contributions to non-domestic assets were unlikely to be reflected in the share of property received. As regards future needs, the needs of dependent children appear to have been a most important consideration, and the financial needs of the former spouse may have been overlooked. The inadequacy of the adjustment made to property interests in recognition of contributions made, and future financial need, is most striking in the case of women who have experienced severe violence. For these women, safety appears to have been given precedence over the right to a fair share of the matrimonial property. This gap between law and reality for many divorcing Australians highlights the crucial role of readily accessible information and legal representation for property matters, to raise awareness of the applicable principles, and to ensure that basic rights to property on divorce are met.

Unfortunately, a remedy for this shortfall is dependent on two factors. The first is the extent of asset wealth available to the parties on divorce; the second is the capacity of the former spouse to pay ongoing support to this spouse in addition to any ongoing financial commitment that he or she may have to their children, or to others, including families from previous or subsequent relationships. *Australian Divorce Transitions Project* findings regarding the asset wealth of couples on separation and the relative value of the assets received at settlement, indicates that for a large minority of women and men the asset wealth available at separation limits the ability of s 75(2) of the Family Law Act to ensure an adequate property adjustment is made in recognition of the future financial need of a former spouse. Thus, for many women addressing this financial need through family law is dependent upon their seeking and obtaining periodic spousal maintenance and having a former spouse whose post-separation financial position can sustain this ongoing financial commitment – a remedy that is at present rare and fraught with difficulties.

An important issue for law reform in Australia is thus how much financial disadvantage a revised family law could prevent and for whom it could be prevented. *Australian Divorce Transitions Project* findings suggest that for a substantial number of couples who divorce in Australia, family law cannot be relied on to have a major impact on the feminization of poverty post-separation and divorce, nor can it be relied on to substitute for anti-poverty government programmes. This is not to say, however, that there are no groups of women and men for whom the financial provisions of the Family Law Act could be employed to make a real difference. Young sole mothers, with primary responsibility for the care of children, appear to be one of the most financially disadvantaged groups. Young and repartnered men, without childcare responsibilities, on the other hand, appear to be the most financially advantaged group at some six years post separation. For divorcing couples in these particular circumstances it would seem that the law and the legal system could do more to ensure that property settlement outcomes, and maintenance orders, impose the financial burden of divorce fairly.

In conclusion, the financial consequences of divorce in Australia today are as they were a decade ago: inequitable division of property and financial resources worth too little to really matter; no or short-term spousal maintenance; and financial disadvantage experienced at the post-separation and divorce stages by sole parents, older women, and women who have experienced severe violence. As our understanding of these financial circumstances continues to grow so also does the importance of challenging and changing the status quo.

NOTES

[1] See, for example, P. Jordan (1996) *The Effects of Marital Separation on Men: Ten Years On*, Family Court of Australia, for evidence of the long-term emotional impact of separation and divorce; and

R. Weston (1993) 'Income circumstances of parents and children: a longitudinal view' in K. Funder, M. Harrison and R. Weston (eds) *Settling Down: Pathways of Parents After Divorce*, Australian Institute of Family Studies, for evidence of the long-term financial impact of separation and divorce.

[2] P. McDonald (1995) *Families in Australia: A Socio-Demographic Perspective*. Australian Institute of Family Studies; Australian Bureau of Statistics (1999) *Children of Australia: A Social Report*, Canberra.

[3] D. DeVaus (1997) 'Divorce' in D. DeVaus and I. Wolcott (eds) *Australian Family Profiles: Social and Demographic Patterns*, Australian Institute of Family Studies, 30–1.

[4] Ibid at 28.

[5] See, for example, McDonald above n 2, and W. Goode (1993) *World Changes in Divorce Patterns, 1950–90*, Yale University Press.

[6] McDonald, above n 2 at 58.

[7] P. McDonald (1986) *Settling Up: Property and Income Distribution on Divorce in Australia*, Prentice-Hall of Australia; K. Funder, M. Harrison and R. Weston (1993) *Settling Down: Pathways of Parents After Divorce*, Australian Institute of Family Studies.

[8] A representative sample is one that displays characteristics across particular variables (such as age, gender, income, and education) in similar proportions and patterns to those found in the wider population.

[9] B. Fehlberg and F. Kelly (2000) 'Jurisdictional overlaps between the Family Division of the Children's Court of Victoria and the Family Court of Australia', 14 *Australian Journal of Family Law* 211.

[10] See above n 7.

[11] The Child Support Scheme was introduced in two stages, the first of which commenced 1 June 1988. Stage One covers children born 1 October 1989 whose parents separated before that date (unless these children have a sibling born on or after that date in which case Stage Two applies; see below). This first stage sought to improve the collection of maintenance covered by court orders. Stage Two reforms specify the amount of child support to be paid according to an administrative formula. This administrative assessment is buttressed by the collection and enforcement powers of Stage One. Where as Stage One can be viewed as an administrative 'transition' phase primarily aimed at the registration of existing court orders, the commencement of Stage Two marks a critical juncture in social policy in Australia insofar as the registration of child support liabilities converts 'a personal obligation into a debt owed to the Commonwealth'. See M. Harrison (1994) 'Child support reforms: the Australia experience', 32 *Family and Conciliation Courts Review* 178. The introduction of the Child Support Scheme is an important aspect of a broad policy shift in Australia towards encouraging continuing parental responsibility after separation and divorce. This shift is also exemplified by changes to the Family Law Act, resulting from the Family Law Reform Act 1995, underlining that parental responsibility is ongoing, despite changes in the parental relationship, and the child's right to know and be cared for by both parents.

[12] I. Wolcott (1997) 'Work and family' in D. DeVaus and I. Wolcott (eds) 'Australian family profiles: social and demographic patterns', Australian Institute of Family Studies; Office of the Status of Women (March 1999) *Facts about Women*, http:/www.dpmc.gov.au/osw/info/facts.htm.

[13] K. Norris and M. Wooden (1996) 'The changing Australian labour market', *Commission Paper No 11*, Australian Government Publishing Service for the Economic Planning Advisory Commission.

[14] D. DeVaus (1997) 'Marriage' in D. DeVaus and I. Wolcott (eds) *Australian Family Profiles: Social and Demographic Patterns*, Australian Institute of Family Studies; DeVaus, above n 4.

[15] The State of Western Australia also has its own Family Law Act: the Family Court Act 1997 (WA). The usual process is that amendments to the Family Law Act 1975 (Cth) are copied over by the WA legislature. However, there are sometimes delays in doing this, which can mean that the applicable law in WA differs, at least temporarily, from the law applicable throughout the rest of Australia. At the time of the *Australian Divorce Transitions Project*, the relevant legislation in WA was the Family Court Act 1975 (WA). That Act was repealed in 1997. The 1975 WA Act contained all the 'old' language in it regarding custody and guardianship. In contrast, the equivalent provisions in the Family Law Act 1975 (Cth) (applicable elsewhere in Australia) had been replaced by the Family Law Reform Act 1995 (Cth) which amended the Family Law Act 1975 (Cth).

[16] To obtain the target samples, a total of 72,308 telephone calls were made. Of these calls, 28 per cent (20,303) of households were not contactable. Of the 52,005 households that were contactable, 28 per cent of people refused to participate at the outset, and 70 per cent did not contain a person who met the screening criteria; 881 households contained a person who fitted the sampling criteria.

[17] The potential follow-up rate thus was 92 per cent (94 per cent of women and 91 per cent of men). At the time the 'Spousal Violence Survey' was being conducted, eight respondents from the long-term marriage sample were still being sought in order to balance quotas in Sydney and Brisbane. Even though six of the eight eventually agreed to be recontacted, these cases were not available for the investigation of spousal violence. The follow-up rate thus uses a base of $n = 642$ (women $n = 354$, men $n = 288$) and the completion rate uses a base of $n = 593$ (women $n = 332$, men $n = 261$).

[18] The first pattern is common to survey research in general: men are often less likely than women to participate in surveys (especially telephone interviews) – not just because they tend to be less available to take calls at home but also because they are more inclined to refuse consent – including doing follow-up interviews. Sampling stratification by gender attempts to offset these patterns. However, the spousal violence sample was not stratified by this element in order to maximize the overall sample size. A second possible pattern of non-response relates to the content of the survey and social desirability: respondents were informed at the outset that the survey covered areas that were 'personal or sensitive, such as domestic violence'. It is possible that men may have perceived this as threatening in a social context where they are typically described as the perpetrators of such violence. Men may also be less likely to participate when they themselves have been victims of violence. While the relatively low completion rate for men in the sample is not necessarily indicative of high level of bias, it is possible that the men's reports of violence are not representative of the Australian divorced male population's experience.

[19] R. Weston (1986) 'Changes in household income circumstances' in P. McDonald (ed) *Settling Up: Property and Income Distribution on Divorce in Australia*, Australian Institute of Family Studies; Weston, above n 1.

[20] For a detailed presentation of the ADTP findings, methodology, measures and statistical analyses relating to the division of property and the treatment of superannuation on divorce, and spousal maintenance see, G. Sheehan and J. Hughes (2001) 'Division of matrimonial property in Australia' *Research Paper No 25*, Australian Institute of Family Studies; J. Dewar, G. Sheehan and J. Hughes (1999) 'Superannuation and divorce in Australia' *Working Paper No 18*, Australian Institute of Family Studies; J. Behrens and B. Smyth (1999) 'Spousal support in Australia: a study of incidence and attitudes', *Working Paper No 16*, Australian Institute of Family Studies. For a detailed presentation of the ADTP findings, methodology, measures and statistical analyses relating to living standards post-divorce for Australian women and men and pathways out of poverty such as repartnering see B. Smyth and R. Weston (2000) 'Financial living standards after divorce: a recent snapshot', *Research Paper No 23*, Australian Institute of Family Studies; J. Hughes (2000) 'Repartnering after divorce: marginal mates and unwedded women', 55 *Family Matters* 16. For a detailed presentation of the ADTP findings, methodology, measures and statistical analyses relating to domestic violence and post-separation financial circumstances, see G. Sheehan and B. Smyth (2000) 'Spousal violence and post-separation financial outcomes', 14 *Australian Journal of Family Law* 102.

[21] McDonald, above n 7.

[22] Sheehan and Hughes, above n 20.

[23] J. Najman, W. Bor, G. O'Callaghan, G. Williams and G. Shuttlewood (July 2000) 'Family form and quality: changes over time'. Paper presented to the symposium: Longitudinal data and family studies, *Seventh Australian Institute of Family Studies Conference*, Sydney.

[24] R. Boheim and Ermisch (1999) 'Breaking up: financial surprises and partnership dissolution', *Working Paper No 99-9*, ESRC Research Centre on Micro-Social Change; R. Conger, M. Reuter and J. Elder (1999) 'Couple resilience to economic pressure', 76 *Journal of Personality and Social Psychology* 54–71; U. Kinnunen and L. Pulkkinen (1998) 'Linking economic stress to martial quality among Finnish couples', 19 *Journal of Family Issues* 705–14.

[25] This figure of $100,000 represents the difference between the average dollar value of the matrimonial assets reported by women and men in the *Australian Divorce Transitions Project* and the average dollar value of household asset wealth for a comparable age cohort from the general Australian population. (See A. King and R. Lloyd (1999) 'Assets of the baby boomers', *Income Distribution Report No 11*, 1–6). To calculate this difference score both figures were adjusted to 1997 dollars.

[26] Respondents were categorized according to the level of asset wealth of the couple at the time of separation. The 1997 social security non-home owner Pension Assets Test was used to assess the reported net asset wealth levels of the couple at the time of separation. As all calculations of assets include the value of couples' net equity in their home, the test for all assets was used rather than the test that excludes the value for the owner-occupied home. This involved deriving the

value of the couple's total net assets excluding superannuation, as superannuation is excluded from calculation of the 1997 social security non-home owner Pension Assets Test. This value was then adjusted to 1997 dollars using the Consumer Price Index to determine whether the real value of assets was above or below the Asset Test cut off: $268, 500.The following three categories of asset wealth were created based on the 1997 social security non-home owner Pension Assets Test: (a) the *high* asset wealth group where asset wealth was greater than the cut off for the assets test (that is, $268,500), (b) the *medium* asset wealth group with asset wealth valued at between $114,000 and $268,500, and (c) the *low* asset wealth group with asset wealth valued at below $114,000. The two 'low asset' groups were determined by a median split for those cases where assets were valued at less than $268,500.

[27] P. McDonald (1986) 'Property distribution: the shares of each partner and their determinants' in P. McDonald (ed) *Settling Up: Property and Income Distribution on Divorce in Australia*, Australian Institute of Family Studies.

[28] Dewar, Sheehan and Hughes, above n 20 at 10.

[29] McDonald, above n 7 at 174–7.

[30] M. Glendon (1981) *The New Family and the New Property*, Butterworths.

[31] Dewar, Sheehan and Hughes, above n 20 at 3, comment that the growth in the number of employees covered by superannuation in Australia is attributable to two factors. The first is the favourable tax treatment accorded to superannuation. Contributions made to a scheme, investment earnings of scheme funds, and payments of benefits to beneficiaries all enjoy favourable tax treatment. Superannuation has become an increasingly important, and tax-efficient, part of salary and wage packages in Australia. The second is the introduction in 1992 of the superannuation Guarantee. This, in effect, requires employers to contribute a minimum amount towards employee's superannuation, where an employee's earnings exceed a certain threshold.

[32] King and Lloyd, above n 25.

[33] These factors are more broadly referred to by the Family Court as the s 75(2) factors – a label that recognizes that this adjustment is not only made on the basis of future financial need. Any other fact or circumstance of a broadly economic nature, which in the opinion of the court the justice of the case requires, can be taken into account (s 75(2)(o)).

[34] P. Parkinson (1999) 'Reforming the law of family property', 13 *Australian Journal of Family Law* 117–39.

[35] Divorce Transitions Project findings indicate that around one third (38 per cent) of those who divorce settle their financial matters without direct court involvement (in other words, privately, without court orders or any agreement registered in court, but perhaps with the assistance of a solicitor).

[36] R. H. Mnookin and L. Kornhauser (1979) 'Bargaining in the shadow of the law: the case of divorce', 88 *Yale Law Journal* 950–97.

[37] Sheehan and Hughes, above n 20. To determine the share of property received by respondents at division, the total net amount (summed across all assets) received by respondents was divided by the total net value of the property. This amount was then calculated as a percentage share received for each respondent.

[38] McDonald, above n 7 at 181–4.

[39] Domestic assets comprise those assets that the vast majority of people have, and that are used in day-to-day family life such as the family home, furniture and cars, bank accounts and non-asset related debts (such as credit card debts and personal or private loans). This distinction is based primarily on usage rather than on current practice in family law in distinguishing between assets for domestic use and other assets when dividing property. The non-domestic assets comprise two different kinds of family wealth: (a) investments such as shares, bonds, debentures or other real estate, and businesses or farms; and (b) financial resources such as superannuation and life insurance.

[40] McDonald, above n 7 at 185–91.

[41] See, for example Sheehan and Hughes, above n 20 at 12, for a detailed analysis of the composition of asset wealth in different types of marriages.

[42] Parties and the Family Court of Australia are currently constrained in the way they deal with financial resources, in particular superannuation entitlements, on divorce. The Family Court only has the power to deal with property that is owned by the parties at the date of the hearing (s 4(1)). Assets that are payable only on retirement, or on some other qualifying event, are not considered 'property' for these purposes, unless that event has occurred and benefits have been paid (*In the Marriage of Crapp* (1979) 5 Fam LR 47). The Federal Government has recently introduced legislation amending the Family Law Act to give the court a new power to divide superannu-

ation benefits on divorce (the Family Law Legislation Amendment (Superannuation) Act 2001). This legislation is expected to come into effect towards the end of 2002. A result of this legal constraint is that, on divorce, financial resources such as superannuation entitlements often remain with the party who contributed directly to the fund – namely the husband (see Dewar, Sheehan and Hughes, above n 20). Parties are, however, able to take superannuation into account by other means such as: (a) increasing the dependent spouses share of property to compensate for the loss of future superannuation rights (ie, offsetting); or (b) adjourning part of the property proceedings until the superannuation becomes payable, then making an order with respect to those benefits once they become payable. However, it is of note that in only 10 per cent of cases was superannuation taken into account via these and other indirect methods of division (ibid at 20).

43 Ibid at 22–3.

44 H. Charlesworth and R. Ingleby (1988) 'The sexual division of labour and family property law', 6 *Law in Context* 29–49; R. Graycar (September 1995) 'Matrimonial property law reform: what lessons have we learnt?', *Enhancing Access to Justice: Family Court of Australia Second National Conference*, Family Court of Australia, Sydney.

45 K. Funder (1986) 'His and her divorce' in P. McDonald (ed) *Settling Up: Property and Income Distribution on Divorce in Australia*, Australian Institute of Family Studies.

46 Sheehan and Hughes, above 20 at 19–27 for information on the measures used and statistical procedures employed to test for the independent influence of each of the s 75(2) factors on share of property received.

47 M. Kaye and J. Tolmie (1998) 'Fathers' rights groups in Australia and their engagement with issues in family law', 12 *Australian Journal of Family Law* 19–68.

48 Sheehan and Hughes, above n 20 at 39.

49 Ibid at 21–4.

50 Behrens and Smyth, above n 20 at 21.

51 This was done by first estimating the annual income that the respondent would receive if he or she had been able to invest their full share of the property. To calculate these values the assumption was made that the dollar share of assets received at settlement, if invested, would yield an income of a simple 7.9 per cent per year (the all ordinaries return on investments for the calendar year 1997: Monthly Index Analysis, December, 1997). The annual income return on these invested assets was then compared with the party's current individual gross annual income (including any child support received) – see Sheehan and Hughes, above n 20 at 17. This procedure of creating a ratio of the estimated income generated from investment of share received to the party's current gross annual income was first adopted by Seltzer and Garfinkel. (See J. Seltzer and I. Garfinkel (1991)) 'Inequality in divorce settlements: an investigation of property settlements and child support awards', 19 *Social Science Research* 82–111) in their investigation of the relative value of property settlement outcomes to American women's and men's financial circumstances post-divorce in the State of Wisconsin.

52 The mean share to the wife in low asset marriages is 58 per cent (see Sheehan and Hughes, above n 20 at 18).

53 The mean share to the wife in high asset marriages is 50 per cent (ibid).

54 B. Chapman, Y. Dunlop, M. Gray, A. Liu and D. Mitchell (1999) 'The foregone earnings from child rearing revisited', *Discussion Paper No 407*, Centre for Economic Policy Research. The value cited here is that derived by Chapman *et al* adjusted to 1997 dollars.

55 L. Bryson (1996) 'Poverty: the gender dimension', *Australian Options* (November) 16–19.

56 Weston, above n 1; Weston, above n 19.

57 Bryson, above n 51; A. Dickinson (1996) 'The financial well-being of women and the family', 24 *American Journal of Family Therapy* 65–73.

58 K. Funder (1986) 'Work and the marriage partnership', in P. McDonald (ed) *Settling Up: Property and Income Distribution on Divorce in Australia*, Prentice-Hall of Australia; Chapman *et al*, above n 50.

59 K. Funder (1992) 'Australia: a proposal for reform' in J. J. Weitzman and M. Maclean (eds) *Economic Consequences of Divorce: The International Perspective*, Clarendon Press; K. Funder (1993) 'Women's post-separation employment and reliance on social security' in K. Funder, M. Harrison and R. Weston (eds) *Settling Down: Pathways of Parents after Divorce*, Australian Institute of Family Studies.

60 McDonald, above n 7; Funder, Harrison and Weston, above n 7.

61 Smyth and Weston, above n 20 at 8–9.

62 Ibid. These rates are based on whether the respondent's current household income places

them above or below the Henderson poverty line. This particular measure of financial disadvantage examines net household income at the time of interview relative to the Henderson poverty line, and is based on the Henderson (1975) equivalence scales and Henderson poverty line estimates for 1997, as updated by the Institute of Applied Economic and Social Research. Smyth and Weston chose this particular measure of financial disadvantage because of its relevance as an indicator of post-divorce economic hardship, and its common usage in the post-divorce living standard literature. For full details on the calculation of these rates, and the strengths and weaknesses of this particular approach to measuring financial disadvantage, see ibid at 6–7.

[63] Ibid at 9.

[64] This pattern in the data is present at below the Henderson poverty line and at less than 73 per cent of the Henderson poverty line, see ibid at 11.

[65] Ibid.

[66] Ibid.

[67] Ibid.

[68] Ibid at 10.

[69] Hughes, above n 20.

[70] Ibid.

[71] In determining property settlement, the general approach adopted by the Family court has been that spousal violence during the marriage is irrelevant, except where it has direct financial consequences, as in cases of dire physical injury. In 1997 in *Kennon (In the Marriage of Kennon)* (1997) 22 Fam LR 1 (Kennon)), however, the Full Court made clear that spousal violence can be relevant, a course of violence conduct must have been present throughout the marriage (conduct related to the breakdown of the marriage will not qualify), and the survivors' contributions must have been made 'significantly more arduous' as a result of the violence. The Court emphasized that the principles set out should only apply to 'exceptional cases'.

[72] For example see H. Astor (1995) 'The weight of silence: talking about violence in family mediation', in M. Thornton (ed) *Public and Private: Feminist Legal Debates*, Oxford University Press; and M. Neave (1995) 'Private ordering in family law: will women benefit?' in M. Thornton (ed) *Public and Private: Feminist Legal Debates*, Oxford University Press.

[73] See, for example, J. Behrens (1993) 'Domestic violence and property adjustment: a critique of "no fault" discourse', 7 *Australian Journal of Family Law* 9–28. Behrens has suggested that economic vulnerability is exacerbated for those women who have experienced spousal violence during marriage or after separation. According to Behrens, the effects of spousal violence on women are long lasting, insidious, and have 'inevitable economic consequences' (at 17). While Behrens' thesis is substantiated by examples of extreme spousal violence charted in case law – cases in which the woman's health and work capacity were clearly affected – the financial consequences of less severe (but perhaps more widespread) forms of spousal violence are difficult to determine and remain largely unknown.

[74] Sheehan and Smyth, above n 20.

[75] See, for example, D. Kalmus and J. A. Seltzer (1986) 'Continuity of marital behaviour in remarriage: the case of spouse abuse', 48 *Journal of Marriage and the Family* 113–20; G. K. Kantor and J. L. Jasinski (1998) 'Dynamics and risk factors in partner violence' in J. L. Jasinski and L. M. Williams (eds) *Partner Violence: A Comprehensive Review of Twenty Years of Research*, Sage.

[76] See, for example J. Giles-Sims (1998) 'The aftermath of partner violence' in J. L. Jasinski and L. M. Williams (eds) *Partner Violence: A Comprehensive Review of Twenty Years of Research*, Sage; Kantor and Jasinski, above n 71.

[77] E. Hore and J. Gibson and S. Bordow (1996) 'Domestic homicide', *Research Report No 13*, Family Court of Australia.

[78] The sort of violence where there is a 'terroristic' control of one party by the other party that involves the systematic use of not only (or necessarily) physical violence, but also economic subordination, threats, isolation, and other controlling and fear inducing tactics, is referred to by Johnson as 'patriarchal terrorism'. This sort of violence is predominantly engaged in by men against women. See M. P. Johnson (1995) 'Patriarchal terrorism and common couple violence: two forms of violence against women', 57 *Journal of Marriage and the Family* 285.

[79] See Sheehan and Smyth, above 20 at 109. The definition of violence adopted by Sheehan and Smyth in calculating these rates is a commonly used definition in the literature on domestic violence, which narrows the range of behaviors considered as abusive. The definition takes a legal approach, and domestic violence refers to actions that could be considered an offence under criminal law, such as any incident involving the occurrence, attempt or threat of either physical or

sexual assault (see Sheehan and Smyth, above n 20 at 108 for further details on the definition of spousal violence adopted).

[80] Ibid at 113. In calculating these rates severe violence was defined as having experienced a wide range of abusive behaviors including physical and sexual violence, emotional abuse and harassment behaviours post-separation such as stalking. In addition, those who were classified as having experienced severe abuse report fearing for their safety and well-being as a result of the violence they experienced (see ibid at 110–11 for details on this definition of violence and the validity of the system adopted for classifying cases on a continuum of abuse severity).

[81] See, for example, A. Dickinson (1996) 'The financial well-being of women and the family', 24 *American Journal of Family Therapy* 65–73; A. Ferrante, F. Morgan, D. Indermaur and R. Harding (1996) *Measuring the Extent of Domestic Violence*, Hawkins Press; R. J. Gelles (1997) *Intimate Violence in Families* (3rd edn), Sage; E. Klein, J. Campbell, E. Soler and M. Ghez (1997) *Ending Domestic Violence: Changing Public Perceptions/Halting the Epidemic*, Sage; United Nations (1989) *Violence Against Women in the Family*, UN.

[82] Sheehan and Smyth, above n 20 at 114–15.

[83] For further details on this classification system and its conceptual validity as a continuum of sabuse severity see ibid.

[84] Several researchers have found the 120 per cent Henderson line cut-off to be a relatively clear threshold of financial disadvantage (see, for example, T. Gilley and J. Taylor (1995) *Unequal Lives: Low Income and the Life Chances of Three Year Olds*, Brotherhood of St Lawrence; H. Brownlee and P. McDonald (1993) 'In search of poverty and affluence: an investigation of families living in two Melbourne municipalities', *AIFS working paper No 10*, Australian Institute of Family Studies; Weston, above n 19; Weston, above n 1). A less stringent cut-off to that which was adopted by Smyth and Weston (above n 20) was used in this analysis because: (a) it maximized the cell sizes for the statistical analysis; and (b) the primary objective of the analysis was to explore between-groups comparisons, not as a means by which to assess the degree of economic wellbeing of any one particular group.

[85] Sheehan and Smyth, above n 20 at 116.

[86] This particular pattern of findings is consistent with the socio-demographic correlates of violence against women found for the general population of Australian women (see Australian Bureau of Statistics (1996) Women's Safety, Australia (Cat no 4128.0), ABS, 17).

[87] Sheehan and Smyth, above n 20 at 115–16.

[88] Ibid at 112.

[89] Ibid.

[11]

CHILD SUPPORT OR SUPPORT FOR CHILDREN? RE-THINKING "PUBLIC" AND "PRIVATE" IN FAMILY LAW

Mary Jane Mossman*

"Who has the power to define social problems? Whose definitions of problems prevail? What sort of social response will be made to those problems?"[1]

These provocative questions introduced a book of essays in the late 1980s in Britain. As the editor's introduction suggested, social problems are identified when "private griefs" that are experienced by individuals are transformed into "public sorrows" because they are experienced more widely. Thus, public sorrows are recognized when "[individual] experience expands to be the common experience of many, even the majority of, individuals".[2] Moreover, whereas solutions to private griefs are considered the responsibility of individuals who are experiencing the problems, public sorrows demand solutions on the basis of societal responsibility for them. As the essays demonstrated, however, exactly how and why particular private griefs become transformed into public sorrows are puzzling questions, in part at least depending on who has the power to define social problems and to implement policy responses to them.

Although this collection of essays focused on changes in social and political ideas about the role of the British welfare state, the same questions are useful in examining social policy debates in Canada in the 1990s. In relation to recent proposals for reforming the law of child support, for example, individuals' concerns about child support awards have been transformed into a more widespread social problem. For many separated custodial parents, inadequacy in levels of child support awards and difficulties in collecting them from recalcitrant payers have been experienced as private griefs for a long time.[3] Recently, however, child support has arguably

---

*Professor, Faculty of Law, Osgoode Hall. Viscount Bennett Memorial Lecture delivered at the Faculty of Law, University of New Brunswick (Fredericton) 7 November 1996. The author is especially grateful to the organizers of the Viscount Bennett Memorial Lecture and to all the panellists who provided excellent comments and suggestions, to Hazel Pollack and Ned Djordjevic at Osgoode Hall Law School for technical and research assistance, and to Professor Harry Glasbeek for help with an early draft.

[1]M. Loney, ed., *The State or the Market: Politics and Welfare in Contemporary Britain*, (London: Sage Publications, 1987) at 7.

[2]N. Manning, "What is a Social Problem?" in *ibid.* at 8.

[3]For an excellent review of the literature documenting the problems, see D. Pask, "The Effect on Maintenance of Custody Sharing" (1989) 3 C.J.W.L. 155. For an account of the limitations of the legal system in ensuring adequate child support for custodial parents, see N. Blown & S. Milliken, "The Failure of the Legal System to Protect the Economic Rights of Children" (1989) 7 Can. J. Fam. L. 366.

become a public sorrow, with a number of different legal and policy responses including more effective enforcement systems in the provinces[4] and the 1996 federal proposals for legislatively-defined child support guidelines.[5] These developments offer an interesting opportunity to identify exactly how and why private griefs that have so long been associated with child support are being re-defined now as public sorrows.

The process of re-defining child support as a public, rather than private, matter for concern demonstrates how the framework for the debate may construct both the problem and the solution. In this lecture, I suggest that governments with the power to define child support as a social problem have constructed the problem as one of "deadbeat dads" and the corresponding solution as a package of mandatory guidelines and more effective enforcement measures. By constructing the child support debate in this way, much critical attention has been focused on complex and highly technical aspects of the proposed solution — child support guidelines — with almost no attention at all directed to the more fundamental question: whether defining the problem as deadbeat dads accurately reflects the dimensions of this social problem as a public sorrow. Although the data about child support awards clearly demonstrate the hardships experienced by custodial parents (frequently mothers) as a result of inadequate awards and late or non-existent payments by payers (frequently fathers), there is less information available about the reasons for fathers' non-payment. Undoubtedly, some fathers fail to make child support payments for no good reason. However, unless we conclude that all fathers fall into this category, a definition of the problem as deadbeat dads oversimplifies a more complicated problem that is not being fully addressed by the solutions being proposed. As Nick Manning has argued, if social problems are characterized in ways that are altogether different from reality, "then policies based on an understanding of the issues only at the level of appearance will fail".[6]

At a more fundamental level, moreover, the choice by governments to define the problem of child support in terms of the failure of deadbeat dads to provide for their children constructs this social problem so that there appears to be no overall societal responsibility for the economic well-being of children whose parents have separated.

---

[4]For an overview of the problems, see F. Steel, "Maintenance Enforcement in Canada" (1985) 17 Ottawa L. Rev. 491. See also Y. Atuobi-Danso & H. Brownstone, "Family Support Enforcement: Dawn of a New Era" (1993) 15 Advocates' Q. 91; and R. Langer "Post Marital Support Discourse, Discretion and Male Dominance" (1994) 12 Can. J. Fam. L. 67.

[5]See Canada, *Backgrounder: New Child Support Strategy* (Ottawa: Department of Justice, March 1996). Child support guidelines were recommended by the Federal/Provincial/Territorial Family Law Committee in *Report and Recommendations on Child Support* (Ottawa: Department of Justice, January 1995). For a critique of the policy-making process, see E. Zweibel, "Child Support Policy and Child Support Guidelines: Broadening the Agenda" (1993) 6 C.J.W.L. 371.

[6]Manning, *supra* note 2 at 21.

Pointing to deadbeat dads as the problem effectively "re-privatizes" this public sorrow, masking the state's abdication of responsibility for children. Instead of recognizing a collective responsibility for child poverty in Canada, governments have assigned blame to deadbeat dads, assuming only the limited responsibility of enforcement and adopting harsh measures to ensure that these private parental obligations are met. In this way, although it appears that the private griefs of child support have been re-defined as public sorrows, the solutions offered by the child support guidelines package will not really transform the continuing reality of child support as private griefs. In terms of the economic well-being of Canadian children, the problem of child support has not been transformed into support for children.

In addition to these concerns about the way that the problem of child support has been constructed in public debates, a focus on the process of its definition shows how difficult it is, in terms of strategy, to confront definitions adopted by those with the power to define social problems. In the context of child support, the definition of deadbeat dads as the problem has all the advantages of simplicity, moral authority, and apparently clear solutions. To suggest that the problem is more complicated and needs more complex solutions is at once a more difficult and more open-ended task. More significantly, such a suggestion risks being misunderstood as supporting the arguments of fathers who do not want to pay child support — for any reasons whatever — and as unsupportive of the real needs of custodial mothers and their children. Indeed, the enormity of these risks, especially for someone who has contributed to public policy debates about the feminization of poverty after divorce for many years, represents a strategic disadvantage, one that I think has contributed to the relative lack of attention to the broader policy implications of the federal proposals concerning child support. In this way, the power to define the social problem of child support and appropriate solutions has been used strategically to narrow the parameters of public critique of these proposals.

In this lecture, I examine how the problem of child support has been constructed in Canada so that the package of child support guidelines appears to be an obvious and appropriate solution. By expanding the context of the debate, the lecture focuses on some aspects of the problem that have been rendered invisible, and some additional issues which would need to be addressed if the private griefs of child support were to be transformed into public sorrows and support for children. In examining the process of defining the social problem of child support, the lecture raises questions about the discourse of privatization as both principle and strategy.

Child Support: Constructing the Problem and the Solutions

The phrase "deadbeat dads" has become widely used in recent years, especially in media stories about child support payments. It has increasingly been adopted by governmental representatives as well. For example, the media report announcing the federal proposals in April 1995 stated: "Parents trying to avoid child support payments will find it much tougher to hide from their obligations under an ambitious plan to be unveiled by Ottawa and the provinces. The offenders are [97%] 'so-called deadbeat dads'."[7] Similarly, Ontario's Premier responded to a proposed federal-provincial programme designed to track debtors using the *Income Tax Act* by suggesting a need to target deadbeat dads as the highest priority: "when you start using the *Income Tax Act* as an enforcement mechanism for repayments, the very top priority ought to be deadbeat parents that are not making their support payments right now to spouses and as you know in many cases that's deadbeat dads."[8]

Both these messages, like others in recent years, convey strongly the importance and magnitude of the problem of non-payment of child support in Canada, while at the same time defining the problem as one of deadbeat dads and the solutions in terms of better arrangements for ensuring that these parental obligations are met. Yet, in spite of the simplicity of these explanations, some research about child support suggests that the issue may be more complicated.

The problem of child support first became apparent in the context of a rising divorce rate in Canada after the enactment of the federal divorce legislation in 1968. The legal principles entitling children to continuing financial support from their parents after divorce were outlined in *Paras* v. *Paras*.[9] The basic principles were that the level of child support should be set so as to maintain a child at the pre-divorce standard of living and that the costs of achieving this standard of financial support should be shared by the parents according to their respective incomes. These legal principles conform to the requirements of section 15(8) of the *Divorce Act, 1985*, now in force.[10] Yet, in practice, the *Paras* objectives have not always been achieved because of the "obvious disjuncture between the principles articulated and the actual outcomes in terms of the quantum of support. ... The end result is that in

---

[7]T. Harper, "Dodgers of Child Support Targeted" *Toronto Star* (27 April 1995) A1. "Sources" were quoted as suggesting a need for tougher enforcement measures to ensure child support payments: "We believe we can make it harder to evade making payments ... . There's a willingness out there to be hard on them."

[8]W. Walker, "Hit Deadbeat Dads with Tax Harris Says" *Toronto Star* (15 August 1995) A8.

[9][1971] 1 O.R. 130 (C.A.). The court stated the principles at 134-135:

> Since ordinarily no fault can be alleged against the children which would disentitle them to support, the objective of maintenance should be, as far as possible, to continue the availability to the children of the same standard of living as that which they would have enjoyed had the family break-up not occurred ...
>
> Ideally, the problem could be solved by arriving at a sum which would be adequate to care for, support and educate the children, dividing this sum in proportion to the respective incomes and resources of the parents and directing the payment of the appropriate proportion by the parent not having physical custody.

[10]S.C. 1986, c. 4.

the majority of child support cases awards are not set at levels which will meet the *Paras* standard''.[11] In her review of reported decisions under the *Divorce Act*, 1985 to mid-1989, moreover, Carol Rogerson concluded:

> With respect to child support, the problem continues to be, as it has been in the past, not with the basic principles of child support but with their implementation. Courts assert that children should, to the extent possible, be guaranteed the standard of living of the pre-divorce family and that the amounts necessary to accomplish that objective should be shared by the parents in proportion to their respective incomes. However, in most cases the amounts transferred do not ensure that .... While the data from the cases reviewed suggests that child support awards may be somewhat higher than they were in the past, in many cases the levels are still not adequate. In cases where mothers have custody, children continue to experience lower standards of living than their non-custodial fathers, and custodial mothers are left bearing a disproportionate share of the costs of child-rearing.[12]

As Rogerson's review suggests, the overall pattern of child support reveals frequent departures in practice from the *Paras* principles in setting awards and clear discrepancies between the financial circumstances of children and their non-custodial parents. This research data is important because it shows how the legal principles have not worked well in practice. Moreover, higher levels of awards would appear to be more consistent with *Paras* and might reduce the discrepancy between the incomes of children's households and those of payer spouses.

However, it is important to consider some of the inherent limitations in this data. As Rogerson herself was careful to explain, her conclusions were based on a review only of reported decisions involving initial applications for, and applications to vary, spousal and child support. Since reported decisions constitute only a small proportion of all divorce cases in Canada, Rogerson expressed caution about an over-reliance on the outcomes in these cases as representative of all child support awards,[13] noting

---

[11]C. Rogerson, ''Judicial Interpretation of the Spousal and Child Support Provisions of the *Divorce Act*, 1985 (Part II)'' (1991) 7 Canadian Family Law Quarterly 271 at 274.

[12]C. Rogerson, ''Judicial Interpretation of the Spousal and Child Support Provisions of the *Divorce Act*, 1985 (Part I)'' (1991) 7 Canadian Family Law Quarterly 155 at 165.

[13]As Rogerson stated, *ibid.* at 158-159:

> Reported cases constitute only a very small subset of divorce cases; in most divorce cases issues of corollary relief are settled by the parties rather than litigated, and even of those cases which are litigated, only a small percentage are reported. Reported cases may be atypical in a number of ways, including the income levels of the parties and the degree of conflict between them, and these factors may affect support outcomes. It is also possible that reported cases are reported for the very reason that they are atypical or unusual.

On the other hand, as Rogerson noted (at 159), it is reported decisions that often establish legal principles used in negotiating spousal and child support so that ''one would expect reported cases to exert a significant influence in shaping support outcomes''. For additional data, see Canada, Department of Justice, *Evaluation of the Divorce Act, Phase II: Monitoring and Evaluation* (Ottawa: Department of Justice, May 1990).

especially that reported cases under the *Divorce Act* probably involved parents with income levels that are higher than average.[14] In light of this limitation in the reported case sample, one that may occur quite frequently in family law, Rogerson's suggestion about using caution in drawing general conclusions about the impact of child support awards is important, perhaps particularly for separated parents who are poor.[15]

If, for example, reported cases generally involve litigants with higher than average income levels, the relative disparity that Rogerson identified between the children's household and that of their non-custodial parent may — or may not — be an accurate picture of the circumstances for other, poorer families at separation. In this way, the construction of the problem as one of deadbeat dads may be inaccurate because it may be over-inclusive, identifying not only those fathers who could afford to pay increased child support and who will not do so, but also those who may have few or no resources and are thus not able to make or increase child support payments. Policy decisions that apparently ignore limitations in the data, lumping together those who won't pay child support with those unable to do so, confirm the need to examine carefully "who has the power to define" child support as a social problem.

In addition to Rogerson's study, other research about the impact of parental separation on the economic well-being of children has tended to confirm a disparity between children's households and those of their non-custodial parents, regardless of overall income levels. For example, Ross Finnie's longitudinal study of income tax returns for couples who divorced in 1982 showed that the incomes of both parents declined in the year of divorce, although women's incomes declined about 2.5 times further than men's, in relation to levels of income in the year of divorce.[16] After three years, Finnie's data showed that men had almost achieved their pre-divorce income levels, and that although women's income levels had also increased, they had returned on average to only three-quarters of their pre-divorce levels. In addition to these comparisons, Finnie's data showed that more women than men had incomes in the transition year (1982) which placed them in poverty and that some women remained in poverty in subsequent years. Although there were some men in poverty

---

[14]Rogerson suggested that applications under the *Divorce Act* which must be decided in superior courts may differ, in terms of parents' income levels, from those decided in provincial courts under provincial legislation. Rogerson, *supra* note 11 at 158.

[15]For an analysis of the extent to which family law principles may be shaped by facts in cases involving litigants with relatively higher incomes and then applied to all family law claimants without regard to their differing economic circumstances, see M.J. Mossman, "'Running Hard to Stand Still': The Paradox of Family Law Reform" (1994) 17 Dalhousie L.J. 5 at 17ff.

[16]R. Finnie, "Women, Men and the Economic Consequences of Divorce: Evidence from Canadian Longitudinal Data" (1993) 30 Canadian Review of Sociology and Anthropology 205. The research used the Longitudinal Administrative Database constructed from Canadian tax files to track a sample of adults from 1982 to 1986.

after separation as well, other men who were poor before separation were no longer poor thereafter.

Finnie's research results clearly identify a "gender gap" in the experience of divorcing couples in Canada. However, he also identified some possible explanations for such a gap, explanations that take account of factors beyond the divorce process itself. Where a woman had earned income prior to divorce, for example, Finnie noted that the post-divorce income of the custodial mother's family was very close to the level of the woman's reported income before divorce, concluding that one factor contributing to the gender gap was women's relatively lower earnings in the paid workforce, in contrast with men's. In this way, women's poverty was "masked" within marriage and more clearly revealed by divorce.[17] Although he also identified low levels of spousal and child support as key factors underlying the patterns of post-divorce disparity between children's households and those of their non-custodial parents, commending proposed governmental policies to reform current child support arrangements, he also identified a need to consider these reforms in relation to broader policies of economic support for poor families, including social assistance policies.[18]

Finnie's interpretation of this research data is interesting. Since the economic consequences of divorce are relatively more severe for women than for men, he concluded that women may be more constrained about choosing to end their marriages, in contrast with men, and that while divorce may reduce women's overall income levels, it may nevertheless increase the degree of their control over available income. On this basis, he stated:

> [These discussions] 1) imply that some of the concern we feel towards the difficult position of women (and their children) in divorced situations should actually be directed towards women still in marriages, and 2) highlight the limitations of conventional measures of well-being based on measured family income, and draw attention to issues of intra-family distributions of income and well-being generally.

---

[17]This argument has also been made in the U.S. context. See M. Fineman, *The Illusion of Equality* (Chicago: University of Chicago Press, 1991).

[18]Unfortunately, the database used in Finnie's research did not take account of child support payments by non-custodial spouses, but the data included unknown amounts of child support in the income of custodial spouses. That is, the data reflected payers' income levels without regard to deductions for child support payments. However, Finnie argued that these omissions would not alter the general disparity between post-divorce households, even though it might reduce the gap a little. In the United States, empirical research by Maccoby and Mnookin also confirmed the continuing disparity between households after separation, concluding that most fathers could afford to pay more. See E. Maccoby & R. Mnookin, *Dividing the Child* (Boston: Harvard University Press, 1992) at 265.

Finnie was subsequently critical of the 1996 federal proposals for child support guidelines, although he supports the idea of guidelines *per se*: see R. Finnie, *Good Ideas, Bad Execution: The Government's Child Support Package* (Ottawa: Calendon Institute of Social Policy, 1996).

> It is especially important to keep in mind that these discussions are relevant not only to actual break-ups, but also to "near divorces" and within-marriage spousal relationships in general.[19]

Finnie's analysis thus confirms that low levels of child support contribute to some extent to the economic hardships experienced by custodial parents and children after divorce. At the same time, the data shows how women's relative inequality in earned income levels is also an important factor in assessing their economic well-being after divorce. Moreover, by showing the relationship of women's relative poverty within marriage as well as post-divorce, his research suggests the relevance of the concept of a "family" economy, including the problems created by traditional, gendered patterns of the division of labour within households. Thus, while Finnie's research shows that child support is a factor that contributes to relative post-divorce economic insecurity for women and children, in contrast with men, his research also demonstrates that solutions focused primarily on reforming child support within the family law context will address only part of a much more complex social problem.

These research studies by Rogerson and Finnie clearly confirm problems with the levels of child support awards, problems that would certainly be worsened by patterns of repeated non-payment. At the same time, the studies reveal how limitations in the data preclude complete separation of these factors from other variables that may affect the economic well-being of post-divorce custodial households. As well, they may not fully capture the reality for poor parents who divorce, by contrast with those who have more assets and income. Increased concerns have also been expressed by some family lawyers that judges routinely discount the proved financial needs of children in setting child support awards. According to Miriam Grassby, for example, an "invisible glass ceiling" enters the courtroom at the moment when a judge calculates a child support award:

> [The glass ceiling is encountered at] the moment in an application for child support where the judge decides, after having applied the tax tables, that it is impossible for the wife to be required to pay as much tax as the tables indicate, that it really cannot cost that much to raise these children, or that the resulting order would be more than is generally ordered. [At that moment] "a glass ceiling" glides invisibly into the courtroom.[20]

This analysis suggests that, in addition to the other variables identified by Rogerson and Finnie, there is a need to assess the impact of societal expectations about what are reasonable levels of child support, the usefulness of judicial and legal education

---

[19]Finnie, *supra* note 16 at 230. See also D. Galarneau, "Alimony and Child Support" (Summer 1992) Perspectives (Statistics Canada) 8.

[20]D. Pask, "Family Law and Policy in Canada: Economic Implications for Single Custodial Mothers and their Children" in J. Hudson & B. Galloway, eds., *Single-Parent Families: Perspectives on Research and Policy* (Toronto: Thompson Educational Publications,: 1993) 185 at 189. See also Judge R. Williams, "Quantification of Child Support" (1989) 18 R.F.L. (3d) 234; and A. Morris & S. Nott, *All My Worldly Goods* (Aldershot: Dartmouth Pub., 1996).

programmes about the costs of raising children,[21] and how the interests of decision-makers may affect reform proposals.[22]

In this context, the choice to define the problem as one of deadbeat dads is too simplistic. The proposed child support guidelines and enforcement measures present only partial solutions to the problem. As Margrit Eichler has argued, the fact that reforms offer only partial solutions is not, of course, a fatal objection, especially if more fairness is achieved for a defined group in society. However, "it is most important to recognize its limitations, and to recognize explicitly what problems will not be solved. It is therefore not the limitations of the proposed solutions which are at issue, but the exaggerated expectation as to what they can deliver."[23]

In the context of Eichler's warning, it is important to limit our expectations of the new proposals for child support guidelines and enforcement measures. Since they are presented as a solution to deadbeat dads, they are likely to increase the level and regularity of payments on the part of payer spouses who can afford to pay child support. However, they will not affect those who cannot afford to pay, or to pay higher levels of, child support. As well, they do not provide a response to the costs and complexity of a public policy of readily-accessible divorce that leads to two households in place of one and corresponding risks of dependency for some family members. Constructing the problem as one of deadbeat dads does not offer much assistance in understanding this larger problem and its relationship to child poverty more generally.

---

[21]For an interesting analysis of the costs of raising children in Canada, see Table XII: The Cost of Raising a Child in Vanier Institute of the Family, *Profiling Canada's Families* (Ottawa: Vanier Institute of the Family, 1994). The data shows *average* costs for children by age and gender, based on average prices for consumer goods and daycare in Winnipeg.

[22]See Finnie, *supra* note 16 at 232-233:

> If it were men who suffered large declines in well-being with divorce, would there be more of a clamour for better documentation of the situation? ... If there were more female judges would there be a shift in decisions commensurate with an alternative perspective regarding inputs to marriages by those who specialize in home production, and to ensure a higher standard of living for the children involved? ... This is part of a more general question: How gender-neutral is our system in terms of identifying and addressing important socio-economic problems?

Finnie's questions are important ones, although there is little agreement about the impact of women as lawyers and judges: see *e.g.* B. Wilson, "Will Women Judges Really Make a Difference?" (1990) 28 Osgoode Hall L. J. 507. For an analysis of gender and family, see S. Moller Okin, *Justice, Gender and the Family* (New York: Basic Books, 1989).

[23]M. Eichler, "The Limits of Family Law Reform or The Privatization of Female and Child Poverty" (1990) 7 Canadian Family Law Quarterly 59 at 81. See also J. Pulkingham, "Private Troubles, Private Solutions: Poverty Among Divorced Women and the Politics of Support Enforcement and Child Custody Determination" (1994) 9 Canadian Journal of Law and Society 73.

Some of the complexity of the child support issue was evident in the judges' differing interpretations of data about the impact of taxation on child support payments in *R.* v. *Thibaudeau.*[24] Although inadequacy in the levels of child support and enforcement measures against payers were not primary concerns in the *Thibaudeau* case, the disparity in living standards of post-divorce custodial mothers and their children, in contrast with their former spouses, was clearly evident in Suzanne Thibaudeau's challenge about taxing child support in the hands of recipient spouses. In the context of applying a *Charter* analysis to the inclusion/deduction system of the *Income Tax Act*, the Supreme Court of Canada reviewed arrangements for child support, including negotiated agreements and court awards, and the impact of taxation arrangements on levels of child support. In their reasons for judgment, members of the court seemed unable to agree about the extent of gendered disparities created by the tax treatment of child support for spouses in separated households, reflecting the great difficulty in applying a *Charter* analysis to a complex policy context. The Court's decision denying Thibaudeau's claim did not really resolve fundamental policy issues about child support in Canada, even though it contributed to the ongoing debate about the plight of children and their custodial parents after divorce. As Lorne Wolfson has stated:

> The decision of the Supreme Court of Canada was unsatisfying for all concerned. Because it was essentially a *Charter* case dealing with the *Income Tax Act*, the legal issues and the language of the judgments are extremely complex and incomprehensible to all but the most sophisticated constitutional law lawyer. Those who look to the Reasons for Judgment for some guidance on the policy issues currently being debated in the public press will be greatly disappointed.[25]

The *Thibaudeau* case was important in Canada, however, in the process of transforming the private griefs of child support into public sorrows. It also ensured that the proposed solutions would include revised arrangements for taxing child support payments for post-divorce parents, although there was little agreement about

---

[24](1995) 12 R.F.L. (4th) 92. For a thorough analysis of the issues arising from the decision in the Federal Court of Appeal (and prior to the decision in the Supreme Court of Canada), see L. Philipps & M. Young "Sex, Tax and the Charter" (1995) 2 Review of Constitutional Studies 221.

[25]L. Wolfson, "Reflections on *R.* v. *Thibaudeau*" (1996) 13 Canadian Family Law Quarterly 163 at 166. Wolfson also expressed disappointment (and embarrassment) that the Supreme Court of Canada divided on gender lines in this case, with the two female members of the Court dissenting, supporting the position of Mme. Thibaudeau, and the male members of the Court in the majority supporting the position of her former husband. Wolfson seemed particularly concerned that this result had occurred as well in a previous challenge under the *Income Tax Act*: *R.* v. *Symes* (1994), 110 D.L.R. (4th) 470 (S.C.C.). For an analysis of the issues in *Symes*, see C. Young, "Child Care — A Taxing Issue" (1994) 39 McGill L. J. 539, and A. Macklin, "*Symes* v. *MNR*: Where Sex Meets Class" (1992) 5 C.J.W.L. 498. For an analysis of family law bargaining, see D. Majury, "Unconscionability in an Equality Context" (1991) 7 Canadian Family Law Quarterly 123.

how these goals might best be accomplished.[26] In addition to these differing views, and especially in light of the disagreements in the Supreme Court of Canada in defining exactly how the current arrangements affected custodial and non-custodial spouses after divorce, the government's continued emphasis on the problem as mainly one of deadbeat dads suggests a rather myopic approach to child support policies.

In formulating proposals to respond to this definition of the problem, however, the federal government had the benefit of similar policy initiatives already in place in the United States, the United Kingdom and Australia.[27] Research and consultation undertaken by a Federal/Provincial/Territorial Family Law Committee resulted in recommendations for the adoption of child support guidelines.[28] These recommendations were reflected in the federal proposals released in early 1996.[29] The most significant aspect of the new federal proposals was the introduction of child support guidelines, based on the income of the payer, with limited discretion to adjust amounts to respond to special child-related expenses and in relation to relative "undue hardship" between the two households. In creating the guidelines, federal and provincial tax rates were taken into account, thus eliminating the current inclusion/deduction system. The proposals included measures to ensure better coordination across Canada for the enforcement of child support, including the withholding of federal licenses for those who persistently fail to pay child support. Finally, the proposals included modest increases in the Working Income Supplement to be phased in over several years.

Not surprisingly, the debate about child support in Canada has shifted to focus on these new federal proposals, with a variety of criticisms about their conception and implementation. Ironically, in light of the defined goals of the new proposals, some lawyers and judges have expressed concern that the levels proposed are not as high as some current child support awards, so that the guidelines may have a negative

---

[26]See *e.g.* Canadian Advisory Council on the Status of Women, *The Tax Treatment of Child Support: Preferred Policy Options* (Ottawa: Canadian Advisory Council on the Status of Women, 1994), National Association of Women and the Law, *Submission to the Federal Task Force on the Taxation of Child Support Payments* (Ottawa: National Association of Women and the Law, 1994), and J. Durnford & S. Toope, "Spousal Support in Family Law and Alimony in the Law of Taxation" (1994) 42 Can. Tax J. 1. In the U.S., see B. Wolfman, "Child Care, Work, and the Federal Income Tax" (1984) 3 Am. J. Tax Pol'y 153 at 174ff.

[27]For a good overview, see A. Kahn & S. Kamerman, eds., *Child Support: From Debt Collection to Social Policy* (Newbury Park, Calif.: Sage Publications, 1988); M. Maclean & J. Eekelaar, "Child Support, Wife Support or Family Support" in L. Weitzman & M. Maclean, eds., *The Economic Consequences of Divorce* (Oxford: Clarendon Press, 1992) 239; and M. Harrison, G. Snider, R. Merlo & V. Lucchesi, *Paying for the Children* (Melbourne: The Australian Institute for Family Studies, 1991).

[28]See Federal/Provincial/Territorial Family Law Committee, *The Financial Implications of Child Support Guidelines* (Ottawa: Department of Justice, 1992); and *Report and Recommendations on Child Support, supra* note 5.

[29]See *Backgrounder: New Child Support Strategy, supra* note 5.

impact on the problem of low levels of child support awards.[30] There have also been concerns about the guidelines because they permit only very limited judicial discretion to achieve fairness in relation to the facts of individual cases, a problem exacerbated by the guidelines' focus on only the income of the payer rather than the incomes of both parents (both incomes can be considered only in assessing standards of living in relation to "undue hardship").[31] Since the guidelines are mandatory after May 1997 for court-ordered child support, but only guidelines for consideration for negotiated agreements, concerns have also been expressed about application of the federal guidelines to negotiated agreements and orders under provincial child support legislation, as well as the need to assess whether variation may be appropriate for existing agreements and awards.[32] Moreover, since the accurate application of the guidelines depends on the payer's income, new practice standards for lawyers are emerging in relation to financial disclosure by clients to enable accurate calculation of child support amounts.[33] The new proposals alter the tax treatment of child support but leave unchanged the inclusion/deduction system for spousal support, creating some uncertainties about how these differences may affect family law bargaining about spousal and child support.[34] In part as a response to so many of

---

[30]For example, Justice Trussler of the Alberta Court of Queen's Bench reported on her own analysis of interim support awards made in Edmonton from January to April 1995, concluding that 40% of the orders would have been lower under the proposed federal child support guidelines. The formula stipulated higher amounts in 29% of the cases and the same amounts in 16% of the cases. (A few cases are apparently missing from the overall total). Justice Trussler particularly noted the more favourable results achieved by judicial child support guidelines established in *Levesque* v. *Levesque*, [1994] 8 W.W.R. 589 (Alta. C.A.) and the approach of the dissenting comments in *Willick* v. *Willick*, [1994] 3 S.C.R. 670. See C. Schmitz, "Proposed Child Support Formula Puts Interest of Parents Over Children: Judge" (8 September 1995) *Lawyers Weekly* at 1. Similar criticisms have been expressed by lawyers in Ontario. According to Ruth Mesbur, for example, the guideline amounts "for low and middle-income families" are lower than "those ordered in court today". See K. Griffin, "Federal Child Support Guidelines take effect in May" (29 July-4 August 1996) *Law Times* at 10.

[31]For example, Justice Trussler suggested that the goal of consistency must be matched by one of fairness, criticizing the guidelines' limits on exercising judicial discretion and their failure to take account of the recipient's income as well as that of the payer:

> Any system that does not take into account the incomes of both parties and apportion support accordingly runs the risk of being inherently unfair, ... noting that the formula is "punitive" for custodial parents who earn more than the non-custodial parent.

See Schmitz, *supra* note 30. See also R. Finnie, "Proposed Child Support Rules Seriously Flawed" *The Ottawa Citizen* (5 November 1996) A13.

[32]See *e.g.* P. Epstein, "Variation Proceedings: The Effect of the Guidelines on Previous Agreements and Orders" in CBAO & LSUC, *Child Support Guidelines: The Mysteries Unravelled* (Toronto, Continuing Legal Education Programme: November 1996).

[33]J. MacDonald & A. Wilton, *The Child Support Guidelines: A Manual* (Scarborough: Carswell, 1997).

[34]See G. Feltham & A. Macnaughton, "Renegotiate Now or Seek a Variation Later? – The New Child Support Rules and Existing Awards" (1996) [unpublished]. See also Feltham & Macnaughton "The New Child Support Rules and Existing Awards: Choosing the Best Tax and Family Law Regime" (1996) 44 Can. Tax J. 1265.

these different issues, there have also been suggestions that the guidelines should be introduced as of May 1997 as presumptive rather than mandatory guidelines for a "trial period" of up to three years.[35]

Like many law reform initiatives, the federal proposals for child support guidelines attempt to respond to the problems as they have been defined: problems about low levels of support, difficulties in collecting support regularly, and the impact of tax consequences that may, or may not, have been taken into account at the outset in computing support entitlement. Not surprisingly, the announcement of the federal proposals for child support guidelines responded to the problem as it had been defined:

> The financial support of children following family breakdown has become an important public issue. Our society is changing, with far more single-parent households today than only a few decades ago. There is widespread recognition that our present child support system has not always been able to ensure that children are properly supported by both parents following divorce. Awards are varied and unpredictable, sometimes inadequate, and too often unpaid.[36]

By defining the problem in this way, the proposed child support guidelines appear to respond directly to the need for higher levels of child support that are predictable and non-taxable, with better measures for ensuring the enforcement of awards on a regular basis. Having defined the problems in these terms, the federal child support proposals respond by offering a modest improvement over current arrangements for some recipients of child support.

At the same time, it is important to understand the more fundamental limitations of child support guidelines and their inadequacy as a response to children's needs for support after divorce, and to the larger problem of child poverty in Canada. Because the proposals do not respond more fully, they fail to accomplish fundamental reform. Moreover, by placing the issues in a broader context, the choice to define the problem as deadbeat dads may reveal governmental unwillingness to take more responsibility for the economic well-being of Canadian children. Instead of proposals that would address these problems, child support has been defined simply in terms of the failure of deadbeat dads to take their responsibilities seriously after family breakdown. In this way, the public problem of "support for children" has been re-privatized as the problem of deadbeat dads.

---

[35] J. Payne, *Critique of Bill C-41 and of a Working Draft of the Federal Child Support Guidelines* (Ottawa: Danreb Inc., 1996).

[36] *Backgrounder: New Child Support Strategy*, *supra* note 5 at 2.

Child Support or Support for Children: Re-Thinking More Fundamental Issues

The federal government's proposed child support package thus offers a solution to the problem of child support as it has been defined. In arguing that the problem has been defined too narrowly, so that the proposals will achieve only a partial resolution of the problem, it is important to avoid "exaggerated expectations" as to what the proposals will accomplish. It is also important to understand what these proposals do not address, and the choices that have therefore been made among competing policy options.

First, since the child support proposals are directed only to children whose parents divorce or separate, the more widespread problem of child poverty in Canada is not addressed by these proposals. This concern is especially significant since the child support package seemed, at least for a while, to divert attention away from the more general problem of child poverty in Canada, much of which exists in two-parent families. Second, the proposals reflect assumptions about the extent of financial support that is available post-separation, without considering issues such as relative access to employment opportunities for men and women or parents' respective obligations for child care in the absence of societal support for those who care for dependents, including children. In this way, the child support proposals assume that support for dependency provided by an intact family can be shared by two households post-separation without real and substantial changes in levels of income and in the face of overall costs that are likely to reduce the standard of living of many post-separation families and to lead to real poverty for some. In addition, the proposals do not provide effectively for the processing of support claims in family law, a context in which there may be need for simple and inexpensive variations as the circumstances of children (and their parents) change over time. Finally, by defining the problem in terms of deadbeat dads, the child support proposals strategically distract attention away from all of these issues, suggesting that solutions directed to payer spouses can solve problems which are much more complex and which require broader societal solutions rather than merely the enforcement of private familial obligations.

The Problem of Child Poverty in Canada

Although statistics on child poverty in Canada are often quite well-known, it appears less obvious that many children in families with incomes below the poverty line live in two-parent families. Thus, as Margrit Eichler has suggested, while the risk of poverty is greater for single-parent, mother-led families, the rate of poverty for two-parent families is also high.[37] In assessing the potential impact of family law reform on child poverty in Canada, therefore, she concluded that "the majority of women

---

[37]Eichler, *supra* note 23.

and children currently living in poverty would not be lifted above the poverty level by reform of the family law, since they are poor within an ongoing marriage."[38] After examining statistics on families in poverty, Eichler argued that broader societal reforms must be undertaken, not just family law reform:

> [Family law reform] cannot eradicate poverty among women and children. Even with further reform, the majority of women and children who are now poor would remain poor. That is an intolerable situation for a society with the resources that Canada has at its disposal.
>
> To the degree that family law reform is seen as a solution for solving the problem of poverty of women and children at the expense of societal reforms, it does us a disservice to focus our energies in that direction.[39]

More generally, Philip Girard has argued that Canada lags behind other western nations in its efforts to ensure the well-being of children. Using comparative statistics, he has suggested that the divergence between rates of poverty for all households and those for single-parent households demonstrates a lack of societal support for children:

> In Italy, where 22 per cent of households fall below the poverty line, 27 per cent of single-parent households fall in this category. There is a discrepancy, but it is not terribly large. In France, the relative figures are of a similar order, 15 per cent and 22 per cent; but in the United Kingdom the disparity rises to 17 per cent and 30 per cent; in the United States 10 per cent and 50 per cent; and in Canada 11 per cent and 62 per cent.[40]

According to Girard, the large divergence in rates of poverty in Canada reflects the absence of public support for children and over-reliance on private, familial resources that too often are unavailable in single-parent households.

---

[38] *Ibid.* at 79. Eichler's analysis started with assumptions that *all* property was shared between spouses at divorce, taking account of the needs of children in their own right, and that *all* support payments were paid.

According to her statistics, 233 000 women heading sole parent families lived in poverty in 1986, as did 16 000 men heading sole parent families. However, there were 309 000 families with two parents who were living in poverty in that year. She also concluded that only 28% of women and children in separated families were likely to be able to live above the poverty line as a result of income-sharing at separation, using the figure of 28% of men in 1985 who were employed in managerial, administrative and professional occupations in Canada.

[39] *Ibid.* at 83. For another perspective, see M. Garrison, "The Economic Consequences of Divorce" (1994) 32 Family and Conciliation Courts Review 10, who has argued (at 22) that even though divorce law reforms cannot overcome all the problems of poverty for women and children, it can strive to "ensure outcomes that impose the burden of divorce fairly on all family members."

[40] P. Girard, "Why Canada has no Family Policy: Lessons from France and Italy" (1994) 32 Osgoode Hall L. J. 579 at 609.

Similarly, Ellen Zweibel has suggested that policy choices in Canada reflect very modest levels of public support for the well-being of children.[41] Zweibel identified different kinds of policy approaches to providing public support for children. Thus, for example, programmes providing direct financial benefits to families with children to ensure a minimum standard of living represent generous levels of public support. By contrast, state assistance in the collection and enforcement of private familial support obligations represents much more limited public support for children. Clearly, the federal proposals for child support, by establishing levels for support awards and enforcement measures for their collection, reflect an approach to child support as a private familial obligation of non-custodial parents. They do not reflect an overall societal interest in children and a level of public support to ensure their well-being. In this way, the child support proposals confirm the privatization of responsibility for children's dependency in Canada, and the absence of significant public societal responsibilities for Canadian children who are poor.

The trend towards the privatization of responsibility for dependency, illustrated by the proposed *Child Support Guidelines*, is evidenced in other recent developments in family law. As Colleen Sheppard has argued, the decision of the Supreme Court of Canada in *Moge* v. *Moge*[42] extended familial responsibility for financial support to a dependent spouse long after the end of the marriage, thereby diminishing Mrs. Moge's need for public assistance.[43] According to Sheppard, the decision in *Moge* was important for its recognition of women's economic insecurity after divorce. At the same time, however, the decision solved the problem of economic insecurity by allocating private responsibility to Mrs. Moge's former spouse. Although it would be difficult in the litigation of a spousal support claim to obtain an order for societal support, Sheppard expressed concern that the decision failed to acknowledge the broader, societal context that resulted in Mrs. Moge's disadvantaged circumstances:

> The *Moge* case does not address social factors beyond marriage that help to account for Zofia Moge's current economic needs. It does not deal with gender, race, ethnic origin, or language discrimination in the labour force. It does not mention patterns of familial dependence reinforced by immigration law and policy. Nor does it touch upon the absence of affordable and accessible child care or social assistance programs. ... [The] larger questions of the social context of Zofia Moge's economic insecurity remain beyond the realm of the court debate. Relegated beyond the margins, they should be occupying the centre of public debate about economic rights and family roles.[44]

---

[41]Zweibel, *supra* note 5 at 384.

[42](1992), 145 N.R. 1 (S.C.C.).

[43]C. Sheppard, "Uncomfortable Victories and Unanswered Questions: Lessons from *Moge*" (1994-95) 12 Can. J. Fam. L. 284. See also S. Boyd "(Re) Placing the State: Family, Law and Oppression" (1994) 9 Canadian Journal of Law and Society 39 at 71ff.

[44]Sheppard, *ibid.* at 329.

Similarly, the extension of the doctrine of constructive trust in *Peter* v. *Beblow* ensured that private, familial resources were available to a dependent spouse who might otherwise have required public assistance.[45] Moreover, statutory definitions of "parent" for purposes of identifying familial responsibilities for child support ensure that there are additional parents with familial support obligations, lessening the likelihood that state assistance may be needed.[46] Recent cases providing for recognition of partners in same sex relationships as "spouses" under provincial family law statutes also have potential to increase "private" responsibilities for economic dependency, decreasing corresponding obligations for "public" support.[47] In the context of these developments, the federal proposals for child support guidelines appear quite consistent with the overall trend towards the privatization of responsibility for economic dependency in family law. Moreover, such a policy approach assumes the existence of adequate private resources to meet all these obligations. In assessing the impact of the trend towards privatization in family law, therefore, it is necessary to examine the reality of private family resources available to meet these obligations, including obligations of child support.

Private Resources for Child Support Payments

Privatization of responsibility for economic security of dependents after divorce requires private, familial resources to meet these obligations in two households instead of one. It also requires at least stability in family income levels and may require higher levels to meet the added costs of two households. However, as Sherri Torjman has suggested, "the well-being of families is tied to the health of the economy", with income levels rising and falling "in line with unemployment and interest rates".[48] Thus, although family income has increased substantially in the past twenty-five years "due primarily to the dramatic rise in the labour force participation rate of women", the overall rise in income levels, in terms of the growth of average "real wages" (wages adjusted for inflation), suggests a very different conclusion.[49] According to Torjman, there were substantial increases in average real wages in the decades between 1920 and 1970. Indeed, average real wages in 1970 were 224 percent higher than in 1920. In contrast, however:

---

[45](1993), 150 N.R. 1 (S.C.C.).

[46]See *e.g. Family Law Act*, R.S.O. 1990, c. F-3, s.1:"'Parent' includes a person who has demonstrated a settled intention to treat a child as a child of his or her family".

[47]*M* v. *H* (1996), 31 O.R. (3d) 417 (C.A.); (1995), 17 R.F.L. (4th) 365.

[48]S. Torjman, "Crests and Crashes: The Changing Tides of Family Income Security" in M. Baker, ed., *Canada's Changing Families: Challenges to Public Policy* (Ottawa: Vanier Institute of the Family, 1994) 69 at 74.

[49]*Ibid.*

> [T]he steady and significant growth in real wages began to slow considerably after 1970, due primarily to rapidly-rising inflation. Between 1970 and 1980, the overall increase in average real wages was less than nine percent. The growth slowed even more dramatically between 1980 and 1990 — years marked by recession at both the beginning and close of the decade. Overall, average real wages rose by only two percent during that period ...[50]

This slow-down of increases in average real wages, moreover, was more dramatic for male workers in Canada than for female workers. According to Torjman, the average real wage of men actually dropped slightly from 1980 ($29 871) to 1990 ($29 757). At the same time, the average real wage for women grew by 14 percent to $17 933 in 1990. Even so, "the wage gaps between the sexes [remained] wide; in 1990, women averaged only 60 percent of men's average wages."[51] As these figures indicate, the average levels of family income available to support two households during the past two decades were declining for men and increasing only within the context of historically-depressed levels for women. Interestingly, it was during these two decades that the issue of non-payment of child support surfaced in policy debates, suggesting a need to take account of these factors in assessing the availability of family resources to meet the needs of two households after divorce.

In addition to the slowing of average real wage increases after 1970, Torjman also concluded that "Canadian families increasingly are insecure as a result of labour market changes", including an increase in both "good" and "bad" jobs, but a decline in "middle-income employment".[52] Stricter eligibility requirements for unemployment insurance and reductions in welfare assistance as well as the repeal of the Canada Assistance Plan have also tended to increase income insecurity for many workers, male and female.[53] In this way, a level of relative security for a family

---

[50] Torjman, *supra* note 48 at 75.

[51] *Ibid.*

[52] *Ibid.* at 75-76:

> "Good" jobs usually are associated with high salaries, a package of benefits and opportunities for training and promotion. "Bad" jobs, by contrast, tend to have limited advancement and on-the-job training opportunities, are often unstable, demand little in the way of formal qualifications and rarely provide private pensions, union membership or job satisfaction, let alone security. Bad jobs not only generate insecurity but also give rise to uncertain, poverty-bound futures.

[53] The relationship between paid work and poverty levels is complex. Thus, although "one of the main reasons for poverty [among families] is a lack of good jobs", some families in which both parents work are still poor. In 1994, "some 71,000 families — or seven percent of all poor families ... — were poor even when husbands and wives together worked for 93 or more weeks during the year." *National Council of Welfare Poverty Profile 1994* (Ottawa: Ministry of Supply and Services Canada, 1996) at 11 and 37.

with both parents in the paid workforce may be quickly and substantially eroded by the costs of two households after divorce, especially if one or other parent loses a job.

Moreover, the existence of two households after divorce may create new problems if both parents wish to continue to work full-time, since child care arrangements for the custodial parent are likely to be more complex than in the original family unit. The lack of an adequate and affordable system of licensed child care in Canada exacerbates these problems for single-parent families, and poorer families generally benefit less than higher-income families from the recently-increased value of child care expense deductions under the *Income Tax Act*.[54] In addition, other changes to taxation arrangements for parents have reduced public support for children's well-being and transferred more responsibility to parents. As Torjman has explained:

> The elimination of family allowances and the non-refundable child tax credit through the introduction of the child tax benefit in 1993 destroyed the principle of horizontal equity — i.e., recognition of the fact that taxpayers who are parents have heavier financial responsibilities than taxpayers at the same income level who do not support children.[55]

As a result of these changes, the real costs of privatized child support have increased and the level of public support for children has declined. As Torjman poignantly concluded, "Canada will have to work hard to make good its signature on the UN Convention on the Rights of the Child that it ratified in 1991."[56]

These factors reveal important connections between family policies and policies affecting labour market activity, connections that are rendered almost invisible in the privatization discourse about child support. In defining guidelines for levels of child support to be paid by deadbeat dads on behalf of their dependent children, the new proposals assume that most non-custodial parents have jobs, that they are likely to have continuing job security and that the levels of real wages available are sufficient to maintain children with little or no help from public support programmes.

These assumptions also contribute to the rather inflexible procedures currently available to reconsider or vary child support awards, either increasing or decreasing

---

[54]The federal government did not adopt the recommendations of the report of the Special Committee on Child Care, *Sharing the Responsibility* (Ottawa: Queen's Printer, 1987). See also Status of Women Canada, *Report of the Task Force on Child Care* (Ottawa: Supply and Services, 1986); National Council of Welfare, *Child Care: A Better Alternative* (Ottawa: Supply and Services, 1988). For a critique, see Teghtsoonian, "Neo-Conservative Ideology and Opposition to Federal Regulation of Child Care Services" (1993) 26 Can. J. Pol. Sci. 97.

[55]Torjman, *supra* note 48 at 78. See also Vanier Institute of the Family, "Investing in Families with Children" (excerpt from a brief concerning child poverty prepared by the Coalition on Child Poverty) (1988) 18(4) Transition 5.

[56]Torjman, *ibid.* at 85.

payments as the circumstances of children and their parents change. In the context of children's changing needs, as well as the rate of change now experienced by many workers, there is need for an efficient, cost-effective means of re-assessing levels of and other arrangements for child support payments. The use of applications to courts, with attendant need for the parties to obtain legal advice and representation, create significant barriers for both custodial and non-custodial parents.[57] In jurisdictions where administrative agencies have been empowered to consider requests for variation, by contrast, there has been greater accessibility to decision-making for separated parents, although there have also been serious problems created by the volume of cases handled by some agencies.[58] It is significant, however, that the new federal proposals for child support allocate funds for the administrative costs of enhanced enforcement measures rather than for the process of defining and varying child support awards. This choice also demonstrates how solutions have responded to the problem as defined in terms of deadbeat dads.

Child Support: Principles and Strategies

> [S]ubstantial and substantive improvements to income programs, and to social programs more generally, are unlikely in these times of fiscal restraint. The problem is more serious than simply a lack of funds; the mindset of restraint also generates a poverty-of-ideas mentality that tends to stifle innovation.[59]

Such a comment seems particularly apt as a description of recent policy-making about child support. The new federal proposals address only one part of the problem of child poverty in Canada, and do so by formulating a response that focuses mainly on the enforcement of private, familial obligations of financial support. The limits of these solutions are obscured by the choice to define the problem in terms of defaulting payers, deadbeat dads, without much regard for the reasons for their non-payment, in spite of ample information about job insecurity, down-sizing of workplaces and wage freezes in many parts of Canada that may affect payers' ability to meet ongoing child support commitments. In the context of governments' difficulties in meeting their own job creation goals, the choice to "privatize" the problem of child support as one of deadbeat dads appears to make child support

---

[57]See M.J. Mossman, "Gender Equality, Family Law and Access to Justice" (1994) 8 Int'l J.L. & Fam. 357.

[58]In the United Kingdom, the caseloads of the Child Support Agency resulted in reforms outlined in United Kingdom, *Improving Child Support* (London: H.M.S.O., 1995). See also G. Craig, K. Clarke & C. Glendenning, "The British Child Support Act in Practice: The State versus Lone Parents?" (Summer 1995) 42 Family Matters 14. In relation to Australia, see L. Alexander, "Australia's Child Support Scheme: Much Promised, Little Delivered?" (1995) 42 Family Matters 6.

[59]Torjman, *supra* note 48 at 84.

payers responsible for all our national economic problems, not just the problems of paying for their children.

Such a strategy of defining problems and solutions is also related to political goals. As Maureen Baker has pointed out, the failure to provide public support for child care and for income security for children shows governmental unwillingness to provide support for the next generation, in spite of frequent words of support:

> Although many politicians have pronounced that children are the nation's future resource, it has not always followed that policies have reflected this attitude. A comparison between federal money spent directly on children and money spent on elderly people indicates that children are obviously not taxpayers or voters![60]

The recent announcement of a federal government proposal to invest in Canadian children, especially children who are poor, suggests a modest effort to define the problem of child poverty more broadly and to address it more directly.[61] However, as some critics have pointed out, "without improved child care and work training for single parents as well, an improved child benefit won't radically alter the face of child poverty" — comments that underscore the complex reasons for economic dependency on the part of some family members, especially after divorce.[62]

The privatization of obligations for ongoing financial support for children after divorce contrasts with public policies permitting freely accessible divorce to adults in Canadian society. In this context, there appears to be public support for private decisions to separate and divorce, thus ending the family unit. At the same time, the continuation of significant private familial responsibilities for child support to ensure children's well-being shows how "the family" continues to exist post-divorce, as well as the limited extent of public support for the consequences of state policies

---

[60]M. Baker, "The Effectiveness of Family and Social Policies" in M. Baker, ed., *Canada's Changing Families: Challenges to Public Policy* (Ottawa: Vanier Institute of the Family, 1994) 127 at 133. In the U.S., Beller and Graham similarly identified a lack of political will to put "children's well-being first" in the context of economic support for them. See A. Beller & J. Graham, *Small Change: The Economics of Child Support* (New Haven: Yale University Press, 1993) at 262.

[61]Finance Minister Paul Martin announced on *Newsworld*, CBC, 27 November 1996: "I think maybe what this generation of politicians ought to do is to say, 'We're going to do for children what the previous generation (of politicians) did for seniors.'"

See also G. Gherson, "Federal Government, Provinces not Prepared for War on Child Poverty" *The Ottawa Citizen* (8 January 1997) A11. There have also been newspaper reports describing the non-partisan national coalition, Campaign 2000, that has been lobbying in favour of the 1989 all-party House of Commons resolution to end child poverty in Canada by the year 2000. See *e.g.* the editorial "Child Poverty Not Insurmountable" *Toronto Star* (27 November 1996) A22: "If we are wealthy enough to contemplate tax cuts, then as Campaign 2000 says, we lose all credibility by pleading collective poverty when it comes to ending the unforgiving poverty in which so many of our children now live."

[62]Gherson, *ibid.* at A11.

ensuring accessible divorce.[63] The strategy of defining the problem as one of deadbeat dads both ensures the continuation of post divorce "private" families and distances the state from any "public" responsibility to respond to the problem.[64]

Yet in spite of all of these concerns, the governmental strategy to define the problem in terms of deadbeat dads is unquestionably effective. The choice to target deadbeat dads identifies all of them as the problem and makes all of them morally blameworthy, with all too little concern for differences in their reasons for non-payment — reasons that might distinguish individuals as more or less at fault. The language used conveys moral authority about family values and parental responsibilities that are difficult to disentangle in relation to more complicated arguments about public and private responsibilities for economic security in the late 20th century. In the face of the simplicity of this definition of the problem (deadbeat dads) and the solution (child support guidelines and more effective enforcement measures), finding an argument that defines the problem and the solutions more broadly, taking into account the economic relationships within families and the role of the family as an economic unit of Canadian society, presents a more complex challenge.

Strategically, however, it is difficult to challenge the accuracy of the label without appearing to support fathers who do not accept any responsibility for their children's economic well-being. In the context of this lecture, it seems critical to record my view that some child support awards are probably much lower than the needs of children and that they are sometimes lower than fathers' ability to pay. Undoubtedly, there are fathers who could pay higher amounts of child support and it is likely that the new federal proposals will enhance the levels of awards and regularity of payments for some fathers, although the data examined earlier suggest some problems in assessing the results very precisely.[65] However, my fundamental

[63]Mary Morton has written about this concept of the "post divorce family unit" from the perspective of gender discrimination. See M. Morton, "Dividing the Wealth, Sharing the Poverty: The (Re)Formation of 'Family' in Law in Ontario" (1988) 25 Canadian Review of Sociology and Anthropology 254.

[64]In research undertaken some years ago, David Chambers concluded that higher standards of living for post-divorce children would not be achieved by reform of spousal and child support arrangements or by implementing more effective enforcement processes. Instead, he suggested that the solutions lay elsewhere: in state policies that ensured children's basic needs were met or that redressed women's inequality in the paid workforce. See D. Chambers, *Making Fathers Pay: The Enforcement of Child Support* (Chicago: University of Chicago Press, 1979).

[65]The assessment of costs and benefits is also complicated, in the U.S. context, according to Harry D. Krause by the fact that a "successful" program will likely increase the rate of voluntary compliance, statistics that may not be included in the enforcement process. In addition, the presentation of figures may sometimes be deceptive if the "easy" cases are skimmed off and the difficult ones left on their own. Finally, as he has argued:

> Enforcement should cease when too large a percentage of AFDC-related support collections goes to the enforcers rather than to the families concerned. When what is billed as child support enforcement turns

concern here is the impact of governments' power to define the problem and the solution. By characterizing the problem as one of deadbeat dads, they have privatized responsibilities for children in post-divorce families and, at the same time, masked the failure of public policies to address the bigger issue of child poverty in Canada. Moreover, the definition of deadbeat dads simplifies the problem without really addressing it, and constrains criticism on the part of those who do not wish to risk being misunderstood by appearing to support men who do not adequately share economic advantages and disadvantages at divorce.

In this context, the real issue is how concerned citizens can regain the power to define the private griefs of child support so as to transform them into collective public sorrows in terms of support for children. As Ellen Zweibel has succinctly stated, there is just one fundamental question at stake for children in Canada: "What are children entitled to expect from the world that they are born into?"[66]

---

into an income transfer program from (mostly rather poor) fathers to lawyers, social workers, and other enforcement personnel, we will have overshot the mark.

See H. D. Krause, "Reflections on Child Support" in A. Kahn & S. Kamerman, eds., *supra* note 27 at 233.

[66]See Zweibel, *supra* note 5 at 382. According to Zweibel, this fundamental question is answered "implicitly by each country's child support strategy when it sets the limits and mix of private (familial) and public (societal) support".

[12]

CHILD WELFARE LAW, "BEST INTERESTS OF THE CHILD" IDEOLOGY, AND FIRST NATIONS©

BY MARLEE KLINE*

Liberalism has structured legal discourse such that racism is most often unintended and rarely explicit. To understand how and why law has an oppressive and discriminatory impact on First Nations and other racialized groups in Canadian society, one must look at some of its more subtle processes and, in particular, its ideological form. The goal of this article is to provide insight into the origins and operation of "best interests of the child" ideology and to illustrate how it structures and constrains judicial decision making in the context of First Nations child welfare. Best interests ideology serves to portray the apprehension and placement of First Nations children away from their families and communities as natural, necessary, and legitimate, rather than coercive and destructive. This is accomplished, in part, through legal processes that appear to be universal and neutral, and to protect children and serve their best interests. As well, the relevance and importance of a First Nations child maintaining her First Nations identity and culture is minimized. After illustrating the difficulty involved in transforming ideology through law reform, the article concludes by suggesting that First Nations must be empowered to develop their own child welfare services outside the framework of existing provincial legislative schemes and in line with more general goals of self-government.

---

* Assistant Professor, Faculty of Law, University of British Columbia. I would like to give special thanks to Joel Bakan and Shelley Gavigan for their invaluable comments on earlier versions of this article and for their support. I would also like to thank Karen Anderson, Susan Boyd, Brenda Cossman, Nitya Duclos, DeLloyd Guth, Didi Herman, Kent McNeil, Patricia Monture-OKanee, Anna Pellatt, Toni Pickard, and J.C. Smith for their helpful comments; Barbara Brown, Christine Deynaka, Deanne Gaffar and Kelly Macdonald for their research assistance; and Christine McKenna for her editorial assistance. The funding support of a Duff Rinfret Scholarship and of the U.B.C. Faculty of Law during the course of research for this article is also gratefully acknowledged.

I. INTRODUCTION 376

II. THE EXTENSION OF CHILD WELFARE LAW TO FIRST NATIONS: A NEW MODALITY OF COLONIALIST REGULATION 382

III. CHILD WELFARE LAW AND ITS APPLICATION TO FIRST NATIONS 388
A. *"Best Interests of the Child" Ideology* 390
B. *"Best Interests of the Child" Ideology in First Nations Child Welfare Cases* 395
1. The First Nations child as abstract individual 395
a) *Individuation and the importance of maintaining a First Nations child's culture and identity* 397
b) *The abstraction of culture* 401
c) *Psychological bonding and permanent placement versus cultural connection* 403
d) *The construction of those who challenge dispositional decisions* 407
2. The "innocence" of law: child welfare law as impartial and universal 414

IV. THE POWER OF BEST INTERESTS IDEOLOGY AND LEGISLATIVE REFORM 419

V. CONCLUSION 423

I. INTRODUCTION

The child welfare system in Canada has had a devastating and tragic impact on First Nations.[1] From the time provincial child welfare schemes were first extended to First Nations on reserves in the late 1950s, large numbers of First Nations children have been removed from their natural parents, their extended families, and their communities.[2] This has had destructive effects on individual children and their extended families.[3] The continuous removal of children has also

[1] I use the term "First Nations" throughout this work to refer to those who are descendants of peoples indigenous to the territory now called Canada, including: First Nations (*e.g.*, Haida, Tlinkit, Mohawk), Métis, and Inuit. The term "Indian" is used in its legal sense to mean a person who falls within the criteria established in the *Indian Act*, R.S.C. 1985, c. I-5 [hereinafter *Indian Act*].

[2] See statistics discussed *infra*, section II, notes 46-56 and accompanying text.

[3] The most serious concern about First Nations children who are apprehended and placed in the care of non-First Nations families is that they tend to lose their "language, identity and culture": S. Bull, "The Special Case of the Native Child" (1989) 47 Advocate 523 at 530. However, racism in the dominant society tends to limit the extent to which these children become assimilated. As a result, they are much more likely than other children to experience "negative adjustment outcomes," including a greater susceptibility to serious identity crises upon reaching adolescence:

hindered the transmission of First Nations culture and traditions from elders to younger generations, thus threatening the very survival of First Nations.[4] Such effects have long been known to First Nations,[5] and several studies have demonstrated empirically that vastly disproportionate numbers of First Nations children end up in the custody of child welfare authorities.[6] As well, highly publicized tragedies

---

see, *e.g.*, P. Hudson & B. McKenzie, "Child Welfare and Native People: The Extension of Colonialism" (1981) 49 Soc. Worker 63 at 64; Ontario Native Women's Association, Ontario Federation of Indian Friendship Centres & Ontario Métis and Non-Status Indian Association, *Remove the Child and the Circle is Broken: A Response to the Proposed Children's Act Consultation Paper* (Toronto: Ontario Native Women's Association, Ontario Federation of Indian Friendship Centres & Ontario Métis and Non-Status Indian Association, 1983) at 18 [hereinafter *Remove the Child*]; T. Sullivan, "Native Children in Treatment: Clinical, Social and Cultural Issues" (1983) 1:4 J. Child Care 75 at 78; S.G. Novosedlik, "Native Children White Law" (1983) 6:3 Perception 27; C. Stuart, "Cross-Cultural Treatment for Native Children: A Point From Which to Begin" (1983) 1:5 J. Child Care 33; and B. Raychaba, *To Be On Our Own With No Direction From Home: A Report on the Special Needs of Youth Leaving the Care of the Child Welfare System* (National Youth in Care Network, 1988). See also W. Warry, *Ontario's First People: Native Children* (Toronto: The Research Policy Nexus: Children, Families, and Public Policy in the 90s, 1989) at 27 (emotional effects on extended family).

[4] *Remove the Child, ibid.* at 17. See also E.F. Carasco, "Canadian Native Children: Have Child Welfare Laws Broken the Circle?" (1986) 5 Can. J. Fam. L. 111 at 115; and J.A. MacDonald, "The Programme of the Spallumcheen Indian Band in British Columbia as a Model of Indian Child Welfare" in J.S. Ismael & R.J. Thomlison, eds, *Perspectives on Social Services and Social Issues* (Ottawa: Canadian Council on Social Development, 1987) 237 at 238. As a result, the removal of children by the child welfare system has been characterized as genocide by many First Nations commentators and others: see, *e.g.*, British Columbia Native Women's Society as quoted in P. Johnston, *Native Children and the Child Welfare System* (Ottawa: Canadian Council on Social Development and James Lorimer & Company, 1983) at 62; P.A. Monture, "A Vicious Circle: Child Welfare Law and the First Nations" (1989-90) 3 C.J.W.L. 1 at 7; Review Committee on Indian and Métis Adoptions and Placements, *No Quiet Place: Final Report to the Honourable Muriel Smith, Minister of Community Services* (Winnipeg: Manitoba Community Services, 1985) at 272 (Chair: Kimelman A.C.J.) [hereinafter *No Quiet Place*]; and Hudson & McKenzie, *supra*, note 3 at 64.

[5] See, *e.g.*, *Remove the Child*, *supra*, note 3 at 3.

[6] H.P. Hepworth, *Foster Care and Adoption in Canada* (Ottawa: Canadian Council on Social Development, 1980); P. Johnston, *supra*, note 4; and Canada, Child and Family Services Task Force, *Indian Child and Family Services in Canada: Final Report* (Ottawa: Indian and Northern Affairs, 1987) [hereinafter *Final Report*]. For a more detailed consideration of this data, see *infra*, notes 48-56 and accompanying text. More recently, various provinces have collected and reported their own data: see, *e.g.*, British Columbia, *An Overview of Family & Children's Services 1990/1991* (Victoria: Ministry of Social Services, 1992).

Prior to these studies, the struggle of First Nations with the child welfare system had not gone entirely unnoticed by the dominant society: see H.B. Hawthorn, ed., *A Survey of the Contemporary Indians of Canada: A Report on Economic, Political, Educational Needs and Policies* (Ottawa: Indian Affairs Branch, 1966) vol. 1 at 327; D. Sanders, *Family Law and Native People: Background Paper* (Ottawa: Law Reform Commission of Canada, 1975); British Columbia, *The Tenth Report of*

in the last decade involving the death of First Nations children receiving foster care in non-First Nations homes have underlined the impact of the child welfare system on First Nations, and have raised questions about the system's legitimacy.[7]

Different approaches have been taken in analyzing the adverse impact of the child welfare system on First Nations. Some commentators attribute the high proportion of First Nations children in care to inadequate parenting and child neglect which, in turn, are understood as resulting from the difficult socio-economic conditions in which many First Nations people live.[8] Others blame over-zealous child welfare authorities who apply culturally biased structures and values in

---

the Royal Commission on Family and Children's Law: Native Families and the Law (Vancouver: Queen's Printer, May 1973) (Chair: T.R. Berger); Canadian Council on Children and Youth, *Admittance Restricted: The Child as Citizen in Canada* (Ottawa: Canadian Council on Children and Youth, 1978); Canada, *Indian Self-Government in Canada: Report of the Special Committee* (Ottawa: Queen's Printer, 1983); and *No Quiet Place*, *supra*, note 4.

[7] For example, *Re*: Cameron Kerley (date of death: 1983), see Monture, *supra*, note 4 at 1, and C. Culhane, "Isn't it time to give this young native a break" (1986) Can. H.R. Advoc. 11. *Re*: Richard Cardinal (date of death: 1984), see Indian Association of Alberta, *Child Welfare Needs: Assessment and Recommendations* (Calgary: Indian Association of Alberta, 1987) at 6 [hereinafter *Child Welfare Needs*], and C. Chartier, *In the Best Interest of the Metis Child* (Saskatoon: University of Saskatchewan Native Law Centre, 1988) at 67. *Re*: Marlon Pippin (date of death: 1989), see G. York, "Teen-ager's Death Seen As Tragic Proof of Need for Native Social Workers" *The [Toronto] Globe and Mail* (24 April 1989) A1; and "Police Shooting of Indian Sparks Call for Inquiry" *The [Toronto] Globe and Mail* (18 April 1989) A3. See, generally, G. York, *The Dispossessed: Life and Death in Native Canada*, 1st ed. (Toronto: Lester & Orpen Dennys, 1989) c. 8.

[8] As discussed in Johnston, *supra*, note 4, and Warry, *supra*, note 3. Poverty is certainly an important factor contributing to the high incidence of First Nations children in protective care. Poor people not only have difficulty paying for necessary daycare and babysitting services, but they are subject to much greater public scrutiny because of their dependence on other social services such as social assistance: F. Stairs, Women and the Child Welfare System (Osgoode Hall Law School, York University, 1989) [unpublished]; and L. Gordon, *Heroes of Their Own Lives: The Politics and History of Family Violence, Boston 1880-1960* (New York: Viking, 1988). This model of child abuse and neglect, however, usually emphasizes individual pathology and ignores broader sociological and historical causes of child abuse and neglect: Warry, *supra*, note 3 at 27. The poverty of First Nations, for example, must be understood as itself a product of the colonialist history of white/First Nations relations which has resulted, among other things, in the destruction of traditional First Nation economies. First Nations poverty is also further exacerbated by the lack of adequate preventive and support services in many First Nations communities that results from ongoing jurisdictional disputes between the federal and provincial governments respecting child welfare services for status Indians: K. McNeil, R. Thompson & C. Bell, *Indian Child Welfare: Whose Responsibility?* (Saskatoon: University of Saskatchewan Native Law Centre, 1981, updated 1984); Monture, *supra*, note 4 at 8-11; Johnston, *supra*, note 4; and B.A. Atwood, "Fighting Over Indian Children: The Uses and Abuses of Jurisdictional Ambiguity" (1989) 36 UCLA L. Rev. 1051 (U.S. context).

their effort to "help" First Nations children.[9] Still other commentators link the operation of the child welfare system to the continuing processes of colonialization[10] in Canada.[11] For these commentators, focusing only

[9] This is understood to play out, for example, in the determination of suitable child-care practices and providers: see Carasco, *supra,* note 4 at 131; Johnston, *supra,* note 4 at 68; and Novosedlik, *supra,* note 3 at 29. See also Sullivan, *supra,* note 3 at 78.

[10] The term "colonialism" is widely used in the literature discussing the impact of European economic development and settlement on the indigenous peoples of North America, yet it is seldom defined. The situation is further complicated by the extensive conflation of the terms "colonialism" and "colonization": see, *e.g.*, J.S. Frideres, *Native Peoples in Canada: Contemporary Conflicts*, 3d ed. (Scarborough, Ont.: Prentice-Hall, 1988) at 367; G. Kellough, "From Colonialism to Economic Imperialism: The Experience of the Canadian Indian" in J. Harp & J.R. Hofley, eds, *Structured Inequality in Canada* (Scarborough, Ont.: Prentice-Hall, 1980) 343 at 343 n. 1 and at 347; R.F. Berkhofer, *The White Man's Indian: Images of the American Indian from Columbus to the Present* (New York: Alfred A. Knopf, 1978) at 123. An early attempt at a general definition of colonialism can be found in R.J. Horvath, "A Definition of Colonialism" (1972) 13 Curr. Anthropology 45. See also the classic consideration of colonizer/colonized relations by A. Memmi, *The Colonizer and the Colonized* (Boston: Beacon Press, 1965). More recent attempts at defining the processes involved in colonialism and/or colonization include: M. Etienne & E. Leacock, "Introduction" in M. Etienne & E. Leacock, eds, *Women and Colonization: Anthropological Perspectives* (New York: Praeger, 1980) at 17 (arguing that each case of colonization is unique depending on the interplay of "the particular mode of colonization, itself determined by the political and economic imperatives of the colonizer and by the nature of the colonized society; the precise strategies of exploitation employed by the colonizer; and the strategies of accommodation or resistance adopted by the colonized."); E.E. Cashmore, *Dictionary of Race and Ethnic Relations* (London: Routledge & Kegan Paul, 1984) at 53-56 (defining colonialism at 53 as "the domination of one group over ... others, culturally unrelated groups which lived in distant territories and had few defences against the conquering powers" and at 55 identifying the process as operating "at many levels, crucially at the level of consciousness." Colonization, in contrast, is defined at 54 as "the process of taking the lands and resources for exploitation."); B.B. Ringer, *"We the People" and Others: Duality and America's Treatment of its Racial Minorities* (New York: Tavistock, 1983) at 7-9 (distinguishing colonization and colonialization as two related, yet distinct processes which have resulted in New World societies of a dualistic nature. As colonists, Ringer argues at 7 that "the English created a society whose institutions were molded in their racial, religious, and national image." Colonization, in other words, refers only to the society created by and for whites. As colonialists, on the other hand, "the English subjected the nonwhites with whom they came into contact to violence, force, and fraud; and they subjugated, killed, or drove them off": at 8. The normative environment of the colonialist society, in other words, was racially bifurcated and "defined by a racial creed which stressed the separateness of the races and the inferiority of the nonwhite." *Ibid.* The inter-connections between these two processes are developed in Ringer's subsequent argument at 9 that "America's historic treatment of its racial minorities has been both an expression and product of the dialectical tension and struggle between these two models."); R.E. Bourgeault, "Race and Class Under Mercantilism: Indigenous People in Nineteenth-Century Canada" in B.S. Bolaria & P.S. Li, eds, *Racial Oppression in Canada*, 2d ed. (Toronto: Garamond, 1988) 41 at 56 (arguing that the "intent of British colonial policy [in nineteenth century Canada] was to create a white colony with political power and re-presentation in the hands of whites."); Frideres, *supra* at 366-72 (developing a "theoretical model" of white/First Nations relations in Canada referred to as "colonialism" by sketching the process of colonization as

on socio-economic factors or social work practices provides a limited and incomplete understanding of the problem. They argue that it is necessary to go beyond these factors and situate child welfare policy and practice in the historical context of the domination of First Nations in Canada by European-based political, legal, and economic systems. Important to such analyses is the question of how law operates in the context of the child welfare system as it applies to First Nations.

Emily Carasco and Patricia Monture have recently addressed this question.[12] Carasco examines child welfare cases from across the country and concludes that "the best interests of the Indian child have not been hitherto protected because of a general failure to give appropriate consideration to the 'indigenous factor'."[13] Monture takes Carasco's analysis further by situating the devaluation of the "indigenous factor" in child welfare cases within the more general context of structures of racism within law. Her analysis focuses on the "*manner* [in] which racism is constituted and implemented within legal structures."[14] She argues that child welfare law is racist in that it applies standards "which are not culturally relevant" to First Nations and that merely

---

involving seven different aspects).

In this article, I use the terms "colonialism" and "colonialization" to refer to the processes of European domination of the First Nations in Canada following the spirit of the analyses of Kellough, *supra*; E.P. Patterson, *The Canadian Indian: A History Since 1500* (Don Mills, Ont.: Collier-MacMillan, 1972) c. 1; and Frideres, *supra*. To avoid confusion, I refrain from using the term colonization except when referring to the process of the establishment of European colonies in the territory now referred to as Canada.

11 Hudson & McKenzie, *supra*, note 3. See also Native People's Resource Centre, B. Loucks & A. Timothy, *Justice-Related Children and Family Services for Native People in Ontario: A Discussion Paper*, rev'd ed. (Toronto: Ontario Native Council on Justice, 1981); and H. Cardinal, *The Unjust Society: The Tragedy of Canada's Indians* (Edmonton: M.G. Hurtig, 1969).

12 Carasco, *supra*, note 4 at 115; and Monture, *supra*, note 4 at 7-8. Others who consider the operation of law in the context of First Nations child welfare include: A. McGillivray, "Transracial Adoption and the Status Indian Child" (1985) 4 Can. J. Fam. L. 437; Bull, *supra*, note 3; Novosedlik, *supra*, note 3; and Chartier, *supra*, note 7. For those who focus on analyzing federal/provincial jurisdictional disputes, see McNeil *et al*, Monture, Johnston, & Atwood, *supra*, note 8. For an analysis of the various legal mechanisms available for arranging the provision of First Nations child welfare services, see D.R. James, "Legal Structures for Organizing Indian Child Welfare Resources," [1987] 2 C.N.L.R. 1.

13 *Supra*, note 3 at 115. Carasco defines the "indigenous factor" as "the disregarded, underemphasized or undervalued factor in child welfare situations involving Indian children." *Ibid.* at 113. For similar analyses, see Bull, *supra*, note 3 at 525 and 530; and Novosedlik, *supra*, note 3.

14 Monture, *supra*, note 4 at 8 n. 29.

"reinforce the status quo."[15] In her view, "fundamental[ly] racist notions ... underpin"[16] judicial interpretations of, for example, the "best interests of the child" test.[17]

My aim in this article is to deepen and complicate this analysis of racist structures in child welfare law by locating such structures historically and ideologically. I will focus my analysis on the courts because their role in First Nations child welfare matters is substantial. Recent data demonstrate that provincial child welfare authorities have tended to rely upon court orders to apprehend First Nations children rather than on the provision of supportive or foster care services to families on a *voluntary* basis.[18] As well, courts have final authority under legislation to determine whether, and in what form and duration, a child should be placed into protective care once apprehended.

I will argue that child welfare law has provided a new modality of colonialist regulation of First Nations in the post-Second World War period. This argument will be developed in two stages. First, I will consider the historical convergence of factors that have led to the extension of child welfare law and services to First Nations on reserves. Second, I will argue that a key to understanding the devastating impact of the child welfare system on First Nations lies in the ideological dimensions of child welfare law.[19] In this article, I will focus on the ideological *form* of child welfare law and, in particular, that of its central legal concept—the "best interests of the child."[20] The historical

---

15 *Ibid.* at 12.

16 *Ibid.* at 8 n. 29.

17 *Ibid.* at 12. See *infra,* note 57 and accompanying text for further consideration of the centrality of the best interests of the child standard to child welfare law.

18 *Final Report, supra,* note 6 at 8-9. I place *voluntary* in italics to indicate that parents, and, in most cases, mothers or female extended family members may be pressured by child welfare authorities into accepting often culturally inappropriate support services by an unspoken threat that court proceedings will be initiated and their children apprehended if they refuse to co-operate. See Stairs, *supra,* note 8.

19 See *infra,* notes 58-60, 78-81, and accompanying text for further consideration of the concept of ideology.

20 In a subsequent, as yet unpublished, paper, I will examine another ideological dimension of child welfare law, namely how ideological thought about First Nations that is formally external to law is relied upon by judges in their decision making: see *infra,* note 60. I have separated consideration of these two types of relations between law and ideology for analytic and illustrative purposes. In actual practice, the two processes are interdependent and mutually reinforcing.

development of best interests ideology will be situated in the context of nineteenth century developments in the ideology of childhood and the role of the state in protecting children. I will then consider how best interests ideology is infused with the basic tenets of liberal legality—individualism, abstraction, universalism, and impartiality—and show how this helps to explain judicial reasoning and results in First Nations child welfare cases. Finally, I will examine the impact of best interests ideology on recent legislative reform efforts in the area of First Nations child welfare.

II. THE EXTENSION OF CHILD WELFARE LAW TO FIRST NATIONS: A NEW MODALITY OF COLONIALIST REGULATION

Child welfare services were not extended to reserves until after the Second World War. The latter part of the 1940s marked the beginning of a significant re-examination of government policies relating to First Nations. The aggressive assimilationist policies of earlier eras[21] came under attack,[22] and debates about First Nations policy were

[21] Beginning around the 1830s in the eastern third of the territory now called Canada, aggressive, assimilationist state policies were developed and instituted which consisted of three main components—reserve systems, political wardship, and residential schools—orchestrated by a complex framework of legislative and administrative structures: see, *e.g.*, A. Tanner, "Introduction: Canadian Indians and the Politics of Dependency" in A. Tanner, ed., *The Politics of Indianness: Case Studies of Native Ethnopolitics in Canada* (St. John's: Institute of Social and Economic Research, Memorial University of Newfoundland, 1983) 1; Frideres, *supra,* note 10; J.S. Frideres, "Policies On Indian People in Canada" in P.S. Li, ed., *Race and Ethnic Relations in Canada* (Toronto: Oxford University Press, 1990) 98; J.R. Miller, *Skyscrapers Hide the Heavens: A History of Indian-White Relations in Canada* (Toronto: University of Toronto Press, 1989); S.M. Weaver, "Segregation and the Indian Act: The Dialogue of Equality vs. Special Status" in W. Isajiw, ed., *Identities: The Impact of Ethnicity on Canadian Society* (Toronto: Peter Martin Associates, 1977) 154; R. Gibbons & J.R. Ponting, "Historical Overview and Background" in J.R. Ponting, ed., *Arduous Journey: Canadian Indians and Decolonization* (Toronto: McClelland and Stewart, 1986) 18; J.L. Tobias, "Protection, Civilization, Assimilation: An Outline History of Canada's Indian Policy" in I.A.L. Getty & A.S. Lussier, eds, *As Long As the Sun Shines and Water Flows: A Reader in Canadian Native Studies* (Vancouver: University of British Columbia Press, 1983) 39; Kellough, *supra*, note 10; R. Fisher, *Contact and Conflict: Indian-European Relations in British Columbia, 1774-1890* (Vancouver: University of British Columbia Press, 1977); and C. Haig-Brown, *Resistance and Renewal: Surviving the Indian Residential School* (Vancouver: Tillacum Library, 1988).

[22] By this time, Ottawa bureaucrats and missionary groups alike could no longer ignore the fact that assimilation and economic development on reserves were not taking place as expected.

increasingly informed by emerging liberal democratic ideologies and discourses.[23] The previous treatment of First Nations as separate from, and inferior to, the dominant Anglo-Canadian culture was challenged by a new concern that First Nations be treated as equals, in particular, by integrating them into developing universal social programs.[24] In this context, a Special Joint Committee of the Senate and House of Commons was appointed in 1946 to "examine and consider" the *Indian Act* and to suggest amendments thereto, with specific terms of reference to include investigation of "any ... matter or thing pertaining to the social and economic status of Indians and their advancement."[25] The Joint Committee sat for three consecutive sessions of Parliament, but only reluctantly began to hear from First Nations constituencies in the middle of the second session after the committee's credibility was called into question over the issue of First Nations representation.[26]

The committee's most significant recommendation was that financial arrangements be developed to integrate Indians into provincial

---

The rise of organized political protest on the part of the First Nations during this period was another important factor contributing to this shift in attitude: Tobias, *supra*, note 21 at 48.

[23] See P. Havemann, "Law, State, and Canada's Indigenous People: Pacification by Coercion and Consent" in T. Caputo *et al.*, eds, *Law and Society: A Critical Perspective* (Toronto: Harcourt Brace Javanovich, 1989) 54. Some of this was the result of a "new social awareness" on the part of the Canadian public and policy makers that had its origins in the war experience. See P. Tennant, *Aboriginal Peoples and Politics: The Indian Land Question in British Columbia, 1849-1989* (Vancouver: University of British Columbia Press, 1990) at 122; Miller, *supra*, note 21 at 220; and Treaties and Historical Research Centre, *The Historical Development of the Indian Act*, 2d ed. (Ottawa: Treaties & Historical Research Centre, P.R.E. Group, Indian and Northern Affairs, 1978) at 133.

[24] For consideration of the development of universal social programs in Canada during the post-Second World War period, see, *e.g.*, D. Guest, *The Emergence of Social Security in Canada* (Vancouver: University of British Columbia Press, 1980); A. Finkel, "Origins of the Welfare State in Canada" in L. Panitch, ed., *The Canadian State: Political Economy and Political Power* (Toronto: University of Toronto Press, 1977) 344; G. Drover & A. Moscovitch, "Inequality and Social Welfare" in A. Moscovitch & G. Drover, eds, *Inequality: Essays on the Political Economy of Social Welfare* (Toronto: University of Toronto Press, 1981) 1; H. Buchbinder, "Inequality and the Social Services" in Moscovitch & Drover, *supra*, 348; and A.W. Djao, *Inequality and Social Policy: The Sociology of Welfare* (Toronto: John Wiley & Sons, 1983).

[25] As set out in Treaties and Historical Research Centre, *supra*, note 23 at 132. See Tobias, *supra*, note 21 at 51-52 for an analysis of the specific factors which gave rise to the appointment of the Special Joint Committee.

[26] I.V.B. Johnson, *Helping Indians to Help Themselves—A Committee to Investigate Itself: The 1951 Indian Act Consultation Process* (Ottawa: Treaties and Historical Research Centre and Indian and Northern Affairs Canada, 1984) at 25-26.

health, education, and social service programs.[27] As in previous years, assimilation of Indians continued to be an important theme in discussions leading to this recommendation, but assimilation was now presented in terms of granting Indians rights equal to those of other Canadians and doing away with their special status.[28] In the end, the committee recommended extension of provincial social services, the goal being "economic assimilation of Indians into the body politic."[29] The government responded to the Report of the Joint Committee by tabling amendments to the *Indian Act*.[30] To distinguish its new initiatives premised on equal status from earlier state policies of assimilation premised on segregation and inferior status, the government attempted to construct a new official discourse of "integration."[31]

---

[27] Treaties and Historical Research Centre, *supra*, note 23 at 144; and Johnson, *supra*, note 26 at 47. Such extensions of services had been advocated in the submissions of some First Nations organizations, Canada, Special Joint Committee of the Senate and the House of Commons Appointed to Examine and Consider the Indian Act, *Minutes of Proceedings and Evidence* (Ottawa: King's Printer, 13 May 1946) at 614, 858; and in a joint brief submitted by the Canadian Welfare Council and the Canadian Association of Social Workers: Canada, Canadian Welfare Council and Canadian Association of Social Workers, Joint Submission to the Special Joint Committee of the Senate and the House of Commons Appointed to Examine and Consider the Indian Act, Special Joint Committee Appointed to Examine and Consider the Indian Act, *Minutes of Proceedings and Evidence*, 1947, app. 30 (Ottawa: King's Printer, 1946-49) at 160-61 [hereinafter *Joint Submission*].

[28] D.E. Ginn, Aboriginal Self-Government (LL.M. Thesis, Osgoode Hall Law School, York University, 1987) at 19 [unpublished]. This is in contrast to old policies which emphasized segregation as a means to "train" First Nations for assimilation: see, *e.g.*, D. Sanders, "Prior Claims: Aboriginal People in the Constitution of Canada" in S.M. Beck & I. Bernier, eds, *Canada and the New Constitution: The Unfinished Agenda*, vol. 1 (Montreal: Institute for Research on Public Policy, 1983) 225; and Tanner, *supra*, note 21 at 16. For example, anthropologist Diamond Jenness introduced his "Plan for Liquidating Canada's Indian Problem Within 25 Years" with the goal "[t]o abolish, gradually but rapidly, the separate political and social status of Indians (and Eskimos); to enfranchise them and merge them into the rest of the population on an equal footing": Canada, Special Joint Committee of the Senate and the House of Commons Appointed to Examine and Consider the Indian Act, *Minutes of Proceedings and Evidence*, app. 30 (Ottawa: King's Printer, 25 March 1947) at 310-11 [hereinafter *S.J.C. Minutes and Proceedings*].

[29] *S.J.C. Minutes and Proceedings, ibid.* 1948 at 189 cited in Treaties and Historical Research Centre, *supra*, note 23 at 144. See also Johnson, *supra*, note 26 at 47.

[30] *Indian Act*, R.S.C. 1952, c. 149 [hereinafter *Indian Act, 1952*].

[31] In introducing the amended *Indian Act* (Bill No. 79, *An Act Respecting Indians*, 4th Sess., 21 st. Parl., 1951) for second reading in the House of Commons, for example, W.E. Harris, the Minister of Citizenship and Immigration, attempted to distinguish between the new policy of "integration" and earlier government policies of "assimilation." After reasserting a statement which he had made earlier in the legislative process that "it was hoped that we could eventually provide for the integration of the Indian into our community life," he said that he had "received many protests

The amendments did not represent a significant structural transformation in government policies towards First Nations,[32] though they did provide a legislative framework which supported and facilitated new modalities of colonialist regulation of First Nations in the ensuing years, most significantly through the application of child welfare law.[33] A new section was added to the *Indian Act* providing that "all laws of general application ... in force in any province are applicable ... except to the extent that such laws are inconsistent with this *Act*."[34] This section was regarded as a necessary precursor to the extension of child welfare services to First Nations. Following the section's enactment, the Indian Affairs Branch and some provincial government officials interpreted it as providing that provincial child welfare laws were applicable to First Nations peoples on reserves.[35] At least in theory, then, there were no longer legal impediments to the extension of provincial child welfare services to First Nations.[36]

In practice, however, the extension of child welfare services to First Nations was not immediately forthcoming. The federal government took the position that it "lacked the authority and capacity to ensure the availability of adequate child welfare services for bands directly" and sought to "arrange for the extension of existing provincial

---

from Indians with respect to that statement because there were many who thought that integration was equivalent to assimilation." In response, he argued "that ... [was] not the meaning of the word in any way; the word was used to indicate the status of having privileges, duties and responsibilities equal to those of other Canadians, and exercising them in the same manner that we do." *House of Commons Debates* (16 March 1951) at 1350. See also N. Dyck, "The Politics of Special Status: Indian Association and the Administration of Indian Affairs" in J. Dahlie & T. Fernando, eds, *Ethnicity, Power and Politics in Canada* (Toronto: Methuen, 1981) 279.

32 Though fifty sections representing "most provisions regarding aggressive assimilation" were repealed by the new *Indian Act, 1952*, "[t]he main elements of the earliest Dominion legislation ... were preserved intact." Johnson, *supra*, note 26 at 51. See also Treaties and Historical Research Centre, *supra*, note 23 at 149.

33 This notion of a "shift ... in the modality of ... regulation" is adopted from S. Hall, "Reformism and the Legislation of Consent" in National Deviancy Conference, ed., *Permissiveness and Control: The Fate of the Sixties Legislation* (Great Britain: MacMillan, 1980) 1 at 2.

34 *Indian Act, 1952*, s. 87.

35 See H.B. Hawthorn, C.S. Belshaw & S.M. Jamieson, *The Indians of British Columbia: A Study of Contemporary Social Adjustment* (Toronto: University of Toronto Press & University of British Columbia, 1960) at 399; A. Pratt, "Federalism in the Era of Aboriginal Self-Government" in D.C. Hawkes, ed., *Aboriginal Peoples and Government Responsibility: Exploring Federal and Provincial Roles* (Ottawa: Carleton University Press, 1989) 19 at 31.

36 Though this was not firmly established until the *Natural Parents* case: see *infra*, note 84.

services on reserves."[37] According to the federal government, the new amendment did not authorize additional federal funding to defray the cost of newly provided services,[38] and provincial service providers were loathe to extend their already overburdened child welfare services to First Nations without such funding.[39] By 1956, only Ontario had entered into an agreement with the federal government to extend provincial children's aid services to reserves.[40] As late as 1959, residential schools were still the primary facility relied on by the Indian Affairs Branch to provide child welfare-like services to First Nations.[41] In 1961, a study of the social work implications of the *Indian Act* described as "entirely inadequate" the commitment of only nine social workers across the country to work with the 179,000 residents of reserves.[42] By 1964, only the Yukon, Nova Scotia, and several children's aid societies in Manitoba had joined Ontario in entering into funding agreements with the federal government.[43]

The uneven provision of child welfare services to First Nations had not significantly improved in 1966 when a federal commission, appointed to examine the social, educational, and economic situation of Indians in Canada, concluded that "the situation [respecting the provision of child welfare services to the First Nations in jurisdictions with no federal/provincial cost-sharing agreements] varies from unsatisfactory to appalling."[44] Nonetheless, the commission's report hailed the limited extension of child welfare services as "one of the most significant achievements in the elimination of discriminatory treatment

---

[37] *Final Report, supra,* note 6 at 3. See also Hawthorn, *supra,* note 6 at 327.

[38] Johnston, *supra,* note 4 at 3.

[39] A.I. Holmes, The Social Welfare Aspects and Implications of the Indian Act (M.S.W. Thesis, University of British Columbia, 1961) at 61 [unpublished].

[40] Holmes, *ibid.* at 60; and Hawthorn, *supra,* note 6 at 327.

[41] Holmes, *ibid.* at 57; and Hawthorn, *supra,* note 6 at 399. But see also W.T. Stanbury, *The Social and Economic Conditions of Indian Families in British Columbia* (Vancouver: British Columbia Family and Children Law Commission, 1974) at 50 providing evidence that the Indian Affairs Branch, at least in British Columbia, also placed Indian children in foster homes in the 1950s and early 1960s.

[42] Holmes, *supra,* note 39 at 60.

[43] Hawthorn, *supra,* note 6 at 327.

[44] *Ibid.*

between Indians and non-Indians in the field of welfare."[45] Despite these limitations, by the time of the report, significant numbers of First Nations children had been brought into state care. In British Columbia, for example, the number of First Nations children in care increased from 29 children in care in 1955 to 39 per cent of the total number in care in 1965.[46]

The introduction of the Canada Assistance Plan in 1966 allowed for a significant expansion of provincial child welfare services by providing federal cost-sharing to offset provincial costs.[47] As a consequence, the proportion of First Nations children in care began to increase dramatically across the country. By 1977, almost 20 per cent (15,500) of the total number of children in care in the country were First Nations children.[48] In the four western provinces, where First Nations populations tend to be larger, the proportions were estimated to be above the average: 39 per cent in British Columbia, 40 per cent in Alberta, 50 per cent in Saskatchewan, and 60 per cent in Manitoba.[49] In particular locales, the percentage of apprehended children was even higher. For example, in 1981 in the Kenora region of Ontario, 85 per cent of children in care were First Nations children, although First Nations people made up only 25 per cent of the local population.[50] According to a 1980 study, status Indian children were placed into state care at a rate of four and one-half times that of other Canadian children.[51] Altogether, in the last twenty-five years, vastly

[45] *Ibid.* at 328-29.

[46] Union of British Columbia Indian Chiefs *et al.*, *A Survey of Adoption and Child Welfare Services to Indians of B.C.* (Vancouver: Department of Human Resources, 1974) at 5-6 [hereinafter *Survey of Adoption*]. At the same time that Indian children were being brought increasingly into the care of provincial authorities, those involved were concerned with the difficulty that they were having in finding "suitable Indian foster homes." Hawthorn *et al.*, *supra*, note 35 at 399. See also *Survey of Adoption*, *supra* at 5.

[47] H.P. Hepworth, "Trends in Provincial Social Service Department Expenditures, 1963-1982" in J.S. Ismael, ed., *Canadian Social Welfare Policy: Federal and Provincial Dimensions* (Kingston, Ont.: McGill-Queen's University Press, 1985) 139 at 140-41.

[48] Hepworth, *supra*, note 6 at 111.

[49] *Ibid.* at 115.

[50] Johnston, *supra*, note 4 at 44.

[51] *Ibid.* at 57.

disproportionate numbers of First Nations children have ended up in the custody of child welfare authorities.

Studies have also documented how First Nations children are much less likely than other children to be returned to their own parents or placed for adoption once admitted into care, and that, if placed in foster homes, they are likely to be situated with non-First Nations families.[52] A 1987 report found that status Indian children were placed into care predominantly outside their community and that they remained in care longer than non-First Nations children.[53] Further, status Indian children were more frequently moved out of care through adoption or by being relinquished into their own custody at age eighteen or nineteen, than through being returned to their familial home.[54] With respect to adoption, the total number of First Nations children adopted by non-First Nations parents increased fivefold from the early 1960s to the late 1970s.[55] From 1969 to 1979, an average of just over 78 per cent of status Indian children placed for adoption each year were adopted by non-First Nations families.[56]

III. CHILD WELFARE LAW AND ITS APPLICATION TO FIRST NATIONS

The above discussion shows that, since the 1950s when provincial child welfare schemes were first extended to First Nations people on reserves, the system has had the effect of removing large numbers of children from their natural parents, their extended families, and their communities. The results of extension have been to further the colonialization of First Nations and to erode their social and political structures. In terms of these effects, child welfare law can be understood as a new modality of colonialist regulation of First Nations, though one less explicit and apparently more "innocent" of colonialist intentions

---

[52] Hepworth, *supra*, note 6 at 118; and Johnston, *supra*, note 4 at 9.

[53] *Final Report*, *supra*, note 6 at 9.

[54] *Ibid.*

[55] Hepworth, *supra*, note 6 at 119; and Department of Indian and Inuit Affairs Program, *Indian Conditions: A Survey* (Ottawa: Ministry of Indian Affairs and Northern Development, 1980) at 24.

[56] Hepworth, *ibid.* at 120. See also Stanbury, *supra*, note 41 at 57.

than the aggressive mechanisms of the past. Canadian child welfare law directs judges to make decisions that are "in the best interests of the child."[57] Unlike earlier colonialist mechanisms that openly segregated Indians and treated them as inferiors, the apprehension of First Nations children from their communities and its negative effects are facilitated and legitimated by a legal system that is based upon ideals of universality and neutrality, and which purports to protect individual children and act in their best interests. In other words, there are ideological dimensions of child welfare law which make decisions arrived at within the system appear natural, necessary, and legitimate, rather than coercive and destructive.[58] These dimensions can be investigated on two different

---

[57] In most jurisdictions, the best interests test applies only in decisions relating to a child at the dispositional stage after it has been determined according to specific statutory criteria that the child is in need of protection. See *Child Welfare Act*, S.A. 1984, c. C-8.1, s. 2 [hereinafter *Alberta Act, 1984*]; *The Child and Family Services Act*, S.M. 1985-86, c. 8, s. 2(1) [hereinafter *Manitoba Act, 1985-86*]; and *Re Greenland* (1984), 50 Nfld & P.E.I.R. 193 (Nfld Unif. Fam. Ct). Some statutes explicitly provide that the best interests of the child is to be the paramount consideration in any interpretation or decision made pursuant to child welfare legislation: *Alberta Act, 1984*, s. 2; *Manitoba Act, 1985-86*, s. 2(1); *Child Welfare Act*, R.S.N. 1990, c. C-12, s. 4(1) [hereinafter *Newfoundland Act, 1990*]; *Child and Family Services Act*, R.S.O. 1990, c. C.11, s. 1(a) [hereinafter *Ontario Act, 1990*]; *Family and Child Services Act*, R.S.P.E.I. 1988, c. F-2, s. 2 [hereinafter *P.E.I. Act, 1988*]; and *Children and Family Services Act*, S.N.S. 1990, c. 5, s. 2(2) [hereinafter *Nova Scotia Act, 1990*]. See also *The Child and Family Services Act*, S.S. 1989-90, c. C-7.2, ss. 3-4 [hereinafter *Saskatchewan Act, 1989-90*]. Of these, some statutes define the best interests of the child, either exhaustively or as an inexhaustive list of considerations: see *Manitoba Act, 1985-86*, s. 2(1); *Newfoundland Act, 1990*, s. 4(2); *Nova Scotia Act, 1990*, s. 3(2); *Ontario Act, 1990*, s. 37(3); *P.E.I. Act, 1988*, s. 1(1)(d); and *Saskatchewan Act, 1989-90*, s. 4. Other statutes establish no overriding best interests of the child principle or specific, defining criteria, but make reference to the best interests of the child or similar terms in a variety of provisions: see, *e.g.*, *Child Welfare Act*, R.S.N.W.T. 1974, c. C-3, ss. 21(2), 26(1), 28(1). In interpreting child welfare provisions, however, courts have generally regarded the best interests of the child as an overriding factor: see, *e.g.*, *Racine* v. *Woods*, [1983] 2 S.C.R. 173, [1984] 1 C.N.L.R. 161 [hereinafter *Racine*, (S.C.C.) cited to S.C.R.]. Even in jurisdictions where the best interests criterion is not legislatively established as overriding, the courts have nonetheless relied on their inherent *parens patriae* jurisdiction to establish it as such: see, *e.g.*, *King* v. *Low*, [1985] 1 S.C.R. 87 [hereinafter *King*]; and Alberta cases discussed *infra*, Section IV.

[58] The works that have been particularly helpful to me in developing an understanding of the concept of ideology are: D. Hay, "Property, Authority and the Criminal Law" in D. Hay *et al.*, eds, *Albion's Fatal Tree: Crime and Society in Eighteenth-Century England* (New York: Pantheon Books, 1975) 17; R. Cotterrell, *The Sociology of Law: An Introduction* (London: Butterworths, 1984); M. Barrett, *Women's Oppression Today: Problems in Marxist Feminist Analysis* (London: Verso, 1980); A. Hunt, "The Ideology of Law: Advances and Problems in Recent Applications of the Concept of Ideology to the Analysis of Law" (1985) 19 L. & Soc. Rev. 11; S. Hall *et al.*, *Policing the Crisis: Mugging, the State, and Law and Order* (London: MacMillan Education, 1978); S. Hall, "The Toad in the Garden: Thatcherism among the Theorists" in C. Nelson & L. Grossberg, eds, *Marxism and the Interpretation of Culture* (Urbana, Ill.: University of Chicago Press, 1988) 35; S.A.M. Gavigan,

levels. First, one can analyze the particular ideological form of the best interests standard and explore how it has affected the interpretation and application of this standard in the adjudication of First Nations child welfare disputes.[59] Second, one can look at how ideological thought about First Nations that is formally external to law is relied upon by judges in child welfare cases and thereby imported into, and reinforced by, law.[60] In this article, I will focus on the former kind of analysis.

A. *"Best Interests of the Child" Ideology*

The ideological form of the "best interests" legal standard in child welfare law is a product of its historical development in the material conditions of nineteenth and twentieth century Canada and Europe. It is premised on liberal notions of law and childhood. Anglo-Canadian law is liberal in form. It is individualistic and abstract, and it claims to be impartial and universal in that all individuals are treated the same without regard to their different social situations.[61] These factors support the appearance of Anglo-Canadian law as incompatible with reproducing and reinforcing social relations of oppression and inequality.[62] There is, however, a substantial literature demonstrating how the liberal form of law serves to obscure, and thereby legitimate and reproduce, oppressive structures.[63] In the context of racial oppression,

---

"Law, Gender and Ideology" in A. Bayefsky, ed., *Legal Theory Meets Legal Practice* (Edmonton: Academic Printing and Publishing, 1988) 283; and T. Eagleton, *Ideology: An Introduction* (London: Verso, 1991).

59 This is an investigation of the form of law which corresponds to the first of two "coextensive" levels of inquiry required by the ideological analysis of law as described by Gavigan, *ibid.* at 292. Gavigan specifically identifies the best interests of the child principle as an example of legal doctrine appropriate for this type of analysis.

60 This is what Gavigan characterizes as the second level of inquiry required by the ideological analysis of law. *Ibid.*

61 See, *e.g.*, S. Picciotto, "The Theory of the State, Class Struggle and the Rule of Law" in P. Bierne & R. Quinney, eds, *Marxism and Law* (New York: John Wiley and Sons, 1982) 169; Hunt, *supra*, note 58; P. Fitzpatrick, "Racism and the Innocence of Law" (1987) 14 J.L. & Soc'y 119 [hereinafter "Innocence of Law"]; P. Fitzpatrick, "Law, Modernization and Mystification" in R.J. Simon & S. Spitzer, eds, *Research in Law and Sociology: A Research Annual*, vol. 3 (Greenwich, Conn.: Ai Jai Press, 1980) 161 at 172; A.C. Hutchinson & A. Petter, "Private Rights/Public Wrongs: The Liberal Lie of the Charter" (1988) 38 U.T.L.J. 278; and *infra*, notes 63-64.

62 See Fitzpatrick, "Innocence of Law," *ibid.* at 122.

63 For recent examples, see H. Glasbeek & M. Mandel, "The Legalization of Politics in

for example, critics have demonstrated how formal equality and universality as central aspects of liberal legality facilitate, rather than counteract, the concrete reality of racial oppression in Canada, the United States, and Britain.[64] I want to argue that the application of the best interests standard in the context of First Nations child welfare can be understood in similar terms. The tragic impact of child welfare law on First Nations can be attributed in part to the liberal form taken by the best interests principle in child welfare adjudication. It has directed judges to focus on the child as an individual abstracted out of her community and cultural contexts, and it has rendered judicial decisions impartial and objective and, thereby, unassailable.[65]

The ideological form of the best interests standard must also be understood in the context of the historical development of the conception of childhood and the role of the state in protecting children. During the sixteenth and seventeenth centuries, childhood emerged as a distinct stage in the life cycle during which time children were recognized as socially, intellectually, and emotionally dependent, and were thus entrusted to their families (and in particular their mothers) for protection, nurturing, and socialization.[66] In the nineteenth century, the

Advanced Capitalism: The Canadian Charter of Rights and Freedoms" (1984) 2 Socialist Stud. 84; J. Fudge, "The Public/Private Distinction: The Possibilities of and the Limits to the Use of Charter Litigation to Further Feminist Struggles" (1987) 25 Osgoode Hall L.J. 485; S.B. Boyd, "From Gender Specificity to Gender Neutrality? Ideologies in Canadian Child Custody Law" in C. Smart & S. Sevenhuijsen, eds, *Child Custody and the Politics of Gender* (London: Routledge, 1989) 126; B. Cossman, "A Matter of Difference: Domestic Contracts and Gender Equality" (1990) 28 Osgoode Hall L.J. 303; J. Bakan, "Constitutional Interpretation and Social Change: You Can't Always Get What You Want (Nor What You Need)" (1991) 70 Can. B. Rev. 307; and the cites *infra,* note 64.

64 See, *e.g.*, Fitzpatrick, "Innocence of Law," *supra,* note 61 at 119; K.W. Crenshaw, "Race, Reform, and Retrenchment: Transformation and Legitimation in Antidiscrimination Law" (1988) 101 Harv. L. Rev. 1331; K.W. Crenshaw, "Demarginalizing the Intersection of Race and Sex: A Black Feminist Critique of Antidiscrimination Doctrine, Feminist Theory and Antiracist Politics" (1989) U. Chi. L.F. 139; A.D. Freeman, "Legitimizing Racial Discrimination Through Antidiscrimination Law: A Critical Review of Supreme Court Doctrine" (1977-78) 62 Minn. L. Rev. 1049; A.D. Freeman, "Racism, Rights and the Quest for Equality of Opportunity: A Critical Legal Essay" (1988) 23 Harv. C.R.-C.L. L. Rev. 295; A. Kobayashi, "Racism and the Law in Canada: A Geographical Perspective" (1990) 11 Urb. Geography 447; and N. Duclos, "Disappearing Women: Racial Minority Women in Human Rights Cases" (1992, forthcoming) 6(1) C.J.W.L.

65 I discuss these aspects separately not to imply that they are distinct or discrete, but to assist in analytical clarity.

66 P. Ariès, *Centuries of Childhood: A Social History of Family Life*, trans. by R. Baldick (New York: Random House, 1962). See also N. Mandell, "The Child Question: Links Between Women and Children in the Family" in N. Mandell & A. Duffy, eds, *Reconstructing the Canadian Family:*

conception of childhood as distinct from adulthood reached a new height, and children's interests became increasingly recognized as severable from, and independent of, those of their parents.[67] As the middle classes assimilated these understandings of childhood, concern developed about the denial of childhood to working-class and poor children. Consequently, a "child saving" movement emerged from what had previously been a more generalized form of poor relief and religious benevolence.[68]

Around this time, courts started to become involved in the protection of children.[69] Judicial concern, increasingly articulated in terms of doing what was necessary for the "welfare" of the child, became a justification for granting custody to mothers or removing children from their families at the expense of previously unquestioned rights of fathers to custody.[70] Reinforced at the end of the nineteenth century by

Feminist Perspectives (Toronto: Butterworths, 1988) 49 at 56. Historical variations in the status and role of children were closely intertwined with changing ideas about the status and role of women within the family and society at large: see J. Ursel, "The State and the Maintenance of Patriarchy: A Case Study of Family, Labour and Welfare Legislation in Canada" in J. Dickinson & B. Russell, eds, *Family, Economy & State: The Social Reproduction Process Under Capitalism* (Toronto: Garamond Press, 1986) 150 at 188.

[67] M.L. Fineman, "The Politics of Custody and Gender: Child Advocacy and the Transformation of Custody Decision Making in the USA" in Smart & Sevenhuijsen, *supra*, note 63, 27 at 30.

[68] P.T. Rooke & R.L. Schnell, *Discarding the Asylum: From Child Rescue to the Welfare State in English-Canada (1800-1950)* (Lantham, Md.: University Press of America, 1983) at 9-10. The child saving movement formed part of a broader range of social and moral reform movements which facilitated the internalization of middle-class conceptions of childhood and family by the dependent poor and working classes: see, *e.g.*, M. Valverde, *The Age of Light, Soap, and Water: Moral Reform in English Canada, 1885-1925* (Toronto: McClelland & Stewart, 1991). For an incisive consideration of the regulatory and coercive legal processes involved in the imposition of bourgeois childhood and family ideology upon the working and dependant poor in the period between the World Wars, see D.E. Chunn, "Rehabilitating Deviant Families through Family Courts: The Birth of 'Socialized' Justice in Ontario, 1920-1940[1]" (1988) 16 Int'l J. Soc. L. 137; D.E. Chunn, "Boys Will Be Men, Girls Will Be Mothers: The Legal Regulation of Childhood in Toronto and Vancouver" in P.A. Adler & P. Adler, eds, *Sociological Studies of Child Development*, vol. 3 (Greenwich, Conn.: Ai Jai Press, 1990) 87; and D.E. Chunn, *From Punishment to Doing Good: Family Courts and Socialized Justice in Ontario, 1880-1940* (Toronto: University of Toronto Press, 1992).

[69] C.B. Backhouse, "Shifting Patterns in Nineteenth-Century Canadian Custody Law" in D.H. Flaherty, ed., *Essays in the History of Canadian Law*, vol. 1 (Toronto: University of Toronto Press, 1981) 212 at 213 and at 240. See also C. Smart, "Power and the Politics of Child Custody" in Smart & Sevenhuijsen, *supra*, note 63, 1 at 5 and at 8-9.

[70] Backhouse, *ibid.* See also Smart, *ibid.* at 6. On the connection between the inherent *parens patriae* jurisdiction of superior courts and the best interest formulation, see M. Reitsma-Street,

provincial legislation aimed at protecting the welfare of the child,[71] state authority to remove children from "unfit" parents continued to grow in the twentieth century.[72] Gradually, the principle of the best interests of the child was adopted by courts and, subsequently, by various legislatures as the central test for resolving child welfare, custody, and other issues involving children.[73]

Today, the best interests of the child standard provides broad discretion to children's aid societies and judges. Such flexibility is considered necessary to allow each case to be treated on its own merits.[74] Though broad, the discretion afforded to judges and other legal actors in the child welfare context is not unlimited. While the best interests standard is conceptually indeterminate, the historical and ideological context in which it is interpreted limits the meanings that will be accepted by courts and other institutions.[75] In the context of First Nations child welfare, the liberal ideological form of the best interests standard has served to constrain judicial decision making so as to minimize, and even negate in some instances, the relevance and importance of maintaining a child's First Nations identity and culture. It provides an interpretive framework in which the removal and placement of First Nations children away from their families and communities

---

"More Control Than Care: A Critique of Historical and Contemporary Laws for Delinquency and Neglect of Children in Ontario" (1989-90) 3 C.J.W.L 510. There is also some judicial authority for this connection: see *Re S.D.* (1989), 100 A.R. 214 (Q.B.), aff'g (1988), 17 R.F.L (3d) 183 (Alta Prov. Ct Fam. Div.); and *Re Adoption of Infant Registration No. 78-09-024190*, [1990] 2 C.N.L.R. 9 (B.C.S.C.).

71 See, *e.g.*, *An Act for the Prevention of Cruelty to, and Better Protection of Children*, S.O. 1893, c. 45., s. 18(3); *An Act Respecting Infants*, S.A. 1913 (2d Sess.), c. 13, s. 6; and, generally, Ursel, *supra*, note 66 at 185 discussing the statutes which provided the "legal apparatus for extending state control over children."

72 Backhouse, *supra*, note 69 at 241; and Reitsma-Street, *supra*, note 69 at 513.

73 N. Bala, "Judicial Discretion and Family Law Reform in Canada" (1986) 5 Can. J. Fam. L. 15 at 22 contrasting this development to the earlier reliance of judges on more rigid rules based on the gender of the parents. See also *supra*, note 57.

74 R.F. Barnhorst, "Child Protection Legislation: Recent Canadian Reform" in B. Landau, ed., *Children's Rights in the Practice of Family Law* (Toronto: Carswell, 1986) 255 at 256.

75 As Alan Hunt argues: "[T]he varieties of social construction of meaning and signification have their limits in the kind of people who construct their social reality, whose language, ideology and consciousness take particular (not just any) historical forms and thus result in determinant limits to the variability of the social." A. Hunt, "The Big Fear: Law Confronts Postmodernism" (1990) 35 McGill L.J. 507 at 532.

appears natural, necessary, and legitimate,[76] thereby giving judges some basis for security and certainty in their decision making. Importantly then, the best interests principle is not simply a mask for unbridled discretion on the part of judges, but is itself "an instrument of regulation."[77]

Certainly, the focus on the best interests of the individual child in child welfare cases is not entirely invalid. The impact on a child will obviously be an important factor in any determination about her placement. This is consistent with the operation of ideology, a central characteristic of which is the potential for "something 'real' " to be gained.[78] The attraction of ideologies like those associated with the best interests standard, even when such ideologies have negative consequences, is partly explained by this dynamic. Moreover, the interpretive framework established by best interests ideology is not so rigid as to preclude occasional acceptance of oppositional interpretations and justifications which do accord with the interests of First Nations. This interplay is illustrated by some of the cases considered below which reveal space within the legal framework of child welfare for judicial decisions that give priority to the maintenance of connections between a First Nations child, her extended family, and her First Nation.[79] Again, such positive results are consistent with the operation of ideology which derives strength precisely because it does not require complete enforcement.[80] Indeed, the very nature of

---

[76] See, *e.g.*, Eagleton, *supra*, note 58 at 58:

> Successful ideologies are often thought to render their beliefs natural and self-evident—to identify them with the 'common sense' of a society so that nobody could imagine how they might ever be different ... [T]he ideology creat[es] as tight a fit as possible between itself and social reality, thereby closing the gap into which the leverage of critique could be inserted. ... On this view, a ruling ideology does not so much combat alternative ideas as thrust them beyond the very bounds of the unthinkable.

I am arguing here only that such decisions will appear natural, necessary, and legitimate in the eyes of the dominant society. I make no claims in the context of this article as to the extent of acceptance of such justifications by First Nations. See M.G. Kline, Child Welfare Law, Ideology, and the First Nations (LL.M. Thesis, Osgoode Hall Law School, York University, 1991) at 130 n. 24 [unpublished]; and Eagleton, *supra*, note 58 at 56.

[77] I. Thèry, " 'The Interest of the Child' and the Regulation of the Post-Divorce Family" (1986) 14 Int'l J. Soc. L. 341 at 345.

[78] See Gavigan, *supra*, note 58 at 292. See also Eagleton, *supra*, note 58 at 45.

[79] See *infra*, notes 102, 110, 124, and accompanying text.

[80] As Douglas Hay has observed about ideology, "[p]rovided that its depths are not explored

dominant ideology is such that it must be continually constructed and reconstructed in the face of challenges by contradictory and oppositional ideologies.[81] Altogether, the determination of what is in the best interests of a child in any given child welfare dispute is a site of ideological struggle. However, once an ideology has assumed dominance as a result of particular material conditions, its authority is difficult to dislodge or shift. Dominant ideology is unlikely to be transformed significantly without a change in the material conditions which gave rise to it in the first place.[82] Understanding this last aspect of ideology provides some insight into the legislative reform experience in Alberta discussed in the fourth section of this article.

Before getting there, the next two sections will investigate the two inter-related aspects of the ideological form of the best interests of the child principle identified above; that is, the focus on the child as an abstract individual, and the purported universality and impartiality of decisions rendered according to that principle.

B. *"Best Interests of the Child" Ideology in First Nations Child Welfare Cases*

1. The First Nations child as abstract individual

The reasoning used by courts to justify First Nations child welfare decisions relies upon a construction of a child's interests as separate from, and abstracted out of, her familial and cultural context. The best interests of the child standard serves in practice to privilege an understanding of children *as decontextualized individuals* whose interests are separate and distinct from those of their families, communities, and

too often or by too many, it remains a reservoir of belief throughout the society and flows into the gaps made by individual acts of protest." *Supra,* note 58 at 55.

[81] D. Macdonell, *Theories of Discourse: An Introduction* (Oxford: Basil Blackwell, 1986) at 33 describing Althusser's position that "no ideology takes shape outside a struggle with some opposing ideology." See also A. Hunt, "Marxism, Law, Legal Theory and Jurisprudence" in P. Fitzpatrick, ed., *Dangerous Supplements: Resistance and Renewal in Jurisprudence* (London: Pluto Press, 1991) 102 at 115 defining ideology as a "contested grid of competing frames of reference"; and Eagleton, *supra,* note 58 at 45.

[82] At bottom, the concept of ideology directs attention to the "material conditions of [transformative] possibility" in any given context. Eagleton, *supra,* note 58 at 223. See also *ibid.* at 30.

cultures.[83] To this extent, it tends to render irrelevant or unimportant the child's cultural identity and heritage, thus helping to justify her separation from it. When judges determine "best interests" in First Nations child welfare cases, facts and arguments are constructed and organized so as to give credence and legitimacy to the removal of First Nations children from their families and communities. By constructing the child *conceptually* as separate from her culture, the *actual* removal of the child from it is made to seem unproblematic.

This abstraction of child from culture happens in a number of ways, some more subtle than others. First, courts may explicitly deny the relevance of maintaining a First Nations child's culture and identity or assign it little weight relative to other factors. Second, courts may hold that culture is important, but treat it as an abstract category that can be filled by any First Nations culture, rather than that of the particular First Nation to which the child belongs. Third, courts may emphasize the child's psychological bonds with her foster parents, but not consider relevant bonds with her culture. Alternatively, the courts may hold that the child needs the stability of a permanent placement, while ignoring the stability that would result from maintaining a connection to her culture. Finally, courts may consider parents, families, or bands who challenge removal orders or placement plans to have interests separate from, and in conflict with, the interests of the child. I will now consider examples of each of these constructions.

---

[83] See Thèry, *supra*, note 77 at 343.

a) *Individuation and the importance of maintaining a First Nations child's culture and identity*

Natural Parents v. *Superintendent of Child Welfare*[84] provides a good illustration of the relationship between an individualistic construction of the child and the deemed irrelevance of concerns about culture. A non-First Nations couple sought to adopt a status Indian child who had been apprehended from his parents and placed in foster care in their home. The natural parents refused to consent to the adoption and asked instead that the child be raised by an aunt and uncle in accordance with Tsartlip and Songhees traditions.[85] In the trial judge's view, the conflict that arose in the case could "only be resolved in the light of the best interests of the child *himself*. He [had to] be considered *as an individual*," and this meant considering the child "not a part of a race or culture."[86] Culture and heritage were thus deemed separate from, and irrelevant to, his best interests as an individual. The judge regarded the complex "claims of native custom" in the case as merely claims of "heredity" which were necessarily in conflict with claims of "environment."[87] In the end, "the best interests of the child himself" were held to require retention of custody by the foster parents through adoption.[88] In a more recent decision,[89] another Court stated that

---

[84] [1976] 2 S.C.R. 751 [hereinafter *Natural Parents*]. The Supreme Court of Canada decided the case on the basis of a constitutional point. The interesting issues from our perspective were addressed at trial and can be gathered from the reasons of the trial judge noted in the judgment of the Supreme Court. The specific constitutional point was whether the application of the provincial *Adoption Act*, R.S.B.C. 1960, c. 4 [hereinafter *Adoption Act*] would extinguish the child's rights to Indian status and was therefore not applicable to the adoption of status Indian children. The Supreme Court held unanimously that the *Adoption Act* applied and thus that the adoption order at issue was valid. A majority of six out of nine judges held that the application of the *Adoption Act* did not interfere with the federally determined question of status. For further commentary on the case, see McNeil *et al., supra,* note 8 at 5; and McGillivray, *supra,* note 12.

[85] *Natural Parents, ibid.* at 768.

[86] *Ibid.* (emphasis added).

[87] *Ibid.*

[88] The trial judge arrived at this conclusion despite his acknowledgement that there was "potential danger to a native child being brought up in a white family, particularly when he reached the later stages of adolescence." This was balanced in his mind by an "intelligently imposed environment" which would in the end be determinative of the child's later adjustment. Although there were relatives in the community wishing to assume the care of the child, the trial judge held not only that it would be in the child's best interests to remain where he was, but also that the foster

"maternal instinct, the wishes of other members of the family *and matters of cultural background and heritage* cannot be allowed to interfere with the paramount consideration of the best interests of the child"[90]—once again separating the analysis of best interests from concerns about maintaining cultural connection. On this basis, an Ojibway mother was denied access to her eight-year-old daughter who had been adopted by her foster parents.

The distinction which courts draw between a child's best interests and the relevance of her "race or culture" is also apparent in cases where courts impose the burden of proving the importance of maintaining cultural connection for the individual child upon parties seeking to regain custody of a child. In *John* v. *Superintendent of Child Welfare*,[91] for example, Perry L.J.S.C. of the British Columbia Supreme Court held that the proposition "that an Indian child has a better chance in life by living among his relatives and among others of his race" could not be accepted unless it was "possible to demonstrate that this [was] so, by way of some cogent evidence, *with particular reference to this child*."[92] Accordingly, the judge attached little weight to evidence demonstrating in *general* terms the experience of identity crisis and dislocation faced by First Nations children raised in white families, and the sense of identity and cultural understanding fostered in First Nations children when raised among their own people.[93] Because this general evidence did not establish the importance of the *particular* child involved in the dispute remaining in his community, Perry L.J.S.C. rejected an attempt by the child's mother to regain custody from a non-First Nations couple who had adopted him. Similarly, in *C.J.K.* v. *Children's Aid Society of Metropolitan Toronto*,[94] a statutory requirement to consider the "racial

parents had established a "right" to the custody of the child. *Ibid.* at 768-69.

89 *Racine* v. *Woods* (1984), [1985] 2 C.N.L.R. 187 (Man. Q.B.). See *infra*, notes 100, 106-109, 113, 131, 132-42, and accompanying text for more detailed consideration of the various judgments in this case including a decision by the Supreme Court of Canada.

90 *Ibid.* at 190-91 (emphasis added). See also *Re J.H. and N.H.* (1988), 3 Y.R. 282 at 291 where the Yukon Territorial Court concluded that, while "[t]he cultural heritage of the children [was] one of the factors and an important factor to be considered[,] ... [t]he welfare of the children ... is the predominant factor."

91 (1979), [1982] 1 C.N.L.R 40, 10 R.F.L (2d) 330 [hereinafter *John* cited to C.N.L.R.].

92 *Ibid.* at 47 (emphasis added).

93 *Ibid.* at 48.

94 [1989] 4 C.N.L.R. 75 (Ont. Prov. Ct Fam. Div.) [hereinafter *C.J.K.*].

culture and origins" of children in the child welfare statute in question[95] was held to have been included only to "underscore the recognized importance, *to any individual*, of familial roots, heritage and tradition."[96] Custody was denied to the First Nations grandmother of three apprehended children because, *inter alia*, there was no evidence that she would "ensure the retention and respect for the Indian culture."[97] It was also important that the children themselves were considered by the judge to have no First Nations identity.[98] These cases demonstrate a heavy and individuated burden on those arguing the importance of maintaining a child's First Nations cultural connection.

More generally, the retention and promotion of First Nations identity has seldom been recognized as an overriding, or even a substantially weighty, factor.[99] In *Racine*, for example, the Supreme Court of Canada rejected the proposition that the search for a home with the identical racial background as the child should be a paramount consideration in making a determination on adoption.[100] The result in *Racine* was followed in *Re W.W.* where the Alberta Court of Queen's Bench indicated that, if the trial judge had "placed greater emphasis on [First Nations heritage considerations] ... than on the issue of bonding," she would have been considered to have applied incorrect legal principles.[101] A few recent decisions suggest some willingness on the part of courts to presume and judicially notice retention of First Nations identity and culture as a relevant factor in determining best interests.[102]

---

[95] *Child and Family Services Act, 1984*, S.O. 1984, c. 55.

[96] *C.J.K., supra*, note 94 at 81 (emphasis added).

[97] *Ibid.* at 81. Having left her reserve at the age of fifteen, the grandmother was considered to be "fully acclimated to urban life in Southern Ontario and to have long ago cast away her own racial heritage and tradition." *Ibid.* at 82.

[98] *Ibid.* "[I]n this case there is no evidence of any recognition by the older children of their Native heritage." Note: this line is reported in the original judgment (28 June 1988), Toronto #C1867/85 (Ont. Prov. Ct Fam. Div.), although it is missing in the C.N.L.R. report of the case.

[99] What I am describing as the importance of maintaining a child's First Nations identity and culture seems to correspond to what Carasco identifies as "the indigenous factor." See *supra*, note 4.

[100] This is the way Kerans J.A. characterized *Racine* in *Re H.I.R.*, [1984] 3 C.N.L.R. 86 at 96 (Alta C.A.).

[101] (1989), 100 A.R. 221 at 232.

[102] In *Re H.I.R., supra*, note 100 at 96, for example, a First Nations mother declared to be

However, the individual and abstract focus of the best interests criterion makes such recognition difficult, and it is usually tenuous.

At best, the retention of First Nations culture and identity by a First Nations child plays an ambiguous role in judicial application of the best interests standard. It is not surprising then that the most legally authoritative description of the meaning of "best interests" fails to even mention the importance of retaining a child's First Nations culture and identity or to indicate the weight to be accorded to this factor.

> [T]he dominant consideration to which all other considerations must remain subordinate must be the welfare of the child. This is not to say that the question of custody will be determined by weighing the economic circumstances of the contending parties. The matter will not be determined solely on the basis of the physical comfort and material advantages that may be available in the home of one contender or the other. The welfare of the child must be decided on a consideration of these and all other relevant factors, including the general psychological, spiritual and emotional welfare of the child. It must be the aim of the Court, when resolving disputes between rival claimants for the custody of a child, to choose the course which will best provide for the healthy growth, development and education of the child so that he will be equipped to face the problems of life as a mature adult.[103]

Thus, in some cases, the importance of maintaining a First Nations child's identity and culture is not taken account of at all; in others, a heavy individualistic burden is placed on those asserting it; and, in still others, it is understood by the courts as being separate from, and irrelevant to, the question of the child's best interests. What ties all of these together, I want to suggest, is a conceptual separation of the individual child in question from her cultural context. That context is

---

unfit as a parent was allowed access to her child in foster care to enable the child, who was being raised in a white foster home, to "have some happy exposure to the native community and culture." The Court recognized that "the simplest and most natural way was for [the child] to maintain a relationship with his natural relatives." See also Carasco, *supra*, note 4 at 126. Similarly, in *King, supra*, note 57 at 103, one of the factors relied on by the Supreme Court of Canada in upholding the decision at first instance and in the Court of Appeal in favour of adoptive parents was that the adoptive mother "share[d] with [the child, whose father was a First Nations man] ... some Indian ancestry." This factor was found to "stand ... in her favour" on the basis that "one would expect that she [would] be enabled to understand and deal with problems the child [might] encounter in [that] respect." While this general recognition of the importance of maintaining a First Nations child's cultural identity and heritage is welcome, the specific application of the importance of this factor in the particular context of this case is problematic. It is relied on in this case to deny custody to the white mother of a First Nations child as opposed to operating in favour of a First Nations mother and against the retention of custody by white *foster* parents. As well, this case can be understood as an example of the "abstraction of culture" discussed in the next section.

103 *King, supra*, note 57 at 101.

portrayed as irrelevant or unimportant to the determination of her best interests.

b) *The abstraction of culture*

When courts do consider culture, they often do so in abstract terms. They reconstruct the concern of First Nations in maintaining the connection between each First Nations child and the heritage and culture of her *particular* First Nation into a concern about maintaining a connection to First Nations heritage and culture in the *abstract*. In other words, the specificity of different First Nations cultures is obscured. This tendency is, I suggest, partly the result of the abstract and individualistic character of best interests ideology. "Cultural connection" cannot be seen as directed to the maintenance of a tie between a child and her particular First Nation when the child has already been constructed as an individual abstracted out of her culture. For example, in *Re A.B.*, Landerkin J. of the Alberta Provincial Court assumed that, because the foster parents of the First Nations children in question lived in a small town "contiguous to a large Indian Reserve ... [i]t would be a fair inference that this physical location would allow this part of their heritage to be explored." This was despite the fact that the reserve in question was not the original home of the children.[104] The Court did not even consider whether the reserve community was part of the children's First Nation.[105]

Similarly, in *Racine*,[106] the Supreme Court of Canada thought that concerns raised about maintaining the Ojibway child's culture and identity were sufficiently met by the "sensitivity" of the adoptive parents (one white, the other Métis) "to the interracial aspect [of the adoption] and their appreciation of the need to encourage and develop in [the child] a sense of her own worth and dignity and the worth and dignity of

---

[104] (1989), 100 A.R. 150 at 154 where permanent guardianship of three First Nations children, aged 6, 3, and 2, was granted to the Director on the basis that the children were thriving in the foster home where they had been for the past two years. The mother from whose care they were removed had substance abuse problems and lived "a transient lifestyle." *Ibid.* at 153.

[105] Tellingly, whether the reserve close to the foster parent's home and the children's home reserve belonged to the same First Nation is not ascertainable from the judgment.

[106] *Supra*, note 57 (S.C.C).

her people."[107] This ruling was made despite Matas J.A.'s concern in the Court of Appeal that the white, adoptive mother could never sufficiently provide the child with the information and role modelling required to transmit successfully to the child an understanding of Ojibway heritage and culture.[108] The Supreme Court was of the view that the Métis adoptive father would be in a position to provide the child with "a model ... of how to survive as a member of a much maligned minority."[109] Though such instruction would obviously be important to the child, the Court was not concerned with finding out whether the adoptive father would be able to provide her with any exposure to the *Ojibway* language and culture that were *her* heritage.

It should be noted that, in some cases, courts have been sensitive to the specificity of First Nations identity and culture, holding that custody should be granted to someone capable of transmitting the identity and culture of the child's First Nation and/or providing for continued access by the child's parents or other extended family members. In *Sandy* v. *Nootchtai*,[110] for example, a First Nations woman sought custody of a fifteen-month-old child who had been in her care for six months following apprehension from his mother who had subsequently died. A custody application was also brought by the child's maternal aunt and supported by the late mother's band. The Court stated that "[t]he assertion of blood relationship and more particularly Indian blood relationship must still be considered in the context of the child's best interests"[111] and came to a determination in favour of the maternal aunt. In addition to the aunt's demonstrated parenting capabilities, the Court appears to have recognized that, with her, the child would also have the benefit of being raised within his own First Nation.[112]

---

107 *Ibid.* at 186 (S.C.C.).

108 *Woods* v. *Racine* (1982), [1983] 2 C.N.L.R. 157 at 187 (Man. C.A.) [hereinafter *Racine* (Man. C.A.)].

109 *Racine, supra*, note 57 at 178 (S.C.C.).

110 [1989] 3 C.N.L.R. 190 (Ont. Prov. Ct Fam. Div.) [hereinafter *Nootchtai*].

111 *Ibid.* at 194.

112 *Ibid.* at 196. See also *Kenora-Patricia Child and Family Services* v. *L. (P.)*, (2 September 1987), Kenora C227/81 (Ont. Prov. Ct Fam. Div.), Wang J. (recognizing that the child's "cultural development" would be "almost a certainty" with the chosen foster mother, an Ojibway woman, and also providing for continued access by the mother); *J.T.K.* v. *Kenora-Patricia Child and Family*

c) *Psychological bonding and permanent placement versus cultural connection*

The above analysis suggests that courts are, at best, ambiguous about the importance of maintaining First Nations identity and heritage in child welfare cases. On occasion, they recognize the importance of a child's connection to his culture, but tend not to give it much weight—let alone see it as central. By way of contrast, the psychological connection—or bond—that a child has developed with her caregivers and/or the permanence of the care situation in which she is placed are generally regarded as crucial to the child's welfare. More often than not, courts find these latter factors to be more consistent with a child's welfare than maintenance of her First Nations identity and culture. Underlying the weighing of these factors by courts is a justifiable concern with the stability of the child's environment and her corresponding emotional security. The problem is that this concern is understood as severable from the maintenance of the child's First Nations identity and heritage, again reflecting the individualistic and abstract focus of the best interests standard.

This point is illustrated by Wilson J.'s reliance in *Racine*[113] on the evidence of a medical expert to the effect that the case had

> nothing to do with race, absolutely nothing to do with culture, ... nothing to do with ethnic background. It's two women and a little girl, and one of them doesn't know her. It's as simple as that; all the rest of it is extra and of no consequence, except to the people involved, of course.[114]

Services, [1985] 4 C.N.L.R. 76 (Ont. Prov. Ct Fam. Div.) (held in favour of placement of the children in the home of relatives on a northern Ojibway reserve their parents came from as opposed to with a more materially well-off Mohawk couple living on a southern Ontario reserve); *Re W.W.*, *supra*, note 101; and *Re W.W.* (1988), 93 A.R. 248 (Prov. Ct Fam. Div.).

[113] *Supra*, note 57 (S.C.C.). The significance placed on bonding is also in evident in *King*, *supra*, note 57 at 87 (headnote), where a mother revoked her consent to the adoption of her child within three months following his birth, and sought to regain custody of him from the prospective adoptive parents whom she had chosen. Though the child had been in the care of the adoptive parents for only seven and a half months at the time of trial, the trial judge held that "[t]he benefits to the child of maintaining the blood ties to his natural mother were outweighed by those resulting from maintenance of his present home stability and his existing parental bonds to the adoptive parents." This decision was affirmed by both the Court of Appeal and the Supreme Court. In *King*, however, it should be recognized that the emphasis placed on bonding served to reinforce rather than counter the importance of maintaining the child's First Nations identity.

[114] *Supra*, note 57 at 188 (S.C.C.) quoting the words of the medical expert.

Accordingly, Wilson J. concluded that "when the test to be met is the best interests of the child, the significance of cultural background and heritage as opposed to bonding abates over time. The closer the bond that develops with the prospective adoptive parents the less important the racial element becomes."[115]

A similar approach is evident in *Re E.J.C.*[116] At issue was whether a two-year-old First Nations boy should be placed with his First Nations maternal grandmother or adopted by his non-First Nations foster mother. The child's mother wanted him to be placed in the care of his grandmother. The Court acknowledged that the child "would benefit from some peripheral contact with his own culture through the special efforts made by the foster parents in that regard,"[117] but recognized that his cultural development would be far greater in his grandmother's home where he would also have the benefit of association with his extended family.[118] Nonetheless, it concluded that the potential placements were, *prima facie*, "relatively equal" because of the potential strength of the child's bond to the foster parents, with whom he had lived for one year, as compared to that of any "remnants of bonding" to his grandmother, with whom he also had lived and who had provided "back-up" care for him prior to his apprehension.[119] Accordingly, a further four months of temporary wardship and continued placement with the foster parents was granted, *inter alia*, to enable further evidence of the extent of the child's psychological attachments to be presented.[120] The difficulty with these cases is not so much that psychological bonding is viewed as important for a child's emotional stability and security, but

---

[115] *Ibid.* at 187. See also *N.P.P.* v. *Regional Children's Guardian* (1988), 14 R.F.L. (3d) 55 (Alta Q.B.) [hereinafter *N.P.P.*] quashing a decision of the Children's Guardian of Alberta to place a child on a reserve with an extended family member because the relevance of disrupting the attachment of the particular child in question to her foster parents was not properly considered. For a more extensive discussion of this case, see *infra*, notes 156-61 and accompanying text.

[116] (1987), 79 A.R. 125 (Prov. Ct).

[117] *Ibid.* at 130. The foster mother had testified that the family "participate[d] in some native cultural and social events." *Ibid.* at 127.

[118] *Ibid.* at 130.

[119] *Ibid.* at 130 and at 126.

[120] *Ibid.* at 130. Increasing the time period during which the child remained with the foster parents, however, would also serve to increase the emotional attachment of the child to them.

rather that a child's connection to her First Nations culture is not understood in similar terms.

In addition to psychological bonding, permanent placement of a child has been accorded greater priority in a number of cases than maintaining a child's connection to her First Nations culture. In *Re S.D.*,[121] for example, the Court was concerned that the provincial Children's Guardian, though requesting the permanent wardship of a First Nations child, had not provided a permanent placement plan. The Children's Guardian had testified that a permanent plan had not yet been determined because the First Nations child welfare worker assigned to the case was in the middle of investigating the possibility of placing the child with a family on the mother's reserve. The child's white father had submitted a plan proposing that the child come to live with him and the child's paternal grandmother in Ontario. Clearly, the Children's Guardian required more time to determine the best placement for the child and, in particular, to make every effort to find a placement for the child with members of his own reserve. Rather than leaving the timing of the preparation of a permanent placement plan to the discretion of the Children's Guardian, however, the Court granted permanent guardianship to the Children's Guardian on the condition that a plan be filed within sixty days. This decision was subsequently upheld on appeal to the Court of Queen's Bench.[122] By favouring quicker assurance of a permanent placement elsewhere, the likelihood of the child being placed with a family on the child's reserve was substantially decreased. The Court's concern with a stable placement for the child, evident in the considerable weight it attached to permanency,[123] appears to have overridden concerns about maintaining the child's First Nations identity and connection to his culture. Indeed,

---

[121] *Supra*, note 70 (Alta Prov. Ct Fam. Div.).

[122] *Re S.D.*, *supra*, note 70 (Alta Q.B.). This decision was subsequently followed in *Re A.B.*, *supra*, note 104.

[123] See also *Re Cherie M.* (1983), 53 A.R. 48 at 56 (Prov. Ct), where the concern with permanent placement was described in this way: "it appears that the latest 'buzz-word' in the child welfare field is 'permanency planning.' The Director is receiving much criticism for permitting children to 'drift' through the system." In that case, however, where the First Nations child in question came into temporary care on the basis of a voluntary agreement between the society and her mother, the Court concluded that "[w]hatever validity there may be to the charge that the Director has permitted that to happen in other cases, ... it would be grossly premature to do other than to work at this time towards the reuniting of [this child] and her mother and her siblings." *Ibid.*

the Court's reasoning strongly implies that these latter concerns are not even related to the child's stability.

Kenora-Patricia Child and Family Services v. *M.M.*[124] provides an encouraging counter example to the tendencies evident in *Re S.D.*, though one that may be explained in part by the express requirement in the governing legislation to take account of culture.[125] The Provincial Court of Ontario considered an application by the Child and Family Services agency proposing the permanent and divided placement of four First Nations siblings, aged six, five, three and two, with two sets of non-First Nations foster parents with whom they had lived for two years. The agency also sought to have the children adopted by the foster parents. The application was opposed by the children's natural parents and band who proposed that the children all be placed with the mother's cousin and her husband and that there be continued contact with the parents. The agency argued that the children's need for "permanency, a stable placement" was a "substantial reason" for placing the children elsewhere than on the reserve.[126] This argument was rejected by the Court on the ground that the factors of stability and maintenance of First Nations identity could not be considered independently of one another. According to the Court, a truly successful permanent placement required that a First Nations child's need for retention of identity and culture be met.

> Although permanency is important, cultural heritage is also important. In fact there is good reason to infer that without cultural heritage being recognized as integral to human growth, permanency will never succeed. One cannot deny what one is; we cannot deny what these children are. They are Ojibway, and unless that is an integral part of our decision making, there is little hope that permanency planning will succeed.[127]

---

[124] (1989), 3 Ont. Fam. L. Rep. 38 (Prov. Ct).

[125] With respect to the protection of the children's First Nations identity accorded by the statute in question, the Court observed, *ibid.* at 39, that "[t]hese are not just bald, technical words but finally recognized [sic] as being of eminent importance to a child's healthy development. Without full respect and recognition of these children's past and cultural heritage, their future will be precarious."

Accordingly, the Court approved the placement of the children with members of their extended family on the reserve on the grounds that this was required by both the *Act* and the best interests standard.

[126] *Ibid.* at 39.

[127] *Ibid.*

d) *The construction of those who challenge dispositional decisions*

To this point, I have focused on how courts tend in many cases to construct the welfare of First Nations children in ways that obscure, or at least undervalue, the maintenance of a First Nations child's culture and identity. Underlying this approach, I have argued, is a conception of the child as an abstracted individual whose interests are severable from those of her extended family, community, and First Nation. In this section, I will analyze the judicial construction of parties who challenge the state's removal of First Nations children. Related to the emphasis on the separate and individual interests of the child considered above is a construction of parents or others who challenge the removal of a child from their care as acting in *their* individual—or selfish—interests.[128] First Nations mothers and members of a child's extended family or band who challenge a determination of a child's best interests are regarded as acting selfishly and as having "vested interests" rendering them incapable of "impartial" consideration of the child's best interests.[129] Moreover, the individualistic emphasis of the best interests analysis tends to preclude consideration of the collective interests and concerns of First Nations, usually represented by particular bands, in preventing First Nations children from being placed outside of their communities.[130]

The judicial construction of First Nations mothers as selfish is well illustrated in *Racine*.[131] The case involved a First Nations child who had spent most of her seven years in the care of a white foster mother and a Métis foster father. The Supreme Court of Canada had to decide between reinstating an adoption order in favour of the foster parents, previously overturned by the Manitoba Court of Appeal, or restoring

---

[128] Thèry, *supra*, note 77 at 347. See, for example, *Re K. and Children's Aid Society of Hamilton-Wentworth* (1989), 70 O.R. (2d) 466 (Unif. Fam. Ct) holding that the right of the parent to raise a child is subordinate to the best interests of the child, implying that the interests of the parent and the child are distinct, and the latter necessarily excludes the former.

[129] Smart, *supra*, note 69 at 24, makes a similar point relating to mothers in general in the context of intra-family child custody disputes.

[130] Monture, *supra*, note 4 at 13, also makes this point. For a discussion of the theoretical basis of the collective rights of the First Nations, see D.M. Johnston, "Native Rights as Collective Rights: A Question of Group Self-Preservation" (1989) 2 Can. J.L. & Jurisprudence 19.

[131] *Supra*, note 57 (S.C.C.).

legal custody or access to the child's natural mother, Linda Woods, an Ojibway woman. Wilson J., in considering the importance of maintaining a child's tie to her natural parents, concluded that this factor was relevant only in relation to its impact on the child, not the parent: "it is the parental tie as a meaningful and positive force in the life of the child and not in the life of the parent that the court has to be concerned about."[132] There is little doubt that considering the significance and meaning of a parental tie from the perspective of the child in question is important. Wilson J. goes further than this, however, and implies that a parent's concern with maintaining a tie is often based on self-interest:

> As has been emphasized many times in custody cases, a child is not a chattel in which its parents have a proprietary interest; it is a human being to whom they owe serious obligations. In giving the court power to dispense with the consent of the parent on a *de facto* adoption the legislature has recognized an aspect of the human condition—that our own self interest sometimes clouds our perception of what is best for those for whom we are responsible. It takes a very high degree of selflessness and maturity—for most of us probably an unattainable degree—for a parent to acknowledge that it might be better for his or her child to be brought up by someone else.[133]

Thus, according to Wilson J., there is a natural self-interest of parents which renders them incapable of distinguishing their own selfish desires from their child's best interests.[134]

The trial judge in *Racine* had found further evidence of the mother's apparent selfishness in her "exploitation of media attention"[135]

---

[132] *Ibid.* at 185. See also *Children's Aid Society of Halifax* v. *C.M.N.* (1989), 91 N.S.R. (2d) 232 at 235-36 (Fam. Ct) stating that "the argument concerning parental rights and the breaking of the bond between parent and child is valid up to a point. However, the best interest of the child has to come first ... the individual rights of the child override all others."

[133] *Racine, ibid.*

[134] See also *Kenora-Patricia Child and Family Services* v. *M.(C.)* (2 February 1989), Kenora C241/83 (Ont. Prov. Ct Fam. Div.), digested at (1989), 15 A.C.W.S. (3d) 78: Little J. sympathizes with an aunt, who wants custody of two First Nations children presently in foster care, but emphasizes that he must decide on the basis of what is best for children, not her. The aunt's reasons for wanting custody are characterized by the Court as "hav[ing] to do with meeting her own needs as opposed to the needs of the children." One would think, moreover, that given the "self-sacrificing ideology of motherhood," and the attendant expectation that mothers generally act in the child's best interest, mothers would be judged with particular severity when challenging determinations based upon the child's best interests. Susan Boyd has demonstrated this point in the context of intra-familial, child custody cases: *supra,* note 63 at 147. This may help to explain the particularly negative construction of the stated interests of the mother in *Racine,* both at first instance and in the Supreme Court.

[135] *Supra,* note 108 at 188 (Man. C.A.).

which was thought to "manifest ... an incredible indifference to the effect such an incident might have on her child."[136] The mother's politicization of the issue, moreover, was regarded by the trial judge, in statements uncritically repeated by Wilson J. in the Supreme Court, as being against the child's best interests. According to Wilson J., the trial judge "saw danger signals in 'the venom of her anti-white feelings' and wondered what effect 'her visible hatred for all things white' would have on her child. She also wondered whether Mrs. Woods' concern was for the child as a person or as a political issue."[137] Implicit in these remarks is a presumption that the mother's political concerns were necessarily inconsistent with the best interests of her child. The trial judge, and possibly Wilson J.,[138] regarded it as not in this child's best interests to have what they viewed as a political First Nations mother, one who acknowledged, confronted, and attempted to resist what she perceived as harsh treatment of herself and her people by the child welfare system.[139] Linda Woods not only failed to conform to the dominant conception of a good mother, but also to that of a " 'good' Indian," one who "is defined in terms of white values and culture and in terms of docile and apolitical behaviour."[140] She defended the importance of her people maintaining an Ojibway way of life, actively resisted the impact of the child welfare system on her daughter and herself, and challenged the threat which the system provided to the survival of her community and First Nation.

---

[136] *Supra*, note 57 at 179 (S.C.C.).

[137] *Racine, supra*, note 57 at 179 (S.C.C.).

[138] Matas J.A. in the Court of Appeal had declared irrelevant concerns about the mother's politicization of the case: *supra*, note 108 at 188. Wilson J. could have done the same.

[139] See also *J.T.K.* v. *Kenora-Patricia Child and Family Services*, *supra*, note 112 where the judge is disparaging of a Chief's threat, prior to the court proceedings, to go to the media; and an unreported case discussed in York, *supra*, note 7 at 221 where a British Columbia Provincial Court judge placed a First Nations child with a Mormon family even though his aunt wanted to adopt him. The judge decided that the aunt was unsuitable "because she was a strong Indian activist who would take the boy to protests and political battles," and thus could not provide "a stable, quiet structured life" for the child. See also K. Arnup, " 'Mothers Just Like Others': Lesbians, Divorce, and Child Custody in Canada" (1989) 3 C.J.W.L 18 at 27-31 for a similar analysis in the context of the effect of lesbian "militancy" in child custody cases involving lesbian mothers. Drawing insight from this latter article, it might be that proud, "confrontational," "militant" First Nations mothers have difficulty regaining custody of their children from the state because they directly flaunt dominant structures and are thus judged to be more likely to raise their children out of accord with dominant values.

[140] Kellough, *supra*, note 10 at 354.

Yet, Linda Woods's anger and frustration were portrayed in the judgments in *Racine* only in a negative light—as a barrier to, rather than evidence of, her continued rehabilitation and commitment to the best interests of her daughter.[141] The judgments do not recognize the strength reflected in her anger, nor the fact that she overcame the adversity in her own life and successfully re-established a life with her other children, nor her determination to take every possible measure to regain custody of her child. Moreover, no attempt is made to perceive Linda Woods's anger as the understandable product of her repeatedly frustrated efforts to regain custody of her daughter prior to initiating the proceedings which resulted in the court case, let alone to situate that anger in the historical context of colonialist white/First Nations relations in Canada. She is presented as acting only for her own (impliedly self-serving and therefore illegitimate) political purposes.[142]

In some cases, it is not only parents or other family members who challenge the removal of children, but also the child's band. The collective concerns of bands in such cases reflect a number of considerations. First, bands often consider the best interests of an individual child to require that the child not be removed from her community and culture.[143] Second, there is concern about the destructive impact that the system has had on First Nations communities, sometimes removing whole generations of children and thereby depriving communities of the capacity to regenerate themselves.[144] Third, and related to the first two considerations, is the traditional priority accorded by First Nations to collective, as well as

---

141 *Racine, supra*, note 57 at 178-79 (S.C.C.).

142 See also *V.S.* v. *M.M.*, [1989] N.W.T.R. 169 at 177 (S.C.) where the Court granted standing to a white, middle-class couple living in Nova Scotia who wanted custody of a twelve-year-old Chipewyan child in foster care in Yellowknife on the ground that there "appear[ed] to be no one else who [was] prepared to put forward the child's wishes, as expressed in her letters, or to ensure that the possibility of her finding a congenial and suitable permanent family environment [was] at least given a chance of realization." To arrive at such a conclusion, the judge must have considered that the child's grandmother and mother, who opposed the application, to represent their own, as opposed to the child's, interests. In contrast, the applicants, who had had only a short-term, long-distance relationship with the child, were thought to represent her best interests.

143 See, *e.g.*, D.J. Goldsmith, "Individual vs. Collective Rights: The Indian Child Welfare Act" (1990) 13 Harv. Women's L.J. 1 at 2.

144 *Ibid.* See also *supra*, note 4; and Johnston, *supra*, note 130 at 32 arguing that "[t]he right of native communities to self-preservation" is the "foundational right accorded to collective entities capable of bearing rights."

individual, concerns.[145] With respect to the latter of these, Patricia Monture has stated, "[t]he structure of First Nation's society is based on cooperation and consensus ... In a community which operates on norms of consensus and cooperation, the collective's rights are the focus. By contrast, the structures of the dominant society operate with the individual as the problem-solving unit."[146] In the context of child welfare, the traditional collective focus takes the form of a recognized communal responsibility for the care of children. An elder in Alberta explained the traditional approach this way:

> The Indian Philosophy is that when you bring a child into this world, you are responsible for that child until that child can look after himself or herself ... For example: like in the family home, if things didn't work out well for that young couple, supposing if there was a sickness in that family, or the mother died or the father died, it is the practice and the cultured belief of our native people that automatically an uncle, an aunt or grandmother, grandfather or a cousin or even a good friend or those people would take over the responsibility for raising that child and that is expected of society in those days ... It's unfortunate now that there is so many things that have entered into the native way of life, that we have lost these values of the family home.[147]

Within the individualistic structure of best interests ideology, however, courts tend not to acknowledge, nor act on, such collective concerns. In particular, as noted above, the individualistic structure of the best interests ideology supports a presumption that the collective interests of First Nations are "inevitably antagonistic"[148] to the individual interests of the child in question. As a consequence, court cases have tended to presume that, if the interests of the First Nations community are met, the child's interests must necessarily be forgone.[149]

This disregard for the collective concerns of First Nations has contributed to the difficulty bands[150] have had in advancing their

---

[145] Monture, *supra*, note 4 at 6.

[146] *Ibid.* See also Bull, *supra*, note 3 at 527. But, see also M.E. Turpel, "Aboriginal Peoples and the Canadian *Charter*: Interpretive Monopolies, Cultural Differences" (1989-90) 6 Can. Hum. Rts Y.B. 3 at 16-17 who writes "I would take issue with some scholars on their projection of 'society' as an either-or [*i.e.*, individualist or collectivist], and caution against an attempt to typify, for example, an Aboriginal society in such a fashion."

[147] *Child Welfare Needs*, *supra*, note 7 at 50-51.

[148] Johnston, *supra*, note 130 at 19.

[149] Smart, *supra*, note 69 at 23, makes a similar point with regard to parental concerns in the context of a discussion of intra-familial child custody issues.

[150] Bands are now generally recognized by First Nations as having a major role in the

interests in child welfare proceedings involving First Nations children.[151] In particular, their concerns about the impact of the child welfare system upon the collective interests of the First Nations or a particular band are liable to be deemed irrelevant, indeed, illegitimate. In *Kenora-Patricia Child and Family Services* v. *Rose F.*,[152] for example, a Band representing the interests of a reserve had made a general argument urging the Court to take seriously its obligation, as set out in section 53(5) of the *Child and Family Services Act*, to place a First Nations child "with a member of the child's extended family; [or] a member of the child's band or native community."[153] The Court ordered costs against the Band because it had advanced only this general position and had not presented a specific plan to the Court with regard to the placement of the particular child in question. According to Little J.:

> I appreciate very much and sympathize with the position of the Islington Band but there are many children of the reserve who have become wards of the state ... [and] the Band is obliged with respect to *every individual case* before the court to develop the position *not based on an opinion with regard to the effect of the child welfare system on the reserve but rather a position based on the facts of the particular case before the court.*[154]

---

articulation and protection of collective interests, and, in child welfare cases, they often take on this role: see, generally, Johnston, *supra*, note 130 at 31, considering whether bands constitute truly representative collectivities.

151 Increasingly, though, courts are recognizing the important contribution of bands to the determination of the best interests of a First Nations child by allowing them to intervene in child welfare proceedings: see, *e.g.*, *Pitzel* v. *Children Aid Society of Winnipeg*, [1984] 5 W.W.R. 474, [1984] 4 C.N.L.R. 41 (Man. Q.B. Fam. Div.) [hereinafter *Pitzel* cited to W.W.R.]; *Nootchtai*, *supra*, note 110; *Re Catholic Children's Aid Society of Metropolitan Toronto and M.* (1986), 57 O.R. (2d) 551 (Prov. Ct Fam. Div.), aff'd (1987), 62 O.R. (2d) 535 (Dist. Ct); and *Children's Aid Society of Nippissing (District of)* v. *Ruby M.*, [1989] 2 C.N.L.R. 21 (Prov. Ct Fam. Div.). However, courts continue to refuse to provide custody of a child to a band. The governing statutes in each province, which emphasize the provision of protective care by specific individuals, are partly responsible for this refusal: *Tom* v. *Winnipeg Children's Aid Society*, [1982] 2 W.W.R. 212 (Man. C.A.); *Re Family and Child Service Act* (1982), (B.C. Prov. Ct) [unreported] cited in Carasco, *supra*, note 5 at 128; and *Simeonoff* v. *J.A.* (14 February 1992), Vancouver CA011869 (B.C.C.A.) arguing that the

> entire thrust of the custody provisions of the *[B.C. Family Relations] Act* is towards [a] person to person relationship ... In its simplest, organic form a tribe is an agglomeration of individuals like a congregation or a club. Regardless of the nature of the tie that binds the members together, the notion that such a group can be regarded as an individual for purposes of child custody is entirely foreign to the concept of custody and to the individual duties and responsibilities implicit in the concept.

152 (19 April 1988), Kenora C102/85 (Ont. Prov. Ct Fam. Div.), Little J. [unreported] [hereinafter *Kenora-Patricia* v. *Rose F.*].

153 S.O. 1984, c. 55, as am. S.O. 1990, c. C-11, s. 57(5).

154 *Kenora-Patricia* v. *Rose F.*, *supra*, note 152 (emphasis added).

The order of costs in this case was clearly meant to discourage bands who wish to advance their collective concerns in First Nations child welfare proceedings.

The judicial approach in child welfare proceedings has also made it difficult for provincial governments and government officials to respond to the First Nations child welfare crisis with decisions and policies that take account of the collective interests of First Nations generally or of particular bands.[155] In *N.P.P.* v. *Regional Children's Guardian*,[156] white foster parents of a nine-year-old Cree child who had been in their care for three years applied for *certiorari* to quash the refusal by the Regional Children's Guardian to consent to their private guardianship order. Instead, the Guardian had decided to place the child with her aunt on her mother's reserve in northern Saskatchewan. This case was the first time a decision of the Regional Children's Guardian of Alberta had been challenged in the courts since the creation of the position in 1984.[157] The Alberta Court of Queen's Bench allowed the application for judicial review on the basis that the Guardian had wrongly interpreted the purpose of the Alberta *Child Welfare Act* respecting First Nations children in care.

The Regional Children's Guardian had interpreted the *Act* as requiring her to place First Nations children receiving care from non-First Nations foster parents, if at all possible, in a First Nations home in the particular band from which the child's mother or parents came.[158] The judge, however, narrowly construed the relevant sections of the *Act* and concluded that the Guardian's approach constituted an error of law. For example, he rejected the Guardian's construction of the word "family" in section 2(a) of the *Act* as including members of a band who share a common ancestry and insisted that "family" included only that group of people who, before intervention by the state, had been responsible for the care and supervision of a child.[159] Thus, since the child in question had been originally apprehended from the custody of

---

155 See *infra*, Section IV for a more extensive consideration of legislative reform efforts in Alberta.

156 *Supra*, note 115.

157 *Alberta Act, 1984*. See also discussion, *infra*, notes 195-98 and accompanying text.

158 *N.P.P.*, *supra*, note 115 at 74.

159 Compare *Re E.J.C.*, *supra*, note 116 at 128, where the centrality of the extended family in Cree social structure is recognized and incorporated into the statutory reference to "family."

her mother, the maintenance of family ties as required by section 2(a) was held not to require the maintenance of ties between the child and an aunt, let alone more distantly related members of her band.

The Guardian had also interpreted a provision emphasizing placement of a child "as close as possible to the child's home community"[160] to mean placement on the particular reserve from which the child's mother had come and on which her aunt and one brother lived. The judge's view, however, was that the phrase meant only the *physical* community in which the child had lived prior to state intervention. On the basis of this interpretation, the Court concluded that it was incorrect to say that the "home community" of the individual child was the reserve. According to Macdonald A.C.J., "there [was] no indication whatever ... that the reserve in Saskatchewan was the home of the child at the time of apprehension," nor could the reserve be considered the mother's home community since she had not lived there for many years.[161] This case places important constraints on administrative officials attempting to address the collective concerns of First Nations regarding the placement of First Nations children.

2. The "innocence" of law: child welfare law as impartial and universal

My analysis up to this point has sought to explain how the alarmingly disproportionate impact of the child welfare system is attributable, at least in part, to the legal form of the best interests standard. This has illustrated one of the subtle ways in which racism operates in the context of law. Now I want to turn to an examination of how this legal form also contributes to a portrayal of the child welfare process as innocent of its disparate and destructive effects on First Nations—an example of what Peter Fitzpatrick refers to as the "innocence" of law relating to racism.[162] Within the liberal, ideological form of the best interests of the child standard, racism is rarely explicit. Instead, the form of law "both substitutes for explicit racism and provides a means of asserting that what is involved is not racism but

160 *Alberta Act, 1984*, s. 2(h)(iii).

161 *N.P.P.*, *supra*, note 115 at 75.

162 Fitzpatrick, "Innocence of Law," *supra*, note 61 at 121.

something different."[163] Thus, law remains not only compatible with racism, but is also a mechanism for its reproduction and reinforcement. "[B]y taking elements of racism into itself and shaping them in its own terms,"[164] the particular form of law establishes "limits beyond which law will not proceed"[165] in addressing or countering racism. In the end, law's claim of innocence obfuscates its role in the reproduction and reinforcement of racism, thereby rendering its racist structures unassailable.[166]

These general insights into the relationship between racism and liberal legality have important bearing on this analysis of the operation of the best interests principle in the context of First Nations child welfare. Here the innocence of law is expressed in terms of the impartiality of the best interests of the child standard—impartiality being a crucial presupposition of liberal legality. The portrayal of law as impartial ensures that it appears innocent of politics, thereby reinforcing its claim to legitimacy. This impartiality is premised upon universality of application: if the law applies equally to everybody, then it must be impartial.[167] In the context of child welfare law, universality is manifest in the application of the same standards and protective mechanisms established in child welfare legislation to all children within each province. The "universalistic pretensions"[168] of child welfare law, in turn, support the putative objectivity of the child welfare system.[169] The system is thus constructed as innocent of the disparate impact and destructive effects that it has had on First Nations.[170] Moreover, universality establishes a particular identity of law that submerges acknowledgement and recognition of unequal power relations between various groups in society. It presumes from the outset the "unity of

---

163 *Ibid.* at 120.

164 *Ibid.* at 122.

165 *Ibid.*

166 *Ibid.* Fitzpatrick illustrates and supports this argument through an analysis of the operation of the British *Race Relations Act 1976* (U.K.), 1976, c. 74.

167 *Ibid.* at 130.

168 *Ibid.* at 129.

169 For a similar observation in relation to racism and law in other contexts, see Kobayashi, *supra,* note 64 at 451.

170 See *supra,* notes 3-4 and accompanying text.

society and nation"[171] that serves to obscure material relations of conflict and oppression.

The "universalistic pretensions" of courts in applying the best interests standard are illustrated by a recent decision of the Supreme Court of Nova Scotia Appeal Division. In *M.K.S.* v. *Minister of Community Services (Nova Scotia)*,[172] a Micmac woman challenged a finding that her two children were in need of protection. She argued under section 15 of the *Canadian Charter of Rights and Freedoms*[173] that she had been discriminated against on the basis of race or ethnic origin, family status, and economic status. In evidence, she submitted a number of studies, characterized by the Court as dealing with the "social-economic problems of native people,"[174] and a federal government report demonstrating the disproportionate impact of child welfare law on First Nations children.[175] Palmeter C.J.C.C. acknowledged that the relevant section of the *Children's Services Act* "may have a greater impact on native people,"[176] but concluded that the "test for children 'in need of protection' [was] standard throughout the province" and "applied equally to all persons."[177] Thus, in his view, there was no discrimination.[178]

---

[171] Fitzpatrick, "Innocence of Law," *supra*, note 61 at 129. See also C. Sumner, *Reading Ideologies: An Investigation into the Marxist Theory of Ideology and Law* (London: Academic Press, 1979) at 293 (arguing that law through its universalistic pretensions provides the "expression of unity in the nation."); E. Lawrence, "Just plain common sense: the 'roots' of racism" in Centre for Contemporary Cultural Studies, ed., *The Empire Strikes Back: Race and Racism in 70s Britain* (London: Hutchinson & Co., 1982) 47 at 59 (arguing that the notion of nation is itself an ideological construction which contributes to the binding of disparate groups in society).

[172] (1988), 86 N.S.R. (2d) 209, [1990] 1 C.N.L.R. 53 (N.S. Co. Ct), aff'd [1990] 1 C.N.L.R. 87 (N.S.S.C.A.D.) [hereinafter *M.K.S.* cited to N.S.R.].

[173] Part I of the *Constitution Act, 1982*, being Schedule B of the *Canada Act 1982* (U.K.), 1982, c. 11 [hereinafter *Charter*].

[174] *M.K.S.*, *supra*, note 172 at 223.

[175] *Ibid.* at 222-23.

[176] *Ibid.* at 223.

[177] *Ibid.*

[178] Given that there was strong evidence of physical abuse of the children in question, this was not a case with a particularly good factual basis for supporting a *Charter* challenge: D.A.R. Thompson, "Why Hasn't the Charter Mattered in Child Protection?" (1989-90) 8 Can. J. Fam. L. 133 at 136 and at 140. Nonetheless, it illustrates the judicial construction of child welfare law as impartial as a result of its universal application.

Evidence of the systemic impact of child welfare law was similarly ignored in *Re Cherie M.*[179] A First Nations mother, seeking the return of her daughter whom she had voluntarily placed into state care some months earlier, called as a witness an expert on child welfare. On the basis of a summary of facts provided to him in a letter prior to the trial, the expert had concluded that "it seem[ed] fairly clear to [him] ... that the 'system' ha[d] through close contact with this kind of work, lost some of its immediate sensitivity with regard to the removal of children from their family."[180] Because the expert had discussed the system in general as opposed to the specific circumstances of the particular case before him and had had "no direct contact with the mother, the child or the child welfare workers involved in the case,"[181] the Court declined to give weight to this evidence. Moreover, according to the Court, the expert's evidence lacked "the neutrality and objectivity that should have been displayed."[182] The judge characterized the views of the expert as follows:

> The thesis of Dr. Bagley as it relates to child welfare and children of native origin is that by and large intervention by child welfare in native families has done more harm than good. According to Dr. Bagley, all kinds of alternatives should be considered before apprehension or ward care, and in his opinion, as an expert in child welfare, "the grounds for apprehending are extremely slender."[183]

According to the Court, Dr. Bagley's testimony and other similar materials "relating to child welfare in general and child welfare and the native community" were "of little assistance ... in conducting this inquiry."[184] The Court's only "duty" was "to inquire into and ascertain the facts of the case, and then apply the law as found in the existing *Child Welfare Act* and the authorities."[185]

The implication in *Re Cherie M.* is that concerns about the systemic impact of the child welfare system are related to policy and therefore not "neutral," while concerns about the best interests of

---

179 *Supra*, note 123.

180 *Ibid.* at 52.

181 *Ibid.*

182 *Ibid.*

183 *Ibid.*

184 *Ibid.*

185 *Ibid.*

individual children are legal, and thus innocent of politics. This point is further illustrated in *Pitzel* v. *Children's Aid Society of Winnipeg*.[186] Anishnaabe Child and Family Services, a First Nations-controlled child welfare agency in Manitoba, applied to intervene in an action addressing the guardianship of a three-and-a-half-year-old child who had been apprehended and placed in the care of foster parents nine days after her birth. The agency had become actively involved in the case with a view to placing the child with her maternal aunt on a reserve. The foster parents, who wanted to adopt the child, opposed Anishnaabe's application for intervenor status. They felt that the agency's involvement would " 'politicize' the case."[187] The Court granted the agency intervenor status and answered the foster parents argument by asserting that it would not allow the case to be "politicized"; rather, it would "confine all parties to the one and only issue—the arrangement that will best serve the needs of the child."[188] In other words, by confining arguments to the child's best interests, the case could not be politicized. Once again, then, the best interests standard is set up as apolitical—as "innocent" of politics.[189]

[186] *Supra*, note 151.

[187] *Ibid.* at 477.

[188] *Ibid.*

[189] Another interesting example of the purported separation of child welfare law from politics can be found in *North West Child and Family Services Agency* v. *B.S.* (1988), 52 Man. R. (2d) 254 (Q.B.). The Court's rejection of a First Nations-controlled child and family services agency's argument that the Court's decision might have undesirable *political* consequences for the agency was reinforced by its implication that the best interests standard and its application thereof were, unlike the agency's practices, above political considerations.

IV. THE POWER OF BEST INTERESTS IDEOLOGY AND LEGISLATIVE REFORM

Child welfare law has been portrayed as impartial and apolitical. Yet, this portrayal has not completely obscured its disparate impact on First Nations. By the late 1970s, the destructive effects of the child welfare system on First Nations were being brought to public light through the lobbying efforts of First Nations, in particular First Nations women's organizations.[190] Demands for legislative change by First Nations and other critics over the past decade have often included recommendations for modification of the best interests standard, and some of these have been adopted in recent legislative reforms.[191] The recent nature of such modifications makes it difficult to properly assess their impact. However, my analysis provides a useful starting point for understanding their potential impact and for developing other transformative strategies in the future. Most importantly, I want to suggest that the power and resilience of best interests ideology may serve to undermine attempts to avoid its destructive effects through legislative reform. Recent experience in Alberta provides a good example of this problem.

Around the time First Nations began to lobby for change to the child welfare system in Alberta, the government initiated an examination of the underlying premises and structures of existing child welfare legislation.[192] First Nations organizations became involved in this process to ensure that any resulting legislation would be responsive to their concerns, although they also continued to pursue other strategies

---

[190] For example, three resolutions were passed by the Ontario Native Women's Association in July 1981 addressing child welfare issues as a priority: see Native People's Resource Centre, *supra*, note 11 at 44-45. See also Native Women's Association of Canada, "Our Children are Our Future" (Presentation to the Special House Committee on Child Care, 10 June 1986); and Monture, *supra*, note 4 at 5 and at 8 discussing the centrality of children's issues for First Nations women.

[191] *E.g.*, Alberta, Ontario, Saskatchewan, Nova Scotia, and the current Child Protection Legislation Review process in British Columbia.

[192] Alberta, Court of Queen's Bench, *Board of Review: The Child Welfare System* (Edmonton: Court of Queen's Bench, 20 October 1983) (Chair: J.C. Cavanagh); and R.J. Thomlison, *Case Management Review: Northwest Region, Department of Social Services and Community Health* (Edmonton: Alberta Department of Social Services and Community Health, Northwest Region, September 1984).

of child welfare reform.[193] Within the consultative process, they and numerous others[194] criticized the broad discretion afforded to agency workers and judges under the best interests standard. They recommended legislative circumscription of this discretion through the introduction of specific criteria to be considered in the determination of any care disposition.

Partly in response to such recommendations, new legislation which provided a more specific formulation of what had previously been a general and undefined best interests standard was drafted and assented to in 1984.[195] Most importantly, the general best interests of the child standard was not established as an overriding consideration. Instead, the revised *Act* began with an extensive list of specific considerations that any court or person exercising decision-making power under the *Act* was required to take into account.[196] That "the interests of the child" be "recognized and protected" was included only as one of the listed considerations.[197] Also explicitly required in "any decision concerning the removal of a child from the child's family" was consideration of "the benefits to the child of maintaining, wherever possible, the child's familial, cultural, social and religious heritage."[198] Finally, in response to failings in the case management processes of the Ministry of Family and Social Services, the *Act* created a new

---

[193] See *Final Report*, *supra*, note 6 at app. 4; and James, *supra*, note 12.

[194] A parallel critique of interventionist child welfare legislation was inspired by the work of American academics: see M. Wald, "State Intervention on Behalf of 'Neglected' Children: A Search for Realistic Standards" (1975) 27 Stan. L. Rev. 985; M. Wald, "State Intervention on Behalf of 'Neglected' Children: Standards for Removal of Children from their Homes, Monitoring the Status of Children in Foster Care, and Termination of Parental Rights" (1976) 28 Stan. L. Rev. 623; R.H. Mnookin, "Foster Care—In Whose Best Interest?" (1973) 43 Harv. Educ. Rev. 599; J. Goldstein, A. Freud & A.J. Solnit, *Beyond the Best Interests of the Child* (New York: Free Press, 1973); and J. Goldstein, A. Freud & A.J. Solnit, *Before the Best Interests of the Child* (New York: Free Press, 1979).

[195] *Alberta Act, 1984*. The previous Alberta legislation, R.S.A. 1980, c. C-8, had set out the best interests of the child as the fundamental consideration and did not specify in any way what was meant by that principle.

[196] *Ibid.* at s. 2.

[197] *Ibid.* at s. 2(b).

[198] *Ibid.* at s. 2(f)(i).

administrative position to perform an advocacy, as opposed to an administrative, role in relation to children in state care.[199]

The absence of a mandatory and general best interests standard in the new legislation became a source of considerable controversy in its subsequent implementation. The question of interpreting the modified guidelines first arose in the context of judicial review of decisions made by the Children's Guardian relating to First Nations children in care. Soon after being appointed, the new Children's Guardian had developed and implemented a policy designed to find permanent homes for First Nations children who were in the long-term, temporary care of the Director.[200] Under this policy, over two hundred First Nations children were returned successfully to the homes of their parents or extended families.[201] However, controversy arose in relation to a few difficult cases in which non-First Nations foster parents challenged the removal of their foster children. Decisions in their favour by the Child Welfare Appeal panel were subsequently overturned by the Children's Guardian. In two such cases, the foster parents then applied to the Court of Queen's Bench for review of the Guardian's decision.[202] The Court quashed the decision of the Children's Guardian in one case, *N.P.P.*,[203] and, in the course of its reasons, drew critical attention to the absence of an overriding best interests of the child principle in the *Child Welfare*

---

199 This new position was called the Children's Guardian. See Alberta, Legislative Assembly, *Hansard* (8 May 1984) at 757.

200 When asked in the Legislative Assembly to comment on the policy of "taking as many native children as possible back to the reserves," Connie Osterman, Minister of Social Services, replied that there was and had never been such a policy. Rather, there was a general concern to find permanent homes for the large number of children who had been in long-term, temporary care, which might involve either private adoption in favour of foster parents or the return of a child to a First Nations community. In her view, that had been achieved quite successfully except for "a small number of cases ... that ha[d] not been achieved with concurrence on both sides." Alberta, Legislative Assembly, *Hansard* (23 March 1988) at 71-72.

201 See G. Koch, "Trying to end the nightmares: Alberta and Manitoba confront failed native child 'repatriation' policies" *Western Report* (7 November 1988) 8. This information could not be verified because the Alberta Ministry of Family and Social Services does not keep a record of the number of First Nations children in state care successfully returned to their communities. Telephone interview with Archie Arcan, Manager of the Child Welfare Information System, Alberta Ministry of Family and Social Services (7 August 1992).

202 *N.P.P., supra*, note 115; and *Tschritter* v. *Sohn* (1987), 83 A.R. 374 (Q.B.).

203 *Supra*, note 115 and accompanying text.

Act.[204] Media reports of this case, along with similar arguments from foster parents' advocacy groups, heightened public concern that the best interests of the individual First Nations children who were being returned to First Nations communities were not being met.[205] Questions posed in the Legislative Assembly relating to the "repatriation" controversies were met with assertions by the government that all decisions had been, and continued to be, made in accordance with the best interests of the individual children in question.[206] Ultimately, the government bowed to political pressure by amending the *Child Welfare Act* to reinstate the best interests of the child standard as an overriding principle and to curtail the broad-ranging powers of the Children's Guardian.[207]

---

[204] See *N.P.P., supra*, note 115 at 65-66:

> The list of considerations set forth in s. 2 does not state that the governing consideration is "the best interests of the child," which before the enactment of the 1984 Act had been regarded as the fundamental consideration. The omission is startling and must be regarded as significant ... Its significance must be that, the legislature having taken the trouble to enact a list of relevant considerations, that list cannot be read as subject to some unstated overriding principle that is neither stated as overriding nor even mentioned as one of the relevant considerations.

See also *Re C.W.L.L.* (1986), 74 A.R. 395, 5 R.F.L. (3d) 53 (Q.B.) where the Court relied on *Racine, supra*, note 57, and *King, supra*, note 57, to read an overriding best interests of the child principle into the Alberta *Act*, notwithstanding its absence. Paying particular attention to those matters mentioned in s. 2(h) of the *Act*, the Court concluded that the best interests principle ought to have governed in deciding whether to return the child in question to the mother or to order permanent guardianship.

[205] See, *e.g.*, J. Cote & T. Philip, "Fostering Heartbreak" *Western Report* (11 May 1984) 37; Koch, *supra*, note 201; and Alberta, Legislative Assembly, *Hansard* (24 March 1988) at 91.

[206] See, *e.g.*, Alberta, Legislative Assembly, *Hansard* (23 March 1988) at 71; Alberta, Legislative Assembly, *Hansard* (24 March 1988) at 92 (Osterman: "I believe there are many processes in place that speak to the best interests of the child, and they are being followed."); Alberta, Legislative Assembly, *Hansard* (21 April 1988) at 576 (Osterman: "certainly the [permanency planning] policy has to speak to the best interests of the child and not the various adults who have wishes to make a permanent home for that child."; and further down: "[I]n all instances—and it's certainly the direction from the minister and the deputy minister and senior staff—the needs of the child must come first and foremost."); and Alberta, Legislative Assembly, *Hansard* (20 June 1988) at 1846 (Osterman: "I think we do have to make a definitive statement about our policy in respect to what interests are to come first and foremost [regarding First Nations children], and it is the interests of the individual children.")

[207] *Child Welfare Amendment Act, 1988*, S.A. 1988, c. 15, reported by the Legislative Assembly of Alberta on 5 July 1988. See Alberta, Legislative Assembly, *Hansard* (30 June 1988) at 2172, in regard to the re-instatement of the best interests standard in the *Amendment Act*, Osterman observes that "obviously, inherent throughout the Bill, that had always been there. But it was

This chain of events demonstrates the strength and resilience of best interests ideology. The original legislative amendments sought to address the First Nations child welfare crisis by, among other things, removing the general best interests standard from the child welfare legislation and creating a child advocate position. The amendments had significant positive effects in that large numbers of First Nations children were returned to their communities. However, these reforms were finally legislatively derailed. I want to suggest that this can be understood in part as a consequence of the continuing power of best interests ideology. While the amendments were a significant victory for First Nations, they were, nonetheless, a fragile and incomplete victory. Without a more direct transformation of the material conditions that gave rise to the development of best interests ideology, even explicit legislative action could not significantly challenge its power and tenacity in the minds of both judges and members of the public.

V. CONCLUSION

Liberalism has structured legal discourse such that racism is most often unintended and rarely explicit. To understand how and why law in its various aspects has an oppressive and discriminatory impact on First Nations and other racialized groups in Canadian society, one must look at some of its more subtle processes and, in particular, its ideological form. My goal in this article has been to provide some insight into the origins and operation of best interests of the child ideology and to illustrate how it structures and constrains judicial decision making in the context of First Nations child welfare. Best interests of the child ideology manifests the basic tenets of liberal ideology. In child welfare cases, this has served to portray the apprehension and placement of First Nations children away from their families and communities as natural, necessary, and legitimate, rather than coercive and destructive. This is accomplished, in part, through legal processes that appear to be universal and neutral, and to protect children and serve their best interests. As well, the relevance and importance of a First Nations child maintaining her First Nations identity and culture is minimized. As a result, I have argued, child welfare law has become a new modality of

important in terms of the way the situation had been addressed in a legal sense to do that."

colonialist regulation of First Nations in the post-Second World War period.

Since best interests ideology has had such a destructive impact on First Nations in the context of child welfare, understanding its nature and operation is crucial in developing effective strategies to address and counter the continuing crisis. At a minimum, the power and effects of best interests ideology in this context should raise concern about any child welfare regime that maintains the best interests standard as central. However, the unsuccessful attempt in Alberta to avoid the power of best interests ideology demonstrates that more needs to be done than simply eliminating explicit legislative requirements to render decisions according to the best interests standard. A number of First Nations child welfare cases have chipped away at assumptions implicit in best interests ideology, but ideology cannot be countered simply through arguments that its assumptions are false or incorrect. To transform ideology substantially, it is necessary to work on changing the material conditions and power relations responsible for its production and reproduction.

In the child welfare context, this means addressing directly the power accorded to institutions of the dominant society to impose destructive child welfare regimes on First Nations in the first place. First Nations must be empowered, financially, politically, and otherwise, to develop their own child welfare services outside the framework of existing provincial legislative schemes. This approach would be consistent with the current, long-term strategies of many First Nations communities which are developing child welfare services with the more general goal of self-government.[208] Autonomous First Nations child

---

[208] See T. Isaac, "Justice for Whom?" *Akwesasne Notes [Rooseveltown, New York]* (Early Fall 1988) 27; and Esse Networks Ltd., *Together Today ... For Our Children Tomorrow: Our Most Valuable Resource: A Discussion of Indian Child Welfare* (Yukon Territories: Council for Yukon Indians, October 1990). See also the recommendations of the Aboriginal portion of the Community Panel established in November 1991 by the Ministry of Social Services in British Columbia to review child protection legislation stating that:

> [t]he first step to righting the wrongs which have been done to us is to limit the authority to interfere in the lives of our families, and to provide remedies other than the removal of our children from our Nations. This must be accompanied by the financial resources which we require to heal the wounds inflicted upon us. At the same time, the responsibilities and jurisdictions vested in your Superintendent and the family courts must be vested in our Nations. Finally, as our Nations rewrite their own family law to meet our contemporary needs, as we rebuild the authority usurped from our Nations, the laws of our Nations must have paramountcy over your laws as they apply to our people.

welfare services, however, will not in themselves be enough. It is necessary as well to challenge (as First Nations are presently doing) the historical and continuing colonialist practices of exclusion, land dispossession, and destruction of traditional First Nations economies. These have resulted in the conditions of poverty, ill-health, and alcohol and drug dependency that, in turn, create much of the need for supportive or substitutional care for First Nations children. Ultimately, then, the welfare of First Nations children cannot be separated from the more general welfare of First Nations. The current crisis in First Nations child welfare will only be effectively resolved if addressed in conjunction with the wider and intersecting social, economic, and political goals of First Nations.

See also A.S. Pellatt, *An International Review of Child Welfare Policy and Practice in Relation to Aboriginal People* (Calgary: Canadian Research Institute for Law and the Family, 1991) at 5-30; Warry, *supra*, note 3 at 31 and at 33; Macdonald, *supra*, note 4 (describing a particularly interesting initiative of the Spallumcheen Indian Band of British Columbia in 1980 to address the child welfare crisis in its own community and develop autonomous, community-based services which involved passage of a by-law assigning exclusive jurisdiction over custody proceedings involving Band children to the Band); B. Wharf, *Toward First Nation Control of Child Welfare: A Review of Emerging Developments in B.C.* (Victoria: University of Victoria, 1989); and R.S. Ratner, *Child Welfare Services for Urban Native Indians* (Vancouver: United Native Nations, 1990).

[13]

JUST FAMILY LAW: A BASIC HUMAN RIGHT OF ALL INDIAN WOMEN

*Archana Parashar**

India is a country of diversity and for the most part we seem comfortable with differences. It is perhaps a part explanation for the existence of many religious personal laws, governing women of various religious communities, differently in family related matters. In this paper however, I wish to argue for one family law that will be non-discriminatory and just for all Indian women. Family law usually is not associated with a discourse of human rights but unless women gain equality of rights in personal matters they cannot be said to have the basic Human Right. In making this argument I am fully aware of the charge of essentialism and universalism. I however, make my argument in the specific context where for more than half a century a post colonial state has failed to guarantee basic equality to Indian women in the area of family relations. All religious personal laws manage to treat women less favorably than men. History of reforms within religious laws is not promising either for the majority Hindu community or the minority communities of Muslims, Christians, or Parsis. The Constitutional guarantees of sex equality and religious freedom have been interpreted by the Supreme Court in such a manner that discriminatory religious personal laws are not found to be unconstitutional. Adequate legislative changes have not been introduced as in a democratic polity the incumbent governments have chosen to politicize religion and play constituency politics. The civil society has failed women as gender and minority identities have been inseparably tied to religious identities. It is in this context that I wish to argue that we are at an impasse. Feminists and everyone else interested in social justice need to move beyond the religious/not religious characterization of the issue of family law and reconceptualise the issue as one about gender justice.

This paper is divided into three broad parts. The first section gives a brief history of the origin of the concept of religious personal laws. A close analysis of the inviolability of religious laws is examined to demon-

* Division of Law, Macquarie University, NSW 2109, Australia. Contact: archana.parashar@law.mq.edu.au.

strate that these arguments are more often reliant on a claim of minority identity. Discourse about the rights of minorities must take into account not only religious but gender claims as well. In the second part an argument is made that the goal of gender justice can be better achieved by law reform. In the third section a tentative model of just family law is developed.

I. Origin of the Concept of Religious Personal Laws

Hindu, Muslim, Christian and Parsi communities are governed by their respective religious personal laws in the matters of marriage, divorce and related issues, as well as succession to property. In all these religious communities women have less than equal rights than men. Hindu law is the only religious personal law that has been extensively modified by the legislature. Hindu women have been the main beneficiaries of these changes but they have not managed to attain a complete parity of rights with men.[1] The starting point of my argument is that denial of equality to women is unjustifiable and we must argue for complete equality. The obvious stumbling block to such a position is that equality is one among many values and equality is supposedly a western value. More specifically, when equality and freedom of religion seem to be in conflict it is far from established that equality should have precedence. I wish to argue that the opposition between gender equality and freedom of religion is a false dichotomy. Religious personal laws as the quintessential expression of religions is a relatively recent development. I will endeavor to establish that religious personal laws have transformed over time and that religious freedom can be enjoyed simultaneously with granting women equality in personal matters.

India was a plural society prior to colonization by western powers. Indian society like other pre-industrial societies, did not make a separation in the institutions of religion and law. Sociological theories of modernization provide that a feudal, agricultural, rural society changes into a modern society with the separation of political, economic and social institutions. In pre-modern societies the place for production and consumption was supposed to be the household, but gradually the production of commodities and household became separated and markets arose for transactions in commodities. Thus Europe transformed into a modern, capitalist system, with the separation of the household from the place of production.[2] The

1. For details see my Women and Family Law Reform (1992).
2. See Linda Nicholson, Gender and History: The Limits of Social Theory in the Age of Family (1986); David Cheal, Family and the State of Theory (1991).

colonization of Indian society by Britain introduced ideas about such separation of institutions. Indian society at that stage had not followed the same path of development as Europe, and when British political and legal ideas were imposed they did not create another English system. The tensions resulting from the imposition of alien concepts is something that we still live with today. One such fundamental idea in European thought: the idea of public and private spheres lies at the root of the concept of Religious Personal Laws (RPLs hereafter). Public/private division is a conceptual means of organizing ideas about the rightful scope of state governance, e.g., how far the state can, or should, regulate our lives; what kinds of laws are justified; and what are the legitimate limits of state laws. The conceptual device of public/private spheres answers these questions by nominating the private sphere as the sphere of freedom - freedom from state regulation. Personal or family relations and religion conventionally fall within the private sphere.

The British administrators came to an Indian society where all aspects of life were subject to religious rules whether enforced by the political rulers or not. The English administrators in the early periods of colonization made a distinction between personal laws and all other laws. All other laws were legitimately made subject to the political state. Only the RPLs were nominated as not subject to state control because of their religious nature.[3] It is worthwhile emphasizing that this legitimization of state intervention was only ever valid for the colonizers. Any Indian in the then contemporary society would have found it incomprehensible that their religion was so constrained that it only regulated the 'personal' affairs or that the colonizers were legitimately regulating other 'non-religious' areas. Once the division between RPLs and other laws was made, it did not necessarily mean that the RPLs were left entirely unregulated. Legislative and judicial actions nevertheless transformed the nature and content of these formerly religious laws. To start with, the exact ambit of RPLs was ambiguous and changed over time. For example, initially contracts were considered a matter for religious rules but later made subject to legislation. The Hindu practice of sati was only gradually came to be regulated as the British administrators initially accepted the religious sanctity argument.[4] So too Hindu widows' remarriage, native converts' remarriage, the removal of caste disabilities, are

3. M. P. Jain, OUTLINES OF INDIAN LEGAL HISTORY 561-2 (1966).
4. Lata Mani, *Production of an Official Discourse on Sati in early Nineteenth Century Bengal* 21 ECON. & POL. WEEKLY WS 32-WS 38 (1986). She persuasively argues that the colonial discourse designated as 'religion' that part of indigenous culture which it did not choose to oppose.

examples of assumption of specific legislative authority.

English law influences came via judicial contact even in the areas of laws that were left unlegislated. The judicial officers were essentially trained in the common law system, and even when applying the rules of Hindu and Muslim laws, they necessarily interpreted them according to their understanding and training. The common law rules of evidence and procedure managed to transform the nature of religious rules. The Privy Council specifically held that the formulae of 'justice, equity and right' and 'justice and right' present in various British charters implied the application of English law if found applicable to Indian circumstances.[5] These decisions in turn formed binding precedent and thus ensured incorporation of the principles of English law into the rules of RPLs. The courts adjudicated personal matters but they gradually came to realize that the religious laws were not necessarily scriptural laws. Thus Hindu law incorporated a complex interrelation of sacred texts and actual usages or customs. While Islamic law did not give a similar importance to custom the courts recognized the customary claims of Muslims.[6] The immunity to change of RPLs thus turns out to be a fiction but it is a fiction that has a strong hold on our collective imaginations. The issue for contemporary legal thinkers is whether it is a sufficient reason for allowing the status quo to remain, especially when women are denied equality in the process.

II. Religious or Legal Change

The dominant discourse in India, since independence from colonial rule has been whether RPLs, as an aspect of religion can be modified by a secular state. There are two kinds of objections to any modification of RPLs, one is a theological argument; the second however, relies on the public/private conceptual device to claim immunity from state regulation. If as argued above, the concept of RPLs is a construct, and the so called religious nature of RPLs does not stand up to scrutiny, it may be possible to transcend the difficulties of determining the relative powers of a secular state vis-à-vis religion.

Theological Argument and Religious Change: Religious autonomy or freedom of faith is undoubtedly an integral part of a Liberal democracy.

---

5. See *Collector of Madura* v. *Moottoo Ramalinga* 1868, 12 Moore's Indian Appeals, 397 at 436; *Mohammad Ismail* v *Lala Sheomukh* AIR 1922 PC 59.
6. *Waghela Rayasanji* v. *Sheikh Masludin* 1887, LR 14 IA at 89. Duncan Derrett, *Justice, Equity and Good Conscience* in J. N. D. Anderson (ed.), Changing Law in Developing Countries (1963) provides a detailed analysis of the effect on RPLs of the formulae of justice, equity and good conscience.

However, like all other freedoms it is not an absolute freedom. The real contention is with regard to determining how far does or should religious freedom extend. Those claiming the immutability of RPLs draw the demarcation so as to put RPLs in the sphere of religious freedom. As a corollary, any change if at all possible, will be religious in nature.

In this argument the modification of RPLs is a task of changing religious rules and the state as well as academics - whether legal, feminist or philosophers - or those seeking social justice, have no *locus standi*. The legitimate authority either to interpret, or modify such rules belongs to specific experts within different religious traditions. If the religious experts or spiritual leaders of a religious community work to 'reform' some aspects of their religious practice or doctrine, the outcome is commonly understood as religious reform. Religious reform movements are a constant feature of history but whenever religious reform happens it struggles for legitimacy vis-à-vis the traditional or orthodox versions and only ever gets partial endorsement.

However, even this partial legitimacy for the changes brought from within a tradition is a welcome development. Outsiders to the tradition, while not authorised to introduce changes, may be able to rely on such changes for pursuing social justice for women. This much is not in dispute. Problems arise when no change is forthcoming from within the religious tradition and it is argued either that the religious rules are sacrosanct and eternal or that no one else but the religious experts may introduce change if they think it is possible and necessary. This is precisely the situation we are faced with in India.

There is no scope for further argument if it is accepted that RPLs represent eternal religious rules which cannot be modified. This is an interpretation I must disregard as it is contrary to the factual evidence of changes in RPLs and as it claims an exclusivity that does not allow any possibility of debate or change. Rather than making religious change the focus of attention it is possible to restate the argument as one about gender justice. The fundamental starting point for discussion then is that gender equality is a desirable goal. It may not be subjected to any other competing goal or right. The obvious next question is whether every religion, in its personal law provisions, can be expected to embrace gender equality? If not, should it be open to the state to modify religious rules or replace them with state enacted laws? I argue that every religious tradition ought to be able to conform to this 'external' standard or lose state protection.

A. Religion and External Standards — Public and Private Spheres

An obvious objection to this proposition is that whether religion is understood as eternal or a product of socio-historical change, either way it is not open to scrutiny and modification by reference to 'external' - non-religious or secular standards. This argument relies on the stance that religion is a private sphere activity and therefore, should remain free of state regulation. The separate spheres ideology has featured in various forms in political theory since the classical times. The conceptual device of public and private spheres helps demarcate the legitimate limits of state regulation and thus helps check the proliferation of state powers. An important aspect of the check on state powers is that the private sphere is the sphere of freedom - admittedly freedom from state regulation. Thus the argument that in matters of religion and therefore, religious laws the state does not have legitimate authority to intervene because these are private sphere activities.

But a vast amount of feminist literature also exists that exposes how the public/private divide keeps women under patriarchal control in the purportedly free private sphere. Carole Pateman is the most well known feminist for analyzing the ideological functions of defining women as the inhabitants of the private sphere and thus not subject to the values operative in the public sphere.[7] Family provides the most familiar illustration of this argument that as a private sphere institution it operates with values of love and altruism rather than those of individualism and competition that operate in the sphere of the market or the values of justice and equality that are supposed to organize the public sphere. Women as the inhabitants of the private sphere of family are thus denied justice and equality, and family relations are expected to be about love and giving rather than about individual rights.

Okin has most convincingly argued that the characterization of family as a private sphere institution does not mean that justice cannot be a relevant value for organizing family relations.[8] Okin's argument, I believe, has a direct relevance to the issue of the private nature of religion and religious rules of personal relations. She provides a detailed argument for making justice an operative principle in the organization of the family. I cannot reproduce the argument in all its detail, but briefly she uses Rawl's

7. Carole Pateman, THE SEXUAL CONTRACT (1988). See also Margaret Thornton (ed.), PUBLIC AND PRIVATE: FEMINIST LEGAL DEBATES (1995).
8. Susan Moller Okin, JUSTICE, GENDER AND THE FAMILY (1989).

argument that justice is the primary moral virtue. This claim is linked to a prior assumption that human society is characterized by the 'circumstances of justice'. These include the condition of moderate scarcity of resources and while people have complementary needs and interests they also make conflicting claims on natural and social resources. These claims need to be resolved by reference to rules that are just. In family relations it is equally relevant that rules of justice apply.

Thinkers who claim that in the family love or altruism and not justice are the highest values misunderstand what is meant by justice as the primary moral virtue. Justice is not the only value, and it is not antithetical to love or altruism, but justice is the most essential value. It is in the conditions of scarcity, and when interests conflict, that justice needs to be operative. For instance, maybe wives would never have an occasion to ask for their fair share of property because of the generosity and spontaneous affection of their husbands, but if they did ask for it they should be entitled to it. There is simply no reason to assume that justice somehow takes away from intimacy, harmony and love that are supposed to prevail within families.

The minority communities in India have consistently put forward this argument with regard to changes in the religious personal laws, namely, that religion, as a private sphere institution, is the exclusive concern of the community. Unlike the earlier theological version of the argument that only those with religious credentials may interpret or modify religious rules the argument here is that it is a matter for the religious community and no one else. Such religious communities making this claim are invariably minority communities as well and maintaining their distinct identity becomes merged with the argument about the religious immutability of personal laws.

B. Religion, Cultural Identity and Essential Capabilities

The concept of essential capabilities is developed by Amartya Sen and utilized by Martha Nussbaum.[9] The idea that religion forms the basis of an ethical life and is an essential capability, in Sen and Nussbaum's terminology, is not controversial. What is controversial is how to balance the claims in the name of religious autonomy with other liberties/freedoms/capabilities. Nussbaum develops a nuanced argument about the scope of legitimate 'interference' with religion.[10] I will explain her argu-

9. Martha Nussbaum, WOMEN AND HUMAN DEVELOPMENT (2000), chap. 1.
10. *Id.* chapter 3 at 167-240.

ment very briefly, but I wish to disagree with her. Nussbaum says that any account of the tension between religion and women's interests that fails to recognize the complexity of both religion and women's interests is worthy of scepticism. She argues for the intrinsic value of religious capabilities then goes on to explore how religious capabilities of each person could be enhanced in constitutional regimes. The US Constitutional principles of non-establishment of religion and free exercise of religion operate together to uphold the citizen's liberty of conscience against the pressures of groups. Nussbaum agrees that we should refuse to give deference to religion when its practices harm people in areas covered by the major capabilities. However, it is difficult to determine this issue with regard to matters internal to the religion itself. When religious actors and groups claim prerogatives it is difficult to judge whether they are really talking about religion. While the principle of moral constraint may allow us to judge such claims, it is only right that such assessment should be made socially rather than by the state or the judiciary. For example, the Indian Constitution uses the political version of the principle of moral constraint, makes no pronouncements of what Hinduism is or is not, but it simply makes untouchability illegal. Socially moral constraint arguments do valuable work.

Nussbaum goes on to examine whether sex discrimination within a religion is permissible. She agrees that the very singling out of women for differential treatment in a central area of human functioning is itself unacceptable. But she then goes on to say that some choices internal to the religion should still be protected. For instance the lesser rights of women within Islam should not be modified by the state. The rationale for this is that even though the non establishment clause is meant to protect the individuals free exercise it is not always the case. In the particular historical and contemporary context of Muslims in India, state support for their religion is essential. In their specific circumstances disestablishment would amount to Muslims not being treated as equal citizens and in fact nonestablishment would be defacto a type of Hindu establishment.

I disagree with Nussbaum's suggestion that in view of the current dominance of Hindus both politically and socially it is imperative that the state refrain from modifying Islamic religious personal laws, firstly because it accepts the 'religious nature' of personal laws. This is at least a contentious issue as I have tried to show above. Secondly, it gives too much ground to the claims of religious leaders, that only they can decide whether something is internal to or an essential core of their religion. Thirdly, it gives too much weight to the claims of minority identity and not enough attention to gender justice.

The makers of the Indian Constitution acknowledged the importance of religion and guaranteed freedom of religion as a fundamental right. The authority to determine whether any matter constitutes an essential or non essential aspect of religion has at times been given to the community but at other times the matter has been scrutinized by the court. As yet there is no clear pronouncement whether RPLs form an essential part of religion that cannot be legitimately modified by the state.[11] The Supreme Court has upheld the validity of social reform legislation even with regard to what are claimed to be the essentials of a religion, e.g. the right of a Hindu denomination to decide who could enter their temple.[12] But when the Supreme Court held that maintenance provisions of the Code of Criminal Procedure 1973 were available to Muslim women as well as other women, the public reaction of a section of the Muslim community compelled legislative intervention by the government of the day.[13] The distinction between the two examples is not in the difficulty of defining the essential or core aspects of religion. Rather it is in the majority and minority status of the Hindu and Muslim communities. So too the legislative history shows that the issue is not about conflicting fundamental rights. It is the claims of minority identity that explain why the 'religious' laws of Hindus could be extensively modified but not those of minority communities. It seems obvious that the debate ought to be framed differently - rather than being about religious sanctity it is really about cultural identity which is linked to the minority status. If this reality can be accepted, then the inquiry is no longer about the legitimate authority of a secular state vis-à-vis religion but is about the responsibility of a state to safeguard the minority identity of certain communities. If so, the reasons put forward by Nussbaum for leaving alone Islamic RPLs need to be read as arguments about the claims of communities to distinct identity.

The right to maintain a distinct cultural identity is however much less clearly theorized than the right to freedom of religion. The question whether the right to a distinct cultural identity is compatible with the fundamental right of sex equality must be answered by reference to different arguments.

---

11. For a detailed analysis of these issues and Supreme Court judgments see Parashar, *supra* n. 1 at 217-222.
12. *Sri Venkataramana Devaru* v. *The State of Mysore*, AIR 1958 SC 255.
13. *Mohammad Ahmad Khan* v. *Shah Bano*, 1985 (1) SCALE 767. See also A. A. Engineer (ed.), THE SHAH BANO CONTROVERSY (1987).

III. Minority Identity

Religious and minority identities intersect and give rise to the argument that whatever may be the case for the majority community at least the minority communities must be allowed immunity from state modification of their religious laws. The claim of autonomy to maintain a distinct religious identity however, simultaneously denies the option of claiming gender equality as part of that identity. This issue of minority/distinct cultural identity can only be meaningfully discussed in conjunction with the factor of gender. Historical evidence in India, and in a number of Islamic countries, is that religious community or political leaders have invariably strengthened patriarchal control over women in the name of Islam. I am not for a moment suggesting that Islam is particularly non-friendly to women. All world religions would be hard pressed to pass this test. But the argument at the moment is about the link between religious and minority status. I suggest that it is naive to believe that the religious community leaders of Muslim, or any other community for that matter, will work for attaining gender equality.

For example, the *Shah Bano* case and the enactment of the Muslim Women's (Protection of Rights on Divorce) Act 1986 (MWA), brought into open the complicity of religious community leaders and political leaders in perpetuating gender discrimination against women in the name of religion.[14] Therefore, any argument that places its faith in the respective religious communities to ensure even basic non-discrimination for women misjudges the alliance between patriarchal interests and religio-political leaders.[15] Minority identity arguments are a version of group rights even if not explicitly characterized as such. In these arguments women's rights become secondary to those of the group. Gender justice therefore, may not be achievable by pursuing distinct cultural identity. With the ascendance of postmodernism in academia, impressive theoretical arguments are made for recognizing differences. In the specific

14. The MWA was supposed to be a protective legislation in so far as divorced Muslim women could not claim ongoing maintenance from their former husbands, the maintenance of such women was declared to be a community responsibility. The claim that the Waqf Boards would discharge this community responsibility was sadly, but predictably an empty claim. Whether and how the wider Indian community might discharge this responsibility has never become an issue of public or scholarly debate.

15. This is not a problem faced only by Indian women. See for an account of women's righs under Islamic law in other contexts, Farida Shaheed, *Networking for Change: The Role of Women's Groups in Initiating Dialogue on Women's Issues* in Mahnez Afkhami (ed.), Faith and Freedom: Women's Rights in the Muslim World 78-103 (1995).

context of political and social theory, there are arguments in favour of recognizing minority cultures.[16] However, as Okin points out there is a distinction between claims of 'identity politics' and group rights. I will rely on her analysis[17] to question how group interests are constituted, whose voices are heard and who is silenced and what are the institutional mechanisms for ascertaining and enforcing such group rights? Significantly, Okin faults not only the male theorists of group rights, but feminists as well for not paying sufficient attention to the consequences flowing from recognizing group rights.

Okin argues that minority cultures that demand special protection make insufficient differentiation amongst those within a group or culture so that gender differences are not acknowledged. Moreover, the content of culture is very significantly constructed in the private sphere and the gender based constructions of cultural identity more often than not disadvantage women. Feminists who shy away from examining these issues show hyper-sensitivity to the charge of cultural imperialism and thus fall into the trap of debilitating cultural relativism.

Many proponents of cultural identity do not even expect the cultural groups to adhere to certain Liberal values, but Kymlicka does. Yet Okin shows that his injunction that any cultural group demanding group rights must not discriminate overtly against its women members does not even acknowledge the reality that most sex discrimination is informal and not overt. In most cultures strict control of women is enforced in the private sphere. For one to be able to make choices about the life one wants to lead it is not enough to have one's culture protected. Okin argues that one's place within one's culture is at least as important to the development of self respect and self esteem as that culture itself . When that culture is patriarchal the healthy development of girls is endangered.[18]

The claim that minority communities and specially women should be free to live by their RPLs places a lot of reliance on the free choice of minority women and demands that the state should enforce such freedom. In the Indian context the religio-political leaders have invariably been men, they manage to be the exclusive voice of the community and have not acquitted themselves particularly well with regard to attaining equality for women. As Uma Narayan says "Feminist commitment to autonomy or equality for women can be portrayed as 'western values' by the same

16. See for example, Will Kymlicka, MULTICULTURAL CITIZENSHIP: A LIBERAL THEORY OF MINORITY RIGHTS (1995).
17. See Susan Moller Okin, *Feminism and Multiculturalism: Some Tensions* in Dan Avnon and De-Shalit Avner (eds.), LIBERALISM AND ITS PRACTICE 81-105 (1999).
18. *Id.* at 97.

fundamentalists who discern no paradox, for instance, in appropriating the language of rights when it suits their interests."[19] But it is still common place to maintain that an 'insecure' minority should be treated with caution.[20] However, that is possible only if the disadvantageous position of women is ignored. The minority identity and religious sanctity discourses come together and their conjunction gives them a 'reality' that is too obvious to be questioned. I argue that this is where deconstruction should be used by Indian feminists and legal feminists in particular, to question the legitimacy of such claims. This should not be read as denying autonomy to minority women but as an effort to make relatively genuine free choice possible.

The postmodernist emphasis on non-essentialising theorizing may help in questioning the categories of minority or religious identity but it also carries with it the danger of relativism.[21] If categories and meanings are always contingent and it is not possible to fix definite meanings for any of them, our knowledge can only be relative and always subject to revision. More over, there is no way normative standards can be posited to judge the legitimacy or even the desirability of any interpretation.[22] Thus, for a postmodernist, in the particular case of minority RPLs it is not an undisputed good to demand gender non-discrimination. Furthermore, if minority women do not ask for such change it is not for anyone else to suggest it to them for that amounts to imposition of universalist ideas. I argue that postmodern positions can and should carry the responsibility of justifying the consequences that follow from any theoretical stance.[23] In the case

19. It is not only the minority community leaders who want to withhold equality form women in the name of tradition. Uma Narayan is here talking about the Hindu fundamentalists. See Uma Narayan, DISLOCATING CULTURES: IDENTITIES, AND THIRD WORLD FEMINISM 22 (1997).
20. Bhiku Parekh, *Balancing Unity and Diversity in Multicultural Societies* in Dan Avnon and De-Shalit Avner (eds.), *supra* n. 17 at 122.
21. There is no uniformly accepted definition of postmodernism but Barrett explains that even though the term has different connotations in different disciplines it generally refers to the trend to critique universalism. Michelle Barrett, *Words and Things: Materialism and Method in Contemporary Feminist Analysis* in A. Phillips (ed.), DESTABILIZING THEORY: CONTEMPORARY FEMINIST DEBATES 210-219 (1992).
22. For example, Seyla Benhabib points out that theorists of difference do not usually point out which differences ought to be recognised. See Seyla Benhabib, *Democracy and Difference: Reflections on Rationality, Democracy and Postmodernism* 2 J. OF POL. PHILOSOPHY 6 (1994).
23. See Nicola Lacey, UNSPEAKABLE SUBJECTS: FEMINIST ESSAYS IN LEGAL AND SOCIAL THEORY 157 (1998). She mentions the following authors who combine an ethical concern with their critical analyses: Christine Littleton, *Reconstructing Sexual Equaliy* 75 CAL. LAW REV. 1279 - (1987); Jennifer Nedelsky, *Reconceiving Autonomy* 1 YALE J.L. & FEMINISM 7-35 (1989); Iris Marion Young, THROWING LIKE A GIRL (1990).

of minority women and RPLs we have no evidence of how many women do want change. But even if, for argument's sake, it was true that minority women do not want change, the role of academics, analysts, or cultural workers[24], can hardly be to sit back and let things be. The enormity of this suggestion would become apparent if the example of RPLs was replaced with that of domestic violence. Even though at one time it was acceptable to 'not interfere' in others' domestic affairs this is no longer the case. Feminists have successfully discredited the idea that private violence is not the concern of everyone. As a consequence it now rings a bit hollow to say that domestic violence legislation amounts to an external imposition of notions of sex equality. Similarly, minority RPLs ought to be the concern of everyone interested in social justice. It has been correctly said that a non-judgmental tolerance of brutality and oppression under the guise of cultural difference or tradition is an ultimate form of ethnocentrism if not an outright ethical surrender.[25] Therefore, I argue that legal thinkers must bear the responsibility of generating a discourse of non-discrimination. The postmodern concern with essentialism and not imposing universal values should not convert into an apology for maintaining the status quo. While some postmodern analysts insist that textual analysis itself is transformative,[26] I am of the opinion that most of them do not construct any argument for social transformation. Thus in most contemporary postmodern legal critiques the existing state of affairs may be analysed but not purposively modified. That is understandable if one is a beneficiary of the present status quo but really debilitating for those unfairly burdened and oppressed.[27] In feminist legal analysis such an argument is presented by African-American writer Patricia Williams who maintains that the trashing of rights is a dangerous game for the oppressed sections of society, for rights based arguments are the only means available to them to redress their wrongs.[28]

Therefore, in the particular context of minority women and RPLs, the role of legal analysts has to be to develop arguments for ensuring gender justice and sex equality. It is worthwhile to remember that the claims of minority status and religious sanctity are also only arguments. We are the

24. The term used by Cornel West in *The New Cultural Politics of Difference* 53 OCTOBER 93-126 (1990).
25. Elizabeth Zechenter, *In the Name of Culture: Cultural Relativism and the Abuse of the Individual* 53 J. OF ANTHRO. RESEARCH 319-347 (1997) at 336.
26. Peter Goodrich, READING THE LAW (1986) esp. 218.
27. Hank Bromley, *Identity Politics and Critical Pedagogy* 39 EDUCATIONAL THEORY 207-223 (1989).
28. Patricia Williams, *Alchemical Notes: Reconstructing Ideals from Deconstructed Rights* 22 HARV. C. R.- C.L.REV. 401-447 (1987).

ones who choose to adopt some of these arguments and not others.[29] The consequences that flow from our choices are most definitely our responsibility. Thus if my theoretical stand helps maintain discrimination against minority women who else but I am complicitous in legitimizing the situation? My feminist credentials or aspirations are not enhanced by absolving myself of the charge of imperialism by not 'imposing' notions of sex equality on minority women. The task is much more complex as it involves responsible reconceptualisation of legal categories of analysis. It should be possible to avoid paternalism but still maintain an open-ended commitment to the ideal of non-discrimination for all women.

Legal feminists are in a unique position to show how the discourse of community or cultural identity holds no more promise of gender equality than that of the private sphere of religion. Therefore, just as Okin argues for extending the value of justice to the private family, I suggest a similar extension of the principle of justice to the private sphere of religion. We meet up again with the issue that 'justice' does not have a unitary meaning. At this point I wish to argue that gender justice as individual autonomy and the right to non-discrimination must be the minimum any religious tradition ought to deliver. Non-discrimination does not have to equate to sameness but at the same time different treatment of men and women must be justifiable and not amount to disadvantage or less favourable treatment.

The implication of this argument is that, in a plural society, claims in the name of religion or religious minority identity ought to be scrutinized for justice, and only then given recognition by the state. This avoids giving a carte blanche to religion, it maintains diversity in the form of distinct minority and religious identities but also opens up the possibility of attaining gender justice.

IV. Legal Change for a Just Family Law

The discussion so far has established that the claims of religious sanctity of RPLs and the minority identity arguments are not valid reasons for refraining from creating a just family law. In a pluralistic, democratic and secular polity that can only be done by the state law. It is therefore, incumbent upon legal feminists and thinkers to create a discourse of a just

---

29. See for a very persuasive argument Seyla Benhabib, *Cultural Complexity, Moral Interdependence, and the Global Dialogical Community* in Martha Nussbaum and Jonathan Glover (eds.), Women, Culture and Development: A Study of Human Capabilities 235-258 (1995).

family law as a basic human right of every Indian woman. This demand for a gender just family law must be radically independent of any religious legitimation.

This is not a particularly onerous move because it treats every one equally. It does not prevent anyone from being a good Hindu, Muslim, Christian or the follower of any other religion. It does not however, invoke state support to be a devout religious person. This is not a novel suggestion either. For example, in most Roman Catholic countries the family law allows divorce while the church does not permit or recognize it.[30] No serious argument is put forward that in these instances some devout Christians' freedom of religion is curtailed. The only difference between this example and the contemporary Indian situation is that in India a dubious legitimacy is granted to the assertion that it is somehow the responsibility of the state to make one a religious person, especially if one belongs to a minority community.

Therefore it is imperative that we create a discourse that compels the state to construct a totally secular family law. In this way the state can walk away from the quagmire of RPLs. The RPLs will not be declared invalid, but nor would they be enforced by the state. This can create the possibility of achieving gender justice in family law while allowing a certain amount of religious autonomy.

Certain assumptions about the nature of law underpin such an argument for legal change and they must be explicitly articulated. Legitimation of legal knowledge is dependent on the ideas about law presented in various theories of law. Jurisprudential theories conceive abstract ideas while sociological theories posit a connection between law and any given society. I suggest that we need to adopt a sociological analysis in order to conceptualise a gender just family law.

The Indian Supreme Court has played a rather disappointing role in that it has declined to address the issue of the compatibility of religious autonomy with sex equality. The reluctance of the Supreme Court however, has not generated sustained academic critique. As a result, the possible compatibility or otherwise of two fundamental rights in the Indian constitution has remained a non-issue even in the legal scholarship. I am here primarily concerned with the failure of the legal scholars, as they are the ones who have the professional role of creating legal knowledge and

30. For a history of divorce reform see Roderick Phillips, PUTTING ASUNDER: A HISTORY OF DIVORCE IN WESTERN SOCIETY (1988); see also Mary Ann Glendon, THE TRANSFORMATION OF FAMILY LAW (1989).

discourse. Their exclusive task is to analyse how the legal system operates and how legal knowledge is constructed. It is disappointing that for the most part legal analysis in India remains doctrinal and focuses on the judicial pronouncements as the last word.[31] This exclusive concern with legal doctrine ignores a very rich tradition of alternative views about the relationship between law and society. Feminists, among others, have focused on the link between the kind and content of law and the prevailing socio economic structures.[32] Laws both construct and reflect social reality and for the most part law and society are mutually influenced and influence the other.

If RPLs are examined in the light of sociological theories of law it is apparent that there exists a serious misfit between such laws and contemporary society. As discussed above, RPLs are a curious amalgam of religious rules and English legal concepts. But these English legal concepts are frozen in time in the RPLs . While the English law has moved on, Indian personal laws are fossilized in the name of religious inviolability. When it is claimed that cultural identity of any minority community is absolutely entwined with such RPLs the feminists should not simply accept any such claim on its face value but they should help to deconstruct these claims. It must be emphasized again and again that we are not dealing with the religious sanctity of personal laws but with family laws that have a connection with religion. The inquiry primarily should be about the nature of law.

Maintenance of wives or former wives under various RPLs provides a suitable illustration of my argument. It is not difficult to argue that post-divorce maintenance is or should be a basic component of a non-discriminatory family law. Every society finds the means of maintaining its members. Across societies and in all historical periods economic dependence of women and children is very often the norm and the responsibility to maintain them typically belongs to the family, or more precisely to the father or the husband. In Indian society there never has been any provision for community support of women or children. Religious and social customs enjoined that a woman was always reliant on the natal or conjugal family for support. However, with time the organic unity of small societies has been eroded and the former social and community con-

31. I develop this argument in greater detail in the *Introduction*, Amita Dhanda and Archana Parashar (eds.), ENGENDERING LAW: ESSAYS IN HONOUR OF LOTIKA SARKAR 1-26 (1999).
32. See for a concise analysis of this literature Roger Cotterrell, THE SOCIOLOGY OF LAW: AN INTRODUCTION (1984).

straints on behaviour do not operate adequately. Many single women who could formerly expect to be maintained by their families now face the likelihood of destitution. Women without family support face an unenviable prospect of hunger and poverty as very often they do not possess any skills or training for economic independence.

What does Indian society have to offer these women? In particular the RPLs present a bleak picture. There are no social welfare or community programs. The ideology of femininity, whether expressed in the ideals of middle and upper class housewife or as seclusion of women, signifying higher social and/or caste membership, prevents women from engaging in economic activity.[33] And the RPLs step in to make a mockery of their need for maintenance. Even the much-reformed Hindu law falls short of securing women's maintenance rights. Substantive provisions vacillate between portraying men and women on par with each other and equally responsible for the other's maintenance (Hindu Marriage Act 1955, Section 25), to acknowledging that the husband has the responsibility of maintaining his wife (Hindu Adoption and Maintenance Act 1956 Section 18). However, in either case the enforcement of court orders granting maintenance are notoriously difficult.[34] The limited rights given in the substantive provisions are taken away by the lack of enforcement. The Code of Criminal Procedure 1973, further makes a mockery of this need by specifying a legislative limit on the maximum amount of maintenance payable.[35] The MWA, goes furthest in capping the right to maintenance to three months or the period of *iddat*. The recent Supreme Court decision in Daniel Latifi's case[36] is a valiant effort at reading the MWA as a progressive Act but this interpretive exercise has severe limitations. It epitomizes the relative disadvantages of introducing change through judicial rather than legislative channels. The Supreme Court in declaring the MWA Constitutional simply disregarded the socio-political storm created by the decision in *Shah Bano's* case. Instead the court has interpreted the MWA as giving legislative form to the judicial view on maintenance for Muslim women incorporated in *Shah Bano* case. It has

33. Martha Chen, *A Matter of Survival: Women's Right to Employment in India and Bangladesh* in Martha Nussbaum and Jonathan Glover (eds.), *supra* n. 29 at 37-60.
34. See N. Gandhi and N. Shah, The Issues at Stake: Theory and Practice in the Contemporary Women's Movement in India (1991).
35. Ss. 125-127. Until recently the maximum amount payable was Rs 500. Amendments to the Code of Criminal Procedure 1973 in 2000 have removed the ceiling of the maximum amount.
36. *Daniel Latifi and Another* v *Union of India*. AIR 2001 SC 3958.

denied any problem with the Supreme Court interpreting the Holy Quran in *Shah Bano* and declared itself bound by the earlier interpretations.

This is all very well if we are in agreement with the interpretation of the Supreme Court and in this instance feminists can only breathe a sigh of relief that the Supreme Court has felt compelled to recognize divorced women's entitlement to a reasonable standard of living. Despite recognizing the dire necessity of adequate maintenance for a divorced woman the Supreme Court still did not articulate what might constitute "adequate" provision for a divorced woman. It also cannot ensure effective execution of maintenance orders and of course there was no occasion to consider whether adequate provision for the divorced wife would take into account the needs of children she may be responsible for.

So too in Hindu law jurisprudence despite legislative provisions maintenance is hard to obtain and generally does not amount to much.[37] In this study a survey of 93 reported cases on maintenance for the period between 1982 to 1987 showed that majority of women received up to Rs 250 per month. Many women had to support their children as well and no separate sum was awarded for the children.

Thus an Indian woman who does not have the support of a husband can expect to live on the benevolence of her father or other family members, but let her not pretend that she has a right to dignity or even subsistence maintenance. Surely this is not an acceptable state of affairs and it is incumbent upon legal feminists to expose how it is justified and explore what may be done to change it.

Legal feminists are not at the forefront of this debate about RPLs and the discourse of religious and minority identities is set by the religious and political leaders. Though the possibility of recasting this debate seems very remote, there is no option but to try. Feminists must abandon their reticence in articulating what might constitute a just family law for all women. Whether Indian laws as represented in RPLs remain frozen in the past or keep in step with a rapidly changing society will depend on how the issues are conceptualised. It is futile to go around in circles about religious sanctity of these laws or their importance in constituting minority identities. The real issue for us is to ask what a gender just family would look like.

37. See for details Neeru Sehgal, *Economic Independence for Women: The Foundation for Eradicating Sex-Based Discrimination*, Ph.D. Thesis, Faculty of Law, University of Delhi, 1991, chap. 7.

V. A Just Family Law Incorporating Economic Independence for Women

A just family law for women in this area would at least recognize the social reality of separation whether by divorce, desertion or death. It would recognize women as the primary care givers and recognize the economic dependence of the primary care giver and the need for adequate financial support. In short, a just family law would ensure economic independence of women.[38]

Thus a just family law would not only provide for adequate maintenance and inheritance rights for women but should also recognize their right to an equal share of matrimonial property. Family law has a limited scope in that it does not create the conditions of employment but it does impact on the possibilities of engaging in such work. And it does have the exclusive role to play in reconceptualising women's care giving work as economically valuable. Economic independence has a direct bearing on women's exit options from unsatisfactory relationships, including their perceived suitability to be the custodial parent.

Two interrelated objections to this proposal are that pursuing economic independence by itself will not change the life circumstances of women. Secondly, family law by itself is an inadequate means of bringing about economic independence. The demand for economic independence for women generates immense hostility and common objections are that economic independence is a middle class urban feminists' issue, that in a poor country like India it is an irrelevant issue for the majority of women as a right to financial assistance is unlikely to be a real safeguard. A family law that accepts the possibility of separation (through divorce) undermines the social fabric as it encourages individualism over concern for family. So too a demand for property rights for all women may not be appropriate. The objections come from other equally committed feminists as well.[39]

This is a serious issue and raises a fundamental question of responsibility - by demanding economic independence for all women do the undeniably elite opinion makers have any right to 'interfere' in the lives of

38. See for a detailed version of this argument my *Human Rights: Imperatives of Theoretical Change*, 40 JILI 6-37 (1998).
39. For example, Nandita Haksar says that the demand of property rights for women in the tribal societies of North-East India, when imposed by urban feminists actually disadvantages these women. Nandita Haksar, *Human Rights Lawyering: A Feminist Perspective* in Amita Dhanda and Archana Parashar (eds.), *supra* n. 31 at 89-116.

poorer or rural women and how can they ensure that the so called just family law will empower rather than disadvantage these women? All I can say in response to such a comment is that for similarly placed men, no one, absolutely no one, makes an argument that they should be denied economic self sufficiency.

Women perform wage and unpaid work. Martha Chen has eloquently argued that gainful employment outside the home, as a wage earner affects the self image and perceived value of women. In addition to providing economic independence it serves as a means of escape from male control over female labour. It often helps increase women's bargaining power within the household and enhances their perceived value both within the household and in society more broadly.[40] Bina Agarwal has also convincingly demonstrated that most rural women show a keen interest in the issues of ownership of land and laws of inheritance.[41] Okin explores the idea that the situation of poor women in poor countries is not qualitatively different from that of most women in rich countries, but rather 'similar but worse'. She uses the concept of differential exit potentials within relationships.[42] She explains that in the affluent western countries the distribution of power within the family is linked to the differential exit factor. The typical asymmetric dependency of wives on husbands affects their potential for satisfactory exit. So too 'when circumstances of severe poverty combine with a lack of paid employment opportunities for women, increasing women's dependency on men, men's power within the family is likely to be greatly enhanced - in many cases legitimized by highly patriarchal cultural norms.'[43] The exit options theory exposes the injustice of a situation in which the assumption that women are responsible for housework and child care, the disadvantaged position of women in wage work and their vulnerability to male violence all come together to give women lesser bargaining power when their interests conflict with those of men. It should therefore, be the goal of a just family law to provide realistic exit options to women.

40. Martha Chen, *supra* n. 33 at 54.

41. Bina Agarwal, A FIELD OF ONE'S OWN: GENDER AND LAND RIGHTS IN SOUTH ASIA, 56-57 and 421-466 (1996)

42. She uses Albert Hirschman's theory of the effects of differential exit potentials on power within relationships. See Susan Okin, *Inequalities Between the Sexes in Different Cultural Contexts* in Martha Nussbaum and Jonathan Glover (eds.), *supra* n. 29 at 274-297.

43. *Id.*, at 287-288. She cites Partha Dasgupta, AN INQUIRY INTO WELL-BEING AND DESTITUTION (1993) and Amartya Sen, *Gender and Cooperative Conflicts* in Irene Tinker (ed.), PERSISTENT INEQUALITIES: WOMEN AND WORLD DEVELOPMENT (1990).

I acknowledge that women are disadvantaged by a complex interaction of economic, social and political power structures and economic independence by itself will not change all other factors. Nor will legal change by itself create economic well being. But as Bina Agarwal has said it is not just an increase in women's command over economic resources but also the process by which such increase occurs that has a critical bearing on gender relations.[44] Law has a specific significance because it sets the normative standards. It is of crucial importance that normatively law upholds the standard of gender equality because then it provides the values for the transformation of other societal arrangements. The present gender hierarchies will not be dismantled by law reform only and the empowerment of women would require a whole complex of changes. But here I am addressing the role of legal thinkers. They can not take shelter behind the argument that law by itself is too insignificant a mechanism of social transformation. Law as one institution among many should uphold the ideal and in that way can be a catalyst for other institutions to transform themselves.

44. Bina Agarwal, *supra* n. 41 at 44 argues that in South Asia women's economic needs have primarily been discussed in the context of employment opportunities but it is crucial to recognise that access to land is one of the most critical factors in empowerment of rural women. She has demonstrated the stability of private land ownership in most of South Asia and how women are excluded from the ownership of this resource.

Part IV
Resolving Family Disputes

[14]

RESOLVING THE DILEMMA OF DIFFERENCE: A CRITIQUE OF 'THE ROLE OF PRIVATE ORDERING IN FAMILY LAW'

Marcia Neave*

I *Introduction*

In their recent article titled 'The Role of Private Ordering in Family Law'[1] Trebilcock and Keshvani suggest that family lawyers could find valuable insights in law and economics scholarship. Wanda Wiegers's subsequent article provides a feminist critique of law and economics.[2] My article also reflects a feminist perspective. However, its major purpose is to examine Trebilcock and Keshvani's proposals for reform of the family law rules governing property division and maintenance after divorce and, in particular, to criticize their contention that private ordering will 'enhance the self-determination and individual fulfilment' of women after marriage breakdown.[3]

Trebilcock and Keshvani refer to the apparent conflict between formal equality, which requires the same rules to be applied to men and women, and substantive equality, which may only be achieved by rules that take account of the ways in which the lives of men and women differ. In recent years family lawyers have recognized that reforms based on the philosophy of formal equality do not produce equality of outcome, because such reforms ignore the effects of marriage and child-rearing on the earning capacity of women. The dilemma for feminists has been how to find ways of recognizing the effects of women's responsibility for bringing up children without entrenching women's dependency. On the one hand, treating women the same as men disadvantages women whose earning capacity has been adversely affected by child-rearing. On the other hand, recognizing women's economic dependency on men reinforces that dependency, thus re-creating women's inequality.[4] Trebilcock and Keshvani argue that a law

* Law Faculty, Monash University.

1 Michael J. Trebilcock and Rosemin Keshvani 'The Role of Private Ordering in Family Law: A Law and Economics Perspective' (1991) 47 *UTLJ* 533.

2 W. Wiegers 'Economic Analysis of Law and "Private Ordering": A Feminist Critique' (1992) 42 *UTLJ* 170.

3 Supra note 1, 538.

4 Cf. supra note 1, 554.

and economics perspective could provide an escape from this 'dilemma of difference.'[5]

The major theme in 'The Role of Private Ordering in Family Law' is that disputes between spouses relating to property division, spousal and child support, and child custody and access, are most satisfactorily resolved by private agreements. But despite their support for private ordering, Trebilcock and Keshvani recognize that pre-nuptial and separation agreements will not improve the situation of women if the legal rules which form the background to spouses' negotiations do not define their entitlements appropriately. Trebilcock and Keshvani argue that the family law rules regulating financial provision on divorce should take account of the effect of marriage on human capital by compensating women for the opportunity costs they incur as the result of withdrawing from the paid workforce to care for children. The first part of this article compares Trebilcock and Keshrani's proposal with a similar proposal made by the Australian Institute of Family Studies and discusses the strengths and weaknesses of this opportunity-cost approach to matrimonial property division.

The second part of this article examines Trebilcock and Keshvani's support for pre-nuptial and separation agreements. As law and economics scholars, Trebilcock and Keshvani believe that private agreements tend to maximize social welfare by ensuring efficient use of resources. Transactions between individuals are Pareto-superior if they produce outcomes which make all parties better off (in economic terms). Alternatively, a transaction is Pareto-efficient if the party who gains from it would remain better off, even if he or she were required to compensate the other party to the extent of that party's loss. Trebilcock and Keshvani argue that agreements between spouses are more likely to produce Pareto-efficient results than outcomes dictated by courts or legislatures. Economists accept that private agreements may not be Pareto-efficient where parties have unequal bargaining power because of transaction-specific failures, for example where one party is overborne or tricked by the other or lacks sufficient information to assess his or her own interests. Trebilcock and Keshvani propose a number of safeguards to overcome these problems.[6] This article examines their view that greater emphasis should be placed on private ordering in the family law con-

5 M. Minow 'Learning to Live with the Dilemma of Difference' (1985) 48 *Law & Contemp. Prob.* 159; M. Minow *Making All The Difference* (Ithaca: Cornell University Press 1990).

6 Supra note 1, 559–60.

text. It is suggested that rather than resolving the 'dilemma of difference' Trebilcock and Keshvani's preference for private ordering takes insufficient account of the fact that men and women who are negotiating pre-marital and separation agreements are often differently situated. Far from enhancing women's individuality and autonomy, such agreements may simply privatize unequal outcomes of divorce for men and women and exacerbate gender inequality. Trebilcock and Keshvani's proposals for procedural safeguards attempt to address this concern, but do not place men and women on an equal footing.

The conclusion of this article briefly re-examines the 'dilemma of difference' posed by Trebilcock and Keshvani at the beginning of their essay. It is argued that the solution to gender inequality does not lie in treating women the same as men or in compensating for their differences, but rather in reinvisioning the relationship between family responsibilities and paid workforce participation. Marriage and child-rearing disadvantage women because the paid workforce is structured on the assumption that workers do not have family responsibilities. The solution to these adverse consequences does not lie in private ordering regimes which treat women's difference as 'given' but rather in changing the social conditions which make it difficult for women to reconcile 'good' mothering and economic self-sufficiency.

II *The problem of background entitlements*

The outcome of agreements between spouses is influenced, at least to some extent, by the family law rules regulating financial provision on divorce. As Mnookin and Kornhauser put it, spouses bargain in the shadow of the law.[7]

Before fault-based divorce was abolished, a central function of the rules regulating matrimonial property division, support, and alimony was (at least in theory)[8] to compensate the 'innocent' party for breach

7 R.H. Mnookin and L. Kornhauser 'Bargaining in the Shadow of the Law: The Case of Divorce' (1979) 88 *Yale LJ* 950. See also R.H. Mnookin 'Divorce Bargaining: The Limits on Private Ordering' in J.M. Eekelaar and S.N. Katz (eds) *The Resolution of Family Conflict: Comparative Legal Perspectives* (Toronto: Butterworths 1984) 364, 366.

8 In practice, however, spousal support awards were usually relatively low. Rogerson has commented that 'one of the shaping forces in spousal support law has always been an unwillingness to adequately compensate women for their domestic labour'; see C.J. Rogerson, 'The Causal Connection Test in Spousal Support Law' (1989) 8 *Can. J. of Fam. Law* 95, 105.

of the marital contract.[9] The introduction of no-fault divorce in most Western countries over the past two decades undermined fault as the basis for resolution of financial disputes after marriage breakdown, prompting a re-examination of the rules regulating matrimonial property division, support, and alimony. In Canada and in the United States, and to a slightly lesser extent in Australia, such changes were influenced by the philosophy of formal equality[10] and the notion of the 'clean break' after marriage breakdown.[11] Marriage is no longer seen as a life-long relationship, but is increasingly regarded as an economic partnership which can be brought to an end by either party, thus restoring both spouses to their pre-marriage situation and, wherever possible, terminating the financial relationship between them.

The major deficiency in the current rules governing matrimonial property division and support is their failure to allow sufficiently for the effects of women's responsibility for child-rearing and domestic labour on their capacity to become financially independent after marriage breakdown. The abandonment of the fault principle, increasing divorce rates, and legislative and judicial acceptance of the view that financial obligations associated with marriage should determine on divorce have meant that the economic costs of marriage breakdown are disproportionately borne by women.

The differential economic impact of divorce on men and women has been widely recognized. Lenore Weitzman's famous research on the effects of 1970 Californian reforms, which provided only limited rights to maintenance and applied a strict equal sharing rule to property acquired during marriage, showed that this approach produced 'unintended but potentially disastrous consequences for women and children.'[12] A year after divorce the living standards of men had risen by 42 per cent while those of women had fallen by 73 per cent. In Weitzman's words:[13]

9 Carbone and Brinig comment that: 'Divorce awards under the old system served as a selective form of specific performance dependent on the inviolability of marital obligations.' J. Carbone and M.F. Brinig 'Rethinking Marriage: Feminist Ideology, Economic Change and Divorce Reform' (1991) 16 *Tulane LR* 953, 955.

10 For a discussion of the effects of this philosophy see M.A. Fineman *The Illusion of Equality* (Chicago: University of Chicago Press 1991) chapters 2, 3.

11 For an interesting discussion on the history of these changes, and a convincing refutation of the view that they were the result of feminist pressure, see C. Bacchi *Same Difference* (Sydney: Allen and Unwin 1991) chapter 8.

12 M. Minow 'Consider the Consequences' (1986) 84 *Mich. LR* 900, 901.

13 L. Weitzman *The Divorce Revolution: The Unexpected Social and Economic Consequence for Women and Children in America* (New York: Free Press 1985) 339. For a critique

[D]ivorce is a financial catastrophe for most women: in just one year they experience a dramatic drop in income and a calamitous drop in their standard of living.[14] It is hard to imagine how they deal with such severe deprivation ...

One of the major effects of the equal division rule was to deprive women and children of housing[15] by forcing sale of the matrimonial home.[16]

In Australia the Family Law Act 1975 confers a broad jurisdiction on the Family Court to make a just and equitable division of all property owned by the spouses at the time of matrimonial breakdown, taking into account their respective past contributions to the marriage (including contributions in the capacity of homemaker and parent) and future needs. Research conducted for the purposes of the Australian Law Reform Commission's reference on matrimonial property showed that this equitable division principle produced similar outcomes to regimes mandating equal division of matrimonial property. The Australian Institute of Family Studies interviewed 825 divorced men and women.[17] The study showed that 3 to 5 years after separation men living alone, as a sole parent, or with a new partner with no children had considerably improved their living standards, while women living alone or as sole parents had 'sustained a drastic fall in living standards.'[18] At the time of interview 41 per cent of women living alone and

of Weitzman's methodology, however, see S.D. Sugarman 'Dividing Financial Interests on Divorce' in S.D. Sugarman and H.H. Kay *Divorce Reform at the Crossroads* (New Haven: York University Press 1990) 130. Sugarman's criticism is mainly directed at the proposition that women have done worse under no-fault regimes than under fault-based divorce laws.

14 In order to measure 'living standards' Weitzman relied on an index of economic well-being developed by the US government. For details see Weitzman, supra note 13, 337–8.

15 See L. Weitzman 'Marital Property: Its Transformation and Division in the United States' in L.J. Weitzman and M. McLean *Economic Consequences of Divorce* (Oxford: Clarendon Press 1992) 101.

16 Weitzman's research has since been replicated in several other US jurisdictions. See Weitzman, supra note 15, 92–3; J.B. McLinden 'Separate But Unequal: The Economic Disaster of Divorce for Women and Children' (1987) 21 *Fam. LQ* 351. Weitzman's work led to some changes to matrimonial property law in California. See Sugarman and Kay, supra note 13, chapter 1.

17 See Law Reform Commission, Report No. 39 *Matrimonial Property Report* (Canberra: Australian Government Publishing Service 1987) 66 for a more detailed discussion of the sample.

18 Ibid, 73. Men and women who had established a new household with a partner and children had returned, roughly, to their pre-separation income level. It should be noted that women living alone or as sole parents were not 'asset-rich' and income-

35 per cent of sole parent women were below the poverty line. In the interview group two-thirds of the women who were single at the time of the study and had been dependent on their husband, or had only low earnings prior to the divorce, were more than 20 per cent below the poverty line and three-quarters were reliant on social security, while only 13 per cent of single men were similarly poor and many were better off than before separation. For many women the only practical means of escaping from poverty after divorce was to enter into a new relationship with another man.

The economic disadvantage experienced by women on divorce is directly related to the sexual segmentation of the paid workforce and the sexual division of labour within the home. The question for feminist law reformers is how this disadvantage can be overcome without entrenching women's economic dependence. A number of commentators have proposed that financial provision on divorce should include compensation for the opportunity costs incurred by women because of interruptions to paid workforce participation due to child-rearing.[19] The Australian Institute of Family Studies justifies this approach on the following grounds:

> Conventionally the function of child rearing leads to a disadvantage for the wife at the breakdown of the marriage because she has forgone the opportunity to develop her income-earning potential. The husband on the other hand has not suffered the same disadvantage. The couple's joint endeavour must therefore bear the cost of the wife's disadvantage because that disadvantage is directly attributable to their joint productive and reproductive endeavour.[20]

Two recent decisions suggest that this approach is gradually gaining judicial acceptance in Canada. In the first case, *Ormerod* v. *Ormerod*,[21] the Ontario Unified Family Court required the husband to compensate his wife for the loss of earning capacity she experienced because of a 12-year interruption to her career as a nurse, while she was caring for the couple's children. In the second case, *Elliot* v. *Elliot*,[22] the husband was required to pay *half* the net income loss of his wife, who had worked

poor. See also K. Funder 'Australia: A Proposal for Reform' in Weitzman and McLean, supra note 15, 146.

19 See, for example, N. Duclos 'Breaking the Dependency Cycle: The Family Law Act Reconstituted' (1986) 44 *U. of T. LR* 1; Carbone and Brinig, supra note 9, 953; H.H. Kay 'Beyond No-Fault' in Sugarman and Kay, supra note, 13, 32–5.

20 Funder, supra note 18, 1147.

21 (1990) 27 RFL (3d) 225 (Ont. UFC).

22 (1993) 42 RFL (3d) 7 (Ont. UFC) and see *The Globe and Mail* 29 August 1992. See also the recognition of the issue in *Moge* v. *Moge* [1992] 3 RCS 813, 853ff.

part-time while the children were under school age, and was unable to obtain a full-time position with her employer after the marriage breakdown. In both cases the court heard expert evidence from economists on the extent of the wife's lost opportunity. The Canadian federal government has since produced a report on the extent of lost earning capacity experienced by women who leave the workforce to care for children.[23]

In Australia, the Institute of Family Studies has also argued that financial provision on divorce should include compensation for loss of earning capacity,[24] although this approach has not yet found favour with the Family Court. Along similar lines, Trebilcock and Keshvani argue that property division and support rules generally fail to take account of the 'impact of marriage upon human capital' and suggest this is an area where 'law and economics scholars and feminist scholars can make common cause.'[25] The remainder of this section compares Trebilcock and Keshvani's proposals with the approach advocated by the Australian Institute of Family Studies and identifies issues which would need to be resolved if a loss of opportunity approach were to be adopted.

One difference between Trebilcock and Keshvani's and the Institute of Family Studies' proposals is that the former suggests that the wife's forgone earnings during marriage should be included, while the latter suggests that compensation should be restricted to future loss of earning capacity after marriage breakdown. In *Ormerod* v. *Ormerod*[26] the wife was not compensated for her loss of earnings during cohabitation. This approach is supported by the Institute, which argues that lost earnings *during marriage* should not be the subject of compensation since such losses represent the investment of both spouses in their children and in the quality of life shared by the family.[27] In the Institute's view, gains or losses experienced during marriage should be ignored, since they are a necessary consequence of the marriage partnership.[28]

23 R. Kerr *An Economic Model to Assist in the Determination of Spousal Support* (Ottawa: Department of Justice 1992) reported in *Lawyers Weekly* 11 July 1992.
24 P. McDonald (ed.) *Settling Up: Property and Income Distribution on Divorce in Australia* (Australia: Prentice Hall 1986) chapter 16; Funder, supra note 18, 143, 152. See also K. Funder 'The Value of Work in Marriage' in D. Ironmonger (ed.) *Households Work* (1989) 173; K. Funder, M. Harrison, and R. Weston *Settling Down: Pathway of Parents After Divorce* (Australia: Australian Institute of Family Studies 1993).
25 Supra note 1, 553.
26 (1990) 27 RFL (3d) 225 (Ont. UFC).
27 Funder, supra note 18, 154. See also 152.
28 Ibid.

One difficulty with compensating women for lost earnings *during* marriage is that this approach fails to take account of the economic benefits the wife may have received because of her husband's higher earning capacity. Trebilcock and Keshvani address this issue by suggesting that the wife's loss of earnings during marriage should be offset by 'gains in consumption benefits that she has obtained up to the date of her divorce, from the incremental income earned by her husband (because she has freed his time to concentrate on his career).'[29] The transaction costs in determining such gains on an individual basis could be considerable. It is not clear how the husband's 'incremental income' would be ascertained, since in most cases the husband's (unlike the wife's) career path will not have been affected by the fact that he has children.

A second difference between the proposals is that Trebilcock and Keshvani suggest that the wife's opportunity costs should be borne by the husband alone, while the Institute proposes that they should be borne equally by the parties, on the ground that 'both parties decided to apportion their roles on the tacit understanding that the benefits and costs be shared.'[30] In *Elliot* the husband was required to compensate the wife for *half* of her net income loss. This approach is less favourable to women than a model under which these costs are borne from the husband's share alone.

For feminists concerned with resolving 'the dilemma of difference' it is important to compare the effects of these proposed reforms on the current division of labour between men and women. Arguably, Trebilcock and Keshvani's proposal has greater potential to disrupt the sexual division of labour. The Institute's proposal is neutral towards the creation of relationships of dependence while the parties remain married (though it compensates women for loss of earning capacity after marriage breakdown). Compensating women for opportunity costs incurred *during* marriage makes economically dependent relationships within marriage 'much more expensive for men in the event of their termination (and more reflective of actual investment).'[31] By taking account of lost opportunity during marriage, and by imposing these costs on the husband rather than on the marriage partnership, Trebilcock and Keshvani's proposal may give husbands (though not wives) an incentive to avoid the creation of relationships of financial

29 Supra note 1, 556.
30 Funder, supra note 18, 155.
31 Supra note 1, 558.

dependence, whilst at the same time protecting women who take primary responsibility for caring for children.

Unfortunately there is little empirical evidence on the extent to which changes to rules regulating the financial consequences of divorce actually affect marriage and divorce behaviour. Many questions remain unanswered. Do rules improving the situation of women in traditional dependent relationships encourage them to remain full-time homemakers? Do such rules discourage men from marrying? Do they make men more prepared to share in the work of child-rearing? Alternatively, do rules which disadvantage 'home-makers' discourage women from marrying or from becoming dependent on their husbands? To what extent is the decision of a person to leave an unhappy marriage affected by rules governing property and support entitlements?

It seems likely that the decisions which couples and individuals make about marrying, divorcing, and dividing labour during marriage are affected by a broad range of emotional and social factors which cannot be reduced to simple computations of costs and benefits. Like other law and economics scholars Trebilcock and Keshvani assume that legal entitlements have a significant impact on marriage and divorce behaviour. But, as La Forest J recognized in *Richardson* v. *Richardson* 'Lawyers and judges alike are prone to exaggerate the influence legal rules ... have on people's behaviour.'[32]

In the absence of clear evidence of the effects of particular reforms on the behaviour of men and women within marriage the best that can be done may be to design rules which rectify injustice in the short term, whilst ensuring that these rules can be rapidly modified if their long-term effects prove undesirable. The opportunity-cost approach could significantly improve the situation of women after divorce and has the symbolic advantage of treating women as creditors of the marriage partnership, rather than as dependents on male breadwinners. It is consistent with the clean-break philosophy and has the virtue of certainty, providing for payment of an ascertainable amount of compensation when the marriage is over (though the difficulties of determining the extent of a spouse's loss of earning capacity should not be underestimated). However, as Trebilcock and Keshvani recognize, the opportunity-cost approach also has some limitations.

First, in cases of long marriages where the wife's loss of earning capacity is significant and the parties have few assets, the property of

32 (1987) 7 RFL (3d) 304, 322 (SCC).

the parties may be insufficient to cover the wife's opportunity costs. To compensate the wife, this amount will have to be met from the husband's future earnings stream, so that the notion of 'clean break' will have to be modified. Historically women have had considerable difficulty in enforcing spousal and child support obligations against their husbands. Compensating women for loss of opportunity will only help them if effective enforcement mechanisms are available.

Second, as Trebilcock and Keshvani acknowledge, the opportunity-cost approach focuses on reductions in the wife's earning capacity, rather than on increases in the husband's earning capacity that may occur over the course of the marriage and may, at least in part, be attributable to it. Because compensation based on loss of opportunity does not take account of the loss of financial security which marriage still provides many women, it does not entirely resolve the dilemma of difference.

Married women often work part-time in the paid labour force, so that wage-earning can be combined with their family responsibilities. Sometimes they refuse promotions or transfers which would advance their own careers, because they put their husbands' careers first. Such decisions are made on the assumption that they will continue to share in increases in the earnings of their spouses. The loss of past and future income experienced by a woman in this situation may be considerably less than the value of her lost expectations. The question for feminist law reformers is whether wives should receive some compensation for loss of expectation, at the possible cost of encouraging them to continue to regard themselves as 'secondary' wage earners, or whether the loss of financial security which many women still rely on marriage to provide should be ignored, thus disadvantaging women who have put their husbands' careers first.

A number of commentators have made proposals for financial provision on divorce which provide some compensation for loss of expectation. Proponents of this approach rely on the notion of the merger of human capital over time. Each spouse brings his or her own earning capacity to the marriage, but over time 'one can less and less distinguish between what was brought into the marriage and what was produced by the marriage. Moreover, the longer the marriage, the longer the spouse in the dependent role has ... submerged her or his independent identity and earning capacity into the marital collective.'[33] At first glance, compensation for loss of expectation seems inap-

33 Sugarman, supra note 13, 131, 160.

propriate in a no-fault system, where the claimant herself may have decided to end the marriage. Trebilcock and Keshvani attempt to deal with this objection by constructing a hypothetical contract under which the parties decide that one party should devote her time to household production. The situation of the spouse who decides to end the marriage and then seeks compensation for lost expectation is compared with the problem of 'moral hazard' which is familiar to insurers. Parties would be unlikely to agree that the wife would have an unlimited right to share in the husband's future earnings, regardless of whether or not they were divorced, since this could make the wife 'largely indifferent to sustaining or terminating the marriage.'[34] By contrast, the costs of marriage breakdown need to be kept sufficiently high to discourage the husband from breaking the contract and appropriating the benefits of the wife's performance.

I am sceptical of reasoning which assumes that couples deciding to marry or to separate calculate the costs and benefits with the degree of precision attributed to owners of widget factories who enter into fire insurance policies. As Wiegers has pointed out, treating couples as entirely self-interested individuals ignores the affection, commitment, and concern for the other spouse's well-being which exists in marriage and sometimes survives divorce.[35] In my view financial incentives and penalties are unlikely to cement failing marriages. Nevertheless I support financial provision on divorce which makes some limited provision for loss of expectation as well as compensating for loss of opportunity. Trebilcock and Keshvani propose that this could be achieved by giving economically dependent spouses a 'percentage of the other spouse's future income on marriage termination for some period after marriage breakdown, calibrated to years of marriage.'[36] The attraction of this model is that it would provide greater benefits to women whose earning capacity had been affected by lengthy periods out of the workforce, compared to women in shorter marriages. Its disadvantage is that it does not allow a 'clean break.'

An alternative approach, supported by some commentators, is to compensate the wife 'for the difference between her reduced earning capacity and her husband's increased earning power resulting from the couple's allocation of their human capital to market and non-market

34 Supra note 1, 556.
35 Wiegers, supra note 2, 170, 203–4.
36 Supra note 1, 558.

labour.'[37] This approach is based on the view that, on the dissolution of the marriage partnership, both parties should share equally in the gains and losses (including gains and losses in earning capacity) occurring during the partnership. The same idea lies behind Lenore Weitzman's suggestion[38] that professional degrees acquired during the marriage should be included in the pool of matrimonial property, but the above proposal would catch enhancements in earning capacity unrelated to the acquisition of professional qualifications. Trebilcock and Keshvani's proposal gives the wife a proportion of any increases in the husband's earnings occurring *after* divorce. By contrast, the alternative approach focuses on increases in earnings occurring *during* the marriage. Hence it is more consistent with the clean-break philosophy. Both approaches may be more favourable to women who have adopted the role of 'secondary' wage earners than compensation provided solely on an opportunity cost basis, and neither approach entrenches dependence for an indefinite period.

A third limitation in the opportunity-costs approach (which would be partly met by providing some compensation for loss of expectation) is that it does not address differences in the level of men's and women's earnings. The Australian Institute of Family Studies explicitly differentiates between gender-related differences in earnings and the opportunity costs associated with withdrawing from the workforce to care for children. In their view, it is not the role of family law to compensate for differences in men's and women's earnings which are not related to marriage. As Funder argues:

> If family law is to play any part in redressing the inequalities which currently exist, that component of inequality which derives from structural features of the ... workforce must be distinguished from that part which derives from the marriage. It is only the latter which may fairly be considered the responsibility of the parties to the marriage, and hence come under the domain of family law.[39]

Consequently the Institute proposes that the opportunity costs of child-rearing should be ascertained by comparing the earnings of women

37 E.S. Beninger and J.W. Smith 'Career Opportunity Cost: A Factor in Spousal Support Determination' (1982) 16 *Fam. LQ* 201, 202. Sugarman has criticized this approach on the ground that the increases in earning capacity of the spouse engaged in market labour may be insufficiently related to the existence of the marriage. See Sugarman, supra note 13, 131, 156–7.

38 L.J. Weitzman 'Marital Property: Its Transformation and Division in the United States' in Weitzman and McLean, supra note 18, 94.

39 Funder, supra note 18, 151.

who withdraw from the work force to care for children with the earnings of women whose participation in paid employment has not been interrupted, rather than with the earnings of childless *men and women*.[40]

I am not convinced that there is any meaningful distinction between the disadvantages experienced by women because of their responsibility for caring for children and the disadvantages they experience as paid workers. Women's dependence on men is constructed and maintained by a complex interaction of social factors. One of the reasons couples may decide that the wife should take care of the children is that she can usually earn less than her husband. Correlatively, one of the reasons that women earn less in the paid workforce is that they are perceived primarily as child-rearers. Women's roles as mothers and as low-paid workers are inextricably interconnected. Family law reforms which place a higher valuation on domestic labour could result in changes in attitudes to the value of women's labour in the paid workforce. This suggests that women's opportunity-cost should be assessed by comparing them with the level of men's and women's earnings rather than by comparison with women's earnings alone.

Finally, the opportunity-cost approach takes insufficient account of costs associated with caring for children. Trebilcock and Keshvani's proposal does not sufficiently differentiate between the obligations owed by husbands to their ex-wives and the obligations owed by fathers to their children. The clean-break principle should not be interpreted as releasing fathers from their parental responsibilities. Changes to family law rules governing property division and spousal support must be accompanied by cheap and effective mechanisms for assessing and enforcing child support obligations. In Australia the situation of women caring for children alone has been improved by a new child support scheme, which provides a statutory formula for the determination of child support and enables child support to be deducted from the liable parent's wages, through the taxation system.[41]

As Funder, Harrison, and Weston explain:

> Inequalities in the standards of living experienced by men and women after separation derive from five major sources: the lower earnings of women generally, the effects on future earnings of the division of labour within marriage which depreciates women's earning capacity (the opportunity costs of children); the continuing indirect costs of children caused by restrictions on resident parents' time and efforts in the labour market; the almost universal

40 Ibid. 147.

41 Child Support (Registration and Collection) Act 1988 (Cth); Child Support Assessment Act 1989 (Cth).

lack of any transfer of resources from the marriage to redress the differential which flows from the marriage partnership and the dependence on public support of sole parents.[42]

All of these problems will need to be addressed if the 'dilemma of difference' is to be resolved.

III *Private ordering*

Under traditional fault-based family law regimes, financial provision on divorce was, at least in theory, intended to compensate the 'innocent' spouse for loss of her expectation of life-long financial support. Courts traditionally refused to enforce pre-marital and separation agreements because such agreements undermined the protection afforded to 'innocent' spouses on matrimonial breakdown and violated the concept of marriage as a life-long relationship.[43] Trebilcock and Keshvani believe that this reasoning is 'squarely challenged by modern visions of the role of marriage and more specifically the paradigm of a partnership between two independent and equally autonomous parties.'[44]

They argue that parties to a marriage should be able to contract out of their statutory entitlements by making pre-nuptial or separation agreements.[45] Subject to certain procedural safeguards and normal contractual doctrines relating to fraud, mistake, and unconscionability, agreements between spouses should be enforceable in the same way as other contracts. Doctrines invalidating pre-nuptial and separation agreements should no longer apply. Trebilcock and Keshvani suggest that pre-nuptial and separation agreements have major advantages over imposed solutions. First, they enable spouses to make arrangements

42 Funder, Harrison, and Weston, supra note 24.

43 See supra note 1, 543–4. At common law, nuptial agreements which provided for a future separation were regarded as contrary to public policy. After breakdown of marriage, or as part of the reconciliation process after a separation, couples could make agreements providing for the financial consequences of separation, but such agreements could not oust the jurisdiction of the courts to resolve property and maintenance disputes. One reason for invalidating such agreements was that they could impose a burden on the public revenue. *Hyman* v. *Hyman* [1929] AC 602; *Bennett* v. *Bennett* [1952] 1 KB 249.

44 Supra note 1, 544.

45 Apparently they contemplate that such agreements should cover child support and custody, as well as property division and spousal support. Supra note 1, 559. Mnookin also argues that divorcing parents should be given considerable freedom to decide custody matters. See infra note 46.

which are mutually beneficial and fit their particular life circumstances. Second, parties are more likely to comply with obligations they have voluntarily assumed than with obligations they have been coerced to accept by court orders. Third, negotiated agreements minimize transaction costs such as legal fees and the trauma of litigation. Finally, separation agreements facilitate a 'clean break' by enabling parties to terminate their relationships and to 'look to the future, to build new relationships, and to undertake new commitments with some confidence in the security of prior arrangements.'[46]

Trebilcock and Keshvani's support for private ordering has its roots in the neoclassical economic view which prefers voluntary agreements to collective decision-making by legislatures or courts.[47] Trebilcock and Keshvani argue that private agreements enhance individual autonomy and freedom of choice for both men and women, affirming in women the ability to operate as 'freely autonomous and self-determining agents, free to bargain and enjoy all the rights and freedoms previously only held by men.'[48] Private agreements are also justified on the utilitarian ground that parties are the best judge of their own interests and, in the absence of transaction-specific failures, will only enter into contracts which make both of them better off in economic terms, so that voluntary agreements maximize social welfare.

Wiegers's article criticizes the view that all matters of social welfare can be monetized and exposes market theory's inability to make ethical distinctions between different types of choices.[49] Moreover, Trebilcock and Keshvani themselves recognize that the extent to which individual autonomy and freedom of choice are valued above more communitarian and egalitarian ideals is ultimately a political decision. However, the purpose of this article is not to engage in a general discussion of the presumption that private agreements enhance social welfare.[50] Rather, my intention is to examine the reasons why, even if a

46 Supra note 1, 550. See also Mnookin, supra note 7.

47 Supra note 1, 534.

48 Ibid. 540.

49 Wiegers, supra note 2. This issue has been taken up in many critiques of law and economics scholarship. See, for example, M. Radin 'Market-Inalienability' (1987) 100 *Harv. LR* 1849; M. Waring *Counting for Nothing: What Women Are Worth* (Wellington: Allen and Unwin 1988).

50 For discussion of the reasons why this may not be the case see R.L. West 'Taking Preferences Seriously' (1990) 64 *Tulane LR* 659; C. Sunstein 'Disrupting Voluntary Transactions' in J. Chapman and J. Pennock (eds) *Markets and Justice* (Nomos XXXI NYU Press 1989) 279; C. Sunstein 'Legal Interference with Private Preferences' (1986) 53 *U. of Chi. LR* 1129; D. Kennedy 'Distributive and Paternalistic Motives in

general presumption in favour of private ordering is accepted, prenuptial and separation agreements are unlikely to provide an escape from 'the dilemma of difference.'

The most obvious response to the argument in favour of private ordering in the family law context is that women seem to have done poorly under private ordering in the past, whether their agreements have concerned the conditions under which they perform domestic labour in the home, financial provision after marriage breakdown, or employment in the paid workforce.[51] Within marriage, where women can 'negotiate' the terms on which they provide domestic services, they continue to take major responsibility for child care and housework, even when they are in the paid workforce as well.[52] After marriage breakdown, empirical evidence shows that the economic costs are disproportionately borne by women.

In all jurisdictions of which I am aware, the majority of property and maintenance claims are already resolved by some form of compromise (although such agreements are not always legally binding). For example, in the Australian Institute of Family Studies research project discussed above, only 3 per cent of the 665 people who had completed their claims had done so in contested legal proceedings.[53] Currently women are disadvantaged by the terms of such compromises. Trebilcock and Keshvani suggest that unequal outcomes on divorce are largely attributable to deficiencies in the rules governing property division and spousal support. In their words:

> In the matrimonial context, a critical threshold question that must be addressed is whether the background entitlements of the parties have been appropriately defined by the legal system ... [M]any reservations that have been

Contract and Tort Law: With Special Reference to Compulsory Terms and Unequal Bargaining Power' (1982) 41 *Maryland LR* 568.

51 In the context of paid employment economists have explained women's lower-paid status in two main ways. First, wage differentials may reflect the existence of discrimination which deprives women of the opportunity to participate in higher-paid occupations. Alternatively it is suggested that women 'voluntarily choose' to enter low-paid occupations. Of course the latter explanation ignores the social and economic factors which constrain women's choices. See D.R. Fischer and E.P. Lazear 'Comparable Worth and Discrimination in Labour Markets' (1986) 53 *U. of Chi. LR* 891 and for a response see M.R. Becker 'Barriers Facing Women in the Wage-Labour Market and the Need for Additional Remedies: A Reply to Fischer and Lazear' (1986) 53 *U. of Chi. LR* 934.

52 M. Bittman *Juggling Time: How Australian Families Use Time* (Office of the Status of Women, 1991).

53 M. Harrison 'Legal Process' in P. McDonald (ed.) *Settling Up: Property and Income Distribution on Divorce in Australia* (Australia: Prentice Hall 1986) 48.

registered with respect to an enlarged role for private ordering in the matrimonial context are in fact misdirected. If all private ordering were to be banned, many of these reservations would continue to obtain, but would instead be directed to court imposed outcomes under the existing legal framework.[54]

But in the paid workforce, where women now negotiate their terms and conditions of employment against the background of equal pay and equal opportunity legislation, they continue to earn substantially less than men. The disparity between men's and women's earnings appears to be lowest in countries which determine wages through centralized wage-fixing mechanisms, rather than by individual negotiation of employment contracts.[55] In New Zealand, the centralized wage-fixing system has recently been abandoned, so that employers and employees now negotiate individual or collective agreements. Preliminary research suggests that the gap between men's and women's earnings is widening, despite a minimum wage guarantee.[56] Given the failure of private ordering to produce equality between men and women in the employment context, where men and women now have similar background entitlements I am sceptical of Trebilcock and Keshvani's claim that it will resolve the dilemma of difference within marriage, even when it is combined with reforms to matrimonial property and support rules.

The Australian Family Law Act already makes some provision for financial agreements.[57] Under section 87 of the Act spouses can make financial agreements in total or partial substitution of their rights to property division or spousal maintenance.[58] If such agreements are

54 Supra note 1, 551.

55 Data comparing men's and women's earnings in ten OECD countries, presented at Academy of Social Sciences Workshop, Women in a Restructuring Australia: Work and Welfare, 17–18 November 1992.

56 R. Du Plessis 'The Gendered Implications of the Welfare/Labour Market Interface.' Paper presented at Academy of Social Sciences Workshop, supra note 55.

57 The Act provides for financial agreements under sections 86 and 87. Section 86 agreements do not oust the court's discretion to make orders dividing property or requiring the payment of maintenance, although when registered they can be enforced as if they are court orders. Section 87 allows parties to make agreements in relation to property and spousal maintenance which, on approval by the court, take the place of their rights under the Family Law Act. Parties also frequently obtain orders by consent, a process which 'rubber-stamps' the terms of their agreement.

58 Such agreements cannot oust the jurisdiction of the court in relation to child custody or access.

approved as 'proper' by the court[59] they can only be set aside in specified circumstances.

Neoclassical economic theory suggests that people only make agreements under which they feel themselves to be better off. Hence, one would have expected that those entering into section 87 agreements would have been satisfied with their outcomes. However, in the Australian Institute of Family Studies project 66 per cent of men and 54 per cent of women[60] who were parties to section 87 agreements said that *at the time they made the agreement* they thought the division was unfair. Interestingly, more men than women subjectively feel unfairly treated. This may reflect the fact that husbands have a greater sense of 'entitlement' to matrimonial property than their wives. The implications of this difference are discussed later.[61] The reported view of a *majority* of both men and women that agreements were unfair may reflect discontent with their background entitlements under existing family law rules, but it also throws doubts on the acceptability to parties of negotiated solutions. Presumably the decision to agree to terms perceived as 'unfair' by one or both of the parties reflects a trade-off between perceived entitlements and concern about the uncertainties of litigation. But this empirical finding suggests that parties making agreements do not experience all choices as equally free and voluntary. The problem of voluntariness is discussed in more detail below.

An additional problem for couples negotiating agreements has been identified by Robert Mnookin. Individuals who are bargaining at arm's length can usually decline to do business with each other, but 'like a monopolist selling to a monopsonist, the two spouses (or their representatives) are locked in a dyadic relationship that cannot be easily avoided.'[62] Because spouses are forced to negotiate with each other, one spouse may 'take advantage' of the other spouse's preferences.

59 The role of the Family Court in approving such agreements is not entirely clear. On one view the court has a responsibility to investigate the circumstances of the parties and the terms of the agreement independently. The alternative view is that the court should sanction such agreements, regardless of their fairness, provided that the parties have independent legal representation. The Family Court has tended to take the latter view. See H.A. Finlay and R.J. Bailey-Harris *Family Law in Australia* (Australia: Butterworths 1989) 368–9. Section 87 agreements can only be revoked by the court in a limited range of circumstances; see Family Law Act 1975 (Cth) s. 87A.

60 M. Harrison, 'Legal Process' in McDonald, supra note 24, 51.

61 The difference between men and women may illustrate the problem of the 'adaptive preference' discussed below.

62 Mnookin, supra note 7, 364, 373.

Emphasis on private ordering avoids questioning the extent to which one spouse should be able to exploit the other spouse's preferences. Perhaps the Australian Institute of Family Studies' finding reflects the feeling of some spouses that the terms of section 87 agreements reflect such unfair exploitation.

Trebilcock and Keshvani also argue that parties are more likely to comply with obligations which 'emerge from an agreed resolution of the issues than one imposed by a third party (a court) where one party will often perceive himself or herself as the loser.'[63] A finding that couples may make agreements they subjectively perceive as unfair throws doubt on the view that parties are more likely to comply with the terms of voluntary agreements than with court-imposed solutions. The research of the Australian Institute of Family Studies suggests that men are only slightly more likely to pay maintenance which they voluntarily agree to, than maintenance required by court order. But enforcement of spousal and child support obligations is a serious problem in most jurisdictions. Historically, women have had great difficulty in persuading their husbands to pay adequate child or spousal support regularly.[64] On an anecdotal level, many family lawyers have encountered spouses who assume obligations they have no intention of satisfying. The solution to problems of default seems to lie in more effective enforcement mechanisms rather than in greater emphasis on voluntary agreements.

For feminists concerned with resolving the 'dilemma of difference' the main difficulty with Trebilcock and Keshvani's proposal is the extent to which family law rules which recognize the effect of marriage and child-rearing on women's earning capacity can be overridden by private agreements.

Consistently with their emphasis on individual autonomy, Trebilcock and Keshvani argue that spouses should be able to bargain away their statutory entitlements. However,

> where the validity of the separation agreement is subsequently challenged, if the petitioner for relief is able to demonstrate that the agreement prima facie generates significantly inferior net benefits for him or her relative to the background entitlements, a presumption of unfairness arises that the other

63 Supra note 1, 550.

64 Attorney-General's Department *Report of National Maintenance Inquiry* (Australian Government Publishing Services 1984). M. Harrison and T. Tucker 'Maintenance, Custody and Access' in McDonald, supra note 24, 259–67.

party bears the burden of rebutting by demonstrating the absence of the factors noted above that may render the bargaining process suspect.[65]

As I understand this proposal, the presumption of unfairness could be rebutted by showing that the making of the contract had not been affected by factors such as fraud, undue influence, or unconscionable conduct. In the absence of such misconduct a court would be unable to override the terms of an agreement simply because the outcome of the agreement was objectively unfair. I will argue below that this provision provides insufficient protection to women caring for children.

Although Trebilcock and Keshvani would allow spouses to override family law rules, they recognize that the capacity of parties to enter into agreements which make them better off may be affected by the circumstances affecting the particular transaction. This concern is particularly relevant to pre-marital and separation agreements. Couples who are contemplating marriage may find it difficult to strike hard bargains which will protect them adequately if, contrary to their expectations, the marriage fails. Divorcing couples usually experience substantial emotional distress,[66] which may take some years to resolve. A spouse's grief or guilt about the marital breakdown may affect his or her ability to assess the implications of a separation agreement. One spouse may suppress information or take advantage of the other spouse's emotional dependence or reluctance to litigate.

Trebilcock and Keshvani suggest that these problems can be overcome by procedural safeguards. Parties should be required to disclose their income and assets and should receive independent legal advice before entering into agreements. A statutory cooling-off period would apply, during which either party could withdraw from the agreement.

In discussing the emotional and relational factors which affect the ability of spouses to make contracts in their own best interests, Trebilcock and Keshvani's language is determinedly gender-neutral. This is consistent with their view that men and women have equal autonomy in assessing and advancing their own welfare and that attempts to provide women with special protection may simply legitimate their unequal position. The broader issue of gender inequality will be discussed in more detail below. But I should point out that some of the factors which Trebilcock and Keshvani recognize as contributing to transaction-specific failures do not apply equally to men and women. Women

65 Supra note 1, 560.
66 Mnookin, supra note 7, 368.

generally have fewer assets and a lower earning capacity than men. They often have difficulty in meeting their short-term living costs, let alone paying legal and accountancy fees. They may be under greater pressure to reach a settlement because of their immediate financial needs.[67] Often they do not have accurate information about their husband's finances.[68] In wealthy households significant assets may be held in complex arrangements involving family companies or trusts established for tax avoidance purposes. The Australian Institute of Family Studies research found that 'wives [feel] outside the club of businessmen, lawyers and accountants. Women have a very distinct sense of absence of control over business information and little sense that the present legal system is of any help.'[69] Procedural safeguards do not necessarily overcome these problems. In Australia spouses seeking court approval of section 87 agreements must file a statement of financial circumstances, but this requirement does not appear to have provided adequate protection for women. The Australian Institute of Family Studies has suggested that the Family Court should make use of independent auditors who could investigate claims of non-disclosure or manipulation of assets.[70] This would go some way towards redressing the imbalance of power caused by lack of information, though if the costs of the service were to be met equally by the parties from the marital property it would also reduce the pool of assets available for distribution.

Finally, Trebilcock and Keshvani recognize that pre-nuptial or separation agreements may not produce Pareto-superior outcomes because of events occurring after such agreements were made. Post-agreement contingencies present major problems for those making pre-marital agreements. Parties entering such agreements cannot predict a variety of factors affecting their financial situation in future, including employment prospects, the number of children they may have, or the effect of marriage on the earning capacity of the spouse who takes responsibility for caring for the children. Parties making

67 R. Ingleby *Solicitors and Divorce* (Oxford: Clarendon Press 1992) 10–11.

68 Edwards has shown that the assumption that household income is pooled between spouses is inaccurate. M. Edwards 'Individual Equity and Social Policy' in J. Goodnow and C. Pateman (eds) *Women, Social Science and Public Policy* (Sydney: Allen and Unwin 1985) 95; M. Edwards *The Income Unit in Australia. Tax and Social Security* (Melbourne: Institute of Family Studies 1984) chapters 6, 7.

69 P. McDonald 'Directions for Law Reform and Social Policy' in McDonald, supra note 24, 320.

70 Ibid.

separation agreements are likely to be more conscious of the need to provide for future contingencies but may still have difficulty in foreseeing events such as loss of employment, which affects a spouse's ability to perform obligations under the agreement, or failure to find work, which may affect a spouse's or child's ability to support him- or herself. Mnookin comments that:

> Informed bargaining requires a divorcing spouse to assess his or her own preferences concerning alternative arrangements. Radical changes in life circumstances complicate such assessments. Within a short period of time, separation and divorce often subject spouses to stresses of many changes ... The past will be a very incomplete guide to the future. Preferences may be based on particular experiences in which child-rearing tasks were performed in an ongoing two-parent family, and dissolution or divorce inevitably alters this division of responsibilities.[71]

Women who are seeking paid work after many years of being supported by their husbands face particularly dramatic changes and may have little basis on which to assess their future financial position. As Cossman points out, 'A woman's lack of experience in the paid labour market may preclude her from an appreciation of her own marketability.'[72] Trebilcock and Keshvani suggest that some of these problems could be overcome by ex ante procedural safeguards such as disclosure, independent legal advice requirements, and provision for cooling-off periods. Their proposals for dealing with events which could not have been foreseen when the contract was made are not altogether clear. However, because of their support for the clean-break principle, they propose limits on the power of courts to re-open pre-nuptial or separation agreements because of changes in the parties' circumstances. In the case of pre-nuptial agreements Trebilcock and Keshvani argue for judicial development of traditional contractual doctrines of frustration, mistake, and unconscionability in order to modify the terms of contracts to take account of changed circumstances, rather than giving courts broader powers to override agreements which result in unjust outcomes for one partner.[73] In the case of separation agreements they suggest that the issue of whether the contractual terms should be reopened should depend on 'considerations of who is the most efficient

71 Mnookin, supra note 7, 365, 368.

72 B. Cossman 'A Matter of Difference: Domestic Contracts and Gender Equality' (1990) 28 *Osgoode Hall LJ* 303, 325.

73 Supra note 1, 565.

risk bearer with respect to that risk, on the assumption that the risk was not foreseen at the time the contract was entered into and therefore not explicitly allocated by the contract.'[74] Under this approach, post-agreement contingencies which could be covered by insurance (such as personal injury of a spouse after divorce) would not permit the court to re-open financial provisions in a contract, but contingencies that the spouses would have provided for if they had addressed their mind to them, such as the serious injury of a child, would justify overriding the parties agreement.

The question whether courts should have power to override pre-nuptial and separation agreements, because of changes in circumstances not contemplated in the agreement, raises policy issues that Trebilcock and Keshvani do not examine in detail. First, it necessarily requires a consideration of the relationship between family law and the social security system, since a spouse who is precluded by agreement from obtaining support from the other spouse despite a change in her circumstances is likely to become dependent on social welfare. This issue is discussed in more detail below. Second, the clean-break principle does not apply to parents and children. But it is doubtful whether changes in circumstances affecting a spouse can be clearly differentiated from changes in circumstances affecting the parties' children.[75] For example, the illness of a spouse may result in a change in custody arrangements, thus making provisions for spousal support in the agreement inappropriate.

It is unsatisfactory to leave it to the courts to develop doctrines relating to the overriding of pre-nuptial and separation agreements. If private ordering is to be encouraged legislation needs to clarify when the terms of such agreements are enforceable and when they may be overridden by the courts. In my view it is more difficult to justify private ordering by pre-nuptial agreements than by separation agreements. In Australia pre-nuptial agreements cannot override family law rules, although separation agreements, if approved as proper by the Family Court, can only be set aside in a limited range of circumstances.[76] Similarly, under the New South Wales De Facto Relationships Act 1984, the court has a broader power to override agreements made by couples contemplating cohabitation, than to override separation agreements.[77]

74 Ibid. 561.
75 Wilson J recognized this in *Pelech* v. *Pelech* (1987) 7 RFL (3d) 225, 266.
76 Family Law Act 1975 (Cth) s. 87(8).
77 De Facto Relationships Act 1984 (NSW), ss 44, 49.

Pre-nuptial agreements are negotiated at a time when couples are more likely to have unrealistic expectations of each other, may be reluctant to consider the possibility of future separation, and may have considerable difficulty in predicting the changes likely to occur in the future patterns of their lives. At this stage of their relationship couples may treat procedural safeguards simply as formalities to be overcome. The statutory cooling-off period of 60 days proposed by Trebilcock and Keshvani is unlikely to lead newly married spouses to re-examine the terms of the agreement. Nor does independent legal advice or a cooling-off period address the difficulty of providing for contingencies which may not occur until many years later. Thus parties should be unable to contract out of family law rules by relying on pre-nuptial or nuptial agreements.

Procedural safeguards and cooling-off periods would be more useful for spouses negotiating separation agreements. Such agreements are negotiated when the marriage is over, so that parties are more likely to take independent legal advice seriously and to consider and negotiate for future contingencies. However, if such agreements were to be encouraged, legislation should specify the circumstances in which separation agreements could be overridden, rather than leaving this to the development of doctrine on a case-by-case basis as is occurring in the Canadian context.[78]

In my view the court should have a relatively broad power to override agreements producing unjust outcomes, because of inequalities in the parties' bargaining power or changes in their circumstances. In deciding whether an agreement should be set aside because of inequalities in the parties bargaining power, compliance with procedural safeguards, such as the fact that a party was independently advised, should be relevant but not decisive. As La Forest J commented in *Richardson* v. *Richardson*,[79] 'What we do know for certain is that many people [in the circumstances of separation] do very unwise things, things that are anything but mature and sensible, even when they consult legal counsel.' Along the lines of the Ontario Family Law Act[80] non-disclosure of significant assets by a spouse should result in the setting aside of the contract.

78 As in the *Pelech* trilogy discussed by Trebilcock and Keshvani; *Pelech* v. *Pelech* (1987) 7 RFL (3d) 225 (SCC); *Richardson* v. *Richardson* (1987) 7 RFL (3d) 304 (SCC); *Caron* v. *Caron* (1987) 7 RFL (3d) 275; see also *Linton* v. *Linton* (1990) 75 DLR (4th) 637 (Ont. CA). The cases are discussed in C.J. Rogerson 'The Causal Connection Test in Spousal Support Law' (1989) 8 *Can. J. of Fam. Law* 95.

79 (1987) 7 RFL (3d) 304, 322.

80 Family Law Act 1986 (Ont.) s. 56(4).

In the case of events occurring after the agreement was made, matters affecting the welfare of the spouses' children (which could include a change in the circumstances of the custodial parent) should allow courts to set aside separation agreements.[81] The court should also be able to override an agreement if a party has breached its terms.[82] This would provide a useful remedy for women who face practical difficulties in enforcing the terms of separation agreements, against their husbands.[83]

I believe that the courts should also be able to disregard the terms of the agreement, where there has been a significant change in the circumstances of the party seeking its revocation, other than a change in circumstances which is entirely unrelated to the marriage. This is a more generous approach than that taken by Canadian courts in the *Pelech* trilogy of cases under which a spouse seeking to override a settlement agreement must show 'a radical change in circumstances' generating needs which are causally connected to the marriage relationship.

Canadian courts appear to have interpreted the causal connection requirement very restrictively.[84] As Canadian commentators have pointed out,[85] this approach has seriously disadvantaged older women whose earning capacity has been affected by interruptions to their workforce participation. Under my proposal the onus would be on the spouse relying on the agreement to show that the other spouse's financial difficulty was *unrelated* to the marriage, before the court could refuse to override an unfair agreement. This approach is justified since women's weaker economic position, both in the paid workforce and in the domestic context, has historically been directly related to their responsibility for housework and child care.

Trebilcock and Keshvani would oppose such a broad power to set aside agreements on the ground that it is inconsistent with the clean-break principle and encourages reliance on court-imposed solutions rather than private ordering. They argue that it is more satisfactory to

81 Cf. Family Law Act 1975 (Cth) s. 79A, which allows property orders to be changed on these grounds. Agreements dealing with child support should always be capable of variation.

82 Cf. Family Law Act 1975 (Cth) s. 79A(1)(c).

83 Cf. *McVeetors* v. *McVeetors* (1985) 49 OR (2d) 225.

84 See, for example, the dissenting judgment of La Forest J in *Richardson* v. *Richardson* (1987) 7 RFL (3d) 304, 324 where the wife's employability had been affected by her spending time out of the workforce caring for children.

85 See, for example, Cossman, supra note 72, 303; C.J. Rogerson 'The Causal Connection Test in Spousal Support Law' (1989) 8 *Can. J. of Fam. Law* 95.

resolve the difficulties faced by women who cannot support themselves after marriage breakdown by altering the family law rules which form the background to parties' negotiations, than by permitting courts to override private agreements.[86] For the reasons discussed below, I am sceptical whether changes in family law rules, which take account of opportunity costs, will prevent women from entering into unfair contracts, even in the presence of procedural safeguards. In the remainder of this section I argue that systemic gender equality will not be resolved by an emphasis on private ordering which treats equality as sameness and ignores the different circumstances of men's and women's lives.

Neoclassical economic theory has frequently been criticised on the ground that, in the absence of factors such as fraud or unconscionability, which vitiate particular transactions, it is assumed that all individuals can make equally free and autonomous choices. This approach perpetuates inequality by ignoring the social and economic factors which constrain individuals' choices. Trebilcock and Keshvani's approach is based on the view that taking account of differences in the bargaining situation of men and women perpetuates women's social subordination. Thus they fail to consider whether women's inferior social and economic position itself constrains their ability to enter into contracts which make them better off in economic terms. In Brenda Cossman's words:

> [T]he focus of the approach is on the importance of the values of individual responsibility and freedom of contract, values which applied equally to women and men. The assumption underlying this approach is that, for the purposes of the enforcement of separation agreements, women are the same as men. They are presumed to be the same in entering into such agreements and in the situations giving rise to enforcement disputes. Therefore, in accordance with the sameness approach, women must be treated the same as men, and the same gender-neutral universal principles of individual responsibility and freedom of choice must be applied, irrespective of gender.[87]

It is the very adoption of the sameness approach to gender equality in this context that can be seen to silence the question of gender equality.

86 Supra note 1, 567–70.
87 Cossman, supra note 72, 303, 316.

Market theory assumes that individuals express preferences which reflect their own interests.[88] Some commentators have suggested that women are more likely than men to express preferences which further the interests of others. Self-sacrifice is often seen as a quintessentially 'feminine' virtue.[89] If this is the case, greater emphasis on private ordering may exacerbate, rather than reduce, gender inequality. The work of the psychologist Carol Gilligan also suggests that men and women bring different values to conflict resolution.[90] Gilligan's research shows that men tend to emphasize individual rights and personal autonomy when resolving moral dilemmas, while women place greater emphasis on cooperation, caring, and the preservation of relationships.

For men, the moral imperative is perceived as 'an injunction to respect the rights of others and thus to protect from interference the rights to life and self-fulfilment.'[91] For women, however, the moral imperative is perceived as "an injunction to care, a responsibility to discern and alleviate"[92] pain and trouble. Moral dilemmas for women are not cast as a conflict of conflicting rights in which one must exercise one's rights without interfering with the rights of others. Rather, women perceive moral dilemmas in terms of conflicting responsibilities.[93]

Such differences may not be innate but rather the product of women's socialization. Moreover generalizations about women's cooperativeness and men's emphasis on rights provide little guidance about how particular individuals will behave. But if, because of social conditioning, these attributes are not equally distributed between men and women, private ordering may increase women's vulnerability to exploitation. A recent article by Professor Carol Rose[94] uses insights from game theory to explore the reasons why women in bargaining situations may end up worse off than men and, in some cases, worse off

88 R. West 'The Difference in Women's Hedonic Lives: A Phenomenological Critique of Feminist Legal Theory' (1987) 3 *Wis. Women's LJ* 81. For further discussion of this issue see Wiegers, supra note 2, 193.

89 Except perhaps in the context of patriotism.

90 C. Gilligan *In a Different Voice: Psychological Theory and Women's Development* (Cambridge: Harvard University Press) 1982. See also Wiegers, supra note 2, 191; R. West 'Jurisprudence and Gender' (1988) 55 *U. of Chi. LR* 1.

91 C. Gilligan *In A Different Voice: Psychological Theory and Women's Development* (Cambridge: Harvard University Press 1982) 100.

92 Ibid.

93 Cossman, supra note 72, 302, 342.

94 C.M. Rose 'Women and Property: Gaining and Losing Ground' (1992) 78 *Va LR* 421.

than they themselves would have been if they had not entered into such agreements. Rose examines the outcomes of employment contracts and domestic agreements on the assumption that (a) women tend to have a greater taste for cooperation than men (Gilligan's theory) or (b) men believe women to have a greater taste for cooperation, whether or not this is actually the case.

Although it is difficult to do justice to Rose's sophisticated analysis, I will attempt to describe it briefly. If the first assumption is correct Rose shows that in a zero-sum game[95] a person with a greater taste for cooperation will inevitably end up worse off because he or she will be prepared to pay a higher price to induce the less cooperative party to enter into the agreement or to abide by its terms. For instance, suppose that wives, in general, tend to place a higher value on the maintenance of an amicable relationship with their former spouse and his relatives than husbands, in general, place on maintaining a continuing relationship with their wives. In this situation wives will be more likely than husbands to 'trade off' matrimonial property or spouse maintenance in order to achieve this goal and will tend to do less well financially as a result. Some support for this hypothesis is supported by Lenore Weitzman's findings. Weitzman found that women generally had a lower tolerance for conflict and were more risk averse than men. Moreover, 'women saw "giving in" on monetary issues as a means of maintaining a relationship with their former husbands, or with his family, or between him and his children.'[96]

Even more interestingly, Rose argues that the same result may follow *even if* the propensity to behave cooperatively is equally distributed between men and women, *but* it is generally believed that women place a higher value than men on cooperative behaviour.[97] Again the argument can be illustrated in the context of marital separation. Suppose that most men assume that women will usually take a smaller share of matrimonial property in order to avoid conflict, or in return for retaining custody of the children. Wives who challenge this assumption will be perceived as acting unreasonably (in comparison with other women) by their husbands, who may take a tougher bargaining posi-

95 A zero-sum game is a game in which a gain secured by one party necessarily results in a loss to the other. Division of property on divorce is normally a zero-sum game rather than a positive-sum game in which cooperation may result in gains for both parties. It is arguable that custody and access arrangements could be positive-sum games. This is discussed in considerable detail by Rose, supra note 94.

96 Weitzman, supra note 13, 313.

97 Rose, supra note 94, 439ff.

tion as a result. They may also be perceived as acting unreasonably by their own legal advisers, who will be influenced by their perception of the 'normal' women's conduct.

Rather than singlehandedly challenging assumptions about the approach which women generally take in these situations,[98] a particular woman may feel pressured to accept a smaller share of the matrimonial property, thus reinforcing the belief that all women are prepared to make such trade-offs. In other words, the effect of the assumption that women are more cooperative than men may be to make them behave more cooperatively.

Rose's discussion of game theory seeks to explain why women as a group do less well than men when negotiating agreements in the paid labour market and in the domestic context. However, she also attempts to explain why some women make agreements under which they are worse off *in absolute terms.* Women are more likely than men to be responsible for caring for children and other family members. Gilligan's work suggests they place a high priority on protecting those in positions of vulnerability and dependence. Rose argues that women may enter agreements under which they are worse off financially in order to protect third parties who can be used as 'hostages' in the bargaining process.[99] Although it is not possible to obtain reliable figures on the extent of domestic violence, women are physically abused in a relatively high proportion of marriages.[100] Violence sometimes continues even after separation and divorce. Women who fear

98 This is an example of the phenomenon of the adaptive preference. See C. Sunstein 'Legal Interference with Private Preferences' (1986) 53 *U. of Chi. LR* 1129, 1146ff.

99 Rose, supra note 94, 447.

100 Family violence has a significant impact on the lives of women. Historically husbands had a legal right to physically chastise their wives. See R. Graycar and J. Morgan *The Hidden Gender of Law* (Leichhardt, New South Wales: The Federation Press 1990) 115. In most common law jurisdictions rape in marriage has only been recognized as a criminal offence in the past decade. See G. Geis 'Rape in Marriage: Law and Law Reform in England, the United States and Sweden' (1978) 6 *Adelaide LR* 284. The extent of domestic violence is difficult to ascertain, but is generally agreed to be a significant problem. See, for example, Women's Policy Co-Ordination Unit, Department of Premier and Cabinet *Criminal Assault in the Home: Social and Legal Responses to Domestic Violence* (Victorian Government Printer 1985) 7–9; Report of the Queensland Domestic Violence Task Force, *Beyond These Walls* (Brisbane 1988) 42–6. Ingleby examined 60 solicitors' divorce files. Twenty-eight of 60 files reported the existence of violence. Ingleby, supra note 67, 9–10. In all but five of the twenty-eight cases it was the survivor rather than the perpetrator of violence who left the home. Physical abuse of husbands by their wives seems to be very rare.

violence from their husbands may bargain away their financial rights in order to protect themselves and their children. It is doubtful whether contractual doctrines dealing with duress can provide practical protection in these circumstances, for women in this situation are often too frightened and powerless to seek to have agreements set aside.

Even where there is no question of physical harm, women may still sacrifice their financial interests in order to retain custody of their children. A third of the divorced women in Weitzman's sample reported their husbands had used threats about custody as ploys in financial negotiations. She commented that:

> Men see custody as part of a total package of divorce issues that are, to some extent, "all up for grabs." Women, by contrast, draw a line when it comes to custody. They are more likely to consider custody on an altogether different level – it is something they simply cannot negotiate about because it is too important – it is worth any price. Since women attach such great importance to their children, they are not only willing to give up financial benefits for custody, they are also willing to lose a great deal just to avoid even the *risk* of losing the children.[101]

Most jurisdictions do not permit parties to make agreements which exclude the jurisdiction of the court to determine issues of custody, access, and child support. Trebilcock and Keshvani contemplate that spouses' agreements could deal with such issues 'subject to a judicial override to ensure that private agreements do not entail custody, support or visitation arrangements that violate the established minimum standards for protecting children from neglect or abuse that the State imposes on all families (an unfitness test).'[102] The use of children as 'bargaining chips' apparently occurs whether or not custody, access, or child maintenance are formally included within separation agreements. Women are often financially disadvantaged in this process. Trebilcock and Keshvani's proposal legitimizes this disadvantage.

A possible response to this objection is that if women wish to 'trade off' custody and access against their financial interests they should be free to do so. Quite apart from the concern that this approach commodifies children,[103] it overlooks the fact that custody, child support, and access are not rights conferred on parents for their own benefit. Even

101 Weitzman, supra note 13, 511–2.

102 Supra note 1, 559.

103 For discussion of the commodification objection see Wiegers, supra note 2, 170, 173; see also Radin, supra note 49.

in cases not involving neglect or abuse there may be strong reasons for finding that one parent, rather than the other, should take responsibility for caring for children. In many jurisdictions children have the right to separate legal representation to ensure that their interests, as opposed to those of their parents, are adequately protected. Similarly, older children have the right to express views on custody and access arrangements. Trebilcock and Keshvani's proposal treats parents and children as if their interests are identical.

Oddly, for law and economics scholars, Trebilcock and Keshvani also fail to examine the question of externalities in detail.[104] Family law is inextricably intertwined with issues of social welfare. The rise in divorce which has occurred in most Western countries over the past three decades has been accompanied by a rise in the numbers of women and families headed by women who are living in poverty.[105] The clean-break principle, with its emphasis on 'one-off' settlements rather than on continuing provision for dependent spouses, has freed men from the continuing costs of supporting ex-wives and children but has resulted in a huge increase in the number of women caring for children who are reliant on social security payments as their main source of income.[106]

If private ordering is to be encouraged, the question is whether the state, or the family, should bear primary responsibility for supporting women whose earning capacity has been affected by child-rearing. For example, if spouses can regulate property division and support obligations in pre-marital agreements, should spouses be able to arrange their affairs so that some of these costs are transferred to the social security system, or should they be obliged to meet externally imposed standards in order to limit welfare expenditure? It is also necessary to determine the approach which should be taken to the provision of public support if a spouse fails to comply with the terms of the agreement and whether the state should introduce special mechanisms (not

104 Brief mention is made of the issue at 563 where the authors comment that: 'By itself, the public charge argument cannot provide sufficient justification to overturn the terms of an otherwise valid and enforceable agreement.'

105 See S.B. Kamerman 'Women, Children and Poverty: Public Policies and Female-Headed Families in Industrialised Countries' (1984) 10 *Signs* 249.

106 In Australia sole parents of children under 16 may be eligible for a means-tested social welfare payment (the sole parent's pension). Of sole-parent pensioners 95 per cent are women (though male sole parents are eligible); 81 per cent of sole-parent pensioners were previously married or living in a marriage-like relationship. Department of Social Security *Annual Report* 1990–91 (Australian Government Publishing Service 1991) 305–6, 317.

applicable to other forms of contract) for enforcing private obligations.

In Australia, recent amendments to the Family Law Act and to social security legislation reflect the view that the family, rather than the state, should take primary responsibility for the costs of marriage breakdown.[107] Such provisions reflect a weakening of commitment to the principle of 'clean break.' Although Trebilcock and Keshvani argue that family law rules should recognize women's opportunity costs, they do not explain why parties should be able to make agreements which throw such costs on to the social welfare. As yet there is little social agreement on the extent to which the state, as opposed to individual men, should be required to support former spouses and children, although some expansion of state responsibility is a logical consequence of the clean-break principle. Policy-makers need to determine the appropriate mix of public and private provision for dependent spouses and children and the role which private agreements can play in achieving this mix.

My final comments go to the heart of Trebilcock and Keshvani's claims that private ordering resolves the 'dilemma of difference.' Feminist theorists have argued that the public/private dichotomy is an important source of women's oppression.[108] Historically women have been disadvantaged by the reluctance of the law to intervene in the private realm of the family to protect women against physical violence and economic exploitation.

Neoclassical economic theory constructs the market as part of the private sphere, where individual choice can be freely exercised. Thus Trebilcock and Keshvani argue that private ordering treats women as autonomous individuals 'free to bargain and enjoy all the rights and freedoms previously held only by men.'[109] But private ordering can also be seen as relegating matrimonial property disputes to the sanctity of the family, where they can be treated as conflicts between particular individuals rather than as disputes raising broader questions about the distribution of power between men and women. As Cossman puts it,

107 Family Law Amendment Act 1987 (Cth); Social Security and Veteran's Entitlements (Maintenance Income Test) Amendment Act 1988.

108 See, for example, C. Pateman *The Discourse of Women* (1989) 118; K. O'Donovan *Sexual Divisions in Law* (London: Weidenfeld and Nicholson 1985) xi. For a discussion of the ambiguities in the public/private dichotomy, see F.E. Olsen 'The Family and the Market: A Study of Ideology and Legal Reform' (1983) 96 *Harv. LR* 1497.

109 Supra note 1, 540.

'The vision that emerges is that if contracts are private, and the family is private, then family contracts must be quintessentially private' and beyond the legitimate sphere of state interest.[110]

Feminist theorists insist that 'the personal is political.' Thus they are wary of proposed resolutions of the 'dilemma of difference' which particularize and privatize conflicts between men and women. In their view private ordering conceals the sexual politics inherent in social arrangements affecting the rules of men and women, thus upholding the status quo. Trebilcock and Keshvani suggest that private ordering allows couples to take account of the circumstances of their particular marriage. In response I suggest that all women, regardless of their circumstances, are affected by gender inequality which includes, but is not confined to, economic inequality.

According to Trebilcock and Keshvani, men and women inhabit a world in which they are equally free, autonomous, and self-interested. Thus decisions made by women to 'trade off' property and spousal maintenance against personal security or the welfare of their children are regarded as autonomous choices. Trebilcock and Keshvani treat individual preferences as emanating from rational thought processes, rather than as wholly or partially conditioned responses to social circumstances. By contrast, I argue that the decisions made by men and women entering into private agreements are inevitably shaped by their social circumstances, including their relative power or powerlessness.

Critics of law and economics have identified the phenomenon of the adaptive preference.[111] Although women have now achieved formal equality with men, they are still unequal in social, economic, and political terms. To reduce cognitive dissonance, those who feel powerless to change their situation tend to express their choices in terms of what they believe they can reasonably expect to get.[112]

Until recently, many legal systems did not recognize the claims of 'home-maker' spouses to any share in their spouse's property. Hence, it is not surprising that women involved in negotiating agreements often have a modest view of their entitlements. As Weitzman comments:

> [M]en and women commonly express differing conceptions of their own entitlement to money and property. Women, especially those who have been

110 Cossman, supra note 72, 338.

111 Sunstein 'Legal Interference with Private Preferences' supra note 50, 1146ff; West, supra note 50, 674–5.

112 D. Rhode 'The "No-Problem" Problem: Feminist Challenges and Cultural Change' (1991) 100 *Yale LJ* 1731.

housewives and mothers throughout marriage, are likely to devalue their entitlement to support, even if it is child support, and their right to share the assets of the marriage. Community property laws notwithstanding, many divorcing women still see the money their husbands have earned as 'his money' and do not feel entitled to it (especially if she is the one who initiated the divorce). In this way women discount their own contributions to marriage and the uncompensated services they provide to make it possible for husbands to earn money.[113]

Improvements in the position of women, including changes to matrimonial property laws which recognize women's contributions to the marriage partnership, may eventually raise women's perceptions of their entitlements. But in the meantime greater emphasis on private ordering may simply maintain women's comparative disadvantage. The ability of courts to override the terms of pre-nuptial and separation agreements may be an important part of the process by which women are given a wider range of choices.

IV *Conclusion*

Trebilcock and Keshvani contend that law and economics scholarship can resolve the 'dilemma of difference' confronted by feminist scholars when they examine reforms to matrimonial property division and support rules. With some reservations I agree that compensation based on opportunity costs incurred during interruption to paid workforce participation will improve the situation of women in the short term, without necessarily entrenching breadwinner/dependent spouse relationships.

I am more sceptical of the view that women will benefit by law reforms which place greater emphasis on pre-marital and separation agreements. Richard Ingleby's work on the role of solicitors in matrimonial disputes has shown that legal rules are filtered through negotiation processes which parties may have different emotional and financial capacities to withstand.[114] I have argued that support for private ordering treats men and women 'the same,' thus ignoring the social and economic factors which constrain women's choices.

113 Weitzman, supra note 13, 315–6.
114 Ingleby, supra note 67.

Catharine MacKinnon[115] has argued that questions of sameness and difference are really questions about political and social power. To paraphrase Cass Sunstein, 'the question of equality is not whether there are "differences" between [men and women] but is instead what sort of political and social difference the difference makes.'[116] Our current social system disadvantages women by forcing them to choose between two equally undesirable alternatives. On the one hand women may choose to behave the same as men, in which case they must compete with men on terms which men have defined. On the other hand they may choose to be 'different' from men by putting child care ahead of career success and financial self-sufficiency. Increasing numbers of women are now attempting to have the best (or worst) of both worlds, while most men are not required to make similar choices.

The 'dilemma of difference' is a dilemma constructed by the social world in which men and women live. Privatization of the economic consequences of the sexual division of labour will not resolve the issue of gender inequality. Rather, the challenge is to transform social structures so that wage-earning can be combined with the essential work of caring for children. Such changes have the potential to liberate men as well as women.

115 C.A. MacKinnon *Feminism Unmodified* (1987) chapter 2; see also E.C.D. Bois, M.C. Dunlop, C.J. Gilligan, C.A. MacKinnon, C.J. Menkel-Meadow 'Feminist Discourse, Moral Values and the Law – A Conversation' (1985–86) *Buffalo LR* 11, 20–1.

116 C.R. Sunstein *Feminism and Political Theory* (Chicago: University of Chicago Press 1990) 6.

[15]

Narratives of divorce

Shelley Day Sclater

Department of Human Relations, University of East London, Dagenham

Abstract: *Divorce is usually traumatic, and the processes involved are almost certainly more complex than current images allow. In this paper, I explore some of the complexities and ambiguities of divorce. These are illustrated with reference to the personal accounts of three divorcing women, produced during in-depth, unstructured interviews, and subjected to narrative analysis. The discussion suggests that we need to look more comprehensively at services for divorcing people and that mediation, as currently envisaged within the provisions of the Family Law Act (1996), pays insufficient attention to the needs of people to make sense of the past. It is suggested that some degree of conflict and polarization may serve a positive psychological function, in enabling a divorcing person to move forward autonomously into the future. Recognition of the emotional content of divorce, however, should be achieved without 'pathologizing' either the experience, the individual or the emotions.*

Keywords: divorce, narrative, litigation, mediation, psychology, adjustment

Introduction

The experience of separation and divorce is almost always traumatic. Numerous research studies over the last thirty years suggest that divorcing people are more likely than those who stay married to succumb to a variety of physical ailments and psychological distress (see, e.g., Riessman and Gerstel, 1985; Gove and Sin, 1989; Booth and Amato, 1991; Bruce and Kim, 1992), although the direction of causation is problematic (Elliott, 1993). The provisions of the Family Law Act, 1996, recognize that the emotional costs of divorce (as well as the financial ones) may be too high. The White Paper (1995) stated that:

> The social, economic and emotional costs are considerable. Apart from the grief to the couple, there is clear evidence that children suffer greatly . . .
>
> (White Paper, 1995: para. 1.9)

However, there is a marked tendency to attribute these high emotional costs, in large part, to the adversarial process by which divorce currently is conducted. The Act, in removing 'fault' and in encouraging mediation over lawyer-led negotiation and litigation, seeks to reduce conflict, to minimize bitterness, to promote co-operation and to encourage future amicable relations between the parties.

Adopting a psycho-dynamic view of the divorce process, I have argued elsewhere (Day Sclater and Richards, 1995) that the reforms may flounder in so far as they overlook the psychological realities of divorce. It may be, as Vaughan (1987) has argued, that a degree of conflict, polarization and imputation of blame is necessary for a true psychological separation from the former partner to be achieved, and a new 'self' established. Thus, it may be that the new law embodies too simplistic a view of psychology. In particular, it does not address the need to revisit the past which divorcing people seem to have, in order to make sense of their experience. 'Looking to the future' may not be possible without first looking back, and the emotions associated with divorce are likely to continue to demand expression.

The aim of this paper is to explore these controversial aspects of the divorce process and I use extracts from the personal accounts of three divorced women to illustrate these points.[1]

Divorce: 'adjustment' or interpretive process?

The traditional approach to the psychology of divorce sees it as a process of 'adjustment' during which the individual gradually comes to terms with 'loss' and adapts to the change. The process of adjustment is seen as having a number of interrelated dimensions (Kaslow and Schwartz, 1987; Kressel, 1985) and in terms of a series of linked 'stages' (Bohannon, 1971; Wiseman, 1975; Chicanola, 1978; Golan, 1981; Ahrons and Rodgers, 1987; Robinson, 1991), although the details and the timing of the various phases vary between studies.

The literature points to a recognition of the 'multiple consequences' of divorce (Kitson and Morgan, 1990), in terms of physical (Riessman and Gerstel, 1985; Elliott, 1993) and mental (Bloom *et al.*, 1978) health. Psychosomatic disorders are common (Bloom *et al.*, 1978). Divorce also frequently has adverse economic consequences, particularly for women (Weitzman, 1985; Maclean, 1991) and adverse social consequences, in terms of changing relationships with friends and family (Weiss, 1975), in relationships with the opposite sex (Arendell, 1986, 1995) and in disruptions at work (Cherlin, 1979, 1981). But although divorce can be acutely emotionally painful in the short term (Spanier and Casto, 1979; Albrecht, 1980; Hetherington, 1989), only a small minority seem to suffer significantly in the longer term (Bloom *et al.*, 1978; Johnston and Campbell, 1988). The well-being of the vast majority improves steadily over a two-to-three-year period (Kelly, 1982), a new 'self' is built (Bohannon, 1971; Weiss, 1975; Vaughan, 1987), and some people emerge as psychologically stronger and as enhanced by having successfully met the challenge; divorce for them offers a new chance to begin again (Kelly, 1982).

Thus, the traditional approach characterizes divorce as a problem of individual adjustment; in doing so it relies on scientific quantification of 'inner states'. In this process, the personal meanings which people bring to bear in making sense of their experiences are overlooked.

However, in recent years, orthodoxy in psychology has increasingly come under critical scrutiny. Those who advocate alternative approaches (see, e.g., Henriques *et al.*, 1984; Potter and Wetherell, 1987; Burman, 1994) have challenged the fundamental *raison d'être* of traditional positivist approaches, namely the very possibility of objectivity in psychological research. On the critical view, objectivity itself appears as a particular mode of representation and as a rhetorical achievement; it is seen, not as permitting privileged access to a pre-existing reality, but as based on social conventions which are realized through particular narrative strategies in which the voice of the empirical researcher commands authority (Mishler, 1991).

The traditional approach (for example, the measurement of 'symptoms' associated with marital breakdown) decontextualizes people's experiences, and personal meanings may be ignored. In other words, the emphasis on objectivity 'eclipses essential information about process' (Riessman, 1991). By contrast, the adoption of a narrative approach allows us to reconceptualize the human subject as a narrator, and interview data is treated as text to be interpreted. Language is no longer assumed to be a transparent vehicle for communicating information (Sandelowski, 1991).

Over the last ten years, an increasing number of researchers in both sociology and psychology have emphasized the 'narrative' nature of human experience (Mishler, 1991) and have advocated a narrative approach as a way of overcoming the limitations of more traditional approaches (White, 1980; Bruner, 1987; Sandelowski, 1991). Mishler (1986) advocates 'treating respondents' answers to questions as stories or narratives, whose meanings may be understood by applying methods of narrative analysis' (p. 234). Sarbin (1986) proposes that 'human beings think, perceive, imagine and make moral choices according to narrative structures' (p. 8). For him, narrative is 'an organising principle of human action' (p. 9).

But the narrative approach is not just a methodological development in the social sciences; rather, it depends also on theoretical formulations which attempt to overcome the old dualisms that separate the 'individual' from 'society' and tries instead to locate 'the self' as a psycho-social phenomenon. According to Giddens (1991), the self-identity of late modernity is the self reflexively understood by the individual in terms of her or his biography, a process which is fundamentally embedded in human relationships. Gergen and Gergen (1983) demonstrate how 'the self' is produced in the process of narrative accounting and Crites (1986) argues that 'to become "a self" is to appropriate the past' (p. 164). According to Mishler (1991), constructing a personal narrative is a critical factor in the establishment and formation of one's identity; through telling one's story, one's experiences can be made coherent and meaningful, and particular identities can be constructed and claimed.

According to Sandelowski (1991), narrative representations of experiences do more than simply re-present those experiences; rather, lives are reconstructed in every act of telling: '[Narrative] studies illustrate how lives can be understood, revealed and transformed *in stories* and *by the very act of story-telling*' (p. 163, italics in original).

Narratives, therefore, are seen as constitutive of reality, rather than as mirroring it:

> In addition to representing the world, being a way to tell a listener 'what happened', narratives are also modes of persuasion, that is, rhetorical strategies that provide a believable explanation for the teller's actions in the light of what happened. Meaning is accomplished interactionally, between teller and listener.
>
> (Riessman, 1991: 45)

A narrative approach thus permits an exploration of individual/social relations and of the ways in which subjectivities are discursively constructed. In the narrative approach to divorce, the sociology of divorce overlaps with the psychology, but neither 'the social' (being the subject matter of traditional sociology), nor 'the individual' (being that of traditional psychology), appear as primary or as privileged, one over the other. Rather, both are reconstituted in relation to each other, in a realm which is neither that of society outside, nor that of personality characteristics inside, but is psycho-social. A narrative approach permits what Rosenwald and Ochberg (1992) call a 'cultural politics of self understanding', where material social conditions and practices interweave with subjectively experienced desires and identities, as people make choices and pursue futures within the range of options available to them.

The complexities and ambiguities of divorce

In what follows, I draw examples from the narrative analysis of the interview transcripts of three divorcing women, to reveal some of the complexities and ambiguities of divorce which it is difficult to discern from more traditional research. A narrative approach, which focuses specifically on how people interpret and make sense of their lives by constructing personal meanings around their experiences, reveals that the stories they tell are not all doom and gloom, as popular images of divorce would lead us to believe. Rather, they can be stories about divorce as a positive and transformative experience; divorce may be (and usually is) emotionally painful, but going through pain can have empowering consequences. However, for this transformative potential to be realized requires that people have the opportunity to piece together their own stories, and that conflicts and polarizations be allowed to emerge so that they can be worked through and integrated into the life history.

In all the women I interviewed, divorce stories appear as part of an ongoing interpretive process, as people strive to make sense of what went wrong in the past, and of what the future might hold for them. In this process, the past of the marriage is revisited and reinterpreted, before it can be left behind and the future faced. Like Riessman (1990, 1991), I found that narrative accounting predominates when people are asked about their experiences of divorce;

people seem to choose this form of representation if given the chance. Analysis of the interview transcripts reveals that divorce is not just a simple process of psychological 'adjustment', and that understanding divorce in terms of a series of more or less well-defined 'stages' may be an over-simplification. There seems to be much more to divorce, psychologically speaking, than coming to terms with 'loss', and the processes involved may usefully be seen in terms of interpretation and reinterpretation, of construction and reconstruction of self, as the subject searches for personal meanings to make a coherent story about what has happened to them.

The participants in my study willingly told their divorce stories. In all cases they recounted a history of the marriage, trying to make sense of what had happened, by constructing a plausible account of the past from the vantage point of the present. The stories also served a rhetorical function; tellings involved the use of literary and linguistic devices which have the effect of drawing the listener into the teller's world, and persuading the listener that the teller's feelings and experiences are comprehensible. It is clear from the interviews that participants felt the need to tell their story of the marriage, of the past, to render the fact of the divorce intelligible.

In all cases, the stories involve a tension between past and present, between the marriage and the divorce, between the self-that-was and the self-that-now-is, which often is expressed metaphorically. The resolution of this tension provides the motor force of the story.

In this interpretive process, new forms of subjectivity are constructed and made available to be claimed. These new subjectivities depend, in large part, on a changing consciousness of the past, and of the subject's own part in it, in which the 'naming' of experience (Riessman, 1992), often through metaphor, appears as significant. Here, history, memory and narrative (Freeman, 1993) interact and recombine in an ongoing process of reinterpretation, from the vantage point of the present.

The 'naming' of experience, which can facilitate a changing subjectivity, may be achieved in relations of opposition; opposition in time (the past versus the present and the future), and opposition in relationships (the husband versus the wife, the self versus the other). A revisiting of the past, and a degree of conflict and polarization appear to be intrinsic parts of the way in which people experience and make sense of the breakdown of their marriage.

In Jane's case, the story of her divorce is built around the metaphor of a 'bubble that burst', which expresses what her story is about. The metaphor condenses and embodies a contradiction between, on the one hand, an idealized image of marriage as a source of happiness and personal fulfilment (with which Jane began her married life) and, on the other hand, the failure of her marriage to realize those expectations in practice, which result in divorce (which is where Jane now is).

In the following extract, Jane is talking about the difficulties which ensued in her marriage to Ed after the birth of her first child:

Jane: and I think looking back now
in hindsight
I think I can see
that actually what happened was
I was pinning all my hopes on my marriage
being kind of fulfilled
and, you know,
actually it just made everything worse
rather than better
it just created more tension
between Ed and I
and it was all just a big bubble that burst
once she was born
and I'd got into the routine
of having a baby, you know,
it was really a [*p*]
you know [*p*]
a disaster

Towards the end of her narrative, Jane invokes the metaphor once again. In the following extract, she is talking about how she understands Ed's view of the divorce. She is highlighting the transformation in Ed from good father and perfect family man (during the marriage) to someone who refuses financially to support her and the children, and who has less and less contact with the children (after the divorce):

Jane: It's almost
as if, you know,
he had this kind of idyllic
kind of view
of what family life would be like
and when the bubble was burst
he just washed his hands of it.
'OK, families are crap
I don't want anything
to do with it,
forget it' [*p*] you know,
it's almost
like he had
that kind of changing attitude

Again the 'bubble' is the ideal marriage and family which was not realized in Jane and Ed's case, and, to Jane, it seems that Ed was unable to contemplate familial responsibilities outside of the traditional family.

These brief extracts show Jane, as a divorcing woman, revisiting the past and reinterpreting her marriage in response to the interviewer's question to 'tell me about your divorce'. They also show something about how the rhetorical functions of narration are achieved; Jane, like other participants, sometimes re-lived specific episodes in an animated way, indicated in the transcript by her use of dramatized speech, drawing the listener into the world the subject is trying to portray. The past is not just left behind, but is revisited and reinterpreted, from the standpoint of the present. These reinterpretations form a basis from which the future may be contemplated.

For Jane, the interpretive process in which she experiences the events of her divorce, and the meanings she constructs within it, are inseparable from her understanding of herself and her needs for personal fulfilment and development. Divorce, for Jane, was an acutely painful experience, but it was also a transformative one, whose positive aspects were linked to her own determination to fulfil her own personal potentials.

In telling her story, Jane draws on wider social discourses about the gender relations of modern marriage. These interact in complex ways with her personal biography and her individual needs, and the availability of alternative discourses offer Jane a range of subject positions (Davies and Harre, 1990) from which she is able to articulate her discontents and envisage a different future and a different subjectivity for herself than that which was offered by the traditional discourse of the ideal marriage. Through an interpretive process, Jane is able to articulate her divorce as personally transformative.

Nina's transcript illustrates how this transformative potential may be realized in the process of narrative accounting. That narrators' stories can themselves be transformative has been remarked on by Bell (1988) in relation to women whose mothers took diethylstilbestrol (DES) during pregnancy, rendering their daughters at risk of cancer, and by Riessman (1992) in relation to a woman who suffered physical and sexual abuse in her marriage.

In my study, a vivid example of a personal transformation occurred in Nina's case. In her story, Nina revisited and reinterpreted her marriage to Harry from the vantage point of someone who was married for twenty years but who now steps into the future alone. In telling her story, Nina creates, and then casts aside, a self which is a 'victim' and replaces it with one which is a survivor. In the following extract, Nina is looking back to a time when she felt she had reached a point of desperation. She concludes the episode by 'naming' herself as a victim, thus paving the way for a new identity as a 'survivor':

> Nina: in the end
> I was very, very beaten down
> worn down
> brutalized
> not too [*unclear*]
> but brutalized
> I was anorexic
> and I was completely traumatized [*p*] ummm
> but there wasn't really any help
> I had to slowly
> put myself together
> and say to myself
> 'you have been *victimized*'
> 'you can't go on
> being a yes-man for this guy'

The point at which Nina identifies herself as a victim is the point at which she begins to free herself from Harry's power to position her as someone to be dominated. The significance of Nina's 'naming' of herself in this way is highlighted in the language that she uses – she stands back from herself, and addresses herself in the second person: 'you have been *victimized*'. She tells herself 'you can't go on being a yes-man for this guy'. This imaginary outside authority has enabled Nina to realize that she has a choice in the matter, that 'no' is a viable alternative to 'yes'.

The transformative effect of this act of 'naming' for Nina is revealed in subsequent episodes of her narrative, where she revisits old themes, and speaks them differently. For example, Nina returns to the question of her own upbringing. Previously in her narrative she has told how her upbringing was 'oppressive' and that her family was 'without understanding'. There, Nina was something of a 'victim' of her own upbringing. After having identified herself as having been 'victimized', Nina takes a different view of her own past.

> Nina: 'I think I had
> a good stable upbringing.
> I've always tended toward depression
> and being isolated
> and introverted,
> but I had a good, stable, eighteen years'

From her new vantage point, having identified herself as a 'victim', Nina is able to articulate her strengths and to recognize the range of supports available to her.

Thus, the act of telling one's story is an interpretive process; it involves 'naming' experiences, which can have transformative consequences for consciousness and for subjectivity. Narrative accounting gives the narrator the opportunity to talk through a change in consciousness and claim a new sense of self.

Significantly, however, the process through which subjectivities are constructed is a social one and involves an opposition between past and present and between self and other. This opposition is evident throughout all of the transcripts and suggests that some form of polarization may be psychologically necessary if a viable new self is to emerge from the experience of divorce. In the process of marital breakdown, the former partner remains central and significant as the 'other' against whom the new self takes shape.

This point is illustrated by Naomi, a woman in her early forties. She was married to John for fifteen years but she left him after he committed adultery. In telling her story, Naomi interprets her experience by giving it a name: she characterizes her divorce as one in which she has had court cases 'thrown' at her by a husband who is a 'bully'. In naming the problem in this way, Naomi is marking her resistance to being positioned by the relations of domination and subjection which characterized both her marriage and her divorce. She is speaking an empowerment for herself which will carry her through the transition from dependent married woman to autonomous selfhood.

Talking about why she suggested mediation as a way of resolving a problem over John's contact with the children, Naomi explains:

> Naomi: it was because it was all over [*p*]
> dates of holidays
> and things like that
> because my ex's family are solicitors
> that any time there is a problem
> I have got a court case thrown at me
> and there was a problem over access
> and contact with the children

Naomi concludes her story thus:

> Naomi: umm, and he's a bully
> and I thought I cannot talk to this man face to face
> so I needed umm a mediator
> so that was why

'Thrown' is a powerful metaphor, and it is one which Naomi invokes several times in her narrative. It alerts the listener to conflict and to what will be revealed in the 'resolution', namely that John is a 'bully'. The metaphor signifies unequal power relations. To throw something at someone is to position them as someone to be dominated. What is thrown at Naomi is the power of John's gendered position, that of his class background, his family, their social network and the power of the formal legal process. The metaphor also signifies the distance between John and Naomi; they are separate, different. The distance is gendered, physical and psychological, and it is important to Naomi; it is the space in which her autonomous subjectivity can be constructed and claimed.

Like Jane and Nina, Naomi returns to the past and revisits her marriage in trying to make sense of her divorce. She tells how her positioning in the gender relations of a middle-class marriage made her 'dead on the inside'; she lost sight of herself and her own needs in her marriage, when she did everything that could have been expected of a wife in her position; she 'went along with everything'.

Naomi's story illustrates the difficulties that the woman narrator has in finding a language in which to articulate her experiences. For her, it is the authority of medicine which legitimates Naomi's desire to articulate her discontents, and psychotherapy helps her to find a meaningful language in which to do it. As a result, Naomi is able to position herself in relation to alternative discourses than the one through which John 'reads' her and through which she has hitherto understood herself. Conflict between them becomes inevitable, as Naomi invokes new interpretations and meanings which challenge the very foundations of her relationship with John. This challenge, and the ensuing conflict, signified by the metaphor 'thrown' very early in the narrative, are preconditions for the establishment of autonomous subjectivity in Naomi's case.

Discussion

The fundamental premise of the approach to divorce which I have adopted is that people come to know the world, and themselves, through stories. But, some qualifications are in order, as neither life nor the self is merely text. Plummer (1995) highlights the necessity of 'decentring the story'; stories are social practices which depend on joint actions (teller–listener–reader), and are located in networks of social power and activities among thinking, feeling, passionate people, living their lives in what Marx described as 'conditions not of their own making'. The meanings of stories are constructed in local contexts, as tellers, listeners and readers draw upon personal biographies, attempting to contain the restlessness of their desires by drawing upon wider cultural discourses, in intersubjective exchanges, which assist, for the moment, in negotiating meanings and closures.

The contemporary importance of 'talking divorce' has recently been illustrated by media coverage of the divorce experiences of the Prince and Princess of Wales, and of Nelson and Winnie Mandela. The divorce reforms reconstitute divorce as constructive dialogue between two people who previously have had nothing except hostilities to express to each other. Mediation falls far short of being a 'talking cure' in the psychoanalytic sense, but it is a talking cure of a kind. In all this talk, divorce leaves the world of private sorrow, and enters the public world of stories, where it intersects the current debates about the 'crisis' in 'the family'. The story of divorce is part of a political process; questions of who has the power to say what, how, where and when, can be addressed.

From such a vantage point, social practices such as the legal process and mediation can be scrutinized. Law occupies an anomalous position in relation to 'truth'; it is a curious mixture of the wholly arbitrary and the atomistically precise. The judicial process has authority to 'find' the truth, which, like a small child hiding beneath a table, taunts from the safety of its location amid a range of competing storied accounts given by plaintiffs, defendants, witnesses and so on. But there is a sense in which the 'truth' of a case, if not wholly predetermined, is at least predictable; it is circumscribed by the legal rules which permit certain stories, and not others, to be spoken. It is circumscribed in the range of permissible discourses through which such stories are heard and their meaning understood.

In family law, the legal forum brings into being a particular kind of story which often bears little relation to the personal meanings of the teller. Emotion is not a relevant issue in the legal divorce, yet the legal process does allow for the expression of conflict and difference, for the polarization of self and other, in a contained way. Both litigation and mediation circumscribe what may legitimately be said; the past cannot be revisited, and the history of the marriage is irrelevant to future arrangements. Yet, my findings show that when people are given the chance to talk about their divorce, they take the opportunity to talk instead about their marriage. It seems that revisiting and reinterpreting the marriage is a necessary precondition for making sense of the divorce. As Freeman (1993) points out, people make sense of their lives by telling stories which look back from the vantage point of the present. Memory, history and narrative become very difficult to separate, one from the other, but all are important if a coherent self is to be claimed which will allow the subject to negotiate the present and move forward into the future.

In divorce, this revisiting of the past has a significantly transformative potential. It is an opportunity to transcend old patterns and experiences by naming them, and by locating them in a framework of meaning in which a new sense of self can be constructed and claimed. In this respect, divorce stories represent a struggle, between the past and the future, between constrained and constraining social structures and individual agency and desire, as subjectivities strain to name themselves in story as autonomous, authentic, coherent and enduring.

If the legal process is productive of particular forms of divorce stories, what about mediation? Mediation advocates a language of amicable co-operation and has the aim of eliminating the polarization of the adversarial process and minimizing conflict. These are laudable aims, but recently a number of authors have begun to question whether mediation is as anodyne as it at first appears (Day Sclater, 1995a).

James (1995) points out that mediation is becoming synonymous with child welfare and that the linking of divorce with mediation may carry with it dangers which should not be ignored. He identifies the dangers in terms of a shift from justice to welfare (see also King and Piper, 1995), where welfarism may be a more covert and insidious form of social control than the overt coercion of law. In a similar vein, Harne and Radford (1994) argue that the welfarism of family law not only eclipses questions of justice in divorce, but has become synonymous with an extension of fathers' 'rights', thus undermining autonomous motherhood and reinforcing traditional notions of the father and of 'the family'. Piper (1996) is worried about the image of the child as 'victim' implicit in the new law, an image which provides the rationale behind the shift towards welfarism and mediation. Dingwall (1988) alerts us to the possibility that the implicit values and assumptions held by mediators may influence both the process and outcome of mediated agreements and Dingwall and Greatbatch (1994) ask whether, in this light, there may be some virtues in the formality of the legal process where 'the framing of the talk and its orchestration are made visible' (p. 396) and the 'talk' occurs within an explicit and visible set of rules and procedures, where the sources of power are more evident. By contrast, the power wielded by the mediator as a new breed of welfare 'expert' (James, 1990) is much less visible. Thus, there is now a range of voices in the academy which express misgivings about the assumptions upon which the new law is based. In this context, and from a psychological point of view, we might ask questions about the ways in which 'talk' and stories are produced in mediation.

One aspect of this relates to a technique called 'reframing', which mediation borrows from family therapy. Reframing is a process whereby the mediator restates something that a person has said in a different frame of reference. For example, a mother's angry assertion that she has no intention of letting her husband see the children because she thinks that he is too selfish and irresponsible to look after them (a common enough assertion in many divorces) and a father's retort that she is too neurotic to be left in sole charge of them anyway (a common enough response) may be reframed as a positive concern on the part of both the mother and the father for the children's welfare. The priority accorded to the welfare of the children in dominant divorce discourses is such that neither the mother nor the father could challenge this reframing without appearing selfish and ridiculous. In this way, 'co-operation' is facilitated in mediation.

According to Walker and Robinson (1990), reframing is a process

> through which the [mediator] positively reframes statements which are presented as accusations or demands by one partner in such a way that the content of the statement does not escalate conflict.
>
> (Walker and Robinson, 1990: 62–3)

They give an example of a conflict over contact with children, similar to the one I have given above, and they see reframing as a way of altering the potentially destructive nature of the exchange, and of breaking the unhelpful cycle, by positively connoting the concerns and abilities of both parents. In this way, the process of reframing bypasses the antagonistic feelings of the parties, and ignores the multiple meanings which may attach to the expression of their conflicting positions. Thus, reframing does not directly address the parties' apparent needs to apportion 'blame', but rather seeks to 'shift the communication to a more productive level' (p. 63). Somewhat paradoxically, this is said to facilitate the parties' abilities 'to retain control of the process' (p. 63).

However, it can be seen that reframing, like the legal process, is about managing emotions, changing the story and creating a new one. In the same way, dangers may lie if the new stories created in mediation draw solely on dominant discourses. For instance, the example of a dispute over contact with children given by Walker and Robinson (1990) draws, quite obviously, on the dominant discourse about parenting which pervades family law in its welfarist orientation. Hooper (1994) considers the limitations of this discourse and points out that academic and judicial thinking on the role of non-resident fathers has swung, over the last twenty years, from one extreme to the other; both extremes, in so far as they are turned into general arguments for all, do a disservice to children. As Piper (1996) points out, they depend on representing the child as 'victim', an image of 'the child' which sits uneasily with the possibility that the multiplicities of children's own voices will actually be heard, and with any notion of children's 'rights'.

The 'presumption' of contact in all cases leaves out of account the fact that, despite the mass of research, we simply still do not know enough about the circumstances in which contact is beneficial for children and those in which it may be harmful (Macoby and Mnookin, 1992); the evidence which we have is inconclusive, and we are unlikely to be able to do what is best for children as long as we continue to conflate their needs, or their rights, with those of their non-resident parent (Hooper, 1994). The operation of these discourses of 'parental responsibility' is what legitimates the disqualification of stories of the past (Piper, 1993; King and Piper, 1995), of old hurts, wrongs and recriminations, stories of conflict, anger and revenge, of emotion and passion, by the non-therapeutic forms of mediation which are favoured in the UK. Stories about the past and stories about conflict will not be heard, but will be transformed by the language co-operation in mediation. If my findings are indicative of any psychological need to revisit and to rewrite the past, or of the necessity for some degree of conflict and polarization to facilitate the emergence of an autonomous, post-divorce self, then the move towards mediation may have psychological consequences which the Government has not considered.

It may be that the time has come to change the way in which we think about divorce, to alter the language that we use to speak about it, and to move away from 'disaster' models which pathologize the experience for adults and children alike. Nothing short of a fundamental challenge to the dominant discourses is what is required. It is possible to acknowledge that divorce is an emotional experience, but emotions are ordinary things and do not have to carry connotations of pathology. It is only when the emotions associated with divorce are read through the framework of the dominant discourses that divorce appears as personal and social disaster. It is only through an appeal to the 'child as victim' (Piper, 1996) that emotions such as anger can be marginalized, and conflictual situations rendered inappropriate.

Yet clinical work with divorcing people shows that anger does have its place and that it is unrealistic to assume that it can be waved away by the magic wand of divorce reform. Isaacs and Leon (1988) argue that anger may serve to ward off a more immobilizing depression and make available energy to reconstruct one's life. Anger is an ordinary emotion and we should not be afraid of it. It may be that the adversarial process has served an important function, that of 'encapsulating' or 'containing' unruly emotions by allowing circumscribed forms of polarization to be worked through. It remains to be seen whether mediation can contain these emotions; if it cannot, the possibility that they will be expressed in other areas of the divorce process must be recognized. Divorcing people often feel mortally wounded by the hurt inflicted by the other. It may be that the expression of anger in these circumstances is vital if any sense of self is to be preserved.

Expressions of anger in some circumstances may be vital to the preservation of 'self' and personal integrity and dignity. Moghissi (1994), for example, writing about racism, sees anger as 'often the only dignity one has' (p. 232). For her, feeling and showing her anger was vital to preserving her sense of self. Similarly, Jordan (1989), also discussing racism, states that 'at a minimum we have the power to stop co-operating with our enemies. We have the power to stop the courtesies and to let the feelings be real' (p. 114). She questions the authority by which dominant discourses seek to marginalize expressions of anger; we might ask the same question in relation to the denial of emotion in divorce.

The implications of my argument are threefold. First, the means whereby which individuals 'adjust' to divorce should be recognized as a complex, psycho-social process in which the history of the marriage is fundamentally re-interpreted and in which some degree of conflict and polarization may be necessary for the re-establishment of an individual identity. If a new identity can be successfully re-established, divorce can be a transformative experience.

Secondly, there is a need to recognize that the feelings associated with divorce cannot be swept away simply because the law has decided that they are undesirable. Feelings will continue to demand expression and we should not be afraid of them.

Finally, there is a need to move away from pathological models which represent divorce as a disaster and in which the expression of these psychological needs is seen as inimical to 'civilized' outcomes. However, as Plummer (1995) argues, all 'stories' have their time and their place. For positive stories about divorce to be successful, there has to be a social world embodying support to receive them. In our current climate, it is a struggle to be positive about divorce when its dominant image is so negative and pathologized. Positive divorce stories may fall into that category of stories which Plummer (1995) sees as 'waiting in the wings for their time, their voice'.

Acknowledgements

I would like to thank 'Nina', 'Jane' and 'Naomi', whose stories are quoted here, and other participants in my pilot study who so generously gave of their time to share their experiences with me. I would have had considerable difficulty in setting up the project without the generous help of Celia and Suzanne. I am grateful to the University of East London for their support of my pilot project. Thanks also to Adrian James, Margaret O'Brien, Julie Jessop, Julia Farrell, and to the two anonymous reviewers for their suggestions.

Note

1 The Pilot Study, out of which this paper arises, was the first part of a larger-scale research project into the Psychology of Divorce. As a small-scale retrospective study into women's experiences of divorce, its main objective was to develop a linked theoretical framework and methodology for the larger project (Day Sclater, 1995b). In depth, unstructured interviews were conducted with eight women whose divorces had been finalized within the previous twelve months, and the transcripts were subjected to narrative analysis. A precise description of the analytic method which ultimately proved to be most fruitful is available on request from the author. For a more general introduction to narrative analysis, adapted for social scientific research, see, e.g., Riessman (1993).

References

Ahrons, C. and Rodgers, R. (1987) *Divorced Families: A Multidisciplinary Developmental View*, New York: Norton.

Albrecht, S. (1980) 'Reactions and adjustments to divorce: differences in the experiences of males and females', *Family Relations* 29: 59–68.

Arendell, T. (1986) *Mothers and Divorce*, Berkeley, CA: University of California Press.

Arendell, T. (1995) *Fathers and Divorce*, London: Sage.

Bell, S. E. (1988) 'Becoming a political woman: the reconstruction and interpretation of experience through stories', in A. Todd and S. Fisher (eds) *Gender and Discourse: The Power of Talk*, Norwood, NJ: Ablex.

Berman, W. (1985) 'Continued attachment after legal divorce', *Journal of Family Issues* 6(3): 375–92.

Bloom, B., Asher, S. and White, S. (1978) 'Marital disruption as a stressor: a review and analysis', *Psychological Bulletin* 85: 867–94.

Bohannon, P. (ed.) (1971) *Divorce and After*, New York: Anchor.

Booth, A. and Amato, P. (1991) 'Divorce and psychological stress', *Journal of Health and Social Behaviour* 32(4): 396–407.

Bruce, M. L. and Kim, L. M. (1992) 'Differences in the effects of divorce on major depression in men and women', *American Journal of Psychiatry* 149(7): 914–17.

Bruner, J. (1987) 'Life as narrative', *Social Research* 54(1): 11–32.

Burman, E. (1994) *Deconstructing Developmental Psychology*, London: Routledge.

Cherlin, A. (1979) 'Work life and marital dissolution', in G. Levinger and O. Moles (eds) *Divorce and Separation: Context, Causes and Consequences*, New York: Basic Books.

Cherlin, A. (1981) *Marriage, Divorce, Remarriage*, Cambridge, MA: Harvard University Press.

Chicanola, S. (1978) 'The process of separation and divorce: a new approach', *Social Casework* 59(8): 494–9.

Clulow, C. F. (1990) 'Divorce as bereavement: similarities and differences', *Family and Conciliation Courts Review* 28(1): 19–22.

Collier, R. (1995) *Masculinity, Law and the Family*, London: Routledge.

Crites, S. (1986) 'Storytime: recollecting the past and projecting the future', in T. Sarbin (ed.) *Narrative Psychology: The Storied Nature of Human Conduct*, London: Praeger.

Crosby, J., Gage, B. and Raymond, M. (1983) 'The grief resolution process in divorce', *Journal of Divorce* 7: 3–18.

Davies, B. and Harre, R. (1990) 'Positioning: the discursive production of selves', *Journal for the Theory of Social Behaviour* 20: 43–63.

Day Sclater, S. (1995a) 'The limits of mediation', *Family Law* 25: 494–7.

Day Sclater, S. (1995b) 'Theory and method for a psychosocial approach to divorce', East London Research Papers, No. 2, University of East London.

Day Sclater, S. and Richards, M. (1995) 'How adults cope with divorce: strategies for survival', *Family Law* 25: 143–7.

Dingwall, R. (1988) 'Empowerment or enforcement? Some questions about power and control in divorce mediation', in R. Dingwall and J. Eekelaar (eds) *Divorce Mediation and the Legal Process*, Oxford: Clarendon Press.

Dingwall, R. and Greatbatch, D. (1994) 'Divorce mediation – the virtues of formality?', in J. Eekelaar and M. Maclean (eds) *A Reader on Family Law*, Oxford: Oxford University Press.

Elliott, B. J. (1993) 'Divorce and well-being: causes and effects?', in *Targeting Health Promotion*, London: Health Promotion Trust.

Fairclough, N. (1992) *Discourse and Social Change*, Cambridge: Polity Press.

Freeman, M. (1993) *Rewriting the Self: History, Memory, Narrative*, London: Routledge.

Gergen, K. and Gergen, M. (1983) 'Narratives of the self', in T. Sarbin and K. Scheibe (eds) *Studies in Social Identity*, New York: Praeger.

Giddens, A. (1991) *Modernity and Self-Identity*, Cambridge: Polity Press.

Golan, N. (1981) *Passing through Transitions: A Guide for Practitioners*, New York: Free Press.

Gove, G. R. and Sin, H. C. (1989) 'The psychological well-being of divorced and widowed men and women', *Journal of Family Issues* 10(1): 122–44.

Harne, L. and Radford, J. (1994) 'Reinstating patriarchy: the politics of the family and the new legislation', in A. Mullender and R. Morley (eds) *Children Living with Domestic Violence*, London: Whiting & Birch.

Henriques, J., Hollway, W., Urwin, C., Venn, C. and Walkerdine, V. (1984) *Changing the Subject*, London: Methuen.

HM Government (1995) *Looking to the Future: Mediation and the Ground for Divorce* (White Paper), Cmnd 2799, London: HMSO.

HM Government (1995) *Family Law Bill [HL]*, London: HMSO.

Hetherington, M. (1989) 'Coping with family transitions: winners, losers and survivors', *Child Development* 60: 1–14.

Hooper, C. A. (1994) 'Do families need fathers?', in A. Mullender and R. Morley (eds) *Children Living with Domestic Violence*, London: Whiting & Birch.

Isaacs, M. B. and Leon, G. (1988) 'Divorce disputation and discussion: communication styles among recently separated spouses', *Journal of Family Psychology* 1(3): 298–311.

James, A. (1990) 'Conciliation and social change', in T. Fisher (ed.) *Family Conciliation within the UK: Policy and Practice*, Bristol: Family Law, Jordans.

James, A. (1995) 'Social work in divorce: welfare, mediation and justice', *International Journal of Law and the Family* 9: 256–74.

Johnston, J. and Campbell, L. (1988) *Impasses of Divorce: The Dynamics and Resolution of Family Conflict*, New York: Free Press.

Jordan, J. (1989) 'Against the wall' (1978), in *Moving Towards Home: Political Essays*, London: Virago.

Kaslow, F. W. and Schwartz, L. L. (1987) *The Dynamics of Divorce: A Life-cycle Perspective*, New York: Brunner/Mazel.

Kelly, J. (1982) 'Divorce: the adult experience', in B. Wolman and G. Stricker (eds) *Handbook of Developmental Psychology*, New Jersey: Prentice-Hall.

King, M. and Piper, C. (1995) *How the Law Thinks About Children*, Aldershot: Arena.

Kitson, G. and Morgan, L. (1990) 'The multiple consequences of divorce: a decade review', *Journal of Marriage and the Family* 52: 913–24.

Kressel, K. (1985) *The Process of Divorce*, New York: Basic Books.

Maclean, M. (1991) *Surviving Divorce: Women's Resources after Separation*, London: Macmillan.

Macoby, E. and Mnookin, R. (1992) *Dividing the Child: Social and Legal Dilemmas of Custody*, London: Harvard University Press.

Mishler, E. G. (1986) *Research Interviewing: Context and Narrative*, Cambridge, MA: Harvard University Press.

Mishler, E. G. (1991) '"Once upon a time . . ."', *Journal of Narrative and Life History* 1(2 & 3): 101–8.

Moghissi, H. (1994) 'Racism and sexism in academic practice: a case study', in H. Afshar and M. Maynard (eds) *The Dynamics of Race and Gender: Some Feminist Interventions*, London: Taylor & Francis.

Piper, C. (1993) *The Responsible Parent*, Hemel Hempstead: Harvester Wheatsheaf.

Piper, C. (1996) 'Divorce reform and the image of the child', *Journal of Law and Society* 23(3): 364–82.

Plummer, K. (1995) *Telling Sexual Stories*, London: Routledge.

Polkinghorne, D. E. (1988) *Narrative Knowing and the Human Sciences*, Albany: State University of New York Press.

Potter, J. and Wetherell, M. (1987) *Discourse and Social Psychology*, London: Sage.

Riessman, C. K. (1990) *Divorce Talk: Women and Men Make Sense of Personal Relationships*, London: Rutgers University Press.

Riessman, C. K. (1991) 'Beyond reductionism: narrative genres in divorce accounts', *Journal of Narrative and Life History* 1(1): 41–68.

Riessman, C. K. (1992) 'Making sense of marital violence: one woman's narrative', in G. Rosenwald and R. Ochberg (eds) *Storied Lives: The Cultural Politics of Self Understanding*, London: Yale University Press.

Riessman, C. K. (1993) *Narrative Analysis*, London: Sage.

Riessman, C. K. and Gerstel, N. (1985) 'Marital dissolution and health: do males or females have greater risk?', *Social Science and Medicine* 20: 627–35.

Roberts, M. (1990) 'The essentials of conciliation', in T. Fisher (ed.) *Family Conciliation within the UK: Policy and Practice*, Bristol: Family Law, Jordans.

Robinson, M. (1991) *Family Transformation through Divorce and Remarriage*, London: Routledge.

Rosenwald, G. and Ochberg, R. (eds) (1992) *Storied Lives: The Cultural Politics of Self Understanding*, London: Yale University Press.

Sandelowski, M. (1991) 'Telling stories: narrative approaches in qualitative research', *Image: Journal of Nursing Scholarship* 23(3): 161–6.

Sarbin, T. (ed.) (1986) *Narrative Psychology: The Storied Nature of Human Conduct*, London: Praeger.

Smart, C. (1991) 'The legal and moral ordering of child custody', *Journal of Law and Society* 8(4): 485–500.

Spanier, G. and Castro, R. (1979) 'Adjustment to separation and divorce: a qualitative analysis', in G. Levinger and O. Moles (eds) *Divorce and Separation: Contexts, Causes and Consequences*, New York: Basic Books.

Vaughan, D. (1987) *Uncoupling: Turning Points in Intimate Relationships*,

Oxford: Oxford University Press.

Walker, J. and Robinson, M. (1990) 'Conciliation and family therapy', in T. Fisher (ed.) *Family Conciliation within the UK: Policy and Practice*, Bristol: Family Law, Jordans.

Wallerstein, J. and Kelly, J. (1980) *Surviving the Breakup*, New York: Free Press.

Weiss, R. (1975) *Marital Separation*, New York: Basic Books.

Weitzman, L. (1985) *The Divorce Revolution: The Unexpected Social and Economic Consequences for Women in America*, New York: Free Press.

White, H. (1980) 'The value of narrativity in the representation of reality', *Critical Inquiry* 7: 5–27.

Wiseman, R. (1975) 'Crisis theory and the process of divorce', *Social Casework* 56(4): 205–12.

[16]

DOMINANT DISCOURSE, PROFESSIONAL LANGUAGE, AND LEGAL CHANGE IN CHILD CUSTODY DECISIONMAKING

*Martha Fineman**

This Article examines the changing relationship between legal and non-legal decisionmakers in custody cases. Although custody determinations historically were viewed as legal events accomplished by legal decisionmakers through legal procedures, the recent trend toward joint custody and mandatory mediation represents an appropriation by the helping professions of authority in this area. Professor Fineman argues that the shared-parenting ideal established by these professional groups facilitated substantive change in long-standing custody policy. These changes have been obscured by the helping professions' focus on the decisionmaking process.

Professor Fineman analyzes the helping professions' presentation of the contrasting therapeutic and legal models and argues that the success of the helping professions in displacing legal divorce in custody matters resulted from their criticism of existing practices, procedures, and decisionmakers and from their success in labeling divorce as an emotional crisis. Professor Fineman suggests a return to a legal model in custody cases and proposes the "primary parent" rule as the way to implement this goal.

I. INTRODUCTION

This Article explores how the rhetoric used by social workers and mediators has been successful in appropriating the business of child custody decisionmaking.[1] An integral part of this process has

---

* Professor of Law and Director of the Family Policy Program of the Institute for Legal Studies, University of Wisconsin.

Completion of this Article was made possible by a research grant from the Graduate Research Committee of the University of Wisconsin and by an Antoine L. Smongeski Bequest administered by the University of Wisconsin Foundation. An earlier version of this Article was presented at the Property and Rhetoric Conference at Northwestern University sponsored by the American Bar Foundation in the summer of 1986.

Many helpful comments were made by my colleagues on earlier drafts of this Article. I would particularly like to thank Anne MacArthur for her assistance and dedication.

[1] The terms used in this Section to describe the competition between social workers and lawyers are related to the metaphor of custody decisionmaking as property. *See infra* Part III.

been an attack on the nature of existing rules and decisionmaking institutions, a phenomenon that can be viewed metaphorically as the claiming by the helping professions[2] of the custody decisionmaking terrain through the rhetoric of reform. The extent to which the concepts and values put forth by the helping professions have been incorporated into and dominate the public and political language of the escalating custody debate illustrates the success of their efforts.

The recent trend in the legal area is to mandate mediation of custody and related post-divorce disputes.[3] Thus, contemporary shifts in custody policy are best understood in the context of the rhetoric and ideology of social workers and mediators, proponents of this trend who, as a professional group, have transformed divorce. In this Article, I argue that the establishment of mandatory mediation as the preferred process, and joint custody or shared parenting as the substantive norm,[4] represents a significant divergence from previously accepted legal doctrine. Yet, because these changes are presented in procedural terms, the rhetoric concerning mediation has masked, at the same time that it has facilitated, the extensive shifts in substantive results. Labeling changes as procedural makes them easier to accept but also obscures the substantive changes that are taking place.

---

[2] In this Article, I use the term "helping professions" to refer principally to social workers, others trained in mental health and/or the behavioral sciences, and mediators, as well as others who have articulated what I describe as "the mediation ideal."

[3] See, for example, CAL. CIV. CODE § 4607(a) (West Supp. 1987), which illustrates changes in procedure (mediation before judicial hearing) and substance (emphasis upon a child's continuing relationship with both parents):

> In any proceeding where there is [a contested] issue . . . [of] custody or of visitation with a minor child . . . the matter shall be set for mediation of the contested issues . . . . The purpose of such mediation proceeding shall be to reduce acrimony which may exist between the parties and to develop an agreement assuring the child or children's close and continuing contact with both parents.

Id.

Under court-associated mandatory mediation programs, existing institutional actors will more likely than not continue to provide services — the (old) "family court social worker" becomes the (new) "family court mediator." *See, e.g.*, Mumma, *Mediating Disputes*, 42 PUB. WELFARE 22, 26–30 (1984) (describing a court-associated mediation program developed in Virginia Beach, Virginia). In addition, a new market may be created for social workers or mediators in private practice, at least under statutes that allow "opting out" (the satisfaction of the statutory mediation requirement through a private service provider). *See, e.g.*, State of Wisconsin Engrossed 1985 Assembly Bill 474, at 4 (on file with the author).

[4] *See, e.g.*, Canacakos, *Joint Custody as a Fundamental Right*, in JOINT CUSTODY AND SHARED PARENTING 223, 224–25 (J. Folberg ed. 1984) (arguing that a presumption of joint custody is constitutionally mandated); Folberg, *Divorce Mediation: A Workable Alternative*, in AMERICAN BAR ASSOCIATION, ALTERNATIVE MEANS OF FAMILY DISPUTE RESOLUTION (H. Davidson, L. Ray & R. Horowitz eds. 1982), *quoted in* KRAUSE, FAMILY LAW CASES, COMMENTS AND QUESTIONS 702 (2d ed. 1983); Robinson, *Joint Custody: Constitutional Imperatives*, 54 U. CIN. L. REV. 27 (1985) (arguing for mandatory joint custody except when a compelling reason for an exclusive award to serve the child's best interests exists); Steinman, *Joint Custody: What We Know, What We Have Yet to Learn, and the Judicial and Legislative Implications*, 16 U.C. DAVIS L. REV. 739 (1983).

My primary concern is with the imposition of these procedural and substantive changes as *mandatory* rules to govern all custody decisionmaking at divorce. This Article, therefore, is not a discussion of the merits of *voluntary* joint custody or *voluntary* mediation as an alternative dispute resolution technique. Similarly, I am not primarily concerned with debating the relative capacity or desirability of legal and nonlegal decisionmakers in custody cases, although, as this Article sets forth, I do not think the solution to the undeniable problems associated with the adversarial model is simply to turn over the decisionmaking task to another professional group. In fact, to do so creates another set of problems. Recognizing that the behavior of attorneys in custody cases has at times been outrageous, it is not my intention to defend legal professionals. Indeed, the adoption of the radical, albeit legalistic, test I propose for resolving custody cases is directed in part at minimizing such abuses.[5]

In addition, it is important to note that my criticism of the mediation process differs from the typical feminist or liberal critiques.[6] I do not necessarily disagree with the literature that points out that the "weaker" partner in a marriage is likely to be disadvantaged within the mediation context.[7] I am concerned, however, that this type of criticism will lead us to look to the wrong methods of "reform." If we focus on inequitable bargaining positions — the continuation of the "woman as victim" model — the solutions that suggest themselves are individualized ones, and ones which are located within the control of the mediators themselves. For example, in response to feminist criticisms that unequal bargaining power mars the process, the mediation profession recently has produced a mass of literature on how practicing mediators can remedy such inequality.[8]

My concern is broader. In this Article, I reveal the shifts in substantive rules that have been the inevitable by-product of changes

---

[5] This test is discussed more fully below in Part VII.

[6] *See, e.g.*, J. AUERBACH, JUSTICE WITHOUT LAW? (1983); Abel, *The Contradictions of Informal Justice*, in 1 THE POLITICS OF INFORMAL JUSTICE 267 (R. Abel ed. 1982); Delgado, Dunn, Brown, Lee & Hubbert, *Fairness and Formality: Minimizing the Risk of Prejudice in Alternative Dispute Resolution*, 1985 WIS. L. REV. 1351 (suggesting that in cases in which there is a wide disparity in the status or power of opponents, methods of alternative dispute resolution may heighten racial and ethnic prejudice); Menkel-Meadow, *Toward Another View of Legal Negotiation: The Structure of Problem Solving*, 31 UCLA L. REV. 754 (1984) (arguing for a problem-solving approach to negotiation); Rifkin, *Mediation From a Feminist Perspective: Promise and Problems*, 2 LAW & INEQUALITY 21 (1984) (arguing that mediation helps to lessen the problem of dominance).

[7] *See generally* Rifkin, *supra* note 6.

[8] *See* Engram & Markowitz, *Ethical Issues in Mediation: Divorce and Labor Compared*, 8 MEDIATION Q. 19, 20–25 (1985); Saposnek, *What is Fair in Child Custody Mediation*, 8 MEDIATION Q. 9, 15 (1985). *But see* Perlmutter, *Ethical Issues in Family Mediation: A Social Perspective*, 8 MEDIATION Q. 99, 103–04 (1985) (suggesting that a solution to the bargaining power dilemma is to bring lawyers into the mediation process).

in the methods and manner of resolving custody disputes. These changes have consequences in all custody decisionmaking. Therefore, the focus of my inquiry is not the power of individuals within any particular mediation context; rather, it is the lack of power that leaves custodial mothers[9] *as a group* disadvantaged in a political process that permits or encourages such changes. This type of power imbalance can only be understood at the macro-level.

I assert that custodial mothers, as a group with shared problems and concerns, have not had access to the political system in any meaningful way. Their voices (at least insofar as they would call for the continuation of sole custody arrangements) are not heard because their concerns cannot be expressed through existing and accepted discourses or rhetorical concepts. The fact that their interests cannot be expressed in acceptable language denies them access to the system that shapes and implements decisions having the most profound impact on their lives. Custodial mothers are unorganized and unrepresented. The groups that should have their concerns in mind are caught up with the political and symbolic implications of the custody debate for their own agendas and platforms.[10]

Perhaps the most significant factor that helps us to understand why custodial mothers lack a discourse with which to voice their concerns is that to the extent that they would argue for sole custody they must fight against a dominant discourse that controls all the terms of the modern custody debate. The professional language of the social workers and mediators has progressed to become the public, then the political, then the dominant rhetoric. It now defines the terms of contemporary discussions about custody and effectively excludes or minimizes contrary ideologies and concepts.[11]

In this Article, I criticize social workers and other members of the helping professions in part because they present themselves as neutral, nonadversarial decisionmakers in contrast to attorneys, whom they characterize as both adversarial and combative. Yet social workers are not neutral; they have a professional bias in favor of a specific substantive result. That result benefits their profession by creating the need for mediation and counseling. It is this bias and self-interest that makes the process one for political consideration. The bias inherent in mediation is different from, but no less suspect than, the

---

[9] I use the term "custodial mothers" to refer to those parents who are or will be the primary caretakers of children after divorce. I realize that sometimes these "mothers" may be men, but it is the primary caretaking role that is stereotypically and statistically associated with mothers that I seek to protect.

[10] *See infra* p. 768.

[11] Ultimately, the existence and consequence of this rhetorical monopoly raises serious questions that are beyond the scope of this Article about the viability of the pluralist model in modern political society.

bias that can result from overt favoritism of one party over another. It is understood from this perspective that if no mutual, objective professional decisionmaker exists, we must confront moral, political and legal questions from which the "experts" cannot save us.[12]

In Parts I and II, I discuss the transformation that has taken place in divorce and custody law. In Part III, I use the metaphor of property to analyze the professional competition between the legal and helping professions over the custody decisionmaking process. I describe in Part IV how social workers have changed from supplementary to substitute decisionmakers. In Part V, I examine the manner in which social workers' rhetoric has enabled them to appropriate the custody decisionmaking process. In Part VI, I discuss the practical consequences of this rhetoric. Finally, in Part VII, I suggest reforms designed to remove coercive custody decisionmaking from social workers' control and return it to the legal profession.

II. Changes and Discourse — An Overview

A. *The Transformation of the Custody Debate*

Divorce and child custody decisionmaking has traditionally been the preserve of legal institutions: legislatures established laws to govern "domestic relations," and judges decided cases presented by attorneys representing adverse parties. Early divorce reforms, which sought changes in legal rules, particularly the movement from a fault-based to a no-fault system, sought adjustments that would mediate the harshness of the legal system.

The current debate about the content and form of child custody law, however, reflects a struggle between two professional ideologies — those of law and social work. Fundamental questions have been raised about the appropriateness of legal institutions, legal solutions, and legal processes in divorce and custody cases.[13] Such objections have culminated in a substantial redistribution of decisionmaking authority from judges and lawyers to the helping professions.

Concomitantly, there has been a transformation in the discourse concerning custody policy. This transformation can be better understood by contrasting the competing discourses of the adversarial model, populated by judges and attorneys, and the therapeutic model, populated by social workers and mediators.

Traditional divorce policy envisioned the termination of the spouses' relationship as its goal, establishing different legal relation-

[12] For a more detailed discussion of this point, see Fineman & Opie, *The Uses of Social Science Data in Legal Policy Making: Custody Determinations and Divorce*, 1987 Wis. L. Rev. 107, 157–58.

[13] *See infra* pp. 746–52.

ships with differing legal consequences for the custodial and noncustodial parents. In this way, the law recognized the status of sole custodian as an institution or legal category and presumed that the law should designate, recognize, and protect the relationship between custodial parent and child.[14] At the same time, the law acknowledged the noncustodial parent's relationship with the child through the imposition of visitation rights.

Helping professionals and other proponents of joint custody asserted that the win/lose philosophy of naming a sole custodian was inappropriate, because parents had equal rights and responsibilities in relation to their children during marriage.[15] In addition, they found the notion of "visiting" one's child ideologically and emotionally offensive.[16] By contrast, the symbolic ideal of parental equality was compelling. Desirable custody policy, therefore, was post-divorce shared parenting. It was this notion of a legally mandated and constructed continuing relationship between divorced parents, so central to joint custody, that was so foreign to traditional family law policy. In essence, the social workers' ideal of shared parenting was a rejection of the desirability of a legally acknowledged sole custodian.

As this view has become accepted, it has altered the way we articulate and conceive of custody issues. The dominant rhetoric no longer describes divorce as a process that terminates the relationship between spouses, establishing one as the custodial parent with clear responsibilities. Rather, divorce is now described as a process that, through mediation, restructures and reformulates the spouses' relationship, conferring equal or shared parental rights on both parents although one, in practice, usually assumes the primary responsibility for care of the children. This is an important substantive shift.

The helping professions' ability to suggest and obtain such radical

---

[14] Traditional practice was to award custody to one parent in order to meet children's need for a permanent, stable relationship. *See* J. GOLDSTEIN, A. FREUD & A. SOLNIT, BEYOND THE BEST INTERESTS OF THE CHILD (1973); *see also infra* note 102 (discussing the post-divorce psychological needs of children).

[15] *See, e.g.*, Ahrons, *Joint Custody Arrangements in the Postdivorce Family*, J. DIVORCE, Spring 1980, at 189, 190 (tracing the gradual downfall of the presumption of maternal custody); Everett, *Shared Parenthood in Divorce: The Parental Covenant and Custody Law*, 2 J.L. & RELIGION 85, 93–94 (1984).

[16] *See, e.g.*, Greif, *Fathers, Children and Joint Custody*, 49 AM. J. ORTHOPSYCH. 311, 319 (1979) (criticizing visitation rights as not maximizing the contact between the child and both parents); Noble, *Custody Contest: How to Divide and Reassemble a Child*, 64 SOC. CASEWORK 406, 411 (1983) (arguing that periodic visitation "does not give sufficient opportunity for the variety and richness of contact that is necesssary to sustain complex family relationships"); *see also* Mumma, *supra* note 3, at 25 ("Perhaps the concepts of custody and visitation are obsolete. The words themselves have become so distorted by stereotypical meanings that they may no longer be useful. New terms, or at least new concepts, are sorely needed.").

change in substantive policy derives in part from their ability to present the debate over divorce and custody as one involving the treatment of an emotional crisis rather than a solution to a legal problem.[17] Custody was merely a "label"; what was really at issue was the states of mind or attitudes of the family members. In this sense, the helping professions ignored the fact of, and the justifications for, the differing legal consequences that flowed from the labels of "custodial parent" and "noncustodial parent."[18] These designations were also considered to be offensive to noncustodial fathers,[19] which added weight to arguments that the terms and rules had to be changed. Terms such as "shared parenting" and "periods of physical placement" replaced "physical custody" and "visitation" as the proper way to discuss custody arrangements.[20]

The attempt to accommodate fathers' interests in a symbolically pleasing manner by changing the language with which custody policy is discussed has had political ramifications, however. Because the change in terminology may alter substantive results, it has worked to reallocate power between parents in custody cases, profoundly affecting bargaining between spouses at divorce.[21] The change in rhetoric disadvantages functioning custodial mothers and their children, the occupants of the shadow institution of sole-custody parenting, who have not had a voice in the reform of custody laws.

The helping professions' concern with symbols overshadowed the fact that in practice joint custody dispositions continue to resemble sole maternal custody and paternal visitation.[22] In fact, the social role and function of a sole custodial parent continues.[23] Whether or not custodial mothers exist as a legal category, they exist as an institution — as a practical reality experienced by many children of divorce and their mothers. The recent rhetorical disapproval of and attempts

---

[17] *See infra* pp. 744–57.

[18] *See infra* pp. 740–44.

[19] *See infra* pp. 741–44.

[20] In material presented to a Wisconsin Legislative Committee considering changes in that state's custody laws, William Johnson Everett expressed the social worker's position: "the child is not some indivisible 'thing' over which a person is to have 'custody' or not. Custody is for criminal suspects, not children. Similarly, children are not guests to be 'visited' by their parents. Visitation is for funeral homes and hospitals." Everett, Shared Parenthood in Divorce: Parental Covenant and Custody Law 12 (1983) (unpublished manuscript on file with the author).

For the legislative response to such pleas, see State of Wisconsin Engrossed 1985 Assembly Bill 474, at 3 (on file with the author), in which "visitation" is abolished in favor of periods of physical placement.

[21] *See infra* note 178.

[22] *See* Phear, Beck, Hauser, Clark & Whitney, *An Empirical Study of Custody Agreements: Joint Versus Sole Legal Custody*, in JOINT CUSTODY AND SHARED PARENTING, *supra* note 4, at 142, 155.

[23] *See id.* at 156.

to abolish formally the institution of the sole custodial parent have not destroyed it, but only placed it in the shadows.

B. The Ideal of Shared Parenting

The helping professions' discourse has presented shared parenting as the only truly acceptable custody policy.[24] This is because they view joint custody as the only "fair" result.[25] Ironically, although they might question the capacity of legal processes and institutions to resolve custody disputes in accordance with this ideal, they view law itself as possessing vast power to transform people's behavior.[26] The helping professions therefore have little hesitation in resorting to law for the implementation of their social policies.

The merits of shared parenting as a legal and social ideal have not been critically debated in political and legal forums in any meaningful way. Although there has been limited criticism of the feasibility

---

[24] *See* Greif, *supra* note 16, at 318–19; *see also* Pruhs, Paulsen & Tysseling, *Divorce Mediation: The Politics of Integrating Clinicians*, 65 SOC. CASEWORK 532, 535 (1984) ("Outside the courtroom there is no such thing as sole custody; divorce requires restructuring of the family but will include continued influence by both parents (even in the absence of one parent).").

[25] See Ababarnel, *Shared Parenting After Separation and Divorce: A Study of Joint Custody*, 49 AM. J. ORTHOPSYCH. 320 (1979), in which the author makes sweeping conclusions based on *four* cases:

> There is no doubt that joint custody yields two psychological parents, and that the children do not suffer the profound sense of loss characteristic of so many children of divorce. The children maintained strong attachments to both parents. Perhaps the security of an ongoing relationship with *two* psychological parents helps to provide the means to cope successfully with the uprooting effects of switching households.

Id. at 328 (emphasis in original). Fairness in this context is seen as having both a practical and a theoretical basis. One commentator found:

> Most supporters of joint custody contend that it significantly improves parental cooperation. The need to reach an agreement on all major child rearing decisions, combined with equalized parental power, fosters an atmosphere of detente rather than hostility. . . .
>
> Joint custody is said to reinforce and facilitate several modern social trends. It is consistent with the movement for sexual equality and its many corollaries, such as the right of the individual to determine his or her own lifestyle. . . . Increasingly, fathers are sharing child rearing and nurturing responsibilities. All of these developments are perfectly conducive to joint custody arrangements in the event of divorce.
>
> . . .
>
> . . . There is also evidence that joint legal custody makes default on child support payments less likely. Several practitioners believe that the involvement in family affairs due to joint custody results in fathers paying child support more readily.

Miller, *Joint Custody*, 13 FAM. L.Q. 345, 364–65 (1979) (citations omitted).

[26] I noted and criticized nonlawyers' tendency to view the law as instrumental in changing people and their behavior in Fineman, *Illusive Equality: On Weitzman's Divorce Revolution*, 1986 AM. BAR FOUND. RES. J. 781. Proponents of joint custody have argued that it creates "behavior modification pressure" on parents to conform to the ideal. *See* Suggestions from Julilly Kohler for Changes in Child Custody Law 4 (Nov. 2, 1984) (submitted to Special Legislative Comm. on Custody Arrangements (Wisconsin)) (on file with the author).

of the ideal,[27] these criticisms do not challenge the degree to which presumptive shared parenting actually reflects pre- or post-divorce family structures. Similarly, there has been uncritical acceptance of the empirical proposition that women and men make undifferentiated, exchangeable contributions to parenting.[28] By focusing on the importance of the father/child relationship, the helping professions' discourse undervalues a mother's real life role, assuming it to be no different than a father's.[29] The extreme presentation of this view is that at times a mother's "mothering" may be characterized as pathological and harmful to children.[30] The creation of such a stereotype has gone largely unchallenged.

The shared parenting discourse of the helping professions found rhetorical compatibility with other family law reform efforts that also incorporated notions of equality, partnership, and gender neutrality.[31] The joint custody rhetoric of the helping professions, like other discourses, assumed and advocated equalitarianism[32] — arguing that there are no differences between women and men, and that none should be promoted through gender-specific laws. Within the context of custody theory, this perspective denied and obscured recognition of anything "special" between mothers and children, innately or in fact. On this level, arguments for joint custody were consistent with feminist discourses that called for increasing male participation in child care to free women from anachronistic roles.[33]

In focusing on ideal sex roles and equalitarian marriage, the helping professions' literature emphasized that traditional custody policy discriminated against men by unjustifiably favoring sole maternal custody.[34] Not unlike the emerging fathers' rights discourse, their rhetoric asserted that there was no basis for maternal preference, which was grounded in the sexist assumption that men could not nurture but that women could.[35] In real life, according to the helping profession, parents shared parenting and "parents are forever."[36]

---

[27] *See infra* note 102; *infra* pp. 762–64.

[28] For an elaborate criticism of both the tendency to view parents as interchangeable and the uncritical use of survey data by legal policymakers, see generally Fineman & Opie, *supra* note 12.

[29] *See* Fineman & Opie, *supra* note 12, at 118–21.

[30] *See infra* pp. 765–66.

[31] *See infra* note 48.

[32] *See infra* pp. 765–66.

[33] *See infra* p. 768.

[34] *See* Pearson, Munson & Thoennes, *Legal Change and Child Custody Awards*, 3 J. FAM. ISSUES 5, 24 (1982).

[35] *See id.*; *infra* pp. 738–39.

[36] Elkin, *Conciliation Courts: The Reintegration of Disintegrating Families*, 22 FAM. COORDINATOR 63, 64 (1973). The phrase has now become a fathers' rights cliche.

III. The Use of Metaphor

A. Control Over Custody Decisionmaking as Property

Control over custody decisionmaking is not typically characterized as a thing or an object. The use of a property metaphor, however, enhances our understanding of the roles of professional discourse and language in legal change. Through the use of the property metaphor, I hope to focus attention on some aspects of custody decisionmaking that need exploration but are often obscured by the tendency to frame the issue as a question of what is in the best interests of children. The use of the metaphor reminds us that what is also at issue (and perhaps more centrally so) is the possession and control of both custody decisionmaking by professionals and children by their parents. The property metaphor therefore helps to illuminate how professional or other ideological presentations may develop into a dominant discourse, which is then allowed to "occupy the field."

In order to become dominant, a discourse often must compete with other potentially dominant discourses — it must exert control over the concepts and ideas that are understood to be the foundation of the area. Language is the medium through which this form of property is appropriated; the ideology and assumptions underlying it are bought or sold by those with the ability to validate one discourse over another. In this way, mediators and social workers have successfully used their professional discourse to appropriate the business of custody decisionmaking.

The helping professions' discourse has two conceptually distinct components. The first component is procedural, focusing on the way in which decisions are made. This component describes the differences between the processes used by the legal and helping professions and is the most visible and prevalent part of the discourse. The second component concerns the substantive nature of the decisions and critiques the different results produced under each decisionmaking method. The substantive discourse is intimately related to and dependent upon the procedural discourse. It is a more obscure and subtle discourse, however, than the one that focuses on procedure and its premises are often not exposed for examination.

Because the substantive component of the discourse is less salient, the real nature of the competition between the legal and therapeutic models for handling divorce has not always been clear. In fact, the debate has been largely confined to the procedural realm, and it therefore is decidedly one-dimensional, with social workers exercising control over the concepts discussed. As characterized, the terms of the debate deter outright opposition by legal professionals, because such criticism can be dismissed as the product of mere "turf" concerns. The focus on process has effectively prevented the emergence of a contrasting "legalistic" narrative, which would develop alternative visions of both procedural and substantive goals. This impediment to the development of a contrasting narrative is an important factor whereby a discourse becomes politically dominant as the vision that captures, incorporates, and expresses existing predominant ideological assumptions.

B. Children as Property

The property metaphor is also illustrative in describing the position of children. Much of the legal language traditionally used to define the custody decisionmaking process adopts implicitly or explicitly the notion of children as property. The term "custody" itself carries with it the idea of a thing susceptible to possession and control. Understanding the ramifications of viewing children as property helps us appreciate how the stage has been set for the competition between rhetorical visions for the business of child custody decisionmaking.

Historically, fathers were entitled to possession of their children. Upon divorce, fathers received custody under the legal doctrine *paternal familius*.[37] In essence, fathers had an absolute right to their children, "owning" them as if they held "title" to them. Ownership brought a corresponding duty to support — to pay for — children.[38]

The notion of paternal possession was successfully challenged during the latter part of the nineteenth century, both through feminist agitation, which stressed the role that mothers played in children's day-to-day upbringing,[39] and through the "enlightened" rhetoric characteristic of the modern welfare state do-gooders.[40] Children were said to be endowed with a right to the best custodial situation, independent of their fathers' property interest in them. The modern, reformist discourse viewed children not so much as individual property to be divided between parents, but as a form of social investment in which custody produced concomitant social duties on the part of each parent, the performance of which the state could supervise.[41]

The legal expression of this view came in the adoption of the best interest of the child standard as the governing substantive principle in custody adjudications. The movement away from the father's ab-

[37] *See* J. SCHOULER, A TREATISE ON THE LAW OF DOMESTIC RELATIONS 61, 333 (1870).

[38] *See* 1 W. BLACKSTONE, COMMENTARIES 435–38 (rev. ed. 1966). In modern practice in cases of divorce, this support obligation is fulfilled through child support payments without the father having actual physical custody of the children.

[39] *See* M. GROSSBERG, GOVERNING THE HEARTH 244–47 (1985).

[40] *See, e.g.*, Grossberg, *Who Gets the Child? Custody, Guardianship, and the Rise of a Judicial Patriarchy in Nineteenth-Century America*, 9 FEMINIST STUD. 235, 239, 246, 254–55 (1983).

[41] For a general description of the development of state supervision of parental duties, see M. GROSSBERG, cited in note 39 above, at 289–91.

solute right to custody to the less absolute guideline of the best interest test and its accompanying tender years presumption can be viewed as a shift in principles governing the distribution of a property interest in children. It can be seen as the state asserting its own proprietary interest in children as future citizens. It can also be understood as the state's recognition that good mothers had "paid for" or "earned" their children through continuous and systematic care of them. This latter view incorporated the notion of children as a "reward" for mothers' socially productive labor in raising future citizens.[42] This test created problems for the legal system, however, because it was indeterminate. In addition, the best interest test required judgments and predictions about psychological and social factors that judges were uncomfortable making.[43]

Courts adopted the "tender years" doctrine as a gloss on the best interest test.[44] The tender years doctrine was a legal presumption that directed the placement of children younger than seven — children of "tender years" — with their mothers, unless their mothers were "unfit" to provide care.[45] Essentially, this presumption gave content to the term "best interest of the child" by assigning "ownership" to the mother. This ownership was not absolute, however. Courts awarded fathers visitation, often for extended periods during school vacations, and placed other limitations on custodial mothers' control over their children.

As the incidence of divorce increased in the early 1970's,[46] fathers' rights groups successfully challenged the tender years doctrine and criticized the nature of child custody decisionmaking as manifesting what they perceived to be a "pro-mother" bias.[47] At the same time that fathers began to reassert ownership interests, mainstream feminists attacked gender-specific legal tests as inherently discriminatory.[48]

---

[42] *See id.* at 237–53.

[43] *See* Levy, *Custody Investigations in Divorce Cases*, 1985 AM. B. FOUND. RES. J. 713, 723–24.

[44] For a discussion of the origins of the "tender years" doctrine, see Zainaldin, *The Emergence of a Modern American Family Law: Child Custody, Adoption and the Courts, 1796-1851*, 73 NW. U.L. REV. 1038, 1072–74 (1979).

[45] Typical grounds for a finding of unfitness included adultery and intemperance. Under such circumstances, mothers forfeited their ownership interests in their children. *See* J. AREEN, FAMILY LAW 433–42 (1985). Recent studies suggest that women's behavior is still examined according to harsher standards than men's. *See* Girdner, *Child Custody Determination: Ideological Dimensions of a Social Problem*, in REDEFINING SOCIAL PROBLEMS 165, 175–76 (E. Seidman & J. Rappaport eds. 1986).

[46] *See* I. ELLMAN, P. KURTZ & A. STANTON, FAMILY LAW 206–07 (1986) (reporting marriage dissolution rates per year for the years 1860–1978).

[47] *See* Folberg, *Custody Overview*, in JOINT CUSTODY AND SHARED PARENTING, *supra* note 4, at 5.

[48] *See* Fineman, *Implementing Equality: Ideology, Contradiction and Social Change: A Study of Rhetoric and Result in the Regulation of the Consequences of Divorce*, 1983 WIS. L. REV.

The fathers' rights movement picked up on the idea of gender neutrality and turned it to fathers' advantage in the custody area.[49] These two forces — male backlash and feminist equality rhetoric — set the stage for more recent challenges to the traditional method and manner of custody decisionmaking.[50]

C. Setting the Stage for Legal and Political Change

The contemporary view could be characterized as holding that it is the biological nexus or relationship between both parents and the child that buys or earns control over the child. In this vision, neither parent has a superior claim to custody based on his or her gender or on the investment in day-to-day care for the child; rather, each parent appropriates an equal interest.[51] Joint and equal interest, embodied most clearly by joint custody, was a virtually inevitable result of the successful attacks on the old rules, because no viable gender-neutral alternative to the tender years doctrine existed. This modern trend illustrates a move backward toward the more explicit treatment of

---

789, 821–22. In the family law context, gender neutrality remains the popular goal of liberal feminist reform. *See id.* at 824; *see also* Ahrons, *supra* note 15, at 189–205. Professor Ahrons has naively concluded:

> More women are entering the labor force rather than devoting themselves to full-time child care roles, and the trend toward more role sharing and egalitarianism in marriage will probably result in increased demands for equality in divorce. . . . As women gain liberation from traditional roles, they will define themselves less as mothers and will have fewer needs for the role to be primary in their lives.

Id. at 203. The gender neutrality debate is also a central focus of British feminism. For a cogent discussion of the historic and contemporary conflict in British feminism between strict or rule equality and special treatment or result equality, see Smart & Brophy, *Locating Law: A Discussion of the Place of Law in Feminist Politics*, in WOMEN IN LAW 1 (J. Brophy & C. Smart eds. 1985).

[49] *See, e.g.*, Folberg, *Custody Overview*, in JOINT CUSTODY AND SHARED PARENTING, *supra* note 4; *see also* Letter from Neal Skrenes, Secretary, Non-Custodial Parents' Rights Coalition, Inc., to Rep. Jeannette Bell, Chair, Special Legislative Committee, Custody Arrangements (Wisconsin) (on file with the author).

[50] For an analysis of the tender years doctrine under the equal protection clause, see *Ex Parte* Devine, 398 So. 2d 686 (Ala. 1981), which held that the doctrine constituted unconstitutional gender discrimination. Most state statutes now specifically provide that both parents are "equal," thus forbidding consideration of gender in custody cases. *See State Divorce Statutes Chart and Summary Sheet Introduction*, Fam. L. Rep. (BNA) 5–6 (Mar. 24, 1986). For example, the relevant Wisconsin statute reads: "In making a custody determination, the court . . . shall not prefer one potential custodian over the other on the basis of the sex of the custodian." WIS. STAT. ANN. § 767.24(2) (West 1981).

[51] A plethora of literature touts the psychological benefits to fathers and children of joint custody. *See, e.g.*, Abarbanel, *supra* note 25, at 320–29 (finding that the benefits of joint custody outweighed the problems it caused for the families studied); Bowman & Ahrons, *Impact of Legal Custody Status on Fathers' Parenting Postdivorce*, 47 J. MARRIAGE & FAM. 481, 481–88 (1985) (arguing that joint-custody fathers are far more active in parenting after divorce than those without custody); Greif, *supra* note 16, at 311–19 (asserting that fathers with joint custody are more likely to remain active in children's development than those with visitation rights).

children as property — only this time the property is to be divided equally.

With the removal of the old custody "rules of thumb,"[52] custody decisionmaking became much more complex. No permissible, easily applied guidelines remain under the best interest test, and questions exist as to which rules should govern. Without the old gender presumption, the legal system is asked to do too much. Judges and attorneys feel ill-equipped to make determinations about what placement will be in the "best interests" of children. This discomfort has set off a search for more determinate rules.[53]

Similarly, new questions are now arising as to who is the best decisionmaker in custody cases. The uncertainty generated by the changing rules has weakened the legal profession's monopoly over custody decisionmaking and has made it easier for social workers to assert increasing power and perhaps eventually to dispossess lawyers. Those in the helping professions have made inroads into this domain with the cooperation and, in some instances, the encouragement of lawyers and judges who feel inadequate to determine what is in the "best interest of the child" in custody cases.[54] To understand this phenomenon, we must consider the changing roles of the lawyer and the social worker in divorce decisionmaking.

IV. Social Workers and Divorce

Under traditional legal rules, the helping professions were confined to a supplemental role in the family court system: agency social workers functioned as counselors or custody investigators.[55] With the cur-

---

[52] The origin of the term "rule of thumb" was the common law rule that a husband could beat his wife without legal sanction if he used a rod no thicker than his thumb. *See* Davidson, *Wifebeating: A Recurring Phenomenon Throughout History*, in BATTERED WOMEN: A PSYCHOSOCIOLOGICAL STUDY OF DOMESTIC VIOLENCE 18–21 (M. Roy ed. 1977).

[53] *See, e.g.*, Chambers, *Rethinking the Substantive Rules for Custody Disputes in Divorce*, 83 MICH. L. REV. 477 (1984) (tentatively recommending a preference for the primary caretaker); Elster, *Solomonic Judgments: Against the Best Interest of the Child*, 54 U. CHI. L. REV. 1 (1987) (comparing and evaluating three alternatives to the best interest of the child standard). For a criticism of the approaches employed in formulating new rules in this area, see Fineman & Opie, *supra* note 12.

[54] A vast body of literature discusses the pros and cons of courts' use of ancillary personnel to aid in making custody decisions. Lawyers have often been assigned to these roles. For an early proposal by a judge, see Hansen, *Guardians Ad Litem in Divorce and Custody Cases: Protection of the Child's Interests*, 4 J. FAM. L. 181 (1964). See also O. STONE, THE CHILD'S VOICE IN THE COURT OF LAW 104–05 (1982), which reviews the suggestion that family court judges be accompanied by "behavioural science 'judges'" trained in the social sciences.

[55] Despite their ancillary role, social workers conducting custody investigations were able to affect case outcome in significant ways, including settlement behavior. *See* Levy, *supra* note 43, at 730–32 & nn. 66–72; *see also id.* at 718–28 (discussing the interventionist philosophy underlying the involvement of social workers in disputed cases).

rent changes in traditional custody decisionmaking ideology, however, social workers are moving from a supplemental role to the role of substitute decisionmaker, displacing guardians ad litem and, ultimately, replacing judges as the final arbiters of child custody.[56]

A. *Opportunity Provided by Changing Legal Rules*

Prior to the enactment of no-fault laws, divorce was seen as a legal event accomplished through adversarial procedures — one spouse, the "innocent" party, instituted a civil suit petitioning for divorce and sought to prove grounds on which divorce could be granted.[57] Social workers therefore had a limited role in the divorce process under fault-based divorce systems.[58]

No-fault legislation[59] worked several significant changes in divorce law that greatly expanded the role of the social worker in divorce cases.[60] Liberalized laws dramatically refocused the inquiry away from the question whether divorce should be allowed to questions about the impact of divorce on the family and society. The mental health professions became more interested in divorce as a psychosocial event — an emotional crisis.[61] As such, social workers argued

---

[56] Other authors have observed the significance of the helping professions in the area of custody. *See* Girdner, *supra* note 45, at 166 ("[Members of the mental health profession] have been critical in defining the custody determination problem and in proposing solutions . . . in the services they offer, in their notions of what is healthy and unhealthy, in their views of what children and parents need, and how families function and change . . . .").

[57] For a discussion of the traditional fault grounds and defenses, see J. AREEN, *supra* note 45, at 245–67.

[58] Because custody was granted to the innocent spouse as a general rule, the fault standard itself resolved custody questions. The movement to no-fault and the best interest standard made the custody question an area of inquiry separate from the determination of entitlement to divorce. This change was seen as mandating a role for behavioral scientists in custody cases. *See infra* note 65.

[59] California was a pioneer in no-fault legislation. *See* J. AREEN, *supra* note 45, at 267–75. No-fault reforms were the product of various forces. See the discussion in L. WEITZMAN, THE DIVORCE REVOLUTION 15–51, 366–78 (1985). The central concept was that divorces were "in reality only symptoms of the ultimate failure of the relationship," and not the result of a single party's fault. *See* THE 1966 REPORT BY THE GOVERNOR'S COMMISSION ON THE FAMILY (California), *reprinted in part in* J. AREEN, *supra* note 45, at 268.

[60] Within the context of divorce, the fault standard was initially seen as a central obstacle to attorney/social worker collaboration. *See* Felner, Primavera, Farber & Bishop, *Attorneys as Caregivers During Divorce*, 52 AM. J. ORTHOPSYCH. 323, 324–25 (1982). Conciliation courts and no-fault were viewed explicitly as increasing the potential for social workers' involvement with divorce cases. *See id.* These reforms were also seen as favoring an expanded mental health role in place of the declining role of attorneys. *See id.* at 324; *see also* Weil, *Research on Issues in Collaboration Between Social Workers and Lawyers*, 56 SOC. SERV. REV. 393, 394–95 (1982) (arguing that the declining role of the social worker in juvenile court was accompanied by an increased role for the social worker in family court); *infra* note 85.

[61] *See infra* pp. 744–57. The early limited attention to divorce as an emotional event was noted by Freund, *Divorce and Grief*, J. FAM. COUNS., Fall 1974, at 40, 40–43. Freund

that divorce should be treated with appropriate therapeutic intervention and even turned into a potentially growth-promoting experience.[62]

The removal of fault did not, however, end the controversy between spouses. Conflict between spouses often was simply displaced, with child custody questions providing one focus. Whereas prior law tended to place children with the party who was not "at fault" for the divorce, the no-fault "irreconcilable differences" determination could not serve as a standard for deciding custody issues.[63] Successful challenges to gender-specific standards like the tender years presumption further increased uncertainty in the area of child custody decisionmaking. The "best interest of the child" standard without the legal presumption of maternal custody, as well as the emergence of concepts like the "psychological parent,"[64] mandated the involvement of mental health professionals in custody decisionmaking.[65] Current

---

presented divorce as a grieving process with stages akin to those experienced during bereavement. *See id.* at 41–43. J. Louise Despert was one of the early authors to characterize divorce as a series of stages, the first of which was "emotional divorce." *See* Wiseman, *Crisis Theory and the Process of Divorce*, 56 SOC. CASEWORK 205, 206 (1975).

[62] *See* Elkin, *supra* note 36, at 64 (noting that divorcing spouses have the ability to "use the crisis of divorce as an opportunity for personal growth and fulfillment"); Kraus, *The Crisis of Divorce: Growth Promoting or Pathogenic?*, 3 J. DIVORCE 107, 111 (1979) (discussing scientific studies suggesting that divorce may precipitate beneficial growth); Mumma, *supra* note 3, at 25 ("The divorcing family must be redefined legally and socially and treated as a family in transition, not as a family in termination. Divorce must be viewed as an opportunity for new growth and success, not defeat and failure.").

[63] Some legal scholars have called for the inclusion of the tender years doctrine in uniform no-fault law. *See, e.g.*, Ellsworth & Levy, *Legislative Reform of Child Custody Adjudication*, 4 LAW & SOC. REV. 167, 202–03 (1969), *quoted in* J. AREEN, *supra* note 45, at 432. Although section 402 of the Uniform Marriage and Divorce Act did not ultimately contain such a provision, the Commissioners' comments concluded that "[t]he preference for the mother as custodian of young children when all things are equal, for example, is simply a shorthand method of expressing the best interest of children." UNIF. MARRIAGE AND DIVORCE ACT § 402, 9A U.L.A. 628 (1970).

[64] *See generally* J. GOLDSTEIN, A. FREUD & A. SOLNIT, *supra* note 14, *passim* (advocating a child-placement standard focusing on the child's relationship with her psychological parent and on other criteria related to the child's psychological well-being); Davis, *"There is a Book Out . . .": An Analysis of Judicial Absorption of Legislative Facts*, 100 HARV. L. REV. 1539, 1547–92 (1987) (describing the psychological parent theory and analyzing its impact in child placement cases). *But see* Radin, *The Psychological Parent Concept in Contested Custody Cases*, 11 J. PSYCHIATRY & L. 503, 512–13 (1983) (arguing that psychological parents may be nonetheless unfit parents and that additional guidelines should also be considered).

[65] One commentator has stated:

> [A]n analysis of the criteria inherent to the recently enacted [custody] statutes reveal [sic] a strong reliance upon factors that can best be evaluated by behavioral science. Among other factors, assessments must be made of the parent's intelligence, morality, knowledge of child development, personality, child-rearing attitudes, emotional ties with the child, and a host of other factors that are of a social and/or psychological nature. The behavioral scientist has essentially been given a societal mandate for involvement and must be prepared to function appropriately in child custody determinations.

Woody, *Behavioral Science Criteria in Child Custody Determinations*, J. MARRIAGE & FAM. COUNS., Jan. 1977, at 11; *accord* Musetto, *The Role of the Mental Health Professional in*

custody reform efforts are in part the product of the mental health profession's success in labeling divorce an emotional crisis, particularly for children.

The first expansion of the social worker's role in divorce was through conciliation courts created by many jurisdictions when they adopted no-fault legislation. These courts were designed to provide "short-contact marital counseling service for couples on the verge of separation and divorce."[66] The proponents of such courts justified them on the ground that divorce was a social problem requiring state services to ease the crisis.[67] These services could be provided by social workers, giving them a new role in the legal system at a time when their role was being limited elsewhere.[68] Conciliation courts thus embodied the notion of a partnership between law and the behavioral sciences.[69]

These courts initially provided reconciliation counseling, but as divorce became more accepted and reconciliation a less important goal, the counseling method was replaced first by a divorce therapy model[70] and ultimately by the contemporary mediation ideal.[71] As the formal role of social workers evolved, so did their ideology and rhetoric. Consistent throughout the evolution of social workers' involvement with divorce, however, has been their perception that their

---

Contested Custody: Evaluator of Competence or Facilitator of Change, J. DIVORCE, Summer 1981, at 72–74 (promoting a more active role for mental health professionals in disputed custody cases).

66 Elkin, *supra* note 36, at 71; *accord* Sitkin, *The California Conciliation Court: An Interdisciplinary Effort to Promote Matrimony*, 2 GLENDALE L. REV. 31 (1977).

67

> The State has an interest in preserving the institution of marriage and restoring peace into the family home; it is in the home where behavior habits are formed which "influence and mold the character of the future citizens in the community and the nation." The Conciliation Court provides the means for the State to actively pursue this interest.

Sitkin, *supra* note 66, at 37 (quoting Henderson, *Marriage Counseling in a Court of Conciliation*, 3 FAM. L.Q. 6 (1969)) (footnote omitted). Another commentator has observed:

> Because of the upsurge of family breakdown and the increasing use of divorce as a solution to marital problems, there has been an increasing awareness in recent years that the responsibility of the law and the courts in divorce cases ought not to be limited to the narrow and traditional considerations of the legal grounds for divorce. Custody of children, division of property, fixing of alimony, and setting of support payments are issues which rarely disclose the real reasons underlying the disintegration of the family.

Elkin, *supra* note 36, at 63–64.

68 At this time, social workers were experiencing a declining role in delinquency proceedings with the movement away from a therapeutic to a more adversarial model. *See* Scherrer, *How Social Workers Help Lawyers*, 21 SOC. WORK 279, 279 (1976) (remarking on the tension between social workers and lawyers in the juvenile court context); Weil, *supra* note 60, at 394–95 (contrasting the trend toward adversarial proceedings in juvenile and dependency courts with a "countertrend . . . in the area of divorce and child custody").

69 *See* Elkin, *supra* note 36, at 63.

70 *See infra* pp. 746–52.

71 *See id.*

appropriate function is to make divorce as conflict-free as possible, or at least to manage the conflict appropriately.[72]

B. Changing Social Work Views[73]

Under early social work ideology, divorce was viewed as pathological.[74] Marriage was to last forever, unless there was legally recognized fault. Divorce was to be avoided if at all possible, and the responsibility of the helping professions was to counsel reconciliation. Under no-fault divorce, by contrast, social workers have moved away from the goal of formally reconciling the couple to reconciling them to their new post-divorce relationship and status. The helping professions adapted to the change in legal rules by creating their own view of reconciling or rehabilitating "the family," in which both parents would continue to "co-parent" after divorce.[75]

Currently, the language of the helping professions portrays divorce as an "emotional crisis" that has to be treated, but that can also be an occasion that provides some "unique opportunities for growth."[76] In the rhetoric of the social workers, divorce is a crisis within the "family system"[77] — a type of "situational" crisis to be "managed."[78]

---

[72] Reducing or managing conflict is a clearly stated goal in many instances of divorce, regardless of the ultimate outcome. For example, in an early and influential writing, the ambitious scope of the social workers' task at divorce was clearly set forth:

> We do not have as a goal the saving of all marriages, but we are concerned with the tragedy of the unnecessary divorce. . . . A conciliation court serves families. If in the course of such service a family does not reconcile, this does not mean that the counselor's concern and responsibility to the family is at an end. In such cases, we still offer a very important and worthwhile service in our counseling efforts to help the family close the book gently rather than bang it shut in anger; to help the family terminate the marriage with dignity, minimal trauma, and without the need to strike back — a need which is often responsible for much of post-divorce litigation.

Elkin, *supra* note 36, at 64.

[73] In this and subsequent sections of the Article, some words and phrases appear in quotation marks in order to highlight them as examples of social work rhetoric. None of these words or phrases should be unfamiliar to the reader, although many are clearly professional jargon. In fact, the dominance of the social work rhetoric is illustrated by the extent to which its terms have been accepted and incorporated into everyday discussions. Specific examples of the professional uses of the terms are provided by the extensive quotes in the footnotes.

[74] *See* Kraus, *supra* note 62, at 108–11 (describing and critiquing the "pathogenic" perspective on divorce); *see also* Girdner, *supra* note 45, at 169–70 (noting that "[t]he ideological definition of divorce as pathology was pervasive until the 1970s").

[75] *See, e.g.*, Girdner, *supra* note 45, at 169–71.

[76] *See* Elkin, *supra* note 36, at 64; Kraus, *supra* note 62, at 108; Mumma, *supra* note 3, at 25.

[77] A family systems approach focuses on the ways that a group of individuals affect and are affected by each other. Divorce, therefore, is a process through which the unit or system moves, not an event that happens to individuals. *See* Mumma, *supra* note 3, at 24–25.

[78] *See generally* Counts & Sacks, *The Need for Crisis Intervention During Marital Separation*, 30 SOC. WORK 146 (1985) (outlining factors that increase stresses of separation and presenting strategies for intervention by mental health professionals).

Although the profession no longer sees divorce as pathological, a negative impact on the family system is viewed as inevitable. The focus of the helping professional, under this view of divorce, is on both alleviating the initial "trauma" of divorce and managing the "external variables" that may affect the family's future "response and adjustment to divorce."

The goal of the helping professional is to bring the parties to the recognition that the "structural dimensions" of their former marital system have not disappeared but must be reshaped into a new, though limited, "post-dissolution organization." This new organization is based on the relationship between the parents — now ex-spouses — with parent-child relationships as "sub-systems" within this paradigm.[79] Divorce requires parents to "decouple from their former marital and nuclear roles and begin to recouple at a level of shared parenting responsibilities."[80]

In this framework, the role of the system is to be therapeutic — to facilitate and assist the family in adapting to a new post-divorce family structure.[81] Attorneys, in this context, are viewed as ill-equipped to handle the crisis because of their adversarial orientation and the ways in which they impede or defeat the therapeutic ideal.[82] By contrast, social workers and others in the helping professions are in possession or control of the therapeutic process.[83]

---

[79] *See* Durst, Wedemeyer & Zurcher, *Parenting Partnerships After Divorce: Implications for Practice*, 30 SOC. WORK 423 (1985) (describing five types of continuing parental partnerships in post-divorce families).

[80] Everett & Volgy, *Family Assessment in Child Custody Disputes*, 9 J. MARITAL & FAM. THERAPY 343, 348 (1983).

[81] Although common sense might indicate both that no mediation or therapy is needed by divorcing spouses who handle their divorces without protracted, acrimonious litigation, and that spouses in strong opposition to one another will not be transformed into conciliatory shared-parenting partners by any amount of mediation or therapy, the advocates of therapy recognize few exceptions. One commentator has stated:

> Virtually all divorcing parents need help in minimizing and managing stress. For this sample, no immunity to stress was afforded by age, sex, socioeconomic status or other background factors. Besides the passage of time, only one other factor led to a significant decrease in stress — the parental use of valued helping resources in coping with the divorce.

Fulmer, *A Structural Approach to Unresolved Mourning in Single Parent Family Systems*, 9 J. MARITAL & FAM. THERAPY 259, 268 (1983); *accord* Counts & Sacks, *supra* note 78, at 149 ("Few people caught up in the process of separation are equipped to deal effectively with the considerable and unique stresses [involved] . . . This is especially true of children and adolescents. Thus, intervention is important and should be the rule, not the exception."). Legal authors, by contrast, characterize the same situation not as a treatment opportunity but as a situation raising questions about the appropriateness of state intervention. For documentation of potential abuses, see Levy, *supra* note 43, at 769–70, 771–75.

[82] *See* Pearson & Thoennes, *Mediation in Custody Disputes*, 4 BEHAV. SCI. & L. 203, 203–05 (1986).

[83] *See* Scherrer, *supra* note 68 (suggesting six areas — interviewing, evaluation, crisis inter-

C. *Opportunity Seized: The Rhetorical War*

As their involvement with divorce cases through conciliation counseling and court-ordered custody evaluations increased, social workers rejected the lawyer/social worker partnership that they had initially espoused.[84] Within the context of divorce generally — and disputed custody cases particularly — helping professionals challenged central aspects of legal ideology. With the elimination of fault-based divorce and the advent of their crisis theory of divorce, helping professionals began to assert that adversarial concepts and procedures were inappropriate for resolving divorce and custody cases.[85] Social workers objected to the very nature of the adversarial process, asserting that it was unnecessary, inappropriate, and indicative of the outmoded notions of "winning" or "losing" custody. Divorce was a crisis to be worked through; conflict was to be recognized and managed. Spouses (with the aid of a social worker) were to be self-determining and exercise their responsibility to each other and their children to settle their differences so they could function as post-divorce parents. There simply was no room for such growth in the traditional adversarial system.[86] Lawyers' use of adversarial procedures was especially criticized for its effect on children.[87] In essence, social workers' attacks

---

vention, short-term case work, negotiation, and referral — in which the social worker can make a significant contribution).

[84] For amplification of the partnership ideal as expressed in 1973, see Elkin, *supra* note 36, at 63. Later mediation literature, however, suggested a complete displacement of attorneys: "At the close of mediation, with a legally binding settlement agreement, either party may obtain an uncontested, no-fault divorce at a nominal cost." McKenry, *Mediation Eases the Split*, PRAC. DIG. Dec. 1979, at 8, 9.

[85] Elkin states:

> [T]he elimination of 'fault' has made it possible for the Court to play a much lesser part in banking the fires of hostility. It is a well-known fact in role theory that people cast in the roles of adversaries probably will live up to those roles. . . . [T]he elimination of adversary proceedings eliminated adversary roles and therefore reduced the need to fulfill antagonistic roles and the need to strike out at each other.

Elkin, *supra* note 36, at 70.

Social workers have frequently expressed their discomfort at working in the legal system because law and social work are perceived as encompassing contrasting frameworks. Whereas both professions "help" clients — lawyers with the client's rights, social workers with the client's emotions — social workers believe their values and principles are compromised by the adversarial model. *See, e.g.*, Fogelson, *How Social Workers Perceive Lawyers*, 51 SOC. CASEWORK 95, 99 (1970); Pruhs, Paulsen & Tysseling, *supra* note 24, at 537; Scherrer, *supra* note 68, at 279. For example, several authors found that "[t]he rational-logical emphasis of the legal system does not provide an ideal atmosphere for the resolution of interpersonal conflict and, in fact, may serve as a catalyst to increased hostilities." Herrman, McKenry & Weber, *Attorneys' Perceptions of Their Role in Divorce*, 2 J. DIVORCE 313, 315 (1979).

[86] *See* Pruhs, Paulsen & Tysseling, *supra* note 24.

[87] *See, e.g.*, Felner & Farber, *Social Policy for Child Custody: A Multidisciplinary Framework*, 50 AM. J. ORTHOPSYCH. 341, 345 (1980) ("One must ask if an adversarial process, in which a child's parents are the adversaries and the child is the prize, is best suited to arrive at a placement that truly serves the child's best interests."); Mumma, *supra* note 3, at 25 (stating

questioned both the appropriateness of the representation ideal and adversariness as a process by which fact-finding and decisionmaking occur.[88]

The helping professions tend to distinguish two aspects of divorce — the emotional divorce, which involves "feelings," and the legal divorce, which involves a division of property, a determination of support, and a decision about custody.[89] Social workers view the legal divorce as secondary to the emotional divorce. Thus, once an emotional divorce has occurred, the legal divorce is pro forma; conversely, without an emotional divorce, no true separation can or will occur and the parties will continue to battle throughout and after the legal divorce. Some form of counseling, therapy, or mediation is seen as essential to a resolution of these emotional issues,[90] with post-divorce shared parenting as the optimal goal.

In this regard, social workers argued that an adversarial role was unnecessary — lawyers were not needed to prove grounds for divorce as they had been under the fault-based system. Similarly, social workers viewed lawyers as unconcerned with, and incompetent to perform,

---

that "the litigation process is little more than an institutionalized form of emotional abuse to children"); Woody, *Preventive Intervention for Children of Divorce*, 59 SOC. CASEWORK 537, 541 (1978) ("For the average family, divorce constitutes a serious crisis situation, and it is likely to be a 'psychological emergency' for the children."). Children were considered the innocent victims of the increasing divorce rate. *See id.* at 541 ("Divorce is certainly a process over which children have no control; inasmuch as possible, they should not become its victims.").

[88] For example, one commentator stated:

> Lawyers represent their clients to the best of their abilities, regardless of the effect that might have on the other party. Thus, they tend to push their particular client to win every possible advantage. This provides the couple with another arena in which to battle out the issues that led to the divorce at the same time that they are trying to negotiate a settlement.

Haynes, *Divorce Mediator: A New Role*, 23 SOC. WORK 5, 5 (1978). Other authors have observed:

> In addition to the universal and unconscious distortions and misunderstandings of relationships by each individual, in custody evaluations everyone is consciously distorting and misinterpreting. The situation precludes total honesty. Each parent is trying to present him- or herself as the best, the other as the worst, and will often censor or distort information to achieve that goal.

Rosenberg, Kleinman & Brantley, *Custody Evaluations: Helping the Family Reorganize*, 63 SOC. CASEWORK 203, 205 (1982).

[89] *See* Oneglia & Orlin, *A Model for Combined Private Practice: Attorneys and Social Workers in Domestic Relations*, J. APPLIED SOC. SCI. Fall/Winter 1978, at 37, 39.

[90] *See supra* note 81; *see also* Herrman, McKenry & Weber, *supra* note 85, at 321 (stating that "[i]t may be necessary in some circumstances for one or both lawyers to undertake the temporary role of listener, but the ultimate goal should be to get the client into the hands of a trained therapist" (citation omitted)). For discussions concerning the role of the therapist in child custody disputes, see generally Counts & Sacks, cited in note 78 above; Everett & Volgy, cited in note 80 above; Sprenkle & Storm, *Divorce Therapy Outcome Research: A Substantive and Methodological Review*, 9 J. MARITAL & FAM. THERAPY 239 (1983); and Woody, Colley, Schlegelmilch, Maginn & Balsanek, *Child Adjustment to Parental Stress Following Divorce*, 65 SOC. CASEWORK 405 (1984).

the needed therapeutic function.[91] Lawyers could not be discarded altogether, however, as some issues still needed legal resolution. The social work literature explicitly expressed the competition between the professions, with legal personnel cast as inappropriate decisionmakers in custody cases due to their lack of training in child development and psychology.[92]

Although it was initially thought that no-fault divorce would eliminate conflict,[93] social workers' involvement with the system convinced them that this legal change had no such transformative effect.[94] In

---

[91] *See, e.g.*, Wiseman, *supra* note 61, at 207 (stating that "[l]awyers do little to lessen the anger that naturally arises; . . . often they appear to heighten it").

Some have viewed the nature of legal training as the cause of attorneys' inadequacies. *See* Oneglia & Orlin, *supra* note 89, at 39 ("Training in contracts, torts and the doctrine of the 'reasonable man' does nothing to prepare the lawyer to handle the human being who is behind the legal problem. . . . [T]he lawyer has no time for non-legal 'trifles' — ironically usually most of the major grievances of the suffering client.").

Others gave advice as to how to handle the attorney involved in the social worker's case:

> [A]n early meeting or telephone contact with the attorneys involved . . . may begin to reduce the adversarial nature of the process . . . . The legal process often seems to have a life and energy of its own; active and repeated attempts . . . are needed to diminish the pressure on the parents to continue their adversarial stance.

Rosenberg, Kleinman & Brantley, *supra* note 88, at 205.

[92] *See, e.g.*, Oneglia & Orlin, *supra* note 89, at 43–44 ("The judge and the lawyers are not qualified to make a determination as to the best placement for a child considering emotional factors. Judges can evaluate financial and physical circumstances — as can almost any layman.").

Some commentators are generous to judges even while criticizing them:

> Although it can be assumed optimistically that most judges are concerned, sensitive, intelligent people who want the best for families, it can also safely be assumed that many of them have limited training in child development, women's issues, psychosocial assessment, or family relations. The reality is that the exercise of judicial discretion is far less a product of the judge's learning than of his or her temperament, background, interests, and biases.

Noble, *supra* note 16, at 407 (footnote omitted). *But see* Charnas, *Practice Trends in Divorce Related Child Custody*, J. DIVORCE, Summer 1981, at 57, 62 (reporting on a study indicating that "there is no interdisciplinary difference in the ability of judges and mental health professionals to select a custodial psychological parent; both overwhelmingly chose as the custodial parent the one which the evaluation reflected as having a more positive and consistent emotional bond with the children").

The competition between the social worker's role and the lawyer's role (as defined by the social workers) becomes apparent:

> The pain, anger, and frustration of divorce are frequently exacerbated by the legal process as it presently works. Frequently, the social worker who has been involved with the family during the period leading up to the decision to divorce is excluded from the proceedings, and the clients are passed onto [sic] a person in another profession. However, it is at precisely this time that the special skills of the social worker are most needed.

Haynes, *supra* note 88, at 5.

[93] *See* L. WEITZMAN, *supra* note 59, at 16–17 (discussing reformers' objectives); Elkin, *supra* note 36, at 69.

[94] One article stated, for example:

> The agency's direct involvement in the divorce process through the preparation of child custody evaluations only served to strengthen the staff's concern with the frequency of unsatisfactory outcomes. Even the most arduous, comprehensive, and conciliatorily

the custody area, in particular, conflict was still apparent. Moreover, the mental health worker, philosophically geared toward cooperation and compromise, experienced great frustration working within a legal system that required the choice of one parent over another and promoted one relationship while "terminating" another.[95] In the task of performing custody evaluations, for example, even the most carefully expressed adverse recommendation might produce pain and anger.[96]

Social workers' criticisms of the existing no-fault system formed the basis of calls for an alternative system, reflecting even more procedural and substantive changes, such as mediation and the establishment of a shared parenting norm. These reforms were urged in rhetoric that embodied their view of litigation, conflict, and what is desirable in the post-divorce family.[97]

> drafted custody evaluation was unsuccessful in significantly reducing the competitiveness, acrimony, and pain within the family system. There continued to be a winner, a loser, and ongoing stress.

Pruhs, Paulsen & Tysseling, *supra* note 24, at 532.

95 *See id.* at 532–33.

96 *See* Derdeyn, *Child Custody Consultation*, 45 AM. J. ORTHOPSYCH. 791, 796–97 (1975); Mumma, *supra* note 3, at 24 (stating that "[t]he adversarial court proceeding and the social worker's investigation and report did not reinforce cooperation and agreement, but rather seemed to generate conflict"); Rosenberg, Kleinman & Brantley, *supra* note 88, at 207.

Social workers' disenchantment with the conflict-reducing potential of no-fault divorce led them toward mediation. Consider the following report about a private agency's transition to a mediation model:

> The agency was uncomfortable in its role [of performing evaluations for use in court] which too often resulted in prolonging, sometimes intensifying, and too seldom resolving the agony of the family. A hypothesis evolved: it was not the characteristics of the decision itself that generated failures but rather the identity of the decision makers. The courts could not hope to *resolve* parental disputes if they did not have the cooperation of the family.
>
> When parents accepted responsibility for restructuring the family, when they used their energy to create a resolution, and when they had an investment in making that resolution work, the outcome had the greatest hope of becoming a true resolution.

Pruhs, Paulsen & Tysseling, *supra* note 24, at 532 (emphasis in original). Another commentator reported:

> In undertaking the role of divorce mediator, social workers must first overcome the difficulty of being party to a family's breakup. Most social workers see their role as a supportive one and use their professional skills in assisting families to resolve their problems and stay together. . . .
>
> Once divorce is inevitable, the social worker's role changes to one of attempting to make the separation as painless as possible, to help the couple maintain their individual dignity, and to assist the children to make the transition by reducing the conflict inherent in the process of divorce.

Haynes, *supra* note 88, at 5.

97

> With half of all first marriages ending in divorce, courtrooms are jammed with hostile parents prepared for battle over the custody or visitation of their mutual children. These parents and children face a destructive adversarial process that will activate a network of court personnel, social workers, and other professionals in a consuming, costly, and stressful human drama that frequently endures for years. For most of these parents the wrangling ends only when one or both litigants become financially or emotionally exhausted and can no longer continue the legal battle. Judges' orders do not seem to settle

The calls for change were accompanied by assertions about what was "really" happening in the divorce context. That reality was psychological, not legal, in its focus. According to mental health professionals, the desire to litigate divorce issues, particularly custody, is the product of unresolved feelings about the termination of the marriage.[98] Intervention by a helping professional is necessary to assist a couple in resolving these feelings so that they do not engage in protracted litigation as the extension of their emotional battles. The helping professionals' view is that litigation is harmful to all, particularly children,[99] and that it is usually undertaken without any true legal or factual justification.[100]

Moreover, results achieved under a sole custody legal doctrine were objectionable from the viewpoint of social workers' "family-systems" theory. Rather than focusing on the best parent, the social worker concentrated on how to "restructure" the family.[101] Restructuring

---

> things, at least for very long. Children suffer and parents blame each other, fueling the confict and maintaining the tragic cycle.
>
> What can be done to help? Parents can voluntarily seek out a mediation center . . . .

Mumma, *supra* note 3, at 22.

[98] This theme is strongly presented in the very influential work of Wallerstein & Kelly, *Children and Divorce: A Review*, 24 SOC. WORK 468 (1979), in which the authors state:

> Psychologically, an individual's rage against an ex-spouse, often expressed in litigation in which the child is the pawn, can apparently remain undiminished by the passage of time or by distance. The fight for a child may serve profound psychological needs in a parent, including the warding off of severe depression and other forms of pathological disorganization.

Id. at 472.

[99] *See* sources cited *supra* note 87.

[100] The literature recognizes few valid bases for custody battles. *See, e.g.*, Musetto, *supra* note 65, at 76, 78 ("Parents who contest custody are usually not emotionally divorced from each other: their struggles with one another are not dead but have disguised themselves as a custody dispute. . . . Custody/visitation disputes are essentially unresolved family conflicts exacerbated by the breakup of the family and the adversarial court procedures . . . ."). Even if some valid reasons for custody disputes were recognized, they were considered "exceptional." *See* Noble, *supra* note 16, at 407.

Conflict in other areas might also be viewed as indicative of pathology:

> Struggles over property may be necessary but they are frequently a manifestation of, if not a metaphor for, security needs. Each parent has a right to have these needs met to the extent of the available resources. It is in the best interest of each parent to see that the other spouse's needs are met.

Pruhs, Paulsen, & Tysseling, *supra* note 24, at 535; *accord* Johnston, Campbell & Tall, *Impasses to the Resolution of Custody and Visitation Disputes*, 55 AM. J. ORTHOPSYCH. 112 (1985) (proposing that interpersonal conflict reflected in the decision to divorce manifests itself in a variety of continuing battles between former spouses).

[101] *See* Rosenberg, Kleinman & Brantley, *supra* note 88, at 204, 207; Wallerstein & Kelly, *supra* note 98, at 468.

Reorganization is clearly the goal:

> Just as the relationship between married spouses is a critical determinant of family interaction, so, too, is the relationship between divorced spouses critical to divorced family reorganization and interaction . . . . The [stressful] process of coparental redefinition requires that divorced spouses separate their spousal and parental roles, terminating

meant allowing both parents to continue their parental relationship with the children.[102] When forced to choose between parents, helping professionals preferred the parent who would most freely allow the child access to the other parent.[103] The notion of "the most generous parent" became synonymous with the determination of who was the better parent.[104]

> the former while redefining the latter. This very difficult and somewhat paradoxical process forms the nucleus of divorced family reorganization and redefinition.

Ahrons, *The Continuing Coparental Relationship Between Divorced Spouses*, 51 AM. J. ORTHOPSYCH. 415, 415 (1981).

Even though the child is characterized as the ultimate beneficiary (as he or she must be for obvious reasons), sometimes it is clear that others are also winners:

> Rather than support the imposition of legal visitation restrictions, we should do everything in our power to maximize contact between the child and both parents. One clear way of doing that is through joint custody arrangements. As suggested by this study, structural arrangements such as custody and visitation are crucial to the post-divorce *adjustment of fathers and, ultimately, of their children.* A different quality of psychological involvement grows out of the opportunity to take care of (*i.e.*, be a parent to) one's child, rather than "visit" with one's child.

Greif, *supra* note 16, at 319 (emphasis added).

102 The debate among mental health professionals over the form of the post-divorce family was perhaps engendered in 1973 by the publication of J. GOLDSTEIN, A. FREUD & A. SOLNIT, BEYOND THE BEST INTERESTS OF THE CHILD, cited in note 14 above. The thesis of the work was that custody placement questions should be resolved according to who was the child's "psychological parent." Perhaps more controversial, however, was the authors' suggestion that the custodial parent be given complete decisionmaking power in relation to the child, including whether the noncustodial parent had visitation privileges. *See id.* at 38.

The research of Wallerstein and Kelly profoundly influenced the contemporary movement toward the view that a child needs both parents after divorce:

> The continuation of contact between the child and the parent who has not retained custody is a crucial issue. Mounting evidence indicates that the maintenance of this relationship between parent and child is of central importance in the psychological adjustment of children within the postdivorce family. [One previous researcher] found that children who spent little time with their fathers during the year after the marital breakup were more likely to develop psychiatric symptomatology than those youngsters who enjoyed more frequent contacts. The findings of the present authors' study point to a significant link between depression in younger children and adolescents and diminished visiting by the children's fathers. Conversely, high self-esteem in all children, especially in older boys, was tied to a good father-child relationship that had been sustained within the structure of visitation.

Wallerstein & Kelly, *supra* note 98, at 471 (citations omitted). *But cf.* Fineman & Opie, *supra* note 12, at 140–43 (criticizing the tendency of these and other social scientists to generalize from limited data and to overlook complex qualifications inherent in their conclusions). Notions of shared parenting also emphasized equality between the sexes and liberal feminist concerns. *See supra* note 48 and accompanying text.

103 *See, e.g.*, Mumma, *supra* note 3, at 30 ("We attempt to base recommendations on the desired changes in the relationship. For example, we may recommend custody be given to the parent who is most likely to allow the most frequent or flexible contact with the other parent and extended family.").

104 Some states have enacted so-called friendly parent provisions. *See, e.g.*, CAL. CIV. CODE § 4600(b)(1) (West Supp. 1987); COLO. REV. STAT. § 14-10-124(1.5)(f) (Supp. 1986); ME. REV. STAT. ANN. tit. 19, § 752.5H (Supp. 1987); MICH. COMP. LAWS ANN. § 722.23(j) (West Supp.

Given social workers' assumptions, their criticisms of the legal system, and their characterization of the divorce, it is no surprise that mediation by those trained in the helping professions emerged as the logical procedural solution.[105] If disputed custody was really an emotional event, and the legal system and lawyers had no ability to address the problems, then a new process and new personnel were necessary. Social workers' criticisms of legal decisionmakers, processes, and results were essential to the formulation of the mediation ideal.[106]

1987). For a discussion of these statutes, see Schulman & Pitt, *Second Thoughts on Joint Child Custody: Analysis of Legislation and its Implications for Women and Children*, 12 GOLDEN GATE U.L. REV. 539, 554–56 (1982).

This version of the shared parenting ideal is being implemented even without statutory authority, as I discovered during my primary research in family court counseling units in Wisconsin during 1984–85. These court-associated social workers were engaged in implementing the shared parenting ideal through the informal adoption of a friendly parent provision and a joint custody norm.

Sometimes these generous parent innovations are justified by the custodial parent's perceived need for assistance from the noncustodial parent: "Parents, like children, benefit from two-parent families. The burdens of being a single parent are unfair not only to the child but also to the parents." Pruhs, Paulsen & Tysseling, *supra* note 24, at 535.

At other times, the children's perceived needs seem paramount. "It is clear that the best interests of the children involve much more than the linear relationships between parent and children. . . . One major consideration often may be the custodial parent's ability to allow an arrangement for an appropriate continuing relationship with the noncustodial parent as well as significant others." Rosenberg, Kleinman & Brantley, *supra* note 88, at 207.

105 The following quotation shows the way in which the helping professions assert this preference for mediation:

> The role of the divorce mediator is to assist the parties to reach a fair settlement in a way that enables them to separate the economic issues from the emotional ones. In the process, he performs the function of helping the clients focus on the future rather than the past. The mediator has another important role. At this critical moment, he may be the only person in the couple's lives who is nonjudgmental and interested in their needs.

Haynes, *supra* note 88, at 6.

106 The mediation ideal seems to have been constructed out of the criticisms of lawyering, denouncing the adversarial model:

> Social workers can understand how damaging [the adversarial] process is. Many of the emotional hurts and feelings of guilt are displayed during the struggle for an economic settlement. The attorney is neither equipped nor interested in dealing with a client's emotional upheaval. He is looking for a settlement that can be taken into court for approval.
>
> . . . .
>
> The concept of mediation is implicit in the role of social worker. Not only because of their professional ethics, but also because of their training and experience, *all social workers*, but particularly those specializing in family therapy, *are uniquely qualified to perform the task of mediation.*

Id. at 6, 8 (emphasis added).

Mediation is often presented as the solution to all sorts of family problems created by the adversary system. *See, e.g.*, Mumma, *supra* note 3, at 24.

This change in procedure is viewed as likely to effect a change in the dynamics of the divorce process: "Managing the process not only provides the instrumental assessment, planning, and ongoing reinforcement of the mediation, but allows the mediator to role-model the 'how to'

Language has played a critical role in the reform process that has shifted decisionmaking authority to mediators and the helping profession. The rhetoric employed criticized the traditional system and established an alternative that called for skills possessed by the helping professionals. Yet the rhetoric has occasioned more than a transfer, formal or informal, of responsibility for making the ultimate decision in contested cases. More importantly, it has invoked changes in the substantive rules by which cases are resolved. The domination of social worker ideology and rhetoric now appears complete. It is inconceivable that one could seriously discuss custody policy and practice today without both using the rhetoric and addressing the concepts and values of the helping professions.

V. The Manner of Appropriation: The Use of Narrative Strategies and the Intersection of Other Interests

I believe that the rhetoric and strategy of the helping professions have been successful for two related reasons. First, the helping professions have presented their arguments in the form of "stories" that contain powerful images that are readily understood by those not familiar with the custody decisionmaking process. Second, the images that they project intersect and are compatible with the interests of significant societal groups that have facilitated the changes suggested by the stories.

A. Narrative Strategies

One of the significant methods by which the helping professions' ideals became dominant in the custody area was through the construction and manipulation of rhetorical visions or narratives.[107] I call these rhetorical devices narratives because they are stories with a beginning, a middle, and an end. There is competition and drama — tension and resolution — in these narratives. Their "morals" are ways of legitimating one type of substantive and procedural result to the exclusion of others. In describing or illustrating a "problem," they also suggest the "solution." This form of presentation makes the professional standards of the helping professions and the legal system concrete, understandable, and susceptible to positive action. This

---

of cooperative conflict resolution, so that when the parties leave, they can emulate the system for their future needs." Barsky, *Strategies and Techniques of Divorce Mediation*, 65 Soc. Casework 102, 105 (1984). Even these idealized presentations, however, recognize that some hostility is inevitable: "Some ventilation of hostility may be necessary so that the individual can move beyond the emotional feeling and not be held back by it. Thus, permitting a display of anger may be useful, if the mediator keeps in mind its effect on the other spouse." *Id.* at 106.

[107] I have discussed this phenomenon within the context of family law reforms elsewhere. *See* Fineman, *supra* note 48.

rhetorical strategy operates by presenting simplistic dichotomous images: negative images or "horror stories" regarding the existing (lawyer-controlled) divorce practice, and corresponding positive images or "fairy tales" of an idealized (social worker-controlled) process for purer and better decisionmaking.

These narratives had an additional characteristic that operated to the helping professions' advantage in securing changes. They were cast in terms of mere substitution of decisionmakers rather than of alteration of results. They focused on divorce as a discrete event that had to be made less volatile through the use of trained mediators. These narratives either assumed or ignored and obscured the desirability of the substantive goal of shared parenting. The narratives confined the discussion to the desirability of a change in procedure without revealing that this would also produce a change in substance compatible with the new decisionmakers' professional ideology and norms.

The use of rhetorical devices serves the institutional interests of those in the mediation business who wish to stake out an area for their own control. Their language, which is cast as neutral and professional, is political.[108] This fact has been obscured, however, because their rhetoric has confined the debate to a procedural level.

1. The Horror Story. — The image of the legal system constructed by the helping professions is adversarial, combative, and productive of divisions, misunderstandings, and hostility.[109] These negative characterizations are understood to be the inevitable product of a system controlled by attorneys and the judiciary. Social workers assert that lawyers focus on rights, claims, due process, and other things "peripheral" to the real issues.

Those who flock to mediation as the ideal decisionmaking mechanism accuse lawyers and the adversary system of increasing trauma, escalating conflict, obstructing communication, failing to perceive the

---

[108] As Professor Edelman discussed in his early work on linguistic theory:

> With [language] we not only describe reality but create our own realities. . . . It is a commonplace of linguistic theory that language, thought, and action shape each other. Language is always an intrinsic part of some particular social situation; it is never an independent instrument or simply a tool for description. By naively perceiving it as a tool, we mask its profound part in creating social relationships and in evoking the roles and the "selves" of those relationships.
>
> . . . .
>
> The most fundamental and long-lasting influences upon political beliefs flow . . . from language that is not perceived as political at all . . . .
>
> The special language of the helping professions, which we are socialized to see as professional and as nonpolitical, is a major example of this level of politics . . . .

Edelman, *The Political Language of the Helping Professions*, 4 POL. & SOC. 295, 296 (1974).

[109] Examples of such labeling are evident in the quotations from Haynes, cited in note 88 above, at 5–6; Herrman, McHenry & Weber, cited in note 85 above, at 314–16; Mumma, cited in note 3 above, at 23, and quoted in note 97 above; and Wiseman, cited in note 91 above, at 207.

need for negotiation and counseling, and generally interfering with the development of a process that could help the parties.[110] In their vision, the adversarial system, with its emphasis on conflict and rationality, is inherently unresponsive to the "emotions" and "feelings" associated with the divorce process,[111] which social workers believe are more important and worthy of concern.

Lawyers in general and judges in particular are viewed as poorly trained to deal with the psychological aspects of divorce. Because they employ what is described as "militant tunnel-vision advocacy" as a result of their "temperament and training," lawyers cannot possibly make a "success of . . . divorce."[112] Lawyers and judges are seen as acting on their own biases and values in determining what is in the best interest of the child.[113] A related criticism is that lawyers replace the parties in the negotiation process and thereby fail to enhance the conflict management skills of the parties and to produce agreements to which the parties are committed.[114] Lawyers are criticized for dwelling on the past, laying blame, finding fault, and failing to focus on future conduct as do mediators.[115] In this way, social workers' rhetoric lays the basis for their claim to control of the process.

---

[110] *See supra* pp. 746–47.

[111] *See, e.g.*, Herrman, McKenry & Weber, *supra* note 85, at 314–15.

[112] *See* Blinder, *Marital Dissolution and Child Custody: A Primer for Family Therapists and Divorce Attorneys*, 9 FAM. THERAPY 1, 5 (1982). Blinder's view of the different roles of attorney and social worker is so remarkable that it is worth quoting in full:

> In short, the attorney has an obligation to point out to the client that the manifest reasons s/he seeks a divorce may not be the real ones, and that the need for professional guidance may not end with marital dissolution. It is the task of the family therapist to help people make a success of their marriage. Should that be impossible, the therapist may still be able to assist the attorney in the latter's responsibility to help the couple at least make a success of their divorce. Attorneys by temperament and training are inclined to see marital and child custody problems as residing entirely within their opponent's client, leaving their own client blameless. The family therapist has the obligation to help the attorney recognize that such problems usually reside not *within* but *between* the contesting parties. I know of no field of law where the tools of militant tunnel-vision advocacy are less appropriate.

Id. (emphasis in original).

[113] *See, e.g.*, Noble, *supra* note 16, at 407 (arguing that lawyers are naturally biased in favor of their clients and that the exercise of judicial discretion is a product of the judge's temperament, background, interests, and biases).

[114] *See, e.g.*, McKenry, *supra* note 84, at 8. Indeed, McKenry views mediation as the only "responsible" choice for couples:

> In the adversary system, couples relinquish nearly all responsibility for decisions about the settlement to their respective attorneys and communicate with each other by proxy. Couples involved in divorce mediation decide on the issues of their divorce settlement themselves. The partners work together under the guidance of an impartial mediator and according to the marital mediation rules of the association.

Id.; *accord* Barsky, *supra* note 106, at 105 ("When the man and woman first entered mediation, their conflict-resolving styles may have consisted primarily of the withdrawing, smoothing, or forcing procedures; by the time their agreement is reached, they have learned the mediator's managerial skills of confrontation and compromise.").

[115] *See* Deis, *California's Answer: Mandatory Mediation of Child Custody and Visitation*

Even social workers and mediators who are friendly to lawyers cannot seem to avoid a negative, stereotypical characterization of them. In a recent article advocating a close working relationship between the professions, one author described how lawyers are committed to "rationality, rights, and conflict solution," whereas social workers are concerned with "feelings, needs, and growth through relationship."[116] In the social work world, of course, to accuse someone of rationality or intellectualism is a criticism, implying an insensitivity to more important emotional concerns.[117]

The generic horror story[118] therefore involves a husband, wife and child(ren) who enter the divorce process, employing two lawyers (his and hers). There is escalating bitterness, pain, and suffering. More and more money is expended. The child(ren) is(are) particularly hurt by the process, particularly since he/she(they) lose(s) a parent in the process (the "noncustodial" parent). It is a process in which there are "winners" and "losers." In other words, it seems inevitable that there will be an unhappy ending to this narrative.

2. *The Fairy Tale.* — In contrast to the negative images embodied in the horror stories describing the legal process, the helping professions present themselves as a distinct and preferable alternative. The ideal is established rhetorically.

Social workers view divorce as occasioning the birth of an ongoing, albeit different, relationship, with mediators and social workers as its midwives and monitors. "Let's talk about it" seems to be the ideal, and the talk is envisioned as continuing for decades. The continued involvement is not only with each other but with the legal system as well. This ideal is obviously very different from the traditional legal system, which seeks an end or termination of a significant interaction at divorce: a division, distribution, or allocation of the things acquired during marriage — an emancipatory model — and with its "ending," the permission for a "new life" for the participants and the withdrawal of active legal interference in their relationship.

The helping professions' ideal process "avoids" or "reduces" conflict and is typified by mediation. Helping professionals believe that mediation,[119] employing a therapeutic process, is within their exclusive

---

Disputes, 1 OHIO ST. J. ON DISPUTE RESOLUTION 149, 163–66 (1985) (discussing the advantages of mandatory mediation); Pearson, *Child Custody: Why Not Let the Parents Decide?*, 20 JUDGES' J. 4, 6 (1981) (outlining the argument "that the adversary system is simply inappropriate for the resolution of many marital disputes," including child custody).

116 Parsloe, *The Interface of Law and Social Work*, 4 CONTEMP. SOC. WORK EDUC. 183, 184 (1981).

117 *See id.*

118 *See, e.g., supra* note 97.

119 There is a large body of literature on family mediation, both in social work and legal publications. For an understanding of the development of family mediation, how it contrasts

domain because lawyers, unlike social workers, ignore the underlying causes of divorce and give little regard to the "real reason" for the split-up. Therapeutic skills can facilitate acceptance of the divorce and foster a positive approach to the crisis.[120]

Lawyers' skills are downgraded and social workers' and mediators' skills are mystified and reified:

> Lawyers or others with legal experience have much to offer, but skills in behavioral science are lacking. It is generally easier for one trained in behavioral sciences to acquire legal and other knowledge required for mediation, than for the legally trained person to gain knowledge and a feel for behavioral science and counseling skills.[121]

In this way, social workers and mediators set apart the concerns of the adversarial system and subordinate them to the more important concerns of their own professions. Caring, sharing, mental health, and concern for future functioning, they assert, are their exclusive preserve and cannot be attained through the adversarial process.

In this contrasting generic fairy tale narrative, husband, wife, and child(ren) consult not two lawyers but one mediator; only one is necessary because the process is nonadversarial. The process is characterized by cooperation, caring and acceptance.[122] It costs less money

---

with what is typically known as "therapy," and "how-to" techniques, see *Dimensions and Practice of Divorce Mediation*, 1 MEDIATION Q. 3 (1983).

There is some debate among mediation practitioners about the extent to which they perform "actual therapy." They analogize private mediation to settlement negotiation, although there is a trend toward viewing child custody mediations — particularly among court-associated services — as more therapy-oriented. *Compare* Haynes, *supra* note 88, at 6–8 (urging the distinction between mediation and therapy) *with* Mumma, *supra* note 3, at 23 (stating that there is no distinction between mediation and therapy in the court-associated program in which Mumma is involved). The process itself, however, is considered "therapeutic" because it uses different procedures and philosophies from the legal model. *See* Haynes, *supra* note 88, at 7–8. Similarly, because its agreements are touted as the product of self-determination, they are considered preferable to those imposed by the court or produced via reliance on third-party advocates (attorneys). *See id.* at 5–8. Paradoxically, although mediation involves a third-party mediator, it is not viewed as relying on outsiders; the process is characterized as the product of each spouse's individual self-determination.

120 *See* sources cited *supra* notes 62, 81.

121 O. COOGLER, STRUCTURED MEDIATION IN DIVORCE SETTLEMENTS 97 (1977), *quoted in* Winks, *Divorce Mediation: A Nonadversary Procedure for the No-Fault Divorce*, 19 J. FAM. L. 615, 646; *accord* CAL. CIV. CODE §§ 4351.5, 4607 (West 1983 & Supp. 1985) (requiring that court-appointed mediators hold a master's degree in social work, marriage counseling, psychology, or a related field); Haynes, *supra* note 88, at 6, 8 (describing mediator's role), quoted *supra* note 106.

122

> Our goal is to divert families from continued litigation, to help them resolve the current issues of dispute by agreement, and to assist them in establishing a more successful way of resolving future disagreements. Our brief intervention is designed to create an envi-

and produces a fairer result. This is obviously a narrative with a happy ending.

B. Intersection with Other Interests

Also significant in regard to the success of the transformation of custody decisionmaking is the fact that the rhetoric of social workers and mediators intersected with and incorporated the concerns and assumptions of several other groups concerned with custody policy. This overlap assisted the mediators' discourse in gaining dominance. The helping professions' views on mediation, for example, have empowered fathers and fathers' rights groups. The rhetoric has offered fathers' groups a legitimate way to argue for their political goal of removing custody cases from the courts,[123] which they view as favoring women. Fathers' rights groups see mediators as more malleable than judges and attorneys, who are concerned with laws and rights.[124] They also see mediators as less powerful and exacting and less likely to focus on embarrassing child support issues when custody and visitation problems exist.[125] Thus, within the fathers' rights discourse, mediators are the preferred decisionmakers.[126]

Some of the nonprocedural implications of the change in process may begin to emerge in the political use by various groups of the helping professions' concepts. There is still no careful or developed assessment of the shared parenting norm, however. Rather, the shared parenting norm is presented as the solution to identified problems. For example, fathers' rights groups have pushed for mediation and

---

> ronment in which parents and children can disengage themselves from conflict and get on with their lives.
>
> . . . .
>
> We were [helping] families negotiate their own custody and visitation arrangements, and they were staying out of court. Children who were displaying symptomatic behavior often began to show improvement — sometimes dramatic — when their parents began to cooperate. It became increasingly clear that parental agreement and cooperation had a greater effect on children than the actual custody or visitation arrangement.
>
> . . . .
>
> The goal [of child custody mediation] is to shift the group from its preoccupation with negatives to a rediscovery of positives, from incompetency to themes of competency, and from conflict to cooperation.

Mumma, *supra* note 3, at 24, 26.

123 *See, e.g.*, Priorities for Dads PAC (Sept. 1984) (on file with the author).

124 See, for example, the primary field research of M. Raschick, Wisconsin Non-Custodial Parents' Groups 17 (May 16, 1985) (unpublished manuscript on file with the author).

125 For a discussion of the various ideological strains within the fathers' rights movement, see M. Shiffman, The Men's Movement: An Exploratory Empirical Investigation 3, 4 (paper prepared for presentation at the 80th Annual Meeting of the American Sociological Association, Washington, D.C., Aug. 26–30, 1985), and M. Raschick, *supra* note 124, at 15–16 which states that fathers' groups believe child support is generally unduly burdensome.

126 *See, e.g.*, M. Raschick, *supra* note 124, at 17 (stating that one fathers' group advocates mediation to settle child support and custody problems).

joint custody because they claim these innovations will encourage men, who now default in alarming numbers,[127] to pay their child support orders.[128] These groups indicate that the legion of fathers who never bother to visit their children will flock to see them if they are empowered with unilaterally exercisable rights with regard to their children.[129] Ironically, the failure of divorced fathers is used as one of the major arguments for giving men more control and power over children and, through them, over their mothers' lives.[130] Joint custody or shared parenting, however, empowers fathers as a group without requiring any demonstration of responsibility. I consider this inappropriate. In no other area does the law reward those who have failed in their duties as an incentive for them to change their behavior.

The rhetoric of mediators also intersects with and complements the concerns of members of the legal profession. This convergence is probably one of the most significant factors in the success of the helping professions' reforms. Mediators have been empowered by judges and court administrators who dislike custody decisionmaking under the best interest test, or who believe that such cases clog up the system.[131] The substantive implications may be lost and the discussion focused merely on the transfer of troublesome custody issues to an "alternative" system. This is particularly true when the alternative system is characterized as "more humane and caring" and appears to resolve everyone's problems.

Further, family law attorneys who are uncomfortable in courtroom settings or bored with their profession may find it attractive to envision themselves as mediators, employing a whole new set of mechanisms that will enhance their prestige, their self-worth, and the quality of what they do on a day-to-day basis. There is a mystique about mediation that many find compelling. Mediators do not choose sides but are counsel for the situation. Mediators are disinterested advisors

---

[127] *See* L. WEITZMAN, *supra* note 59, at 283–307.

[128] Some argue that increased power in the form of mandatory joint custody will inspire fathers to pay their child support orders. *See supra* note 25; Suggestions from Julilly Kohler for Changes in Child Custody Law, *supra* note 26, at 4. *But see* Bartlett & Stack, *Joint Custody, Feminism and The Dependency Dilemma*, 2 BERKELEY WOMEN'S L.J. 9, 35 n.109 (1986) (suggesting a lack of causal link between custody arrangements and compliance with child support orders).

[129] *See, e.g.*, Bruch, *Making Visitation Work: Dual Parenting Orders*, FAM. ADVOC. Summer 1978, at 22, 25–26.

[130] One example of direct control over the custodial parent's life is found in "permission to leave the state" statutes, which have become popular. These require a custodial parent to get consent of either the non-custodial parent or the court before moving out of the state. *See, e.g.*, WIS. STAT. ANN. § 767.245(6) (West 1981). These statutes have been criticized. *See* Sheehan, *Post-Divorce Child Custody and Family Relocation*, 9 HARV. WOMEN'S L.J. 135 (1986).

[131] *See* Zolla & Alexander, *Report of the Family Law Mediation Program of the Los Angeles County Superior Court (Western District)*, 14 BEVERLY HILLS BAR ASS'N J. 87, 88–90 (1980).

whose only role is to assist the family in making nonadversarial decisions. Family lawyers have a bad image in the press, in the eyes of the public, and in their own eyes;[132] mediation may be a way of rehabilitating that image.

Legislatures also have found the reallocation of decisionmaking power attractive. The reallocation can be accomplished by using existing court-associated personnel — the social workers who previously performed custody investigations can now try their hand at mediation. Further, it has symbolic appeal.[133] Because the goal of shared parenting leads to equal division or joint custody,[134] it is consistent with the recent trend in all of family law toward mathematical formulas for decisionmaking.[135]

To those uncertain about or upset with the function of the present family law system, the mediators' vision presents a more coherent and more encompassing ideal referencing deeply held beliefs and assumptions. In the procedural context, it offers a process free of conflict. In the substantive context, it appeals to ideals of equality, sharing, and caring. The mediators' view is also one that seems distinctly utopian. Its underlying premise is that one can seek personal happiness and fulfillment by terminating a marriage relationship, yet not lose any of the benefits that marriage provides. The hidden message is that divorce can be painless. One can retain one's children, even one's "family," although the family structure may be slightly altered. It is a grand dream: everybody wins, nobody loses.

VI. Practical Consequences

The issue arises why anyone (except those involved) should care about the rhetorical "competition" I have described between lawyers and social workers in this area. In fact, some lawyers join the mediators and fight for the very reforms that will take divorce and custody decisionmaking out of the legal system.[136] The rhetorical "competition" I have described has important implications for many people who are or will be involved in the family law process, particularly custodial mothers.[137] The ideological shifts described may in

---

[132] *See, e.g.*, J. Heinz & E. Laumann, Chicago Lawyers: The Social Structure of the Bar 90–94 (1982) (showing "divorce" and "general family" as the two areas ranking lowest in a "Prestige Ranking of Thirty Fields of Law").

[133] *See, e.g.*, Fineman, *supra* note 48, at 872–75 (tracing the acceptance of divorce reform by the Wisconsin legislature).

[134] *See id.* at 875–80 (concluding that the search for symbolic equality has led to a sacrifice of equity).

[135] *See, e.g.*, *id.* at 839 (stating the presumption of mathematical equality in property division).

[136] *See, e.g.*, Folberg, *supra* note 4.

[137] *See id.*

fact result in a process that produces bad decisions for many women and children.[138] Joint custody can be a disaster if parents are unwilling or unable to cooperate.[139] Such an arrangement may give a man continued control over his children (and through the children, control over his ex-wife's life), yet not result in increased assumption of responsibility on his part. Anecdotal evidence indicates that many women view joint custody as "losing" — whereas many men view it as "winning" — the divorce wars;[140] as a result, many women bargain away needed property and support benefits to avoid the risk of "losing" their children. The negative implications of the shift to a therapeutic model and mediation remain largely unexplored.

Proponents of the therapeutic model have defused possible political controversy and opposition to these changes by casting themselves as neutral, disinterested professionals in their advocacy of mediation and the substantive goal of shared parenting. But they are *not* neutral. They have an institutional and professional bias for certain procedural and substantive results that promote their own interests and that will produce changes designed to enhance and ensure their continued centrality in custody decisionmaking.

A. Assessing the Narratives

The discourse of the helping professions has created rather than reflected reality. In part, helping professionals have been successful in appropriating the divorce business for themselves because, in the abstract, they offer hope to those who have been hurt by divorce and custody battles. The "reality" that they construct through their rhetoric is one that many want to believe exists.

The realistic assessment of the "fairy tale" narrative, however, is that there will be no happy ending; in fact, there will be no ending at all. The narrative assumes an ongoing relationship between the spouses — not an ending — a fact that is not apparent in the presentation of the typical adversary system versus mediation.

---

[138] *See, e.g.*, Benedek & Benedek, *Joint Custody: Solution or Illusion?*, 136 AM. J. PSYCHIATRY 1540, 1541–42 (1979) (pointing out the risk of instability inherent in joint custody); *see also* Schulman & Pitt, *supra* note 104, at 570–71 (concluding that joint custody is only appropriate when both parents desire it and are willing to cooperate).

[139] *See* Benedek & Benedek, *supra* note 138, at 1543 (stating that "[w]hen the requisite cooperation is not forthcoming, as is often the case following divorce, joint custody can be calamitous").

[140] This anecdotal information comes from lawyers and legal academics working in the area. *See, e.g.*, Neely, *The Primary Caretaker Parent Rule: Child Custody and the Dynamics of Greed*, 3 YALE L. & POL'Y REV. 168 (1984).

Women and men seem to view the custody issue differently, with women regarding it as more central. *See* L. WEITZMAN, *supra* note 59, at 310–12 (concluding that "[w]omen . . . draw a line when it comes to custody"). Joint custody has also been the focus of fathers' rights reformers.

The costs associated with such non-endings are also hidden. Traditional divorce was an emancipatory process that terminated the relationship and freed lives for rebuilding. The social workers' ideal of an ongoing co-parental relationship may leave little room for the formation of new relationships by parents or by children. Children may in fact suffer more from these non-endings.[141] They may never be able to overcome the quite typical fantasy that mommy and daddy will get back together. It is not clear that non-endings will in fact be "happy" in any significant number of family situations.

Non-endings do benefit mediators, however, who assert that only they can achieve reorganization of families (the process that produces happy non-endings). In the view of the social worker, mediation is in the first instance designated as a superior *process*[142] — one based on informality that can therefore give full protection to the privacy and autonomy of the parties by allowing them to make important decisions for themselves. The ideal process takes place within a context of open communication and protects against the parties having issues decided for them through lawyers' adversarial tricks.

Yet the supposed benefits of mediation are not all process related. It is also argued that the *purpose* of mediation — to reorient the parties toward one another — is substantially different from, and superior to, the legal ideal.[143] Mediation discourages the focus on legal rights and seeks to help the divorcing parties achieve a new and shared post-divorce relationship, in which they redirect their attitude and disposition toward one another for post-divorce shared parenting. The ideal product of the process, in the rhetoric of the helping professions, is a *restructuring* of the relationship of the adults, rather than its termination.[144]

Some processes, according to the helping professions, facilitate the adjustment of the "family system" for post-divorce parenting; others, such as adversarial processes, interfere with it. The professions believe that the process for awarding sole custody, for example, is indicative of the win/lose mentality that social workers seek so desper-

---

141 *See* J. Goldstein, A. Freud & A. Solnit, *supra* note 14, at 12 (noting that children "become prey to severe and crippling loyalty conflicts" when parents are hostile to each other); *see also* Chambers, *supra* note 53, at 550–57 (cautioning that research on joint custody arrangements is incomplete and suggesting possible problems with such arrangements); Felner & Farber, *supra* note 87, at 343–44 (questioning the wisdom of joint custody when parents cannot resolve important issues concerning their children).

142 *See, e.g.*, Pruhs, Paulsen & Tysseling, *supra* note 24, at 537 ("Comprehensive mediation is a *superior absolute system* which with careful nurturing *may ultimately supplant the adversarial process* in the majority of divorce cases." (emphasis added)).

143 *See id.*; *see also* Sprenkle & Storm, *supra* note 90, at 240, 252 (describing mediation as superior to traditional adversarial methods for resolving custody and visitation disputes, and citing "an increase in joint custody arrangements" as one of the favorable results of mediation).

144 *See* Mumma, *supra* note 3, at 24–26.

ately to purge from the system.[145] Implicitly, within the helping professions' rhetorical framework, the mediator-social worker is the appropriate, preferred decisionmaker, who dispenses the appropriate, preferred result.[146] The social worker's old role as dispenser of "treatment" to deter divorce or, failing this, of advisor to the court about what placement would be in the "best interest of the child," has evolved into a new role. Social workers are now in charge of reordering and maintaining the family system. Their role has evolved into one that begins by managing the initial trauma, then attempts to achieve acceptance of the changes caused by the divorce, and ultimately seeks to restructure the family from "married couple with children" to "divorced co-parents."

Although "system stability" has remained a constant goal under early and contemporary social work practice, the new ideal focuses on building the post-divorce relationship between both parents, rather than ensuring that there is one "custodial parent" with whom the children have a primary relationship.[147] In this process, the relationship of the "noncustodial" parent to his or her children has assumed great importance, and facilitating continual contact between children and "noncustodial" parents is the paramount pragmatic goal.[148]

The implications of this approach are enormous. Not only does this represent a serious decision about who it is that ultimately makes

---

[145] *See* Johnston, Campbell & Tall, *supra* note 100, at 119; Pruhs, Paulsen & Tysseling, *supra* note 24, at 533.

[146] *See, e.g.*, Barsky, *supra* note 106, at 105 (discussing the importance and influence of mediators).

[147] *See* Durst, Wedemeyer & Zurcher, *supra* note 79, at 423.

[148] *See* Abarbarnel, *supra* note 25, at 321; Greif, *supra* note 16, at 318–19; Noble, *supra* note 16, at 411; Wallerstein & Kelly, *supra* note 98, at 471. Social workers are aware that the operative legal standard in a given jurisdiction constrains the extent to which they can implement their ideal post-divorce family structure of shared parenting. Many jurisdictions still require the selection of a custodial parent when, for example, no statutory authority exists for joint custody. Even in those instances, however, social workers' rhetoric suggests ways to achieve post-divorce shared parenting in fact if not by law. Commentators have described social workers' responsibility to achieve post-divorce shared parenting in such situations as follows:

> Clinical research in the area of the divorce process is pointing to the importance of the child's need for a continuing relationship with both parents; legal systems are shifting to accommodate this recognized need.
>
> . . . .
>
> The end result of [the] painful procedure [of a court-ordered custody evaluation] is a recommendation regarding which parent is the "best" or the "psychological parent" and therefore the one who should have custody of the child. . . .
>
> Professionals must use the evaluation and subsequent recommendations to convey [the value of not terminating the relationship with the non-custodial parents] to the family and to attempt to shift the focus from a contest over the "best" parent to a redefinition of roles and a restructuring of the children's family. Such a use of custody evaluations goes beyond the legal process, for which any therapeutic outcome is irrelevant. . . .
>
> Thus there are dual goals in the evaluation process — prompt resolution of custody issues and the restructuring of the children's family with continued contact with both parents.

Rosenberg, Kleinman & Brantley, *supra* note 88, at 203–04.

custody decisions — judge, attorney, or mediator-social worker — but, because of the inherent nature of the mediator/shared parenting ideal, adoption of this approach represents a significant opportunity for continuous and substantial intervention by social workers or other court-associated personnel. The goals of the helping professions are at odds with the traditional legal goal of divorce. Nothing is "terminated," except the formal marital bond between the adults. Because the family unit theoretically continues, it may often be in need of the services and communication skills provided by the mediator alternative to the adversarial system. Potentially, therefore, the legal system's involvement will not end either, at least until all the children reach adulthood. Coercive and continuous supervision of the restructured unit is compatible with this view. There are no legal or doctrinal impediments to reactivating the mediation system.[149] If things are not operating to the satisfaction of one ex-spouse, the mediation mechanism can be reengaged to work things out.

This narrative non-ending has been uncritically incorporated into reform rhetoric concerning the legal system. Recent changes in custody rules, particularly those setting forth presumptions of joint custody, are consistent with the rhetoric and the non-ending it advocates. The acceptance of this nontermination ideal is also associated to some extent with the imposition of other ideals onto family law, including the goals of equality, gender neutrality, and social restructuring. Concern with these abstract goals may overtake the desire to reach workable and practical decisions upon divorce. The entire area is permeated with symbolism that relates only tangentially to the realities of divorce.[150]

Ultimately, the helping professions' discourse has encompassed and absorbed traditional legal dialogue concerning custody. "Sharing" became identified as the public and political language of the escalating debate over the appropriate concept and process for resolving custody disputes.[151] The political victory of the helping professions is mani-

---

[149] After a traditional divorce, if one party wants to change custody or visitation arrangements, he or she may do so in cooperation with the other parent or may apply to the courts for changes. If the route is through the courts, doctrines such as the "substantial change in circumstances" test operate to deter non-custodial parents from using the legal process to harrass custodial parents continually. *See, e.g.*, UNIF. MARRIAGE & DIVORCE ACT § 409, 9A U.L.A. 197 (1979) (precluding modification of custody decrees for a two-year period unless evidence is presented that the current arrangement may endanger the child's health).

[150] *See* Fineman, *supra* note 48.

[151] Compare Edelman's discussion of the public's tendency to adopt the point of view of professional experts:

> The lay public by and large adopts the professional perspective; for its major concern is to believe that others can be trusted to handle the problem . . . . This public reaction is the politically crucial one, for it confers power upon professionals and legitimizes their norms for society generally. The public reaction, in turn, is a response to the language

fested by the conferring of legally significant rights and obligations, through the explicit delegation of decisionmaking authority to the social workers and mediators. Legislatures[152] and the judiciary[153] have delegated this power both on an institutional level, as with the creation of mandatory mediation or counseling services staffed with social workers and connected to the court system, and in individual cases, in which judges seek and accept the advice of "experts" in the helping profession. This formal recognition of the helping professions' role places the state's imprimatur on their appropriation of custody decisionmaking.

B. The Politics of Rhetoric

The rhetorical symbolism employed by social workers and mediators is politically powerful. It empowers the helpers and may allow them to eclipse the interests of those who are designated as the very ones to be helped. For example, although the helping professions' vision portrays mediation as allowing custody decisions to be made with sharing and caring rather than with conflict and contention, mediation may in fact merely hide rather than eliminate conflict, allowing the stronger of the two parents to dominate and control the weaker.[154]

The adoption of the mediators' image has important substantive implications with significant political and social ramifications. One of the most harmful assumptions underlying social workers' discourse is that a parent who seeks sole custody of a child has some illegitimate motivation.[155] Mediators may acknowledge exceptions to this generalization in situations in which one parent is a drunkard or drug addict or in which a child is abused, but the general assumption is

---

> of the professions and to the social milieu that gives that language its authoritative meaning.

Edelman, *supra* note 108, at 304.

152 *See, e.g.*, CAL. CIV. CODE § 4607 (West 1983 & Supp. 1987) (providing for mandatory mediation when a petition for order of custody or visitation is contested). Other states allow judicial discretion in ordering mediation. *See, e.g.*, FLA. STAT. § 61.138 (Supp. 1986); *see also* New York Law Revision Commission Bill before the N.Y. Assembly Judiciary Committee A.7315-S.5127 (1985); State of Wisconsin Engrossed 1985 Assembly Bill 474, at 4 (on file with the author).

153 *See* Mumma, *supra* note 3 (illustrating a judicial delegation of power to court-associated social workers to mediate custody disputes).

154 *See, e.g.*, Lefcourt, *Women, Mediation and Family Law*, 18 CLEARINGHOUSE REV. 266, 269 (1984) (concluding that unequal financial and social power of men and women makes mediation an unfair process); Woods, *Mediation: A Backlash to Women's Progress on Family Law Issues*, 19 CLEARINGHOUSE REV. 431 (1985) (arguing that mediation fails to protect battered women and produces unequal financial results).

155 For an example of the presentation of conflict as "illegitimate," see Wallerstein & Kelly, *supra* note 98.

that the parent who is willing to live up to the ideal of shared custody and control is the one with the child's real interests at heart.[156]

Mediation advocates often characterize opposition to shared custody as pathological.[157] The assumption in the social workers' discourse is that the parent who rejects the shared parenting ideal and seeks sole custody of his or her child has an illegitimate motive. A mother who resists sharing her child with her ex-husband is characterized as having "issue overlay"; she protests too much.[158] Such women may be characterized as clinging and overly dependent on the role identification as wife and mother; social workers and mediators assert that these women can be helped through the mediation process only if they are cooperative. Other women are seen as greedy, merely using the children in order to get larger property settlements; it is claimed that an "effective" mediator can block these women from achieving their evil ends. A third stereotype focuses on vindictive mothers who use the children to get back at their ex-husbands; it is perceived that these are the type of women who should be punished by having their children taken away and sole custody awarded to the fathers.

Lost in the rhetoric of the social worker are real concerns. There is little or no appreciation of the many real problems that joint custody and the ideal of sharing and caring can cause. The prospect of a continued relationship with an ex-spouse may be horrifying to contemplate,[159] but the sharing ideal assumes that a relationship between the noncustodial parent and the child cannot proceed without it. Also unsettling is the extent to which allegations of mistreatment, abuse, or neglect on the part of husbands toward either their wives or children are trivialized, masked, or lost amid the psychological rhetoric that reduces mothers' desires to have custody and control of their children to pathology.[160]

---

[156] *See supra* note 104.

[157] *See, e.g.*, Kelly, *Further Observations on Joint Custody*, 16 U.C. DAVIS L. REV. 762, 769 (1983).

[158] The characterizations in this paragraph are based in part on interviews with social workers conducted by the author. In addition, the negative image of mothers is reflected in the literature. Sometimes the formal characterizations are "gender-neutral," although it is clear that it is the primary caretaker or custodial parent who is being criticized. *See* Musetto, *supra* note 65; Wallerstein & Kelly, *supra* note 98. Others, however, are more explicit in their gendered view of the situation. *See* Abelsohn, *Dealing with the Abdication Dynamic in the Post Divorce Family: A Context for Adolescent Crisis*, 22 FAM. PROCESS 359, 364–66 (1983); Greif, *supra* note 16; Hancock, *The Dimensions of Meaning and Belonging in the Process of Divorce*, 50 AM. J. ORTHPSYCH. 18 (1980); Kelly, *supra* note 157; Lerman, *Mediation of Wife Abuse Cases: The Adverse Impact of Informal Dispute Resolution on Women*, 7 HARV. WOMEN'S L.J. 57 (1984).

[159] The prospect of continued contact is especially troubling in cases of spousal or child abuse. *See, e.g.*, Lerman, *supra* note 158, at 107; Schulman & Pitt, *supra* note 104, at 555–56 (pointing out the danger of continuing contact with an abusive father).

[160] *See, e.g.*, Kelly, *supra* note 157, at 769 (recognizing some problems of abuse but empha-

We should be deeply skeptical of these views of women and mothers. They are not accurate and the visions they present are deeply misogynous.[161] Most mothers love their children and would not willfully deprive them of contact with a caring and responsible father. In fact, if the children are old enough to assert their own interests, it is unlikely that mothers could deprive them of contact with their fathers even if they wanted to. By making these observations, I do not mean to suggest that abuses never occur, but rather to point out that they are not typical, or even common, and that it is irrational to base custody policy on the deviant rather than the typical post-divorce situation.

Because social workers and others sympathetic to mediation have created and controlled the presentation of both narratives, the real nature of the competition between the legal and therapeutic models has been hidden. Notably, there are no parallel scenarios involving vindictive or greedy husbands in the mediation literature. No alternative narrative, sympathetic to single parent or sole custody and control, has gained any credibility in the literature. Nor do many stories assign different characters to the stock "victim" and "villain" roles.

Further, by branding opposition to mediation and joint custody as the manifestation of a psychological problem to which mediation is

---

sizing the problem of "emotionally disturbed women who, due to their own pathology, vigorously fight a father's desire to be involved in the children's lives"). *But see* Lemon, *Joint Custody as a Statutory Presumption: California's New Civil Code Sections 4600 and 4600.5*, 11 GOLDEN GATE U.L. REV. 485, 527–31 (1981) (suggesting that the stereotype of the manipulative and vindictive mother opposing joint custody is overstated). The therapist is viewed as having a potentially powerful role in the process in correcting pathological behavior. *See* Abelsohn, *supra* note 158, at 364–66 (stating that "[t]he therapist delivers this basic message to the mother — you lose, you do not win, if you succeed in keeping your children from their father").

[161] Mothers tend to get a "bad rap" in the literature of the helping professions in general. In a recent survey of the literature of mental health professionals published between 1970 and 1982, one author found "mother-blaming" in "epidemic proportions." Caplan, *Take the Blame Off Mother*, PSYCHOLOGY TODAY, Oct. 1986, at 70. "In the 125 articles in [the] study, mothers were held responsible for 72 different types of psychological disorder in their children . . . . [N]ot a single mother was ever described as emotionally healthy, although some fathers were, and no mother-child relationship was said to be healthy, although some father-child [relationships] were described as ideal." *Id.*

Although the bulk of the literature discussed in this Article has presented the recent scholarly and professional focus on fathers as a "natural" evolution, some authors have argued that this shift has not necessarily been the product of neutral, detached observation or analysis:

> In my five years of professional experience in an academic pediatric hospital, divorced women with children occasioned little comment, other than negative. They were dealt with routinely, given appointments without asking about their schedules, handed instructions imperiously without a thought as to how they would carry them out amidst the conflicting demands of work and child care. Yet when any father with custody of his children appeared, the staff went out of its way to praise his efforts and laud his heroism. They agonized over the conflicts he must face in the exigencies of caring for his child and managing his life. In both situations, one adult had sole responsibility for parenting and work. What differed was the way the parent was viewed.

Hancock, *supra* note 158, at 23.

itself the solution, mediation rhetoric forecloses any effective expression of women's legitimate concerns. As things now stand, the cries of protest over the imposition of a joint custody or shared parenting solution from mothers who will be assuming primary care for their children (but sharing control) are attributed to the fact that these mothers have not accomplished an "emotional divorce." As soon as they are able to get over "their issues" they will be able to begin "rational problem solving" and will cooperate agreeably.

The social workers' discourse accepts without criticism the superiority of "rational decisionmaking" within the new, reconstructed family structure. Through this method, the "vindictive" woman is thwarted, the "victimized" man allowed to continue to operate as *paternal familius* (in an altered form, of course) by being given "equal rights" without the formal imposition of responsibility. The helping professionals believe this approach remedies the pro-mother imbalance that has existed in custody decisionmaking.[162]

VII. An Alternative Vision

A. The Perspective of the Custodial Mother

Custodial mothers currently have no spokesperson. Feminist groups might have picked up their cause. However, mothers' desire for sole custody or claims for preferential consideration based on maternal status or on the functions they stereotypically perform are incompatible with the symbolic presentation of equality by liberal mainstream feminism.[163] In fact, some feminists argue for joint custody because they view it as a means of ensuring that men take equal responsibility for their children.[164] Lawyers are another group of potential spokespersons for custodial mothers' perspective that past parenting behavior is the relevant consideration. Yet they, too, have failed to present mothers' concerns. Indeed, family law specialists seem to favor transferring decisionmaking from judges, attorneys, and the legal system to mediators and social workers.[165]

Custodial mothers' experience as primary caregivers during marriage and after divorce should have figured significantly in the establishment of new rules to govern the process and content of custody decisionmaking. Yet because of the domination of the social workers'

---

162 *See, e.g.*, Pearson, Munson & Thoennes, *supra* note 34, at 18–20 (arguing that fathers bear a greater burden of proof and face a longer struggle in their attempts to gain custody).

163 *See* Fineman, *supra* note 48, at 820–26 (criticizing feminist efforts to make decisions concerning the family gender-neutral).

164 *See, e.g.*, Bartlett & Stack, *supra* note 128, at 33–35 (arguing that men should have to earn co-parenthood).

165 *See* Folberg, *supra* note 4.

rhetoric, which stressed shared parenting, custodial mothers' concerns were excluded. Thus, reform is occurring with the exception, rather than the norm, providing the prototype for change.

In most marriages, one parent, normally the mother, assumes day-to-day primary care.[166] Shared parenting in these situations seldom means equally divided responsibility and control; typically one parent sacrifices more than the other in order to care for the child. The sense of sharing in this context is not based on the actual assumption of divided responsibilities by the parents. Rather, the shared parenting can be viewed as based on the relationship between the parents who, because of the intimacy of their situation, share the potential for jointly exercising important decisionmaking responsibility for their children. Yet an unrealistic and idealized vision of shared parenting *independent* of the relationship (or lack thereof) between parents is now imposed on couples after divorce. This vision assumes that they will work out their relationship to make shared parenting successful. It is one thing for divorcing parents voluntarily to choose the shared parenting ideal,[167] but quite another to impose it on parents who do not or cannot live up to its demands. There may be substantial costs to treating the deviant as the norm and fashioning rights outside the context of responsibility. In the divorce context, this amounts to furthering the interests of noncaretaking fathers over the objections and, in many instances, against the interests of caretaking mothers. The legal system should not participate in, let alone facilitate, this unjust result.

We must ask a number of questions. Why are we as a society condoning the imposition of this ideal? Don't we, and the legal system, have a responsibility for the form and content of these decisions? The mediators' interest in the acceptance of this alternative system is clear, but why should those of us who are lawyers and family law policy makers acquiesce in this transfer of decisionmaking power? Are we comfortable with the social workers' assertions that mediation is a superior process and shared parenting the appropriate goal? For lawyers, the central question may be whether there is any role for law — for a legalistic approach — in the custody area. Further, we should consider whether the legal model, although imperfect, may be superior to the therapeutic model.

A legal model that relies on both legislative and judicial institutional roles in formulating custody rules would have to give some

---

[166] Even when the mother works, it is typical for her to assume control of child care. *See* Maret & Finlay, *The Distribution of Household Labor Among Women in Dual-Earner Families*, 46 J. MARRIAGE & FAM. 357, 360 (1984).

[167] There is even substantial debate about the impact of voluntary joint custody and its benefits for children and parents. *See* Chambers, *supra* note 53, at 550–58; Fineman & Opie, *supra* note 12, at 121–23.

credence to traditional legal values such as procedural due process: the right to a hearing, the right to cross-examine witnesses, and so on. Mediators are free to criticize or to ignore these aspects of the adversary system. Yet these legalisms are not vestiges of an arcane system; they embody a consensus about important values in our society. In fact, because there seems to be greater consensus about the importance of due process values than about what constitutes an ideal, or even an acceptable family, shouldn't custody decisionmaking rules comport with *these* values? The public nature of the legal process means that the basis for decisions will be explained, debated, and publicly considered. This process may not be foolproof, but it is better than one in which substantive rules and standards evolve and are implemented behind closed office doors without any possibility of checks from the political system.

B. The Role of Law: Creating a New Rule from the Discarded Discourse

As it has evolved, legal doctrine cannot adequately address the difficult problems inherent in custody decisionmaking. The best interest of the child test must be replaced. The task is to find a rule that both avoids moralizing in making choices between parents and is determinate enough to be applied within the traditional legal system. The rule would have to eliminate the need for predictions about the future psychological well-being of children or speculations about how best to ensure their developmental potential.[168] It must remove the potentially abusive social worker-mediator, yet guard against potentially abusive lawyers or judges. Thus, what we need is a more definite rule that will nonetheless have at its core an appreciation of what we as a society agree will be in the "best interests" of children.

One recent suggestion is that custody courts should apply a "primary caretaker" rule.[169] This rule has been characterized in different

---

[168] *See generally* Mnookin, *Child-Custody Adjudication: Judicial Functions in the Face of Indeterminacy*, 39 LAW & CONTEMP. PROBS. 226 (1975) (arguing that psychological theories cannot accurately predict the effects of alternate custody determinations and arguing for less discretionary custody award standards).

[169] *See, e.g.*, Chambers, *supra* note 53; Neely, *supra* note 140; Polikoff, *Why Are Mothers Losing: A Brief Analysis of Criteria Used in Child Custody Determinations*, 7 WOMEN'S RTS. L. REP. 235 (1982).

I might be willing to settle for a more initially ambiguous rule that provides for termination of parental rights if the non-custodial parent refuses to visit or participate in a child's upbringing. The analogy, of course, is to neglect or abandonment statutes, which govern the custodial parent's interaction with the child. Reforms that place responsibilities on fathers to correspond with the increased rights they seek have not been forthcoming.

ways,[170] but the essence of the primary caretaker standard is that children need day-to-day care and that the parent who has performed this primary care during the marriage should get custody.[171] The primary caretaker standard does not ignore the less essential, secondary contributions of the other parent:[172] they are rewarded by the establishment of visitation periods with the children. Custody can be viewed as a reward for past caretaking behavior.

This test implicitly recognizes that no one can confidently predict the future and that the past may in fact be the best indication we have of future care and concern. I think it is essential that only the past performance of the parents be considered. Helping professionals should not speculate about which parent would be able to produce the best future environment for the child. The only relevant inquiry should be which parent has already adapted his or her life and interests to accommodate the demands of the child.

Further, in determining custody, there should be no speculation as to the quality or extent of emotional bonding between parents and children. The primary caretaker test assumes that these bonds exist between the primary caretaking parent and the child; they are evidenced by the caretaker's sacrifice and devotion to the child. The test also assumes that the child reciprocates this devotion.

In addition, I would apply the rule to all contested custody cases, not just to those involving children of "tender years" as is sometimes

---

[170] *See* Chambers, *supra* note 53, at 527 (confining the application of the primary caretaker rule to children of "tender years"); Neely, *supra* note 140, at 180–82 (advocating application of the primary caretaker rule unless the child is old enough to decide for him or herself who should be the custodial parent).

[171] A version of this test was set forth in Garska v. McCoy, 278 S.E.2d 357 (W.Va. 1981). One commentator has hypothesized that such a standard would encourage fathers to co-parent during marriage. *See* Polikoff, *supra* note 169, at 241–43. Which party is the primary caretaker would be established by "lay testimony by the parties themselves, and by that of teachers, relatives, and neighbors. Which parent does the lion's share of the chores can be demonstrated satisfactorily in less than an hour of the court's time in most cases." Neely, *supra* note 140, at 181. Thus, this test is very different from the one for determining the psychological parent, which relies heavily on expert testimony.

[172] It is my position that there are qualitative differences between the contributions of primary caretakers (typically mothers) and primary earners (typically fathers) to the upbringing of their children. The income contributions fathers make for their families cannot be classified as "sacrifices." In the process of generating family income, fathers are simultaneously establishing themselves in their professions, a benefit they retain throughout their careers. Although this undeniably affords advantages to the entire family during marriage, the sharing of the benefit generally diminishes significantly at divorce, as evidenced by data relative to fathers' post-divorce child support payment patterns. *See* L. WEITZMAN, *supra* note 59, at 262–322. By contrast, mothers' sacrifices in providing daily care to children yield no collateral advantages, except in terms of the attachment that forms between mother and child. Children consume the services mothers provide to them, with the years spent in child-rearing representing a depletable amount of the mother's non-renewable resources. Similarly, the time a woman spends away from career development probably disadvantages her throughout her work life.

suggested.[173] I believe that limiting the rule to children under the age of seven unrealistically assumes that nurturing ends when a child begins school. This limitation would also send the message that if a parent fails to nurture during a child's early years, he need not worry, because there will be no negative consequences with respect to later custody determinations.

The primary caretaker rule is particularly susceptible to legal analysis because it involves past fact-finding, an inquiry traditionally performed by courts. It has the advantage, therefore, of being a rule that judges can comfortably apply and that lawyers can easily understand and use. More importantly, however, the criterion for selecting a custodial parent is clear enough that in most instances parents will be able to predict what the result would be if they litigated the custody issue. Such predictability reduces the need for litigation. Avoidance of litigation does more than save the system from an overload of family law cases. Custody disputes are expensive and time consuming for the parties to litigate. The current set of rules, which requires individualized hearings to determine a plethora of facts and to parade a bevy of experts on the issue of what is in a child's best interest,[174] does not provide "justice," particularly for women, who tend to be less well-off economically than their husbands, and who cannot afford such expensive procedures.[175]

Further, the mere fact that both parents work does not, in the vast majority of cases, mean that both are primary caretakers (or that neither is). This is an additional benefit of the primary caretaker rule: appropriate application should seldom result in very different parental sacrifices being considered equal.[176] It is important to take account of the fact that although most mothers work, they choose careers (or more likely, "jobs") that accommodate their children in ways most fathers do not.[177] Their jobs are usually the ones that must be flexible

---

[173] *See, e.g.*, Chambers, *supra* note 53, at 560–65.

[174] The potential drawbacks of expert testimony were well demonstrated in the recent *Baby M.* case. *See Nothing Surrogate About the Pain*, N.Y. Times, Mar. 9, 1987, at A14, col. 1 (noting potential class biases in testimony by experts in the case).

For a scholarly discussion of the use of expert testimony in child custody decisionmaking, see Okpaku, *Psychology: Impediment or Aid in Child Custody Cases?*, 29 RUTGERS L. REV. 1117, 1144–50 (1976).

[175] *See* Weitzman, *The Economics of Divorce: Social and Economic Consequences of Property, Alimony and Child Support Awards*, 28 UCLA L. REV. 1181, 1251 (1981). The Weitzman study found that in the first year after their divorces under the equal division rules, men in California experienced a 42% *increase* in their standard of living, as measured by income in relation to needs. Divorced women, by contrast, experienced a 73% *decline*. This post-divorce economic analysis indicates how marriage masks the subordinate economic position of women.

[176] *See* Neely, *supra* note 140, at 180 (noting that the situation in which neither parent is clearly the primary caretaker is rare).

[177] Moreover, women experience parenthood differently than men in the sense that they are more willing to arrange their lives, even in the anticipation of motherhood, to accommodate

enough to permit time off — initially for the bearing and breast feeding of an infant and later for other day-to-day obligations such as school conferences or the care of a sick child. Thus, even though both parents work, mothers' career sacrifices for their children would often qualify them as the primary caretakers.

One possible objection to this test is that it will produce even more maternal custody arrangements than has the best interest of the child test. Even if this objection were valid, it should not be the basis for rejecting the test. The primary caretaker test is not designed to remove the potential for fathers to obtain custody at divorce. The rule is gender neutral on its face. As with most gender-neutral rules, its impact may not be gender neutral,[178] but this result only reflects the fact that women are the primary nurturers of children in our society. The rule may currently operate to the advantage of mothers, but, if we value nurturing behavior, then rewarding those who nurture seems only fair. If fathers are "left out," they can change their behavior and begin making sacrifices in their careers and devoting their time during the marriage to the primary care and nurturing of children. Men can exercise the same "free" choice that women traditionally have in these matters, adjusting their outside activities to care for their children. Men who choose not to devote their time and attention to the children during the marriage but wish to care for them after the marriage ends can bargain against the mother's entitlement as primary caretaker by making financial or emotional concessions at divorce. In cases in which both parents acted as true primary caretakers, I predict that few custody battles would ensue and the cooperative patterns concerning the children established during the marriage would continue.

The system should reward demonstrated care and concern for children. If we merely want to further the goal of symbolic "equality" between parents, custody could be decided by the flip of a coin.[179] If we aspire beyond rhetoric, however, we need a more sensitive and realistic rule. The primary caretaker test is an attempt to ensure a good future for children in our culture. It encourages nurturing and

childrearing responsibilities. *See* Project, *Law Firms and Lawyers with Children: An Empirical Analysis of Family/Work Conflict*, 34 STAN. L. REV. 1263, 1274 (1982).

[178] *See* Fineman, *supra* note 48, at 832–42 (describing the gender-specific impact of the gender-neutral equal property division reform in Wisconsin); *see also* Neely, *supra* note 140, at 180–81 (arguing that the unequal impact of the rule on fathers is justified because women are in an unequal bargaining position and often trade economic advantages because they fear losing custody). In any case, many family law rules have a gender-specific impact; joint custody norms certainly have gender-specific implications.

[179] For a discussion of the coin-flip approach that includes some indication of why we as a society would view this as inappropriate, see Mnookin, *supra* note 168, at 289–91. Compare Elster, *supra* note 53, at 41, which argues that random custody decisionmaking minimizes the harm done to children by protracted litigation and appeals to equity concerns.

concern for children in a concrete way. The positive message that the rule sends to parents about what is valued by the legal system and by society at large is clear and unambiguous.

VIII. Conclusion

In this Article, I have explored the rhetoric with which social workers have urged reforms in divorce and child custody decisionmaking. I have also suggested several problems with these reforms. I challenge the notion that these professionals are neutral and disinterested and that their vision represents "truth" or "progress."

The important substantive implications of these reforms for divorce and child custody cases are obscured by viewing mediation simply as an "alternative procedure" that is preferable to settlement negotiations previously performed by attorneys. Such a perspective misses the more fundamental challenges mediation presents to central aspects of the legal model, particularly the traditional notion that representation by competing adversaries is the most reliable method of establishing the necessary facts upon which to base subsequent decisionmaking. The ability of the helping professions to label divorce a psycho-social crisis has been pivotal in this regard — what was once a legal event handled through legal procedures by lawyers and judges has become an emotional crisis to be managed by mental health professionals. That substantive changes have resulted from this procedural shift should not be surprising. This trend should be reversed.

The legal system should initially award custody based on factors that encourage nurturing and care of children. After the initial determination, however, the law should leave subsequent decisionmaking over the course of the child's minority to parents, the most interested parties. Absent abusive situations, parents should be left to work out arrangements concerning their children. If the law takes this approach, then the legal system will fulfill its responsibility by making an initial custody determination when the parties cannot agree and the basis for ongoing coercive intervention will clearly terminate with the marriage.

[17]

Neither justice nor protection: women's experiences of post-separation violence

Cathy Humphreys
School of Health and Social Studies, University of Warwick
Ravi K. Thiara
School of Health and Social Studies, University of Warwick

Abstract: *Post-separation violence is an issue for a significant group of domestic violence survivors (and their children) leaving abusive relationships. This article draws on research conducted with women who have experienced post-separation violence. It explores definitions and the nature of post-separation violence experienced by women and often their children. More than three-quarters (76 per cent) of the 161 separated women in the study initially suffered further abuse and harassment from their former partners. Much of the violence ceased after the first 6–12 months, often due to the woman moving. However, more than one-third (36 per cent) of the women suffered continued post-separation violence. Against this background, women's experiences of legal routes to protection are examined and the effectiveness of the law in tackling the issue of post-separation violence explored. In so doing, post-separation violence is used to exemplify and further explore Smart's contention that there are many contradictions and complexities in the practice of the law, particularly as it relates to the on-going oppression of women (1995: 145). For a group of women, violence escalated over time. These women and their children were seriously at risk of harm. Poor law enforcement, the ineffectiveness of civil protection orders and inadequate prosecution and sanctions left these women (and their children) vulnerable to further assaults and harassment. Child contact was a point of vulnerability for on-going post-separation violence and abuse. The implications for future policy and practice are highlighted.*

Keywords: post-separation violence, stalking, child contact, domestic violence, protection orders

Introduction

> It has been a nightmare. I had no idea what a hell-hole I was living in until I left. Only I thought when I left it was a fresh start, but I didn't realize that my difficulties were just beginning.
>
> (Julie)[1]

'Why doesn't she leave?' is probably one of the most frequently asked questions for those who witness a woman suffering domestic violence. Implicit in this question is frustration and mystification that women are failing to 'look after themselves', and often their children, by remaining caught in a web of violence and abuse. This individualizing discourse places the responsibility on the woman for leaving herself open to continued violence and abuse. It further implies that there is a clear line separating her life in the abusive relationship and the safety and security which awaits her once she separates.

Post-separation violence is a fear and frequently a reality for women[2] and children who attempt to escape from abusive and violent relationships. However, it is often over-looked as a danger and remains an area where the failure of effective intervention leaves women and children vulnerable and unprotected. The effect of this failure is not neutral, but compounds the abuser's control and the woman's sense of entrapment.

This article focuses on post-separation violence by drawing on research conducted with women who have experienced this violence. It begins by looking at definitions and the nature of post-separation violence experienced by women and often their children. Against this background, women's experiences of legal routes to protection are examined and the effectiveness of the law in tackling the issue of post-separation violence explored. In so doing, post-separation violence is used to exemplify and further explore Smart's contention that there are many contradictions and complexities in the practice of the law, particularly as it relates to the on-going oppression of women (Smart, 1995: 145). Indeed, we argue that any analysis needs to highlight the ambiguities in the practice of the law and acknowledge that discourses and practices within the legal arena operate differentially and not as an 'homogeneous entity'.

In writing this article, we have had to recognize the temptation to construct the legal arena as a hegemonic discourse in relation to post-separation violence. While failure of law enforcement and implementation leads to further abuse and violence, and stands out in the women's narratives in which this discussion is grounded, there is also a significant amount of evidence from our research, which shows that women's experiences of both policing and judicial processes are more varied. There exists testimony to the effectiveness of the law and practice in this area alongside its abject failure to either prosecute violence or secure safety. There is also evidence of the use of the law to facilitate the abuser's continued access to women and children and hence to continue his violence and control.

Further evidence of the shifting nature of the discourse is provided by new policy guidance which has been introduced since the research was undertaken and which has the potential to impact on areas discussed in the article. This policy guidance relates to: the police *(Home Office Circular 19/2000 – Domestic Violence)*, the Crown Prosecution Service (*Domestic Violence: Guidance on Prosecuting Cases of Domestic Violence, 2001*) and to private law proceedings under the Children Act, 1989 (*Guidelines for Good Practice on Parental Contact in Cases Where There is Domestic Violence, 2001*).

While each of these initiatives has the potential to increase protection for women and children from post-separation violence, this article highlights the deeply entrenched nature of the problems which need to be overcome if significant changes to practice are to occur.

Defining the problem and definitional problems

The extent of post-separation violence is difficult to ascertain; particularly in the UK, where there has been no national prevalence study. The Canadian Violence Against Women Survey found that 19 per cent of women were physically assaulted following separation and for 35 per cent the violence escalated upon separation (Johnson, 1998). A London-based study identified that one-third of police calls for domestic violence incidents came from women who were separated and who were being harassed by their ex-partners (Kelly *et al.*, 1999). Wilcox (2000), in a qualitative study of twenty working class women leaving situations of domestic violence, found that one-third of the women suffered persistent and systematic violence and a further third experienced continued harassment. Moreover, it has been shown that women are at greatest risk of homicide at the point of separation or after leaving a violent partner (Wilson and Daly, 1992). The increased attention being given to stalking brings to light further evidence relevant to the issue of post-separation violence. Canadian data suggests that 57 per cent of stalkers are former partners (METRAC, 1998). Moreover, those people most in danger from a violent assault as a result of stalking are women who have previously been in a relationship with the stalker (Palarea *et al.*, 1999; Tjaden and Thoennes, 1998; Shaum and Parrish, 1995).

The emphasis being placed on stalking raises interesting definitional issues. The term 'stalking' has been so imbued with stranger and celebrity discourses that it is hard to claim the terminology fully within the framework of domestic violence and, more specifically, post-separation violence. For example, the Protection From Harassment Act (PFHA) (1997) was designed to cover cases of 'stranger danger', with ex-partner stalking virtually invisible within the popular media and the public policy arena when the legislation was being drafted. The government estimated that only 200 criminal prosecutions a year would be brought using this legislation (Kelly and Humphreys, 2000). In fact, in its first year of implementation in 1998, 5,788 defendants were proceeded against under different sections of the PFHA (Edwards, 2001). Although currently available data does not specify how many cases involve post-separation violence, a Home Office study (Harris, 2000), drawing on a random sample of reviewed cases, indicated that the legislation was most frequently used by complainants who had ended an intimate relationship (43 per cent of cases).

In this article, stalking is understood as one element of post-separation violence, especially as actual physical and sexual violence is often seen to be beyond 'the course of conduct' implied by terms such as stalking and harassment. This is both a legal and a cultural distinction. Academic discourse has tended to reflect and reinforce different categories of stalkers highlighted in popular debates (Kelly and Humphreys, 2000). Stalkers who have a previous relationship with the victim are categorized separately from obsessional stalkers and sociopaths who are defined as men with criminal records for other anti-social behaviour or mental health problems (Zona *et al.*, 1993; Meloy, 1997). Such typologies fail to recognize the overlap between categories, including the fact that former partners may also have obsessional personalities and a history of criminal behaviour; especially if domestic violence is understood as a crime. Within these typologies, the ex-partner category is under-theorized and under-investigated.

A further definitional problem is raised by the term 'post-separation violence', which implies that there is a clear point of separation in a relationship. While we recognize that this boundary is blurred, it is difficult to find a language that does not imply a binary concept. Separation does not always imply leaving. Some women leave and return many times, negotiating many complex emotional and logistical difficulties in this process and making a clear point of separation hard to define. However, the notion of 'separation violence' suggests that it occurs within the separation process and is equally problematic as many women have suffered violence, abuse and stalking years after they considered themselves to have separated. The tendency has also been to use the more general terms 'stalking', 'harassment' or 'domestic violence'. However, these terms conflate women's experiences of violence and abuse by ex-partners with many others. This has had the effect of marginalizing these experiences and setting them outside the focus of policy and practice. We have therefore opted for the term 'post-separation violence'.

Methodology

This article draws on research commissioned by Women's Aid Federation, England and carried out in 2000/2001 (Humphreys and Thiara, 2002). One of the key aims of the research was to explore the issues that women face when they end a violent relationship, including their experiences of legal, health and welfare professionals. Twelve projects for women and two projects for children, all affiliated to Women's Aid, which offered non-refuge based domestic violence intervention services (outreach), provided the research sites. Two services were specialist projects for black and minority ethnic women, while a further two specialized in providing a service to rural women.

Lengthy questionnaires were distributed through project outreach workers and completed by women with their support. In total, 180 questionnaires were completed by women, representing an average return rate between projects of 80 per cent. Twenty-five percent of the samples were Asian and other minority ethnic women. Half of the women had lived in a refuge at some stage, while the other half had only ever used the outreach service. Each of the twelve projects was asked to identify two women (who had not completed questionnaires) to be interviewed in-depth by the researchers. This was a purposive sample selected on the basis of experiences of post-separation violence. Twenty women were interviewed, of whom four were from black and minority ethnic groups. One woman was currently living with her partner, while the others were all separated at the time of interview. This article presents the women's perspectives on their situation. Evidence to corroborate these experiences was not sought within this project.

Women's experiences of post-separation violence

Echoing previous research, high levels of violence and abuse were found to be experienced by women when they attempted to separate. More than three-quarters (76 per cent) of the 161 separated women who completed questionnaires suffered further abuse and harassment from their former partners after they ended the relationship.

For many, the abuse ceased after the first 6–12 months of separation. Sometimes this was due to women moving to a further safe address (25 per cent of the total sample were at a secret address). In other cases, some men ceased their abuse of the woman. However, more than a third (36 per cent) of women reported that the abuse was continuing. Post-separation violence and abuse appeared to be less of a problem proportionally for black and minority ethnic women (BME) in the first 6 months. However, more white women found that post-separation violence reduced over time, while BME women who experienced it in the short term continued to experience it for longer. The in-depth interviews shed further light on these figures and highlight several important issues. First, for all the women who were interviewed, post-separation violence was part of a continuum of abuse and violence (Kelly, 1998) and can be understood as an on-going part of the man's efforts to continue his control over the lives of women and children. Second, processes of separation and leaving need to be understood in the context of the myriad of ways in which post-separation violence occurs. Third, women's experiences of post-separation violence were diverse and the application of the law and law enforcement and, especially, the lack of effective action by public authorities, such as the police and courts, often contributed to the women (and children's) lack of safety. These issues are explored in detail below.

The escalation of violence and abuse

> It's just their way of continuing to control you.
>
> (Elaine)

Women who were interviewed had all been subjected to severe physical violence and emotional abuse within the relationship. Twelve had been sexually assaulted and at least fourteen had sought medical attention for injuries due to the man's violence. All twenty described the effects that this abuse had had on their mental health, including six women who reported incidents of self-harm and suicide attempts (Humphreys and Thiara, 2003). Their experiences resonate with the findings of other research studies, which indicate that the women most vulnerable to post-separation violence are those who suffer more serious abuse prior to separation; this included both physical violence

(Morrison, 2001; Coleman, 1997; Burgess *et al.*, 1997)[3] and serious psychological abuse (Davis and Andra, 2000; Mechanic *et al.*, 2000). The women who were interviewed all spoke of an escalating pattern of violence and abuse that can be termed 'intimate terrorism' (Johnson and Ferraro, 2000), where violence is used as part of a regime of control. Many women reported the obsessional jealousy of the abuser or stalking (being followed, watched and having phone calls monitored) when they were still living together.

Data from the 161 women who completed the questionnaire and who had left their former partners was also indicative of the gravity of the situations that many women left. When asked 'Why did you leave?' the following responses were given (percentages total greater than 100 per cent, since multiple responses were possible to this pre-coded question): 69 per cent feared for their emotional well being; 66 per cent said that the abuse was becoming worse; 60 per cent of women feared they would be killed; 60 per cent feared for their mental health; 54 per cent left when they could see the abuse affecting their children; 25 per cent said they feared for their children's lives; 25 per cent said they feared they would kill their abuser.

Forms of post-separation violence

> He still wants me to live in fear.
>
> (Kate)

It was apparent from women's narratives that separation was an extremely difficult state to achieve. Less than a quarter (24 per cent) achieved this step without being subjected to post-separation violence in a myriad of different forms. All of these forms of violence and abuse had the effect of continuing the abuser's control over the woman, and often the children's lives, making it emotionally and physically difficult to find a place of safety.

Women outlined a range of ways in which stalking, violence and harassment occurred. The questionnaire indicates the most commonly used tactics (see Table 1).

Verbal abuse and physical threats were more frequently reported than physical and sexual assault. However, threats, verbal and emotional abuse

Table 1 Forms of post-separation violence

	(%)	*n*
Verbal and emotional abuse	76	105
Serious threats*	41	64
Physical assault	23	37
Financial abuse	23	37
Threats to other family members	18	30
Threats from other family members	14	23
Threats to new partner	11	18
Sexual violence	6	10

Percentages total greater than 100% as multiple responses were possible. *Examples included threats to: kill; rape; abduct the children; commit suicide; harm family pets.

are often experienced as terrifying and some women commented that they found this harder to cope with than actual physical violence. Research has also suggested that there is a significant relationship between threats and subsequent violence (Brewster, 2000) and women generally had no way of knowing whether threats would actually be carried through and could no longer read and predict the situation in ways which were possible when they were co-habiting. Women who were interviewed also cited a range of other threatening tactics, including abuse at work (either over the phone or in person), which resulted in several women being forced to leave their jobs. BME women with uncertain immigration status were particularly vulnerable to threats to undermine their claims for residency, alongside threats to abduct the children. With child abduction escalating to more than ten children a week in the UK (Kilsby, 2001), women were right to fear that these threats could become a reality.

Other women reported a range of incidents: being followed; run off the road; reported to child protection authorities; threatened with outing the woman's sexuality; abusive letters from prison; threatening the neighbours; suicide threats. When women managed to re-locate to a secret address, several abusers, especially within BME communities, began a concerted campaign of undermining and discrediting the woman within her community and her extended family through spreading rumours. Women also reported being particularly frightened and entrapped when other people were enlisted to participate in the abuse. Sometimes these were other family members (see Table 1), but could also be new girlfriends, the abuser's friends and possibly 'hit men':

> My ex-partner asked a friend of his to come to my home and beat me up because I had left him. I did not know this man. I opened the door to a knock one night, a man asked my name. I told him and basically he kicked and punched the hell out of me. He got hold of my three-year-old son and literally threw him into the glass door, which smashed. My son needed his head injuries glued at hospital. I had a fractured skull and extensive bruising to my body and a couple of broken ribs. I had to get immediate hospital attention for both of us ... the police were a waste of time ... they never even questioned my ex-husband ... I moved about six times in all.
>
> (Rose)

Rose's experience highlights intrusions into the home, which leave women and children feeling terrorized, unsafe and subject to the continued control of the abuser, particularly when police support is inadequate. Other reported invasions of safety included the following: breaking down doors; breaking in when the woman was absent and 'trashing' her home; stealing items from the house, including personal items such as underwear; watching the house; breaking windows; throwing paint and/or writing graffiti on the house; getting other relatives to watch the house; verbally abusing her when she was in the house or leaving the house; breaking in and physically or sexually assaulting her; leaving bouquets of dead flowers; hate notes; harassing and threatening phone calls.

While one group of women reported that post-separation violence diminished over time, another group reported serious escalation. Five of the interviewed women eventually testified against men for serious offences – rape, attempted murder or indecent assault. This resulted in lengthy jail sentences for three of the men. Others were involved in criminal prosecutions, but their perception was that the eventual charges failed to reflect the serious nature of the violence. This evidence of escalation is supported by Mechanic *et al.* (2000), who found that the length of time since separation was the strongest predictor of increased stalking.

The qualitative data suggested that women who experienced less violence and abuse could instead be subjected to a 'charm offensive'. This could involve persistent letters, phone calls, flowers and general attempts to renew courting behaviour. As part of this process, the abuser continually promised to change, often apologized for his behaviour and sought to make the woman feel special, loved and wanted. At the same time, most women also reported being blamed and held responsible for causing him to be abusive and violent. Alternatively, the man played on their guilt by pointing to their role in undermining the family by leaving and depriving the children of a father.

The 'charm offensive' raises the blurred line, at least for some women, between 'intrusive' and unwanted behaviour that falls within dominant discourses of romance and courtship. This blurring, particularly in the early stages of separation, could be confusing. In our study, just over half (53 per cent) of the women who completed the questionnaire said that they never considered returning, while others reported various levels of ambivalence including returning and leaving again, or actively resisting returning (ambivalent responses were not only the outcome of pressure from the man to return, but also the woman's depleted social and economic circumstances on leaving). Where women had succumbed to pressures to return this made it more difficult for them to ask for help when abuse continued and/or escalated.

Resisting post-separation violence

Both the interview and the quantitative data reveal that women did not act passively in the face of abuse and violence but sought help from a range of formal and informal sources. In this section, women's experiences of using the law as a resource are briefly discussed; particularly its effectiveness in securing safety, and/or justice. This includes their use and experience of the following: civil protection orders under the Family Law Act, 1996, Part IV (non-molestation orders and occupation orders); the Children Act, 1989, Part 8 with particular attention to contact and residency; the Protection From Harassment Act, 1997; and criminal proceedings. Criminal proceedings and civil remedies clearly have different functions. However, the lack of integration between most criminal and civil proceedings in the UK (with the exception of the PFHA) often means that one rather than both strategies are pursued. Usually, where a criminal case is being prosecuted, women do not take out non-molestation and occupation orders.

The women in this study tended to conflate their experiences of law enforcement and court proceedings and were frequently unclear about the nature of criminal charges (particularly as many charges were changed just before the court appearance) and whether violence was post-separation. Therefore, this discussion does not concern itself with the details of criminal prosecutions (for more details on those, see Cretney and Davis, 1997 and Burton, 2000). Suffice to say, just under half (46 per cent) of women had had the experience of their partner or ex-partner being arrested at some stage and half of these arrests ($n = 42$) culminated in a court case. While ten men were jailed, most women reported being unhappy when under-charging occurred (for example, men charged with common assault when strangulation or rape was reported) and when men were found not guilty, given cautions, conditional discharges, other community based orders or very short jail terms.

Ironically, the women often reported feeling more endangered than protected by the prosecution process, illustrating the costs to women of the separation between prosecution and protection. New policies for police and the prosecution service have now been developed which should impact on practice in this area. For example, the Police Circular expects police to be involved in enhanced evidence gathering, a positive arrest policy, the use of custody and bail provision to protect women and children from continued abuse, keeping women informed of police and legal proceedings and avoiding cultural relativism. The proposed Domestic Violence Bill should also have some impact in the area. Experience, however, suggests that there is a difference between a written policy, legislation and its implementation. An integrated criminal justice response requires both resourcing and pro-active work to overcome the traditional barriers which allow women in situations of domestic violence to fall into the chasm between police and prosecution services (Barron, 2002; Holder, 2001).

Non-molestation and occupation orders

The use of civil protection orders[4] has been considered controversial by some feminist lawyers and activists, largely due to fears that they have been used as a substitute for legitimate criminal prosecution (Edwards, 1989). It is frequently noted that there are barriers to women accessing or following through with their application for protection (Zoellner *et al.*, 2000; Egger and Stubbs, 1993), not least due to financial barriers in England and Wales for any women in paid employment (Edwards, 2001). The questionable effectiveness of the orders for some women (Harrell and Smith, 1996), combined with the issues of either attachment to the abuser (Zoellner *et al.*, 2000) or threats from him (De Maris and Swinford, 1996) are just a few of the many issues which create problems of attrition in the process of gaining an order. On top of this, problems of access may be created for black and other minority ethnic women through language, cultural isolation and fears of racism (Patel, 1997).

In our quantitative sample, non-molestation orders had been used by 32 per cent of separated women, 13 per cent of separated women had used occupation orders (Family Law Act, 1996: Part IV) and 16 per cent of women had used injunctions under previous legislation. The data suggest that there was a group of women who found protection orders effective. In fact, over one-third (36 per cent) of those who used protection orders said that they were very helpful and the abuse stopped. A further 39 per cent said that they were of some help; that although they were breached, the abuse may have been less or they felt more protected.

The following extract from an interview with a young woman who had taken out a non-molestation order after continued phone harassment illustrates the successful use of a non-molestation order where a breach was acted upon:

> I did call the police. After that, he got locked up for two nights; it was the weekend. He got arrested on the Saturday, stayed there the whole day Sunday and then Monday, half a day. I feel that sort of made him think, then he stopped completely and he still hasn't, even to this day, harassed me.
>
> (Razia)

In this case, the breach of the order was immediately acted upon with custodial action by the police, which had the effect on the abuser of checking his offending behaviour. The case does, however, raise the question of the police's assertive action on a first reported breach by an Asian man and whether a white man would have received the same treatment. This is not to suggest that the action should not have happened, but rather that similar responses should also occur in all similar situations. It should also be noted that the young woman had extensive advice and support from outreach services in gaining the order and contacting the police to act on the breach.

There is evidence in both the quantitative and qualitative data that a significant group of women are finding effective (or some) protection using civil remedies. A total of 73 per cent of this sample of women said that they would apply for an order if they needed one in the future, though many (60 per cent who answered the question) said that they would have preferred a third party to take the order on their behalf to relieve them of the dangers and responsibilities of invoking legal proceedings against their partner or ex-partner. This latter provision is available in other countries (Humphreys and Kaye, 1997), though recent government consultation has not resulted in steps towards implementing Section 60 of the Family Law Act (1996); which would have made this process possible in the UK (Burton, 2003).

The most important point in this context, however, was that for those women who were suffering chronic post-separation violence, civil protection orders had little impact. Over a third of the women (36 per cent) completing the questionnaire found that abuse was continuing. Twenty five percent of those who used orders found them of no help; the abuse continued and police or the courts were unhelpful in acting upon breaches. These women experienced themselves to be outside protection, a finding mirrored in other research which indicates significant disillusionment with the effectiveness of orders (Barron, 2002).

Women who were unable to access orders also failed to gain protection. This included women who found them too expensive, who lacked knowledge of the orders, who were afraid to take court proceedings for fear of making the abuse worse, and whose immigration status precluded them from access. Interestingly, the data on the use of non-molestation orders shows that in spite of significant improvements to protection orders under the Family Law Act, 1996, and a very substantial increase in orders with a power of arrest,[5] there has not been an increase in the actual number of civil protection orders granted under the legislation. 26,029 orders were granted in 2000 as against 32,781 in 1993 and 28,000 in 1994 (Home Office Research and Statistics, 2001). The increasing financial cost of legal services is posited as a significant factor inhibiting use (Edwards, 2001).

Protection from Harassment Act, 1997

A small group of women had used the Protection From Harassment Act, (PFHA) 1997. This involved only 7 per cent of the sample of separated women and less than half ($n = 5$) of these cases had resulted in court action. Given that such a large part of the sample suffered post-separation violence, 36 per cent of which was on-going, the lack of action under any section of the PFHA confirms Edwards (2001) research that, in spite of significantly more action than was predicted under this legislation, its use throughout the country is very uneven.

Problems lay not just with under-utilization of the law. Although the number of women using the PFHA is extremely small ($n = 5$), three of them were unhappy with outcomes which neither stopped the harassment nor resulted in a custodial sentence:

> After the outreach service was involved, my ex-husband was eventually arrested six times under the Harassment law. But magistrates failed to make a restraining order and so the harassment went on.
>
> (Sheena)

Sheena's experience is mirrored in the case review research by Harris (2000), which found that 43 per cent of offenders were given a conditional discharge and in only half of the cases where a conviction was given were restraining orders issued. Harassment cases under Section 2 (harassment) were brought three times more frequently than cases under Section 4 (fear of violence). This suggests an under-utilization of this section of the PFHA (Edwards, 2001), particularly in the light of the numbers of women reporting 'fear of violence' in the British Crime Survey, 1998 (Budd *et al.*, 2000). The serious violence and threats which women in this research reported also suggest that escalating violent incidents may have been forestalled had Section 4 been used.

Ineffective action and protection

The lack of action under the PFHA and the ineffectiveness of both criminal proceedings and protection orders for women suffering chronic post-separation violence, and also ineffective action under other aspects of the criminal law, left a significant group of women (and often their children) unprotected. Sixteen of the women interviewed had been very reluctant to re-locate, for various reasons: they owned their house; they held sole rental; they had already moved at least once; or, in two cases, they had Occupation Orders. Generally speaking, these women felt that the abuser had no right to be on their property. Also, women with children did not want their children's schooling disrupted or to move away from supportive family networks.

The interview data demonstrate that the reasons for the lack of effective protection were complex and involved an inter-play of many factors. The accounts of two women presented below are typical of those who attempted to use the police and courts to secure both protection and justice:

> They took him to the end of the estate where I lived and dropped him off. He came straight back and because he had had to walk back he was angrier than what he was before he went and he beat me for ringing the police. I didn't bother then to re-ring. They weren't doing anything anyway, just dropping him at the end of the estate. . . . a favourite of the police is to say, 'She'll take him back'. And they say that in front of you to their colleague. So they're basically just reinforcing what my husband used to say all the time we were together . . . that I was weak . . . you know if they'd given me some support or made injunctions work, or made conditional bail work I don't think the final violent incident would have happened. (Elaine, who has five children and wanted to stay in her own home. The violent harassment continued for 3 years until he was charged with grievous bodily harm and sentenced to 9 months in prison. He served 4 months and moved to another area from which he harasses her intermittently).

> I had my house and he had his. . . . I'd call them out and they'd come and they'd say, 'Oh, is it here again?' and they were talking to each other on the radio. 'Oh, I was there last week. She'll take him back.' I could hear this. . . .I'd think, 'They're right, I shouldn't have taken him back.' And he'd sort of trash my house, throw paint all over it, beat me, pull my curtains down. I'd run out of the house and he'd just start on me outside. . . . I gave up ringing the police . . . when it was really bad, I'd run out onto the street so that it would be somebody else that'd contact the police on my behalf when they heard me shouting and screaming. . . . I finally got one good officer. He said, 'I've arrested him and we're going to charge him, and if you get any hassle let me know.' ... then I seemed to charge him with everything he did after that. . . . I've had him charged about nine times. Four or five times he got fined, probation, bound over. Then he did the prison sentence [3 months for common assault that had resulted in her hospitalization, as a result of plea bargaining.]. He's on a charge again now. (Mary, whose current practice of taking action on every incident including serious assaults and breaching protection orders has gone on for 2.5 years).

The women's accounts illustrate that it was not one single action or inaction which left them unprotected but an interconnected set of issues that varied for individuals. While lack of effective police action was evident, both police and women experienced barriers to the prosecution of violence due to the unwillingness of prosecutors to take forward serious charges.[6] The attitude of the abuser to breaking the law was also significant and could be compounded by the court's unwillingness to severely sanction breaches of non-molestation and occupation orders.

Women often felt blamed for 'taking him back', when poor law enforcement often meant that they had no effective way of 'keeping him out'. The interviewed women continually commented on the centrality of outreach support and advocacy, which encouraged them to resist the abuser's emotional control tactics; including 'the charm offensive' described earlier. Such support was crucial in helping them to regain their confidence and have the courage to assert their rights to protection.

In all, sixteen of the twenty women's narratives involved women talking with great distress or resignation about their inability to access effective protection, particularly when their address was known to the abuser. Many of these women had young children. Their cases illustrate the dangerous nature of post-separation violence and the escalation that can occur when no effective early intervention occurs.

Re-location and the issues of child contact

> He said to me that if he can't get to me then he will go after the children.
>
> (Hilary)

The severe problems of post-separation violence reported in previous sections highlight that for some women and children re-location to a secret address is the only answer when they fail to secure protection in their own homes. However, a secret location may be equally difficult to achieve and maintain. Wilcox (2000) reported that two-thirds of women in her qualitative sample were unable to keep a secret address. Friends of the ex-partner, family members, public agencies manipulated by the abuser, and women themselves, under sustained pressure from the abuser or his networks, gave away their address. It was child contact arrangements, however, which provided the most consistent vulnerability to post-separation violence and under-mined re-location as a safety strategy.

Within the quantitative sample, forty-nine women (49 per cent of those women with potential child contact arrangements) had contact arrangements with the abusive ex-partner. They reported the first six months after separation as the most dangerous. Only four of the forty-nine women who had child contact arrangements reported no problems with post-separation violence. Several women reported that they stopped contact either through the courts (6 per cent) or informally. Also, a small group of men ceased their abuse over time. In the longer term, over a quarter (27 per cent) of women reported on-going, chronic problems associated with abusive child contact arrangements. Fourteen per cent of women said that child contact had been used to track them down. Not all contact was court-ordered. Solicitors often negotiated contact arrangements which women agreed to, fearing their ex-partners or an unsympathetic hearing by the court and welfare officers, or believing that their children should have contact with their fathers. Women reported that two-thirds of court ordered contact was for unsupervised contact with the woman's abusive ex-partner.

Three women who completed the questionnaire reported that, in spite of their experiences of domestic violence and abuse directed at the children, they were currently in contempt of court or threatened with prison for not meeting the court-ordered child contact arrangements. In these situations, women experienced the law as undermining their safety and minimizing their experiences of violence and the impact of this violence on their children; particularly when they lack significant, corroborative evidence of violence and abuse (Harrison and Humphreys, 2003). The initiation of child contact proceedings and the associated court orders were effectively closing down re-location as a major safety strategy for many women. All of the interviewed women with child contact reported serious problems and commented on what they perceived as the negative effects on their children:

> The last message I got from him was, 'Tell her she's a fucking big, fat bastard'. That's off my son. And that's a nine-year-old. (Jenny, whose ex-husband refuses to allow her contact with her two children and where the solicitors and courts have failed to take effective action to ensure either contact or her claim for residency).

> . . . over the last few months, Janie started having tantrums, having nightmares after she's seen him and he's been sending me threats as well. (Gill, whose ex-partner sexually assaulted her on a number of occasions and she reports showed no interest in the child until she left. Contact is currently court-ordered).

Interviewed women also commented on the way in which stalking and harassment through child contact arrangements provided several abusers with the leverage which they needed to violate the separation and move back home (at least temporarily):

> It was mental harassment which got him back in the house, to be quite honest . . . He was looking after the children all weekend (child contact) . . . he would just come round (to return the children). It was basically, 'I'm moving back in anyway, this is my house. If I can't come in as your husband, I'm going to come back as a lodger. (Karen, who had previously taken an overdose following unremitting stalking and harassment from the abuser).

In summary, our study supports the findings of other research (Hester and Radford, 1996; Wilcox, 2000) which shows child contact as a vulnerable point for continued post-separation violence and one which also has direct and negative consequences for children. While a small group of women found support for their safety through no contact and highly supervised contact, the majority of those with child contact experienced the opposite. Child contact proceedings were used as a legal means to track the woman and sanction unsafe child contact arrangements, leaving both women and children unprotected.

New guidelines for the use of seek and find orders, changes to the definition of harm in the Adoption and Children Act, 2002 – which now include witnessing harm to another person – and the implementation of new guidelines on child contact where there is domestic violence (Lord Chancellor's Department, 2001), have the potential to subvert these continuing abusive practices. The guidelines specifically state that the safety of the resident parent and child before, during and after contact must be secured. Moreover, assessment needs to ascertain whether child contact is being used as a further opportunity for harassment, and whether the abuser has recognized and taken responsibility for the harm his behaviour has caused.

Feedback from Women's Aid refuges (Saunders, 2001; Barron, 2002) suggests that practice in this area is slow to change and that even some women living in refuges are still being subjected to intense pressure to agree to unsafe contact arrangements. A recent study of 300 case files in contested contact cases showed that while 58 per cent of men had some contact when they came into the court arena, this had risen to 94 per cent by the end of the legal proceedings. In 61 per cent of these cases, there were allegations of domestic violence. In one third of cases the allegation was proved. In only 5 per cent of these cases was the order for indirect contact (Fletcher, 2002). Such data suggest that the implementation of the new guidelines is making little progress, at least in some areas.

Concluding comments

The experiences of post-separation violence reported in our study point to the difficulties faced by many women and their children when they attempted to separate from abusive men. These findings demonstrate that women's experiences of the law and its enforcement were varied, thereby supporting Smart's thesis (1995) that the law does not operate hegemonically in this field. There was a group of women who found civil protection orders (mainly non-molestation and occupation orders) effective. Similarly, there was a very small minority of women and children whose safety was promoted by 'no contact' orders or supervised contact. For the majority, however, this area of the law facilitated the man's capacity to continue abuse rather than curtailing it. The research also identified a significant group of women suffering chronic post-separation violence who currently fail to receive either justice or protection.

The effectiveness of protection orders for some women suggests that there is a group of men who respond to cultural norms and the legislative framework and do not want to be seen to step outside the law. The shame bought to the family or the impact on employment provide significant restraining factors. More assertive action on breaches could impact relatively quickly on making more of these orders effective. It is also important to recognize that all the women in this study had the support of outreach services and that they therefore had access to information, advocacy and on-going support. It needs to be recognized that it is difficult in the extreme for women to take legal action and give evidence about violence and abuse without support. In other countries, extensive court support services are in place and evaluations suggest that these are essential services for both gaining protection orders and pursuing criminal proceedings (Holder, 2001).

What was also evident was that a smaller group of chronic and serious offenders were unresponsive to normative frameworks. 'Brushes' with the law which result in being charged with minor offences, cautions, binding over or short custodial sentences had no effect and in fact served to reinforce the abuser's belief that there are no effective constraints or sanctions on his behaviour. They can increase the dangers to women, who will be seen to have 'transgressed' by having called the police or given evidence against the abuser. Moreover, poor and ineffective action from law enforcement and prosecution services may serve to confirm a woman's belief that she is outside help and, therefore, has no option other than to seek to appease the abuser.

While it is unrealistic to expect the law to be an instrument of social transformation, it should not be beyond the limits of law enforcement and prosecution to deliver greater protection and justice than is currently experienced by women and children suffering chronic post-separation violence. The lack of effective action currently places them on the margins of society and further compounds their social exclusion. The new policy developments flagged at the beginning of the article have the potential to shift practice and at least provide a framework where police forces, prosecution services and family proceedings can proactively tackle the problems of protection and justice in their areas. However, the uneven and inconsistent approach to post-separation violence in the UK, including the unsatisfactory disconnection between criminal and civil action, suggests that co-ordinated programme approaches to community support, civil protection and criminal justice that have shown positive results elsewhere (Holder, 2001) need to be developed alongside the new policies and guidelines. The serious and chronic nature of the post-separation problems identified in this article suggest that immediate and concerted action is required to create further inroads into the problem.

Notes

1 Names have been changed to preserve anonymity.

2 Gendered terminology is used in this article to reflect dominant patterns of domestic violence and the fact that the research sample was drawn from women's services. However, it needs to be noted that within these services there were women abused in same sex relationships and women who were abused by female members of the man's family or his new girlfriend.

3 However, care needs to be taken about over-stating this relationship. Statistics Canada (1994) in the most comprehensive prevalence study of domestic violence found 8 per cent of women reported violence commenced at separation.

4 Protection orders is used as a generic term to cover non-molestation orders, occupation orders (Family Law Act, 1996, Part IV), exclusion

orders (Children Act, 1989) and restraining orders (Protection From Harassment Act, 1997).

5 In 2000 there were still 3,372 non-molestation orders and 2,008 occupation orders with no power of arrest. This represents 20 per cent of occupation orders without power of arrest attached, even though this is a much more dangerous situation for the women (and often children) involved (LCD Research and Statistics, 2000).

6 In some areas, there has been effective de-criminalization of domestic violence. Surrey had 5,000 incidents of domestic violence reported to the police and three prosecutions, which proceeded and many other areas showed equally poor rates (Surrey Domestic Violence Project Criminal Justice Response Group (2001).

References

Barron, J. (2002) *Five Years On: A Review of Legal Protection From Domestic Violence*, Bristol: Women's Aid Federation.

Brewster, M. (2000) 'Stalking by former intimates: verbal threats and other predictors of physical violence', *Violence and Victims* 15: 41–54.

Budd, T. and Mattinson, J., with Myhill, A. (2000) *The Extent and Nature of Stalking: Findings from the 1998 British Crime Survey*, London: Home Office.

Buchanan, A., Hunt, J., Bretherton, H. and Bream, V. (2001) *Families in Conflict: Perspectives of children and parents on the Family Court Welfare Service*, Bristol: Policy Press.

Burgess, A., Baker, T., Greening, D., Hartman, C., Burgess, A., Douglas, J. and Halloran, R. (1997) 'Stalking behaviours within domestic violence', *Journal of Family Violence* 12: 389–403.

Burton, M. (2003) 'Implementing third party applications for protection orders in England and Wales', *Journal of Social Welfare and Family Law* 25: 137–50.

Burton, M. (2000) 'Prosecution decisions in cases of domestic violence involving children', *Journal of Social Welfare and Family Law*, 22: 175–91.

Coleman, F. (1997) 'Stalking behaviour and the cycle of domestic violence', *Journal of Interpersonal Violence* 12: 420–32.

Counts, D., Brown, J. and Campbell, J. (eds) (1992) *Sanctions and Sanctuary: Cultural Perspectives on the Beating of Wives*, Boulder, CO: Westview.

Cretney, A. and Davis, G. (1997) 'Prosecuting 'Domestic Assault': victims failing courts or courts failing victims?', *Howard Journal of Criminal Justice*, 36: 24–35.

Davis, K. and Andra, M. (2000) 'Stalking perpetrators and psychological maltreatment of partners: anger-jealousy, attachment insecurity, need of control and break-up context', *Violence and Victims* 15: 407–25.

De Maris, A. and Swinford, S. (1996) 'Female victims of spousal violence: Factors influencing their level of fearfulness', *Family Relations* 45: 98–106.

Edwards, E. (2001) 'Domestic violence and harassment: an assessment of the civil remedies', in J. Taylor-Brown (ed.) *What Works in Reducing Domestic Violence?* London: Whiting and Birch.

Edwards, E. (1989) *Policing Domestic Violence*, London: Sage.

Egger, S. and Stubbs, J. (1993) *The Effectiveness of Protection Orders in Australian Jurisdictions* Canberra: Australian Publishing Service.

Fletcher, 2002. Contact, Separation and the Work of Family Court Staff: A Briefing from NAPO the Trade Union and Professional Association for Family Court and Probation Staff, London.

Harrell, A. and Smith, B. (1996) 'Effects of restraining orders on domestic violence victims', in Buzawa, E. and Buzawa, C. (eds) *Do Arrests and Restraining Orders Work*, Thousand Oaks, CA: Sage.

Harris, J. (2000) 'An evaluation of the use and effectiveness of the Protection From Harassment Act: Summary of Home Office Research Study 203', in T. Budd and J. Mattinson, with A. Myhill (eds) *The Extent and Nature of Stalking: Findings from the 1998 British Crime Survey*, London: Home Office.

Harrison, C. and Humphreys, C. (2003) 'Child contact and domestic violence: how safe is it?' *SAFE, The Domestic Abuse Quarterly*, 5 (Spring): 10–13.

Hester, M. and Radford, L. (1996) *Domestic Violence and Child Contact Arrangements in England and Denmark*, Bristol: Policy Press.

Holder, R. (2001) *Domestic and Family Violence: Integrated Criminal Justice Responses*, Issue 3, University of New South Wales, Sydney: Clearinghouse, www.austdvclearinghouse.unsw.edu.au.

Home Office (2000) *Circular 19/2000 – Domestic Violence*, London: Home Office.

Humphreys, C. and Thiara, R. K. (2003) 'Domestic violence and mental health: 'I call it symptoms of abuse', *British Journal of Social Work* 33: 209–26.

Humphreys, C. and Thiara, R. K. (2002) Routes to Safety: Protection Issues Facing Abused Women and Children and the Role of Outreach Services, Bristol: Women's Aid Publications, PO Box 390, Bristol BS99 7WS.

Humphreys, C. and Kaye, M. (1997) 'Third-party applications for protection orders: opportunities, ambiguities and traps', *Journal of Social Welfare and Family Law*, 19: 403–21.

Johnson, H. (1998) 'Rethinking survey research', in R. Dobash and R. Dobash (eds) *Rethinking Violence Against Women*, London: Sage, pp. 23–51.

Johnston, J., Kline, J. and Tschann, J. (1989) 'On-going post-divorce conflict: effects on children of joint custody and frequent access', *American Journal of Orthopsychiatry*, 59: 190–200.

Johnson, M. and Ferraro, K. (2000) 'Research on domestic violence in the 1990s: Making distinctions', *Journal of Marriage and the Family* 4: 948–63.

Kelly, L. and Humphreys, C. (2000) 'Stalking and paedophilia: ironies and contradictions in the politics of naming and legal reform', in J. Radford, M. Friedberg and L. Harne. *Women, Violence and Strategies for Action*, Buckingham: Open University Press.

Kelly, L. with Bindel, J., Burton, S., Butterworth, D., Cook, K. and Regan, L. (1999) 'Domestic violence matters: an evaluation of a development project', *Home Office Research Study 193. Research, Development and Statistics Directorate*, London: Home Office.

Kelly, L. (1988) 'How women define their experiences of violence', in K. Yllo and M. Bograd (eds). *Feminist Perspectives on Wife Abuse*, London: Sage.

Kilsby, P. (2001) *Aspects of Crime: Children as Victims*, London: Home Office Crime and Criminal Justice Unit Research, Development and Statistics Directorate.

Lord Chancellor's Department (2001) *Domestic Violence: Guidance on Prosecuting Cases of Domestic Violence*, London: Lord Chancellor's Department.

Lord Chancellor's Department (2001) *Guidelines on Good Practice on Parental Contact in Cases Where There is Domestic Violence*, London: Lord Chancellor's Department.

Lord Chancellor's Department (2002) Summary report on findings from the Lord Chancellor's Department's survey to monitor awareness of the: Guidelines for Good Practice on Parental Contact in Cases Where There Is Domestic Violence. www.lcd.gov.uk/family/abfla

Mechanic, M., Weaver, T. and Resick, P. (2000) 'Intimate partner violence and stalking behavior: exploration of patterns and correlates in a sample of acutely battered women', *Violence and Victims* 15: 55–72.

Meloy, R. (1997) 'The clinical risk management of stalking', *American Journal of Psychotherapy*, 52: 174–84.

METRAC, Metropolitan Action Committee on Violence Against Women and Children (1998) *Stalking: Facts and Issues*, Toronto, Canada: METRAC.

Morrison, K. (2001) 'Predicting violent behaviour in stalkers: a preliminary investigation of Canadian cases in criminal harassment', *Journal of Forensic Science* 46: 1403–10.

Palarea, R., Zona, M. Lane, J. and Langhinrichsen-Rohling, J. (1999) 'The dangerous nature of intimate relationship stalking: threats, violence and associated risk factors', *Behavioural Science and Law*, 17: 269–83.

Patel, M. (1997) *Domestic Violence and Deportation*, London: Southall Black Sisters.

Saunders, H. (2001) *Making Contact Worse*: Report on a National Survey of Domestic Violence Refuge Services into the Enforcement of Contact Orders, Bristol: Women's Aid Federation, England.

Schwartz-Watts, D. and Morgan, D. (1998) 'Violent versus non-violent stalkers', *Journal of American Academy of Psychiatry and Law*, 26: 241–5.

Shaum, M. and Parrish, K. (1995) *Stalked: Breaking the Silence of the Crime of Stalking in America*, New York: Pocket Books.

Sinwelski, S. and Vinton, L. (2001) 'Stalking: the constant threat of violence', *Affilia* 16: 46–65.

Smart, C. (1995) *Law, Crime and Sexuality*, London: Sage.

Statistics Canada (1994) *Violence Against Women, Survey Questionnaire*, Toronto, Canada: Statistics Canada.

Tjaden, P. and Thoennes, N. (2000) 'The role of stalking in domestic violence crime reports generated by the Colorado Springs Police Department', *Violence and Victims* 15: 427–41.

Tjaden, P. and Thoennes, N. (1998) 'Stalking in America: Findings from the National Violence Against Women Survey', in *National Institute of Justice/Centres for Disease Control and Prevention*. Washington, DC: US Department of Justice.

Wilcox, P. (2000) 'Me mother's bank and me nanan's, you know, support! Women who left domestic violence in England and issues of informal support', *Women's Studies International Forum* 23: 35–47.

Wilson, M. and Daly, M. (1992) *Homicide*, New York: Aldine de Gruyter.

Zoellner, L., Feeny, N., Alvarez, J., Watlington, C. O'Neill, M., Zager, R., and Foa, E. (2000) 'Factors associated with completion of the restraining order process in female victims of partner violence', *Journal of Interpersonal Violence* 15: 1081–99.

Zona, M., Sharma, K. and Lane, J. (1993) 'A comparative study of erotomanic and obsessional subjects in a forensic sample', *Journal of Forensic Sciences*, 38: 894–903.

[18]

Incomplete Citizens: Changing Images of Post-Separation Children

Felicity Kaganas* and Alison Diduck**

The image of the child as the victim of separation or divorce is well-established in legal, socio-legal and popular discourse. However, the authors argue, alongside this traditional image of the child, there is a different image of the child emerging, that of the autonomous, responsible child. This is apparent in academic discourse, policy documents and legal pronouncements. This child is included in the project of 'remoralising' the family by building the 'good' post-separation family. The 'good' child of separation or divorce is responsible for safeguarding his or her own welfare and is expected to make those choices that are assumed to best protect his or her best interests. In order to ensure that the child makes the 'right' decisions, he or she, like the adults concerned, is the target of education, information and therapeutic intervention. There is a blending of paradigms in which the ideal child is both an autonomous social actor and a vulnerable object of concern.

INTRODUCTION

Many have observed that law's constructions of families, parents and children are constantly subject to change. The images of 'good' post-separation parents, for example, that are currently discernible in law are very different from the images promoted only 20 years ago.[1] These changes are not merely the result of changing fashion or fad. Rather, law's constructions adapt and respond to prevailing social, political and economic conditions and, in turn, are implicated in policy and law reform incentives designed to promote and entrench those constructions. The images of 'good' parents that populate law's discourse, therefore, are very close to those apparent in the dominant discourse espoused by policy-makers and within popular culture. Yet the new ideals embodied in these constructions do not necessarily supplant the old in dominant discourse but may co-exist, albeit uneasily in some cases, with them. And so, we see changing images of the 'good' post-separation family that take into account the newer political, sociological and cultural ideals of individual responsibility, equality and negotiated fluidity alongside the traditional ideals of family stability, familial roles and predetermined obligation.[2]

* Centre for the Study of Law, the Child and the Family, Dept of Law, Brunel University.

** Faculty of Laws, University College London. We are grateful to Christine Piper, Shelley Day Sclater and the two anonymous referees for their helpful comments on earlier versions of this paper.

1 C. Smart and B. Neale, *Family Fragments?* (Cambridge: Polity Press, 1999) 37–39, discuss the importance of the Children Act 1989 as an experiment to promote 'a new style of child-centred post-divorce parenting' (37); and see also B. Neale and C. Smart, 'In Whose Best Interests? Theorising Family Life Following Parental Separation or Divorce' in S. Day Sclater and C. Piper (eds), *Undercurrents of Divorce* (Aldershot: Ashgate, 1999) in which they note the shift in the 1980s in legal and political discourse from the 'lone/reconstituted family' to the 'co-parenting, biological family'.

2 A. Diduck, *Law's Families* (London: ButterworthsLexisNexis, 2003). H. Reece, *Divorcing Responsibly* (Oxford: Hart, 2003) regards changes in political and legal ideals of autonomy and responsible behaviour as evidence of a shift to post-liberalism, in which the post-liberal subject exercises

Changing Images of Post-Separation Children

In general, it has been the adults in the family who have been targeted in the drive to ensure that these ideals are realised. Law and policy-makers alike have undertaken the task of impressing on parents their duty to arrange their post-separation family lives in a way that conforms to the image of the 'good' post-separation family, one in which parents are exclusively concerned with the welfare of their children and who therefore co-operate in sharing time with and responsibility for them. Reece, for example, suggests that in the 'good' divorce, couples become 'divorced to each other not divorced from each other; divorce is not the destruction of the nuclear family but the creation of the bi-nuclear family, and so a potential growth experience for the extended family'.[3] And it is not simply a matter of imposing these norms of continuing and co-operative parenting. Academic writing has not only identified the images of 'good' fathers and 'good' mothers that are being purveyed, but it has also observed the ways in which parents have been co-opted into the project of *becoming* those parents, of *making* those 'good' post-separation families,[4] which are to resemble as closely as possible the 'intact' family.

Unlike his or her parents, the child of the family traditionally has not been the focus of such legal or policy strategies. The image of the post-separation child, it has been observed, is that of victim.[5] This child is an object of concern, is passive, vulnerable, and always at risk. He or she is at the mercy of the vagaries of parental conduct and so, in this account of the 'broken home', it is the parents alone who are charged with the responsibility of alleviating that risk by making the good post-separation family.

In this paper, however, we suggest that evidence is emerging of a metamorphosis in this dominant image of the child. It seems that we may be seeing the genesis of a new concept: the 'good' post-separation child. This child is no longer simply a victim, but is one who, like his or her parents, has an important role to play in shaping the post separation/divorce life of the family and thus has some responsibility for the consequences of separation or divorce. The change may reflect that which Reece has described as 'official government policy'[6] promoting post-liberal responsibility, but because the autonomy of the child subject cannot be expressed in the same terms as that of the adult subject, it also appears to reflect a combination of modern and traditional mythologies incorporated into the discourse about families. In consequence, there is a paradox inherent in this new image of the child. The traditional child of divorce or separation, who is vulnerable and the passive victim of his or her parents' choices, must also fulfil the role of the modern child, who shares responsibility for him-or herself. The child, then, bears

his or her autonomy and freedom through reflection, deliberation and participation so as to achieve self fulfillment and serve the public good. Hendrick in turn identifies what he refers to as 'neo-liberal governance [which] puts the emphasis on individuals being responsible for their actions and communities' (H. Hendrick, *Child Welfare. Historical Dimensions, Contemporary Debate* (Bristol: The Policy Press, 2003) 225–226.

3 Reece, n 2 above, 159.

4 Smart and Neale, n 1 above; C. Smart, *The Ties That Bind* (London: Routedge, 1984); C. Piper, *The Responsible Parent: A Study in Divorce Mediation* (Hemel Hempstead: Harvester Wheatsheaf, 1993).

5 See for example Piper *ibid*; C. Piper, 'Divorce Reform and the Image of the Child' (1996) J of Law and Society 23–36.

6 Reece, n 2 above, 179.

responsibility for promoting his or her *own* welfare by helping to build the 'good' post-separation family in which he or she will be safe. Like his or her parents, this child is cast as a decision-maker, but the decisions he or she makes must be channelled and constrained to comply with the demands of welfare; education and information within the new culture of therapeutic family law[7] are key. To us, this paradoxical child embodies not so much a paradigm shift, as a blending of formerly divergent paradigms that conforms to dominant political and cultural imperatives.

AN EMERGENT, BLENDED PARADIGM

The newly complex paradigm child incorporates two previously competing images of the child. The first is the child as incompetent and dependent. This child is vulnerable because he or she is in the process of development toward self or personhood. This child is one whose welfare is to be prioritised over rights because he or she is not yet fully capable of exercising rights competently. This child needs to be protected. The image is rooted in philosophical ideas of the child as 'becoming' a fully rational subject, and incorporates images of the child as evil, innocent or as a blank slate. It also incorporates socialization theory as well as ideas in developmental psychology suggesting that there is a teleological progression through various and fixed developmental stages of maturation. It can be described as a romantic developmentalist view of the child[8] and has a veneer of common sense about it. It appears to be the dominant paradigm in which educationalists, psychologists and child welfare professionals, including the Children and Family Court Advisory and Support Service (CAFCASS) practitioners, work[9]

However, in contrast to this, sociologists studying childhood have begun to take seriously the idea of the child as 'being'.[10] Rather than seeing childhood as a 'biologically determined'[11] and universal stage, which is characterised by incompetence or irrationality, and through which all children pass on their way to completion as autonomous adults, they see it as a socially constructed space or as a variable concept.[12] On this view, children need not necessarily be conceived of as inactive mounds of clay to be formed by socializing agents, by nature or by structural forces over which they have no control. Instead, it becomes possible to put forward alternative images of children and these, according to James and Prout,[13] have gained currency: 'Looking at children not only as outcomes of social

7 *ibid*, 89.

8 Diduck, n 2 above.

9 A. L. James and A. James, *Constructing Children's Welfare: A Comparative Study of Professional Practice* Research Report to ESRC (2003).

10 C. Smart, B. Neale and A. Wade, *The Changing Experience of Childhood* (Cambridge: Polity Press 2001).

11 A. Prout and A. James, 'A New Paradigm for the Sociology of Childhood? Provenance, Promise and Problems' in A. James and A. Prout (eds), *Constructing and Reconstructing Childhood* (London: Routledge, 2003).

12 *ibid*, and see also D. Archard, *Children: Rights and Childhood* (London and New York: Routledge, 1993).

13 James and Prout, n 11 above, Preface to Second Edition.

processes but as actors within them has gained widespread acceptance'.[14] Indeed, they highlight this as an 'emergent paradigm' for the study of childhood[15] and identify as one of the key features of this approach the need to see children 'as active in the construction and determination of their own social lives, the lives of those around them and of the societies in which they live'.[16] With this kind of paradigm, it becomes possible to ascribe to children the characteristics of reflexivity and agency and to see them as participants in the project of late modern individualization.[17] In this paradigm, children have the capacity to exercise a form of agency, a type of post-liberal autonomy, and to affect and influence their environment, conditions, attachments, detachments and self-identity. More than this, they are assigned an increasing degree of responsibility for doing so.[18]

Both the romantic developmentalist child and the autonomous reflexive child are idealised constructs. While they are in many ways dichotomous ideals, we suggest that both contribute to the new ideal child of law. Their simultaneous presence reflects an ambivalence within the legal ideal, an ambivalence most clearly apparent in criminal law.[19] And, while there can be little doubt that it is the dependent, romantic child that is still dominant in private family law,[20] we are of the view that it is possible to detect in this field of discourse too increasing references to children's autonomy and responsibility.

This blending of paradigms is more than a way for law to reconcile the long-standing tension between the child as subject and as object. While that attempted reconciliation is important, we suggest that what is also important is the process and the discourse through which it is pursued. It may, in other words, reflect a more general drive to recruit children into a broader social project of promoting 'active citizenship'[21] and individual responsibility for actions and their conse-

14 *ibid*, xiv.

15 *ibid*, 'Introduction' 3.

16 *ibid*, 8. See also M. Freeman, 'The Child in Family Law' in J. Fionda (ed), *Legal Concepts of Childhood* (Oxford: Hart, 2001).

17 See, for example, U. Beck and E. Beck-Gernsheim, *The Normal Chaos of Love* (Cambridge: Polity Press, 1995); U. Beck and E. Beck-Gernsheim, *Individualization* (London: Sage, 2002).

18 See Hendrick, n 2 above, 243. His perspective is somewhat different but he also notes the emphasis on responsibility. He argues that New Labour 'desires a passive child citizen – full of responsibilities, but with very few rights'.

19 See, for example, B. Vaughan, 'The Government of Youth: Disorder and Dependence?' (2000) 9 (3) *Social and Legal Studies* 347; Hendrick, n 2 above, 238–244.

20 Freeman observes that 'we have shown ourselves more willing to impose criminal . . . responsibility on children before granting them participatory rights' (Freeman, n 16 above, 200).

21 Vaughan, n 19 above. See also S. Day Sclater and C. Piper, 'Re-moralising the Family? – family policy, family law and youth' (2000) CFLQ 135. That children and young people are being brought into in this project is manifest in a recent Green Paper, *Every Child Matters* (DfES, 2003). In this document, the Government has declared its intention of developing a 'strong partnership with [its] stakeholders', which it defines as including 'children and young people' (Executive Summary para 22). As part of this drive, consultation with children and young people has become a priority. The goals identified within the Green Paper are the product of such a consultation exercise and these goals are described as being important not only for children's well-being but for society as a whole (paras 1.5–1.6). Children's involvement in the 'planning, delivery and evaluation of government services' is said to bring benefits in that it promotes 'citizenship and social inclusion' (*Learning to Listen. Core Principles for the Involvement of Children and Young People* (CYPU, 2001) 6.) See also P. Kirby, C. Lanyon, K. Cronin and R. Sinclair, *Building a Culture of Participation* (DfeS, 2003) and Department of Constitutional Affairs, *Involving Children and Young People: Action*

quences. In the criminal justice context, the project is expressed in the paradox whereby children are seen both as being at continual risk from others and as a constant source of risk to others and, as such, responsible for extricating themselves from this state of dangerousness.[22] In the family law context, it means that maintaining the good post-separation family is no longer the exclusive responsibility of parents but that children can now be brought on board in the project to mitigate the damage divorce does to them and to society. The new good child of divorce is held at least partly responsible for protecting him or her *self*.

We explore the idea of the new 'good' post-separation child of law by looking at three different fields of discourse about post-separation contact with children. We turn first to academic work reporting the outcome of research conducted with children experiencing parental separation or divorce. Psychologists and others within the 'psy' professions speak with a particularly authoritative voice in family and child law, and their observations are influential in shaping not only family policy, but also legal doctrine and procedure.[23] A notable example is the Sturge/Glaser report[24] which has played a significant role in influencing judicial decision-making on contact. Social science research too is influential on occasion and some, like the recent report published by the Joseph Rowntree Foundation[25] setting out recommendations relating to interventions and services for children of divorce, is clearly intended to be. We draw on these two documents and identify in them a newly ambiguous image of children.

We then examine policy statements made by government and, in particular, by the Lord Chancellor's Advisory Board on Family Law. In 2002 the Lord Chancellor's Department published a report entitled *Making Contact Work*[26] and the Government responded to it later that year. *Making Contact Work* was issued pursuant to extensive consultation and it reports that responses were received from all the disciplines working within the Family Justice system as well as from a number of those directly affected by it, namely post-divorce families themselves. These responses displayed, says the Report, 'remarkable unanimity'[27] and the document

Plan 2003–2004 (2003). In the latter document children are identified as 'customers' of the department's services and its strategy is stated as being to 'involve children in the development and evaluation of all policies and services that affect them where this is appropriate' (*ibid*, 6).

22 See Vaughan, n 19 above; Diduck, n 2 above, 206–208.

23 See M. King and F. Kaganas, 'The Risks and Dangers of Experts in Court' (1998) *Current Legal Issues* 221; F. Kaganas, 'Contact, Conflict and Risk' in S. Day Sclater and C. Piper (eds), *Undercurrents of Divorce*, n 1 above; Reece, n 2 above, 195.

24 C. Sturge in consultation with D. Glaser, 'Contact and Domestic Violence-The Experts' Court Report' [2000] *Fam Law* 615. This report was endorsed and adopted by the Court of Appeal in *Re L (Contact: Domestic Violence); Re V (Contact: Domestic Violence); Re M (Contact: Domestic Violence); Re H (Contact: Domestic Violence)* [2000] 2 FLR 334.

25 J. Hawthorne, J. Jessop, J. Pryor and M. Richards, *Supporting Children Through Family Change. A Review of Interventions and Services for Children of Divorcing and Separating Parents* (Centre For Family Research, University of Cambridge; York: Joseph Rowntree Foundation, 2003).

26 The Advisory Board on Family Law: Children Act Sub-Committee, *Making Contact Work. A Report to the Lord Chancellor on the Facilitation of Arrangements For Contact Between Children and their Non-Residential Parents and the Enforcement of Court Orders For Contact* (London: The Stationery Office, 2002).

27 *ibid*, Letter to the Lord Chancellor, 2.

can be read, therefore, as embodying both professional and everyday dominant discourse on contact with children.

Finally, we examine the sometimes subtle shifts discernible in the case law regarding children's capacity to litigate. In part, these shifts may be attributable to the increasing importance of rights discourse in UK law, but they may also be attributable to an equally significant discourse of individual responsibility and active citizenship. It is important in any society committed to principles of equality, justice, fairness and the rule of law that the rights and autonomy of all of its members are respected and it is possible to characterise these shifts as evidence of a transition in which children are being admitted into the margins of this democratic ideal. Moreover there appears to have developed among the judiciary, as there has among policy makers, a heightened consciousness of the potential for young people, in practical terms and irrespective of formal status, to exercise volition and to take it upon themselves to resist the norms on which the ideal post-separation family is built. Children therefore have to be included within the project of citizenship. But they also have to be taught to exercise their autonomy in such a way as to make choices responsibly and in a way that does not jeopardise their welfare. Recently the courts appear to have been playing their part in this education.

ACADEMIC AUTHORITY

Increasingly, research into divorce has begun to focus on children's experiences of the process and its outcome. Researchers, both in the field of the social sciences and from the ranks of the 'psy' professions, have begun to ask children themselves about their parents' divorce. Children's responses indicate that they want to be informed and consulted about the divorce and separation process.[28] Most importantly, they wish to be consulted about their living arrangements post-separation.[29]

Involving children in this way traditionally has been thought to be antithetical to their interests; children were thought to be too immature to cope with such momentous decisions or to identify or be able to express their interests. Wallerstein and Kelly, for example, took this view in *Surviving the Breakup*,[30] a book that was published in 1980 and that has had a profound impact on law and policy concerning post-divorce arrangements for children. They warned that pre-adolescent children are 'not reliable judges of their own best interests and that their attitudes at the time of the divorce crisis may be very much at odds with their usual feelings and inclinations'.[31] They doubted the capacity of children between 9 and 12 to make informed judgments and pointed to their susceptibility to adult manipulation. Freeman,[32] in 1983, criticised this assessment as paternalistic. However, he

28 See, for example, A. Buchanan, J. Hunt, H. Bretherton and V. Bream, *Families in Conflict. Perspectives of Children and Parents on the Family Court Welfare Service* (Bristol: The Policy Press, 2001) 67, 93, 98.

29 See Smart, Neale and Wade, n 10 above; Diduck, n 2 above, ch 4, and sources cited therein.

30 J. S. Wallerstein and J. B. Kelly, *Surviving the Breakup: How Children and Parents Cope with Divorce*, (London: Grant McIntyre, 1980).

31 *ibid*, 314.

32 M. D. A. Freeman, *The Rights and Wrongs of Children* (London: Pinter, 1983) 214.

too noted that '[t]here are undoubtedly problems with relying on the wishes of children'. He too referred to 'questions of competence',[33] the danger that the child might have been coached or manipulated and the potential for damage to the parent-child relationship. By contrast one of the most influential documents relating to children's contact with non-residential parents after divorce to be published in recent years acknowledges the importance of children as social actors in relation to decision-making.

Produced for the court in the form of a report by child welfare experts,[34] the Sturge/Glaser Report sets out the 'psychiatric principles' of contact as well as the benefits and risks of contact for children. It draws on child welfare knowledge in the form of 'developmental and psychological knowledge, theory and research'.[35] It focuses primarily on the issue of whether and how children's current well-being or future welfare is affected by contact or lack of it. While much of the Report is concerned with children's emotional and developmental needs, it also adverts to children's roles as active participants in settling the arrangements for contact and putting them into effect.

The Report states that children's needs should be assessed within the context of their wishes and that the older the child, the more weight those wishes should carry.[36] But the Report goes further and recommends that children who do not want contact for what are regarded as cogent reasons, such as the unreliability of the non-resident parent, should be heeded.[37] Children who adamantly resist contact must be taken seriously and any decision to go against their wishes must take account of the potentially damaging effect of disregarding those wishes or feelings. In addition, such a step should not be taken unless there is some indication of the possibility that the child will change his or her mind.[38] The Report goes on to explore ways of '[o]vercoming fear and resistance where this appears to be ill-founded'.[39] It suggests the use of a one-way screen in interviews with parents, thus enabling the child to retain some 'control', or the use of proxy contact by means of a go-between.

The Report, then, takes into account the emotional response of children to contact in assessing its value. But it also makes it clear that decisions should be made in the light of children's views and that to ignore these might be counterproductive. Rather than being compelled to participate in contact arrangements, ostensibly for their own good, children should be permitted to veto them. Alternatively, in some cases, efforts might be made to persuade them to accept contact. In any event, the Report clearly contemplates that children should have a significant influence on whether contact takes place and what form it should take. Notably, the Report seems to accept that decisions should take account of the possibility that reluctant children can sabotage contact.

33 *ibid*, 206.
34 See Sturge and Glaser, n 24 above.
35 *ibid*.
36 *ibid*, 624. This, in itself is not new. See *Gillick* v *West Norfolk and Wisbech Area Health Authority* [1986] AC 112.
37 Sturge and Glaser, *ibid*, 618–619.
38 *ibid*, 621.
39 *ibid*, 625.

Changing Images of Post-Separation Children

Social science researchers have long been concerned with documenting the effects on children's welfare, whether physical or emotional, of parental divorce or separation. Most studies have focused on outcomes and how these are affected by external factors such as gender, age, contact and conflict. In addition, as Rodgers and Pryor comment in their review of a wide range of research, the majority have 'relied on accounts from adults'.[40] 'Insufficient attention' they say, 'has been paid to [children's] perspectives'.[41] There has been a 'paucity of qualitiative studies . . . which examine the experiences of separation for individual family members.'[42] And there has been little research into the impact on outcome of factors such as the personal resources of and support available to children.[43]

However a few recent studies appear, like the Sturge/Glaser Report, to be focusing on children as active protagonists in the story. In *Families in Conflict*,[44] the researchers highlight what they appear to perceive as the ability, or at least the potential ability, of young people themselves to manage their own difficulties. The authors recommend a 'comprehensive preventative strategy' to alleviate children's distress and indicate that it is crucial to provide them with information on how to 'handle their situation and how to cope'.[45] Education and therapeutic intervention are key. To these authors, children are not merely passive victims, suffering the effects of outcomes over which they have little or no control. Rather they are active survivors of family conflict: 'Many of these children have developed sophisticated coping strategies for surviving in an environment where, for some, family conflict and violence has been an everyday reality'.[46] That the researchers believe that these survival skills can potentially extend to the experience of separation or divorce is apparent in their chapter entitled 'How to make it better – what the children and parents said'.[47]

Another recent report, *Supporting Children Through Family Change*,[48] is directed even more closely at exploring issues around how children can be helped to 'cope'. It contains detailed recommendations and also bears testament to a growing perception that the needs of children arising from the divorce or separation of their parents have to be addressed independently of the needs of the adults concerned.[49] Children, the authors assert, 'have separate needs for support'.[50]

40 B. Rodgers and J. Pryor, *Divorce and Separation: The Outcomes for Children* (York: Joseph Rowntree Foundation, 1998) 15.
41 *ibid*, 45.
42 *ibid*, 44.
43 *ibid*, 40.
44 Buchanan et al, n 28 above.
45 *ibid*, 98.
46 *ibid*, 82.
47 Indeed, the young people themselves who were interviewed thought it possible to help others in their position by providing 'top tips' for children, parents and Family Court Welfare Officers (*ibid*, 82–84).
48 Hawthorne et al, n 25 above.
49 The authors point out that the traditional support systems have tended to concentrate on the adults on the assumption that children will benefit indirectly and that parents often function as 'gatekeepers' for their children (*ibid*, 3). Despite the fact that '[r]esearchers and service providers have united in arguing that children have a right to be involved in decisions and that they have the capacity to act as agents in their own lives', they say, much support and advice continues to be targeted at parents (*ibid*, 4).
50 *ibid*, 3.

The reasons for this conclusion are revealing. While it is acknowledged that, in the long term,[51] the majority of children and young people emerge from the separation or divorce of their parents relatively unscathed, 'most . . . experience upset during periods of parental conflict and separation, and for some, there may be persistent negative consequences'.[52] And although 'the separation or divorce in itself is not always a major explanatory factor',[53] children whose parents separate or divorce are 'undoubtedly at increased risk for negative outcomes in the medium- and long-term'.[54] Economic problems lead to poor 'outcomes';[55] impaired parenting capacity such as lack of support is 'associated with behaviour problems and antisocial behaviour';[56] and, in particular, post-separation parental conflict gives rise to 'ongoing risk for low self-esteem and psychological distress'.[57] The language used is suffused with notions of harm, risk and negative outcomes and it clearly evokes the image of the child as the passive victim of parental separation or divorce. It also conjures up the figure of the child as victim turned threat, a child so damaged by events that he or she is at risk of becoming dysfunctional to the point of being antisocial.

Yet there is also another image of the child inhabiting this world. This is the child who is entitled to be involved in decisions, a child who is able to articulate views and who has the capacity for agency. This child is not merely the product of parental actions and the embodiment of externally forged 'outcomes'. Children are deemed to be able to choose to seek help, to use that help constructively and so to avert the negative outcomes to themselves and to society that could otherwise materialise. Through their *own* efforts, they can promote their own welfare, their own psychological well-being. Not only will this optimise their chances of becoming responsible citizens in the future, it is also an immediate exercise of responsible citizenship.

Research studies, the authors tell us, show that children want to know 'what is happening and to be given explanations that are appropriate for them'; they want to maintain good quality relationships with both parents; and they often want to participate in decision-making about living arrangements.[58] Children, they say, benefit from knowing about absent parents and, depending on its quality, from contact.[59] They also have more positive feelings about the division of their time between parents if they have had some input into the decision.[60] Generally, it is in children's best interests that they be listened to.[61] Furthermore, 'an understanding of children's perspectives is essential if support and intervention for them is to be effective'.[62]

51 *ibid*, 16.
52 *ibid*, 1. See also 9.
53 *ibid*, 16.
54 *ibid*, 15.
55 *ibid*, 17.
56 *ibid*, 19.
57 *ibid*, 18.
58 *ibid*, 13. They go on to point out that children who do not understand why family change is occurring may suffer from symptoms such as 'anxiety, depression and conduct disorder' (14).
59 *ibid*, 14–15.
60 *ibid*, 15.
61 *ibid*, 21.
62 *ibid*, 14.

In what way children's best interests are served and what is meant by 'effective' intervention is not made clear. However, some idea of what is intended can be derived from an examination of the recommendations made by the Report and the reasons supplied for these. First, it is clear that children's welfare is considered best served by conflict-free parental relationships and by sustained contact with the non-resident parent.[63] This is not new, and reiterates the standards of the 'good' post-separation parent. But importantly, the report states that children should be helped to help themselves. They need coping strategies that will enable them to negotiate the change in a way that 'avoid(s) long-term adversity'.[64] Services should 'help children understand and manage conflict in intact families and in stepfamilies'.[65]

The aims and outcomes suggested for these services include a number directed at increasing children's well being, but also a number that implicate children themselves in that project. Children should be helped 'to develop skills for appraising and coping with conflict and distress', the Report says. They should be encouraged to seek support; they should be consulted about intervention and their wishes and needs should be respected. If these recommendations are followed, the authors maintain, the outcomes are likely to be good communication with parents; ongoing relationships with both parents, where appropriate; coping with loss of a parent; minimal disruption of school attendance and performance; and avoidance of behavioural problems,[66] all outcomes that characterise the responsible child citizen in the ideal post-divorce family.

Intervention, then, according to this Report, should be aimed at alleviating distress, but that is not all. It should be directed at supporting, informing and equipping children with the skill to do this for themselves. Children are perceived as capable of shaping the consequences of divorce both in terms of their own emotional stability and behaviour and in terms of their relationships with their parents. Implicit in the report, it seems, is the child as social actor, capable of, and responsible for, influencing his or her own life as well as the lives of other family members. And the way in which that influence is exerted has to be directed. In many ways this report envisions a type of post-liberal child, one who becomes an active participant in securing the 'good' divorce or separation where contact continues and, if conflict occurs, 'copes' with it. This is the 'good' child of divorce or separation: a well-adjusted, adequately educated child who eschews antisocial activity.

MAKING CONTACT WORK

The concern to mitigate the negative consequences of family breakdown by promoting the 'good' post-separation family has also been expressed in policy

63 Conflict before, during and after divorce is said to be 'important in outcomes' (*ibid*, 23).

64 *ibid.* Children 'cope' better if they have 'appropriate' information and involvement (*ibid*, 22). Children should be helped to understand the changes and to 'cope actively and effectively' (*ibid*).

65 *ibid*, 23.

66 *ibid*, 65–66.

documents.[67] Perhaps the most important of these in recent years is *Making Contact Work*. The Report not only contains prescriptions for state provision of services but also prescriptions for good conduct by individuals. Implicit in both of these strands are normative images of parents and children. Parents are encouraged to exercise their autonomy and to assume individual responsibility for achieving the norm by negotiating and reaching extra-legal agreements about residence and contact. However the message is clear as to how that autonomy is to be exercised; contact with both parents is considered crucial for children's welfare, and conflict is bad. In this version of the post-separation family, then, parents are meant to make those choices that will help to sustain family relationships and a family form that is socially and politically desirable. Since they cannot always be trusted to do so, they must be steered in the right direction with the aid of information, education or counselling sessions.[68]

It is true that exhortation or coercion of parents may not be entirely new but, as is the case in relation to the academic research, we see in this document a new treatment of children. This change becomes apparent when it is compared with earlier documents.

In 1988, for example, the Law Commission published a report dealing with guardianship and custody.[69] It stated that there were obvious dangers in giving children's views 'too much recognition'.[70] Children's views should be discovered in a way that did not embroil them in parental disputes, force them to choose between parents or feel responsible for the eventual decision. Also, children's views 'may not be reliable'.[71] 'Nevertheless', it continued, 'experience has shown that it is pointless to ignore the clearly expressed wishes of older children'.[72]

Similar concerns are voiced in *Making Contact Work*. But while the Law Commission focused on children's vulnerability, their unreliability and their potential for intractable opposition, *Making Contact Work* is different in that it sets out also to bring children into the process of making the 'good divorce'.

Admittedly it is parents who are at the centre of the document[73] but children are included in the plans to inform and educate. According to *Making Contact Work*, the rôle of the state is to 'help' not only adults, but also children, to achieve

67 See, for example, Home Office, *Supporting Families: A Consultation Document* (London: The Stationery Office, 1998). Relationship support, relationship education and the avoidance of negative outcomes as a result of separation or divorce are all dealt with in Advisory Group on Marriage and Relationship Support, *Moving Forward Together* (Lord Chancellors Department, 2002).

68 Reece states that *Making Contact* Work is an 'outstanding example of the influence of post-liberal information within family law' (n 2 above, 200) and it is also a good example of how this form of information seems to have become 'official government policy' (*ibid*, 179).

69 The Law Commission, *Family Law. Review of Child Law: Guardianship and Custody*, Law Com no 172 (London: HMSO, 1988).

70 *ibid*, para 3.23.

71 *ibid*.

72 *ibid*.

73 They in particular, as one respondent put it, need information about the difficulties of post-separation parenting and the 'effect of continuing parental hostility on their children' to ensure that their views on contact would be 'better informed' (The Advisory Board on Family Law n 22 above, para 3.9). They need to realise that contact is a process of negotiation demanding patience, tolerance and a commitment to the nostrum that 'contact is of positive value to their children' (para 3.21) The main focus should always be the needs of the child (para 3.29. See also para 3.20).

the desirable outcome. One of the themes identified as having emerged from the Consultation was 'the need at an early stage to provide information for separating parents *and their children* about the likely effects of the separation, the difficulties they are likely to encounter, and the means whereby those difficulties can be addressed'.[74] Respondents agreed[75] that children should have access to 'age-appropriate information'.[76] Children should be given both substantive information and information about the process of how to become better responsible subjects: they should be given 'advice about their rights and about how they can make their voices heard in any dispute between their parents'.[77] They should be told that contact can be difficult and be encouraged to talk to parents about their views.[78] Parents should be advised of the necessity of 'informing and consulting children about arrangements'.[79] At the same time, however, any information imparted as well as the consultation process must take into account children's vulnerability. One of the clear messages to be communicated to them must be that they are not responsible for the separation.[80] And while parents must inform and consult, they have to ensure that they shield their children from conflict.[81]

The image that emerges from the report, like that painted by the Law Commission, is one of children who are fragile and in need of protection. Information and communication are said to be necessary to protect their well-being. However, providing information and education for children is also indicative of another image of children, one in which they are at least partly *responsible* for the successful implementation of contact arrangements.

Evidently the aim is to get children to accede to contact. Where 'a child or one of the children is resisting contact', the Report says, CAFCASS should make provision for supervised contact.[82] And families or children might be referred to CAFCASS where contact has broken down. Echoing the Sturge/Glaser Report, *Making Contact Work* suggests that recalcitrant children can often be 'persuaded' to view a parent through a screen, giving the child 'control' in deciding whether to meet and this measure might 'at best' lead to face-to-face contact.[83] Therapy is important here as well; child counselling is included among the measures recommended to facilitate enforcement of contact.[84] The policy is to 'protect and enhance' the child's relationship with both parents[85] and it seems that children's co-operation in achieving this goal is acknowledged to be necessary. And older children might even be empowered in contact orders to renegotiate contact with parents.[86]

74 The Advisory Board on Family Law, n 26 above, para 1.2, emphasis added.
75 *ibid*, para 4.3.
76 *ibid*, para 6.12. One of the tasks for CAFCASS was seen to be that of providing children with information. The information given to them, said one expert, should include advice on practical strategies to manage problems arising in relation to contact (*ibid*, para 3.22).
77 *ibid*, para 4.1.
78 *ibid*, para 4.5.
79 *ibid*, para 3.23.
80 *ibid*, para 4.4.
81 *ibid*, para 3.23.
82 *ibid*, para 8.18.
83 *ibid*, para 13.9.
84 *ibid*, para 14.50.
85 *ibid*, para 8.17.
86 *ibid*, para 13.21.

While children are portrayed in the Report as objects of concern, they are, at the same time, given the status of potentially active participants in the process of divorce and the making of contact arrangements. The paradoxical 'good' child of divorce is discernible here. On one hand, the Report makes it eminently clear that what is being striven for is the securing of children's best interests through the facilitation of conflict-free contact; the ultimate goal is therefore founded on a particular construction of welfare. On the other hand, the Report endorses a strategy of making increased concessions to the child's role in achieving that goal. Parents and children alike are to be counselled and provided with the necessary education and information so that they can better understand and heed the message 'radiated'[87] by the law and by policy makers. Children are vulnerable and in need of protection, but at the same time, they carry the disruptive potential for resistance to contact. This is something to be avoided. Information and consultation is not only necessary to protect children's best interests, it is important also to secure their compliance.[88] They, like their parents, are constructed as being in need of tutelage so that they can make responsible choices about their behaviour. For the post-liberal or communitarian, 'education and participation march hand in hand'[89] to make the good post-divorce family.

The Government's response to *Making Contact Work*[90] is unsurprising in many ways. It states at the outset that government's target is to increase contact on parental separation.[91] Under the heading 'Communication and Information', the response accepts in principle recommendations to develop a coordinated communication and information strategy that would encompass not only CAFCASS, but also other government departments and information providers. The government appears committed to a belief in the value of education for families and anticipates that information on family breakdown and the practicalities of post-separation parenting will be aimed at both parents and children.

This, coupled with the government's agreement with recommendations[92] concerned to facilitate the private ordering of contact arrangements,[93] conveys the message that family members themselves are to bear the primary responsibility for increasing post-separation contact. Thus, information and education about separation, counseling services and dispute resolution are crucial to promote children's well-being and also to promote children's involvement in the process of arranging and implementing contact, at least at the informal, private level.

87 See J. Dewar, 'The Normal Chaos of Family Law' (1998) MLR 467–470.

88 The 'good' post-separation child accepts the need for contact and co-operates in achieving this objective. The image of the 'good' post-separation family has in turn to be modified to accommodate the perceived need to secure this co-operation. Not only must parents communicate with each other to achieve harmony, they must also communicate, and possibly negotiate, with their children. Arguably the need for co-operation by children also underlies the importance attributed in the Report to tailoring contact orders to take account of children's changing wishes and aspirations (para 13.15); presumably orders that do so are more likely to survive.

89 Reece, n 2 above, 142.

90 *Government's Response to the Report of the Children Act Sub-Committee of the Lord Chancellor's Department's Advisory Board on Family Law "Making Contact Work"* (Lord Chancellors Department, 2002).

91 *ibid*, 1.

92 *ibid*, Recommendations 14, 16, 17 and 31.

93 *ibid*, 7.

What is more, children are seen as having a wider role; they have a part to play in the compilation of the information to be disseminated. The document records the fact that children have been involved in the development of leaflets and website information,[94] and declares that children 'too have views' and that government 'must listen to them'.[95] It goes on to say that 'we want to hear children's ideas as to how they can be involved in decision making about their future'.[96] Children's role here as both producers and consumers of information designed to promote their welfare evidences again an amalgamation of the child as 'being', as responsible agent, and the child as 'becoming', as passive victim whose welfare must take priority.

Yet while empowering children is apparently seen as necessary, it is also seen as a risky business. This concern is particularly pronounced in the views expressed about children's participation in the *formal* process of decision-making on divorce or separation. *Making Contact Work* reports that questions about the functioning of the court system in relation to contact disputes prompted responses indicating general dissatisfaction. Much of this dissatisfaction focused on images of children as victims of the system.[97] Children were perceived as harmed or damaged by the legal process and, to make things worse, the outcome of the process could not guarantee protection of their best interests. Although there was some support for greater participation by children in legal proceedings,[98] it was their needs and welfare that were at the forefront of discussion. Most respondents agreed with the law on children's representation as it is at present and considered the existing rules of court sufficiently flexible.

The government response also indicates that hearing children's unmediated voices in court is not a priority. The document states:

> One issue that has clearly emerged from the scoping study is that there are many different ways of ensuring children and young people can be and are heard - it is not just about legal representation. Our consultation will therefore explore the wide range of options available.[99]

The tension between autonomy and welfare appears strongest, then, in the context of children's participation in formal court proceedings.[100] The tension is partly resolved by the fact that the rules of court appear to allow a role for children, but usually require it to be exercised through, and with the assistance of, adult professionals. It might be that to concede rights to children as protagonists in litigation contradicts too strongly the traditional image of the child of divorce;

94 *ibid*, 4.
95 *ibid*, 3.
96 *ibid*, 11.
97 See, for example, para 10.11.
98 One former judge, for example, said children should be much more involved in decision-making and the Report notes that there was generally a 'strong feeling' among respondents that children should be represented separately more often in difficult cases (paras 12.6–7. See also Recommendations 20).
99 *Government's Response*, n 90 above, 11.
100 It is doubtful whether there is any room in a formal courtroom setting for the exercise by adults or children alike of post-liberal autonomy which, according to Reece, is characterised by party control and behaviour modification (Reece, n 2 above, 181),

the litigation process is portrayed as 'corrosive'[101] for children and exposure to it is regarded as too damaging.[102]

LEGAL STATEMENTS ABOUT CONTACT

We have endeavoured to show that 'extra-legal', that is, policy and social scientific, discourse relating to the ideal post-separation child is ambivalent and reveals the paradoxical nature of that child. We now go on to argue that legal statements manifest a similar ambivalence.[103]

The legal system traditionally has been uncomfortable with the prospect of dealing directly with children in court, but the significance accorded to children's views and wishes in private law proceedings appears to be on the rise. To some extent, this new focus may be attributed to International Conventions such as Art 12 of the United Nations Convention on the Rights of the Child and to the incorporation of the European Convention on Human Rights into the Human Rights Act 1998. And, presumably, the notion of children's rights will be further entrenched in judicial consciousness by the European Constitution, Art 24. We may increasingly, therefore, see rights relied upon as the basis for paying attention to children's views in court.

The UK courts, of course, have to deal with the concept of rights now in the context of the European Convention. Referring to this and to other international instruments, courts in the UK do not shy away from invoking children's rights. Although the European Court of Human Rights has focused on children's 'best interests' rather than rights in its efforts to 'strike a fair balance',[104] and although the paramountcy test in section 1 of the Children Act 1989 has been held by domestic courts to be compatible with the Convention,[105] they appear to be acknowledging that the Human Rights Act attributes rights to children as well as to their parents. For instance, in *Re S*,[106] a case concerning contact, the court stressed the need to ascertain children's wishes and feelings and, in doing so, referred to the Convention and 'other . . . enactment[s] that relate to the rights of children'.[107] Similarly,

101 *Government's Response*, n 90 above, para 12.12.

102 More cynically, it might be suggested that this portrayal may assist in diverting family disputes away from the courts and towards (cheaper) private negotiation.

103 As do extra-judicial statements. The President of the Family Division, for instance, has recently said that to advocate 'child power or child decision-making' would be 'clearly wrong'. Even older children might not have 'sufficient maturity'. However, she stated, 'children have a right to be informed as to what is going on and to have their views taken into account – even if, on many occasions, what they want cannot be achieved' (Dame Elizabeth Butler-Sloss, Paul Sieghart Memorial Lecture, 'Are we failing the family? Human rights, children and the meaning of the family in the 21st century' (LCD Speeches, 3 April 2003).

104 *Elsholz* v *Germany* [2000] 2 FLR 486 para 50; *TP and KM* v *United Kingdom* [2001] 2 FLR 549 para 71; *Yousef* v *The Netherlands* [2003] 1 FLR 210 para 66; *Sahin* v *Germany*; *Sommerfeld* v *Germany; Hoffman* v *Germany*: *Sahin* v *Germany* [2002] 1 FLR 119 paras 40 and 42.

105 See eg *Dawson* v *Wearmouth* [1999] 1 FLR 1167, 1182; *Re KD (A Minor) (Ward: Termination of Access)* [1998] 1 All ER 577, 587 and 588. See, for discussion, F. Kaganas and C. Piper, 'Grandparents and Contact: "Rights v Welfare" Revisited' (2001) *Int J of Law, Policy and the Family* 250.

106 *Re S (Contact: Children's Views)* [2002] 1 FLR 1156.

107 At 1170. See also *Re T (Contact: Alienation: Permission to Appeal)* [2003] 1 FLR 531. There the Court of Appeal indicated that, when considering parental alienation cases it might be necessary, in the

the court in *Re A*[108] considered that the incorporation of the Convention into domestic law might have to lead to change.[109] However, this concern with human rights legislation has not been the only impetus for change. Domestic courts have increasingly come to adopt a general view that 'the children should be seen and heard in child cases',[110] and that they have a role to play even in the formal court process. It is the growing prevalence of this view that we suggest provides further evidence of the new child of divorce.

As long ago as 1987, King observed that older children, dissatisfied with court orders concerning arrangements after divorce, would simply 'vote with their feet'.[111] The Law Commission expressed a similar opinion in 1988.[112] Now courts' perceptions of children appear to be developing along the same lines and they seem to be placing greater emphasis on taking children's views into account. While there are examples of courts in the past refusing contact or access orders in the face of determined opposition by children,[113] there are also examples of cases where the courts have tended to discount children's distress at having to have contact with the non-resident parent.[114] More recent decisions have generally afforded greater prominence to children's emotional state[115] and to their wishes.[116] In one notable case, *M* v *M (Defined Contact Application)*,[117] an 8-year old girl was found to be too immature to make decisions, yet the court was loath to make an order that would effectively compel her to accept contact. There was the danger that she might 'flout'[118] an order and without her agreement, a court decision would not be effective.[119] Judicial rejection of coercion is apparent also in *Re S (Contact: Children's Views)*[120], a case concerning three young people aged 12, 14 and 16. The court said that the older children needed to be accepted as young adults[121] who could make decisions without being pressurised, while the youngest also needed 'space'.[122] As regards the youngest child, an order was inadvisable in the light of his attitude and emphasis was placed on the desirability of allowing him

light of Arts 6 and 8, for judges to interview children and to allow them separate representation (para 25). This discussion was not concerned with the child's right however. What was being considered was a possible infringement of the father's rights.

108 *Re A (Contact: Separate Representation)* [2001] 1 FLR 715.

109 At para 22.

110 *ibid.*

111 M. King, 'Playing the Symbols: Custody and the Law Commission' (1987) *Fam Law* 186.

112 Law Commission n 69 above.

113 For example, in *Churchard* v *Churchard* [1984] FLR 635, the court accepted that there was nothing it could do to compel boys of 10 and 8 to have contact with their father. It made an order for no access. In *M* v *M (Minor: Transfer of Custody: Appeal)* [1987] 2 FLR 146, the child's views were crucial. The 12 year old child would be likely to resist a court order to which she was opposed and might run away (153).

114 See, for example, *M* v *M (Child) (Access)* [1973] 2 All ER 81, *Re H (Minors) (Access)* [1992] 1 FLR 148.

115 *Re M (Contact: Welfare Test)* [1995] 1 FLR 274.

116 *Re F (Minors) (Denial of Contact)* [1993] 2 FLR 677.

117 *M* v *M (Defined Contact Application)* [1998] 2 FLR 244.

118 *ibid*, 249.

119 *ibid*, 250.

120 *Re S (Contact: Children's Views)* [2002] 1 FLR 1156.

121 *ibid*, 1170, 1171.

122 *ibid*, 1165.

some 'choice commensurate with his age'.[123] The older children would react with 'sullen resentment' to compulsion and would comply 'with bad grace and with a counter-productive result'.[124] The court added that orders should not be made in the expectation that they would not be enforced if disobeyed, particularly in the light of the introduction into the national curriculum of instruction in citizenship. Young people had to be brought up to 'respect the law' and so 'the law must respect them and their wishes, even to the extent of allowing them, as they occasionally do, to make mistakes'.[125] In effect, they must be allowed to learn from their mistakes.

What emerges from this decision is the notion of children as fledgling citizens. What also emerges from both *M* v *M* and *Re S* is that courts are now directing their efforts at finding ways to persuade children and young people, and not just parents,[126] to choose the 'good' post-separation family; while children's choices should be respected, they should be given a clear indication of what the 'correct' choice would be. In *M* v *M*, the court stated that the parents should express an expectation that contact should take place[127] and, in seeking to achieve this aim, they should seek to provide 'guidance and support'.[128] In *Re S*, the court declared contact to be in the children's best interests and its orders, while stressing the need for agreement on the part of the older children and some choice for the younger, endorsed various arrangements designed to enable contact to take place.[129] While compulsion was undesirable, persuasion was the way forward.[130] Similarly, in *Re W (Contact: Joining Child as Party)*,[131] the court saw the need to convince the child, even though he was young, of the 'right' course to take. It stated that the 7 year old had a right to a relationship with his father whether he wanted it or not. With the help of CAFCASS and a health professional, it might be 'possible for the boy to see it as right and proper that he should see his father'.[132]

There is some evidence then, that the courts may be more concerned than in the past to consider children's wishes and to take them seriously, particularly where older children are involved.[133] And, correspondingly, more and more emphasis is being placed on canvassing what those wishes and views might be.[134] Some children may have an account of their views included in a report

123 *ibid*, 1172.
124 *ibid*, 1170.
125 *ibid*, 1171.
126 Compare *Churchard* v *Churchard*, n 113 above, where Ormrod LJ's disapproval was reserved for the parents. He rebuked them for engaging in a protracted dispute and indicated that they should behave like adults.
127 n 117 above, 250.
128 *ibid*, 251.
129 n 120 above, 1171–1172.
130 *ibid*, 1170.
131 [2003] 1 FLR 681.
132 *ibid*, 685.
133 See C. Smart and V. May, 'Residence and Contact Disputes in Court' [2004] *Fam Law* 36, 42. Cf C. Humphreys and C. Harrison, 'Squaring the Circle – Contact and Domestic Violence' [2003] *Fam Law* 419, 422.
134 Compare *M* v *M* (1977) 7 *Fam Law* 17. However J. Fortin, *Children's Rights and the Developing Law*, (London: ButterworthsLexisNexis, 2003) reports that the Committee on the Rights of the Child (2002) expressed concern about the inadequacy of the present system regulating separate representation for children (para 29, cited by Fortin, *ibid*, 201). It recommended reforms, including

prepared, at the court's request, by a child and family reporter (CFR)[135] and this has generally been the court's preferred option. Others may be given party status and separate representation if the court considers this appropriate.[136] Normally, the child must be represented by an adult: a next friend or, if the child is a respondent, either a CAFCASS officer or some other person appointed by the court to act as a guardian ad litem. In all of these options, the ideal is to ensure that the child's views are mediated through professional or at least adult assistance.

Even so, the courts allow children party status only infrequently, and despite the Family Proceedings Rules having been altered in ways that might make it more common in future,[137] judicial reluctance to use this procedure seems to mirror government reluctance to encourage it. A recent study into the application of Rule 9.5, conducted by two District Judges,[138] found that the power to order separate party status for children is used relatively sparingly; it tends to be exercised only in particularly complex or difficult cases: 'In each case the judge will have to exercise his discretion according to the seriousness of the case and the welfare need of the child'.[139] Yet views on separate representation also appear to be changing. The authors go on to note, citing a speech by the Parliamentary Secretary in the LCD and reported in Hansard, that it appears to be government policy that children should be 'directly represented in more private law cases than has hitherto been the case'.[140] In addition, there are some within the judiciary who seem to accept that this would be a desirable development; it has been said that children need information, they need a voice, someone to listen and even someone to 'orchestrate an investigation of the case on their behalf'.[141]

According to Fortin, there is some potential for change in the legal system.[142] In particular, she notes that while in the past it may have been exceptional for courts

changes to divorce proceedings, to ensure that children capable of forming their own views should have the right to express them and have them taken into account (para 30, cited by Fortin, *ibid*).

135 See Buchanan et al, n 28 above. For a critique of the practice of CFRs, see A. L. James, A. James and S. McNamee, 'Constructing Children's Welfare in Family Proceedings' [2003] *Fam Law* 889.

136 Family Proceedings Rules 1991 rule 9.5.

137 The Family Proceedings Rules provide that the CFR is under a duty in every case to advise the court whether it 'is in the best interests of the child to be made a party to the proceedings' (FPR 1991 rule 4.11B (5) and (6)). And a new s 41(6A) CA 1989 (inserted by s 122 of the Adoption and Children Act (2002)) means that some children involved in contact and residence cases may have the possibility of separate representation by a children's guardian together with a legal advocate, rather than simply by a guardian ad litem (See for discussion Fortin, n 134 above, 221–222). But, as Fortin points out, the guidance produced by CAFCASS Legal as to when the services of its officers for the purposes of separate representation should be offered are restrictive (*ibid*, 223; CAFCASS Practice Note [2001] 2 FLR 151 at [4]).

138 District Judge Clifford Bellamy and District Judge Geoff Lord, 'Reflections on Family Proceedings Rule 9.5' [2003] Fam Law 265.

139 *ibid*, 267.

140 *ibid*; see also Department for Constitutional Affairs n 21 above, 5. Reaching the department's aim of ensuring children have a voice in all services affecting them includes working with courts, judges and lawyers, among others.

141 *Re A (Contact: Separate Representation)* [2001] 1 FLR 715 at 721.

142 She suggests that the possibility of appointing a children's guardian may induce judges to afford children party status more readily. Also, she observes, courts are already tending to order separate representation in a wider range of cases than those contained in the CAFCASS guidelines (Fortin, n 134 above, 223). Indeed, policy expressed in the *Action Plan 2003 – 2004* (Department for Constitutional Affairs n 21 above) may also encourage such changes.

to allow separate representation, judges are now more receptive to applications even in relation to young children. Certainly they are mindful of the fact that to refuse such representation could invite a challenge under the Human Rights Act.[143]

There is also another route to separate representation and Fortin describes this as 'a legal acknowledgement of [mature children's] capacity to make important choices in their lives and to take responsibility for certain aspects of their own upbringing'.[144] With the leave of the court under section 10(8) of the Children Act 1989, children themselves may initiate proceedings. And under rule 9.2A FPR 1991, the child can apply to begin such proceedings without an adult representative or, if one is in place, to dispense with that person's services. A successful application enables a child to instruct a solicitor directly.

However when it comes to the prospect of children exercising these rights, the courts have, to date, shown themselves to be particularly cautious.[145] In order to obtain leave under section 10(8), children have to satisfy the court that they have 'sufficient understanding' to apply for an order. To proceed without a next friend or guardian, the minor must persuade the court that he or she has sufficient understanding to participate in the proceedings without adult assistance.[146] To have sufficient understanding, the child must demonstrate the intellectual capacity to instruct a solicitor and to participate in litigation.[147]

While the courts appear willing in principle to open their doors to minors without prejudging[148] the case, they remain hesitant to expose children to what they perceive as the dangers of litigation. So, in *Re H (Residence Order: Child's Application for Leave)*,[149] for example, the court refused leave to a 12 year old boy to apply for residence order in his father's favour. In the course of his judgment, Johnson J referred to the disadvantages of a child seeing all the evidence in a case between the parents. He also doubted whether the boy would have been permitted to attend court. Nevertheless the judge did hasten to reassure the minor that his views would not be discounted: 'judges who have to decide these difficult matters are experienced in weighing up the considerations that are relevant and are very conscious that it is never desirable to impose on a child a result, be it as to contact or residence, contrary to the wishes of the child'.

In relation to a child's application to instruct a legal representative directly, the court in *Re S*[150] held that '*Gillick* competence' was the appropriate test for the child's understanding.[151] However the protectionist stance of the court is again evident. Sir Thomas Bingham MR observed that:

143 Fortin, n 134 above, 213.
144 *ibid*, 224.
145 For evidence of similar unease in the face of child autonomy, see for example the cases demonstrating what has been termed a retreat from *Gillick*: *Re R (A Minor) (Wardship: Medical Treatment)* [1992] 1 FLR 190; *Re W (A Minor) (Medical Treatment: Court's Jurisdiction)* [1992] 3 WLR 758.
146 r 9.2A Family Proceedings Rules 1991.
147 See *Re SC (a minor)(leave to seek residence order)* [1994] 1 FLR 96; *Re H (Residence Order: Child's Application for Leave)* [2000] 1 FLR 780.
148 Section 10(8) applications are not governed by the welfare principle although, of course, s 1(1) does apply in the substantive hearing.
149 [2000] 1 FLR 780, 783.
150 *Re S (A Minor)(Independent Representation)* [1993] 2 FLR 437.
151 *ibid*, 447.

> where any sound judgement on these issues calls for insight and imagination which only maturity and experience can bring, both the court and the solicitor should be slow to conclude that the child's understanding is sufficient.[152]

In *Re H (a minor)(guardian ad litem: requirement)* Booth J set a high standard for the level of understanding required by the courts:

> Participating as a party . . . means much more than instructing a solicitor as to his own views. The child enters the arena among other adult parties. He may give evidence and he may be cross-examined. He will hear other parties, including in this case his parents, give evidence and be cross-examined. He must be able to give instructions . . . Thus the child is exposed and not protected . . . The child also will be bound to abide by the rules . . . including rules as to confidentiality.[153]

Again, there is a tension between autonomy and welfare. In *Re S* the court put it this way:

> [C]hildren are human beings in their own right with individual minds and wills, views and emotions, which should command serious attention. A child's wishes are not to be discounted or dismissed simply because he is a child. He should be free to express them and decision-makers should listen. Second is the fact that a child is, after all, a child. The reason why the law is particularly solicitous in protecting the interests of children is that they are liable to be vulnerable and impressionable, lacking the maturity to weigh the longer term against the shorter, lacking the insight to know how others will react in certain situations, lacking the experience to match the probable against the possible . . . [154]

Judges thus tend to agree with government policy makers: children's active participation in litigation and, in particular, the prospect of allowing them to run a case unmediated by the judgment of welfare professionals or other concerned adults is seen as being fraught with danger. Children, in the view of the courts, lack the capacity for reflection on self and others; they need to be shielded from their own inexperience and lack of judgment. They also need to be shielded from hurtful knowledge.

However, in *Re H (a minor)(guardian ad litem: requirement)* the court seems to have come down on the side of autonomy. It considered it important that the 15-year old boy concerned be given the opportunity to present his case and the decision to allow him to do so should not be affected by welfare considerations.[155] Significantly, in our view, the court went on to say, 'Unless H is able to put his case it is, I think, unlikely that he would accept any decision which was contrary to his wishes'.[156] This comment appears to acknowledge a need to secure the co-opera-

152 *ibid*, 444.

153 [1994] 4 All ER 762, 765. This test was endorsed in *Re N (Contact: Minor Seeking Leave to Defend and Removal of Guardian)* [2003] 1 FLR 652. It reaffirms the view that children should not lightly be permitted to dispense with the guardian's services and to bring applications on their own behalf.

154 n 150 above, 448.

155 n 153 above, 767.

156 *ibid.*

tion of the young person. For if he rejected the decision of the court, this would, it is implicitly conceded, have consequences. It may well be that the consequences in the mind of the judge included the risk that any order of court would be resisted and so undermined.

Overall, in Fortin's opinion, the ways in which children's wishes are at present conveyed to the court are 'fragmented and arbitrary'[157] and, she says, 'legal changes have produced little real support' for children.[158] The changes that are supported by government, such as the '*Parenting Plan*', [159] remain focused upon altering private and informal behaviour and apparently endorse the reluctance of the formal legal system to accommodate more decisively the active, responsible child.

Nevertheless, while the child's means of making his or her wishes known to the court are circumscribed, there appears to be some flexibility, dependent upon the court's construction of the child's welfare and his or her competence or ability to understand and reflect upon it. In any event, the child's *co-operation* both during and after the divorce and separation is seen as important for the smooth functioning of the post-divorce family and judges, accordingly, consider it necessary on occasion to seek to persuade children, even younger children, of the benefits of contact.

CHILDREN AS MORALLY RESPONSIBLE VICTIMS

There may be a number of explanations for the (re)surgence of interest in children and childhood within the law, the 'psy' professions, social science research and the field of policy-making. One of these seems to be that children constitute a particular type of social problem in contemporary times, requiring a refocus of the regulatory and explanatory gaze upon them. This is not to say that childhood has not constituted a social problem historically,[160] only that its nature has shifted somewhat.

In the 'old' children 'as becoming' paradigm, the problem was centred around their potential citizenship and productivity, their *futurity*.[161] Their development and moral socialization therefore required control and adequate guidance, usually by the family.[162] John Bowlby's maternal deprivation theory and Parsonian socialization theory captured perfectly the post-war political concern for humanitarian

157 Fortin, n 134 above, 211.

158 *ibid*, 210.

159 National Council of Voluntary Childcare Organisations, *The Parenting Plan* (London: LCD, 2002). This document advises parents that children need age-appropriate information and opportunities to express their views. They also need their views to be taken into account (2), particularly in relation to contact (3). 'Above all,' it states, 'discuss arrangements with your children and listen to their views' (4). The Parenting Plan recommends communication between children and parents for a number of reasons such as showing children that they are still important. One notable reason, however, is that '[c]lear communication will also help make the changes run as smoothly as possible' (4).

160 R. Dingwall, J. Eekelaar and T. Murray, 'Childhood as a Social problem: A Survey of the History of Legal Regulation' (1984) 11 J of Law and Society 207.

161 C. Jenks, *Childhood* (London: Routledge, 1996).

162 *ibid*.

intervention, moral surveillance and economic reconstruction.[163] These theories 'gave [and continue to give] a scientific basis for concentrating policy attention both on the family as an institution and on individual family members in terms of allocating responsibility for the moral and mental health of children'.[164] Indeed, Hendrick contends, in the context of juvenile justice, that socialization continues to be 'relevant to the modernisation project in the sense that [children] are . . . regarded as an investment in futurity'.[165]

We are not suggesting, through this overview of the research literature, policy documents and the law, that a radical reconstruction of children and childhood is taking place. While the discourse is replete with references to the importance of communication with and listening to children, it does not mean that children are in the process of being elevated to the status of autonomous rights holders to the extent that they are able to litigate untrammelled by adult conceptions of welfare. Nor are we suggesting that they are endowed with agency in the sense of being empowered to shape moral or public policy agendas directly.[166] We are not even suggesting that they are permitted in a formal or even, often, in a practical sense to make important decisions. What we do suggest, however, is that there is a new project in the making centring on the promotion of 'citizenship' and that children are being included in this project. In other words, in our view children are not seen simply as passive 'vessels awaiting the correct input' as Hendrick puts it.[167] Rather, they are now perceived to have a role to play in 'making a positive contribution to the community and to society',[168] and it is one they play *immediately*, rather than in the future.

More particularly, children have a role to play in shaping the post-separation family. Like their parents, they are expected to internalise the prevailing norms underlying the 'good' post-separation family. Like their parents, they are expected to be open to information, education, therapeutic intervention and persuasion. And like their parents, they are expected to act on the advice and information offered to them. These expectations, along with the emphasis on the development by children of individual coping skills and their co-operation in implementing contact arrangements suggests also that, like their parents, they are capable of and therefore have responsibility for the building of 'good' post-separation families.

While giving a voice to any previously disempowered or marginalised constituency is important, and listening to children is long overdue, we must be alert to the discourse through which that voice is heard and interpreted. In this case, the discourses of rights, responsibility, education and welfare that dominate talk about the post-separation family fit in well with what has been termed a project to 'remoralise' the family.[169] And in our view, this is a project to which children are

163 J. Brannen, 'Reconsidering Children and Childhood: Sociological and Policy Perspectives' in E. Silva and C. Smart (eds), *The New Family?* (London: Sage, 1999).
164 Day Sclater and Piper, n 21 above, 140.
165 Hendrick, n 2 above, 243 and 253.
166 Children's views and needs do inform policy, but always indirectly as interpreted by adults.
167 Hendrick, n 2 above, 220. His comment was, however, made in the context of education.
168 DfES, n 21 above, para 1.3. Reece (n 2 above) would describe this a post-liberal civic responsibility.
169 Day Sclater and Piper, n 21 above.

now expected to make a contribution. The aim of this enterprise is to encourage individual reflection, negotiation and autonomy within the family and to promote responsible decision-making in favour of those arrangements that, it is thought, will lead to the best possible outcomes for children and for society. Responsibility for achieving these outcomes has for some time been privatised. Now this responsibility has also been extended to the young. Now *all* family members, adults and children, bear primary responsibility for easing the perceived 'crisis' of the family.

The remoralisation project, it seems, allows for some form of resolution to the so-called rights versus welfare dilemma within family and child law. It legitimises both rights and welfare by appealing to children's rights/responsibility as a device to promote the version of their welfare that is important for the 'good' post - separation family. By appealing to a form of (post-liberal) autonomy, any threat or potential threat to that family posed by unruly childish behaviour or unschooled decisions can be defused. The remoralisation project demands that children should not be given the opportunity of sabotaging arrangements that are, it is assumed, designed to promote their welfare. Provided they, like their parents, are educated and guided in the right direction so that they make the 'right' decisions, the damage assumed to be caused by divorce or separation can be avoided or minimised.

The nuclear family has long been accorded an idealised status and the 'good' post-separation family has been moulded in its image. In consequence, adherence to the model of the 'bi-nuclear' or separated but continuing family renders 'family breakdown' safe(r). Information, education and therapeutic intervention aimed at persuading all the family members to adopt this model enhances its legitimacy; it has, after all, the cachet of being the model that is freely chosen because it is best for everyone. That children have a role in the newly privatised remoralisation project further adds to its legitimacy while leaving relatively little to chance. Children are listened to and their participation is solicited. At the same time, the choices they are permitted to make are confined to those which are regarded as most likely to secure their own best interests. As Hendrick[170] says, children as 'being' pose risks. They have to be shown the way. And the 'right' way leads back to the child as object of concern, a vulnerable child whose welfare must be protected.

170 Hendrick, n 2 above, 253.

Name Index

Agarwal, Bina 362–3
Anderson, Michael 83
Andrews, Karen 67
Aristotle 36
Arnup, Katherine xv

Baker, Maureen 287
Barlein, Michael 221
Barrett, Michelle 71
Bauman, Zygmunt 106
Beck, U. 106, 107
Beck-Gernsheim, E. 106, 107
Behrens, J. 248
Bell, S.E. 409
Bellah, Robert 106
Bingham, Sir Thomas 509
Blackstone, Sir William 180
Bonnet, Catherine 225
Bowlby, John 511
Boyd, Susan B. xv, 79, 81–2, 91, 95–6
Butler, Judith 77

Carasco, Emily 296
Chen, Martha 362
Chunn, Dorothy xviii
Cohen, Morris 31
Collier, Richard xiv, xviii, 175–98
Cossman, Brenda xv, 63–101, 388, 392, 398

Dahl, Robert 41
Day Sclater, Shelley xxii, 403–421
Dekeuwer-Defossez, Francoise 217–8
Dewar, John xi, xvii, xxi, xxiii, 109, 243
Diduck, Alison xiii, xvi, xxiii–xxiv, 491–513
Donzelot, J. xiv, 42
Dubois, W.E.B. 61
Duclos, Nitya 84, 85
Durkheim, Emile 41

Eagleton, Terry 81
Edwards, E. 481
Eekelaar, John xvi, 105–133
Eichler, Margrit 275, 281
Eisenstein, Zillan 80

Fehlberg, Belinda xvi–xvii, xix, 135–58
Felstiner, William xxiii
Finch, Janet 107, 162–3
Fineman, Martha xvii, 423–470
Finnie, Ross 272–4
Fitzgibbon, Scott 105, 128
Fitzpatrick, Peter 330
Fortin, J. 508–511
Foucault, Michel xiv, 33, 41, 81
Freeman, M. xiii, 34, 413, 496
Freud, A. xxi, 37
Frug, Mary Jo 92
Funder, K. 238, 378–9
Fuss, Diana 74

Galanter, Marc xvii
Gavigan, Shelley 91, 97
Gergen, K. 405
Gergen, M. 405
Giddens, A. 106, 109, 122, 131, 405
Gilligan, Carol 161–3, 172, 393
Gillis, John xvi
Girard, Philip 281
Glaser, D. 495, 497–8
Goldstein, J. xxi, 37
Graham, H. 162–3
Gramsci, Antonio 41
Grassby, Miriam 274
Graycar, Reg xiv
Greatbatch, D. 413
Groves, D. 162–3

Hale, Robert 5
Hall, Stuart 81
Harrison, M. 379
Hekman, Susan 77
Hendrick, H. 512–3
Herman, Didi 72, 84
Hooper, C.A. 414
Hughes, J. 238, 242–3, 245–9, 252–6
Humphreys, Cathy xxi, xxii, 471–490

Ingleby, Richard 400
Issacs, M.B. 415

James, A. 413, 493
Jordan, J. 415

Kaganas, Felicity xii, xxiv, 491–513
Kelly, J.B. xv, 496
Keshvani, Rosemin xxi, 367–9, 373–400
King, M. 506
Kline, Marlee xii, xx, 291–341
Kornhauser, L. xxi, xxii, xxiii, 369
Kymlicka, Will 353

Laws, Sir John 109
Lefaucheur, Nadine 217, 224–5
Leon, G. 415
Lewis, Jane 108, 124
Lipovetsky, Gilles 106
Locke, John 36

McDonald, P. 243
MacIntosh, Mary 71
MacKinnon, Catharine 401
Maclean, Mavis xi, xvi, 105–133
Marx, Karl 36, 41
Mechanic, M. 478
Mill, J.S. 36
Mishler, E.G. 405
Mnookin, R.H. xxi, xxii, xxiii, 369, 384
Moghissi, H. 415
Monture, Patricia 296, 327
Morgan, David xvi
Mossman, Mary Jane xix, 267–289
Moyisch, Jurgen 225

Narayan, Uma 353
Neale, Bren 107
Neave, Marcia xxi, 367–401
Neirinck, Claire 223
Nussbaum, Martha 349–50

Ochberg, R. 406
O'Donovan, Katherine xiii, xvi, 41, 201–31
Okin, Susan Moller 348, 353, 356
Olsen, Frances E. xiii, 3–32, 35

Pahl, Jan 139
Parashar, Archana xx, 343–63
Parker, Stephen 109
Pashukanis, Evgeny 41
Pateman, Carole 348
Perry, Twila L. xiv, xvi, 49–62
Plummer, K. 412, 416
Piper, C. 413, 414
Prout, A. 493
Pryor, J. 498

Raz, J. 111
Reece, H. xvii, xxi, xxiii, 492
Resick, P. 478
Rhoades, Helen xii
Rixen, Stephen 221
Riessman, C.K. 406, 409
Roberts, Dorothy xv–xvi
Robinson, M. 414
Rodgers, B. 498
Rogerson, Carol 271–4
Rose, Carol 393–5
Rose, Nikolas xi, xiii, xiv, 33–48
Rosenwald, G. 406

Sandelowski, M. 405
Sarat, Austin xxiii
Schlag, Pierre 77
Scott, Joan 73, 89, 93
Sen, Amartya 349
Sheehan, Grania xi, xix, 235–66, 242–3, 245–9, 253, 255–7
Sheldon, Shelley xix
Sheppard, Colleen 282
Smart, Carol xi, xiv, xv, xvii–xviii, xxiii, 95, 107, 159–74, 485
Smythe, B. 238, 248, 252–3, 255–7
Solnit, A. xxi, 37
Sturge, C. 495, 497–8

Thery, Irene 217–8
Thiara, Ravi K. xxii, 471–490
Thibaudeau, Suzanne 276
Thomas, W.I. 164
Torjman, Sherri 283
Trebilcock, Michael J. xxi, 367–9, 373–400
Tronto, J. 161–3, 166

Vaughan, D. 404

Wallbank, Julie xx
Walker, J. 414
Wallerstein, J.S. 496

Weaver, T. 478
Weber, Max 41
Weedon, Chris 76, 78, 88
Weitzman, Lenore xix, 370, 394, 399
Weston, Kath 89, 252
Weston, R. 379
Wiegers, Wanda 367, 377, 381
Wilcox, P. 483
Williams, Patricia 355
Wolfson, Lorne 276

Yngvesson, Barbara 203, 222

Zweibel, Ellen 282, 289

For Product Safety Concerns and Information please contact our EU representative GPSR@taylorandfrancis.com Taylor & Francis Verlag GmbH, Kaufingerstraße 24, 80331 München, Germany

Batch number: 10704229

Printed by Printforce, the Netherlands